Lecture Notes in Artificial Intelligence   1510

Subseries of Lecture Notes in Computer Science
Edited by J. G. Carbonell and J. Siekmann

Lecture Notes in Computer Science

Edited by G. Goos, J. Hartmanis and J. van Leeuwen

T0223208

Springer
Berlin
Heidelberg
New York
Barcelona
Budapest
Hong Kong
London
Milan
Paris
Singapore
Tokyo

Jan M. Żytkow   Mohamed Quafafou (Eds.)

Principles of
Data Mining and
Knowledge Discovery

Second European Symposium, PKDD '98
Nantes, France, September 23-26, 1998
Proceedings

 Springer

Series Editors

Jaime G. Carbonell, Carnegie Mellon University, Pittsburgh, PA, USA
Jörg Siekmann, University of Saarland, Saarbrücken, Germany

Volume Editors

Jan M. Żytkow
Wichita State University, Department of Computer Science
Wichita, KS 67260-0083, USA
E-mail: zytkow@wise.cs.twsu.edu

Mohamed Quafafou
Université de Nantes, IRIN
2, rue de la Houssinière, F-44322 Nantes Cedex 3, France
E-mail: quafafou@irin.univ-nantes.fr

Cataloging-in-Publication Data applied for

Die Deutsche Bibliothek - CIP-Einheitsaufnahme

Principles of data mining and knowledge discovery : second
European symposium ; proceedings / PKDD '98, Nantes, France,
September 23 - 26, 1998. Jan M. Żytkow ; Mohamed Quafafou
(ed.). - Berlin ; Heidelberg ; New York ; Barcelona ; Budapest ; Hong
Kong ; London ; Milan ; Paris ; Singapore ; Tokyo : Springer, 1998
  (Lecture notes in computer science ; Vol. 1510 : Lecture notes in
  artificial intelligence)
  ISBN 3-540-65068-7

CR Subject Classification (1991): I.2, H.3, H.5, G.3, J.1

ISBN 3-540-65068-7 Springer-Verlag Berlin Heidelberg New York

© Springer-Verlag Berlin Heidelberg 1998
Printed in Germany

Typesetting: Camera ready by author
SPIN 10692663   06/3142 – 5 4 3 2 1 0   Printed on acid-free paper

Preface

Knowledge Discovery in Databases (KDD), also known as Data Mining, has emerged in the last decade in response to the challenge of turning large and ubiquitous databases into knowledge that can be used in practice.

KDD has been able to grow very rapidly by drawing its techniques and data mining experiences from a combination of many existing research areas: databases, statistics, machine learning, automated scientific discovery, inductive logic programming, artificial intelligence, visualization, decision science, and high performance computing. While each of these areas can contribute in specific ways, the strength of KDD comes from the value that is added by creative combination of techniques from the contributing areas.

The practical successes of KDD in a broad range of application domains have led to very high expectations. In the long run, KDD can meet or fail those expectations. In order to maintain its status of interdisciplinary research of great practical payoff KDD has to establish its own theoretical principles that go beyond each of the contributing areas, and demonstrate how they jointly create a broad and exciting area of research. Such principles will be instrumental in maintaining the identity of KDD research, in effective communication and in guiding the practitioners.

Seeking the principles has always been a part of the European research tradition. Thus "Principles of KDD" (PKDD) make a suitable focus for the annual meetings of the KDD community in Europe. The main long-term interest is in theoretical principles for the emerging discipline of KDD. Another goal of the PKDD series is to provide a European-based forum for interaction among all theoreticians and practitioners interested in data mining and knowledge discovery as well as fostering the interdisciplinary collaboration. The first meeting was held in Trondheim, Norway, in June 1997.

This volume contains papers selected for presentation at the Second European Symposium on Principles of Data Mining and Knowledge Discovery in Databases – PKDD'98, held in Nantes, France, September 23-26, 1998. The University of Nantes hosted the symposium. The symposium was sponsored by the Ville de Nantes, Université de Nantes, MENRT, Conseil Régional des Pays de Loire, Centre de Recherche et Développement de France Télécom (CNET). We wish to express our thanks to the sponsors of the symposium for their generous support. The contributed papers were selected from 73 full draft papers by the following program committee:

Pieter Adriaans (Syllogic, The Netherlands), **Pawel Brazdil** (U. Porto, Portugal), **Henri Briand** (U. Nantes, France), **Leo Carbonara** (British Telecom, UK), **A. Fazel Famili** (IIT-NRC, Canada), **Ronen Feldman** (Bar Ilan, U. Israel), **Patrick Gallinari** (U. Paris VI, France), **Jean Gabriel Ganascia** (U. Paris VI, France), **Attilio Giordana** (U. Torino, Italy), **David Hand** (Open U. UK), **Bob Henery** (U. Strathclyde, UK), **Mikhail Kiselev**

(Megaputer Intelligence, Russia), **Willi Kloesgen** (GMD, Germany), **Yves Kodratoff** (U. Paris VI, France), **Jan Komorowski** (NTNU, Norway), **Nada Lavrac** (Josef Stefan Inst. Slovenia), **Heikki Manilla** (U. Helsinki, Finland), **Steve Muggleton** (Oxford U. UK), **Zdzislaw Pawlak** (Warsaw Technical U. Poland), **Gregory Piatetsky-Shapiro** (Knowledge Stream, Boston, USA), **Lech Polkowski** (U. Warsaw, Poland), **Mohamed Quafafou** (U. Nantes, France), **Zbigniew Ras** (UNC Charlotte, USA), **Lorenza Saitta** (U. Torino, Italy), **Wei-Min Shen** (U. South Calif. USA), **Arno Siebes** (CWI, Netherlands), **Andrzej Skowron** (U. Warsaw, Poland), **Derek Sleeman** (U. Aberdeen, UK), **Nicolas Spyratos** (U. Paris XI, France), **Shusaku Tsumoto** (Tokyo Medical & Dental U. Japan), **Raul Valdes-Perez** (CMU, USA), **Thierry Van de Merckt** (CSC, Belgium), **Rudiger Wirth** (Daimler-Benz, Germany), **Stefan Wrobel** (GTE, Germany), **Ning Zhong** (Yamaguchi U. Japan), **Wojtek Ziarko** (U. Regina, Canada), **Djamel A. Zighed** (U. Lyon II, France), **Jan M. Żytkow** (UNC Charlotte, USA).

PKDD was truly international: papers came from 24 countries, including Australia (2), Belgium (1), Brazil (1), Bulgaria (1), Canada (1), China (1), Cuba (1), Czech Republic (3), Finland (2), France (18), Germany (6), Israel (3), Italy (2), Japan (5), Norway (1), Poland (4), Portugal (2), Russia (1), Singapore (2), Spain (5), Sweden (1), Switzerland (1), United Kingdom (6), United States of America (3). Many thanks to all who submitted papers for review and for publication in the proceedings. The accepted papers were divided into two categories: 26 oral presentations and 30 poster presentations. In addition to poster sessions each poster paper was allocated 4 minutes highlight presentation. All papers were allocated the same number of 9 pages in the proceedings.

Three tutorials were offered to all symposium participants on September 23rd: Scalable, High-Performance Data Mining with Parallel Processing by Alex Alves Freitas, Industrial Applications of Data Mining by Gholamreza Nakhaeizadeh, and Practical Text Mining by Ronen Feldman.

The members of PKDD'98 local organizing committee: Emmanuelle Martienne, Laurent Ughetto, and Abdellatif Saoudi, all of the University of Nantes, did an enormous amount of work and deserve the special gratitude of all the participants. We wish to express our thanks to the following colleagues for their reviewing participation: M.R. Amini, J-F. Boulicaut, V. Corruble, A. Giacometti, A. Jorge, A. Leger, D. Laurent, F. Mitchell, H.S. Nguyen, D. Slezak, N. Valette, H. Zaragoza, J-D. Zucker.

Special thanks are due to Alfred Hofmann of Springer-Verlag for his help and support.

July 1998   Mohamed Quafafou and Jan M. Żytkow

Table of Contents

Communications

Session 1. Rule evaluation

Session 2. Visualization

Session 3. Association rules and text mining

Session 4. Clustering and discretization

Posters

Tutorials

On Objective Measures of Rule Surprisingness

Alex A. Freitas

CEFET-PR (Federal Center of Technological Education), DAINF (Dept. of Informatics)
Av. Sete de Setembro, 3165, Curitiba - PR, 80230-901, Brazil
alex@dainf.cefetpr.br
http://www.dainf.cefetpr.br/~alex

Abstract. Most of the literature argues that surprisingness is an inherently subjective aspect of the discovered knowledge, which cannot be measured in objective terms. This paper departs from this view, and it has a twofold goal: (1) showing that it is indeed possible to define *objective* (rather than subjective) measures of discovered rule surprisingness; (2) proposing new ideas and methods for defining objective rule surprisingness measures.

1 Introduction

A crucial aspect of data mining is that the discovered knowledge (usually expressed in the form of "if-then" rules) should be somehow interesting, where the term interestingness is arguably related to the properties of surprisingness (unexpectedness), usefulness and novelty of the rule [Fayyad et al. 96]. In this paper we are interested in quantitative, objective measures of one of the above three properties, namely rule *surprisingness*.

In general, the evaluation of the interestingness of discovered rules has both an objective (data-driven) and a subjective (user-driven) aspect. In the particular case of surprisingness, however, most of the literature argues that this property of the discovered rules is inherently subjective - see e.g. [Liu et al. 97].

Hence, objective measures of rule surprisingness seem to be something missing, or at least underexplored, in the literature, and this is part of the motivation for the discussion presented in this paper. Another motivation, of course, is that objective measures of rule surprisingness have one important advantage. Objectiveness is strongly related to domain independence, while subjectiveness is strongly related to domain dependence. Hence, objective measures of rule surprisingness are, in principle, more generic than subjective measures. (However, subjective measures are still necessary - see below.)

We should emphasize that the aim of the paper is *not* to propose a new rule surprisingness measure. Note that any rule interestingness measure is part of the bias of the corresponding data mining algorithm, and it is well-known that any data mining bias has a domain-dependent effectiveness.

Hence, instead of investigating the effectiveness of any particular rule surprisingness measure, the aim of this paper is rather to suggest and discuss ideas that can be used to objectively measure the degree of rule surprisingness, in a generic way. We hope that this discussion will be a useful reference for other researchers who have a specific data mining problem to be solved, since these researches could use the ideas discussed in this paper to design their rule surprisingness measure.

It should be noted that the goal of our work is to complement, rather than to replace, the existing subjective measures of rule surprisingness. Actually, in practice both objective and subjective approaches should be used to select surprising rules. In our case, the new ideas for objective rule suprisingness measures proposed in this paper can be used as a kind of filter to select potentially surprising rules, among the many rules discovered by a data mining algorithm. We can then return to the user a much smaller number of potentially surprising rules, and let him/her judge the ultimate surprisingness of those rules only. Obviously, the user will be able to save a lot of his/her rule analyzis time with this approach, particularly when the data mining algorithm discovers a large number of rules.

This paper is organized as follows. Section 2 discusses how to measure the surprisingness of small disjuncts. Section 3 discusses how to measure the degree of surprisingness associated with individual attributes in a rule antecedent. Section 4 discusses how we can discover surprising knowledge by detecting occurrences of Simpson's paradox. Finally, section 5 concludes the paper.

2 On the Surprisingness of Small Disjuncts

A rule set can be regarded as a disjunction of rules, so that a given rule can be regarded as a disjunct. The size of a disjunct (rule) is the number of tuples satisfied by the rule's antecedent – i.e. the "if part" of the rule. Thus, small disjuncts are rules whose number of covered tuples is small, according to some specified criterion (e.g. a fixed threshold, or a more flexible criterion).

At first glance, it seems that small disjuncts are undesirable, since they have little generality and tend to be error-prone (see below). Based on this view, most data mining algorithms have a bias favoring the discovery of large disjuncts.

However, small disjuncts have the potential to capture truly unexpected relationships, in the data. For instance, [Provost & Aronis 96] report an application where a small disjunct discovered by a data mining algorithm was considered truly interesting and led to substantial new research in the application domain. Hence, it would be nice if the data mining algorithm could automatically evaluate the surprisingness of small disjuncts, reporting to the user only the most promising ones.

The remaining of this section is divided into two parts. Subsection 2.1 reviews previous research on small disjuncts, while subsection 2.2 proposes our idea to objectively measure the surprisingness of small disjuncts.

2.1 A Review of Small Disjuncts

As mentioned above, small disjuncts are error-prone. Since they cover a small number of tuples, it is possible that they cover mainly noise. At first glance, it seems that this problem can be solved by simply discarding small disjuncts.

Unfortunately, however, prediction accuracy can be significantly reduced if all small disjuncts are discarded by the data mining algorithm, as shown by [Holte et al. 89]. This is a particularly serious problem in domains where the small disjuncts collectively match a large percentage of the number of tuples belonging to a given class [Danyluk & Provost 93]. The main problem is that a small disjunct can represent either a true exception occurring in the data or simply noise. In the former case the disjunct should be maintained, but in the latter case the disjunct is error prone and should be discarded. Unfortunately, however, it is very difficult to tell which is the case, given only the data.

[Holte et al. 89] suggested that one remedy for the problem of small disjuncts was to evaluate these disjuncts by using a bias different from the one used to evaluate large disjuncts. Hence, they proposed that small disjuncts be evaluated by a maximum-specificity bias, in contrast with the maximum-generality bias (favoring the discovery of more general rules) used by most data mining algorithms. [Ting 94] further investigated this approach, by using an instance-based learner (as far as we can go with the maximum-specificity bias) to evaluate small disjuncts.

It should be noted that the above literature has studied the effect of small disjuncts mainly in the classification accuracy of the discovered knowledge. In this paper we are rather interested in the effect of small disjuncts in the surprisingness of the discovered knowledge, as will be discussed in the next subsection.

2.2 Measuring the Surprisingness of Small Disjuncts

We propose that a small disjunct be considered as surprising knowledge to the extent that it predicts a class different from the class predicted by the minimum generalizations of the disjunct. The minimum generalizations of a disjunct are defined as follows. (Henceforth, we use simply the term disjunct to refer to small disjuncts.)

Let the disjunct be composed by the conjunction of m conditions, of the form $cond_1$ AND $cond_2$ AND ... $cond_m$, where each $cond_k$, k=1,...,m, is a triple of the form <Att op Val>, where Att is an attribute, op is a relational operator in the set $\{<,>,\geq,\leq,=\}$ and Val is a value belonging to the domain of Att. Also, following a common practice in data mining algorithms, if the attribute Att is continuous (real-valued), then op is in the set $\{<,>,\geq,\leq,\}$; whereas if the attribute Att is categorical then op is the "=" operator.

A disjunct has m minimum generalizations, one for each of its m conditions. The k-th minimum generalization of the disjunct, associated with $cond_k$, k=1,...,m, is defined as follows. If Att in $cond_k$ is categorical, then the k-th minimum generalization of the disjunct is achieved by removing $cond_k$ from the disjunct. If Att in $cond_k$ is continuous, then the k-th minimum generalization of the disjunct can be defined in two ways, namely: (a) by removing $cond_k$ from the disjunct; (b) by adding a small value α to the value of the "cut-point" Val in $cond_k$, when op in $\{<,\leq\}$, or subtracting α from Val in $cond_k$, when op in $\{>,\geq\}$; where α is a user-defined, problem-dependent constant. It is up to the user to choose one of these two definitions of minimum generalization for continuous attributes, depending on the application.

To clarify the above definition (b) of minimum generalization, let us consider, as an example, the following rule condition: "Age < 23". Supposing that α is specified as 5, the minimum generalization of this condition would be "Age < 28". In practice there might be several continuous attributes, and different absolute values for α would be necessary, due to differences of scale among the attributes - for instance, for the attribute "Yearly Income", $\alpha = 5$ is too small. Obviously, it would be tedious to specify a different absolute value of α for each continuous attribute. A solution is to specify a relative value of α, such as 5%. Then, for each continuous attribute, the actual absolute value for α would be automatically calculated as 5% of the highest value observed for that attribute. An alternative definition of minimum generalization for continuous attributes could use some kind of percentile-based approach.

In any case, note that a minimum generalization produces a new disjunct which covers a superset of the tuples covered by the original disjunct. As a result, the class distribution of the tuples covered by the new disjunct (produced by minimum generalization of the original disjunct) can be significantly different from the class distribution of the tuples covered by the original disjunct.

Therefore, after a new disjunct is produced by minimum generalization, its predicted class (i.e. the consequent of the rule) is re-computed. More precisely, the class predicted by the new disjunct is determined by using the same procedure used by the data mining algorithm that discovered the original disjunct. (Typically, picking up the class with largest relative frequency among the tuples covered by the disjunct.)

We are now ready to define a way to objectively measure the surprisingness of small disjuncts discovered by a data mining algorithm. Let C be the class predicted by the original disjunct and C_k be the class predicted by the disjunct produced by the k-th minimum generalization of the original disjunct, k=1,...,m, as explained above. We then compare C against each C_k, k=1,...,m, and count the number of times C differs from C_k. This result, an integer number in the interval 0...m, is defined as the raw surprisingness of the original disjunct, denoted $DisjSurp_{raw}$. The higher $DisjSurp_{raw}$, the more surprising the disjunct is.

Note that the value of $DisjSurp_{raw}$ is significantly influenced by the number of conditions m in the disjunct, which is in turn a measure of syntactic complexity. Several data mining algorithms already use a measure of syntactic complexity as part of their inductive bias. In this case, to avoid confusion between measures of syntactic complexity and measures of disjunct surprisingness, we can render the latter somewhat more independent from the former by defining a normalized disjunct surprisingness measure, as follows: $DisjSurp_{norm} = DisjSurp_{raw} / m$; where m is the number of conditions of the disjunct. Clearly, $DisjSurp_{norm}$ takes on values in the interval [0..1]. The higher $DisjSurp_{norm}$, the more surprising the disjunct is. However, it should be noted that this normalized measure has a bias towards rules with fewer conditions, since it will probably be difficult for rules with many conditions to hold a high normalized value. The suitability of this bias depends on the application domain.

Finally, note that the above measure of small disjunct surprisingness is being proposed as a post-processing approach, applied once the rules have been discovered. This approach seems consistent with top-down, specialization-driven rule induction algorithms, that iteratively add conditions to a candidate rule, in order to specialize it. Note that this is the most common kind of rule induction algorithm used in practice.

3 On The Surprisingness of a Rule's Individual Attributes

Most rule surprisingness measures (or, more generally, rule interestingness measures) consider the rule antecedent as a whole, without paying attention to the individual attributes occurring in the rule antecedent - see e.g. the well-known rule interestingness measure proposed by [Piatetsky-Shapiro 91].

In some sense, these rule surprisingness measures are coarse-grained. However, two rules with the same value of a coarse-grained rule surprisingness measure can have very different degrees of interestingness for the user, depending on which attributes occur in the rule antecedent.

In order to evaluate the surprisingness of predicting attributes in a rule antecedent, denoted AttSurp, we propose an information-theory-based measure, as follows - see [Cover & Thomas 91] for a comprehensive review of information theory. First, we calculate InfoGain(A_i), the information gain of each predicting attribute A_i in the rule antecedent, using formulas (1), (2) and (3). In these formulas, Info(G) is the information of the goal (class) attribute G, Info(G|A_i) is the information of the goal attribute G given predicting attribute A_i, A_{ij} denotes the j-th value of attribute A_i, G_j denotes the j-th value of the goal attribute G, Pr(X) denotes the probability of X, Pr(X|Y) denotes the conditional probability of X given Y, and all the logs are in base 2. The index j in formulas (2) and (3) varies in the interval 1..n, where n is the number of goal attribute values. The index k in formula (3) varies in the interval 1..m, where m is the number of values of the predicting attribute A_i.

$$\text{InfoGain}(A_i) = \text{Info}(G) - \text{Info}(G|A_i) \tag{1}$$

where
$$\text{Info}(G) = -\sum_{j=1}^{n} \Pr(G_j) \log \Pr(G_j) \tag{2}$$

$$\text{Info}(G|A_i) = \sum_{k=1}^{m} \Pr(A_{ik}) \left(-\sum_{j=1}^{n} \Pr(G_j|A_{ik}) \log \Pr(G_j|A_{ik}) \right) \tag{3}$$

Attributes with high information gain are good predictors of class, when these attributes are considered individually, i.e. one at a time. However, from a rule interestingness point of view, it is likely that the user already knows what are the best predictors (individual attributes) for its application domain, and rules containing these attributes would tend to have a low degree of surprisingness for the user.

On the other hand, the user would tend to be more surprised if (s)he saw a rule containing attributes with low information gain. These attributes were probably considered as irrelevant by the users, and they are kind of irrelevant for classification when considered individually, one at a time. However, attribute interactions can render an individually-irrelevant attribute into a relevant one, and this phenomenon is intuitively associated with rule surprisingness. Therefore, all other things (such as the prediction accuracy, coverage and completeness of the rule) being equal, we argue that rules whose antecedent contain attributes with low information gain are more surprising than rules whose antecedent contain attributes with high information gain. This idea can be expressed mathematically by defining AttSurp as follows:

$$\text{AttSurp} = 1 / \left(\sum_{i=1}^{\#att} \text{InfoGain}(A_i) / \#att \right), \tag{4}$$

where $\text{InfoGain}(A_i)$ is the information gain of the i-th attribute occurring in the rule antecedent and #att is the number of attributes occurring in the rule antecedent. The larger the value of AttSurp, the more surprising the rule is.

4 On the Surprisingness of the Occurrence of Simpson's Paradox

4.1 A Review of Simpson's Paradox

Simpson's paradox [Simpson 51] can be defined as follows. Let a population be partitioned into two mutually exclusive and exhaustive populations, denoted Pop_1 and Pop_2, according to the value of a given binary attribute, denoted 1stPartAtt (First Partitioning Attribute). Let G be a binary goal attribute, which takes on a value indicating whether or not a given situation of interest has occurred in a population, and let G_1 and G_2 be the value of the attribute G in each of the respective populations Pop_1 and Pop_2. Let $\Pr(G_1)$ and $\Pr(G_2)$ denote the probability that the situation of interest has occurred in Pop_1 and Pop_2, respectively. Assume that $\Pr(G_1) > \Pr(G_2)$.

Let us now consider the case where both the populations Pop_1 and Pop_2 are further partitioned, in parallel, according to the value of a given categorical attribute, denoted 2ndPartAtt. Let this attribute have m distinct categorical values. We can now compute the probability $\Pr(G)$ in each population, for each of these m categories, which we denote by G_{ij}, where i=1,2 is the id of the population and j=1,...,m is the id of the value of 2ndPartAtt. Let $\Pr(G_{1j})$ and $\Pr(G_{2j})$ denote the probability that the situation of interest has occurred in Pop_1 and Pop_2, in the j-th category of 2ndPartAtt, j=1,...,m.

Finally, Simpson's paradox occurs when, although the overall value of $\Pr(G)$ is higher in Pop_1 than in Pop_2, i.e. $\Pr(G_1) > \Pr(G_2)$, in *each* of the categories produced by 2ndPartAtt the value of $\Pr(G)$ in Pop_1 is lower than or equal to its value in Pop_2, i.e. $\Pr(G_{1j}) \leq \Pr(G_{2j})$, j=1,...,m. The paradox also occurs in the dual situation, i.e. when $\Pr(G_1) < \Pr(G_2)$ but $\Pr(G_{1j}) \geq \Pr(G_{2j})$, j=1,...,m.

Some real-life examples of the occurrence of this paradox are mentioned in [Wagner 82]. For instance, the paradox occurred in a comparison of tuberculosis deaths in New York City and Richmond, Virginia, during the year 1910. Overall, the tuberculosis mortality rate of New York was lower than Richmond's one. However, the opposite was observed when the data was further partitioned according to two racial categories: white and non-white. In both the white and non-white categories, Richmond had a lower mortality rate. In terms of the above notation, the 1stPartAtt was *city*; the situation of interest measured by attribute G was the *occurrence of death* in a tuberculosis case; and the 2ndPartAtt was *racial category*.

Some authors have drawn attention to Simpson's paradox in the context of data mining - see e.g. [Glymour et al. 97]. However, most of this literature regards this paradox as a kind of danger, or obstacle, for data mining algorithms. In particular, the existence of this paradox in a given data set can easily fool a data mining algorithm, causing the algorithm to misinterpret a given relationship between some attributes. For instance, decision-tree learners usually build a tree by selecting one attribute at a time. Hence, they can select an attribute that seems to have a certain relationship with a given class, when in reality the true relationship (taking into account attribute interactions) is the reverse of the apparent one.

Instead of considering Simpson's paradox as an obstacle, in this paper we are interested in the potential that the occurrence of Simpson's paradox offers for the discovery of truly surprising knowledge, as discussed in the next subsection.

4.2 Discovering Surprising Knowledge via the Detection of Simpson's Paradox

We suggest to make a data mining algorithm to explicitly search for occurrences of Simpson's paradox and to report the discovered occurrences for the user, as a kind of surprising knowledge.

This search can be performed by the Algorithm 1 below. The input for the algorithm is a list L_G of user-defined binary goal attributes, each of them indicating whether or not a given situation of interest has occurred. The algorithm below is specified in a high level of abstraction, so the two statements that identify the attributes to be put in lists L_1 and L_2 can be expanded in different procedures, using different criteria, as long as three conditions hold: (a) all attributes in L_1 are binary; (b) all attributes in L_2 are categorical; (c) any goal attribute contained in L_G does not appear in L_1 nor in L_2. Note that these conditions are not very strict, and in particular they allow the possibility that an attribute is contained in both L_1 and L_2 (since binary attributes are a particular case of categorical attributes). This possibility justifies the use of the condition $A_2 \neq A_1$ in the third FOR EACH statement of Algorithm 1. In practice, this and other more strict conditions may be directly implemented in the two statements that identify the attributes to be put in lists L_1 and L_2, when Algorithm 1 is refined to achieve a particular implementation.

Algorithm 1 only detects occurrences of Simpson's paradox. Extending the algorithm to explain why the paradox has occurred is beyond the scope of this paper.

```
INPUT: list of user-defined goal attributes, denoted L_G
BEGIN
    identify attributes that can be used as 1stPartAtt and put them in list L_1
    identify attributes that can be used as 2ndPartAtt and put them in list L_2
    FOR EACH goal attribute G in L_G
        FOR EACH attribute A_1 in L_1
            partition population into Pop_1 and Pop_2, according to the values of A_1
            Pr(G_1) = Pr(G="yes"|A_1=1)
            Pr(G_2) = Pr(G="yes"|A_1=2)
            FOR EACH attribute A_2 in L_2 such that A_2 ≠ A_1
                FOR i=1,2
                    partition Pop_i into m new populations Pop_{i1} ... Pop_{im},
                    according to the values of A_2
                    FOR j=1,...,m
                        Pr(G_{ij}) = Pr(G="yes"|A_1=i,A_2=j)
                    IF ( Pr(G_1) > Pr(G_2)  AND  Pr(G_{1j}) ≤ Pr(G_{2j}), j=1,...,m )
                    OR ( Pr(G_1) < Pr(G_2)  AND  Pr(G_{1j}) ≥ Pr(G_{2j}), j=1,...,m )
                    report the occurrence of the paradox to the user
END
```

Algorithm 1: Search for occurrences of Simpson's paradox.

5 Conclusion

We cannot overemphasize that a rule surprisingness measure (or, more generally, a rule interestingness measure) is a bias, and so there is no universally best rule surprisingness measure across all application domains. Each researcher or practitioner must adapt/invent a rule surprisingness measure to his/her particular target problem.

Hence, as mentioned in the introduction, in order to render the contribution of the paper generic, the main goal of this paper was not to introduce yet another rule surprisingness measure. Rather, this paper had the twofold goal of: (1) showing that it is possible to define *objective* (rather than subjective) measures of discovered rule *surprisingness*, unlike what we might infer from the literature; (2) proposing new ideas for defining objective rule surprisingness measures, which will hopefully be useful for other data mining researchers.

More precisely, the main new ideas proposed in this paper were: (a) a method for measuring the surprisingness of discovered small disjuncts, essentially based on how much the prediction of the *small disjunct* differs from the predictions of its *minimum generalizations*; (b) an information-theoretic, *fine-grain* method for measuring the surprisingness of a discovered rule by considering the surprisingness of *individual attributes* in the rule antecedent, rather than the rule antecedent as a whole (the conventional coarse-grain approach); (c) a method for discovering surprising knowledge via the *explicit detection* of occurrences of *Simpson's paradox*, in the form of a high-level algorithm specifically designed for this task.

One limitation of this paper is that our discussion has not taken into account the interaction between rules in the discovered rule set. In principle, however, the issue of rule interaction is somewhat orthogonal to the issue of individual rule surprisingness, in the sense that the measure of rule interaction (typically a measure of rule overlapping) is often independent of the measure of individual rule surprisingness (or, more generally, interestingness). Hence, it should be possible to use the rule surprisingness measures proposed in this paper together with rule interaction measures. The reader interested in rule selection procedures taking into account rule interaction is referred to [Gebhardt 91], [Major & Mangano 95].

A natural direction for further research is to implement the new ideas for defining objective rule surprisingness measures proposed by this paper in some data mining algorithm(s), in order to evaluate their effectiveness in some real-world data sets.

References

[Cover & Thomas 91] T.M. Cover and J.A. Thomas. *Elements of Information Theory*. John Wiley & Sons, 1991.

[Danyluk & Provost 93] A.P. Danyluk & F.J. Provost. Small disjuncts in action: learning to diagnose errors in the local loop of the telephone network. *Proc. 10th Int. Conf. Machine Learning*, 81-88, 1993.

[Fayyad et al. 96] U.M. Fayyad, G. Piatetsky-Shapiro and P. Smyth. From data mining to knowledge discovery: an overview. In: U.M. Fayyad, G. Piatetsky-Shapiro, P. Smyth and R. Uthurusamy. *Advances in Knowledge Discovery & Data Mining*, 1-34. AAAI/MIT, 1996.

[Gebhardt 91] F. Gebhardt. Choosing among competing generalizations. *Knowledge Acquisit.*, 3, 1991, 361-380.

[Glymour et al. 97]. C. Glymour, D. Madigan, D. Pregibon and P. Smyth. Statistical themes and lessons for data mining. *Data Mining and Knowledge Discovery* 1(1), 11-28. 1997.

[Holte et al. 89] R.C. Holte, L.E. Acker and B.W. Porter. Concept learning and the problem of small disjuncts. *Proc. Int. Joint Conf. AI (IJCAI-89)*, 813-818.

[Kamber & Shinghal 96] M. Kamber & R. Shinghal. Evaluating the interestingness of characteristic rules. *Proc. 2nd Int. Conf. Knowledge Discovery & Data Mining*, 263-266. AAAI, 1996.

[Liu et al. 97] B. Liu, W. Hsu and S. Chen. Using general impressions to analyze discovered classification rules. *Proc. 3rd Int. Conf. Knowl. Disc. & Data Mining*, 31-36. AAAI, 1997.

[Major & Mangano 95]. J.A. Major and J.J. Mangano. Selecting among rules induced from a hurricane database. *J. Intelligent Information Systems* 4(1), Jan./95, 39-52.

[Piatetsky-Shapiro 91] G. Piatetsky-Shapiro. Discovery, analysis and presentation of strong rules. In: G. Piatetsky-Shapiro and W.J. Frawley. *Knowledge Discovery in Databases*, 229-248. AAAI, 1991.

[Provost & Aronis 96] F.J. Provost and J.M. Aronis. Scaling up inductive learning with massive parallelism. *Machine Learning* 23(1), Apr./96, 33-46.

[Simpson 51] E. H. Simpson. The interpretation of interaction in contingency tables. *Journal of the Royal Statistical Society, series B, 13*, 1951, 238-241.

[Ting 94] K.M. Ting. The problem of small disjuncts: its remedy in decision trees. *Proc. 10th Canadian Conf. Artificial Intelligence*, 91-97. 1994.

[Wagner 82] Simpson's paradox in real life. *The Amer. Statist.*, 36(1), Feb./82, 46-48.

Discovery of Surprising Exception Rules
Based on Intensity of Implication

Einoshin Suzuki[1] and Yves Kodratoff[2]

[1] Electrical and Computer Engineering, Yokohama National University,
79-5 Tokiwadai, Hodogaya, Yokohama 240-8501, Japan
[2] Equipe Inference et Apprentisage, Université de Paris-Sud,
91405 Orsay Cedex, France

Abstract. This paper presents an algorithm for discovering surprising exception rules from data sets. An exception rule, which is defined as a deviational pattern to a common sense, exhibits unexpectedness and is sometimes extremely useful. A domain-independent approach, PEDRE, exists for the simultaneous discovery of exception rules and their common sense rules. However, PEDRE, being too conservative, have difficulty in discovering surprising rules. Historic exception discoveries show that surprise is often linked with interestingness. In order to formalize this notion we propose a novel approach by improving PEDRE. First, we reformalize the problem and settle a looser constraints on the reliability of an exception rule. Then, in order to screen out uninteresting rules, we introduce, for an exception rule, an evaluation criterion of surprise by modifying intensity of implication, which is based on significance. Our approach has been validated using data sets from the UCI repository.

1 Introduction

Rule discovery [1, 2, 6, 7, 8, 9, 10] is, due to its generality and simplicity, one of the most important research topics in Knowledge Discovery in Databases (KDD). In KDD, a rule can be classified into two categories: strong rules and weak rules. A strong rule is a description of a regularity for numerous objects with high confidence. On the other hand, a weak rule represents, for a relatively small number of objects, a regularity with high confidence. Typically, strong rule discovery, while useful in recognizing general trends in a data set, results in a set of overly general rules. Finding a widely known rule, such as "most people who buy butter also buy bread", is uninteresting. On the other hand, weak rule discovery can produce extremely interesting results.

Various methods for weak rule discovery have been proposed in KDD community. Some of them [2, 7] try to capture interestingness by using a criterion. Others [6, 8, 9, 10] assume a knowledge representation for this purpose, and seek for chunks of knowledge which deviate from strong rules. Among such rules, an exception rule, which represents a deviation to a strong rule, exhibits unexpectedness and is often useful. For instance, the rule "using a seat belt is risky for a small child", which represents exceptions to the well known regularity "using a seat belt is safe", exhibited unexpectedness when it was discovered from car accident data several years ago, and is still useful. Moreover, an exception rule is often beneficial since it differs from a common sense rule which is often a basis for people's daily activity. For instance, suppose a species of poisonous mushrooms has a small number of exceptions. The exact description of the exceptions is highly beneficial since it enables the exclusive possession of the edible mushrooms.

Simultaneous approach [8, 9, 10], which was proposed by one of us (E. Suzuki), discovers a set of rule pairs each of which is a common sense rule and its exception rule. This approach deserves special attention since it requires neither domain specific criteria nor background knowledge to obtain interesting rules. Especially, the most recent system PEDRE [10], obtains reliable rule pairs.

Careful observation of historical discovery, however, shows that surprise, which was not directly considered in the previous systems represents an important aspect in exception knowledge discovery. For instance, antibiotics are widely known to cure diseases, however, MRSA, a kind of staphylococci, is often resistant to antibiotics in a hospital. Although MRSA is not a dangerous bacteria, people in a hospital, often weakened by other causes, die by taking antibiotics which kill other bacteria and favor MRSA. This phenomenon, when it was observed in the U.S. for the first time, lacked reliability in its generality since only a small number of patients were found in this situation. However, it showed an astonishment to people because it is represented by the conjunction of two very rare events: dying from MRSA and dying by taking antibiotics.

Here, this rule is not easily discovered by PEDRE since a huge number of rule pairs are more reliable. In other words, PEDRE is too conservative in evaluating rules with low reliability to discover surprising exception rules. In order to discover such kind of knowledge, we propose a modified approach of PEDRE which is based on intensity of implication [3]: an evaluation criterion of surprise with several desirable properties. Preliminary results with data sets from the UCI repository [5] are promising.

2 Discovery of Reliable Exceptions: PEDRE [10]

2.1 Reliable Exception

Consider a data set D with n examples each of which is expressed by m discrete attributes. An event representing, in propositional form, a single value assignment to an attribute will be called an atom. We define a conjunction rule as the production rule of which premise is represented by a conjunction of atoms and conclusion is a single atom. Another interesting class of rules is an association rule [1], in which premise and conclusion are a set of examples and all attributes are binary. Conjunction rules have been chosen in PEDRE since they do not assume such restrictions on attributes.

In PEDRE, we consider the problem of finding a set of rule pairs each of which consists of an exception rule associated with a common sense rule. Let a_i, b_j, c and c' be a single atom, where c and c' have the same attribute with different values, then a rule pair $r(\mu, \nu)$ is defined as a pair of conjunction rules as follows:

$$r(\mu, \nu) \equiv \begin{cases} A_\mu & \to c \\ A_\mu \wedge B_\nu \to c'. \end{cases} \tag{1}$$

$$\text{where} \quad A_\mu \equiv a_1 \wedge a_2 \wedge \cdots \wedge a_\mu, \ B_\nu \equiv b_1 \wedge b_2 \wedge \cdots \wedge b_\nu. \tag{2}$$

We hereafter call $A_\mu \to c$, $A_\mu \wedge B_\nu \to c'$ and $B_\nu \to c'$ a common sense rule, an exception rule, and a reference rule respectively.

In discovery of reliable exception rules, both a common sense rule and an exception rule should be general and accurate with some confidence level. It should be also noted that, in an exception rule, the extra condition B_ν should not contribute to the prediction of the conclusion c', unless the exception rule is easily predicted from $B_\nu \to c'$ and is thus uninteresting. Let $1 - \delta$ be a user-provided confidence level, and $\theta_1^S, \theta_2^S, \theta_1^F, \theta_2^F, \theta_2^I$ and M be a user-provided threshold, then the constraints considered in PEDRE for a discovered rule pair are given as follows.

$$\Pr\{ \ p(A_\mu) \geq \theta_1^S, \ p(c|A_\mu) \geq \theta_1^F, \ p(A_\mu, B_\nu) \geq \theta_2^S, \ p(c'|A_\mu, B_\nu) \geq \theta_2^F,$$
$$p(c'|B_\nu) \leq \theta_2^I \ \} \geq 1 - \delta. \tag{3}$$
$$\mu, \nu \ \leq M. \tag{4}$$

For resolving (3), we should estimate the confidence region of the probabilities related to (3). Normal approximations of a multinomial distribution is a natural choice for this purpose. It is shown that the following equations are equivalent to (3) [10].

$$G\left(A_\mu\right)\hat{p}(A_\mu) \geq \theta_1^S, \ F(A_\mu, c)\hat{p}(c|A_\mu) \geq \theta_1^F, \ G(A_\mu, B_\nu)\hat{p}(A_\mu, B_\nu) \geq \theta_2^S,$$
$$F\left(A_\mu B_\nu, c'\right)\hat{p}(c'|A_\mu, B_\nu) \geq \theta_2^F, \ F(B_\nu, c')\hat{p}(c'|B_\nu) \leq \theta_2^I, \tag{5}$$

where,

$$G(x) \equiv 1 - \beta\sqrt{\frac{1 - \hat{p}(x)}{n\hat{p}(x)}}, \ F(x, y) \equiv 1 - \beta\sqrt{\frac{\hat{p}(x) - \hat{p}(x, y)}{\hat{p}(x, y)\{(n + \beta^2)\hat{p}(x) - \beta^2\}}}, \tag{6}$$

and β is a positive constant related to the confidence level [10].

2.2 Search Algorithm

In PEDRE, a discovery task is viewed as a search problem, in which a node of a search tree represents a rule pair $r(\mu, \nu)$. Let $\mu = 0$ and $\nu = 0$ represent the state in which the premises of a rule pair $r(\mu, \nu)$ contain no a_i and no b_i respectively, then we define that $\mu = \nu = 0$ holds in a node of depth 1, and as the depth increases by 1, an atom is added to the premise of the exception rule or the common sense rule. A node of depth 2 is assumed to satisfy $\mu = 1$, $\nu = 0$, and a node of depth $l \ (\geq 3)$, $\mu + \nu = l - 1 \ (\mu \geq 1, \ \nu \geq 0)$.

A depth-first search method is employed to traverse this tree, and the maximum value M of μ and ν is given by the user. To improve search efficiency, a node which satisfies at least one of the stopping criteria (7) in theorem 1 is not expanded without altering the algorithm's output.

Theorem 1. *Let the rule pair of the current node be $r(\mu', \nu')$. If the rule pair satisfies an equation in (7), no rule pairs $r(\mu, \nu)$ of the descendant nodes satisfy (5).*

$$G\left(A_{\mu'}\right)\hat{p}(A_{\mu'}) < \theta_1^S, \;\; G(A_{\mu'})\hat{p}(c, A_{\mu'}) < \theta_1^S\theta_1^F, \;\; G(A_{\mu'}, B_{\nu'})\hat{p}(A_{\mu'}, B_{\nu'}) < \theta_2^S,$$

$$G\left(A_{\mu'}, B_{\nu'}\right)\hat{p}(c', A_{\mu'}, B_{\nu'}) < \theta_2^S\theta_2^F, \;\; G(A_{\mu'}, B_{\nu'})\hat{p}(B_{\nu'}) < \frac{\theta_2^S\theta_2^F}{\theta_2^I}. \tag{7}$$

Proof Each equation can be proved by contradiction using that the function $G(x)$ increases monotonously for $\hat{p}(x)$ since $n, \beta > 0$. $\square$

3 Measures for Surprising Exceptions

3.1 Reformalization of Problem

As mentioned in Introduction, PEDRE is appropriate for the discovery of reliable exceptions, but fails to capture the surprise of an exception rule. For instance, table 1 [10] shows a rule pair discovered by PEDRE, where the edibility class is the only attribute allowed in the conclusions and the parameters were set to $M = 3$, $\delta = 0.1$, $\theta_1^S = 0.2$, $\theta_2^S = 0.05$, $\theta_1^F = 0.7$, $\theta_2^F = 1.0$ and $\theta_2^I = 0.5$.

Table 1. A rule pair with its associated reference rule discovered by PEDRE from the mushroom data set, where the edibility class is the only attribute allowed in the conclusions. Here, $\uparrow p$ and $\downarrow p$ represent the upper and lower bound of p respectively.

common sense rule exception rule rererence rule	$\downarrow p(A_\mu)$ $\downarrow p(A_\mu B_\nu)$	$\downarrow p(c\|A_\mu)$ $\downarrow p(c'\|A_\mu B_\nu)$ $\uparrow p(c'\|B_\nu)$
b=f, gs=b, sts=e → class=p	0.213	0.703
b=f, gs=b, sts=e, str=v → class=e	0.051	1.000
str=v → class=e		0.318

We see that the rule pair in the table shows interesting exceptions. However, the accuracy of the common sense rule is relatively small: its lower bound value is 0.703. We attribute this to the high reliability of the exception rule since it has a negative effect on the accuracy of a common sense rule. In PEDRE, a common sense rule cannot have a high accuracy unless the user assumes a low value for δ, θ_1^S and θ_1^F. In other words, PEDRE has lost surprise while gaining reliability.

In order to discover truly surprising exception rules, we reformalize the constraints (3), and consider point-estimated probabilities $\hat{p}(A_\mu, B_\nu)$ and $\hat{p}(c'|A_\mu, B_\nu)$ instead of true probabilities $p(A_\mu, B_\nu)$ and $p(c'|A_\mu, B_\nu)$.

$$\Pr\left\{p(A_\mu) \geq \theta_1^S, \ p(c|A_\mu) \geq \theta_1^F, \ p(c'|A_\mu, B_\nu) \leq \theta_2^I\right\} \geq 1 - \delta. \tag{8}$$

$$\hat{p}\ (A_\mu, B_\nu) \geq \theta_2^S, \ \hat{p}(c'|A_\mu, B_\nu) \geq \theta_2^F, \tag{9}$$

$$\mu + \nu \leq M. \tag{10}$$

While this modification makes our approach less tolerant to noise, it generates an increasing number of rule pairs due to the looser restrictions on the generality and accuracy of an exception rule. Constraints on the length of premises are slightly modified in order to keep the computation time reasonable. Similarly as in the previous section, the following equations are equivalent to (8).

$$G(A_\mu)\hat{p}(A_\mu) \geq \theta_1^S, \ F(A_\mu, c)\hat{p}(c|A_\mu) \geq \theta_1^F, \ F(B_\nu, c')\hat{p}(c'|B_\nu) \leq \theta_2^I. \tag{11}$$

3.2 Evaluation of Surprise

Since this reformalization of the problem increases the numbers of discovered rule pairs, an evaluation criterion of surprise is introduced to screen out rule pairs of minor interest.

Intensity of implication [3] is an evaluation criterion of surprise for a rule. It represents the degree of surprise that a rule $A_\mu \to c$ has so few counter examples. Let U and V be a randomly-selected set whose number of observation $|U|$ and $|V|$ in data set D is equal to those of $|c|$ and $|A_\mu|$ respectively

$$|U| = |c|, \ |V| = |A_\mu|, \tag{12}$$

then an intensity of implication $\varphi(A_\mu, c, D)$ for this rule is given as follows.

$$\varphi(A_\mu, c, D) \equiv 1 - \Pr(|\overline{U}V| \leq |\overline{c}A_\mu|). \tag{13}$$

Assuming that U and V are independent, the random variable $|\overline{U}V|$ follows the hypergeometric law. Poisson approximations can be applied when $|\overline{U}V|$ is small [4], which is often the case in rule discovery.

$$\varphi(A_\mu, c, D) = 1 - \sum_{k=max(0,|A_\mu|-|c|)}^{|\overline{c}A_\mu|} H(A_\mu, c, D, k) \tag{14}$$

$$\approx 1 - \sum_{k=0}^{|\overline{c}A_\mu|} \frac{\lambda^k}{k!} e^{-\lambda}, \tag{15}$$

$$\text{where } H(A_\mu, c, D, k) \equiv \frac{\binom{|c|}{|A_\mu| - k}\binom{|\overline{c}|}{k}}{\binom{n}{|A_\mu|}}, \qquad \lambda \equiv \frac{|A_\mu|(n - |c|)}{n} \tag{16}$$

Since intensity of implication is based on a statistical significance $\Pr(|\overline{U}V| \leq |\overline{c}A_\mu|)$, its definition is easier to be interpreted than an information-based criterion such as J measure [7]. This definition shows that intensity of implication increases as the number of counter examples $|\overline{c}A_\mu|$ decreases. Moreover, intensity of implication has the desirable property of evaluating the reliability of a rule according to the size of a data set: it increases as n increases. Also, it evaluates the rareness of the conclusion that a rule predicts: it increases as $|c|$ decreases. A detailed analysis of this criterion is given in [2].

Let consider a direct application of intensity of implication to the evaluation of an exception rule. First, we should replace n by $|A_\mu|$ since the premise of a common sense rule can be considered as the universe for an exception rule. Similarly, A_μ and c are replaced by $A_\mu B_\nu$ and $c'A_\mu$ respectively. Therefore, the intensity of implication for an exception rule in a rule pair $r(\mu,\nu)$ is given by $\varphi(A_\mu B_\nu, c'A_\mu, A_\mu)$.

$$\varphi(A_\mu B_\nu, c'A_\mu, A_\mu) = 1 - \sum_{k=0}^{|\overline{c'}A_\mu B_\nu|} \frac{\lambda'^k}{k!} e^{-\lambda'} \tag{17}$$

$$\text{where } \lambda' \equiv \frac{|A_\mu B_\nu|(|A_\mu| - |c'A_\mu|)}{|A_\mu|} \tag{18}$$

Let examine this criterion in the context of exception knowledge discovery. If we have a large number of exception rules each of which covers more than 20 examples $|A_\mu B_\nu| \geq 20$, then its λ' is also nearly 20. If these rules have few counter examples $|\overline{c'}A_\mu B_\nu|$, which is often the case, their intensity of implication is all equal to 1. Therefore, the intensity of implication $\varphi(A_\mu B_\nu, c'A_\mu, A_\mu)$ is inappropriate for ranking exception rules according to their degree of surprise.

To overcome this problem, we propose a modified version of this criterion. The idea is to take the logarithm of the probability of having so few counter examples in order to have a precise view when this probability is nearly 0. The criterion of surprise $\varphi'(A_\mu B_\nu, c'A_\mu, A_\mu)$ for an exception rule in this paper is given as follows.

$$\varphi'(A_\mu B_\nu, c'A_\mu, A_\mu) \equiv -\ln\left(\sum_{k=0}^{|\overline{c'}A_\mu B_\nu|} \frac{\lambda'^k}{k!} e^{-\lambda'} \right) \tag{19}$$

where $\ln(x)$ represents the natural logarithm of x. Note that this criterion is equal to λ' when an exception rule has no counter examples ($|\overline{c'}A_\mu B_\nu| = 0$).

3.3 Search Algorithm

Similarly to PEDRE, the proposed approach employs a depth-first search to traverse a search tree for obtaining rule pairs which satisfy (9) $\sim$ (11) and which have the K highest $\varphi'(A_\mu B_\nu, c'A_\mu, A_\mu)$. A theorem similar to theorem 1 holds in this search problem.

Theorem 2. *Let the rule pair of the current node be $r(\mu', \nu')$. If the rule pair satisfies an equation in (20) or (21), no rule pairs $r(\mu, \nu)$ of the descendant nodes satisfy (9) and (11).*

$$G\left(A_{\mu'}\right)\hat{p}(A_{\mu'}) < \theta_1^S, \ G(A_{\mu'})\hat{p}(c, A_{\mu'}) < \theta_1^S\theta_1^F, \tag{20}$$
$$\hat{p}\left(A_{\mu'}, B_{\nu'}\right) < \theta_2^S, \ \hat{p}(c', A_{\mu'}, B_{\nu'}) < \theta_2^S\theta_2^F \tag{21}$$

Proof First, the proof for (20) is equivalent to theorem 1. Second, (21) is derived from $\hat{p}(A_{\mu'}, B_{\nu'}) \geq \hat{p}(A_{\mu}, B_{\nu})$ and $\hat{p}(c', A_{\mu'}, B_{\nu'}) \geq \hat{p}(c', A_{\mu}, B_{\nu})$. $\square$

An improvement to PEDRE is that a node represents not only a rule pair $\{A_\mu \rightarrow c \ \& \ A_\mu, B_\nu \rightarrow c'\}$, but also $\{A_\mu \rightarrow c' \ \& \ A_\mu, B_\nu \rightarrow c\}$, $\{B_\nu \rightarrow c \ \& \ B_\nu, A_\mu \rightarrow c'\}$, and $\{B_\nu \rightarrow c' \ \& \ B_\nu, A_\mu \rightarrow c\}$. Since these 4 rule pairs employ similar atoms in calculating (9) $\sim$ (11) and (20) $\sim$ (21), this fourfold representation improves time efficiency. A 4-bit flag is employed to represent which rule pairs are considered in a node of a search tree.

4 Application to Data Sets

The proposed method was implemented and tested with data sets from several domains. The results were quite successful. Here, we show the results using the mushroom data set and the shuttle data set from the UCI Repository [5].

The mushroom data set includes 22 descriptions and the edibility class of 8,124 mushrooms, each attribute having 2 $\sim$ 12 values. Table 2 shows the rule pairs discovered by our approach, where the edibility class is the only attribute allowed in the conclusions and the parameters were set to $M = 3$, $\delta = 0.1$, $\theta_1^S = 0.2$, $\theta_2^S = 40/8124$, $\theta_1^F = 0.8$, $\theta_2^F = 1.0$, $\theta_2^I = 0.5$ and $K = 5$.

The discovered rule pairs in the table show very interesting exceptions. According to the first rule pair, with 90 % confidence level, at least 86.6 % of the mushrooms whose "gs" is "n" are poisonous but 100 % of them are actually edible if "sts" is "e" and "p" is "y". The first rule holds for at least 2,388 mushrooms (29.4 %). Note that, from the reference rule, only at most 28.0 % of the mushrooms whose "sts" is "e" and "p" is "y" are edible. This shows that the discovered exception rule is truly unexpected. Compared with the rule pair discovered by PEDRE (table 1), each rule pair in this table has a stronger common sense rule, and thus a more surprising exception rule. These results confirm the validity of our approach.

The shuttle data set includes 10 descriptions of 58,000 examples, each attribute having 3 to 8 values. Table 3 shows the rule pairs discovered by our approach, where the parameters were set to $M = 3$, $\delta = 0.1$, $\theta_1^S = 0.2$, $\theta_2^S = 50/58,000$, $\theta_1^F = 0.7$, $\theta_2^F = 1.0$, $\theta_2^I = 0.5$ and $K = 5$.

The discovered rule pairs in the table also show very interesting exceptions. According to the second rule pair, with 90 % confidence level, at least 83.6 % of the examples whose "att9 = 2" have "att8 = 1" but 100 % of them actually have "att8 = 0" if "att2 = 1" and "att7 = 0". The first rule holds for at least 19,836 examples (34.2 %). Note that, from the reference rule, only at most 27.7 % of

Table 2. The rule pairs discovered from the mushroom data set, where the edibility class is the only attribute allowed in the conclusions.

No.	common sense rule exception rule reference rule	$\downarrow p(A_\mu)$ $\lvert c'A_\mu B_\nu\rvert$ $\varphi'(A_\mu B_\nu, c'A_\mu, A_\mu)$	$\downarrow p(c\lvert A_\mu)$ $\hat{p}(c'\lvert A_\mu B_\nu)$ $\uparrow p(c'\lvert B_\nu)$
	gs = n → class = p	0.294	0.866
1	gs = n, sts = e, p = y → class = e	72	1.000
	sts = e, p = y → class = e	63.7	0.280
	gs = n → class = p	0.294	0.866
2	gs = n, b = f, p = y → class = e	72	1.000
	b = f, p = y → class = e	63.7	0.156
	gs = n → class = p	0.295	0.868
3	gs = n, gsp = c, ssb = f → class = e	48	1.000
	gsp = c, ssb = f → class = e	42.4	0.339
	gs = n → class = p	0.294	0.866
4	gs = n, str = b, scb = n → class = e	48	1.000
	str = b, scb = n → class = e	42.4	0.175
	gs = n → class = p	0.295	0.868
4	gs = n, spc = h→ class = e	48	1.000
	spc = h→ class = e	42.4	0.041

Table 3. The rule pairs discovered from the shuttle data set.

No.	common sense rule exception rule reference rule	$\downarrow p(A_\mu)$ $\lvert c'A_\mu B_\nu\rvert$ $\varphi'(A_\mu B_\nu, c'A_\mu, A_\mu)$	$\downarrow p(c\lvert A_\mu)$ $\hat{p}(c'\lvert A_\mu B_\nu)$ $\uparrow p(c'\lvert B_\nu)$
	time = 0 → att7 = 2	0.678	0.729
1	time = 0, att3 = 2 → att7 = 3	2,400	1.000
	att3 = 2 → att7 = 3	1766.3	0.343
	att9 = 2 → att8 = 1	0.342	0.836
2	att9 = 2, att2 = 1, att7 = 0 → att8 = 0	555	1.000
	att2 = 1, att7 = 0 → att8 = 0	511.0	0.277
	att9 = 2 → att8 = 1	0.342	0.836
3	att9 = 2, att2 = 1, Class = 4 → att8 = 0	554	1.000
	att2 = 1, Class = 4 → att8 = 0	510.1	0.276
	att5 = 2 → att7 = 2	0.861	0.736
4	att5 = 2, att8 = 2 → att7 = 3	94	1.000
	att8 = 2 → att7 = 3	73.9	0.058
	att7 = 2 → time = 0	0.681	0.726
5	att7 = 2, att2 = 1, att3 = 3 → time = 2	59	1.000
	att2 = 1, att3 = 3 → time = 2	46.0	0.127

the examples which satisfy "att2 = 1" and "att7 = 0" have "att8 = 0". This shows that the discovered exception rule is truly unexpected and surprising.

5 Conclusion

This paper has described a novel approach for discovering surprising exception rules using a simultaneous estimation method and a modified version of intensity of implication. The approach depends on neither a subjective evaluation nor an inspection of the reliability by a human. An exception rule discovered in this approach deviates from a strong common sense rule, has few counter examples and predicts a rare conclusion. Consequently, our exception knowledge discovery system, compared with PEDRE [10], is oriented to the discovery of surprising exception rules rather than reliable exception rules. We believe that both approaches are valuable, and should be used according to the goal of discovery.

Our approach has been applied to several benchmark data sets in the machine learning community. Experimental results show that our system is promising for the efficient discovery of surprising exception rules. Ongoing research is focused on the comparison of various rule evaluation criteria and practical applications of our approach to large databases.

References

1. Agrawal, R., Mannila, H., Srikant, R. *et al.*: Fast Discovery of Association Rules, *Advances in Knowledge Discovery and Data Mining*, AAAI Press/The MIT Press (1996) 307–328
2. Fleury, L., Djeraba, C., Briand, H. and Philippé, J.: Rule Evaluations in a KDD System, *Database and Expert Systems Applications*, Springer-Verlag (1995) 405–414
3. Gras, R. and Lahrer, A.: L'Implication Statistique: une Nouvelle Methode d'Analyse de Données, *Mathematiques, Informatique et Sciences Humaines*, **120** (1993) 5–31.
4. Lerman, I. C., Gras, R. and Rostam, H.: Elaboration et Evaluation d'un Indice d'Implication pour Données Binaire, *Mathematiques, Informatique et Sciences Humaines*, **74** (1981) 5–35
5. Merz, C. J. and Murphy, P. M.: UCI Repository of machine learning databases, *http://www.ics.uci.edu/~mlearn/MLRepository.html*, Univ. of California, Dept. of Information and Computer Sci. (1998)
6. Silberschatz, A. and Tuzhilin, A.: On Subjective Measures of Interestingness in Knowledge Discovery, *Proc. of KDD-95* (1995) 275–281
7. Smyth, P. and Goodman, R. M.: An Information Theoretic Approach to Rule Induction from Databases, *IEEE Trans. on Knowledge and Data Eng.*, **4** (4) (1992) 301–316
8. Suzuki, E. and Shimura, M.: Exceptional Knowledge Discovery in Databases based on Information Theory, *Proc. of KDD-96* (1996) 275–278
9. Suzuki, E.: Discovering Unexpected Exceptions: A Stochastic Approach, *Proc. of RSFD-96* (1996) 225–232
10. Suzuki, E.: Autonomous Discovery of Reliable Exception Rules, *Proc. of KDD-97* (1997) 259–262

A Metric for Selection of the Most Promising Rules

Pedro Gago[1,2] and Carlos Bento[2]

[1] Escola Superior de Tecnologia e Gestão do Instituto Politécnico de Leiria
Morro do Lena, Alto Vieiro, 2400 Leiria
pgago@estg.iplei.pt
[2] CISUC - Centro de Informática e Sistemas da Universidade de Coimbra
Polo II, 3030 Coimbra
pgago,bento@eden.dei.uc.pt

Abstract. The process of Knowledge Discovery in Databases pursues the goal of extracting useful knowledge from large amounts of data. It comprises a pre-processing step, application of a data-mining algorithm and post-processing of results. When rule induction is applied for data-mining one must be prepared to deal with the generation of a large number of rules. In these circumstances it is important to have a way of selecting the rules that have the highest predictive power. We propose a metric for selection of the n rules with the highest average distance between them. We defend that applying our metric to select the rules that are more distant improves the system prediction capabilities against other criteria for rule selection. We present an application example and empirical results produced from a synthesized data set on a financial domain.

1 Introduction

The process of Knowledge Discovery in Databases pursues the goal of extracting useful knowledge from large amounts of data. It comprises a pre-processing step, application of a data-mining algorithm and post-processing of the results.

When rule induction is applied for data-mining one must be prepared to deal with the generation of a large number of rules. In these circumstances it is important to have a way of selecting the rules that have the highest predictive power.

The selection of interesting rules faces an essentially subjective problem. It is not likely that two different users will find the same rules to be interesting. Some authors support decisions on interestingness on subjective information provided by the user (Liu, Hsu and Chen [4], Klementinen, Mannila, Ronkainen, Toivonen and Verkamo [3]; Piatesky-Shapiro and Matheus [7]; Silberschatz and Tuzhilin [8]), other authors (Kamber and Shinghal [2]; Piatesky-Shapiro [6]; Major and Mangano [5]; Srikant and Agrawal [9]) choose to look for objective measures for rule interestingness. Some of those measures are simplicity, statistical significance, coverage and confidence.

Within our work the goal is not to decide on the individual interestingness of rules. Our aim is to build a set of rules that together gives a good coverage of the search space. We build on work on creativity (Gomes, Bento, Gago and Costa [1]) where a measure for the distance between cases is developed. We propose a metric for distance between two rules and use it to select the most heterogeneous set of rules that is possible in the assumption that this set has high predictive capabilities.

We present an example on a database of fictional data on bank clients. From the client database, rules are generated describing the 'good' and 'bad' clients. We use our metric on the rules to select n heterogeneous rules supposed to be the n rules that globally have the highest prediction power. Finally we present the results obtained using these rules and compare them with the use of the same number of rules selected randomly.

2 A Metric for Distance Between Two Rules

The rules are of the form 'IF *conditions* THEN *conclusion*'. *Conditions* is a conjunction of terms in the form $a_1 s_1 v_1 \wedge ... \wedge a_n s_n v_n$ with A={$A_1, ..., A_t$} a set of attributes and S={$<, <=, >, >=, =$} a set of comparison operators, $a_i \in$ A, $s_i \in$ S and v_i being a numeric value. *Conclusion* is a class $c_i \in$ C with C={$c_1, ..., c_m$}, a set of classes.

The measure we propose for distance between two rules with the same conclusion is based on three factors:

1. the number of attributes in one rule and absent in the other,
2. the number of attributes in both rules with overlapping values,
3. the number of attributes in both rules with values slight or null overlapping.

Based on these features we propose the following distance metric:

$$dist\,(r_i, r_j) = \begin{cases} \dfrac{\alpha \ \#DA_{i,j} + \beta \ \#DV_{i,j} - \omega \ \#EV_{i,j}}{\#F_i + \#F_j} & \text{if } \#NO_{i,j} = 0 \\ \\ 2 & \text{otherwise} \end{cases}$$

In this metric we have:

$\#DA_{i,j}$ Number of attributes in rule i and not in rule j plus the number of attributes in rule j and not in rule i.

$\#NO_{i,j}$ Number of attributes both in rule i and in rule j but with non overlapping values.

$\#DV_{i,j}$ Number of attributes both in rule i and in rule j, but with slightly overlapping values (we consider an overlapping bellow 66%).

$\#EV_{i,j}$ Number of attributes in both rules, with overlapping values (we consider an overlapping above 66%).

$\#F_i + \#F_j$ Number of attributes in rule i plus the number of attributes in rule j.

For attributes appearing in both rules we check the intersection of their values. If there is no intersection we know the two rules cannot be applied to the same cases and thus we assign a value of two for the distance between the rules. We chose value two as it is a value higher than the one assigned in any other situation. In the case we have an intersection in less than 66% of the range of the rules values we consider the respective attributes to behave as if they were different attributes. We consider an attribute in two rules to be equal if the intersection of values in these rules is over 66% of the range of possible values.

To illustrate this concept of overlapping attributes consider that we have the attribute A appearing in two rules (Rule #1: A>=20 AND A<=70, Rule #2: A>=40): We can apply rule 1 when the values for attribute A are between 20 and 70 and can apply rule 2 if the values for attribute A are over 40 (see Fig. 1). Consider that the upper and lower limit for this attribute value is, respectively, 0 and 100.

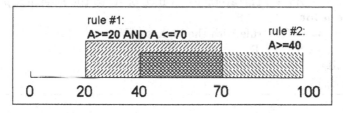

Fig. 1. Overlapping of an attribute in two rules.

We want to know if we can consider the conditions in both rules as equal. Suppose we have more rules with attribute A and that the highest value attribute A has in any of those rules is 100. For attribute A in rule 1 the range of possible values is 70-20 = 50. In rule 2 the range is 100-40 = 60 (100 is the maximum value for attribute A). The overlapping range for values in both rules is 70-40 = 30. This overlapping happens in 30/50 = 60% of the range of possible values for attribute A in rule 1 and in 30/60 = 50% of the range of possible values for attribute A in rule 2. If we average the intervals of overlapping in the two rules we get 55%. As this value is below 66% we consider attribute A in rule 1 and attribute A in rule 2 as if they were different attributes.

In the distance metric the characteristics which are strongly different between the two rules ($\#DA_{i,j}$ and $\#DV_{i,j}$) increase the value returned by the function. The ones appearing in both rules ($\#EV_{i,j}$) decrease the function value. The terms $\#DA_{i,j}$, $\#DV_{i,j}$ and $\#EV_{i,j}$ are weighed by constants α, β and ω. We use $\alpha=1$, $\beta=2$ and $\omega=2$, making the metric take values between minus one and one. A value of one relates to two rules that have few things in common whereas a value of minus one indicates that the rules overlap strongly. When we are absolutely sure that the rules do not overlap the metric returns a value of two.

3 Rule Selection

We use the metric described in the previous section for selection of the n rules that provide the highest coverage for a data set. We pursue this goal by looking for the rules most different from the ones selected till now. We believe those rules to be the ones that provide, in general, the best coverage for the data set.

Considering the original set of classification rules to be S we must apply the following algorithm in order to build the set of n rules which are more distant between each other. We use as distance criteria the one provided by the distance function described in the previous section. We name this set of rules S_R.

Algorithm RuleSelect(S, n)
    R ← The rule with the highest average distance to the other rules in S;
    S_R ← R;
    While #S_R < n **do**
        for each rule R' in S and not in S_R
            AV ← The average distance of R' to the rules in S_R ;
        endfor
        R_{max} ← The rule with the highest AV;
        S_R ← S_R ∪ { R_{max} };
    endwhile
    return(S_R) .

If we look for the rules with the lowest average distance we get the set of the rules closest to each other and we assume this set to be the least representative ruleset S_L.

4 Domain Description

Our rule selection heuristic was tested in the domain of loan analysis. We synthesized a database with 3000 entries describing bank clients. The database was split in 2000 cases for training and 1000 for testing. For each client we know its yearly income, size of household, assets owned and amount to be paid per year. The database contains also information on whether the client presented a surety and on whether he is on a contract. The classification field in the database tells us if the client is a 'good' or 'bad' client. The following table shows the available information for three clients.

The independent attribute values were generated using the uniform distribution. The dependent attribute status is labeled 'Good' or 'Bad'. Status is assigned 'Good' or 'Bad' accordingly to two simple criteria: (1) if a client's available money (income minus loan) is over 500 units per household member then the client will honor his debts ((Income-Loan)/Household > 500); (2) 10% of the clients on a contract are 'Bad' clients. We do not consider noisy data.

C4.5 is used on this database for rule generation.

23

Table 1. Three cases

Income	Household	Assets	Loan	Surety	Contract	Status
7000	4	21000	3100	No	No	Good
4100	1	3000	400	No	No	Good
7500	4	8000	2300	No	Yes	Bad

5 An Example

We considered the 14 rules generated by C4.5 (see appendix) for illustration of
our approach. We describe how the distance between two rules is calculated on
three rules in the set of 14 initial rules and show the results returned by the
distance function (see Fig. 2).

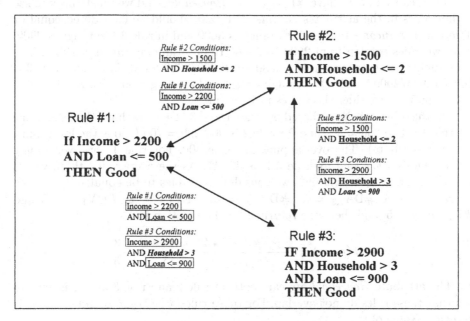

Fig. 2. Three rules generated by C4.5.

In order to determine the overlapping percentage for each attribute in the
rules we need to know the range of values for this attribute. From the ruleset we
have that the lowest value for *Income* is 1500, the highest being 5800. The *Loan*
attribute ranges between 200 and 2900.

Rules 1 and 2 have two distinct attributes - *Loan* and *Household*. The attribute *Income* appears in both rules. We have to determine the intersection for
the values for this attribute.

Rule 1 may be used when *Income* is between 2200 and 5800 (the upper
limit). For this rule the range is 5800 - 2200 = 3600. For rule 2 the range is

5800 - 1500 = 4300. Rules 1 and 2 overlap from 2200 to 5800. The overlapping range of these rules is 5800 - 2200 = 3600. The rules overlap in all the range of the first rule. The overlapping percentage for attribute *Income* in rule 1 is 3600 / 3600 * 100 % = 100%. For rule 2 the overlapping takes place in 3600 / 4300 * 100% = 83.7 % of the range covered by the attribute *Income*. When we average these values we get (100 % + 83.7 %) / 2 = 91.85 %. As the value obtained is over 66% we consider the values in both rules to be equal.

We can now calculate the value returned by the distance function considering that $\#DA_{1,2} = 2$ (*Household* and *Loan*), $\#NO_{1,2} = 0$, $\# DV_{1,2} = 0$, $\#EV_{1,2} = 1$ and $\#F_1 + \#F_2 = 4$.

The value returned for $dist(r_1, r_2)$ is:

$$dist(r_1, r_2) = \frac{2 + 2 * 0 - 2 * 1}{4} = \frac{2 - 2}{4} = 0$$

For rules 1 and 3 we have $\#DA_{1,3} = 1$ (*Household*) and we must check to see if the values in the attributes *Income* and *Loan* should be considered equal or different. For *Income* in rule 1 the range is 3600 and in rule 3 the range is 2900. The two rules overlap from 2900 to 5800 (the overlapping range is 2900). The overlapping percentage for rule 1 is 80.5% (2900/3600 * 100 %) and for rule 3 is 100% (2900/2900 * 100 %). Averaging these values we get 90.25%. As the value is over 66% we consider the values to be equal.

For the other attribute shared by rules 1 and 3 (*Loan*) we have that the range for rule 1 is 500-200 = 300 and for rule 2 is 900-200 = 700 (200 is the lower limit for this attribute). The overlapping range is 300. For rule 1 the overlapping percentage is 100% and for rule 3 it is 42.8%. As the average for these values (71.4%) is once again over 66% we consider the values to be equal.

So, we have $\#DA_{1,3} = 1$, $\#DV_{1,3} = 0$, $\#EV_{1,3} = 2$, $\#OV_{1,3} = 0$ and $\#F_1 + \#F_3 = 5$, and the value returned by the function is:

$$dist(r_1, r_3) = \frac{1 + 2 * 0 - 2 * 2}{5} = \frac{1 - 4}{5} = -\frac{3}{5}$$

The attribute *Household* appears both in rule 2 and rule 3 and it is easy to see that these rules do not overlap. For these rules $\#NO_{2,3} \neq 0$ and the metric returns a value of two.

$$dist(r_2, r_3) = 2$$

Rules 1 and 2 share one attribute with values very much alike. Rules 1 and 3 have two attributes with almost equal values and only one that is different. These results agree with our intuitive knowledge that rule 2 is "much farther" from rule 3 than from rule 1 and that rules 1 and 3 are very close.

In our example, the rule with the highest average distance to the others is rule 2 (the average distance is one) and it will be the first in set S_R. The second rule in S_R will be rule 3 as it is the rule with the highest distance to the rule already in S_R (rule 2).

6 Empirical Results

We applied our algorithm for rule selection to 14 rules (see appendix) to get the set S_R of the most promising rules. We also considered a set with the least representative rules S_L and several sets of rules chosen at random S_{RA}.

Using our program we built sets S_R and S_L with sizes from 1 to 8. Using the 1000 cases for testing we measured the coverage for S_R and S_L function of the number n of rules in these sets. We also determined the average coverage of randomly chosen groups of rules denominated S_{RA}. The results are presented in the graph in Fig. 3.

When considering the sets S_R, S_{RA} and S_L with a number n of rules near half the number in the original ruleset we see that the rules in S_R have a higher prediction power than those in S_{RA} and in S_L. We also note that the rules in S_L are consistently the ones with the lowest predictive power.

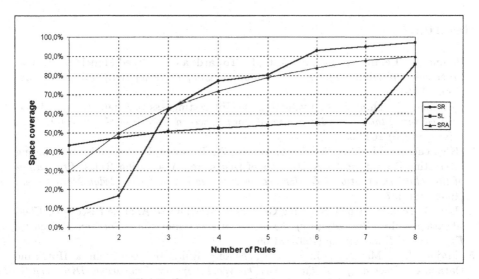

Fig. 3. Comparison of the sets coverage.

7 Conclusions and Future Work

We developed a method for rule selection that consistently outperforms random choice. Using this method one can reduce the time spent analyzing uninteresting rules and concentrate on the best ones. Unlike previous work (Kamber and Shinghal [2]; Piatesky-Shapiro [6]; Major and Mangano [5]; Srikant and Agrawal [9]) we do not try to measure the interestingness of a rule. We use our metric to measure the distance between any two rules in order to build a set with the rules with the highest predictive power.

One of the problems found within our framework is the difficulty in the assignment of weights for our metric. For now this selection is guided by the fact that these values make the metric take values between minus one and one. We believe our approach is domain independent as long as the underlying data are uniformly distributed.

This method for rule selection works well if the underlying data follow a uniform distribution. If the data follow other distributions one must adjust the algorithm that allows us to calculate the range of the interception between two rules. One of the next steps is to adapt the metric to make it work with normally distributed data. It would also be interesting to explore the behavior of the metric when it has available domain knowledge concerning the upper and lower limits for the values of each attribute without having to guess them from the induced rules. For now our program looks at the rules in order to find values it may use as limits. We will probably get better results if we ask the user to provide us with an upper and lower limits for the attributes values.

References

1. Gomes, P., Bento, C., Gago, P., Costa, E.: Towards a Case-Based Model for Creative Processes. *Proceedings of the 12 th European Conference on Artificial Intelligence* (1996) 122-126.
2. Kamber, M., Shingal, R.: Evaluating the Interestingness of Characteristic Rules. *Proceedings of the Second International Conference on Knowledge Discovery & Data Mining* (1995) 263-266.
3. Klementinen, M., Mannila, H., Ronkainen, P., Toivonen, H., Verkamo, A.: Finding Interesting Rules from Large Datasets of Discovered Association Rules. *Proceedings of the Third International Conference on Information and Knowledge Management* (1994) 401-407.
4. Liu, B., Hsu, W., Chen, S.: Using General Impressions to Analyse Discovered Classification Rules. *Proceedings of the Third International Conference on Knowledge Discovery & Data Mining* (1997) 31-36.
5. Major, J.A., Mangano, J.: Selecting Among Rules Induced from a Hurricane Database. *Proceedings of the AAAI-93 Workshop on Knowledge Discovery in Databases* (1993) 28-44.
6. Piatesky-Shapiro, G.: Discovery, Analysis and Presentation of Strong Rules. *G. Piatesky-Shapiro & W.J. Frawley, eds., Knowledge Discovery in Databases. Menlo Park, CA: AAAI/MIT Press.* (1991) 229-248.
7. Piatesky-Shapiro, G., Matheus, C.J.: The Interestingness of Deviations. *Proceedings of the AAAI-94 Workshop on Knowledge Discovery in Databases* (1994) 25-36.
8. Silberschatz, A., Tuzhilin, A.: What Makes Paterns Interesting in Knowledge Discovery Systems. *IEEE Trans. On Know. and Data Eng. 8(6)* (1996) 970-974.
9. Srikant, R., Agrawal, R.: Mining Generalized Association Rules. *Proceedings of the 21st VLDB conference* (1995) 407-419

Appendix - The rules generated by C4.5.

Rule #1:
  if Income > 5600
  and Contract = 0
  then Good

Rule #2:
  if Income > 4100
  and Assets <= 28000
  and Surety = 0
  and Contract = 0
  then Good

Rule #3:
  if Income > 5800
  then Good

Rule #4:
  if Income > 3600
  and Loan <= 1800
  then Good

Rule #5:
  if Income > 4500
  and Loan <= 2900
  then Good

Rule #6:
  if Income > 3100
  and Loan <= 1300
  then Good

Rule #7:
  if Income > 2900
  and Household <= 3
  then Good

Rule #8:
  if Income > 2900
  and Household > 3
  and Loan <= 900
  then Good

Rule #9:
  if Income > 1500
  and Household <= 3
  and Loan <= 200
  then Good

Rule #10:
  if Income > 1500
  and Household <= 2
  then Good

Rule #11:
  if Income > 2300
  and Household <= 3
  and Loan <= 1100
  then Good

Rule #12:
  if Income > 1900
  and Household <= 3
  and Loan <= 700
  then Good

Rule #13:
  if Income > 2200
  and Loan <= 500
  then Good

Rule #14:
  if Household <= 1
  then Good

For Visualization-Based Analysis Tools in Knowledge Discovery Process: A Multilayer Perceptron versus Principal Components Analysis: A Comparative Study

Xavier Polanco, Claire François, Mohamed Aly Ould Louly

Programme de Recherche en Infométrie (PRI) - Informetric Research Program
Institut de l'Information Scientifique et Technique (INIST)
Centre National de la Recherche Scientifique (CNRS)
2 allée du Parc de Brabois - 54514 Vandœuvre-lès-Nancy Cedex, France
claire.francois@inist.fr, polanco@inist.fr

Abstract. Mapping knowledge structures is a key task in Knowledge Discovery in Databases (KDD). In order to display the thematic organization of knowledge, we compare and evaluate two different cartography approaches: principal components analysis (PCA) and a multilayer perceptron (MLP) in "self-association" mode. This kind of MLP can be used to perform a PCA when the activation function is set to the identity function. This allows us to look for the non-linear activation function which best fits the data structure. We present an evaluation criterion and the results and maps obtained with both methods. We notice that the MLP detects a non-linearity in the data structure that the PCA does not detect. However, the MLP does not express the non-linearity completely. Finally we show how a related component analysis (RCA), based on graph theory, provides representations of the inter-clusters relationships, compensating for the approximate nature of the maps, and improving their readability.

1. Introduction

We are concerned with the design and development of information analysis tools in which informetrics, computational linguistics and artificial intelligence techniques are combined. In particular, *informetrics* address the issue of applying metric or quantitative information analysis methods (i.e., statistics, probabilities and multivariate data analysis) to produce useful information (for a general statistical perspective on KDD, see [3]). The aim of our activity is to perform the analysis of information by computer using cluster analysis and cartography algorithms which represent the generated clusters in the form of maps. We apply this approach to the domain of scientific and technical information, i.e., publications and patents stored in databases (for details, see [7]; [10]; [11]; [9]).

In this article, we avoid using the terms *classification* and *classes*; rather we use *cluster analysis* or *clustering* and *clusters*, in order to distinguish at the conceptual level two different techniques: a supervised method that classifies data into predefined classes or taxonomy, and a descriptive unsupervised technique that seeks to produce statistically some aggregations from data themselves. We use the terms *cartography* and *maps* to mean our statistical-based process of knowledge representation, that is *knowledge mapping*, as opposed to the knowledge representations and the processing of representations in logically-inspired ways (see, [8], ch. 6).

1.1 Process Overview

Clustering, cartography, and hypertext generation are the three main components of our approach. Informetric analysis of the information is divided into two phases: the first involves the generation of clusters using clustering procedures, in which learning is unsupervised (the user does not define classes), while the second consists of positioning the clusters on a global map in order to display the topical organization of knowledge. These two phases are data driven. A hypertext interface generator provides the user with a user-friendly interface displaying the global map, the topics or clusters and the documents themselves. The global map consists in an overview of the target documents set and then gives access to useful information organized by topics (clusters). This approach is implemented in the NEURODOC system.

The NEURODOC system uses the axial k-means method (AKM), i.e., an unsupervised winner-takes-all algorithm producing overlapping clusters, and a principal components analysis (PCA) for mapping. Our research is currently oriented to develop NEURODOC into a platform which can be used to apply artificial neural networks (ANNs) on bibliographic and textual data for clustering and mapping ([12]). Our interest in ANNs algorithms lies in the links which exist between multivariate data analysis and connectionist approach.

This article covers the cartography issue only, and concentrate on work concerned explicitly with mathematical means for comparing two different cartography techniques: PCA and a MLP. In the process of KDD, the maps are "visualization-based analysis tools". As Brachman and Anand ([2], p. 45) note: "The visualization produced is by itself a model, and the user can examine the visualization to determine its explanatory power (...) Appropriate display of data points and their relationships can give the analyst insight that is virtually impossible to get from looking at tables of output or simple summary statistics. In fact, for some tasks, appropriate visualization is the only thing needed to solve a problem or confirm a hypothesis, even though we do not usually think of picture-drawing as a kind of analysis".

1.2 Application Domain

The target data set used here for mapping knowledge structures was built for an unpublished study on "prion diseases" which was carried out in 1997 by PRI/INIST for the Life Science Department of the CNRS. The corpus consists of 1855 bibliographic records taken from the Science Citation Index CD-ROM (SCI). This data set represents essentially the past five years of research published in 453 journals covered by the SCI. Documents (*n* objets) are indexed by 1750 keywords (*p* attributes) generated by an in-house linguistic engineering platform (ILC platform) applied on titles and abstracts. Using the AKM, the NEURODOC cluster analysis generates 30 clusters (*m*) described by a cluster matrix X ($m * p = 30 * 1750$) which is very multi-dimensional and sparse, that is essentially composed of null values.

In this paper, the clusters, that are obtained, are the data to be positioned on the global map. In documentary data analysis, the representativeness of the two axes of the map measured as an inertia percentage, is always very weak. In the case of the "prion diseases" corpus, the factorial plane of the PCA explains only 17.77 % of the inertia.. The MLP is of interest since it is able to detect non-linearities in the data structure and therefore produces a more representative cartography in theory.

2. A Non Linear MLP with One Hidden Layer

This section presents the MLP used for mapping the clusters obtained by the AKM. We do not use the MLP for its "associative properties" which perform a discriminant factorial analysis, but for its "spatial projection properties" which can be used to map the data. The learning is defined by the gradient back-propagation algorithm, which is both stochastic and incremental.

2.1. Network Architecture

The network architecture corresponds with the task that the MLP has to perform. Bourret *et al.* [1], continuing the work of Gallinari *et. al* [6] show that a linear MLP using the "identity" activation function ($f = Id$) can perform a PCA. To do this, the input and output layers have an equal number of neurons and the hidden layer has only two neurons. This MLP takes vectors of size *p* as input and compresses them in 2-dimensional vectors before restoring the information at the output. Once the convergence has been carried out, the outputs of the hidden neurons are used for a 2-dimensional map representation.

The data (clusters) are centered before to be passed through the MLP, implying that the network does not contain a polariser neuron, i.e., a neuron the output of which is always equal to 1, which would give as result a affine line. In this case, we know that the best-fit plane passes through the origin now situated at the center of gravity of the clusters.

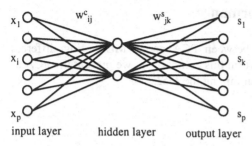

For an input x, the output x^c_j of neuron j of the hidden layer is given by :

$$x^c_j = f(\sum_{i=1}^{p} w_{ij} x_i)$$

Similarly, the output s_k of neuron k of the output layer is given by :

$$s_k = f(\sum_{j=1}^{2} w_{jk} x^c_j)$$

Fig. 1. MLP architecture. Notation: l is the indice for the m clusters of the learning set; i, j and k are the indices for the first, second and third network layers respectively; X is the cluster matrix in which each row x is one of the input vectors, $x = [x_1, ..., x_i, ..., x_p]$; x^c is the output vector of the hidden layer, $x^c = [x^c_1, x^c_2]$ (in French "c" for "cachée" or hidden); s is the output vector of the network, $s = [s_1, ..., s_k, ..., s_p]$ (in French s for "sortie" or output); W^c is the weighting matrix of the hidden layer, each element of which denoted by w^c_{ij} represents the ith weight of the jth neuron of the hidden layer; W^s is the weighting matrix of the output layer, each element of which denoted by w^s_{jk} represents the jth weight of the kth neuron of the output layer; and lastly, f is the network neuron activation function

2.2. Learning Algorithm

The learning mode is a "self-association" supervised learning algorithm, that is to say that the network is trained to adjust its output as close as possible to the input. For each input, the individual squared error (*ISE*) corresponds to the Euclidean distance between the input and output vectors. The learning level of the network is known due to the mean squared error (*MSE*) which is calculated periodically. Its evolution has three phases: a relatively long plateau, a step-wise descent, and a final stabilization. The *MSE* is given by the following formula:

$$MSE = \frac{1}{m} \sum_{l=1}^{m} ISE(l) \text{ where for a data x : } ISE = \|s - x\|^2$$

The learning is stochastic, the network connections are corrected after processing each data x. Moreover, the standard gradient back-propagation algorithm is not incremental, and the connections of the two neurons of the hidden layer are calculated simultaneously. In order to perform a PCA, we must apply an incremental algorithm [5], and so once the connections of the first neuron have been calculated and have stabilized, the connections of the second neuron are then calculated. Once convergence has been achieved, the outputs of the two hidden neurons define the coordinates on the map for each cluster.

3. Statistical Assessment of Performance

This section presents the comparisons between PCA and a MLP using different activation functions. In attempting to perform this comparison, we present the PCA as a means of approximating a matrix by minimizing the *MSE*.

3.1. MSE definition for PCA

To place the clusters on a map (defined in the space R^2), the best result obtained using multivariate data analysis methods is the set of data projections on the first two factorial axes, also defined by the set of the coordinates of the first two principal components, the vectors c_1 and c_2. This corresponds to the second rank approximation of the cluster matrix X, that is $X*(2)$:

$$X^*(2) = X \sum_{k=1}^{2} u_k u_k'$$

where u_k is the unit eigenvector of the matrix $X'X$ associated with the kth largest eigenvalue λ_k, or the unit vector of the kth factorial axis. This approximation is the result of the maximization of the squares of the projections of the m individual points (row vectors representing the clusters) onto the factorial plane created by the vectors u_1 and u_2, and which represents the visualization plane. This approximation also corresponds to the minimization of the sum of the squares of the distances of the m individual points from this factorial plane. But the sum of the squares of the distances corresponds to what is called the general squared error (*GSE*) in the field of ANNs. Once the PCA has been performed and the two principal components determined, we will be able to evaluate the *GSE* and then *MSE* is defined by:

$$MSE = \frac{1}{m} GSE = \frac{1}{m} \sum_{i=3}^{m} \lambda_i$$

where m is the number of clusters, λ_i is the ith eigenvalue associated with the ith factorial axis. This *MSE* corresponds therefore to the sum of the eigenvalues of the complementary space to the first factorial plane, which is defined by the two factors associated with the two largest eigenvalues. This *MSE* is the *minimum MSE* that the PCA can achieve, and is thus our means of evaluating the MLP.

3.2. PCA and linear and non-linear MLP

The MLP performs the approximation S_f for the cluster matrix $X(m,p)$. For the identity function $f = Id$, the network output becomes:

$$S_{Id} = Id\left(Id\left(XW^c\right)W^s\right) = XW^c W^s$$

The network must then find two weighting matrices W^c and W^s with sizes $(p,2)$ and $(2,p)$ respectively such that the matrix $XW^c W^s$ is the best possible approximation of the matrix X. This is equivalent to finding a matrix M of size (p,p) and rank 2 such that XM is the best approximation of X. This matrix is $X^*(2)$ (cf. § 3.1).

The weighting matrix $W^c W^s$ must therefore converge to this matrix M. In other words, the self-associative linear MLP (where $f = Id$) with two hidden units projects the data in the 2-dimensional space corresponding to that which would have been found by the PCA. This linear MLP then performs a PCA which will be used as a basis for comparison with the behavior of a non-linear MLP. The only difference between the two networks is the non-linearity provided by the activation function. The aim is now to verify that this function detects a non-linearity in the data structure, and therefore performs a better cartography, which can be qualified as a non-linear projection of the clusters.

3.3. Determination of the activation function

The intrinsic data structure is unknown *a priori*. We are looking for a sigmoid function f which produces a better approximation of the data S_f at the output than the result obtained via the factorial plane (S_{id}). The comparison criterions that we define for evaluating the results are *MSE* and Quality. Quality is defined in terms of global relative error and is expressed as a percentage. Thus, for all m clusters, the global relative error (GRE) is:

$$GRE = \frac{\sum_{l=1}^{m} ISE(l)}{\sum_{l=1}^{m} \|X_l\|^2}$$

The quality is thus: $Qualiy = (1 - GRE) \times 100$. In the case of PCA, this corresponds to the quality of the data global projection on the first factorial plane, which is also called the percentage of explained inertia. Table 1 shows the results summarized in three columns: [1] Initial $MSE = MSE$ before learning; for PCA, Initial MSE is comparable to the sum of the normalized squares of the vectors ; [2] Final $MSE = MSE$ after learning; [3] Quality.

Table 1. Results obtained with different activation functions on the "prion diseases" data set

Function	Number of iterations by thousand	Initial *MSE*	Final *MSE*	Quality
PCA		0.8418	0.6922	17.77
x	100	0.8640	0.6962	17.29
f(x)	100	8.307	1.027	-22.00
$g_1(x)$	4000	0.8418	0.6943	17.52
$g_{15}(x)$	100	0.8842	0.6740	19.93
$g_{15}(x)$	160	0.8842	0.6694	20.47

The first row of table 1 presents the result obtained with PCA, and provides the basis for estimating the quality of the results obtained with the MLP. A study of table 1 allows us to verify that the identity activation function: $Id(x) = x$ gives results which are very close to the PCA. We then use the sigmoid activation function f. The function f brings out the problem that the output s is positive for all neurons, while the input x does not need to be (the data are centered). We introduce the additional term $(-1/2)$ to make the function odd, and thus preserve positive and negative signs. By analogy with numerical methods used to find eigenvectors and eigenvalues, we introduce a factor acc to spread out the spectrum of the covariance matrix. The function thus defined is the function g_{acc} given by:

$$g_{acc}(x) = f(acc \times x) - \frac{1}{2} \text{ with } f(x) = \frac{1}{\left(1 + e^{-x}\right)}$$

The functions g_{acc} allows the MLP to obtain an initial MSE comparable to the initial MSE of the PCA (= 0.8418) while for the function f, the initial MSE is high (8.307). The function g_1 provides better results than the function Id but with a slow rate of convergence (4 million iterations). The factor acc speeds up the convergence: 160 thousand iterations with $acc=15$, moreover, this factor provides the lowest value of final MSE (0.6694), and the highest Quality of 20.47%. Thus we have adopted the function g_{15} which enables the optimal minimum obtained by the PCA to be passed, and to find a final MSE between a 2-dimensional PCA and a 3-dimensional PCA.

In conclusion, we can observe that the results obtained with the MLP are at least similar to the PCA results, therefore the learning process may be considered to be achieved. This process carries out a minimization whose result depends on the correlations between the data. Nervertheless, the large dimension of the data implies a low final quality with MLP as well as with PCA.

4. Mapping Knowledge Organization

Before examining the maps obtained by the two methods, we present an approach that we call Related Components Analysis, for validating and explaining the map obtained in a format better suited for human reading. Indeed, one of the objects of KDD is to generate a visualization of knowledge in a form suitable for verification or interpretation providing users with useful or interesting knowledge.

4.1. Related Components Analysis (RCA)

This method is based on graph theory. It defines the related components which represent the relative closeness between clusters. These related components are not defined according to predefined thresholds, but 10 proximity levels are calculated from the distances between clusters. The highest level is defined by the minimum distance between clusters and the lowest by the maximum distance between clusters. At a given level, two clusters are connected if their distance is lower than the maximum threshold of that level. Once the connections are calculated, sets of clusters linked up by a connection path, named "related components", are defined. This operation is repeated for each level. While this method does not have the means to project the individual points (clusters), it clearly shows their closeness and separation in multidimensional space.

The maps obtained by PCA and MLP do not allow a complete representation of the position of the clusters, because their quality value is not superior to 21% as we can see in table 1. To compensate for this, we use the RCA. This technique gives the analyst the means of verifying if maps respect the distances between the clusters, and therefore the concentration of some clusters and the isolation of others. Moreover, the RCA facilitates the interpretation of the maps by allowing the clusters configuration to be visualized.

4.2. Presentation of the maps

The function g_{15} makes the MLP to converge on the plane giving the best account of the non-linearity. Once this plane has been determined, its axes can be interpreted in the same way as standard factorial axes. While this activation function gives a better approximation of the data than the PCA, it is less easy to visualize, because the clusters are close together at the centre of the space. To solve the visualization problem, we added a scale factor to the function g_{15} that is $g_{15}(scale*x)$. This operation is performed after the convergence of the MLP and can be thought of as unfolding the Kohonen map.

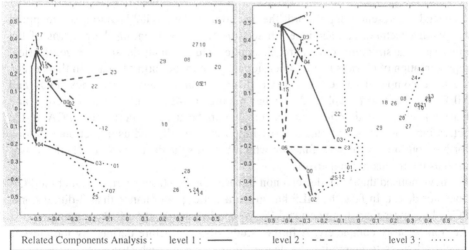

Related Components Analysis :   level 1 : ——   level 2 : - - -   level 3 : ······

Fig. 2. MLP Map of the 30 clusters with function « g_{15} » and scale = 10

Fig.3. PCA Map of the 30 clusters. For the titles of clusters see table 1.

Figure 2 shows the map obtained by the MLP for our example of "prion diseases" with *scale=10*. Figure 3 shows the map obtained with the same set of data using the PCA. The related components of the three highest levels are shown on these figures. In figure 2, the left-hand side of the map groups together two very strong related components (level 1). According to our expert, these two components correspond to the domains of the "molecular biology of the prion protein" (component

[17,16,11,15,4,9]) and "scrapie" (component [6,0,2]). If we also look at the related components of levels 2 and 3, these two components are grouped together in a large set taking up the whole of the left-hand side of the map. This confirms the proximity of the two level 1 components. At the bottom right in figure 2, we note a level 3 related component (component [14,24,28]) which, according to our expert, corresponds to the problem of the "transmission of Creutzfeldt Jacob and Spongiform Encephalopathy Diseases". At the top right of the MLP map are the clusters more isolated in the multidimensional space. The map therefore respects the relationships between the clusters. In figure 3, the related components representing the "molecular biology of the prion protein" and the "scrapie" are also found on the left-hand side of the PCA map, but they are further away from each other, which is not justified by the RCA. The related component [14,24,28] representing "transmission of Creutzfeldt Jacob and Spongiform Encephalopathy Diseases", appears less well grouped on this map.

The above discussion shows that knowledge organization designate by the clusters can be represented in the forms of maps in which relations (proximities) can be examined by users or experts. A user-friendly hypertext interface allows to explore the knowledge organization interactively.

5. Conclusions and Open Problems

This study represent a step towards the development of a reliable automated mapping knowledge method. As mentioned in section 1, for representing the patterns of the inherent data structure, our approach applies cluster analysis and the geometrical representation of clusters in a 2-dimensional space in the form of maps. In this article, we have compared and evaluated two different cartography approaches: PCA and MLP. We have also explained in what manner a MLP, with the architecture and learning algorithm described in section 2, can be used to perform a PCA if the activation function is set to the identity function. This allowed us in section 3 to look for the non-linear activation function which best fits the data structure. The *MSE* was used as the means of comparison.

We have noticed that MLP detect a non linearity in the clusters structure that the PCA does not detect. In fact, the MLP has given a better performance than 2-dimensional PCA, but lower than 3-dimensional PCA. In other words, the MLP does not express the non linearity completely. A further study of the structure defined by the clusters would allow us to determine the degree of freedom of such structure, and to know whether it can be described by two factors. Such results could be used to create maps which better represent the knowledge content of the data.

The maps studied in this article are not only means of visualization. They also represent an analysis tool insofar as they allow us to evaluate the relative position of clusters (or topics) in the multidimensional space of representation. As observed in section 4, we must deal with the problems of readability of such maps. In the case of the MLP map, we have added a scale factor for improving its readability. A RCA, based on graph theory, was also used to show and evaluate best-fit distances and proximities in multidimensional space, and compensating the approximate nature of the maps obtained by the MLP or the PCA.

Finally, as regards of the remark that KDD process involves "the evaluation and possibly interpretation of the patterns to make the decision of what constitutes useful or interesting knowledge and what does not" [4, p. 9], all that can be said currently is that generating maps easily understood by people is a promising field that calls for further studies. Furthermore, cartography may indicate an interesting new domain of research and development in knowledge discovery systems.

References

1. Bourret, P., Reggia, J., Samuelides, M.:Réseaux neuroneaux, une approche connexionniste de l'intelligence artificielle, Toulouse, TEKNEA (1991).
2. Brachman, R.J., Anand, T.:The Process of Knowledge Discovery in Databases, in Adavances in Knowledge Discovery and Data Mining. Fayyad, U.M., Piatetsky-Shapiro, G., Smyth, P., and Uthurusamy, R. Editors. Menlo Park, Calif. AAAI Press / The MIT Press, (1996) 37-57.
3. Elder, J., Pregribon, D.: A Statistical Perspective on Knowledge Discovery in Databases, in Databases, in Adavances in Knowledge Discovery and Data Mining. Fayyad, U.M., Piatetsky-Shapiro, G., Smyth, P., and Uthurusamy, R. Editors. Menlo Park, Calif. AAAI Press / The MIT Press (1996) 83-113.
4. Fayyad, U.M., Piatetsky-Shapiro, G., Smyth, P.: From Data Mining to Knowledge Discovery: An Overview, in Adavances in Knowledge Discovery and Data Mining. Fayyad, U.M., Piatetsky-Shapiro, G., Smyth, P., and Uthurusamy, R. Editors. Menlo Park, Calif. AAAI Press / The MIT Press (1996). 1-34.
5. Gallinari, P., Fogelman-Soulié, F.: Progressive Design of MLP Architecture", Neuro-Nïmes (1988) 171-182.
6. Gallinari, P., Thiria, S., Fogelman-Soulié, F.: Multilayer perceptrons and data analysis, International Conference on neural networks, IEEE 1 (1988) 391-399.
7. Grivel, L., François, C.: Une station de travail pour classer, cartographier et anlyser l'information bibliographique dans une perspective de veille scientifique et technique, in Noyer, J.M. Editor, Les sciences de l'information: Bibliométrie, Scientométrie, Infométrie, Rennes, SOLARIS II, Presses Universitaires de Rennes (1995) 81-112.
8. Holsheimer, M., Siebes, A.P. Data Mining: The Search for Knowledge in Databases. Amsterdam, CWI Report CS-R9406, ISSN 0169-118X. (1994)
9. Muller, Ch., Polanco, X., Royauté, J., Toussaint, Y.: Acquisition et structuration des connaissances en corpus : éléments méthodologiques. Rapport de recherche INRIA N° 3198, available in postcript format ftp.inria.fr (192.93.2.54) (1997)
10. Polanco, X., Grivel, L., Royauté, J.: How to Do Things with Terms in Informetrics: Terminological Variation and Stabilization as Science Watch Indicators, Proceedins of the Fifth International Conference of the International Society for Scientometrics and Informetrics. Edited by M.E.D. Koening and A. Bookstein. Medford, NJ: Learned Information Inc (1995) 435-444.
11. Polanco, X.: Extraction et modélisation des connaissances : une approche et ses technologies, Premières Journées du Chapitre Français de l'International Society for Knowledge Organization (ISKO), à Lille, France, les 16-17 octobre 1997 (1997)
12. Polanco, X., François, C., Keim, J-P.: Artificial Neural Network Technoloy for the Classification and Cartography of Scientific and Technical Information, Scientometrics, vol. 41, n° 1(1998) 69-82

Trend Graphs: Visualizing the Evolution of Concept Relationships in Large Document Collections

Ronen Feldman, Yonatan Aumann, Amir Zilberstein, Yaron Ben-Yehuda

Department of Mathematics and Computer Science
Bar Ilan University
Ramat-Gan, 52900 Israel
{feldman,aumann,zilbers,benyehdy}@cs.biu.ac.il

Abstract. The proliferation of digitally available textual data necessitates automatic tools for analyzing large textual collections. Thus, in analogy to *data mining* for structured databases, *text mining* is defined for textual collections. A central tool in text mining is the analysis of *concept relationship,* which discovers connections between different concepts, as reflected in the corpus. Most previous work on text mining in general, and concept relationship in particular, viewed the entire corpus as one monolithic entity. However, large corpuses are often composed of documents with different characteristics. Most importantly, documents are often tagged with *timestamps* (e.g. news articles), and thus represent the state of the domain in different time periods. In this paper we introduce a new technique for analyzing and visualizing differences and similarities in the concept relationships, as they are reflected in different segments of the corpus. Focusing on the case of timestamped documents, we introduce *Trend Graphs*, which provide a graphical tool for analyzing and visualizing the dynamic changes in concept relationships over time. *Trend Graphs* thus provide a tool for tracking the evaluation of the corpus over time, highlighting trends and discontinuities.

1. Introduction

Most informal definitions [4] introduce *knowledge discovery in databases* (KDD) as the extraction of useful information from databases by large-scale search for interesting patterns. The vast majority of existing KDD applications and methods deal with structured databases, for example - client data stored in a relational database, and thus exploits data organized in records structured by categorical, ordinal, and continuous variables. However, a tremendous amount of information is stored in documents that are nearly unstructured. The availability of document collections and especially of online information is rapidly growing, so that an analysis bottleneck often arises also in this area. Thus, in analogy to *data mining* for structured data, *text mining* is defined for textual data. *Text mining* is the science of extracting information from hidden patterns in large textual collections.

Text mining shares many characteristics with classical data mining, but also differs in some. Thus, it is necessary to provide special tools geared specifically to text mining. A central tool, found valuable in text mining, is the analysis of *concept relationship* [5,7], defined as follows. Large textual corpuses are most commonly composed of a collection of separate *documents* (e.g. news articles, web pages). Each document refers to a set of *concepts* (*terms*). Text mining operations consider the distribution of concepts on the *inter-document* level, seeking to discover the nature and relationships of concepts as reflected in the collection as a whole. For example, in a collection of news articles, a large number of articles on politician X and "scandal" may indicate a negative image of the character, and alert for a new public-relations campaign. Or, for another example, a growing number of articles on both company Y and product Z may indicate a shift of focus in the company's interests, a shift which should be noted by its competitors. Notice that in both of these cases, the information is not provided by any single document, but rather from the totality of the collection. Thus, *concept relationship* analysis seeks to discover the relationship between concepts, as reflected by the totally of the corpus at hand.

Most previous work on detecting concept relationships viewed the entire textual corpus as one monolithic entity. However, large corpuses are often composed of documents with different characteristics. In this case, we seek a mining tool which can aid in analyzing the similarities and differences between the different segments of the corpus. For example, news-articles are often gathered over an extended period of time, and each document is timestamped with a date. In this case, the mining process should not only provide analysis of the corpus as a whole, but also describe the temporal behavior of events, and provide an analysis of the evaluation of the concepts and their relationships, as reflected in the collection. In this paper we introduce a new technique for analyzing and visualizing differences and similarities in the concept relationships, as they are reflected in different segments of the corpus. Focusing on the temporal case, we introduce *Trend Graphs*, which provide a visual representation of the time-dependent behavior and evaluation of concepts and their inter-relationships, as reflects in the corpus. Trend Graphs provide a global overall picture of the dynamic behavior of corpus, highlighting important changes, trends, and discontinuities. Our notion of Trend Graphs complements the trend analysis technique of Lent et. al. [11], providing an overall picture of all major trends, and focusing on concept relationships, rather than sequences.

Document Explorer System. The *Trend Graphs* tool we describe here is part of an integrated text mining system, developed at Bar-Ilan University, named *Document Explorer*. The system gets as input a set of text documents, and provides a full suite of analysis and mining tools. As a first step, the system analyzes each document, and, using a special *Term Extraction* module, generates a set of *terms* representing the document. This process is performed only once for each document, and all subsequent analysis is performed upon the term-representation of the document.

Outline. The rest of this paper is organized as follows. Following, we provide a brief summary of related work. Next, in Section 2, we give some preliminary definitions and describe the notion of *Context Graphs*, which is the basis for the definition of *Trend Graphs*. In Section 3, we introduce *Trend Graphs*. In Section 4, we discuss the application of our methods to general inter-collection comparisons. We conclude in Section 5 with open research directions. The examples provided in the paper are based on application of the system to a set of 52,000 articles of Reuters Financial News from 1995-1996.

Related Work.

A data mining approach to analyzing large textual collections was presented by Feldman and Dagan [5]. Mining for association rules in texts is discussed be Feldman and Hirsh [6]. Visualization techniques for text mining are presented by Feldman et. al. [7]. Hahn and Schnattinger [8] describe the SYNDIKATE system for "deep KDD from natural language texts" which is aimed at extracting knowledge from real-world texts and assimilating them into a knowledge base.

The problem of discovering trends in textual collections was first considered by Lent, Agrawal, and Srikant [11]. They present a method for detecting and presenting trends in word phrases (where phases are taken to have a very broad meaning). Their method is based on a two-phase process. In the first phase they construct frequent *sequences* of words, using a sequential patterns mining algorithm [14]. Then, the user can query the system to obtain all phases whose trend matches a given pattern (such as "recent upward change"). Our Trends Graph tool presents a totally different approach and solution to the problem. Trend Graphs present *all* major trends in the corpus (not only of a given type), and are based on a visualization technique. The appreciation of trends emerges from their visual appearance.

Sequences and trends in structured databases are considered in many papers. Srikant and Agrawal [14] define *sequential patterns* and provide an efficient algorithm for mining such patterns. Mannila et. al. [12] define the notion of *episodes*, and provide an efficient algorithm for mining them. Frequent episodes are used to discover behavior patterns, and to generate behavior rules. Other work on knowledge discovery from sequential data includes [2,3,9] and others. Time series analysis is discussed in [1,10].

2. Context Graphs

Taxonomy. All operations are performed using a *taxonomy,* which is defined by the user (or preloaded together with the system). The taxonomy is a hierarchy of the terms generated by the term extraction module. Each node of the taxonomy corresponds to a set of terms. The taxonomy is necessary in order to allow the system to focus on the relevant set of concepts. The *Document Explorer* system provides several tools to aid the user in creating the taxonomy.

Context Graphs. The basis for the definition of Trend Graphs is the notion of a *Context Graph.* A Context Graph is a visual representation of the relationship between a set of terms (e.g. "companies"), as reflected in the corpus with regards to a given context *(*e.g. "merger"). In order to specify a Context Graph the user chooses two sets of terms. The first set, called the *connection nodes,* defines the terms for which the user is interested in finding the inter-relationship. The second set, called the *context,* defines the context in which the relationship must be found. Both sets may be defined using the taxonomy. The context set can be treated either as an AND set, i.e., all terms must occur in the document, or as an OR set, i.e., at least one of the terms must occur in the document.

We now formally define a Context Graph, starting with some necessary notations:

- *Context Phrase:* For a collection of documents, D, and a set of terms, T, we denote by $D/A(T)$ the subset of documents in D that are labeled with *all* of the terms in T. Similarly, $D/O(T)$ is the subset of documents in D that are labeled with *at least one* of the terms in T. $A(T)$ and $O(T)$ are called *context-phrases.*

- *Context Relationship:* For D, a collection of documents, t_1, t_2 individual terms, and C a context phrase, we denote by $R(D, t_1, t_2|C)$ the number of documents in D/C which include both t_1 and t_2. Formally, $R(D, t_1, t_2|C) = |(D/A(\{t_1,t_2\}))/C|$.

- *Context Graph:* For D, a collection of documents, T, a set of terms, C a context phrase, and threshold k, the Context Graph of D,T,C is a weighted graph $G = (T,E)$, with nodes in T and set of edges $E = \{\{ t_1, t_2\} \mid R(D, t_1, t_2 \mid C) > k \}$. For each edge $\{t_1,t_2\}\in E$, we define the *weight* of the edge, $w(\{t_1,t_2\})= R(D, t_1, t_2 \mid C)$.

Intuitively, a context graphs is a graph where vertices represent the terms, and there is an edge between vertices terms if both terms co-occur in the given "context" sufficiently many times. Figure 1 shows the Context Graph for "companies" in the context of "merger talk" (i.e. $T=\{$"companies"$\}$, $C=A(\text{"merger talk"})$). The threshold was set to 7. The weights of the edges are noted alongside the edge. Nodes with no edges are not depicted.

The graph clearly exposes the main industry clusters, which are shown as disconnected components of the graph: the computer industry cluster, the broadcasting cluster, a banking cluster, and a telephony cluster. The Context Graph provides a powerful way to visualize relationship encapsulated in thousands of documents.

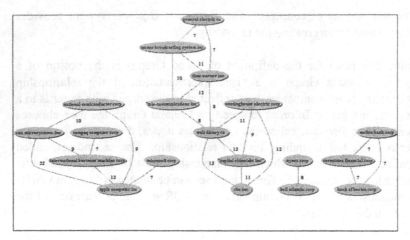

Fig. 1. Context Graph – Companies in the context of merger.

3. Trend Graphs

Each document is assumed to be tagged with a time-stamp, which indicates its creation time. For example, in the running example for this paper, each Reuters' document is tagged by its publication date.

Context Graphs, as defined in the previous section, provide a static visualization of relationship of terms in the collection as a whole. We now show how to go beyond the notion of Context Graphs, and provide a tool that tracks the *evolution* and *changes* of relationships over time. Thus, we obtain a tool that aids the user in finding trends and discontinuities. The user can select the time granularity, and then, using the visualization tool, see how the relationships change and evolve over time. The system automatically highlights new connections, and alert for changes.

We start with several formal definitions:

- *Temporal Selection*: If D is a collection of documents and I is a time range, D_I is the subset of documents in D whose time stamp is within I.

- *Temporal Context Relationship*: If D is a collection of documents, t_1 and t_2 are individual terms, C is a context phrase, and I is a time Interval, then $R_I(D, t_1, t_2|C)$ is the number of documents in D_I in which t_1 and t_2 co-occur in the context of C, i.e., $R_I(D, t_1, t_2|C)$ is the number of D_I/C which include both t_1 and t_2.

- *Temporal Context Graph:* If D is a collection of documents, T is a set of terms, C is a context phrase, I is a time range, and k is a threshold, the Temporal Context Graph of D,T,C,I, is a weighted graph $G_I = (T,E_I)$, with set nodes in T, and set of edges E_I, where, $E_I=\{\{t_1,t_2\}|R_I(D, t_1, t_2 | C) > k \}$. For each edge $\{t_1,t_2\}\in E$, we define the *weight* of the edge, $w_I(\{t_1,t_2\})= R_I(D, t_1, t_2 | C)$.

Intuitively, a Temporal Context Graph is a Context Graph for a specific time slice. Given these definitions, a *Trend Graph* is obtained by partitioning the entire time span covered by the collection into a series of consecutive time intervals, and taking the corresponding sequence of Temporal Context graphs. The *changes* in edge weights reflect the changes in relationships over time.   In order to emphasis the temporal effect, we mark each edge with information on the difference between the weight of the edge in the current time interval, and that of the previous interval.   The edges are categorized into four classes:

1. New edges: edges that did not exist in the previous graph.
2. Increased edges: edges that have a much higher weight compared to the previous time interval.
3. Decreased edges: edges that have a much lower weight compared to the previous graph.
4. Stable edges: edges that have approximately the same weight as the corresponding edge in the previous graph.

When depicting the Trend Graph, each edge is marked as being a member of one of the classes.   The notions of "much higher" and "much lower" can be defined according to the context.   Currently we require a 1.25 factor increase or decrease as the minimum for a *significant* change.

Trend graphs can be visualized in several ways. We chose to visualize the category of each edge by either using a color scheme or by changing the width of the edge. The layout of the graph was chosen so as to minimize the changes in the layout of the nodes and edges. Thus, we first precompute the Context Graph for the entire period and determine its layout. This layout determines the position of all nodes and edges in all graphs. Thus, the entire sequence of Temporal Context graphs is defined, together with the class definition for each edge.   The system now provides the user with several ways to view the sequence.   The best way is by animation, where one graph transforms into the next, and the changes become most apparent. Another way the user can chose to view the sequence is by using a listbox, which contains all the periods (in the selected granularity).   The user can then flip between periods and see a Trend graph that compare between the context graph of the current period and the average of the previous *n* periods.

Figure 3 shows the interface for the user to define a Trend Graph. In this case, the user chose to examine trends in the relationship between companies in the context of included the word "merger". In this case there are three such terms: "merger", "merger agreement", and "merger talk".   The time granularity was chosen to be quarters.

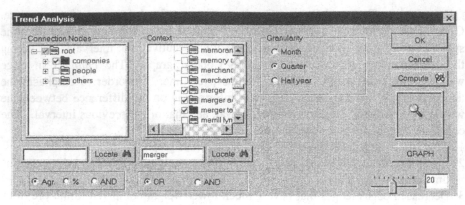

Fig. 2. Specifying a Trend Graph

Figures 4 and 5 depict the trend graphs for the forth quarter of 1995 and the first quarter of 1996. New and increased edge are depicted with a fat line, other edges are depicted with a regular line. Each edge is labeled with the difference of the edge in this graph, with regards to the average of previous quarters. A *n label represents a new edge with weight n. A >n label represents an edge with an increase in weight. A <n label represent an edge with a decrease in weight.

The 1996 1ˢᵗ quarter graph unveils several clear trends. First, there is an overall increase in connections. More specifically, there is a sharp increase in the connection between Nynex and Bell Atlantic, and an altogether new connection between Sun and Apple. In the banking industry, the connection has decreased.

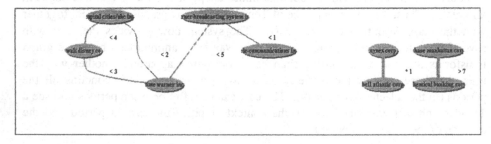

Fig. 3. Trend Graph for 4ᵗʰ Quarter 1995 (Companies in the context of "merger")

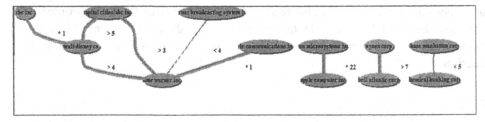

Fig. 4. Trend Graph for 1ˢᵗ Quarter 1996 (Companies in the context of "merger")

4. Inter-Collection Comparisons

Trend Graphs represent only one type of comparison, which can be performed using Context Graphs. In this case, the comparison is made between the documents written at different time intervals. In a similar fashion, one can use Context Graphs to find similarities and differences between any sets of document, e.g. documents coming from different sources, or different segments of the same corpus. For example, a company may wish to analyze the similarities and differences between the email message it gets from its US based customers, and its European customers. Or, one can compare the way two different newspapers reflect on a given domain. In these types of applications, the graphs shall represent the concept relationships as reflected in one collection in comparison to the other. There are several ways to present the comparison results. The first is to use the same representation used for Trend Graphs, i.e., using several graphs and labeling the edges with the differences. However, since there is no natural order of the segments, other representation may also be considered. If the comparison is only between two segments, a single graph showing the differences and similarities is possible. If there are more than two segments, one can superimpose the edges using a color-coding scheme to distinguish the segments.

Comparisons using Context Graphs can performed on the set of clusters generated by a clustering algorithm, thus obtaining a better understanding of the clusters.

5. Conclusions and Future Work

Temporal affects are central to the understanding of many systems. Thus, data mining tools, which aspire to analyze the behavior of systems, must take the time factor into account as a major component. In this paper we presented a new tool, called Trend Graphs, which captures to temporal behavior of concept relationships in large textual collections. The tool provides the user with an easy to understand graphical representation of the changes in the collection over time, highlighting trends, directions, and discontinuities.

The tools we provide can also be used to analyze differences and similarities between different segments of a given collection, or of separate collections.

An interesting research direction is the issue of the graph layout in Trend Graphs. The approach adopted in this paper is to use a static layout for all the graphs in the sequence. The layout is obtained from the union of all the graphs in the sequence. Thus, nodes are always located in the same place, and differences are depicted by varying edge weights, or edge colors. An alternative method is to have a dynamic graph layout. In this case, the relative node locations shall correspond to their relationship, e.g. closer nodes describing a stronger connection. Using this approach, the differences between the graphs are visualized by the changes in the graph layout. In this approach, animation techniques should be used to help the user follow the changes.

References:

1. Agrawal, R.; Lin, K. I.; Sawhney, H. S.; and Shim, K.: Fast Similarity Search in the Presence of Noise, Scalling and Translation in Time-Series Databases. In: Proceeding of the Annual Symposium on Very Large DataBases (VLDB), (1995) 490-501.
2. Bettini, C.; Wang, X. S.; and Jajodia, S.: Testing Complex temporal relationships Involving Multiple Granularities and its Application to Data Mining. In: Proceedings of the 15th ACM Symposium on Principles of Database Systems (PODS), (1996) 68-78.
3. Dousson, C.; Gaborit, P.; and Ghallab, M.: Situation Recognition: Representation and Algorithms. In: Proceedings of the 13th International Joint Conference of Artificial Inteligence (IJCAI), (1993) 166-172.
4. Fayyad, U,; Piatetsky-Shapiro, G.; and Smyth P.: Knowledge Discovery and Data Mining: Towards a Unifying Framework. In: Proceedings of the 2nd International Conference of Knowledge Discovery and Data Mining (KDD), (1996) 82-88.
5. Feldman, R.; and Dagan, I.: KDT - Knowledge Discovery in Texts. In: Proceedings of the 1sr International Conference of Knowledge Discovery and Data Mining (KDD), (1995).
6. Feldman, R.; and Hirsh, H.: Mining Association Rules in Text in the Presence of Background Knowledge. In: Proceedings of the 2nd International Conference of Knowledge Discovery and Data Mining (KDD), (1996).
7. Feldman, R.; Klosgen, W.; and Zilberstein, A.: Visualization Techniques to Explore Data Mining Results for Document Collections. In: Proceedings of the 3rd International Conference of Knowledge Discovery and Data Mining (KDD), (1997) 16-23.
8. Hahn, U.; and Schnattinger, K.: Deep Knowledge Discovery from Natural Language Texts. In: Proceedings of the 3rd International Conference of Knowledge Discovery and Data Mining (KDD), (1997) 175-178.
9. Hotanen, k.; Klemettinen, M.; Mannila, H.; Ronkainon, P.; and Toivonen, H.: TASA: Telecommunication Alarm Sequence Analyzer, or "How to Enjoy Faults in Your Network". In: Proceedings of the 1996 IEEE Network Operations and Management Symposium (NOMS), (1996) 520-529.
10. Keogh, E.; and Smyth, P.: A Probabilistic Approach to Fast Pattern Matching in Time-Series Databases. In: Proceedings of the 3rd International Conference of Knowledge Discovery and Data Mining (KDD), (1997) 24-130.
11. Lent, B.; Agrawal, R.; and Srikant, R.: Discovering Trends in Text Databases. In: Proceedings of the 3rd International Conference of Knowledge Discovery and Data Mining (KDD), (1997) 227-230.
12. Mannila, H.; Toivonen, H.; and Verkamo, A.I.: Discovering Frequent Episodes in Sequences. In: Proceedings of the 1st International Conference of Knowledge Discovery and Data Mining (KDD), (1995) 210-215.
13. Mannila, H.; and Toivenen, H.: Discovering Generalized Episodes Using Minimal Occurances. In: Proceedings of the 2nd International Conference of Knowledge Discovery and Data Mining (KDD), (1996) 146-151.
14. Srikant, R.; and Agrawal, R.: Mining Sequential Patterns: Generalizations and Performance Improvements. In: Proceedings of the 5th International Conference on Extending Database Technology (EDBT), (1996).

Ranked Rules and Data Visualization[1]

Leon Bobrowski[2,3], Tomasz Sowiński[2]

[2] Institute of Computer Science of Technical University of Białystok, Poland
[3] Institute of Biocybernetics and Biomedical Engineering PAS, Warsaw

Abstract. The design of non-linear visualizing transformations of data sets that allow for a good separation of classes (categories) on the diagnostic maps is considered. The proposed transformations are based on a model of the ranked family of decision rules. Such family of rules could be generated by separate and conquer algorithms.

Key words. Extraction of rules from data, ranked decision rules, visualization of multivariate data, diagnostic maps

1 Introduction

Knowledge discovered in databases is usually represented in the form of logical rules which can be used, for example, in expert systems [1]. A chain of rules is a convenient manner of explanation and justification of decisions suggested by a computer system. The graphical representation of the information contained in a database is also important because it allows for deeper involvement of users in a decision making process.

Pattern recognition methods could be often adopted to solving the data mining problems [2] Neural networks models can be also used in the design of computational tools for data mining and knowledge discovery in databases ([3], [4]). We are referring here to the so-called neural ranked networks [5]. The ranked layers could be generated in accordance with separate-and-conquer or covering strategy ([6], [7]). Such layers may be used in the design of non-linear visualizing transformations of data sets in the form of the diagnostic maps [8].

The diagnostic maps constitute a graphical representation of data, which results from the compression of data sets which greatly preserves their separability. The selected groups of patients (classes, categories) could be well separated on the map.

[1] This work was partially supported by the grant 8T11E00811 from the State Committee for Scientific Research (KBN) in Poland, and by the grant W/II/1/97 from Technical University of Białystok

The diagnostic maps constitute the main tool of diagnosis support in the computer system "Hepar" ([9], [10]). In this paper, the design of the visualizing transformations based on a family of logical rules is described.

2 The learning sets and the ranked decision rules

Let us assume that we have access to a database with descriptions of some objects O^j ($j=1,....,m$). In result of some measurements, a set of n discrete or continuous numbers (*features*) x_i could be related to the each object O^j ($x_i \in \{0,1\}$ or $x_i \in R^1$). The data describing objects O^j are represented in the form of column *feature vectors* $x^j = [x_{j1},....,x_{jN}]^T$ belonging to N-dimensional *feature space*. We assume that the objects' descriptions in the database are *labeled*, which means that each object O^j is related to one of the *classes* (category) ω_k ($k = 1,....,K$). The k-th learning set C_k contains m_k feature vectors $x^j(k)$ associated with the class ω_k:

$$C_k = \{x^j(k)\} \ (j = 1,......,m_k) . \tag{1}$$

The learning sets are *separable* if they are disjoined in the given feature space:

$$(\forall k' \neq k) \quad C_{k'} \cap C_k = \varnothing . \tag{2}$$

This means, that the elements $x^j(k')$ and $x^j(k)$ are always different if they belong to two different learning sets C_k.

In the framework of pattern recognition, the learning sets C_k are used to solve the classification problem. During the classification process, the feature vectors x of unknown origin are allocated into one of the classes ω_k in accordance with an *allocation rule* $d_w(x)$ which may depend on some vector of parameters w ($w \in R^N$):

$$\{d_w(x) = k \} \Rightarrow \{ x \text{ is allocated into class } \omega_k\} . \tag{3}$$

The choice of the vector $w = [w_1,....,w_N]^T$ could be made on the basis of the learning sets C_k in accordance with the *reclassification postulate*:
The parameters w (3) should be chosen in such a manner that each feature vector x from the learning sets is properly classified:

$$(\forall k \in \{1,......,K\}) \ (\forall x \in C_k) \ d_w(x) = k . \tag{4}$$

The above demand characterizes the *deterministic approach* to the design of the classifiers. In a *statistical approach* we are satisfied if only a *dominant* $(1-\alpha)$-part of the feature vectors x^j from the learning sets is properly classified.

The allocation rule $d_v(x)$ could be based on the layer of n' *formal neurons* FN_i described by the following decision rule $r_i'(w,\theta;x)$:

$$r_i' = r_i'(w,\theta; x) = 1 \ if \ <w,x> \geq \theta . \tag{5}$$

$$r_i' = r_i'(w,\theta; x) = 0 \ if \ <w,x> < \theta .$$

where $w = [w_1,.......,w_N]^T \in R^N$ is the weight vector, θ is the threshold, and $<w,x> = \Sigma \ w_i \ x_i$ is the inner product.

The formal neuron FN_i is excited ($r_i' = 1$) if and only if the weighted sum of inputs x_i is greater then the the threshold θ.

Let us consider also the layer build from the n' *logical elements* E_i operating in a parallel manner on the same feature vectors $\mathbf{x}$ in accordance with the following decision rule:

$$r_i = r_i(\mathbf{w}, \theta; \mathbf{x}) = 1 \ if \ w_i x_i \geq \theta. \tag{6}$$

$$r_i = r_i(\mathbf{w}, \theta; \mathbf{x}) = 0 \ if \ w_i x_i < \theta.$$

The above decision rule could be treated as a special case of the formal neuron rule (5) which depends on only two parameters w_i and θ.

The element E_i partitions the feature space $\mathbf{X}$ into two regions separated by the following hyperplane:

$$H_i(\mathbf{w}, \theta; \mathbf{x}) = \{\mathbf{x}: \ w_i x_i = \theta \}. \tag{7}$$

The hyperplane $H_i(\mathbf{w}, \theta; \mathbf{x})$ is parallel to all but the i-th coordinate axis of the feature space $\mathbf{X}$. The feature vector $\mathbf{x}$ excites the element E_i ($r_i = 1$) if and only if $\mathbf{x}$ is located on the positive side ($w_i x_i > \theta$) of the hyperplane $H_i(\mathbf{w}, \theta; \mathbf{x})$.

The allocation rule $d_\mathbf{v}(\mathbf{r}(\mathbf{x}))$ (3) of the classifier based on the layer of n' logical elements E_i is determined by the output vector $\mathbf{r} = [r_1, ..., r_n]^T$ of this layer. In a particular case, *the ranked allocation rule* could be used.

Definition 1: The ranked allocation rule has the following general structure:

$$\textit{if} \ ((r_1(\mathbf{x})=0) \wedge (r_2(\mathbf{x})=0) \wedge ... \wedge (r_l(\mathbf{x})=1)) \tag{8}$$
$$\textit{then} \ (\mathbf{x} \text{ is allocated into the class } \omega_{k(l)})$$

where the number $k(l)$ of the chosen class $\omega_{k(l)}$ is determined by the assigned number ("*rank*") l of the first excited element E_i in the layer ($l \leq n'$).

Definition 2: The layer of n' elements E_i (formal neurons FN_i) is *ranked* with respect to the learning sets C_k if and only if there exists a decision rule (8) which allows for correct classification of the all elements $\mathbf{x}^j(k)$ of these sets.

The elements constituting the ranked layer are indexed (ordered) in such a manner that the elements E_i (or their decisions rules $r_i(\mathbf{x})$) with low values of the index i are the most "important". For example, the rule $r_2(\mathbf{x})$ is more important than $r_3(\mathbf{x})$. In accordance with (8), the allocation is based on the most important, excited element E_1.

The order among the elements E_i results from described later the separate-and-conquer procedure of the layer design. Let us define, for the moment, the *support set* A_i of the decision rule $r_i(\mathbf{x})$, as the set of such feature vectors $\mathbf{x}$ which excite the element E_i ($r_i(\mathbf{x}) = 1$). We can remark that if the support sets A_i are disjoined ($A_i \cap A_j = \emptyset$), then the elements E_i could be ranked in an arbitrary manner.

Definition 3: The layer of n' elements E_i is α-*ranked* with respect to the learning sets C_k if and only if there exists a decision rule (8) which allows for correct classification of at least the dominant $(1-\alpha)$-part of the all elements $\mathbf{x}^j(k)$ of these sets.

The last definition will be used in a statistical approach to classification, when we are satisfied with only a dominant part of the feature vectors $\mathbf{x}^j(k)$ from the learning sets being properly classified.

The procedure of designing a layer of formal neurons FN_i which is ranked with respect to the learning sets C_k has been described in the papers [8] and [12]. This multistage procedure could be used also in design of the ranked layer from the logical elements E_i. The procedure is based on finding the sequence of so called *admissible* hyperplanes $H_i(\mathbf{w}^*, \theta^*; \mathbf{x})$ (7).

Definition 4: The hyperplanes $H_i(\mathbf{w}^*, \theta^*; \mathbf{x})$ are *admissible* with respect to the family of learning sets $\{C_k\}$ if and only if the vectors $\mathbf{x}^j(k)$ from only <u>one</u> set C_k are situated on its positive side. This means that:

$$(\exists k)\,(w_i^* \, x_{ji} \geq \theta^*) \Rightarrow (\mathbf{x}^j \in C_k). \tag{9}$$

Definition 5: The hyperplanes $H_i(\mathbf{w}^*, \theta^*; \mathbf{x})$ are α-*admissible* with respect to the family of the learning sets $\{C_k\}$ if and only if at least the $(1-\alpha)$-part of the vectors $\mathbf{x}^j(k')$ situated on its positive side belongs to only one learning set C_k.

The vectors $\mathbf{x}^j(k)$ which are situated on the positive side of the admissible (α-admissible) hyperplane $H_i(\mathbf{w}^*, \theta^*; \mathbf{x})$ (7) are removed before the next stage of the design procedure. In other words, the learning sets C_k are reduced during successive n stages of the design procedure. This procedure could be treated as a special case of the separate-and-conquer strategy [2]. Generally, the separate-and-conquer algorithm searches for a rule that explains a part of the learning sets C_k, separates these examples and recursively conquers the remaining examples by designing more rules until no examples remain.

The separate-and-conquer procedure allows us to find the sequence of admissible or α-admissible hyperplanes $H_i(\mathbf{w}, \theta; \mathbf{x})$ (7). As a result, the ranked allocation rule (8) can be established. Note that this rule could be represented in the following form:

$$\textbf{\textit{if}}\ ((\gamma_{i(1)}\, x_{i(1)} < \theta_{i(1)}) \wedge (\gamma_{i(2)}\, x_{i(2)} < \theta_{i(2)}) \wedge ... \wedge (\gamma_{i(l)}\, x_{i(l)} \geq \theta_{i(l)}) \tag{10}$$
$$\textbf{\textit{then}}\ (\mathbf{x}\ \text{is allocated into the class}\ \omega_{k(l)})$$

where $\gamma_i \in \{1, -1\}$ and θ_i is the threshold value of the i-th element E_i.

Each of the above subrules or hyperplanes $H_i(\gamma_i, \theta_i; \mathbf{x})$ (7) is defined by two parameters γ_m and θ_m. These parameters are to be found in accordance with the postulate of *admissibility* or α-*admissibility* with respect to a given family of the learning sets $\{C_k\}$. An α-*admissibility* is taken into consideration in the case of the statistical approach to design of the ranked layers. From a computational point of view it is relatively easy to find the numbers γ_m and θ_m using a discrete, exhaustive search. The basis exchange algorithms, similar to linear programming methods, have been developed for the purpose of finding the admissible hyperplanes related to the formal neurons FN_i [12]. These algorithms allow to find the solution in efficient manner even in the case of large learning sets C_k.

3 Data transformations based on the ranked layer

The feature vectors $\mathbf{x}^j$ from the learning sets C_k are transformed by the ranked layer built from n' elements E_i into n'-dimensional vectors $\mathbf{r}^l$, with binary components $r^l{}_i$. This transformation has the following general form:

$$\mathbf{r}^l = F(\mathbf{W}; \mathbf{r}) . \qquad (11)$$

where $\mathbf{W}$ is the vector of the layer parameter.

A few feature vectors $\mathbf{x}^j$ could be integrated into one vector $\mathbf{r}^l$ in accordance with the transformations (15) (we can enumerate the vectors $\mathbf{r}^l$ in such a manner that they are different: $l \neq l' \Rightarrow \mathbf{r}^l \neq \mathbf{r}^{l'}$). As a result, the data sets are compressed and the number m' of the different vectors $\mathbf{r}^l$ could by significantly less than m. Let us define the *active fields* $S_l(\mathbf{W})$ of the layer with the transformation function $F(\mathbf{W}; \mathbf{x})$:

$$S_l = S(\mathbf{W}; \mathbf{r}^l) = \{ \mathbf{x}^j : F(\mathbf{W}; \mathbf{x}^j) = \mathbf{r}^l \text{ and } (\exists \, C_k : \mathbf{x}^j \in C_k) \} . \qquad (12)$$

The feature vectors $\mathbf{x}^j$ belonging to one active field S_l are integrated into one vector $\mathbf{r}^l$ by the ranked layer.

Definition 6: The active field S_l is of the *clear* type if and only if it contains the feature vectors $\mathbf{x}^j$ from one learning set C_k. Equivalently, the *mixed* active field contains the elements of more than one learning set C_k (1).

Definition 7: The learning set C_k is *dominant* in the active field S_l if most of the feature vectors $\mathbf{x}^j$ constituting S_l belong to C_k. Let symbol $S_l(k)$ mean the active field with the dominant set C_k, or in other words, the active field related to the class ω_k.

The class membership of the vectors $\mathbf{r}^l$ could be defined (*assigned*) in the following manner:

$$\{ \text{the learning set } C_k \text{ is dominant in the active field } S_l \} \Rightarrow \{ \mathbf{r}^l \in \omega_k \} \qquad (13)$$

The labeled vectors $\mathbf{r}^l$ constitute the transformed learning sets D_k:

$$D_k = \{ \mathbf{r}^l(k) \} \ (l = 1,...., m'_k) . \qquad (14)$$

where m'_k is the number of transformed vectors $\mathbf{r}^l(k)$ belonging to the class ω_k ($m'_k \leq m_k$).

The most important property of the ranked layer is its (*separable*) *linearization* of the learning sets ([11], [12]). This means that the sets D_k of the vectors $\mathbf{r}^l$ transformed by the ranked layer are linearly separable:

$$(\forall \, k = 1,......,K) \, (\exists \, \mathbf{w}_k , \theta_k) \, (\forall \, \mathbf{r}^l \in D_k) \ \langle \mathbf{w}_k, \mathbf{r}^l \rangle \geq \theta_k \qquad (15)$$
$$\text{and } (\forall \mathbf{r}^l \in D_i, i \neq k) \ \langle \mathbf{w}_k, \mathbf{r}^l \rangle < \theta_k$$

The family of the sets D_k is *linearly separable* if each set D_k can be separated in the feature space from the sum of all remaining sets D_i by some hyperplane $H'(\mathbf{w}, \theta; \mathbf{x})$ (9). This linearization property could be used, among other applications, in the design of the visualizing transformations.

4 Design of the ranked visualizing transformations

We consider special nonlinear transformations from the N-dimensional feature space $\mathbf{X}$ onto a plane (two dimensions):

$$y_1 = F_1(\mathbf{W}_1; \mathbf{x}) \qquad (16)$$

$$y_2 = F_2(\mathbf{W}_2; \mathbf{x})$$

where $\mathbf{y} = [y_1, y_2]^T$ and $\mathbf{W}_k$ ($k = 1,2$) are parameters of the transformations. Each of the above two transformations is related to one axis of the plane and will be based on a separate layer of the elements E_i, ranked with respect to some sets G_1 as described below.

The feature vectors $\mathbf{x}^j(k)$ are transformed and visualized as the points $\mathbf{y}^l(k')$ on the plane. The vectors $\mathbf{y}^l(k)$ belonging to one class ω_k constitute the transformed learning sets F_k (14).

$$F_k = \{ \mathbf{y}^l(k) \} \ (l = 1,...., m'_k) \tag{17}$$

The so called *diagnostic maps* of the learning sets C_k can be generated by the transformations (16). A diagnostic map visualizes the data in such a manner that the selected sets F_k are well separated. In other words, the feature vectors $\mathbf{x}^j(k)$ belonging to the selected sets C_k are transformed and visualized as the points $\mathbf{y}^l(k)$ located in the separate regions of the map. A decision support rule could be based on the diagnostic map in the following manner:

if *the transformed feature vector* $\mathbf{y}(\mathbf{x})$ (16) *is located on the map* (18)
in the region of the well separated set(-s) F_k
then *the vector* $\mathbf{x}$ *should be allocated into the class(-es)* ω_k.

Let us divide the data set twice into some subsets G_{k1} and G_{k2} ($k = 1,2$) of the feature vectors $\mathbf{x}^j$ in order to design the transformations (16). Two ranked layers of the elements E_i, are designed by using the subsets G_{ki}. The first layer is ranked with respect to the sets $\{G_{11}, G_{12}\}$ (G_{11} *vs* G_{12}), and the second layer is ranked with respect to the sets $\{G_{21}, G_{22}\}$. The sets G_{k1} and G_{k2} will be transformed by the k-th ranked layer into the sets D_{k1} and D_{k2} of the vectors $\mathbf{r}^j$. In accordance with the previous consideration, the sets D_{k1} and D_{k2} are linearly separable (19). Let (v_k^*, θ_k^*) be the parameters of a hyperplane which separates the sets D_{k1} and D_{k2}. These parameters can be used also in definition of the linear transformation of the transformed vectors $\mathbf{r}_k^j$ from the sets D_{k1}:

$$y_{1j} = \langle v_1^*, r_1^j \rangle + \theta_1^* \tag{19}$$
$$y_{2j} = \langle v_2^*, r_2^j \rangle + \theta_2^*$$

The transformed vectors $\mathbf{y}^j = [y_{j1}, y_{j2}]^T$ will constitute points on the diagnostic maps which represent the feature vectors $\mathbf{x}^j$.

In summary, the transformation of the feature vectors $\mathbf{x}^j$ into the points $\mathbf{y}^j$ on the diagnostic maps is done in two steps. During the first step, each feature vector $\mathbf{x}^j$ is transformed by two parallel ranked layers into two vectors $\mathbf{r}_1^j$ and $\mathbf{r}_2^j$. During the second step, the vectors $\mathbf{r}_1^j$ and $\mathbf{r}_2^j$ are transformed linearly (19) into the point $\mathbf{y}^j$.

Note that the diagnostic map designed in this way is divided into the following quarters:

the upper-right quarter - $G_{11} \cap G_{21}$ (20)
the lower-right quarter - $G_{11} \cap G_{22}$
the lower-left quarter - $G_{12} \cap G_{22}$

the upper-left quarter - $G_{12} \cap G_{21}$

The *Iris* data sets have been visualized in this manner (Fig. 1).

5 An example of the diagnostic map design

The Fisher's *Iris* data sets contain 150 four-dimensional feature vectors x^j from three classes ω_k (learning sets C_k): ω_1 -*Iris setosa*, ω_2 - *Iris versicolor*, ω_3 - *Iris virginnica* [3]. Each learning set C_k contains in this case exactly 50 feature vectors x^j. The transformation (16) related to the first axis of the diagnostic map has been defined by the layer of 7 elements E_i with the rule (14) ranked with respect to two sets C_2 and $C_1 \cup C_3$ (*partition* C_2 *vs.* $C_1 \cup C_3$) (Tab. 1). Similarly, the layer of the second axis was ranked with respect to sets C_2 and $C_1 \cup C_3$ (Tab. 2).

Table 1. Ranked layer designed for the partition C_2 *vs.* $C_1 \cup C_3$ (first axis)

Rule index	Index of control feature x_i	Threshold θ_i	Direction γ_i	Dominant Classes ω_i	Numbers of the separated feature vectors
1	3	2.45	-1	$\omega_1 \cup \omega_3$	50 (34 %)
2	4	1.8	1	$\omega_1 \cup \omega_3$	43 (29 %)
3	3	4.5	-1	ω_2	36 (24 %)
4	2	3.05	1	ω_2	5 (3 %)
5	3	5.1	1	$\omega_1 \cup \omega_3$	5 (3 %)
6	1	6	1	ω_2	9 (6 %)
7	1	6	-1	$\omega_1 \cup \omega_3$	2 (1 %)

Table 2. Ranked layer designed for the partition C_3 *vs.* $C_1 \cup C_2$ (second axis)

Rule index	Index of control feature x_i	Threshold θ_i	Direction γ_i	Dominant Classes ω_i	Numbers of the separated feature vectors
1	4	1.4	-1	$\omega_1 \cup \omega_2$	84 (56 %)
2	4	1.8	1	ω_3	40 (27 %)
3	3	5.1	1	ω_3	7 (5 %)
4	1	6	1	$\omega_1 \cup \omega_2$	11 (7 %)
5	2	3	1	$\omega_1 \cup \omega_2$	4 (3 %)
6	2	3	-1	ω_3	3 (2 %)
7	1	3	1	$\omega_1 \cup \omega_2$	1 (< 1 %)

The linear transformations (19) related to each of the two axis has been defined by the following parameters:

$$\mathbf{v}_1^* = [v_1,......, v_7]^T = [-10, -2, 6, 2, -2, -10, -10]^T, \; \theta_1^* = 11$$
$$\mathbf{v}_2^* = [v_1,......, v_7]^T = [-10, 2, 2, 0, -10, -10, 0]^T, \; \theta_2^* = 9$$

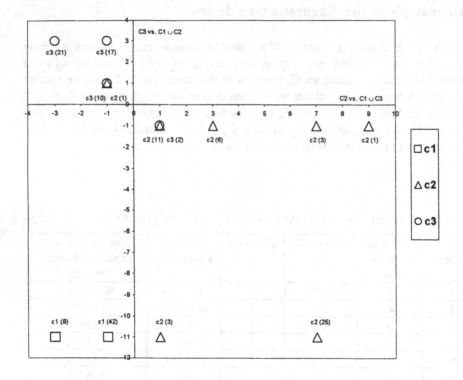

Fig. 1. Diagnostic map for Iris data

The characteristic feature of the map is that one set C_k of the objects $\mathbf{x}^j$ is located in the one quarter of the visualising plane. Any four separable data sets could be transformed in this way on the plane

6 Concluding remarks

The procedure for designing the visualising transformations has been described here. These non-linear transformations can be based on the ranked layer of the decision rules which are extracted from the learning data sets. The visualising transformation defines a new structure (topology) of the feature space **X**.

The described procedure can be applied to the design of diagnostic maps, which can be used in the decision support (18) to complement logical formulas. The maps make possible the interactive user involvement in the decision making process.

Another possible application of the maps is a search for (non-linear) interactions among a groups of objects. The visualizing transformation designed on the base of the selected four categories (groups) of objects could be used to visualize the same or another object divided into other categories. We could observe in which way the selected partitions of the feature space X interact.

One of the problems which should be avoided during the design of the non-linear visualizing transformations is data overfitting. The transformation based on ranked networks may depend on a large number of parameters which have to be estimated from the learning data sets. The large number of estimated parameters could diminish the generality of the design transformations and the decision rules.

The design of the ranked layers from the logical elements E_i (6) allows the number of the estimated parameters to be decreased in comparison with the formal neurons FN_i (5). Also, the computation of the ranked rules is easier for the elements E_i (6). On the other hand, this diminishes the discrimination power of the decision rules and it may be impossible to design the fully separable, ranked layer for some data sets by using only the elements E_i (6). This fact could be observed even for the Iris data sets.

References

1. U. M. Fayyad, G. Piatetsky-Shapiro, P. Smyth, *Advances in Knowledge Discovery and Data Mining*, AAAI Press/ The MIT Press 1996
2. O. R. Duda and P. E. Hart: Pattern Classification and Scene Analysis. New York, J. Wiley 1973
3. Ch. M. Bishop, *Neural networks for pattern recognition*, Clarendon Press, Oxford 1995
4. B. D. Ripley *Pattern Recognition and Neural Networks*, Cambridge University Press, 1996
5. L. Bobrowski, "The Ranked Networks of Formal Neurons". *Biocybernetics and Biomedical Engineering*, Vol. 12, Nr. 1 - 4, pp.61-75, 1992
6. J. Fuhrkranz: Separate-and-Conquer Rule Learning, Austrian Research Institute for Artificial Intelligence, Technical Report OEFAJ-TR-96-25
   http://www.research.att.com/~wcohen/cs536/oefai-tr-96-25.ps
7. M. Mizard and J.-P. Nadal: Learning in Feedforward Layered Neural Networks: The Tiling Algorithm, J. Phys. A22, 2191 (1889)
8. L. Bobrowski, H. Wasyluk, "Neural networks in discrimination of liver diseases", *Biocybernetics and Biomedical Engineering*, 1998 (in a press)
9. L. Bobrowski (Ed.): "Hepar - computer system for diagnossis support and data analysis" (in Polish), *Prace IBIB*, 31, 1992
10. H. Wasyluk, The Four Year's Experience with HEPAR - Computer Assisted Diagnostic Program" in *MEDINFO 95* Proceedings, R. A. Greenes et al. (Eds.)
11. L. Bobrowski, "*Piecewise-Linear Classifiers, Formal Neurons and separability of the Learning Sets*", Proceedings of ICPR'96, pp. 224-228 (*13th International Conference on Pattern Recognition*", August 25-29, 1996, Wienna, Austria)
12. L. Bobrowski: "Design of piecewise linear classifiers from formal neurons by some basis exchange technique". *Pattern Recognition*, 24(9), pp. 863-870, 1991.

TextVis: An Integrated Visual Environment for Text Mining

David Landau, Ronen Feldman,
Yonatan Aumann, Moshe Fresko, Yehuda Lindell,
Orly Lipshtat

Oren Zamir

Department of Mathematics and Computer Science
Bar-Ilan University
Ramat-Gan, Israel
{landuad,feldman}@cs.biu.ac.il

Department of Computer Science
University of Washington
Seattle, WA
zamir@cs.washington.edu

Abstract. TextVis is a visual data mining system for document collections. Such a collection represents an application domain, and the primary goal of the system is to derive patterns that provide knowledge about this domain. Additionally, the derived patterns can be used to browse the collection. TextVis takes a multi-strategy approach to text mining, and enables defining complex analysis schemas from basic components, provided by the system. An analysis schema is constructed by dragging functional icons from a tool-pallette onto the workspace and connecting them according to the desired flow of information. The system provides a large collection of basic analysis tools, including: frequent sets, associations, concept distributions, and concept correlations. The discovered patterns are presented in a visual interface allowing the user to operate on the results, and to access the associated documents. TextVis is a complete text mining system which uses agent technology to access various online information sources, text preprocessing tools to extract relevant information from the documents, a variety of data mining algorithms, and a set of visual browsers to view the results. This paper provides an overview on the TextVis system. We describe the system's architecture, the various tools, and discuss the advantages of our visual environment for mining large document collections.

1. Introduction

Knowledge discovery in databases (KDD) is informally defined as the extraction of useful information from databases by large-scale search for interesting patterns [4]. The vast majority of existing KDD applications and methods deal with structured databases, e.g. client data stored in a relational database, and thus exploit the predefined organization of the data in the database. However, a tremendous amount of information is also available in unstructured, textual form. The availability of document collections and especially of online information is rapidly growing. The vast amounts of information prohibit manual analysis and effective exploration. Thus, it is necessary to provide automatic tools for analyzing large textual collections. Accordingly, in analogy to *data mining* for structured data, *text mining* is defined for textual data. The goal of text mining is to extract information from patterns in large textual collections. The results can be important both for the analysis of the collection, and for providing intelligent navigation and browsing methods.

Text mining shares many characteristics with classical data mining, but also differs in many ways. On the one hand, many classical data mining tasks and algorithms, such as value prediction or decision trees, are irrelevant or ill suited for the textual application. On the other hand, there are special mining tasks, such as concept relationship analysis, which are unique to text mining. In addition, the unstructured form of the raw data necessitates special preprocessing for extracting the main features of the text. Thus, it is necessary to provide special tools and systems geared specifically to text mining.

Current text mining systems (e.g., the KDT system [7,8], FACT [6] and WEBSOM [11]) have a rigid architecture. The system provides the user with one or more fixed analysis tools, with no ability to combine between tools, or to construct new analysis paths. Thus, the analysis process is limited to the small predefined analysis tasks envisioned by the creator of the system.

In this paper we describe TextVis, a new integrated visual system for text mining. TextVis takes a multi-strategy approach to text mining, allowing the formation of arbitrarily complex analysis tasks. The system provides the user with a set of *basic-tools* as building blocks, and complex analysis tasks are constructed by combining the basic tools. The process may be interactive, defining and refining the analysis process ad-hoc. The system provides a visual interface for constructing the analysis path. Using the visual interface, basic-tools are represented as drag-and-drop icons (from an icon pallet), and the combination of tools is executed by drawing arrows between icons on the workspace. In addition, TextVis provides an elaborate set of browsers, including IR (Information Retrieval) tools, for viewing the data and the analysis results. The browsers are integrated into the analysis process, and may be used as active filters. Thus, TextVis provides a knowledge discovery framework which integrates advanced mining tools with traditional IR.

TextVis is a complete knowledge-discovery-in-texts suite, supporting the entire discovery process, from the data collection step, through the linguistic analysis of the text, to the mining analysis, and the visual presentation of results.

The TextVis System builds upon the experience that was gained from building the KDT system [7,8], FACT [6], and Explora [9,10].

Outline. The rest of this paper is organized as follows. We start by providing a general overview on the architecture of the system. Next we describe the different components of the system, including analysis tools and visual browsers. Finally, we describe the formation of complex analysis paths, using the visual workspace. The examples we provide were created using a set of 52,000 articles of Reuters Financial News from 1995-1996.

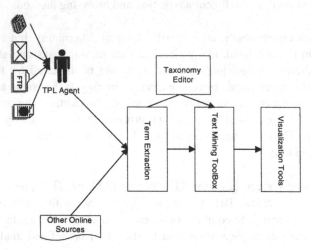

Fig. 1. TextVis System Architecture

2. System Architecture

TextVis takes a multi-strategy approach to text mining, and enables building complex text analysis schemas based on the basic components provided. The schemas are built by dragging functional icons from a tool-palette onto the workspace and connecting them according to the desired flow of information. TextVis is a complete text mining system supporting the entire mining process, starting with obtaining the documents from various online information sources and ending with a set of visual browsers to view the results of the various data mining tools. The architecture of the TextVis system is show in Figure-1.

The TextVis system is comprised of four main components: an information gathering agent, a document preprocessing module, mining tools, and visualization tools. It further contains a taxonomy editor to aid in creating taxonomies which support the term extraction and mining tools. We now describe each of the four system components.

Information Gathering: The TPL (Text Parsing Language) Agent is used for gathering information. This agent can access various types of information sources including FTP Sites, WWW Sites, email messages, and newsgroups. The agent has a special script language for specifying the exact task to be performed. Each script includes the URL of the information source, a control mechanism for interacting with the specific site and some parsing guidelines for identifying the relevant information. TPL packages the information extracted in a format suitable for further analysis by the TextVis system. We have experimented with accessing the results of a search engine(Alta Vista), a news wire (Reuters) and a special knowledge sources (IBM Patent Server).

Document Preprocessing: After the document collection is identified, the system starts by preprocessing and extracting terms from the documents. Each document is represented by a set of terms which characterize its content. The terms can be accompanied by their frequencies in the document and a weight signifying their importance. The system stores the following attributes with each document: the date, title, author/source, body of text, and a set of extracted terms. The system handles two types of terms: Tagged Terms and untagged Terms. Tagged Terms are terms that are already categorized, like "<Inventor>: David Lewis". Usually tagged terms are fetched from HTML or SGML files where the HTML tag is used as the tag of the term. The TPL agent is able to extract such tagged terms. Untagged terms are terms that were extracted from an untagged portion of the document, usually the document text itself. The output of the preprocessing phase may be saved as a flat file, SGML file, binary file or in a relational database. The data module of TextVis supports data sources in any of these formats and presents a uniform interface to the mining tools. The original source type is invisible to the rest of the system. The data module implicitly builds an inverted file upon loading any source. This is relied upon by different modules of TextVis enabling fast retrieval of all documents containing a set of entities. The module further supports fast retrieval of a given document's term list and original text via its identification number. The free interaction of the data module with the different mining tools emphasizes the modularity unique to TextVis.

Mining Tools: The text mining tools provided by TextVis can be grouped into two classes: Filters and Analyzers. *Filters* are modules which output a subset of the document set. They are typically coupled with a visualization tool for exploring the input set and choosing subsets for further mining. As text corpora are usually very large and diverse, filters are essential for reducing the size of the input and achieving efficient data mining. The output of a filter is handled by TextVis as any other document source, and can be the subject of further analysis. *Analyzers* typically apply a mining algorithm on their input set and extract information regarding that set. The format of this information differs for the different mining tools. Whereas filters are usually used to aid in further mining, analyzers are often results within themselves containing important analytical information.

The Filters currently offered in TextVis are:
1. Query Tools: the output is a set of documents that satisfy a given query.
2. Clustering Tools: the tool gets as input a collection of documents and produces a set of clusters. Each cluster contains documents that are similar to each other using a predefined metric.

The analyzers currently offered in TextVis are:
1. Distribution Based Tools: the system can compute the *profile* of any entity found in the document collection. Typically entities are people, companies, organizations, concepts, countries etc. A profile is the co-occurrence distribution of the given entity with closely related entities. The system can also compare between a set of profiles to find similarities and differences.
2. Frequent-Set Based Tools: the system can generate all frequent sets or only those that satisfy a set of content based constraints. See Section 3 for details.
3. Association Based Tools: the system can generate all associations [1,2] that meet a set of constraints.

Visualization Tools: TextVis offers a set of visual browsers to aid the user in the interactive process of analyzing the data. The system offers browsers for each entity type (e.g., documents, clusters of documents, frequent-sets, association rules, concept distribution trends etc.). Entities may have multiple browsers to allow different visualization capabilities. When browsing a pattern found by the system, the list of the documents, and actual documents, that support the pattern may be viewed.

TextVis is an object-oriented visual system that enables the user to draw visual analysis diagrams. Each diagram starts with one or more document collections. The system is able to read documents from various sources including flat files, SGML files, binary files and files stored in databases that support the ODBC standard. In addition to the document collections, each diagram may include a sequence of filters, analyzers and visualization tools. Each operation produces an intermediate object, which can then be the input for another tool. This enables the spontaneous building of analysis schemas where, upon seeing an interesting pattern, the user may further research that pattern by using it for input to other tools. Intermediate objects may be a collection of frequent sets, a set of association rules, a distribution, or simply an intermediate document collection. Each object has an associated input and output format. The system will allow connecting objects only if the output of one object will match the input of the other object. Trying to combine incompatible objects will result in changing the cursor to a no-entry sign.

3. Text Mining Operations

As was mentioned above, TextVis provides the user with a palette of tools that can be used for building complex text analysis schemas. In this section we highlight a number of the tools, some of them new, provided by the TextVis System.

3.1. Query Module

This module provides the basic functionality of an information retrieval system. The user can enter a query and receive all documents satisfying that query. The resulting

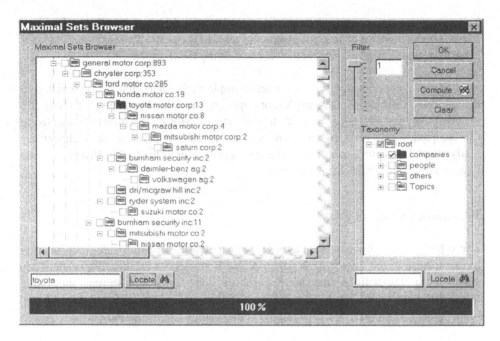

Fig. 2. *Maximal Set* browser

set of documents can then be "exported" for further analysis. The export operation creates a new icon in the graphical work area, representing the new sub-collection of documents. This new sub-collection is handled by the system as any other document source. It can therefore be subject to further analysis.

3.2. Clustering

Any set of documents (either an original set, or the result of any of the other tools) can be clustered by the system. The user may choose from one of four classical clustering algorithms: Hierarchical, k-means [12], Buckshot, and Fractionation [3]. Following the clustering, the user can select any number of documents, either individual documents or whole clusters, and export them for further analysis.

3.3. Frequent-Set Based Tools

Frequent Sets [1] are sets of terms that co-occur frequently in the collection (above a user defined threshold). Although originally defined as an intermediary step in finding association rules, we found that frequent-sets contain much interesting information within themselves. *Maximal sets* [5] are sets of items relating to a user specified topic. We say that a document supports a given set if the document contains the terms of the set and there is no larger set which the document supports. The maximal sets browser in TextVis presents the output in a tree format, giving an effect similar to clustering.

The root of the tree contains the term which appears in the most sets. The sub-tree of any node is comprised of sets containing the term in the node. The first son of a node is the term which appears most in the sets containing the term's node.

In Figure 2 (previous page) we see an example of the maximal sets associated to the subject "companies". General Motors appeared in 893 documents, of them 353 included Chrysler and so on. The sub-tree of General Motors is a cluster connected to car companies and their co-occurrences. The documents relevant to a cluster are easily viewed by double-clicking on the appropriate node. This tool is also used to aid in generating taxonomies for the system.

3.4. Association-Based Tools

These tools accept frequent sets as input, and output association rules. Association rules are rules of the type $A \Rightarrow B$ where A and B are sets of entities. The system can generate all associations that meet a set of constraints. Constraints are either threshold-based (confidence and support) Some constraints are threshold-based (confidence and support) and relate to the contents of the association.

4. Text Analysis Schema

The uniqueness and power of TextVis is its ability to build elaborate analysis schemas. Each such schema is combined of Data Sources, Analyzers, Filters and Visualizers. The user builds an analysis schema by dragging icons from pallets and connecting them with arrows. Each icon represents one of the TextVis modules and has its own particular settings, depending on the nature of the object. Data Source objects settings define the files from reach to read the data. Algorithmic components settings are used to set the appropriate parameters needed to run the algorithms.

In Figure 3 we see a sample analysis schema. We started by selecting a Data Source and attaching it to the Reuters Financial Collection from the years 1995-96. We used two analysis paths. In the upper path we first applied clustering of the entire collection. Examining the clusters, we identified a cluster consisting of documents regarding "joint ventures". We where interested in analyzing this cluster. However, the cluster was too large for efficient exploration. Thus, we exported it to a Subset Data Source which was then re-clustered. The resulting clusters provided us with a grouping of the articles regarding "joint ventures" by industries. In particular, the system identified a cluster of documents about joint ventures of cable TV companies, and another cluster on oil companies (due to lack of place, the results are not shown). In the bottom path we used an IR filter to select all documents regarding high-tech industries. We obtained a subcollection (marked Data Set in the visual environment). We then applied a clustering algorithm to this subcollection, and exported two sub-

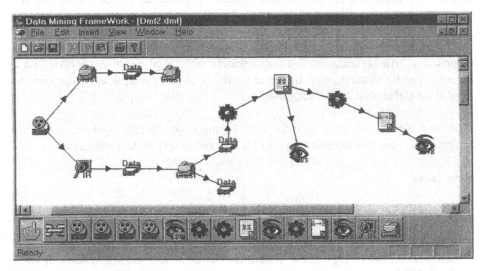

Fig. 3. Analysis Schema

collections of documents. One of these collections was used for analysis by data mining tools. Frequent sets were built and association rules generated. Browsers were attached to icons storing the frequent sets and rules at the end to enable viewing the intermediate and final results.

5. Conclusions

TextVis is a second-generation text mining system in that it provides an integrated environment for text mining. The system enables the user great flexibility in combining a variety of different tools. A key feature of the system is the ability to construct complex analysis paths comprising of both classical information retrieval tools for filtering and powerful data mining tools for extracting interesting information. The analysis process is interactive, so that the analysis path may be refined based on the output of the previous steps. At any point in the analysis, several non-exclusive options are available to the user. More than one tool may be used originating from a single point. Another strength of the system is the clear separation between algorithmic tools and browsers. This enables each user to view the results of the algorithmic tools with a browser that suits his/her needs. The major benefit of this approach when compared to previous first-generation text mining systems such as KDT, FACT, and WEBSOM is that the user is no longer limited to the individual tools provided by the system. The ability to combine tools provides an unlimited number of analysis schemas that can be built. Due to the high level of modularity, adding new components to the system is quick and simple, making the system readily expandable. New modules are added with ease and interact with the overall system according to defined uniform interfaces. The system is equipped with a TPL agent which enables a constant feed of articles and documents. The tight integration between the agent and the text mining modules provides a very powerful tool for mining the vast information available on the Internet.

The system allows storing schemas in a library. The schemas can then be reused by other users. An organization can thus create a library of common analysis tasks. Schemas can be customized to fit the exact needs of each user, without the need to rebuild the full analysis path each time.

In the future, we plan to add more components to the system, including information extraction tools and support for a larger variety of data sources

References

1. Agrawal A., Srikant R.: Fast algorithms for mining association rules. In: Proceedings of the VLDB Conference, (1994).
2. Agrawal A., Imielinski T., Swami A.: Mining association rules between sets of items in large databases. In: Proceedings of the ACM SIGMOD Conference on Management of Data, (1993) 207-216.
3. Cutting D. R., Karger D. R., Pederson J. O., Tukey J. W.: Scatter/Gather: a cluster-based approach to browsing large document collections. In: Proceedings of the 15th International ACM SIGIR Conference on Research and Development in Information Retrieval, (1992) 318-329.
4. Fayyad, U,; Piatetsky-Shapiro, G.; and Smyth P.: Knowledge Discovery and Data Mining: Towards a Unifying Framework. In: Proceedings of the 2nd International Conference of Knowledge Discovery and Data Mining (KDD), (1996) 82-88.
5. Feldman R., Aumann A., Amir A., Zilberstein A., Kloesgen W.: Maximal Association Rules: a New Tool for Mining for Keyword Co-occurrence in Document Collections. In Proceedings of the 3rd International Conference on Knowledge Discovery (KDD),(1997) 167-170.
6. Feldman R., and Hirsh H. "Exploiting Background Information in Knowledge Discovery from Text, ", Journal of Intelligent Information Systems, (1997).
7. Feldman R., Dagan I., Kloesgen W.: Efficient Algorithms for Mining and Manipulating Associations in Texts. In: Proceedings of EMCSR96, (1996).
8. Feldman R., Dagan I.: KDT - knowledge discovery in texts. In: Proceedings of the First International Conference on Knowledge Discovery (KDD), (1995).
9. Klösgen W.: Efficient Discovery of Interesting Statements. The Journal of Intelligent Information Systems, 4(1) (1995).
10. Klösgen W.: Explora: A Multipattern and Multistrategy Discovery Assistant. In: U. Fayyad, G. Piatetsky-Shapiro, P. Smyth, R. Uthurusamy, (Eds.) Advances in Knowledge Discovery and Data Mining, MIT Press, Cambridge, MA (1996).
11. Lagus, K., Honkela, T., Kaski, S., Kohonen, T.: Self-organizing maps of document collections: A new approach to interactive exploration. In: Proceedings of the 2nd International Conference on Knowledge Discovery and Data Mining (KDD), (1996) 238-243.
12. Rocchio, J. J.: Document retrieval systems – optimization and evaluation. Ph.D. Thesis, Harvard University, (1966).

Text Mining at the Term Level

Ronen Feldman[1], Moshe Fresko[1], Yakkov Kinar[1], Yehuda Lindell[1], Orly Liphstat[1],
Martin Rajman[2], Yonatan Schler[1], Oren Zamir[3]

[1] Department of Mathematics and Computer Science, Bar-Ilan University,
Ramat-Gan, Israel
{feldman, fresko, kinary, ylindell, okatz, schler}@cs.biu.ac.il
[2] Artificial Intelligence Laboratory (LIA), Swiss Federal Institute of Technology,
Lausanne, Switzerland
martin.rajman@epfl.ch
[3] Department of Computer Science, University of Washington,
Seattle, WA
zamir@cs.washington.edu

Abstract. Knowledge Discovery in Databases (KDD) focuses on the computerized exploration of large amounts of data and on the discovery of interesting patterns within them. While most work on KDD has been concerned with structured databases, there has been little work on handling the huge amount of information that is available only in unstructured textual form. Previous work in text mining focused at the word or the tag level. This paper presents an approach to performing text mining at the term level. The mining process starts by preprocessing the document collection and extracting terms from the documents. Each document is then represented by a set of terms and annotations characterizing the document. Terms and additional higher-level entities are then organized in a hierarchical taxonomy. In this paper we will describe the Term Extraction module of the Document Explorer system, and provide experimental evaluation performed on a set of 52,000 documents published by Reuters in the years 1995-1996.

1 Introduction

Traditional databases store information in the form of structured records and provide methods for querying them to obtain all records whose content satisfies the user's query. More recently however, researchers in *Knowledge Discovery in Databases* (KDD) have provided a new family of tools for accessing information in databases [1,3,15,19,20]. The goal of such work, often called *data mining*, has been defined as "the nontrivial extraction of implicit, previously unknown, and potentially useful information from given data" [15]. Work in this area includes applying machine-learning and statistical-analysis techniques towards the automatic discovery of patterns in databases, as well as providing user-guided environments for exploration of data.

Most efforts in KDD have focused on knowledge discovery in structured databases, despite the tremendous amount of online information that appears only in collections of unstructured text. Previous approaches to text mining have used either tags attached to documents [11,12,13] or words contained in the documents [21].

Standard Text Mining systems do not usually operate on unprepared documents but rather on "categorized documents", i.e. documents that were (manually or automatically from a set of examples) tagged with terms identifying their content. Such systems can of course be extended to use the full text of the document by systematically tagging the documents with *all* the words they contain. This process however, does not provide effectively exploitable results, as has been shown for association generation [22]. For example, in the experiment just mentioned, the association generation process detected either compounds, i.e. domain-dependent terms such as [wall, street] or [treasury, secretary, james, baker], which cannot be considered potentially useful associations or extracted uninterpretable associations such as [dollars, shares, exchange, total, commission, stake, securities] that cannot be considered easily understandable.

The exploitation of untagged, full text documents therefore requires some additional linguistic pre-processing, allowing the automated extraction from the documents of linguistic elements more complex than simple words. We use *normalized terms*, i.e. sequences of one or more lemmatized word forms (or lemmas) associated with their part-of-speech tags. "stock/N market/N" or "annual/Adj interest/N rate/N" are typical examples of such normalized terms.

In this paper, we present our approach to text mining, which is based on extracting meaningful terms from documents. The system described in this paper begins with collections of raw documents, without any labels or tags. Documents are first labeled with terms extracted directly from the documents. Next, the terms and additional higher-level entities (that are organized in a hierarchical taxonomy) are used to support a range of KDD operations on the documents. The frequency of co-occurrence of terms can provide the foundation for a wide range of KDD operations on collections of textual documents, such as finding sets of documents whose term distributions differ significantly from that of the full collection, other related collections, or collections from other points in time.

The focus of this paper is on the Term Extraction module of our term-based text mining system. In particular, we will describe the term extraction algorithms and the organization of the terms in a taxonomy. We begin this paper with the description of the Term Extraction module of the Document Explorer system. We then describe how we construct a hierarchical taxonomy of the extracted terms. Next, we present experimental results from the Reuters financial news from 1995-1996. We conclude by comparing the term-based approach to the tag-based approach and outline the strength and weaknesses of each.

2. The Term Extraction Module

The Term Extraction Module is responsible for labeling each document with a set of terms extracted from the document. An example of the output of the Term Extraction module is given in Fig.1. The following excerpt is taken from an article published by Reuters Financial on 5/12/96. Terms in this excerpt that were identified and designated as interesting by the Term Extraction module are underlined.

```
     Profits at Canada's six big banks topped C$6 billion
($4.4   billion)   in   1996,   smashing   last   year's
C$5.2    billion    ($3.8    billion)    record    as
Canadian   Imperial   Bank   of   Commerce   and
National Bank of Canada  wrapped up the earnings season
Thursday. The six banks each reported a double-digit jump
in  net income for a combined profit of C$6.26 billion
($4.6 billion) in fiscal 1996 ended Oct. 31.
     But a third straight year of record profits came
amid growing public anger over perceived high service
charges  and  credit card  rates,  and  tight  lending
policies.
     Bank officials defended the group's performance,
saying that millions of Canadians owned bank shares
through mutual funds and pension plans.
```

Fig. 1. Example of the output of the Term Extraction Module. Terms chosen to label the document are underlined.

The overall architecture of the Term Extraction module is illustrated in Fig.2. There are three main stages in this module: Linguistic Preprocessing, Term Generation and Term Filtering.

The documents are loaded into the system through a special reader. The reader uses a configuration file that informs it of the meaning of the different tags annotating the documents. In such a way, we are able to handle a large variety of formats. The TPL reader packages the information into a standardized SGML file.

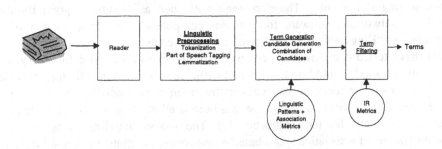

Fig. 2. Architecture of the Term Extraction Module

The next step is the Linguistic Preprocessing that includes Tokenization, Part-of-Speech tagging and Lemmatzations (i.e., a linguistically more founded version of

Stemming [17]). The objective of the Part-of-Speech tagging is to automatically associate morpho-syntactic categories such as *noun, verb, adjective*, etc., to the words in the document. In our system, we used a rule-based approach similar to the one presented in [4] which is known to yield satisfying results (96% accuracy) provided that a large lexicon (containing tags and lemmas) and some manually hand-tagged data is available for training.

The Term Generation and Term Filtering Modules are described in the following subsections.

Term Generation

In the Term Generation stage, sequences of tagged lemmas are selected as potential term candidates on the basis of relevant morpho-syntactic patterns (such as "Noun Noun", "Noun Preposition Noun", "Adjective Noun", etc.). The candidate combination stage is performed in several passes. In each pass, association coefficient between each pair of adjacent terms is calculated and a decision is made whether they should be combined. In the case of competing possibilities (such as $(t_1\ t_2)$ and $(t_2\ t_3)$ in $(t_1\ t_2\ t_3)$), the pair having the better association coefficient is replaced first. The documents are then updated by converting all combined terms into atomic terms by concatenating the terms with an underscore. The whole procedure is then iterated until no new terms are generated.

The nature of the patterns used for candidate generation is an open research question. In [8] and [9] specific operators (such as overcomposition, modification, and coordination) are proposed to select longer terms by using combinations of shorter ones. In [7] candidate terms are taken to be Noun-Noun* sequences (i.e. Noun sequences of length 2 or more). This technique improved the precision but reduced recall. [18] suggests to accept prepositions as well as adjectives and nouns. This approach generate a much larger number of term candidates, while in [14] only (Noun|Adjective)-Noun sequences are accepted to reduce the amount of "bad" terms.

In Document Explorer we used two basic patterns: Noun-Noun and Adjective-Noun, but we also allowed the insertion of any kind of Determiner, Preposition or Subordinating Conjunction. Therefore sequences such as "health program for the elderly", "networking software for personal computers", "operating system of a computer" or "King Fahd of Saudi Arabia" are accepted as well.

We have tested 4 different association coefficients: co-occurrence frequency, ϕ^2, Association Ratio [5], and Log-Likelihood [9,10]. The co-occurrence frequency is the simplest association measure that relies on the number of times that the two terms match one of the extraction patterns. ϕ^2 has been used to align words inside aligned sentences [16] and for term extraction [9]. The Association Ratio was used for monolingual word association and is based on the concept of mutual information. Log-Likelihood is a logarithmic likelihood probability. Our candidate combination phase uses two thresholds. The first is a threshold T_{freq} for the co-occurrence frequency. The second is a threshold T_{metric} for additional filtering on the basis of a complementary association coefficient.

Term Filtering

The Term Generation stage produces a set of terms associated with each document without taking into account the relevance of these terms in the framework of the whole document collection. A consequence of this is a substantial over-generation of terms. Additional filtering is therefore necessary and several approaches can be tested.

The goal of the Term Filtering stage is to reduce the number of term candidates produced by the Term Generation stage on the basis of some statistical relevance-scoring scheme. After scoring all the terms generated in the Term Genration stage, we sort them based on their scores and select only the top M terms.

For Example, the following are all two-word terms that were identified in the Term Generation stage but later filtered out in the Term Filtering stage: right direction, other issue, point of view, long way, question mark and same time. These terms were determined not to be of interest in the context of the whole document collection either because they do not occur frequently enough or because they occur in a constant distribution among different documents.

We have tested 3 approaches for scoring terms based on their relevance in the document collection:

1. **Deviation-Based approach:** The rationale behind the deviation-based approach is the hypothesis, often used in lexicometry, that terms with a distribution uniform over a collection of documents correspond to terms with few semantic content (i.e., "uninteresting" words to be filtered out [2]). We use the standard deviation of the relative frequency of a term t over all the documents of the collection as its score.
2. **Statistical Significance approach:** The underlying idea is to test whether the variation of the relative frequency of a given term t in the document collection is statistically significant. This is done using the χ^2 significance test on the relative frequency of a given term t.
3. **Information Retrieval approach:** The notion of term relevance with respect to a document collection is a central issue in information retrieval [23]. We assign each term its score based on maximal *tf-idf* (term frequency - inverse document frequency, maximal with respect to all the documents in the collection).

An example of the results of the Term Filtering stage for tf-idf scores is given in Fig.3. The table shows the scores of the terms found in the excerpt given in Fig.1. Terms appearing in the shaded region were discarded in the Filtering stage.

Term	Score	Term	Score
net_income	17.17	record_profit	5.63
bank	14.88	canadian_imperial_bank_of_commerce	5.56
earnings	11.41	big_bank	5.39
canada	10.39	canadian	5.29
mutual_fund	8.22	lending	4.73
national_bank_of_canada	7.68	credit_card	4.56
bank_official	6.56	jump	4.03
pension_plan	6.34	season	3.86
profit	6.20	group	3.77
performance	6.09	policy	2.84
anger	5.82	share	1.50

Fig. 3. Scores of the terms found by the Term Generation stage for the document in Fig.1.

3. Taxonomy Construction

One of the crucial issues in performing text mining at the term level is the need for a term taxonomy. A term taxonomy enables the production of high level association rules which are similar to General Association Rules [24]. These rules capture relationships between groups of terms rather than individual terms. A taxonomy is also important in other text mining algorithms such as Maximal Association Rules and Frequent Maximal Sets [12].

A taxonomy enables the user to specify mining tasks in a concise way. For instance when trying to generate association rules, rather then looking for all possible rules, the user can specify interest only in the relationships of companies in the context of business alliances. In order to do so, we need two nodes in the term taxonomy marked "business alliances" and "companies". The first node contains all terms related to alliance such as "joint venture", "strategic alliance", "combined initiative" etc., while the second node is the parent of all company names in our system (we used a set of rules and knowledge extracted from WWW directories to generate company names).

Building a term taxonomy is a time consuming task. Hence we provide a set of tools for semi-automatic construction of such a taxonomy. Our main tool is a taxonomy editor. This tool enables the user to read a set of terms or an external taxonomy, and use them to update the system's term taxonomy. The user can drag entire subtrees in the taxonomies or specify a set of terms via regular expressions. In our case, the initial set of terms is the set of all terms extracted from the Reuters 52,000 document collection. The terms matching any user-specified pattern is represented as a subtree, and can be dragged to an appropriate place in the target taxonomy.

The taxonomy editor also includes a semi-auomatic tool for taxonomy editing called the Taxonomy Editor Refiner (TER). The TER compares generated frequent sets against the term taxonomy. When most of the terms of a frequent set are determined to be siblings in the taxonomy hierarchy the tool suggests adding the remaining terms as siblings as well. For example, if our taxonomy currently contains 15 companies under the "tobacco companies" and the system generated a frequent set containing many tobacco companies, one of which does not appear in the taxonomy, the TER will suggest adding this additional company to the taxonomy as a tobacco company. The TER also has a term clustering module again suggest that terms clustered together be placed as siblings in the taxonomy.

4. Experimental Evaluation

We have used 51,725 documents from the Reuters financial news of years 1995-1996. This collection is 120M RAM in size and contains over 170,000 unique words. Each document contained on average 864 words. In the Term Generation stage, 1.25M terms were identified (25M RAM), 154K of them unique. After the Term Filtering stage we were left with 975K term (approximately 45 terms per document), 16,847 of them unique. Our feature space was therefore reduced by more than a factor of 10 and the average document length was reduced by a factor of 20.

In the example presented below the user is interested in business alliances between companies. She therefore specifies a filter for the association rules generation algorithm, requesting only association rules with companies on the LHS of the rule and business alliance topics on the RHS.

Using the Reuters document corpus described above, Document Explorer generates 12,000 frequent sets that comply with the restriction specified by the filter (with a support threshold of 5 documents and confidence threshold of 0.1). These frequent sets generated 575 associations. A further analysis removed rules that were subsumed by other rules, resulting in a total of 569 rules. A sample of these rules is presented in Fig.4. The numbers presented at the end of each rule are the rule's support and confidence.

---

america online inc, bertelsmann ag $\Rightarrow$ joint venture 13/0.72
apple computer inc, sun microsystems inc $\Rightarrow$ merger talk 22/0.27
apple computer inc, taligent inc $\Rightarrow$ joint venture 6/0.75
sprint corp, tele-communications inc $\Rightarrow$ alliance 8/0.25
burlington northern inc, santa fe pacific corp $\Rightarrow$ merger 9/0.23
lockheed corp, martin marietta corp $\Rightarrow$ merger 14/0.4
chevron corp, mobil corp $\Rightarrow$ joint venture 11/0.26
intuit inc, novell inc $\Rightarrow$ merger 8/0.47
bank of boston corp, corestates financial corp $\Rightarrow$ merger talk 7/0.69

Fig. 4. A sample of the association rules found by TextVis with companies on the LHS of the rule and business alliance topics on the RHS.

The example above illustrates the advantages of performing text-mining at the term level. Terms such as "joint venture" would be totally lost if we worked at the word level. Company names, such as "santa fe pacific corp" and "bank of boston corp", would not have been identified as well. Another important issue is the construction of a useful taxonomy such as the one used in the example above. Such a taxonomy cannot be defined at the word level as many logical objects and concepts are, in fact, multi-word terms.

5. Conclusions

Previous approaches to text mining have used either tags attached to documents or words contained in the documents. Tags were either assigned manually like in some of the on-line services (Dialog, Reuters), which is a very expensive and time consuming process, or by using machine learning algorithms. These text-categorization algorithms must be provided with a training set of pre-tagged documents. The main drawbacks of the machine learning approach are that it requires an expert to go and tag hundreds of training documents and that the accuracy is not high enough. The break-even point of these algorithms is below 80% [6]. This tag-based approach is characterized by a relatively small and controlled vocabulary. This has many implications on the results of the mining operations. On the one hand, the tags are meaningful and are often organized in a taxonomy, thus the mining results are often of high quality. On the other hand, much of the information present in the documents is not captured by the tags and thus is lost for the mining process.

Systems that use the full texts of the documents tend to produce a huge number of often meaningless results. In one example, the association generation process detected either compounds, i.e. domain-dependent terms such as {treasury,secretary,james} ⇒ {baker}, or extracted uninterpretable associations [22]. There is an additional disadvantage when using the full text of the documents and that is the execution time and the memory requirements of the mining algorithms.

Term level text mining attempts to benefit from the advantages of these two extremes. On the one hand there is no need for human effort in tagging document, and we do not loose most of the information present in the document as in the tagged documents approach. Thus the system has the ability to work on new collections without any preparation, as well as the ability to merge several distinct collections into one (even though they might have been tagged according to different guidelines which would prohibit their merger in a tagged based system). On the other hand the number of meaningless results and the execution time of the mining algorithms are greatly reduced. Working on the term level also enables the construction (with the help of semi-automatic tools) of a hierarchical taxonomy which is extremely important to a text mining system. We are currently working on an empirical evaluation of the Term Extraction process in which we shall compare the results obtained by different methods to a set of terms designated as important by Human indexers.

One of the future directions is to use a hybrid approach that represents the document as a combination of tags and terms. In such a way we can benefit from both approaches.

References

1. Anand, T.; Kahn, G.: Opportunity Explorer: Navigating Large Databases Using Knowledge Discovery Templates. In: Proceedings of the 1993 workshop on Knowledge Discovery in Databases, (1993).
2. Bookstein, A.; Klein, S.T.; Raita, T.: Clumping Properties of Content-Bearing Words. In: Proceedings of International Conference on Research and Development in Information Retrieval (SIGIR), (1995).
3. Brachman, R. J.; Selfridge, P.G.; Terveen, L.G.; Altman, B.; Borgida, A.; Halper, F.; Kirk, T.; Lazar, A.; McGuinness, D.L.; Resnick, L.A.: Integrated Support for Data Archaeology. International Journal of Intelligent and Cooperative Information Systems, (1993)2(2):159-185.
4. Brill, E.: Transformation-based error-driven learning and natural language processing: A case study in part-of-speech tagging. Computational Linguistics, (1995) 21(4):543-565.
5. Church, K.W.; Hanks, P.: Word Association Norms, Mutual Information, and Lexicography. Computational Linguistics, (1990) 16(1):22-29.

6. Cohen, W.; Singer, Y.: Context Sensitive Learning Methods for Text categorization. In: Proceedings of International Conference on Research and Development in Information Retrieval (SIGIR), (1996).
7. Dagan, I.; Church K.W.: Termight: Identifying and Translating Technical Terminology. In: Proceedings of the European Chapter of the Association for Computational Linguistics, EACL, (1994) 34-40.
8. Daille, B.; Gaussier, E.; Lange, J.M.: Towards Automatic Extraction of Monolingual and Bilingual Terminology. In: Proceedings of the International Conference on Computational Linguistics (COLING), (1994) 515-521.
9. Daille, B.: Study and Implementation of Combined Techniques for Automatic Extraction of Terminology. In: Resnik, P.; Klavans, J. (eds.): The Balancing Act: Combining Symbolic and Statistical Approaches to Language, MIT Press, Cambridge, MA, USA, (1996) 49-66.
10. Dunning, T.: Accurute Methods for the Statistics of Surprise and Coincidence. Computational Linguistics, (1993) 19(1).
11. Feldman, R.; Hirsh, H.: Exploiting Background Information in Knowledge Discovery from Text. Journal of Intelligent Information Systems, (1996).
12. Feldman, R.; Aumann, Y.; Amir, A.; Klösgen, W.; Zilberstien, A.: Maximal Association Rules: a New Tool for Mining for Keyword co-occurrences in Document Collections. In: Proceedings of the 3rd International Conference on Knowledge Discovery (KDD), (1997).
13. Feldman, R.; Dagan, I.: KDT – Knowledge Discovery in Texts. In: Proceedings of the First International Conference on Knowledge Discovery (KDD), (1995).
14. Frantzi, T.K.; Incorporating Context Information for the Extraction of Terms. In: Proceedings of ACL-EACL, (1997).
15. Frawley, W.J.; Piatetsky-Shapiro, G.; Matheus, C.J.: Knowledge Discovery in Databases: an Overview. In: Piatetsky-Shapiro, G.; Frawley, W. J. (eds.): Knowledge Discovery in Databases, MIT Press, (1991), 1-27.
16. Gale, W.A.; Church, K.W.: Concordances for parallel texts. In: Proceedings of the 7th Annual Conference of the UW Centre for the New OED and Text Research, Using Corpora, (1991) 40-62.
17. Hull, D.: Stemming algorithms - a case study for detailed evaluation. Journal of the American Society for Information Science, (1996) 47(1):70-84.
18. Justeson, J.S.; Katz, S.M.: Technical Terminology: Some linguistic properties and an algorithm for identification in text. Natural Language Engineering, (1995) 1(1):9-27.
19. Klösgen, W.: Problems for Knowledge Discovery in Databases and their treatment in the Statistics Interpreter EXPLORA. International Journal for Intelligent Systems, (1992) 7(7):649-673.
20. Klösgen, W.: Efficient Discovery of Interesting Statements. The Journal of Intelligent Information Systems, (1995) 4(1).
21. Lent, B.; Agrawal, R.; Srikant, R.: Discovering Trends in Text Databases. In: Proceedings of the 3rd International Conference on Knowledge Discovery (KDD), (1997).
22. Rajman, M.; Besançon, R.: Text Mining: Natural Language Techniques and Text Mining Applications. In: Proceedings of the seventh IFIP 2.6 Working Conference on Database Semantics (DS-7), Chapam & Hall IFIP Proceedings serie, (1997) Oct 7-10.
23. Salton, G.; Buckley, C.: Term-weighting Approaches in Automatic Text Retrieval. Information Processing and Management, (1998) 24(5):513-523.
24. Srikant, R.; Agrawal, R.: Mining generalized association rules. In: Proceedings of the 21st Very Large Databases (VLDB), (1995).

A New Algorithm for Faster Mining of Generalized Association Rules

Jochen Hipp[1], Andreas Myka[1], Rüdiger Wirth[2], and Ulrich Güntzer[1]

[1] Wilhelm Schickard Institute, University of Tübingen, 72076 Tübingen, Germany
{hippj, myka, guentzer}@informatik.uni-tuebingen.de
[2] Daimler Benz AG, Research & Technology FT3/KL, 89081 Ulm, Germany
wirth@dbag.ulm.daimlerbenz.com

Abstract. Generalized association rules are a very important extension of boolean association rules, but with current approaches mining generalized rules is computationally very expensive. Especially when considering the rule generation as being part of an interactive KDD-process this becomes annoying. In this paper we discuss strengths and weaknesses of known approaches to generate frequent itemsets. Based on the insights we derive a new algorithm, called Prutax, to mine generalized frequent itemsets. The basic ideas of the algorithm and further optimisation are described. Experiments with both synthetic and real-life data show that Prutax is an order of magnitude faster than previous approaches.

1 Introduction

Association rules were introduced in [1] and today the mining of such rules can be seen as one of the key tasks of KDD. The intuitive meaning of an association rule $X \Rightarrow Y$, where X and Y are sets of items, is that a transaction containing X is likely to also contain Y. The prototypical application is the analysis of supermarket basket data where rules like "34% of all customers who buy fish also buy white wine" may be found. Obviously, association rules can be quite useful in business applications. But even the above example shows a severe shortcoming: Rather than containing an item like "white wine" the transactions will typically contain item identifiers derived from a barcode which distinguishes the items quite accurately. So instead of finding a few useful rules a huge set of rules like "Smoked Irish Salmon, 500g $\Rightarrow$ Augey, Bordeaux White, 1993" will be generated.

One approach is to substitute all items with their generalizations, but this leads to a loss of information. A more elaborate solution are the generalized association rules introduced in [3, 4]. These rules extend the simple ones to contain items from arbitrary levels of a taxonomy. However this leads to an enormous increase in itemsets that have to be evaluated, because many more generalized items are frequent than simple ones. At the same time when considering the rule generation as being part of an interactive KDD-process performance becomes very important. To address this problem, we present Prutax, a new algorithm for fast mining of generalized association rules.

The problem of mining association rules is formally described in Section 2. In Section 3 the common approaches to generate boolean frequent itemsets are sketched. In addition we explain how the performance of each of the approaches is differently affected by the characteristics of the database. We show that, when mining boolean rules, choosing a superior algorithm is not as straightforward as supposed in literature. In Section 4 we present the algorithm Prutax to mine generalized frequent itemsets. Based on the insights of Section 3 we conclude that in the presence of a taxonomy a considerable performance gain can be expected when determining supports by tid-intersections instead of counting actual occurrences. In order to avoid the overhead of partitioning the database, as done eg in [5], we use a special kind of depth-first search. Our approach differs from [7] in so far as it is able to prune candidates that have an infrequent subset and is not restricted to mine frequent k-itemsets only for $k \geq 3$. In addition our modified depth-first search makes it possible to add further optimisations to the basic algorithm which are described in the remainder of Section 4. In Section 5 the performance of the new algorithm is compared to former algorithms on both synthetic and real-life data. The paper ends with a short summary in Section 6.

2 Problem Description

Let $\mathcal{I} = \{x_1, \ldots, x_n\}$ be a set of distinct literals, called items. A set $X \subseteq \mathcal{I}$ that contains k items is said to be a k-itemset or just an itemset. Let $\mathcal{D}$ be a set of transactions T, $T \subseteq \mathcal{I}$. A transaction T supports an itemset X if $X \subseteq T$. The fraction of transactions from $\mathcal{D}$ that support X is called the support of X, denoted by $\mathsf{supp}(X)$. An association rule is an implication $X \Rightarrow Y$, where $X, Y \subseteq \mathcal{I}$ and $X \cap Y = \emptyset$. In addition to $\mathsf{supp}(X \Rightarrow Y) = \mathsf{supp}(X \cup Y)$ every rule is assigned the confidence $\mathsf{conf}(X \Rightarrow Y) = \mathsf{supp}(X \cup Y)/\mathsf{supp}(X)$, cf [2].

A set of taxonomies $\mathcal{T}$ is coded as an acyclic directed graph with the items as nodes. An edge (x, y) means that x "is-a" y. x is the child and y the parent. $\mathsf{ancestors}(x)$ denotes the set of all items $\hat{x}$ for which an edge $(x, \hat{x})$ exists in the transitive closure of $\mathcal{T}$. A non-leaf item is called a generalized item. Accordingly, a transaction T supports an item $x \in \mathcal{I}$ if $x \in T$ or $\exists y \in T : x \in \mathsf{ancestors}(y)$. T supports an itemset $X \subseteq \mathcal{I}$ if T supports every item in X. A generalized rule may contain items from arbitrary levels of the taxonomy, cf [4].

To obtain all association rules that achieve minimal thresholds for support and confidence, minsupp and minconf respectively, it suffices to generate the set of all frequent itemsets, cf [2].

3 Generation of Frequent Itemsets

Since the introduction of association rules in [1], several algorithms for the generation of frequent itemsets have been developed, eg Apriori [2], Partition [5] or Eclat [7]. In this section we give a general survey and discuss the pros and cons.

3.1 Basics

Except for the empty set all $2^{|\mathcal{I}|}$ subsets of the itemset $\mathcal{I} = \{1, 2, 3, 4, 5\}$ are shown as a lattice in Figure 1(a). The thin lines indicate the subset relations. The bold line is an example of actual itemset support and separates the frequent itemsets in the upper part from the infrequent ones in the lower part. The goal

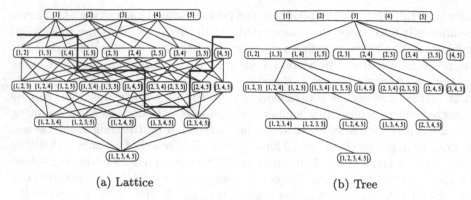

(a) Lattice   (b) Tree

Fig. 1. Subsets of $\mathcal{I} = \{1, 2, 3, 4, 5\}$

is to traverse the lattice in such a way that all frequent itemsets are found but as few infrequent itemsets as possible are visited. To achieve this the algorithms use the downward closure property of itemset support: All subsets of a frequent itemset must also be frequent.

Let map: $\mathcal{I} \to \{1, \ldots, |\mathcal{I}|\}$ be a mapping that maps all items $x \in \mathcal{I}$ one-to-one onto natural numbers. Now the items are totally ordered by the usual relation "<". In addition, for $X \subseteq \mathcal{I}$ let $X.\text{item} : \{1, \ldots, |X|\} \to \mathcal{I} : n \mapsto X.\text{item}_n$ be a mapping with $X.\text{item}_n$ denoting the n-th item of the items $x \in X$ increasingly sorted by "<". The n-prefix of an itemset X with $n \leq |X|$ is then given by $P = \{X.\text{item}_m \mid 1 \leq m \leq n\}$. The common strategy of the recent algorithms is to join every two frequent $(k-1)$-itemsets which have a $(k-2)$-prefix in common. Such a join results in a candidate k-itemset. In Figure 1(a), eg, $\{2, 3, 4\}$ and $\{2, 3, 5\}$ form the candidate $\{2, 3, 4, 5\}$. After the support of a candidate is counted, it will by pruned or will be added to the set of frequent itemsets. This approach starts with the 1-itemsets as the set of candidate 1-itemsets. Whenever a candidate turns out to be frequent, it may be used for further candidate generation. This strategy ensures that all frequent itemsets are visited. At the same time the number of infrequent itemsets that are visited is reduced.

3.2 Lattice Traversal

Let the classes $E(P), P \subseteq \mathcal{I}$ with $E(P) = \{H \subseteq \mathcal{I} \mid |H| = |P| + 1$ and P is a prefix of $H\}$ be the nodes of a tree. Two classes are connected by an edge, if all itemsets of the first class can be generated by joining two itemsets of the second class, eg Figure 1(b).

When traversing the tree by breadth-first search – BFS – as done by Apriori and Partition, all frequent $(k-1)$-itemsets are known when generating the candidate k-itemsets. Therefore both algorithms improve performance by pruning those candidates that have an infrequent subset before counting supports.

The algorithms introduced in [7] use depth-first search – DFS – to traverse the tree but are restricted to mine only frequent k-itemsets with $k \geq 3$. Furthermore, a fundamental drawback is not mentioned in [7]: Arbitrary DFS does not guarantee that the infrequent $(|C| - 1)$-subsets of a candidate C are known at the time the support of C has to be determined. Therefore, candidates having infrequent subsets cannot be pruned by the algorithms from [7] and usually must be counted at large expenses instead. Especially when mining generalized rules this problem becomes impeding because the pruning is required by an important optimization. In Section 4 we show how to integrate the pruning into DFS.

3.3 Support Counting

Counting actual occurrences of candidates as done by Apriori relies on a hashtree structure, cf [4]. Obviously counting candidates that occur quite infrequently is fairly cheap. But with growing candidate sizes, this approach gets more and more expensive because the number of levels of the hashtree increases.

Counting support by intersecting tid-sets as done in Partition and Eclat requires for every item in $\mathcal{I}$ the tid-set, i.e. the set of transactions containing this item, to be provided. Tid-sets also exist for every itemset X and are denoted by X.tids. The support of a candidate $C = X \cup Y$ is obtained by the intersection C.tids $= X$.tids $\cap Y$.tids and evaluating $|C$.tids$|$. Intersecting tid-sets does not suffer from large candidate sizes. Yet, there is another problem: Regardless of the actual support of a candidate, the cost of an intersection is at least $\min(\{|X$.tids$|, |Y$.tids$|\})$ operations. In addition, memory usage may become critical but solutions to this problem are given in [5, 7].

3.4 Conclusion

Obviously the performance of the algorithms is affected differently by the characteristics of the database. Whereas the inability to prune candidates that have an infrequent subset is an obvious disadvantage of DFS, the performance studies in literature seem to be contradictory concerning the different approaches of support counting: According to [5] the algorithm Partition that relies on tid-intersections achieves a much better performance than Apriori that counts actual occurrences (both use BFS). On the other hand in [6] it is shown that tid-intersections usually are more expensive than counting actual occurences. Our own experiments support [6]: Even when extending Eclat to prune candidates that have an infrequent subset – cf Subsection 4.2 – Eclat does not perform better than Apriori for k-itemsets with $k \geq 1$ on datasets comparable to those in [5].

4 Algorithm Prutax

Based on the insights from the boolean case described in Section 3, the basic approach to mine generalized association rules is derived in Section 4.1. The resulting algorithm is then further optimised in Sections 4.2 - 4.4.

4.1 Basic Idea

One perception of Section 3 is that determining supports by tid-intersection instead of counting actual occurrences is favoured under certain conditions:

(a) A shrinking average gap between the number of actual occurrences of a candidate $C = X \cup Y$ and $\min(\{|X$.tids$|, |Y$.tids$|\})$.
(b) A growing average size of candidates and frequent itemsets.

Experiments showed that both conditions typically become true when introducing a taxonomy. The reason is that, usually, the more general an item is, the higher is its support. Therefore our algorithm Prutax uses tid-intersections and combines them with DFS for two reasons: With DFS only the tid-sets of the frequent 1-itemsets that need roughly the same amount of memory as the original transactions must be maintained in memory permanently and partitioning, as done in [5], is not necessary under normal conditions. In addition it allows to prune candidates by taxonomy information as described later.

4.2   Optimisation i: Prune Candidates with infrequent subsets

As noticed in Section 3.2 arbitrary DFS does not allow the pruning of candidates by their infrequent subsets. This is due to the fact that in general not all infrequent $(|C| - 1)$-subsets of a candidate C are already known at the time its support must be determined. In order to cope with this problem, the following relation is defined for all pairs of itemsets $X, Y \in K_m = \{H \subseteq \mathcal{I} \mid |H| = m\}$:

$$X < Y :\Leftrightarrow \exists n, n \in \mathbb{N}, n \leq m : X.\text{item}_n < Y.\text{item}_n \wedge$$
$$\forall n', n' \in \mathbb{N} \wedge n' < n : X.\text{item}_{n'} = Y.\text{item}_{n'}$$

"$<$" imposes the lexicographic order on the itemsets of each K_m. Consequently for every subset K' of K_m there exists exactly one largest itemset. Let $C = \{c_1, \ldots, c_n\}$ with $c_i = C.\text{item}_i$ be a subset of $\mathcal{I}$ and let $P = \{c_1, \ldots, c_{n-1}\}$ be the $(|C| - 1)$-prefix of C. For all $S \subseteq C$ with $|S| = |C| - 1$ follows:

$$S \neq P \Rightarrow S = \{c_1, \ldots, c_{j-1}, c_{j+1}, \ldots, c_n\}$$
$$\Rightarrow P.\text{item}_j < S.\text{item}_j \wedge \forall n', n' \in \mathbb{N}, n' < j : P.\text{item}_{n'} = S.\text{item}_{n'}$$
$$\Rightarrow P < S.$$

When generating a candidate $C = X \cup Y$ with $X < Y$ as supposed in Section 3, the $(|C| - 1)$-prefix of C is X. Consequently, all $S \subseteq C, |S| = |C| - 1, S \neq X$ have the property $S > X$. To assure that all infrequent itemsets $S > X$ are known at the time C is generated, it suffices to realize a right-most DFS by choosing the largest itemset according to "$<$" whenever there is the choice of:

(a) different candidates to be counted,
(b) different prefixes P that determine the next class $E(P)$ to descend to.

4.3   Optimisation ii: Avoid counting redundant supports

In [4] the following property of itemsets containing generalized items is described:

> The support of an itemset X that contains both an item x and its ancestor $\hat{x}$ will be the same as the support of the itemset $X \setminus \{\hat{x}\}$.

As a consequence, counting the support of an itemset that contains both an item and an ancestor of this item is redundant. If our optimisation i) is applied to DFS, the only thing that has to be done in order to avoid determining redundant supports is to treat redundant 2-itemsets as infrequent, cf [4].

4.4 Optimisation iii: Prune by taxonomy

The itemset $\hat{X}$ is an ancestor of X if $|\hat{X}| = |X|$ and $\hat{X}$ can be generated by replacing one or more items from X with one of their ancestors. $\hat{X}$ is a parent of X if there is no X' with X' being an ancestor of X and $\hat{X}$ being an ancestor of X'. Obviously those candidates can be pruned that have an infrequent parent. In the context of BFS the use of this approach is rather limited, cf [4], but not when using our optimised right-most DFS lattice traversal: As a prerequisite, it has to be guaranteed that at the time the support of a candidate is to be determined all its infrequent ancestors are known. Accordingly, a certain ordering among itemsets of the same size has to be followed when traversing the subsets of $\mathcal{I}$. This can be realized by introducing the depth of each itemset:

$$\text{depth} : 2^{\mathcal{I}} \to \mathbb{N} : X \mapsto \begin{cases} 0, \text{ if } \{\hat{X} \mid \hat{X} \text{ is ancestor of } X\} = \emptyset \\ \max(\{\text{depth}(\hat{X} \mid \hat{X} \text{ is parent of } X\}) + 1, \text{ else} \end{cases}$$

For all ancestors $\hat{C}$ of a candidate C $\text{depth}(\hat{C}) < \text{depth}(C)$ holds. Consequently determining the support of all candidates C with $\text{depth}(C) = i$ before counting the support of a candidate C' with $\text{depth}(C') = i+1$ ensures that all infrequent ancestors of a candidate are known when its support has to be counted.

Pruning candidates by their infrequent subsets requires to follow the order imposed by the mapping map, cf optimisation i). On first sight, this order may seem to be contradictory to the one imposed by depth. But whereas depth is determined by the taxonomy, map only serves as a common base for the relation "$<$" no matter what specific kind of order it actually implies. Let x_n be the n-th element of the list generated by sorting all items $x \in \mathcal{I}$ according to descending depth. Now map is chosen so that $\text{map}(x_n) = n$ holds for all x_n. It follows:

$$\text{map}(x) < \text{map}(\hat{x}) \Leftrightarrow \text{depth}(\{x\}) \geq \text{depth}(\{\hat{x}\})$$

For arbitrarily chosen $X, \hat{X} \subseteq \mathcal{I}$ with $|X| = |\hat{X}|$ that means:

$$X < \hat{X} \Rightarrow \exists n, n \in \mathbb{N} : X.\text{item}_n < \hat{X}.\text{item}_n$$
$$\Rightarrow \text{depth}(\{X.\text{item}_n\}) \geq \text{depth}(\{\hat{X}.\text{item}_n\})$$
$$\Rightarrow X.\text{item}_n \text{ is not an ancestor of } \hat{X}.\text{item}_n$$
$$\Rightarrow X \text{ is not an ancestor of } \hat{X}$$

In other words, $\hat{C} > C$ holds for all ancestors $\hat{C}$ of C. Accordingly, if choosing map as indicated above, applying optimization i) will ensure that all infrequent ancestors are known when processing a candidate.

4.5 Algorithm

The algorithm Prutax that incorporates the described ideas is given in Figure 2. The parameters $H_1, \ldots, H_n$ are initialized with the frequent 1-itemsets, considering $H_i < H_{i+1}, \forall H_i, 1 \leq i < n$. The part to enrich the tid-sets of the generalized items with the tid-sets of their children has been left out but its implementation is straightforward as a recursive function. The set of frequent itemsets, F, should be implemented as a hashtree [2] in order to allow fast lookup.

```
(1)    function prutax(H₁, ... , Hₙ)
(2)       for i = n − 1 down to 1 do
(3)          E.ClearArray();
(4)          for j = n down to i + 1 do
(5)             C = Hᵢ ∪ Hⱼ;
(6)             if not (|C| = 2 ∧ C.item₂ ∈ ancestors(C.item₁)) then
(7)                if not (|C| ≠ 2 ∧ ∃S, S ⊆ C, |S| = |C| − 1 : S ∉ F) then
(8)                   if not (∃Ĉ, Ĉ ⊆ I, Ĉ is parent of C : Ĉ ∉ F) then do
(9)                      C.tids = Hᵢ.tids ∩ Hⱼ.tids;
(10)                     if|C.tids| ≥ minsupp · |D| then do
(11)                        E = C.Append(E);
(12)                        F = F ∪ {C};
(13)                     endif;
(14)                  endif;
(15)            endfor;
(16)         prutax(E);
(17)         endfor;
(18)   end.
```

Fig. 2. Algorithm Prutax

5 Performance Study

Prutax is evaluated and compared with the algorithm Cumulate, cf [4], that uses BFS and counting of actual occurences. For EstMerge, a variation of Cumulate that uses sampling, only a performance gain up to 30% and no fundamental different performance behaviour is detected in [4]. So due to the difficulties in duplicating the circumstances of sampling only "pure" Cumulate was taken into account. In addition the algorithms from the ML-family, cf [3], are not considered: They perform badly because of the extra pass over the database done for every level of the taxonomy and excessive data pre-processing. To make the comparison fair the time to generate the tid-sets of the generalized items is added to the total time when generating frequent itemsets with Prutax.

The first part of the performance evaluation relies on synthetic datasets similar to those from [4]. They were generated by the tool gen but with slightly modified default values. We decreased the number of items on level 2 of the taxonomy – the number of roots in terms of gen – from 250 down to 64. Even this seems to be quite large, eg if thinking of level 2 representing the different departments of a supermarket. Yet, this number could only be slightly decreased because of Cumulate performing badly on lower values as shown in Figure 3(b). In addition we decided to double the default value of the minimal support from 0.5% to 1% in order to decrease the gap between the algorithms. Furthermore the number of transactions has been decreased from 1000K to 100K. This does not affect the overall results because the needed time grows linearly with the number of transactions for both algorithms.

According to our evaluation Prutax is more than 3 times faster than Cumulate at minsupp=0.25%. As shown in Figure 3(a), the gap is even increasing with decreasing support. This is due to the fact that, when lowering minsupp, the average size of the candidates and frequent itemsets increases and the average gap between the number of actual occurrences of a candidate $C = X \cup Y$ and $\min(\{|X.\text{tids}|, |Y.\text{tids}|\})$ shrinks. Fewer items at level 2 of the taxonomy mean

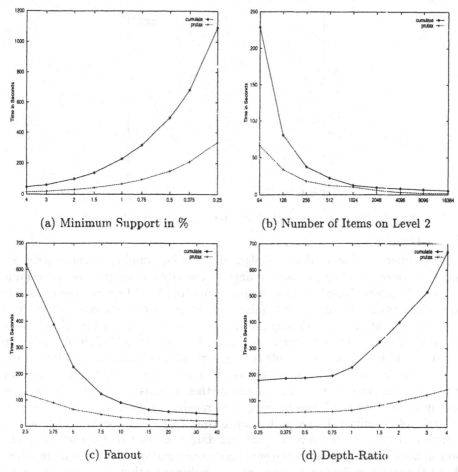

(a) Minimum Support in % (b) Number of Items on Level 2

(c) Fanout (d) Depth-Ratio

Fig. 3. Experiments on Synthetic Data

that the support of these items increases. The effects are the same as when lowering minsupp, cf Figure 3(b). Decreasing the parameter fanout, cf Figure 3(c), corresponds to increasing the number of taxonomy levels. At lower values Prutax is able to prune quite a lot of candidates by their infrequent parents and at fanout=2.5 performs nearly 6 times faster than Cumulate. With higher depth-ratio the support of frequent itemsets that contain items from the lower levels of the taxonomy increases and more candidate counting is done on lower levels. Again Prutax is able to prune quite many candidates by their infrequent parents. At depth-ratio=4 Prutax achieves a performance gain of almost factor 5 over Cumulate. In addition to the experiments from Figure 3 both algorithms scale linearly with the number of transactions and showed to be independent from the number of items when the number of frequent itemsets stays roughly constant.

A further evaluation is done on a real-life dataset. It consists of about 70,000 customer transactions from a supermarket. There is a total number of about 60,000 different items with an average of 10.5 items per transaction. Again Prutax outperforms Cumulate being even 10 times faster at minsupp = 0.6%.

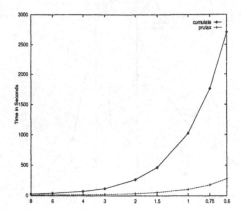

Fig. 4. Comparison on a Real-life Dataset (Minimum Support in %)

6 Summary

In this paper we described a new algorithm for fast mining of generalized association rules. First we discussed todays commonly known approaches to mine frequent itemsets. Based on this, support counting by tid-set intersections was recognised as the best approach to mine generalized association rules. In order to avoid the overhead of partitioning the database, as it is proposed in [5], we introduced right-most DFS to traverse the lattice. In contrast to DFS, as described in [7], the resulting algorithm is able to prune candidates that have an infrequent subset and in addition is not restricted to mine frequent k-itemsets only for $k \geq 3$. Furthermore we were able to add further optimisations that use the taxonomy to improve candidate pruning. The resulting algorithm Prutax achieves an order of magnitude better performance than former approaches. This performance gain was shown on both synthetic data and on a real-life dataset. The overall benefit from Prutax is the enhanced consideration of taxonomic relationships: the stronger the taxonomy dominates rule generation the more significant is the performance gain, especially at lower values of minimum support.

References

1. R. Agrawal, T. Imielinski, A. Swami: Mining Association Rules between Sets of Items in Large Databases, In *Proc. of ACM SIGMOD '93*, 1993, Washington, USA.
2. R. Agrawal, R. Srikant, Fast Algorithms for Mining Association Rules, In *Proc. of the VLDB '94*, 1994, Santiago, Chile.
3. J. Han, Y. Fu, Discovery of Multiple-Level Association Rules from Large Databases, In *Proc. of the VLDB '95*, 1995, Zürich, Switzerland.
4. R. Srikant, R. Agrawal, Mining Generalized Association Rules, In *Proc. of the VLDB '95*, 1995, Zürich, Switzerland.
5. A. Savasere, E. Omiecinski, S. Navathe, An Efficient Algorithm for Mining Association Rules in Large databases, In *Proc. of the VLDB '95*, 1995, Zürich, Switzerland.
6. M. Holsheimer, M. Kersten, Heikki Mannila, Hannu Toivonen, A Perspective on Databases and Data Mining, In *Proc. of the KDD '95*, 1995, Montreal, Canada.
7. M. J. Zaki, S. Parthasarathy, M. Ogihara, W. Li, New Algorithms for Fast Discovery of Association Rules, In *Proc. of the KDD '97*, 1997, Newport Beach, California.

Knowledge Discovery with Clustering Based on Rules. Interpreting Results

Karina Gibert[1], Tomàs Aluja[1] Ulises Cortés[2]

[1] Dep. of Statistics and Operation Research. {karina, aluja}@eio.upc.es
[2] Departament of Software. ia@lsi.upc.es
Universitat Politècnica de Catalunya***
Pau Gargallo, 5. Barcelona. 08028. SPAIN.

Abstract. It is clear that nowadays analysis of complex systems is an important handicap in Statistics, Artificial Intelligence, Information Systems, Data visualization, and other fields.

Describing the structure or obtaining knowledge of complex systems is known as a difficult task. The combination of Data Analysis techniques (including clustering) , Inductive Learning (knowledge-based systems), Management of Data Bases and Multidimensional Graphical Representation must produce benefits on this field.

Clustering based on rules (*CBR*) is a methodology developed with the aim of finding the structure of complex domains, which performs better than traditional clustering algorithms or knowledge based systems approaches. In our proposal, a combination of clustering and inductive learning is focussed to the problem of finding and interpreting special patterns (or concepts) from large data bases, in order to extract useful knowledge to represent real-world domains. This methodology and its behaviour as a *Knowledge Discovery* has been, in fact, presented in previous papers ([3], [5], [2]...).

The aim of this paper is to emphasize the *reporting* phase. Some tools oriented to the interpretation of the clusters are presented; automatic rules generation is presented and applied to a real research. Actually, in a *KD* system, data preparation and interpretation of the results is as important as the analysis itself. In this paper, missing data treatment is analysed; a statistical test, based on non parametric techniques, for comparing several classifications is presented. Also, a method for finding characteristic values of the classes is presented; this is based on the prototype of each class. Finally, these characterizations allow automatic generation of decision rules, as a predictive tool for future items.

Keywords: Combining many methods in one system, statistical tests in *KDD* applications, medicine: diagnosis and prognosis, from concept learning to concept discovery, Prior domain knowledge and use of discovered knowledge.

*** This research has been partially financed by the project *TIC'96–0878*.

1 Introduction

The formation of and distinguishing between different classes of objects (clustering) has been in use for very long. This process has been studied from the point of view of Statistics, AI, and other areas. The classes may be interpreted as diagnoses, predictions, etc. From a Machine Learning point of view, clustering is useful for the automated generation of classification rules, which is extremely interesting in knowledge-based environments, in particular the diagnosis oriented ones.

However, in real applications, it is usual to work with very complex domains [2], such as mental disorders, sea sponges[4]..., where data bases with both qualitative and quantitative variables appear; and expert(s) have some prior knowledge (usually partial) of the structure of the domain — which is hardly taken into account by clustering methods.

Clustering based on rules is a methodology developed in [4] with the aim of improving the process of finding the structure of an *ill-structured domain*. A combination of clustering and inductive learning is focussed to the problem of finding and interpreting special patterns (or concepts) from large data bases, in order to extract useful knowledge to represent real-world domains. Actually, *CBR* can be seen as a process of building a knowledge model for a given domain. That is why it is also connected with Knowledge Discovery of Data (*KDD*) and Data Mining (*DM*) [1]. In fact, we agree with the idea that a number of real applications in *KDD* either require a clustering process or can be reduced to it [8]. From this point of view, clustering techniques are an important pile for what is known as *KDD*.

CBR is a new way to perform classifications of any heterogeneous data matrix, as well as building a set of rules to describe the knowledge contained in the domain. Especially good results are obtained when analyzing data from complex domains. If we consider that Fayyad defines a *KDD* process as the "*overall process of finding and interpreting patterns from data, typically interactive and iterative, involving repeated application of specific data mining methods or algorithms and the interpretation of the patterns generated by these algorithms*"[1], it is clear that *clustering based on rules* fits this definition very closely. Following Fayyad, two important key points of *KDD* are: *i*) using domain knowledge and *ii*) domain characterization. It can be seen that these elements play an important role in the methodology presented here.

2 The methodology: Clustering based on rules

In this section, *clustering based on rules* (or rule-based clustering, *CBR*) is described. As most *KDD* systems, it combines, integrated in the same system, acquisition and management of prior knowledge from the expert with a Data Mining method (in this case, automatic clustering) [2] and some interpretation tools to analyze the results. It is an *iterative* and *interactive* process, structured in two major phases which finally organize the set of objects into a set of classes that are presumed to be *semantically* interpretable: initially, there is a process of acquisition of the available background knowledge, followed by the clustering process *strictu sensu*.

On the one hand, this methodology helps the user to make explicit his prior knowledge relevant to the problem. The main idea is to allow the user to introduce *constraints*, which may be based on *semantic* arguments..., on the formation of classes; the expert provides them in form of *logic–rules*. It is important to note that no complete definition of the domain may be provided; this implies a great difference with classical Knowledge-Based systems, where the completeness of the Knowledge Base determines the predictive capacity.

The use of rules in the clustering process contributes (acting as a semantic bias) to increasing the classification quality (and to decreasing the computational cost). In fact, the rules act as selectors that cluster objects which could be considered similar in the expert's experience. So the resulting classes (and therefore their prototypes) tend to be more meaningful to the expert's eye.

After a previous phase of detecting and solving the rule conflicts, the conditions imposed by the expert are used to induce a sort of *super-structure* on the domain, the *classes induced by the rules*. A *residual* class is formed with all the objects for which no prior knowledge is given. Clustering will be performed *within* each class induced by the rules and prototypes are built for each one of them. Another important feature is that different kind of variables are considered. So, mixed distances are needed for clustering in order to evaluate distances between objects partially described by numerical variables and partially described by qualitative ones. In [3] details are given of a new family of *mixed-metrics* used in our applications. This distance has given good results until now, but others could also be used [6].

Finally, the elements of the residual class and the prototypes of the rules–induced classes are clustered together and a a global structure is found. Hierarchical clustering is especially suited to our purposes, mainly because the expert can provide heterogeneous knowledge, *i.e.* very specific knowledge of small parts of the domain, together with more general knowledge about other parts and the prototypes will join global hierarchy at different levels.

The idea is to obtain *cooperation* between a knowledge-based process and a clustering one so as to analyze a complex domain. The part not described by the Knowledge Base is analyzed by the Data Mining method. Final description of the domain is the result of combining the clustering with the Knowledge Base. Several real applications show how including rules improves the quality of the results, in the sense that it produces classes with clear meaning.

At the end of this process, the system has *acquired* the knowledge needed to organize the domain, and the expert has succeeded in making explicit his knowledge in a relatively friendly way (see [2] for a complete and detailed description of this methodology). To some extent, the system can act in a similar way to a supervised learning method.

After that, interpretation–oriented tools help the expert to *understand* which clusters were formed and *why*. Automatic generation of final reports is available;

prototype generation is the basis for describing the classes. Our idea is to provide human interpretable descriptions of the classes.

There is a last step oriented to the consolidation of the discovered knowledge related to automatic rules generation. This is useful for later predictive goals.

3 About definition and preprocessing the data

Firs of all, we would like to point out that the system is able to store *metadata*, such as the modalities of each categorical variable, or the range of definition of certain numerical ones. This will make the interpretation of the results, and the data cleaning process easier.

During data cleaning, an important aspect is *missing* data treatment. At the begining, imputation was carries out, as usual, *before* processing data. It was observed that this introduced some incoherencies in the classes induced by the rules, and other possibilities were considered. In this paper, results imputing missing data *after* rule evaluation are presented in §5.

The system is prepared to deal with missing values during the rules evaluation: rules are evaluated only on the present information. Then, the knowledge provided by the expert can be taken into account to substitute for the missing values. Involving the Knowledge Base in inputation is, of course, better that carrying out the imputation under absolute lack of knowledge, as happens when imputation is a previous step to the analysis. Indeed, improvement in the quality of the final clusters appears, in the sense that more compact classes are obtained (see §5). Several real applications show the same behaviour referring this point.

4 Interpreting tools

Actually, given a partition (classification) of a large set of objects it seems necessary to introduce tools for assisting the user in the interpretation tasks, in order to establish the *meaning* of the resulting classes. Often it is not enough for the user to automatically obtain the classes, but to understand *why* those classes where detected. This is also another important point of a *KDD* system and this section presents some ideas concerning our own approach to this topic.

4.1 Class characterization and automatic rules generation

Some statistical packages include several tools to orient the interpretation of a given classification, such as the *contribution* of a certain variable to the formation of a given class, but finally, the interpretation itself must be done by the user in a non-systematic way. We provide a system, based on the use of the representative of each class (see [3]), to find a characterization of a given class, automatically. The idea is to identify, if possible, the variable X_k and the values $\mathcal{D}_k^{\mathcal{C}}$ that allow identification of each class ($i \in \mathcal{C} \Leftrightarrow x_{ik} \in \mathcal{D}_k^{\mathcal{C}}$). Sometimes, pairs of variables are needed to distinguish a certain class from the others. Intersection analysis is required. Even three or more variables may be needed to characterize a class. In this case, the analysis has a combinatory complexity. Our proposal is to introduce negative information and a recursive method based on consecutive conditioning of descriptions. Characterizations are given in logic terms and the *semantics* of the classes is then obvious to the expert.

With these characteristic descriptions, a method for automatic generation of classification rules is designed. The resulting Knowledge Base can be used as a predictive tool for new items.

To provide details on these techniques is not the purpose of this paper. In the application (§5) an example of them can be found.

4.2 Comparing two classifications

The index: Sometimes it is interesting to compare two classifications $\mathcal{P}_1 = \{C_i^1, i = 1 : n_1\}, \mathcal{P}_2 = \{C_j^2, j = 1 : n_2\}$ (including the case $n_1 < n_2$) of the same set of n objects. When several methods are used in parallel for processing the same dataset, it is interesting to evaluate whether results differ widely or not. Also, if two prior Knowledge Bases are provided by different experts, it is interesting to quantify if the degree of discordance is important or not.

Statistical literature provides some tests relative to the independence of two classifications. The most known is, may be, the χ^2 independence test; others are the test of Akaike. .... But we are not really interested in testing the independence of two classifications, but in assessing when differences between two classifications may be disregarded. One natural measure for that is the index $\delta(\mathcal{P}_1, \mathcal{P}_2) \in [0, 1]$ (from now on, it will be noted as δ for short). If $n_{ij} = card\ C_i^1 \cap C_j^2$:

$$\delta(\mathcal{P}_1, \mathcal{P}_2) = 1 - \frac{\sum_{(ij) \in \mathcal{N}} n_{ij}}{n}, \qquad \mathcal{N} = \{(ij) : n_{ij} = \max_i n_{ij} = \max_j n_{ij}\} \quad (1)$$

Grosso modo, it can be interpreted as the percentage of cases not equally classified by $\mathcal{P}_1$ and $\mathcal{P}_2$. If $\mathcal{P}_1$ is a reference partition of the objects — provided by the expert or some other source —, then $1-\delta$ may also act as a quality coefficient. In [2], formal definition and details on that index are provided. For short, it can be said that δ is adimensional (which allows comparisons), $0 \le \delta \le 1$, if $\mathcal{P}_1 = \mathcal{P}_2 \Leftrightarrow \delta = 0$.

The test: Anyway, in real applications, the index by itself is not enough to decide if small differences between two partitions of a given large set of objects can be dismissed or not. A significance test on that index isconstructed to decide when two partitions can be considered statistically equal or not. The test is

$H_0 : \mathcal{P}_1\ different\ from\ \mathcal{P}_2$
$H_1 : \mathcal{P}_1\ equal\ \mathcal{P}_2$ **The decision rule:** *if $P_{H_0}(\delta < d_0)too\ small \Rightarrow reject\ H_0$*

To built a statistical test, the reference distribution for the statistic δ supposing H_0 true must be known (p_δ). This distribution can be calculated theoretically, but it involves a combinatory probability problem; it suggests the use of a non parametric technique to estimate it. A prove is designed on the basis of the permutation test proposed by Fisher. The main idea is to simulate a sample of δ values for building its empirical distribution $(\hat{p}_\delta)$ as an estimate of p_δ.

To achieve this, a random sample of k pairs of classifications (which will be represented in the form of rectangular tables) is built and δ is calculated upon each of them. Tables are generated by permuting the n objects through the different classes. However, some precautions are needed for these permutations, since p_δ changes depend on several conditions. In order to obtain comparable values for δ, factors n, n_1, n_2 and marginal distributions will be fixed for permutations. Given the estimate of p_δ, an estimation of the p-value for the observed value of δ, namely d_0, can be calculated and the test can be solved. Even a 95% confidence interval for that p-value can be calculated: $p - value \pm 1.96 \sqrt{\frac{p-value(1-p-value)}{k}}$.

Figure 1 illustrates how permutations are well designed: two different tables with equal characteristics (*i.e.* $n, n_1 \ldots$) give, indeed, the *same* $\hat{p}_\delta$.

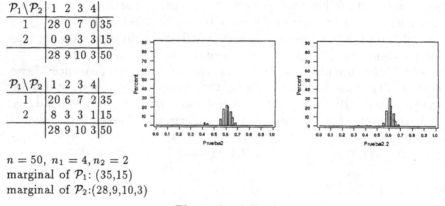

$\mathcal{P}_1 \backslash \mathcal{P}_2$	1	2	3	4	
1	28	0	7	0	35
2	0	9	3	3	15
	28	9	10	3	50

$\mathcal{P}_1 \backslash \mathcal{P}_2$	1	2	3	4	
1	20	6	7	2	35
2	8	3	3	1	15
	28	9	10	3	50

$n = 50$, $n_1 = 4$, $n_2 = 2$
marginal of $\mathcal{P}_1$: (35,15)
marginal of $\mathcal{P}_2$:(28,9,10,3)

Fig. 1. Good fit of p_δ.

The analysis of the test: An additional experiment was designed in order to obtain more information on the behaviour of the p_δ. The experimental conditions include the factors and levels listed in table 1. Among the 3125 possible tables, 40 were randomly generated for our study.

n (sample size)	$n_1(= card\ \mathcal{P}_1)$ $n_2(= card\ \mathcal{P}_2)$	Matrix type	Type of marginals (of $\mathcal{P}_1$ and $\mathcal{P}_2$)
25	2	Independent-like	uniform
50	4	Diagonal	uniform-like
100	7		two modalities greater than the rest
250	11		one modality greater than the rest
1000	15		one modality much greater than the rest

Table 1. Experimental factors considered in the experiment.

For each table, the proposed non parametric technique was used to obtain a reference distribution for δ under the hypothesis H_0. Some characteristics of this reference distribution were recorded: mean, standard deviation, minimum, maximum, symmetry and kurtosis. The observed value for δ, (d_0) and the $p-value(d_0)$ which allows resolution of the test are also calculated.

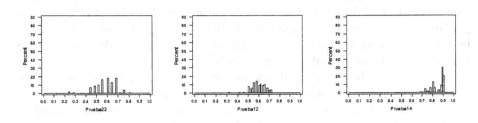

Fig. 2. Different forms of $\hat{p}_\delta$.

Resulting reference distributions have very different forms (see figure 2). A global analysis of the relationships among variables was made using Multivariate Analysis Techniques. The conclusions are the following:

- Changes in factor values $(n, n_1, \ldots)$ change the form of p_δ.
  - Variance decrease with n, since δ is defined as a proportion $\delta \propto \frac{1}{n}$.
  - Kurtosis decrease with n.
  - Symmetry increase with n.
  - In some cases (some rectangular tables) n-modality can be presented.
  - Big n_1, n_2 and small n produce uniform distributions for p_δ.
- In general, as n increases, p_δ becomes symmetric, less pointed, more continuous: it tends to a normal distribution.
- The form of p_δ is orthogonal to d_0: reference distribution of δ is found independently of the observed table.
- Localization of p_δ depends on d_0. This is a consequence of maintaining the marginal distributions and sample size for permutations constant. Non comparable elements will be found otherwise.
- Diagonal tables give null p-values: When the two partitions are similar, significant p-values are found, as wanted.

5 An application in medicine: Thyroid dysfunctions

Among other real applications, an application to medicine was selected for this paper. The data base comprises results of the routine assays performed at Clinical Hospital *Setre Milosrdnice*, Zagreb (Croatia), and it has been collected over a period of two years.

A sample of 1002 patients was described by 12 laboratory tests and 3 factors, relevant to the outcome of diagnosis. The study took place using a subset of 6 variables — total triiodothyronine ($T3$), total thyroxine ($T4$), thyroid stimulating hormone (TSH), gender (male, female), age and drug therapy (thyrosuppresion, thyroid hormone, without therapy) —, in order to allow future comparison with previous classifications performed by other methods [9] on the same sample (and the same variables).

By means of physical examination, experienced physicians decided on diagnosis of thyroid function state of each patient: euthyreosis (842 cases), hyperthyreosis (104 cases) or hypothyreosis (56 cases). Predictions are based on laboratory tests results, gender age and information about possible drug therapy. Laboratory tests are described in detail in [9].

The variable *Diagnosis* could act, in some sense, as the *response* variable. In consequence, it was not considered in the clustering process. So, the key in this application is not discovery of classes, but their *characterization* and the possibility of establishing a Knowledge Base to identify the diagnosis of a new case. This is one of the applications in which *CBR* can perform, to some extent, as a supervised learning method.

A first study was presented in [5] where interest of including rules was shown. *CBR* was used with a simple set of rules provided by the expert:

$If\ T3 = $ Normal $\wedge\ T4 = $ Normal $\wedge\ TSH = $ Normal $\longrightarrow Euthyreosis$ (non-ill patients)
$If\ T3 = $ High $\wedge\ T4 = $ High $\wedge\ TSH = $ Low $\qquad \longrightarrow Hyperthyreosis$

Final classes obtained by using the rules were semantically interpretable, while classes obtained by classical hierarchical clustering were difficult for the expert to interpret (see tree in figure 3 (*left*), details in [5]). An automatic characterization for the partition was found and interpretation of the classes was clear:

$(C_1, (Therapy = No) \wedge (Age \in [30, 60]) \wedge (Gender = Female) \wedge (T3 = Normal))$,
$(C_2, (T3 = High)), (C_3, (Age > 60)), (C_4, (Age \in [16, 30]))$,
$(C_5, (Therapy = Thyrosuppression)), (C_6, (Therapy = Thyroidhormone))$,
$(C_7, (Gender = Male)), (C_8, (T3 = Low))$

It can be seen that the cluster criteria is a combination of the variables *therapy, age, gender* and *levels of T3* and *T4*, and it is obvious that classification rules can be derived for this characterization.

In a second phase of this research, missing data treatment was considered. Instead of carrying out the missing data imputation as a previous step *before* evaluating the rules, it was done, as indicated in §3, *after* building the rules induced partition. Figure 3 (*right*) shows the structure of the resulting tree. Characterization of classes is, in this case, directly related to diagnosis (see expression 2) and comparison between the resulting partition and variable Diagnosis produces table 2. The accuracy was 92%, which means about 75 misclassified objects out of 1002. Part of this misclassification cannot be avoided at present, since there are several identical cases with contradictory diagnostics in the sample, owing to the existent delay between the moment when the physician decides the diagnostic and the arrival of some relevant tests results. The observed value of δ, $d_0 = 0.0928$

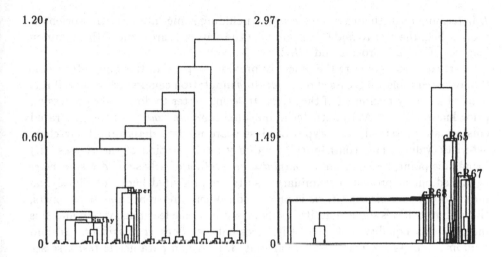

Fig. 3. *(left)* Hierarchical tree obtained with global missing data imputation; *(right)* Hierarchical tree obtained with local missing imputation.

and the permutation test presented in §4.2 produces a $p - value(0.0928) = 0$: partitions produced by the CBR method and variable $Diagnosis$, provided by the physicians, are significantly equal, though few discordances are observed.

$$((C_1, (TSH = Normal)), (C_2, (TSH = High)), (C_3, (TSH = Low))) \qquad (2)$$

The other interesting feature to comment is that it seems to be possible to predict diagnosis using only the level of hormone TSH. This will have to be confirmed whith a more extensive study, actually in progress.

6 Conclusions and future work

CBR successfully combines AI techniques with Statistical Methods, for finding the structure of complex domains (see §2). In this paper, its properties as a KD system are presented: taking prior knowledge into account, applying a repeated

Class Diagnosis	1	2	3	
Hiperthyreosis	31	3	70	104
Hypothyreosis	10	42	4	56
Euthyreosis	797	26	19	842
	838	71	93	1002

$d_0 = 0.0928$

$p - value(0.0928) = 0.000$

Table 2. Relationship between Diagnostic and results of CBR with missing inputation *after* rules evaluation.

DM technique (in this case, clustering), including some interpretation-oriented tools to help the user to find the *meaning* of the classes... are some of the common features of a *KDD* process and *CBR*.

Particular aspects were the object of previous papers. In this one, interpretation oriented tools are focussed on:*i*) *Missing* inputation can disturb results if it is done at the very beginning of the study. It seems better to do it after processing prior knowledge. *ii*) Automatic techniques for *characterization* of the generated clusters are presented; prototypes of classes are used to determine their characteristic values. This contributes to an easy interpretation of the classes. *iii*) From this point, research on *autommatic generation* of a base of *decision rules* is carried out at present. Preliminary results are presented here. *iv*) Finally, an index to *compare classifications* is presented. When a reference partition exists, the system behaves somewhat like a supervised machine learning system and this index acts as a quality coefficient. Distances between "*expert classifications*" and "*automatic classifications*" can be calculated. *v*) A non parametric *test* assesses the significance of this index (equality of classifications). An experiment was designed to study the form of p_δ in different situations. Conclusions are reported in §4.2.

In the last section an application to the domain of thyroid diagnostics is presented. For this application, *CBR* inputing missing data after rules evaluation can improve the quality of the results, even when a small set of very simple rules is used. From other applications, it has also been seen that the introduction of *semantic* information in the form of rules into the clustering process, generally produces clusters which are easy for the user to interpret.

Acknowledgements: To Dr. Zdenko Sonicki for providing data and for his collaboration. To Juan Carlos Martín, to Juan José Márquez for implementing part of the system.

References

1. Fayyad, U., *et al. From Data Mining to Knowledge Discovery: An overview* **Advances in KD and DM**, Fayyad, U.,*et. al.* R. AAAI/MIT, 1996.
2. Gibert, K, Cortés, U. (98) Clustering based on rules and knowledge discovery in ill-structured domains, Computación y Sistemas, México, 1998. (in press).
3. — Weighing quantitative and qualitative variables in clustering methods, *MATH-WARE* **10**(4), January 1997.
4. — Combining a knowledge based system with a clustering method for an inductive construction of models in: P. Cheeseman *et al.* (Eds.), *Selecting Models from Data: AI and Statistics IV*, LNS n° 89 (Springer-Verlag, New York, 1994) 351 – 360.
5. Gibert, K., Sonicki, Z. (97) Classification based on rules and medical research. Proc Applied Stochastic Models and Data Analysis. Ed. Lauro *et al.*. Napoli. pp 181–186.
6. Gower,J. C., A general coefficient for similarity, *Biometrics*, (27) 857–872.
7. Lebart, L *et al.* **Traitement statistique des données**. Dunod, Paris.
8. Nakhaeizadeh, G. *Classification as a subtask of of Data Mining experiences form some industrial projects.* In *IFCS'96*. Kobe, Japan (*in press*). pp. 17–20
9. Sonicki, Z. *et al.* (93) The use of induction in routine laboratory diagnostics of thyroid, *LIJECNICKI VJESNIK* **115**, pp 306–309 (in Croatian).

Efficient Construction
of Comprehensible Hierarchical Clusterings

Luis Talavera and Javier Béjar

Departament de Llenguatges i Sistemes Informàtics
Universitat Politècnica de Catalunya
Campus Nord, Mòdul C6, Jordi Girona 1-3
08034 Barcelona, Catalonia, Spain
{talavera,bejar}@lsi.upc.es

Abstract. Clustering is an important data mining task which helps in finding useful patterns to summarize the data. In the KDD context, data mining is often used for description purposes rather than for prediction. However, it turns out difficult to find clustering systems that help to ease the interpretation task to the user in both, statistics and Machine Learning fields. In this paper we present ISAAC, a hierarchical clustering system which employs traditional clustering ideas combined with a feature selection mechanism and heuristics in order to provide comprehensible results. At the same time, it allows to efficiently deal with large datasets by means of a preprocessing step. Results suggest that these aims are achieved and encourage further research.

1 Introduction

Clustering is one of the primary data mining tasks aiming to the goal of finding a useful set of categories or clusters to summarize the data. As in other inductive tasks, clustering results may serve for two different purposes, namely, *prediction* and *description*. As pointed out in [2], in the context of Knowledge Discovery on Databases (KDD), description tends to be a more important task, since the main focus in this discipline is on finding interpretable patterns. Traditionally, when applying clustering algorithms, the interpretation step is usually left to users. So, they have to evaluate the results and change the appropriate settings of the clustering system if the results does not suit their needs. However, the settings of a clustering system may be difficult to interpret for an average user who has not deep knowledge about metrics or control strategies.

Therefore, it may be desirable to have clustering methods which not only perform a partition of the data, but also facilitate the interpretation task. The weaknesses of traditional statistical clustering methods to cope with this requirement, gave raise to the development of *conceptual clustering* methods in the Machine Learning (ML) community [3, 5, 6, 8]. These methods are intended to combine the clustering and interpretation tasks thus making easy the later to the external user.

Furthermore, data mining poses additional problems for the inductive tasks such as *database size, high dimensionality* or the need for *user interaction*, which make the process even harder. We present the ISAAC system, an approach that combines traditional clustering concepts with some heuristic procedures in order to provide comprehensible results and, at the same time, efficiently deal with large amounts of data. It also allows the user to decide the structure of the cluster hierarchy with regard to the number of levels and their generality.

2 Isaac

ISAAC is a conceptual clustering system that accepts vectors of nominal attribute-value pairs and summarizes these objects in probabilistic concept hierarchies. A probabilistic concept is represented by a summary description that lists attribute values and its associate probabilities. For each concept C_k, a *prototype* stores $P(A_i = V_{ij} \mid C_k)$, the conditional probability that a value V_{ij} for a feature A_i will occur in an object of the cluster C_K. Probabilistic descriptions are not traditionally used in statistical clustering approaches, but they are more common in conceptual clustering systems [3, 5]. This sort of representation allows gradual updating of clusters descriptions and should be more robust than logic-based representations in the face of noise or graded concepts.

ISAAC is intended to allow users to model the construction of the cluster hierarchy which better suits their needs. Typically, hierarchical clusterings are arranged in a binary tree or dendrogram. From this tree, the user has to extract a useful partition, or apply some automatic procedure to select the best level or levels. In our approach, the system allows the user to specify the number of levels of the hierarchy and their generality. This is done via the NG parameter which is in the [0,1] range. As the NG value increases, the system creates more general partitions with few concepts. Lower NG values instruct the system to build more specific partitions. A complete hierarchy is built by specifying a set of increasing NG values to indicate the desired levels. The user can interact with the system experimenting with different sets of values for this parameter. Since the effect of modifying the NG values is semantically clear to the user, it should be relatively easy to deal with this parameter.

The ISAAC clustering process, which is depicted in Fig. 1, consists of three stages: Preprocessing, Reflection and Refinement which will be detailed in the following sections.

2.1 Preprocessing

Typically, complexity of hierarchical clustering algorithms is $O(n^2)$ where n is the number of objects in the dataset. This complexity may be acceptable if one desires just a 'one-shot' clustering. However, for large datasets, it may result in a relatively slow processing, particularly if the user needs to interact with the clustering system by changing some setting in order to obtain interesting results.

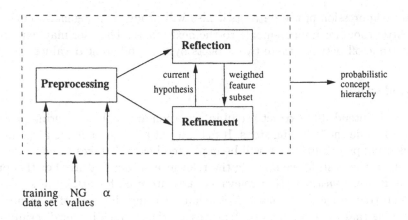

Fig. 1. Stages of the ISAAC system

The Preprocessing stage is intended to cope with this problem. We can see this stage as similar to the typically used feature selection steps which reduce the set of features used in the learning process. The difference here lies in that, instead of selecting objects, the Preprocessing step transforms the initial data vectors into new vectors summarizing compact groups of objects. Particularly, we exploit *incremental* clustering algorithms, which can efficiently deal with large datasets. An incremental clustering algorithm can construct a flat partition in a $O(nk)$ time, where k is the number of clusters created. Note that this complexity is equivalent to $O(n^2)$ only if $k \approx n$. The problem with incremental algorithms is that they are sensitive to ordering effects. To cope with this problem while maintaining the efficiency of incremental processing, we are working on a buffering strategy which has shown to be fairly robust under bad object orderings and it is detailed in [10].

We chose a nearest neighbor algorithm with uses a similarity measure and an α threshold to form clusters. For each instance the similarity with every existing cluster is computed. If the maximum similarity found is greater than α then the instance is incorporated into the cluster. Otherwise, a new cluster is created. With this preliminary step, the size of the database can be compressed in a variable amount dependent on the value of α. Intuitively, similarity is obtained by computing the intersection between the cluster prototypes for each feature. Specifically, similarity for two clusters C_m and C_n with respect to a feature i is computed by the expression:

$$Sim(C_m, C_n, i) = \sum_j min\{P(A_i = V_{ij} \mid C_m), P(A_i = V_{ij} \mid C_n)\} \qquad (1)$$

The total similarity between two clusters is the average similarity computed for each feature, normalized by dividing for the total number of features considered.

This procedure helps to detect very similar -or even identical- objects in a fast manner. It is worth to notice that although very low α values will result in a greater compression of the dataset, it also will produce very general clusters, letting little room for improvements to the next stages. The user may explore a suitable trade-off between these two aspects by using different α values.

2.2 Reflection

This stage is intended to extract useful information about the clustering process in order to guide the following steps. It actuates at every step of the agglomerative clustering procedure which will be explained below. It takes the current set of clusters as the basis for computing the relevance of each feature. For this purpose the *distance measure* [7], a relevance measure used for attribute selection in decision tree induction, is used. Note that by using this sort of measure we are assuming that the more relevant features are those which better discriminate among the clusters of a given partition. As a result of the process, an ordered set of features is obtained and those which do not score high enough are discarded. A heuristic procedure is used to determine this subset of useful features. The rationale behind this procedure is the assumption that the set of attributes which can discriminate among the clusters of a given partition is smaller for more general levels than for specific ones. The level of generality of the level which is being built is indicated by the NG value specified by the user, so it can be used to heuristically define the set of useful features $\mathcal{U}$ as follows:

$$\mathcal{U} = \{a \in \mathcal{A} \mid Rel(a) \geq m \cdot NG\} \tag{2}$$

where $\mathcal{A}$ is the initial set of features, $Rel(a)$ is the relevance of feature a and m is the maximum computed relevance for features in $\mathcal{A}$. This procedure does not guarantee in any case that the selected subset is neither the best nor the minimal for any particular task. We are just using a relatively naive approach to make a conservative selection in an unknown domain allowing the system to dynamically discard features which are very likely to be irrelevant.

2.3 Refinement

This stage consists of an agglomerative procedure which iteratively selects the best two candidates to merge and creates a new cluster. However, a number of differences with traditional clustering procedures exist. First, the starting point for this procedure is not the original dataset, but the clusters obtained in the Pre-processing stage or in the previous generalization if a set of NG values is given. Secondly, the procedure ends when the level of generality indicated by current NG value is achieved and the resulting level does not store all the intermediate pairs of mergings. Therefore, the system does not necessarily produces binary trees. And finally, at each merging step, the current set of clusters is passed to the Reflection step to obtain a weighted subset of useful features which is used in the following computations.

To be able of determining when a given level of generality is reached, we need a measure to characterize cluster generality. ISAAC measures the generality of a cluster using probabilistic analogs of logical sufficiency and necessity. These measures are interpreted as degrees of sufficiency and necessity of the probabilistic descriptions used by the system. From this point of view, they represent a continuous valuation over the sufficiency and necessity properties analogous to the binary one of classical logic, but allowing a greater flexibility. These measures are called *continuous sufficiency* (CS), and *continuous necessity* (CN), and are defined, for a cluster C_k as follows:

$$CS(C_k) = \sum_i \sum_j P(C_k \mid A_i = V_{ij})^2 \tag{3}$$

$$CN(C_k) = \sum_i \sum_j P(A_i = V_{ij} \mid C_k)^2 \tag{4}$$

i indexes the features of the objects, and j indexes the values of each feature. Both measures can be easily generalized to partitions by simply averaging the results for the set of clusters. These two measures evaluate the average degree of sufficiency or necessity for the features contained in the prototypes of the clusters of a given partition.

Each of the measures is biasing the selection of partitions in a different direction as regards the generality of a partition. Favoring CS over CN tends to reward partitions with more general concepts and favoring CN over CS tends to reward partitions with more specific concepts. This property allows the user to bias the process towards the type of partition required, linking the bias to the NG parameter by means of the formula:

$$Gen(P, NG) = (1 - NG) \times CS(P) - NG \times CN(P) \tag{5}$$

This measure indicates whether a given level of generality defined by a given NG value has been achieved and measured is used to allow merging until a certain level of both CN and CS measures is reached. The initial partition usually will have a negative Gen value due to the high score of CN and, as the generalization progresses, the generality of the partition will tend to zero according to the evolution of the CS and CN measures.

The control structure for the Refinement stage is shown in Table 1. As mentioned before, it follows a typical agglomerative schema which merges pairs of clusters until the desired NG level is reached. However, unlike most of its statistical counterparts, our algorithm does not construct a similarity matrix to decide which pair of clusters should merge. Instead, the algorithm takes advantage of the generality measure defined above and always chooses as the first cluster to merge the one who has the lower generality score. The similarity of this cluster with the rest of the clusters in the partition is then computed, by means of the similarity measure previously defined, to find the most similar one and perform the merging operation. All of this computations (similarity and generality) are done in the context provided by $\mathcal{U}$, the subset of useful features obtained in the Reflection stage. This means that only features included in $\mathcal{U}$ are considered when computing both measures, which also use the available weights.

Let P be a partition
Let NG be the level of generality desired
Let U be the weighted subset of useful features

Function Refinement(P, NG)
  U=Reflection(P, NG)
  while Generality(P, NG, U) < 0 **do**
    Let C be the least general cluster in P
    Compute the similarity between C and the rest of clusters in P using U
    Merge C with the most similar concept in P
    U = Reflection(P, NG)
  endwhile

Table 1. Algorithm for the Refinement stage of ISAAC

The reason for using the generality measure as a heuristic to decide one candidate to merge is twofold. If we use a similarity matrix, since we want to dynamically adjust similarity computations with feature weights, we are forced to update the whole matrix at each step of the process. These computations will result in a cubic complexity for the algorithm with respect to the number of clusters initially considered. The heuristic used, allows to maintain a quadratic complexity for the algorithm. On the other hand, the heuristic should bias the algorithm to reach levels in which each cluster approximately corresponds to the same level of abstraction, and hence improve the understandability of the obtained clusters.

3 Empirical evaluation

The framework outlined in this paper may suggest several lines for evaluation, but in our experiments we focused on two aspects, the effect of the Preprocessing stage, and the effect of the feature selection mechanism. Particularly, we want to check the degree of compression that can be achieved in the first stage of the process and if this compression can decrease the quality of the final results. Also, we are interested in analyzing the results from the point of view of comprehensibility of the results to confirm the utility of feature selection.

The experiments were carried out using the mushroom dataset from the UCI repository. The mushroom dataset consists of 8124 mushroom descriptions represented by 22 nominal features belonging to two classes, edible and poisonous. ISAAC was run with a set of NG consecutive values with an 0.1 increment until achieving a two-class top level partition. Depending of the initial partition considered, the number of levels ranged between 7 and 9 in order to get the desired number of clusters.

To evaluate the quality of the discovered hierarchies, we measured the degree of fit of the resulting clusters in the top level with the original mushroom division into edible and poisonous. We measured cluster purity by using the measure suggested in [4].

α	# clusters	time	feat./node	Purity	Pur$\geq$0.85
0.75	29.18 ± 1.10	5.66 ± 0.17	4.94 ± 0.43	0.78 ± 0.10	40 %
0.77	33.82 ± 1.14	6.81 ± 0.15	4.50 ± 0.39	0.79 ± 0.10	46 %
0.80	54.10 ± 1.96	10.42 ± 0.24	4.08 ± 0.26	0.77 ± 0.09	26 %
0.82	82.50 ± 2.18	15.30 ± 0.29	3.85 ± 0.23	0.81 ± 0.10	58 %
0.85	157.54 ± 3.98	27.25 ± 0.51	3.64 ± 0.22	0.81 ± 0.09	58 %
0.87	263.04 ± 4.70	43.09 ± 0.80	3.45 ± 0.16	0.76 ± 0.11	36 %
0.90	610.28 ± 7.92	99.58 ± 1.80	3.10 ± 0.09	0.75 ± 0.11	26 %
0.92	1072.18 ± 12.89	202.60 ± 2.57	2.83 ± 0.05	0.74 ± 0.13	36 %
0.95	2327.36 ± 14.81	512.84 ± 4.65	2.15 ± 0.03	0.84 ± 0.09	66 %

Table 2. ISAAC results for different α values.

Table 2 shows the results for 50 ISAAC runs on the mushroom dataset using different α values. Some data from the table is graphically depicted in figure 2, showing that a great amount of compression may be achieved by just using α values around 0.85, which are relatively high. As expected, decreasing the α value allows for greater data compression. Obviously, the amount of data compression is directly correlated with the running times of the system. Figure 2 also shows the average purity scores and stardard deviations achieved by the system for each different α value. Clearly, there is no relationship between these two factors since results appear to be somewhat variable. In fact, we cannot expect to find such a relationship because different initial partitions may bias the subsequent feature selection steps in a different and not easily predictable manner. Actually, the interest here was in demonstrating that the system is able to reach high scores with some of the compressed datasets. The impact of the compression in the final results may vary between different datasets and users should experiment with different α values until obtaining a suitable partition.

For comparison purposes, we also run the well-known AUTOCLASS program [1], obtaining a purity score of 0.90. Since ISAAC results do not appear to follow a very homogeneous distribution, table 2 shows an additional column with the percentage of 'good clusterings' obtained with each α value, considering as good clusterings those with a purity score over 0.85. It is not possible to establish a direct comparison between the two systems, since ISAAC generates hierarchical clusterings as opposed to the flat clusterings of AUTOCLASS. However, the AU-TOCLASS score indicates that, despite the variability of its results, our approach may achieve good quality clusterings with a reasonable amount of compression.

Table 2 also give us a picture of the capabilities of the feature selection mechanism. In average, the system only uses between a 10-20 % of features from the initial feature set in order to discriminate between the different hierarchy nodes. This demonstrates the ability of ISAAC to bias the clusterings towards simplicity and, hence, provides results which should be easier to interpret.

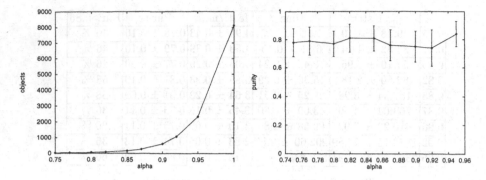

Fig. 2. Data compression (left) and purity of top level partitions (right) as a function of α.

4 Concluding remarks

We have presented ISAAC, a conceptual clustering system which combines statistical procedures with symbolic learning oriented heuristics. The system partitions the clustering process into three stages. The first one, accomplishes two goals, namely, to achieve a compression of the dataset, and to provide an initial set of hypotheses for the rest of the process. The following stages are performed in a collaborative manner. One of them is responsible of obtaining a weighted subset of features from the actual cluster structure. The second, uses this information to generalize the current partition and generates new cluster structures, from which new weights may be computed.

One novel feature in our approach is the definition of a cluster generality measure. This measure allows to parameterize the system in order to allow the user to bias the resulting structures towards the desired level of generality. We think that this sort of parameters are more meaningful to users than those in traditional statistical clustering. Users should be more comfortable interacting with systems which have parameters with a semantically clear interpretation [9].

Our preliminary experiments suggest that this approach achieves two interesting goals from the standpoint of data mining tasks. First, the system should efficiently deal with large datasets by means of the initial Preprocessing step. Second, the resulting hierarchical clusterings should be easy to understand since the system provides descriptions with an important reduction in the number of features used.

On the other hand, results seem to show a large variability with respect to the original labeling in the used dataset. However, we cannot assume the original labeling to be the only interesting underlying structure present in the dataset. Also, variability may be due to the global interaction between the different biases provided by the preprocessing and the feature selection mechanisms. This suggests a future research to explore the isolate and joint influences of all these biases.

Some aspects of the system deserve further research such as the similarity metrics used, the feature weighting measure or the feature selection strategy. Currently, some of these components are chosen largely based on intuitions and empirical results. Probably, a more accurate study of the properties of the different measures used can lead to a better understanding of the behavior of the system.

The modular design of ISAAC easily allows to extend the system. We plan to explore different feature selection measures and their impact in performance tasks like prediction. Also, a set of discretization procedures will be added to the Preprocessing stage to provide the system with the ability to deal with numerical valued features. Finally, we are working on extending the Reflection stage in order to constraint the Refinement process using declarative knowledge provided by the user.

Acknowledgments. This work has been supported by the Spanish Research Council (CICyT) project TIC96-0878.

References

1. P. Cheeseman and J. Stutz. Bayesian classification (autoclass): theory and results. In U. M. Fayyad, G. Piatetsky-Shapiro, P. Smyth, and R. Uthurusamy, editors, *Advances in knowledge discovery and data mining*, pages 153–180. AAAI Press, Menlo Park, CA, 1996.
2. U. M. Fayyad, G. Piatetsky-Shapiro, and P. Smyth. From data mining to knowledge discovery: An overview. In U. M. Fayyad, G. Piatetsky-Shapiro, P. Smyth, and R. Uthurusamy, editors, *Advances in Knowledge Discovery and Data Mining*, pages 1–34. AAAI Press, Cambridge, Massachusetts, 1996.
3. D. H. Fisher. Knowledge acquisition via incremental conceptual clustering. *Machine Learning*, (2):139–172, 1987.
4. D. F. Gordon, P. M. Tag, and R. L. Bankert. Unsupervised classification procedures applied to satellite cloud data. Technical Report AIC95-005, Navy Center for Applied Research in Artificial Intelligence, 1995.
5. S. J. Hanson and M. Bauer. Conceptual clustering, categorization and polymorphy. *Machine Learning*, (3):343–372, 1989.
6. M. Lebowitz. Experiments with incremental concept formation: UNIMEM. *Machine Learning*, (2):103–138, 1987.
7. R. López de Mántaras. A distance based attribute selection measure for decision tree induction. *Machine Learning*, (6):81–92, 1991.
8. R. S. Michalski and R. E. Stepp. Learning from observation: Conceptual clustering. In R. S. Michalski, J. G. Carbonell, and T. M. Mitchell, editors, *Machine Learning: An Artificial intelligence approach*, pages 331–363. Morgan Kauffmann, 1983.
9. L. Talavera and U. Cortés. Exploiting bias shift in knowledge acquisition. In *10th European Workshop on Knowledge Acquisition, Modeling, and Management*, Lecture Notes in Artificial Intelligence, Sant Feliu de Guixols, Barcelona, Spain, 1997. Springer.
10. L. Talavera and J. Roure. A buffering strategy to avoid ordering effects in clustering. In *Proceedings of the Tenth European Conference on Machine Learning*, volume 1398 of *Lecture Notes in Artificial Intelligence*, Chemnitz, Germany, 1998. Springer.

Cost Sensitive Discretization of Numeric Attributes

Tom Brijs[1] and Koen Vanhoof[2]

[1]Limburg University Centre, Faculty of Applied Economic Sciences, B-3590 Diepenbeek, Belgium
tom.brijs@rsftew.luc.ac.be

[2] Limburg University Centre, Faculty of Applied Economic Sciences, B-3590 Diepenbeek, Belgium
koen.vanhoof@rsftew.luc.ac.be

Abstract. Many algorithms in decision tree learning are not designed to handle numeric valued attributes very well. Therefore, discretization of the continuous feature space has to be carried out. In this article we introduce the concept of cost sensitive discretization as a preprocessing step to induction of a classifier and as an elaboration of the error-based discretization method to obtain an optimal multi-interval splitting for each numeric attribute. A transparant description of the method and steps involved in cost sensitive discretization is given. We also evaluate its performance against two other well known methods, i.e. entropy-based discretization and pure error-based discretization on a real life financial dataset. From the algoritmic point of view, we show that an important deficiency from error-based discretization methods can be solved by introducing costs. From the application point of view, we discovered that using a discretization method is recommended. To conclude, we use ROC-curves to illustrate that under particular conditions cost-based discretization may be optimal.

1 Introduction

Many algorithms which focus on learning decision trees from examples are not designed to handle numeric attributes. Therefore, discretization of continuous valued features must be carried out as a preprocessing step. Many researchers have already contributed to the issue of discretization, however as far as we know, no efforts have been made to include the concept of misclassification costs to find an optimal multi-split. Discretization also has some additional appeals. Kohavi & Sahami [1996] mentioned that discretization itself may be considered as a form of knowledge discovery in that critical values in a continuous domain may be revealed. Catlett [1991] also reported that, for very large data sets, discretization significantly reduces the time to induce a classifier.

Traditionally, five different axes can be used to classify the existing discretization methods: *error-based* vs. *entropy-based*, *global* vs. *local*, *static* vs. *dynamic*, *supervised* vs. *unsupervised* and *top-down* vs. *bottom-up*. Our method is an error-based, global, static, supervised method combining a top-down and bottom-up approach. However, our method is not just an error-based method. Through the introduction of a misclassification cost matrix, candidate cutpoints are evaluated against a cost function to minimize the overall misclassification cost of false positive and false negative errors instead of just the total sum of errors. False positive (resp. false negative) errors, in our experimental design, are companies incorrectly classified as not bankrupt (bankrupt) although actually they are bankrupt (not bankrupt).

The objective of this paper is to evaluate the performance of our cost sensitive discretization method against Fayyad & Irani's entropy-based method. First, we evaluate the effectiveness of both methods in finding the critical cutpoints that minimize an overall cost function as a result of the preprocessing knowledge discovery step. Secondly, both methods will be compared after induction of the C5.0 classifier to evaluate their contribution to decision tree learning.

In section 2, we introduce the concept of cost sensitive discretization and a transparant description of the several steps that have been undertaken to achieve cost sensitive discretization will be given. In section 3, we elaborate on related work in the domain of discretization of continuous features. In section 4, an empirical evaluation of both methods is carried out on a real life dataset. Section 5 is reserved for a summary of this work.

2 Cost Sensitive Discretization

Cost sensitive discretization signifies taking into account the cost of making errors instead of just minimizing the total sum of errors. This implies that discretizing a numeric feature involves searching for a discretization of the attribute value range that minimizes a given cost function. The specification of this cost function is dependent on the costs assigned to the different error types. Potential interval splittings can then be generated and subsequently evaluated against this cost function. To illustrate the process of cost sensitive discretization we consider a hypothetical example of a numeric attribute for which 3 boundary points are identified (see figure 1). In each interval the number of cases together with their class labels are given. Intuitively, a boundary point is a value V in between two sorted attribute values U and W so that all examples having attribute value U have a different class label compared to the examples having attribute value W, or U and W have a different class frequency distribution. Previous work [Fayyad and Irani 1992] has contributed substantially in identifying potential cutpoints. They proved that it is sufficient to consider boundary points as potential cutpoints, because optimal splits always fall on boundary points. Formally, the concept of a boundary point is defined as:

Definition 1 [Fayyad and Irani 1992] *A value T in the range of the attribute A is a boundary point iff in the sequence of examples sorted by the value of A, there exist two examples $s_1, s_2 \in S$, having different classes, such that $val_A(s_1) < T < val_A(s_2)$; and there exists no other example $s' \in S$ such that $val_A(s_1) < val_A(s') < val_A(s_2)$.*

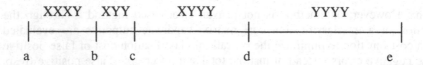

Fig. 1. an example (numeric-valued) attribute and its boundary points.

Now suppose $C(Y|X) = 3$, i.e misclassifying a class X case as belonging to class Y costs 3 and $C(X|Y) = 1$. For a real life dataset these cost parameters may be found in the business context of the dataset. However, in many cases, exact cost parameters are not known. Usually the cost parameters of true positive and true negative classifications are set to null but the cost-values for false positive and false negative errors reflect their relative importance against each othter. This results in what is called a cost matrix. The cost matrix indicates that the cost of misclassifying a case will be a function of the predicted class and the actual class. The number of entries in the cost matrix is dependent on the number of classes of the target attribute. Consequently, for each potential interval the minimal cost can be calculated by multiplying the false positive cost (respectively false negative cost) by the false positive (respectively false negative) errors made as a result of assigning one of both classes to the interval and picking the minimal cost of both assignments. For example, the total minimal cost for the overall interval (from a to e) is 10 which can be found as follows:

> the number of X cases in interval a-e is 5
> the number of Y cases in interval a-e is 10, so
> classifying all cases in a-e as 'X' gives a cost of $10 * C(X|Y) = 10 * 1 = \mathbf{10}$
> classifying all cases in a-e as 'Y' gives a cost of $5 * C(Y|X) = 5 * 3 = 15$
> therefore, the minimal cost for the overall interval a-e is *10*.

Suppose the maximum number of intervals k is set to 3, now a network can be constructed as depicted in figure 2 (not all costs are included for the sake of visibility). The value of k may be dependent on the problem being studied, but Elomaa & Rousu [1996] advise to keep the value of k relatively low. Increasing parameter k reduces the misclassification cost after discretization but it has a negative impact on the interpretability of the classification tree after induction because the tree will become wider.

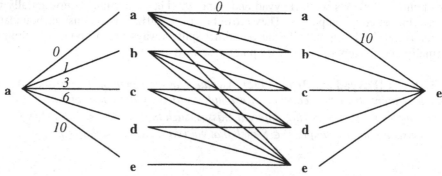

Fig. 2 Shortest route network.

The shortest route linear programming approach can be used to identify the optimal number and placement of the intervals that yields the overall minimal cost for the discretization of this numeric attribute.

This short illustration shows that several phases are to be undertaken to discretize numeric attributes in a cost sensitive way. First, all boundary points for the attribute under consideration must be identified. Second, a cost matrix must be constructed to specify the cost of making false positive and false negative errors. Third, costs must be calculated and assigned to all potential intervals. Fourth, the maximum number of intervals k must be specified. Fifth, a shortest route network can be constructed from all potential intervals with their corresponding minimal costs. Finally, this shortest route network can be solved using the shortest route linear programming routine.

3 Related Work

Traditional error-based methods, for example Maas [1994], evaluate candidate cutpoints against an error function and explore a search space of boundary points to minimize the sum of false positive and false negative errors on the training set. Entropy-based methods, for example Fayyad and Irani [1993], use entropy measures to evaluate candidate cutpoints. Our method is an *error-based* discretization method. However, through the introduction of a misclassification cost matrix, candidate cutpoints are evaluated against a cost function to minimize the overall cost of false positive and false negative errors instead of just the total sum of errors. Kohavi and Sahami [1996] show that the error-based discretization method has an important deficiency, i.e. it will never generate two adjacent intervals when in both intervals a particular class prevails even when the class frequency distributions differ in both intervals. Our cost sensitive discretization method however does not suffer from this deficiency because it takes into account these class frequency differences. By increasing the error-cost of the minority class, the frequency of the minority class is leveraged so that, eventually, different class labels will be assigned to both intervals, indicating a potential cutpoint.

For previous work on other discretization methods we refer to [Holte 1993: static discretization] versus [Fulton, Kasif & Salzberg 1994: dynamic discretization] and [Van de Merckt 1993: unsupervised discretization] versus [Holte 1993 or Fayyad and Irani 1993: supervised discretization] and [Fayyad and Irani 1993: top-down discretization] versus [Kerber 1992: bottom-up discretization].

4 Empirical Evaluation

4.1 The Data Set

To carry out our experiments we used a real life dataset of 549 tuples, all tuples representing a different company. Each company is described by 18 continuous valued attributes, i.e. different financial features on liquidity, solvability, rentability, and others. The entire set is not included because of space limitations. The target attribute is a 2-class nominal attribute indicating whether the company went bankrupt (class 0) or not (class 1) during that particular year. The class distribution in this data set is highly unbalanced, containing only 136 (24.77%) companies that went bankrupt. This data set was gathered from the official financial statements of these companies which are available at the National Bank of Belgium. In Belgium medium to big enterprises are obliged to report their financial statements in large detail.

4.2 Position of Cutpoints and Induced Cost

In a first experiment we evaluated the performance of Fayyad & Irani's discretization method against our cost sensitive method relative to a specified cost function. We know our method yields optimal results, i.e it achieves minimal costs given a maximum of k intervals. Now, we are interested if Fayyad & Irani's entropy-based method is able to come close to this optimal solution by using the same cost function. We discretized all numeric attributes seperately for different misclassification cost matrices ranging from false positive cost parameter 1 (uniform cost problem) to 8 (false positive errors are severely punished relative to false negative errors). For the sake of simplicity we call this cost parameter the *discretization cost*. Parameter k was arbitrarily set to $2n+1$, i.e 5, with n the number of classes. We are particularly interested in to what extent our cost sensitive method is able to achieve significantly better results on the overall cost function compared to the method of Fayyad & Irani. Our experiments revealed that for all attributes, cost sensitive discretization achieved significantly better results than Fayyad & Irani's entropy-based discretization. On average, for all discretization costs and for all attributes, entropy-based discretization resulted in a 8.7 % increase in cost relative to our method. Table 1 shows the percentage increase in cost of Fayyad & Irani's method against our method for different discretization costs.

Table 1 Average percentage increase in cost Fayyad vs. cost sensitive

Discretization Cost	1	2	3	4	5	6	7	8
	6.3	6.9	7.1	7.1	8.7	9.0	11.4	13.1

This large performance gap is mainly due to the fact that our cost sensitive method exploits local class differences to achieve lower costs whereas the entropy-based method finds thresholds to minimize the entropy function and, as a consequence, it is not so heavily distracted by local differences.

Experiments revealed that on average entropy-based discretization results in fewer cutpoints (2) compared to cost-sensitive discretization (4). For low false positive costs, cost-sensitive discretization only subdivides the range where the frequency of the minority class equals that of the majority class or small frequency differences exist, resulting in sensitivity to local class frequency differences. For high false positive costs only the common range with high class frequency differences is subdivided.

4.3 Comparison of entropy-based versus cost-based discretization

False positive(FP) and false negative(FN) error rates We induced the C5.0 classifier and used repeated 3-fold cross validation on the discretized data sets to compare the FP and FN error rate for both discretization methods. The C5.0 algorithm has been used with increasing FP cost. Increasing this cost results in a lower FP error rate and a higher FN error rate. In order to visualize the differences between the different discretization methods, we normalized the error rates and used entropy-based discretization as the base line. This means that a given percentage is the cost sensitive error rate divided by the entropy-based error rate. First, we want to investigate the interaction effect of a given discretization cost and changing the C5.0 cost parameter on the FP and FN error rates. When the discretization cost equals 1, the method is an error-based method. On figure 3 it can be seen that for this method the FP error rate is higher but the FN error rate is lower than the base line (entropy-based).

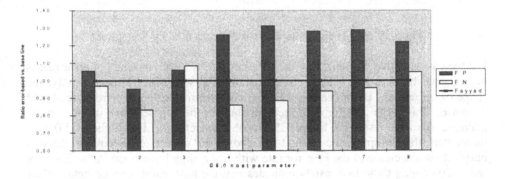

Fig. 3 FP and FN error rates discretization cost 1 vs. Fayyad & Irani

This higher number of FP errors results from the fact that some attribute value ranges are highly dominated by non-bankruptcy cases and thus will be classified as non-bankrupt while this range can still contain a large proportion of bankruptcy cases. Calculation of the frequency of FP errors (43.6%) confirmed this observation. With the given class distribution, the global accuracy is higher with the error based discretization. The following figures (4 and 5) give the error rates for other discretization costs (resp. 2 and 6).

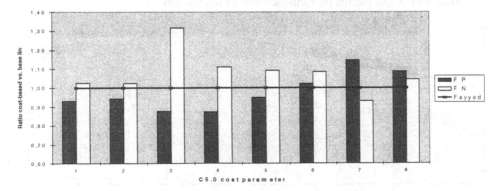

Fig. 4 FP and FN error rates discretization cost 2 vs. Fayyad & Irani

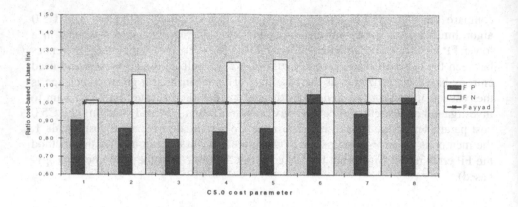

Fig. 5 FP and FN error rates discretization cost 6 vs. Fayyad & Irani

For the cost sensitive discretization the FP error rate is lower and the FN error rate is higher than the base line. These figures show two surprising results. Firstly, the shape of the curves. By increasing the C5.0 cost parameter, the FP error rate should decrease. This is the case for both methods, but for the cost sensitive discretizer the decrease is much faster (at lower C5.0 cost parameter). For higher C5.0 cost parameters, the entropy-based method has a lower FP error rate. Secondly, the first bar(s) show a decrease of the FP error rate with just a slightly increase in the FN error rate. Combining these two results indicates that the best results can be obtained by using a low C5.0 cost parameter.

Misclassification costs We will compare the performance of the classifiers obtained with the different discretization methods in a ROC graph [Provost & Fawcett 1997]. On a Roc graph the true positive rate (TP) is plotted on the Y axis and the false positive rate (FP) on the X axis. One point in the ROC curve (representing one classifier with given parameters) is better than another if it is to the north-west (TP is higher, FP is lower or both). A ROC graph illustrates the behaviour of a classifier without regard to class distributions and error cost, so that it decouples classification performance from these factors. Figure 6 shows the ROC graph for the different sets of classifiers. We decided not to show all classifiers, only the most relevant classifiers with respect to the performance evaluation are shown.

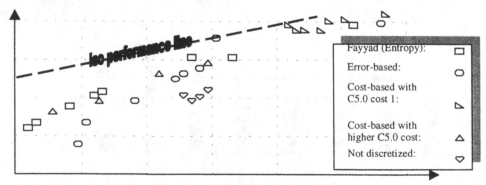

Fig. 6 Roc curve for different classifiers

Provost has shown that a classifier is potentialy optimal if and only if it lies on the northwest boundary of the convex hull [Barber, Dobkin and Huhdanpaa 1993] of the set of points in the ROC curve. From the figure we can see that the set of classifiers with the entropy-based and cost-based discretization method are potentialy optimal. From a visual interpretation, we can rank the methods for the region with a FP rate lower than 35 as follows: entropy, better than cost-based, better than error-based discretization. For the region with a FP rate higher than 35: firstly cost-based and secondly entropy and error-based discretization. To choose the optimal (minimal misclassification cost) classifier we need to know the error cost and the class distributions. In Belgium, the FP error cost is estimated to be 30 to 50 times higher than the FN error cost and the prior probability (this is the true distribution) of negative classes versus positive classes is estimated to be approximately 1 in 95. With this information a set of iso-performance lines [Provost & Fawcett 1997] with a slope of 30/95 can be constructed. On an iso-performance line all classifiers corresponding to points on the line have the same expected cost and the slope of the line is dependent on the a priori cost and class frequency distributions. This provides us with an instrument to choose the optimal classifier of the given sets of classifiers. If only the single best classifier is to be chosen, under the known cost and class frequency distributions, the error-based classifier (indicated by a circle) slightly outperforms the cost-based discretization methods with C5.0 cost 1 (indicated by a right triangle), as can be seen on figure 6. Altogether, it can be seen on the same figure that discretization of numeric attributes prior to induction is always better than discretizing while inducing the C5.0 classifier.

Overfitting With our dataset, by using a discretization method, better estimated accuracies are obtained due to the fact that overfitting is reduced. When using the C5.0 cost functionality this observation is even strengthened. Increasing the C5.0 cost parameter results in increasing resubstitution error rates as illustrated in table 2. The overfitting pattern is similar to that of the false negative error rates shown in the first paragraph of section 4.3. From these observations, it can also be seen that cost sensitive discretization is less robust compared to entropy-based discretization, but more robust than C5.0 without discretization. So, cost sensitive discretization is more able to lower the false positive error rate but is more sensitive to overfitting than entropy-based discretization.

Table 2 Overfitting in absolute percentages

C5.0 cost parameter	1	2	3	4	5	6	7	8
Not discretized	11.96	15.06	13.68	15.07	14.48	13.88	12.87	11.93
Fayyad	10.95	12.31	10.69	9.77	9.45	8.53	8.00	7.83
Average of all cost sensitive	9.16	11.75	12.54	11.39	10.94	10.48	9.88	9.42

5 Conclusion

The concept of misclassification costs is an important contribution to the work of error-based discretization because in many real world problems, the cost of making certain mistakes is not equal. As a consequence, false positive and false negative classifications were treated equally. A discretization method that is cost sensitive has been implemented, tested and compared with a well known discretization method on a real life financial dataset. From an algoritmic point of view, it has been shown that an important deficiency from error-based discretization methods can be solved by introducing costs, i.e. two adjacent intervals with different class labels can be generated even when in both intervals a particular class prevails. From the application point of view, we may conclude that using a discretization method is recommended. C5.0 is overfitting the financial dataset. It is easier to reduce this overfitting by a priori discretization than by tuning the C5.0 pruning parameter. Choosing the optimal discretization method is more difficult. Firstly, the results are only valid for this small dataset. Secondly, dependent on the evaluation procedure and distributions used, different choices are possible. The three methods considered are all potentialy optimal, but cost sensitive discretization of numeric attributes has showed to be worth considering further research.

References

1. Barber C., Dobkin D., and Huhdanpaa H. (1993). The quickhull algorithm for convex hull. Technical Report GCG53, University of Minesota.
2. Catlett J. (1991). On changing continuous attributes into ordered discrete attributes. In *Proceedings of the Fifth European Working Session on Learning*, 164-178. Berlin: Springer-Verlag.
3. Dougherty J., Kohavi R., and Sahami M. (1995). Supervised and unsupervised discretization of continous features. In *Machine Learning: Proceedings of the Twelfth Int. Conference*, 194-202. Morgan Kaufmann.
4. Elomaa T., and Rousu J. (1996). Finding Optimal Multi-Splits for Numerical Attributes in Decision Tree Learning. Technical Report NC-TR-96-041, University of Helsinki.
5. Fayyad U., and Irani K. (1992). On the handling of continuous-valued attributes in decision tree generation. In *Machine Learning 8*. 87-102.
6. Fayyad U., and Irani K. (1993). Multi-interval discretization of continuous-valued attributes for classification learning. In *Proceedings of the Thirteenth Int. Joint Conference on Artificial Intelligence*, 1022-1027. Morgan Kaufmann.
7. Fulton T., Kasif S., and Salzberg S. (1995). Efficient algorithms for finding multi-way splits for decision trees. In *Proceedings of the Twelfth Int. Conference on Machine Learning*, 244-251. Morgan Kaufmann.
8. Holte R. (1993). Very simple classification rules perform well on most commonly used datasets. In *Machine Learning 11*, 63-90.
9. Kerber R. (1992). Chimerge: Discretization of numeric attributes. In *Proceedings of the Tenth Nat. Conference on Artificial Intelligence*, 123-128. MIT Press.
10. Kohavi R., and Sahami M. (1996). Error-based and Entropy-Based Discretization of Continuous Features. In *Proceedings of the Second Int. Conference on Knowledge & Data Mining*, 114-119. AAAI Press.
11. Maas W. (1994). Efficient agnostic PAC-learning with simple hypotheses. In *Proceedings of the Seventh Annual ACM Conference on Computational Learning Theory*, 67-75. ACM Press.
12. Provost F., and Fawcett T. (1997). Analysis and Visualization of Classifier Performance: Comparison under Imprecise Class and Cost Distributions. In *Proceedings of the Third Int. Conference on Knowledge Discovery and Data Mining*, 43-48, AAAI Press.
13. Van de Merckt T. (1993). Decision Trees in Numerical Attributes Spaces. In *Proceedings of the Thirteenth Int. Joint Conference on Artificial Intelligence*, 1016-1021, Morgan Kaufmann.

Handling KDD Process Changes by Incremental Replanning

Ning Zhong[1], Chunnian Liu[2], Yoshitsugu Kakemoto[3], and Setsuo Ohsuga[4]

[1] Dept. of Computer Science and Sys. Eng., Yamaguchi University
[2] Dept. of Computer Science, Beijing Polytechnic University
[3] RCAST, The University of Tokyo
[4] Dept. of Information and Computer Science, Waseda University

Abstract. Within the framework of our GLS (Global Learning Scheme) system that is a multi-strategy and cooperative KDD (Knowledge Discovery in Databases) system, this paper reports new research progress, by addressing one deeper issue concerning KDD process planning: *change management,* and giving our solution for it. The problem on change management can be largely solved by an incremental replanning technique. With the issue being properly handled, the GLS system is more complete in KDD process modeling, and more flexible and robust for practical use.

1 Introduction

Our previous work in the GLS system has set up the KDD process framework as an organized society of intelligent agents, and solved the basic problem in a multi-strategy and cooperative KDD system: how to choose appropriate KDD techniques to achieve a particular discovery goal in a particular domain [9, 10]. The solution has been based on AI planning techniques, and increased both autonomy and versatility of the GLS system [11, 12]. However, KDD process and its planning is a new research field, there are more challenging and deeper issues demanding further research such as

- How to manage changes in a KDD process?
- How to handle KDD process iteration?

In particular, during the (long) lifetime of a KDD application session, there may be many kinds of changes which demand replanning the KDD process, such as changes in the databases, introducing new KDD techniques and/or new strategies to coordinate various discovery steps, etc. As replanning from scratch is in most cases unpleasant and unnecessary, we need a method to reuse the exiting KDD process plan, with local adjustment adapted to the changes.

The major contributions of this paper are addressing and solving the first one of the two important issues that have been essentially untouched in KDD literature, that is, handling KDD process changes by incremental replanning. The second problem (process iteration) can be solved by a mechanism integrating process planning with process controlling. We would like to discuss this problem in our other papers. The remaining part of this paper is organized as follows:

Section 2 gives a short summary of the GLS system and its planner; Sections 3 describes how to handle KDD process change by incremental replanning techniques; Finally Section 4 gives the concluding remarks.

2 An Overview of GLS and Its Planner

In this section, we give a brief summary of the GLS architecture and its planner. Here we only present the materials which are strictly needed in understanding the core part of the paper. The reader may refer to (Zhong et al 1997a; Zhong et al 1997b, Zhong et al 1997c) for more details.

2.1 GLS Architecture

The GLS system is divided into three levels: two meta-levels and one object level. On the first meta-level, the *planning meta-agent* (*KDD planner*, for short) sets the discovery process plan that will achieve the discovery goals when executed. On the second meta-level, the KDD agents are dynamically generated, executed, and controlled by the *controlling meta-agent* (*KDD controller*, for short). On the object level, the KDD agents are grouped into three learning phases: *(1) Pre-processing, (2) Knowledge-elicitation, (3) Knowledge-refinement*. Each phase includes a set of KDD techniques modeled as KDD agents, such as *CBK, QDR, FSN, SCT* in phase (1); *KOSI, DBI, GDT-RS* in phase (2); and *IIBR, HML* in phase (3). Each KDD agent represents a simple discovery step, and when they are organized into a society, more complex discovery tasks can be accomplished. The KDD planner is just a meta-tool to automatically build such a society.

2.2 Formal Description of KDD Agents

In terms of AI planning, a KDD agent is an *operator*. We must formally describe the KDD agents as operators in order to apply AI planning techniques here. The formalism for this purpose is the OOER (Object-Oriented Entity Relationship) data model, which extends the traditional ER concepts (entity/relation, type/instance, instance-level attributes) with object-oriented concepts (subtyping, multiple inheritance, procedures, type-level attributes/procedures, and so on).

There are two kinds of types: *D&K* types (describing passive objects – various data and knowledge presented in a KDD system) and *Agent* types (describing active objects – various KDD techniques used in the GLS system). Types are organized into a hierarchy by the OO *subtyping* mechanism. *D&K* and *Agent* are the supertypes for all passive and active objects respectively. In the text of this paper, an *"Agent* type" means any subtype of *Agent*, modeling a particular KDD technique.

Types have ordinary instance-level attributes. As for *Agent* types, there are additional properties defined as *"type-level" attributes* with information that is used by the planning meta-agent:

- In/Out: specifying the types of the input/output of an *Agent* type.
- Precond/Effect: specifying the preconditions for an agent (an instance of the *Agent* type) to execute, and the effects when executed. Note that a large part of the *Precond/Effect*, concerning constraints on input/output of the *Agent* type, has been specified implicitly by the *In/Out* attribute.
- Action: a sequential program performing real KDD actions upon agent execution.
- Decomp: describing possible *subtasking*. When a "high-level" agent (with dummy *Action*) is to be executed, it is decomposed into a network of subagents (i.e. a subplan). *Decomp* specifies the candidate *Agent* types for the subagents.

2.3 The KDD Planner

AI planning in general works on the goal, the pool of operators, and the world state descriptions (WSD). In KDD planning, the goal is a knowledge discovery task, the operators are the KDD *Agent* types, and the WSD is the description of the structure and status of the databases (the source of learning) and the knowledge bases (the results of learning). Given a discovery goal, the KDD planner reasons on operators and WSD to build a KDD process plan – a network of KDD agents that will achieve the discovery goal when executed. It has three layers as shown in Figure 1.

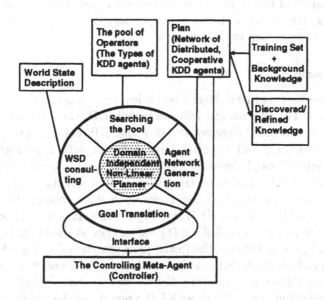

Fig. 1. The planning meta-agent coupled with the controlling meta-agent

- The Inner Layer: A Domain-Independent Non-Linear Planner.
  Given the initial world state description (WSD), the discovery goal and the pool of operators (KDD agents), it starts with a dummy partial plan, then expands the partial plan until finds a complete and consistent plan that achieves the goal when executed. The Planner is implemented by a production system which will be extended/modified in this paper to cope with new issues (iteration/changes). We will (re)present its original (meta-)rule set and searching strategy before introducing any extension/modification in the following sections.
- The Outer Layer: The Interface with the KDD Controller to Realize Hierarchical Planning.
  Hierarchical planning is necessary for real-world application, which means alternatively adding detailed steps to the plan and actually executing some steps until the overall goal is achieved. In GLS, this is accomplished by the cooperation of the two meta-agents – planner and controller. The interface between them is the outer layer.
- The Middle Layer: KDD Specific Issues.
  Because the core of the planner is domain-independent, we provide a middle layer to deal with all KDD specific issues including: (1) To transform the KDD goals into AI goals (conjunctions of logical literals); (2) To search the pool of operators for suitable KDD agents achieving a subgoal, hence being introduced into the plan; (3) To consult the world state description (WSD) to see if a subgoal is already satisfied by the WSD, or to translate the *In/Out* specification in an agent into logical literals that are added to *Precond/Effect* of the agent; (4) To represent the resulting plan as a network of KDD agents, so the controller can dynamically generate and execute the KDD agents according to the network.

2.4 A Scenario

Assume that we have a central, large space science database, each record (tuple) describing a star. The interesting attributes include CD (cluster designation), ET (effective temperature), LU (luminosity), B-V and U-B (color indexes). The facts such as we have already had a central, large database with *CleanData*, and the nominal attribute CD can be used for forming *Scopes*, etc. are explicitly stated in the initial-state (WSD). The discovery goal is to find structural characteristics hidden in the database and to refine them upon data change. Based on the specifications of WSD, goal, and KDD agent types, the planner and the controller cooperate and come up with a full KDD process plan as shown in Figure 2.

The process goes as follows. The initial plan consists of a single KDD agent *Kdiscover* to produce *RegreTree* that is a subtype of *Krefined*. It is decomposed into the sequential phases: *Preprocess, Kelicit,* and *Krefine* (in Figure 2, we also show the input/output types for these KDD agents). As the WSD contains the fact that we have already got *CleanData, Preprocess* can be simply done by *Select* (no need of *Collect* and *Clean).* Because the nominal attribute CD designates star clusters, and we need clustering other attributes as preparation for the next

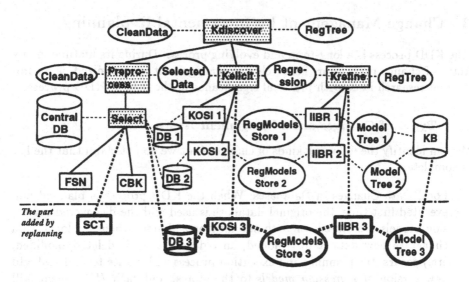

Fig. 2. A sample KDD process plan and replan

learning phase, *Select* is decomposed into *FSN* and *CBK* that can be executed in parallel and cooperatively. The result of the execution of *Select* (or its subplan) is two subdatabases.

Then the second learning phase *Kelicit* is under consideration. Here we show how to transform the In/Out of *Kelicit* into part of Precond/Effect. The original In/Out specification,

$SelectedData \rightarrow Kdiscovered,$

is first refined to subtypes:

$\$Scope \rightarrow \$Regression,$

where \$ means unspecified number of. Then, by consulting the current WSD that contains two subdatabases, we have got the precondition "there are two Scopes" and the effect "there will be two regression model stores" (represented as conjunctions of literals). The result of decomposing *Kelicit* as shown in Figure 2 is that two *KOSIs* are needed in the subplan of *Kelicit* to learn from the two *subdatabases* separately and in parallel. (But in terms of implementation, we may install only one *KOSI* tool with multiple executions, just as in software development process, one compiler may be used simultaneously to compile several source files). In the third learning phase *Krefine,* we have a similar situation: there are two *IIBRs* to refine and manage the knowledge (regression models) discovered by the two *KOSIs* in parallel.

3 Change Management by Incremental Replanning

The KDD process is a long-term and evolving process. During its lifetime, many kinds of change may occur, hence change management is recognized as an important research issue with practical significance in the field of KDD process.

3.1 Types of Changes and Management Issues

We can identify the following kinds of changes (but we do not claim that the list is complete):

- Local Data Changes in Databases: When the KDD process is planned and executed first time, the original database is used and the discovered regression models are stored for each subdatabases. Later, whenever local data change (a new data item is added, an old data item is deleted/modified, etc.) occurs, the planning and execution process will iterate to find and add new version of *regression models* to the stores, and each *IIBR* agent will manage and refine the corresponding tree of regression models. This is a universal and important problem in all real world KDD applications, as the contents of most databases are ever changing.
- Large-Scale and/or Structural Changes in Databases: Some changes in the data could be big and structural, resulting in different decomposition of the central database, for example. In this case, the process plan itself should be changed accordingly. This is called *process evolution.*
- Changes in the Process Schema: The formal description of all available KDD techniques (i.e. the *Agent* types) in the KDD system is called the *process schema*. Process schema could change during the lifetime of the KDD process. For example, new KDD techniques can be introduced into the KDD system; existing KDD techniques could become obsolete, or remain in the system but with new parameter settings; new/modified strategies coordinating various discovery steps are adopted; and etc. These changes should be reflected in the process schema accordingly: some new *Agent* types are added, while some old *Agent* types are either removed, or modified in their "type-level" attributes (*In/Out, Precond/Effect, Decomp*). Finally, process schema changes in turn cause process plan changes. That is, we see process evolution here again.

For some of the changes mentioned above, the KDD meta agents (the KDD planner and the KDD controller) presented in the previous section can be further extended to deal with them. For example, if we add the following Monitoring Rule:

Monitoring Rule:
IF   there is local change in the databases
THEN restart the process according to the same process plan

With this new (meta-)rule, the databases are under monitoring. Whenever their contents change locally, (a new data item is added, or an old data item is deleted/modified), the KDD process is restarted according to the same process plan.

However, in the case of process evolution, changes are difficult to be handled in this way. Because here the problem we are facing is not the re-execution of (part of) the existing plan. Rather, we should replan the KDD process to reflect the changing environment. More precisely, we have the following observations:

- If we insist in solving the problem of process evolution and process replanning by further extending the set of (meta-)rules, our production system will become too complicated. As (Jonsson & Backstrom 1996) points out, the integration of planning and execution is suitable only for some restricted classes of planning problems (the 3S class, for example). As we are not sure if the KDD planning problem in its full-scale can be solved properly by the ever-expanding set of (meta-)rules, we may try to realize replanning as an additional component of the searching strategy of the production system.
- As replanning from scratch is in most cases unpleasant and unnecessary, we need a method to reuse the existing KDD process plan, with local adjustment adapted to the changes. In other word, we need an *incremental replanning algorithm*.
- The big variety of possible changes does not mean that we need a separate replanning algorithm for each kind of changes. In fact, all possible changes can disturb an existing plan only in the following ways:
  - Some new preconditions come in;
  - Some old preconditions become unsupported;
  - Some old effects become obsolete;
  - *Decomps* of some agents change when new (old) *Agent* types are added into (removed from) the schema;

  A general incremental replanning algorithm just needs to consider all these situations and take proper replanning activities.
- Because of the hierarchical planning, the KDD process plan has a hierarchical structure. Incremental replanning always works on a particular part at particular levels of the existing plan, and at a particular time. So we should specify when, where and how to replan.

3.2 Incremental Replanning for Change Managements

In light of the above observations, we have designed a general, incremental replanning algorithm. In the following, we present the algorithm in the context of the original coupling mode.

First we recite the searching strategy of the production system implementing the non-linear planning as a *non-linear planning algorithm* which is called by the KDD controller when it tries to "execute" a high-level KDD agent A:

ALGORITHM-1: Non-Linear Planning
INPUT: (1) High-level agent A to be decomposed
                 (2) Current WSD
OUTPUT: Plan of A (a network of agents carrying out A's job)
METHOD:
 1. Create AI goal G from the $Out/Effect$ attributes of A, consulting WSD;
 2. Build the initial partial-plan of A: $< START\{WSD\}, GFINISH\{\} >$
 3. Inspect the current partial-plan P to find all flaws, order them
    according to heuristics about flaw priority, and store them in $AGENDA$
 4. IF $AGENDA$ is empty /* P is flaw-free, hence a plan of A */
    THEN stop /* P is returned to the KDD controller */
 5. Try to fix up the flaw $AGENDA[top]$:
    IF there is no more applicable (meta-)rule for the flaw
    THEN backtrack
    ELSE (1) choose (using heuristics) a rule to fix up the flaw;
         (2) transform P into a new partial-plan P';
         (3) set a backtrack point;
 6. Inspect the new current partial-plan P' to re-adjust $AGENDA$;
    /* remove the fixed flaw and add newly introduced flaws */
 7. Goto $step4$.

Next we present the *incremental replanning algorithm* which is also called by
the KDD controller. Recall that one of the main tasks of the KDD controller is
to monitor the execution of the process plan. Concerning change management,
we charge it with the following extra responsibilities:

 − Detecting changes in the databases
 − Receiving and approving changes in the process schema
 − Determining the starting point of replanning − the high-level KDD agent A
   that is the root of the affected part in the existing, hierarchical plan.
 − Calling the replanning algorithm (ALGORITHM-2 below) with agent A and
   the changes as the input parameters.

ALGORITHM-2: Incremental Replanning
INPUT: (1) High-level agent A and its existing plan
                 (2) Changes demanding replanning from A
                 (3) Current WSD
OUTPUT: Re-adjusted plan of A, coping with the changes
METHOD:
 1. IF there is any change in WSD (databases), or in Out/Effect of A
    THEN re-create the AI goal G' for A;
 2. IF there is a change in Decomp of A
    THEN delete those agents whose types disappear in the new Decomp of A;
    /* New agents of new types may be added in step 6 below */
 3. For each agent A_i in the existing plan of A :
    IF there is any change in WSD, or in Out/Effect of A_i
    THEN re-adjust Effect of A_i according to the change;
    /* specially, START will have new WSD as its $Effect$ */
 4. For each agent A_i in the existing plan of A :
    IF there is any change in WSD, or in In/Precond of A_i

THEN re-adjust Precond of Ai according to the change;
/* specially, FINISH will have new goal G' as its Precond */
5. Delete all "dead" agents in the existing plan;
/* an agent supporting no Precond of other agents becomes "dead" */
6. /* Now the existing plan is disturbed, because *step 1-4*
above have introduced various flaws into it. */
Invoke the planner to resume its work at *step3* of ALGORITHM-1
to find and fix up new flaws, returning a new plan of A;
7. For each high-level subagent HA_j in the new plan of A :
IF HA_j is newly introduced,
or though HA_j was in the old plan but had not been expanded
THEN do nothing here
/* planning of HAj will be done later when controller tries to execute it. */
ELSE Apply this ALGORITHM-2 recursively to HA_j
/* because HA_j may need replanning as well as its parent A */

Note that the replanning algorithm (ALGORITHM-2) is a recursive procedure, and it in turn calls the non-linear planning algorithm (ALGORITHM-1).

Let us look at an example of replanning. Back to Figure 2, supposing that we have got the following events:

- Time-serious data, come implying possible structural changes in the *central DB*;
- A new KDD technique *SCT* (stepwise Chow test to discover structural changes in time-series data) is introduced into the KDD system;
- *Decomp* of *Select* type is modified from $< FSN, CBK >$ to $< FSN, CBK, SCT >$

.

When the KDD controller detects and approves these changes, it determines that the high-level agent *Kdiscover* in Figure 2 is the starting point of replanning, and calls ALGORITHM-2 to recursively re-adjust the existing, hierarchical plan, resulting in the following changes in the plan, which are marked in Figure 2 by bold lines and boxes:

- The subplan of the *Select* agent has an additional *SCT* subagent to discover possible structural changes in time-series data;
- The *Select* agent has more subdatabases as its output;
- There are more *KOSIs* in the subplan of *Kelicit* to learn *Regression Models* from the new *subDBs*;
- There are more *IIBRs* in the subplan of *Krefine* to build *Model Trees* from the new *Regression Models*.

4 Concluding Remarks

KDD process and its planning is a new research field, there are more challenging and deeper issues demanding further research. The major contributions of this paper is addressing and solving one of two important issues that have been essentially untouched in KDD literature:

– Incremental replanning to manage process changes.
– Integrating KDD process planning with process controlling to automate process iteration;

The second problem (process iteration) can be solved by a mechanism integrating process planning with process controlling. We would like to discuss this problem in our other papers. With the issues being properly handled, the GLS system is more complete in KDD process modeling, and more flexible and robust for practical use.

In comparison with related systems, GLS is mostly similar to INLEN [6] where there are also several existing methods of machine learning integrated and a toolkit like in GLS. However, GLS can dynamically plan and organize the KDD process performed in a distributed cooperative mode. As for KDD process planning, so far we have seen in the KDD literature only one paper [8] devoted to this topic, emphasizing user-guided task-decomposition (corresponding to the hierarchical planning in our context). In contrast, we apply various AI planning techniques to the area of KDD, taking broader view, and addressing deeper issues such as process iteration and change management.

References

1. Brachman, R.J. and Anand, T. 1996. "The Process of Knowledge Discovery in Databases: A Human-Centered Approach", in *Advances in Knowledge Discovery and Data Mining*, MIT Press, 37-58.
2. Fayyad, U.M., Piatetsky-Shapiro, G, and Smyth, P. 1996. "From Data Mining to Knowledge Discovery: an Overview", in *Advances in Knowledge Discovery and Data Mining*, 1-36.
3. Jonsson, P. and Backstrom, C. 1996. "Incremental Planning", in *New Directions in AI Planning*, IOS Press, 79-90.
4. Liu, C 1991. "Software Process Planning and Execution: Coupling vs. Integration", *Proc. the 3rd International Conference on Advanced Information Systems (CAiSE91)*, LNCS 498, Springer, 356-374.
5. Liu, C. and Conradi, R. 1993. "Automatic Replanning of Task Networks for Process Evolution in EPOS", *Proc. the 4th European Software Engineering Conference (ESEC'93)*, LNCS 717, Springer, 437-450.
6. Michalski, R.S. et al. 1992. Mining for Knowledge in Databases: The INLEN Architecture, Initial Implementation and First Results. *J. of Intell. Infor. Sys.*, KAP, 1(1):85-113.
7. Russell, S.J. and Norvig, P. 1995. *Artificial Intelligence - A Modern Approach* Prentice Hall, Inc.
8. Engels, R. 1996. "Planning Tasks for Knowledge Discovery in Databases - Performing Task-Oriented User-Guidance", *Proc. Second Inter. Conf. on Knowledge Discovery and Data Mining (KDD-96)*, AAAI Press, 170-175.
9. Zhong, N. and Ohsuga, S. 1995. "Toward A Multi-Strategy and Cooperative Discovery System", *Proc. First Inter. Conf. on Knowledge Discovery and Data Mining (KDD-95)*, 337-342.
10. Zhong, N., Kakemoto, Y., and Ohsuga, S. 1997a. "An Organized Society of Autonomous Knowledge Discovery Agents", Peter Kandzia and Matthias Klusch (eds.) *Cooperative Information Agents*. LNAI 1202, Springer, 183-194.
11. Zhong, N., Liu, C., Kakemoto, Y., and Ohsuga, S. 1997b. "KDD Process Planning", *Proc. Third Inter. Conference on Knowledge Discovery and Data Mining (KDD-97)*, AAAI Press, 291-294.
12. Zhong, N., Liu, C. and Ohsuga, S. 1997c. "A Way of Increasing both Autonomy and Versatility of a KDD System", Z.W. Ras and A. Skowron (eds.) *Foundations of Intelligent Systems*, LNAI 1325, Springer 94-105.
13. Zytkow, J.M. 1993. "Introduction: Cognitive Autonomy in Machine Discovery", *Machine Learning*, KAP, 12(1-3) 7-16.

Object Mining:
A Practical Application of Data Mining for the Construction and Maintenance of Software Components

Anders Torvill Bjorvand

Department of Informatics, University of Oslo.

P.O. Box 1080 Blindern, 0360 Oslo

Email: torvill@trolldata.no

Abstract. This paper adresses the issue of automatic construction and maintenance of software components by utilizing data mining techniques. Some methods are shown, and more specifically, an implementation on an IBM PC is demonstrated. This approach is particularly useful for the synthesis of embedded decision support components and intelligent agents.

1 Introduction

In the following, a working knowledge of the object-oriented paradigm and data mining is recommended.

The object-oriented paradigm, invented at the Norwegian Computing Center in the 1960s ([5]), has gained a tremendous momentum in both academia and industry, and is now widely regarded as the most important current methodology for the construction of large information systems.

Compared to previous approaches, these information systems are easier to both build and maintain since they are divided into autonomous parts; making delegation of responsibilities easier. A lower degree of coupling between different parts of the system is a natural consequence of this approach.

This paper introduces the notion of Object Mining which is the process/idea of using data mining for both creation of and maintenance of such components. This concept was first published in [4] . The current paper, however, emphasizes the practical aspects of using this technology. The example is based on a smaller example in [4] . It will become clear that this approach merges creation and maintenance in a way that gives full support to the entire life cycle of the system. Most practical investigations show that maintenance of a software system represents a greater cost than the initial creation.

1.1 Structure of this Document

I will explain how the Object Mining technology merges these techniques to become a powerful tool for both development and maintenance of computer software. Much of this technology is explained through an example from real life showing the entire process from data analysis to the finalized component.

First we will introduce Object Mining, then we will illustrate it with some examples, then we will describe an implementation of it.

1.2 Related Research

The idea of synthesizing software into components is new, but its ancestors are many.

The most important are the fields of embedded and distributed expert systems and intelligent agents. A fair overview of this can be seen in [9] .

The Object Mining technology is, as will become evident, related to the field of expert systems. Traditional expert systems were constructed as monolithic applications that corresponded with the world through a human being, but the adaptation to an embedded expert system seems a natural one, where the expert system automatically interacts with the rest of the system. This, however, would require changes to the intended object model of the system with respect to communications, interpreters, etc. The Object Mining technology produces components that fit easily into the existing object model. This is crucial to maintaining an elegant, understandable and therefore maintainable design.

2 Object Mining

An object can be viewed as a set of attributes/variables and a set of methods to set/get and/or analyze those attributes. For the great class of objects where this definition of an object holds true in a strict fashion, our method is applicable (some known exceptions are typical user interface objects and objects with attribute-values that are hard to discretize (typically mathematical functions and computational objects)). Data mining techniques take sets of attributes and their combinations of values as input. The product is a set of rules. By putting these attributes and rules together, we have an automatically produced object (also called software component in more modern terminology).

The Object Mining technology is the idea of utilizing data mining techniques to produce software objects. The choice of data mining techniques will vary with the domain that is being modelled, and is not part of the Object Mining technology.

To formalize, the Object Mining technology is best applied through the following five steps:

- Given an object model of your system, check which objects you either have or can easily sample data/measurements about.
- Given the databases for these objects, choose the parameters for which you want the component to supply you with results. These parameters are called the decision parameters. The set of decision parameters can very well be the entire set of parameters. This will often be the case in components intended to perform simulations.
- Apply data mining techniques to produce a set of rules on the form "if $param\_1=6$ and $param\_2=34$ and .... and $param\_n = 56$ then decision_param_1=4 and ... and decision_param_m=75". The initial number of parameters should also decrease because the dependency analysis performed by the data mining system should prove some parameters redundant/superfluous. This is provided for very nicely in many data mining techniques - a common one is the reducts of rough set theory.
- Create a component with the following features:
  - Internal variables representing all the parameters and decision parameters.
  - A data structure for the ruleset.
  - Methods for setting and reading the values of each variable, eg set_param_1(), get_param_1(), etc.
  - Methods retrieving the values of the decision parameters. These methods rely on data mining strategies for applying the ruleset.

- Incorporate these objects in your system according to the object model - interfaces might be an issue here.

The component described would be relatively simple. To use it, you set its conditional values and every time you want a decision value you ask for it explicitly - upon which it is calculated and returned. These tasks of interacting with the object might of course be delegated to several objects. Some objects might provide with data acquisition, some want to read the decisions etc.

A natural extension is an "active component" where the objects that rely on information from the component can be automatically informed of changes. This is accomplished by letting the dependent objects register with the component. Every time one of the parameters of the component changes, the set of decision parameters are immediately recalculated (without an explicit method invocation). If the values of one or more of the decision values have changed, an event informing of the change is automatically posted to the objects that have registered themselves.

Active objects fit well into the framework of process control and other systems where the object plays an active part. An obvious application domain where this sort of functionality would be required, is the field of intelligent agents. A more advanced way of registering for notification might be subscription lists with detailed information when each object should be notified. An object in charge of crisis situations might for instance only be noticed when the parameters reach a critical level.

3 Examples

We have a simple example concerning dogs. This example was introduced in [4] , but is elaborated on here.

3.1 Dog Recognizer Model

Figure 1 shows the UML () sequence diagram for a simple system for visual recognition of breeds of dogs. The system consists of a camera, a feature recognizer and the Object Mining generated component Dogs. The camera component supplies the feature recognizer with a picture of a dog, the feature recognizer extracts the characteristics of the dog's tail and hair and initializes the Dogs component with it. The Dogs component is then capable of informing the system of the breed of the dog. A more realistic example would of course have to handle exceptions and ambiguities.

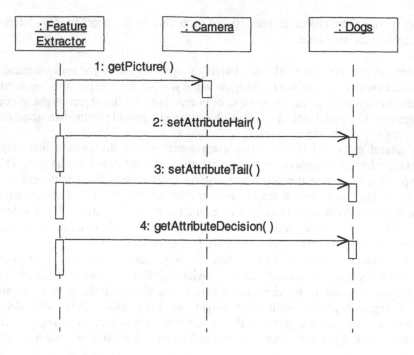

Figure 1 UML Sequence diagram for the dog recognition process

3.2 Development of the Dogs Component

We have a database of 10000 dogs. Each dog is stored in a record with several parameters like hair length, color, length of tail, breed etc. We have an image processing system that automatically extracts/recognizes all of these features except breed. We want a component that in each case can classify a dog based on certain features. Following the process outlined above, we get the following:

- We have a dog database, we choose the breed parameter as our only decision parameter.
- We apply data mining techniques and obtain the ruleset for determining the breed of dogs based on the information/experience in the database. Let's oversimplify and say that in our case, all other parameters than size and color are proved redundant in order to decide the breed. We get a ruleset with rules of the form: "if color=black and size=big then breed=Doberman Pincher"
- We can then automatically create a component with the following features:
  - Variables: color, size and breed.
  - A data structure for the rules.
  - Methods setting and reading the values of each variable:
    - set_param_size(), get_param_size()
    - set_param_color(), get_param_color()
    - The method: get_decision_breed() relying on data mining strategies for applying the ruleset.

To summarize, the Object Mining technology applies the techniques of data mining to the task/problem of producing objects/components.

4 Implementation

The crucial parts of the technology have already been implemented as an add-on to the data mining system "Rough Enough" which is also copyrighted by the author of this paper. "Rough Enough" as a pure data mining tool (without the Object Mining capabilities) was developed in 1995 at the Nowegian University of Science and Technology in Trondheim, Norway. The Object Mining capabilities have been added during 1997 and parts of 1998 and are part of version 4.0 of the Rough Enough system. Rough Enough is a general purpose data mining tool based on rough set techniques. It is further described in [1] , [2] and [3] .

The system can be downloaded from the internet address http://www.trolldata.com/.

4.1 Component Creation

The system will produce components conforming to the JavaBean standard from Sun Microsystems which is the most popular component standard right now built upon the Java language ([8]). OMG's CORBA² IDL³ files will also be automatically produced to allow the components more easily to be a part of an open distributed system.

The Java event model also supports the listener registration interface so that objects can register with the components developed through Object Mining so as to receive updates through the event system. Active objects, as explained in section 2, are therefore straightforward in Java.

4.2 The Dog Example Revisited

We will now return to the dog example and show a practical case of applying these methods.

Case

We have a table of information about dog breeds (Table 1). We want a component that can classify between these breeds, which makes the breed-attribute our decision attribute.

---

[1] OMG - Object Management Group - a consortium of leading information technology companies creating and maintaining industrial standards for object oriented development

[2] CORBA - Common Object Request Broker Architecture - an OMG standard for distributed access to objects

[3] IDL - Interface Definition Language - a middle language between the CORBA server and the different objects which may be implemented in Java, C++, Smalltalk, Cobol etc.

Table 1 . Dog Information System

Object number	Breed	Tail	Hair	Size
1	Doberman Pincher	Short	Short	Big
2	Dalmatian	Long	Short	Big
3	Cocker Spaniel	Short	Long	Small
4	German Shepherd	Long	Medium	Big

Processing with Data Mining Techniques

First, we import the data into a data mining system.

By applying data reduction methods, we get the result that tail and hair are sufficient with respect to deciding the breed. This makes the size parameter superfluous in our case.

By utilizing a method for synthesising rules, the ruleset is obtained. Each class of data mining techniques has its own methods of rules creation, so I will leave that alone for now.

Creation of a Component

A component is created from the rules. Currently, the system only supports JavaBeans conforming to the JDK 1.1 standard (the most recent Java standard at time of writing).

The system supports both passive and active objects and several rules-application strategies.

The particular component created in this example was a passive one called Dogs. It contains the following structure:

- Internal variables: AttributeTail, AttributeHair, AttributeDecision and Ruleset (double array)
- Methods:
  - Dogs(): constructor
  - getAttributeTail and setAttributeTail: sets and gets the tail attribute
  - getAttributeHair and setAttributeHair: sets and gets the hair attribute
  - calculateDecision: sets the value of the AttributeDecision variable utilizing the Ruleset variables
  - getAttributeDecision: invokes the method calculateDecision and then returns the value of the variable AttributeDecision

Listing of the Source for the Dog Component

The following code shows that each conditional attribute has an internal variable with external methods for setting and getting its value. The rules are represented with a double array, and the decision is calculated on demand. Due to space limitations, the full text of the method calculateDecision() could not be included. It is not part of the general framework either, so displaying it would not be very interesting - the method for applying rules should be chosen from the domain, possibly even on a situation to situation basis.

```java
public class Dogs implements java.io.Serializable
{
    // Property declarations
    protected int AttributeDecision = 0;
    protected int AttributeTail = 0;
    protected int AttributeHair = 0;

    // Ruleset
    protected int[][] ruleSet = {
        {-1, 2,  4},
        {-1, 3,  3},
        {1,  1,  1},
        {1,  3,  3},
        {2,  1,  2},
        {2,  2,  4},
    };

    // Constructor
    public Dogs()
    {
    }

    protected void calculateDecision()
    {
        // here, different schemes for
        // rule-interpretation can be
        // implemented
    }

    public void setAttributeTail(int attribute_value)
    {
        AttributeTail = attribute_value;
    }

    public int getAttributeTail()
    {
        return AttributeTail;
    }

    public void setAttributeHair(int attribute_value)
    {
        AttributeHair = attribute_value;
    }

    public int getAttributeHair()
    {
        return AttributeHair;
    }

    public int getAttributeDecision()
    {
        calculateDecision();
        return AttributeDecision;
    }
}
```

Using the Component

Figure 2 shows a Java Applet utilizing the Dogs component. The Applet was created in the Symantec Visual Cafe Java environment. The Applet consists of textfields, a button, the Dogs component and a component that translates between the domain (tail-lengths, breeds) and our discretized component working internally in integers. The Dogs component was used as is, and did not need manual refinement. When the Tail and Hair parameters are given, pressing the Calculate-button gives the name of the Breed.

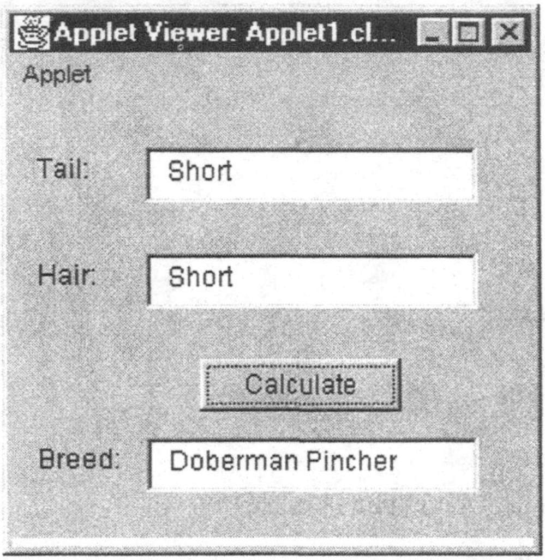

Figure 2 Java Applet using the Dogs JavaBean

5 Conclusion

We have identified the possibilities and importance of utilizing data mining techniques for synthesis of objects from experimental data. Several examples have been given, and an implementation is described.

The application of data mining to software engineering, called Object Mining in this paper, shows great promise, and will hopefully be further investigated in the future.

6 Future Research

The techniques outlined here suggests that a central system and a database might generate components based on the latest information with regular intervals. The next logical step would be to let these components enhance themselves through rule improvement   by feedback. This opens up several important applications for embedded decision support systems and autonomous intelligent agents. A problem, especially with embedded systems, is that a lightweight object like the ones outlined in this paper often will be the only feasible way to go. A single superobject might sound glorious, but it might be too large or too inefficient.

By automating software construction relying on experimental data, the issue of correctness immediately becomes a major one. Completeness, inconsistency and handling of indeterminate decisions should be further investigated. There is a great potential for automating several of these tasks more easily than in traditional approaches to correctness preservation of programs.

Creating general "superobjects" with their own rule storage and techniques for exploring their own domain, a total system can be created with only one object class. In many ways, this is only a different perspective on agent oriented programming. I believe that an integration of that approach and the principles of genetic programming would be a fruitful direction of research.

Ways of integrating the Object Mining approach with modelling is an important field of study; especially within the new UML standard ([6] and [7]).

Acknowledgements

I would like to thank my wife Annette for her support and my little daughter Susanne for her cheerful smile. I would also like to thank the people at Oslo Research Park for fruitful discussions concerning the Object Mining technology.

References

[1] Bjorvand, Anders Torvill (1997). *'Rough Enough' - A System Supporting the Rough Sets Approach.* Proceedings of the Sixth Scandinavian Conference on Artificial Intelligence 1997. Helsinki, Finland. IOS Press, Amsterdam.

[2] Bjorvand, Anders Torvill and Komorowski, Jan (1997). Practical Applications of Genetic Algorithms for Efficient Reduct Computation. Proceedings of the 15th IMACS World Congress 1997 on Scientific Computation, Modelling and Applied Mathematics. Wissenschaft & Technik Verlag, Berlin.

[3] Bjorvand, Anders Torvill (1997). *Rough Enough - Software Demonstration.* Proceedings of the 15th IMACS World Congress 1997 on Scientific Computation, Modelling and Applied Mathematics. Wissenschaft & Technik Verlag, Berlin.

[4] Bjorvand, Anders Torvill (1998). *Synthesis of Objects: A Rough Sets Approach to Automatic Construction and Maintenance of Software Components.* European Conference on Artificial Intelligence, August, 1998. Workshop entitled Synthesis of Intelligent Agent Systems from Experimental Data.

[5] Dahl, O.J., Myrhaug, B. and Nygaard, K. (1968). *SIMULA 67 Common Base Language.* Norwegian Computing Center, Oslo.

[6] Douglass, Bruce Powell (1998). Real-Time UML - Developing Efficient Objects for Embedded Systems. Addison-Wesley.

[7] Fowler, Martin and Scott, Kendall (1997). UML Distilled - Applying the Standard Object Modeling Language. Addison-Wesley.

[8] Gosling, James and Joy, Bill and Steele, Guy (1996). *The Java Language Specification.* Addison-Wesley.

[9] Kaelbling, Leslie Pack (1993). Learning in Embedded Systems. MIT Press.

A Relational Data Mining Tool
Based on Genetic Programming

Lionel MARTIN, Frédéric MOAL, Christel VRAIN

LIFO, Université d'Orléans,
rue Léonard de Vinci, BP 6759, 45067 Orleans cedex 02, France
{martin,moal,cv}@lifo.univ-orleans.fr

Abstract. In this paper, we present a Data Mining tool based on Genetic Programming which enables to analyze complex databases, involving several relation schemes. In our approach, trees represent expressions of relational algebra and they are evaluated according to the way they discriminate positive and negative examples of the target concept. Nevertheless, relational algebra expressions are strongly typed and classical genetic operators, such as mutation and crossover, have been modified to prevent from building illegal expressions. The Genetic Programming approach that we have developed has been modeled in the framework of constraints.

1 Introduction

In this paper, we propose a Data Mining tool based on Genetic Programming. At present, most systems rely on the universal relation assumption which hypothesizes that a database is composed of a unique relation scheme [FPSSU96]. This is not realistic for real applications, since this leads to a huge relation which is hardly tractable. The Data Mining task we address in this paper is a discrimination task that can be stated as follows.

Given:
- a database scheme $\mathcal{R}$ over a set U of attributes
$\mathcal{R} = \{r_1(a_{11}:d_{11}, \ldots, a_{1k_1}:d_{1k_1}), \ldots, r_p(a_{p1}:d_{p1}, \ldots, a_{pk_p}:d_{pk_p})\}$, where r_i is a relation of arity k_i, a_{ij} is the jth attribute of the relation r_i and d_{ij} is the domain of the attribute a_{ij},
- a concept to learn defined by:
  - a positive example relation e^+ defined by the schema :
  $e^+(a_1:d_1, a_2:d_2, \ldots a_n:d_n)$
  - a negative example relation e^- defined by the same schema as e^+,
find a SQL request which recognizes the positive examples and rejects the negative ones.

Table 1: The Discrimination Task

As has been stated in the task, we aim at analyzing complex databases, involving several relation schemes and therefore, we relax the classical "universal relation scheme assumption"[FPSSU96]. To achieve this and considering the size of the search space, we have chosen a Genetic Programming approach [Koz92, Koz94, SJB+93], that enables to stochastically explore the search space. Genetic-based approaches have already been proposed for Data Mining but, most of them use genetic *algorithms* encoding attribute-value representations [GSB97] and consequently, relying on the universal relation assumption. Some approaches [AVK95] have extended genetic algorithms to first order representations, but examples are represented by conjunctions of atoms before execution, which allows to code them with strings of fixed length. In our case, examples are only given by a relation and we must find the relations that are involved in the definition of the given concept. To our knowledge, the only Data Mining approach based on Genetic Programming is described in [RE96], but it is applied to object-oriented databases.

Let us first shortly recall the basic principles of Genetic Programming. It is an optimization method used for finding nearly optimal solution(s) to a problem, given a *fitness function*. The hypotheses are coded by trees and are called individuals; initially, a population of individuals is randomly built and then new populations are iteratively generated from the previous one by applying one of the 3 following operations:

- **reproduction:** an individual of the generation i is added to the generation $i + 1$,
- **mutation:** before an individual of the generation i is added to the generation $i + 1$, one of its sub-trees is replaced by a randomly generated sub-tree,
- **crossover:** given 2 individuals belonging to the generation i, 2 new individuals are added to the generation $i + 1$ obtained by exchanging one sub-tree of each initial individual.

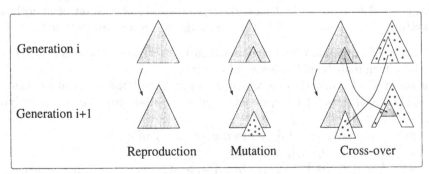

Fig. 1. Genetic operations ($\triangle$ represent trees and sub-trees)

The number of individuals in a population, the number of generations and the rate of each operation performed during a generation are fixed by parameters before learning. Moreover, for each genetic operation, individuals are chosen according to a probability proportional to their fitness.

The solution of the problem is given by the best individual that has been built. Let us notice that this result depends heavily on the values of the given parameters and on the generation of the initial population.

For our purpose, we have chosen to represent individuals of the genetic program by relational algebra expressions which enable to get results that can be both easily understood by an expert and easily translated into SQL requests for evaluation. Nevertheless, this leads to an important drawback from the point of view of Genetic Programming: relational algebra expressions are strongly typed, each node of a tree represents a relation with a fixed arity and predefined domains, therefore crossover or mutation operators can lead to syntactically or semantically incorrect expressions. Let us consider for instance, a tree representing a projection on the attribute *age* of the relation *customer* : a mutation which changes the relation *customer* into the relation *purchase* leads to an incorrect tree.

Typed Genetic Programming as defined by [Koz94] or by [Mon95] could not be used here, since a node of a tree represents a relation and its type is a list of domains: the probability to randomly select two trees with the same type is very low.

We have developed a new Genetic Programming approach and formalized it in the framework of constraints.

The paper is organized as follows. In Section 2, we present how the Data Mining task, given in Table 1, has been formalized in a Genetic Programming framework. Section 3 presents some experiments. Section 4 concludes and discusses futher works.

2 A constraint based model

2.1 Individual Representation

A tree (also called an individual) is the basic structure of our approach. The language used to build trees defines the search space, i.e. the set of hypotheses the system will be able to build. This language is syntactically defined by:

- a set $\mathcal{T}$ of terminals which is included in the database relations set, $\mathcal{T} \subset \mathcal{R}$. These terminals label the leaves of the trees ;
- a set $\mathcal{NT}$ of non-terminals which is composed of the following relational algebra operators : (A_i represents a *variable* that will refer to underlying attributes)
  - projection $\pi[A_1, \ldots, A_n]$, where n is the arity of e^+,
  - selection $\sigma[A_1 \ Op \ A_2]$, where $Op \in \{=, >, <\}$,
  - selection $\sigma[A_1 \ Op \ V]$, where $Op \in \{=, >, <\}$ and V is a value occurring in the database,
  - join $\bowtie [A_1, A_2]$,
  - product $\times$.
  $\bowtie [A_1, A_2]$ and $\times$ are the only operators with arity 2 ; such nodes require two subtrees. The A_i are *variables* that will refer to underlying attributes.

Let us notice that a same result can be expressed by different trees, e.g. $\bowtie [A_1, A_2](r_1, r_2)$ and $\sigma[A_1 = A_2](r_1 \times r_2)$. Such trees are not equivalent since applying mutation and crossover operator does not lead to the same individuals.

Each tree and each subtree represent a relation. For sake of simplicity, we refer to an attribute in a relation by an integer representing the position of that attribute in the underlying relation. It is called the attribute name or the attribute reference.

To deal with the problem of semantically incorrect trees, we add a set of constraints to each node of the tree, constraints that must be satisfied to get semantically correct expressions. In a first step, the expressions A_i appearing in a tree represent *variables* that must be instantiated by attribute references in a second step. A tree will be correct, if the instantiation of the variables A_i satisfies the constraints associated to each node.

The set of constraints associated to a node is defined as follows: (*arity* and *dom* are functions which respectively give the arity of a relation and the domain of a given attribute reference k)

A node	Its set of constraints
$\pi_{[A_1,...,A_n]}(S)$	$\{1 \leq A_i \leq arity(S) \mid \forall i \in [1..n]\}$
$\sigma_{[A_1 Op V]}(S)$	$\{1 \leq A_1 \leq arity(S), dom(A_1, S) = dom(V)\}$
$\sigma_{[A_1 Op A_2]}(S)$	$\{1 \leq A_1 \leq arity(S),$
	$1 \leq A_2 \leq arity(S), dom(A_1, S) = dom(A_2, S)\}$
$\bowtie_{[A_1,A_2]}(S_1, S_2)$	$\{1 \leq A_1 \leq arity(S_1), 1 \leq A_2 \leq arity(S_2),$
	$dom(A_1, S_1) = dom(A_2, S_2)\}$
$\times(S_1, S_2)$	$\emptyset$
r_i	$\emptyset$

An individual is therefore a tree over $\mathcal{T} \cup \mathcal{NT}$ and a valuation ϑ which associates an attribute reference to each variable A_i and which satisfies the constraints over each of its node. This ensures that the relational algebra expression, represented by the tree is correct. In the following and without loss of generality, we suppose that each variable appearing in a tree t has been renamed in order to be unique. Consequently, satisfying the constraints of each node of t is equivalent to satisfying the set of all constraints of t. From a logical point of view, ϑ is one of the solutions to the set of constraints of t.

2.2 Individual generation

The individual generation algorithm is a recursive function. A node is randomly generated and subtrees are generated for this node, until a tree and a satisfiable set of constraints is completely built. We use a constraint solving system which is supposed to be correct, i.e., not to reject satisfiable set of constraints. The major advantage of using a constraint solving system is that the generation immediately stops when a partial tree leads to a deadlock. Once a tree has been completely constructed, the constraint solving system is called to get a set of correct instantiations of the variables of the tree. We then randomly choose *one* valuation, given a set ϑ of instantiations *variable = value*.

The result of the generation process is a pair (t, ϑ), where t is a tree over $\mathcal{T} \cup \mathcal{NT}$ which contains variables denoted by $A_1, \ldots, A_k$, and where ϑ is a set

$\{A_1 = ref_1, \ldots, A_k = ref_k\}$, where ref_i are references to attributes of relations that appears in t.

Let us notice that the system has some initial constraints, namely the domains of the target concept given by the relation e^+. Such constraints must always be satisfied and cannot be relaxed.

2.3 Crossover and mutation : a constraint solving problem

Let us consider an individual (t, ϑ) and a subtree s of t. The main problem when dealing with mutation and crossover operators occurs when replacing the subtree s by another individual defined by the tree s' and the valuation $\vartheta_{s'}$ (which comes from another individual in case of crossover, or has been randomly generated in case of mutation) given the tree t', since the new set of constraints thus obtained must be still satisfiable.

Notations:

- ϑ_s denotes the restriction of ϑ to variables of s,
- ϑ_o denotes the restriction of ϑ to the rest of the tree $(t - s)$,
- ϑ_o is decomposed into two sets: ϑ_{o1} is restricted to the variables that do not refer to attributes occurring in the subtree s and ϑ_{o2} is restricted to variables which refer to attributes occurring in s (cf figure 2).

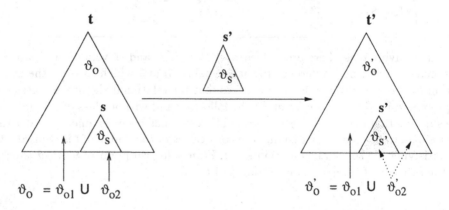

Fig. 2. Crossover and mutation: subtrees and valuations exchange

There are three possible cases :

- Case 1: there exists a valuation ϑ', which is consistent with the set of constraints defined in t' and which extends $\vartheta_{o1} \cup \vartheta_{s'}$; in other words, ϑ' gives only new values to the variables occurring in ϑ_{o2}. The result is therefore the individual (t', ϑ').
- Case 2: there exists a valuation ϑ', which is consistent with the set of constraints defined in t' and which extends $\vartheta_{s'}$ (but which does not extend ϑ_{o1}). It is no longer possible to, even partially, keep the previous valuation ϑ_{o1}. The result is therefore the individual (t', ϑ').

– Case 3: the new tree t' has no solution, even when relaxing all the valuations. In that case, the operator applied to this individual with the subtree s' fails.

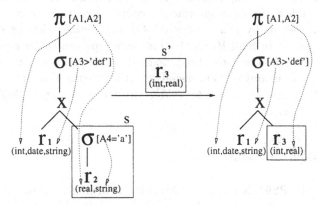

Fig. 3. ϑ_{o1} ($A_1 = 1, A_3 = 3$) remains valid (Case 1)

For instance, in Figure 3, the resulting valuation is constructed with ϑ_{o1} which assigns to A_1 the first attribute of r_1 and to A_3 the third attribute of r_1 and with a new valuation for A_2 to the second attribute of r_3 (the fact that A_4 is assigned the second attribute of r_2 is no longer useful).

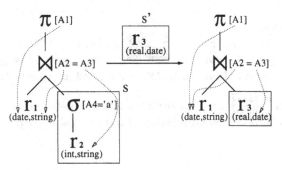

Fig. 4. ϑ_{o1} ($A_1 = 1, A_2 = 2$) must be changed. (Case 2)

Figure 4 illustrates the second case: the initial valuation ϑ_{o1} is no longer consistent, because A_2 refers to a string attribute, and there is no string in the new tree s'. So, keeping this valuation makes the constraint ($dom(A_2) = dom(A_3)$) on the join node not satisfiable. To solve this problem, we relax the valuation ϑ_{o1}, and the new set of constraints becomes satisfiable with $dom(A_2) = dom(A_3) = date$.

The last case is similar to the previous one, but even after relaxing ϑ_{o1}, the constraint set remains unsatisfiable.

In our application, a less random version of the mutation operator has also been implemented: it allows to generalize or specialize an individual.

3   Preliminary results

This approach has been implemented in C. The evaluation of individuals is performed through a standard interface. According to the choice of the user, either Oracle is called (by means of PRO*C) and requests are executed, or a module implemented in SWI-PROLOG for data represented by ground atoms is used. The fitness function has been defined so that it penalizes individuals that cover negative examples. The usual genetic programming parameters are the Reproduction rate (here set to 20%), the Crossover rate (60%) and the Mutation rate (20%).

3.1   Michalski's 10 trains

This example [MMPS94] is a classical Machine Learning example. It has only a few instances, but it allows to test the convergence of the algorithm in a relational case : there are 8 relations (*car, load, in-front, ccont, ...*) with redundancies.

The dataset is composed of 10 trains, and the goal is to discriminate between 5 trains (positive examples) going in the east direction and 5 trains (negative examples) going in the west direction. The population contains 1000 individuals and selection is restricted to the equality operator. The algorithm converges to the following *conjunctive* definition for east trains :

```
SELECT r0.idtrain
FROM ccont r0, infront r1, load r2, load r3
WHERE (r0.idwagon=r1.idwagon) AND (r2.idwagon=r1.idwagon)
   AND (r3.idwagon=r1.idwagon2) AND (r2.load_shape='triangle');
```

It is important to notice that this definition is a complete and consistent solution and that it does involve several relations (and several occurrences of the same one).

3.2   The mushrooms

This database [Sch87] has only *one* relation, called *mush*, which contains all data about 8124 mushrooms. The *mush* relation has 22 attributes with discrete values. The goal is to discriminate the edible mushrooms (4208) from the poisonous one (3916).

Here the set of non-terminal is restricted to projection and constant selection (since there is a single relation). The trees are linear, crossover and mutation operators always succeed. Such an experiment enables to test the performance of the system in an attribute/value case, with much more instances. Two conjunctive solutions emerge, depending on the relative weight given to the number of negative covered examples in the fitness function : $3408e^+/120e^-$ covered by the first one (80%/3%), and $2496e^+/0e^-$ by the second one (59%/0%).

3.3 The 100 trains example

This example [MMPS94] is similar to the 10 trains example, but there are 100 unclassified trains, and about 300 cars. The dataset is *a priori* unclassified. We have invented a concept and then tested how our system could learn the right definition of this concept.

We have chosen the following partially defined concept:
– the positive examples $e+$ are defined by the relation "SELECT r1.idtrain FROM car r1 WHERE (r1.position = 1) AND (r1.wheels = 3)" (16 trains),
– the negative examples $e-$ are defined by "SELECT r1.idtrain FROM car r1, car r2 WHERE (r1.wheels $\neq$ 3) AND (r1.idtrain = r2.idtrain) AND (r2.shape = 'rectangle') AND (r2.roof_shape = 'flat')" (38 trains).

Here, the population contains 250 individuals. Since the target concept is a "simple" conjunctive one, the best solution is reached after five generations in average.

4 Conclusion

The experiments show that the system that we have developed is able to handle several relations, even on quite important collections of data. Further experiments must still be achieved to test the efficiency on very large collection of data and to improve the quality of the fitness function.

The method proposed in this paper brings two kinds of contribution:
– a formalization of the search space in terms of relational algebra,
– an exploration of such a search space by a Genetic Programming approach.

The first point has already been studied in [BR97]. Nevertheless, the two approaches differ: in [BR97], a normal form of relational algebra expression is used and the algorithm relies on an exhaustive evaluation of all possible products of relations in the database.

The approach that we have chosen associates to each node of a tree a set of *internal* constraints, which defines the space of all correct individuals. When dealing with a particular problem, the user usually has knowledge about the solution, or knowledge about what is not a solution. This is usually coded by biases. A first method to express biases is to restrict the set $\mathcal{T} \cup \mathcal{NT}$, but this can be too drastic and this does not allow to express fine knowledge. Another method would be to extend the set of constraints with *external* constraints, defined by the user and associated to the root of each tree. For instance, limiting the height of the trees would be simply written by adding the constraint $height(t) < 7$ at the root of a tree t (where *height* is a function recursively defined over the nodes). This approach has two major interests:
– extensibility: this would allow the user to define new biases over the initial search space,
– simplicity: this would provide us with an unified way to express the search space (constraint trees) and biases over it.

Nevethess, we must now study the class of biases that can be represented by constraints.

Another important point is learning disjunctive concepts. For the time being, we have focused on conjunctive concepts, and a parallel architecture, splitting the whole population into subpopulations (islands), was mainly used to promote species formation, i.e. the emergence of different solutions. We would like to use such an architecture for learning disjunctive concepts, as done in the system Gnet [GSB97]. The final solution will be the union of *some* of the best conjunctive ones.

References

[AVK95]   S. Augier, G. Venturini, and Y. Kodratoff. Learning first order logic rules with a genetic algorithm. In *Proceedings of the First International Conference on Knowledge Discovery & Data Mining (KDD'95)*, pages 21–26, Canada, August 1995.

[BR97]   Hendrik Blockeel and Luc De Raedt. Relational knowledge discovery in databases. In Stephen Muggleton, editor, *Proceedings of the 6th International Workshop on Inductive Logic Programming (ILP-96)*, volume 1314 of *LNAI*, pages 199–211, Berlin, August 26–28 1997. Springer.

[FPSSU96]   U. M. Fayyad, G. Piatetsky-Shapiro, P. Smyth, and R. Uthurusamy, editors. *Advances in Knowledge Discovery and Data Mining.* MIT Press, Mento Park, 1996.

[GSB97]   A. Giordana, L. Saitta, and G. Lo Bello. A coevolutionary approach to concept learning. In Zbigniew W. Raś and Andrzej Skowron, editors, *Proceedings of the 10th International Symposium on Foundations of Intelligent Systems (ISMIS-97)*, volume 1325 of *LNAI*, pages 257–266, Berlin, October 15–18 1997. Springer.

[Koz92]   J. R. Koza. *Genetic Programming On the programming of computers by means of natural selection.* MIT Press, Cambridge, Massachusetts, 1992.

[Koz94]   J. R. Koza. *Genetic Programming II Automatic Discovery of Reusable Programs.* MIT Press, Cambridge, Massachusetts, 1994.

[MMPS94]   D. Michie, S. Muggleton, D. Page, and A. Srinivasan. To the international computing community: A new East-West challenge. Technical report, Oxford University Computing laboratory, Oxford,UK, 1994.

[Mon95]   David J. Montana. Strongly typed genetic programming. *Evolutionary Computation*, 3(2):199–230, 1995.

[RE96]   Tae-Wan Ryu and Christoph F. Eick. Deriving queries from examples using genetic programming. In Evangelos Simoudis, Jia Wei Han, and Usama Fayyad, editors, *The Second International Conference on Knowledge Discovery and Data Mining (KDD-96)*, pages 303–306, Portland, Oregon, USA, August 2-4 1996. AAAI.

[Sch87]   J. C. Schlimmer. Concept acquisition through representational adjustment. Technical Report ICS-TR-87-19, University of California, Irvine, Department of Information and Computer Science, July 1987.

[SJB+93]   W. M. Spears, K. A. De Jong, T. Bäck, D. B. Fogel, and H. de Garis. An overview of evolutionary computation. In Pavel B. Brazdil, editor, *Proceedings of the European Conference on Machine Learning (ECML-93)*, volume 667 of *LNAI*, pages 442–459, Vienna, Austria, April 1993. Springer Verlag.

Inducing Cost-Sensitive Trees
via Instance Weighting

Kai Ming Ting

School of Computing and Mathematics, Deakin University, Vic 3168, Australia.

Abstract. We introduce an instance-weighting method to induce cost-sensitive trees in this paper. It is a generalization of the standard tree induction process where only the initial instance weights determine the type of tree to be induced—*minimum error* trees or *minimum high cost error* trees. We demonstrate that it can be easily adapted to an existing tree learning algorithm. Previous research gave insufficient evidence to support the fact that the greedy divide-and-conquer algorithm can effectively induce a truly cost-sensitive tree directly from the training data. We provide this empirical evidence in this paper. The algorithm incorporating the instance-weighting method is found to be better than the original algorithm in terms of total misclassification costs, the number of high cost errors and tree size in two-class datasets. The instance-weighting method is simpler and more effective in implementation than a previous method based on altered priors.

1 Introduction

Cost-sensitive classifications have received much less attention than minimum error classifications in empirical learning research. Classifiers that minimize the number of misclassification errors are inadequate in problems with variable misclassification costs. Many practical classification problems have different costs associated with different types of error. For example, in medical diagnosis, the errors committed in diagnosing someone as healthy when one has a life-threatening disease is usually considered to be far more serious (thus higher costs) than the opposite type of error—of diagnosing someone as ill when one is in fact healthy.

A line of research in cost-sensitive tree induction employing the greedy divide-and-conquer algorithm demands further investigation. Breiman *et al.* (1984) describe two different methods of incorporating variable misclassification costs into the process of tree induction. These methods adapt the test selection criterion in the tree growing process. Pazzani *et al.* (1994) reported negative empirical results when using one of the Breiman *et al.*'s formulation to induce cost-sensitive trees. They found that the cost-sensitive trees do not always have lower misclassification costs, when presented with unseen test data, than those trees induced without cost consideration. Using a post-processing approach, Webb (1996) shows that applying a cost-sensitive specialization technique to a minimum error tree can reduce its misclassification costs by about 3% on average. Employing the greedy divide-and-conquer algorithm, the research so far does not show convincingly that a truly cost-sensitive tree can/cannot be effectively learned directly from the training data. We investigate this issue specifically in this paper.

This paper presents the instance-weighting method to induce cost-sensitive trees that seeks to minimize the number of high cost errors and total misclassification costs. This method is inspired by instance weight modification in boosting decision trees by Quinlan (1996). Boosting generates multiple classifiers in sequential steps. At the end of each step, the weight of each instance in the training set is adjusted to reflect its importance for the next induction step. These weights cause the learner to concentrate on different instances in each step and so lead to different classifiers. These classifiers are then combined by voting to form a composite classifier. Boosting begins with *equal* initial weights in the first step. The intuition for the cost-sensitive induction in this paper is to have *different* initial weights which reflect the (given) costs of misclassification. This effectively influences the learner to focus on instances which have high misclassification costs. We demonstrate that this is a viable method and can be easily adapted to an existing learning algorithm. We show convincingly that a truly cost-sensitive tree can be effectively learned using this method—an algorithm incorporating the instance-weighting method achieves a substantial reduction in misclassification costs, the number of high cost errors and tree size over the same algorithm without it in two-class domains.

The proposed instance-weighting method changes the class distribution such that the tree so induced is in favor of the class with high weight/cost and is less likely to commit errors with high cost. This usually reduces the total misclassification costs as a consequence. Smaller trees are a natural product of the tree induction procedure when presented with training dataset of skewed class distribution, which is a result of weighting instances in dataset with relatively balanced class distribution. We present the proposed instance-weighting method in the next section.

2 Cost-Sensitive Tree Induction via Instance-Weighting

Let N be the total number of instances from the given training set, and N_j be the number of class j instances. Similarly, let $N(t)$ and $N_j(t)$ be the number of instances and class j instances in node t of a decision tree. The probability that an instance is in class j given that it falls into node t is given by the ratio of the total number of class j instances to the total number of instances in this node.

$$p(j|t) = \frac{N_j(t)}{\sum_i N_i(t)}. \tag{1}$$

When node t contains instances that belong to a mixture of classes, the standard greedy divide-and-conquer procedure for inducing trees (e.g., Breiman *et al.* (1984) and Quinlan (1993)) uses a test selection criterion to choose a test at this node such that the training instances which fall into each branch, as a result of the split, become more homogeneous. One of the commonly used criterion is entropy i.e., $-\sum_j p(j|t)log[p(j|t)]$. At each node, the tree growing process selects a test which has the maximum gain in entropy until the node contains only a single-class collection of instances.

To avoid overfitting, a pruning process is employed to reduce the size of the tree such that the estimated error is minimum. In short, the standard tree induction procedure seeks to produce a *minimum error* tree.

Our intuition for cost-sensitive tree induction is to modify the weight of an instance proportional to the cost of misclassifying the class to which the instance belonged, leaving the sum of all training instance weights still equal to N. The last condition is important because there is no reason to alter the size of the training set, which is equivalent to the sum of all training instance weights, while the individual instance weights are adjusted to reflect the relative importance of instances for making future prediction with respect to cost-sensitive classification.

Let $C(j)$ be the cost of misclassifying a class j instance, then the weight of a class j instance can be computed as

$$w(j) = C(j)\frac{N}{\sum_i C(i)N_i}, \tag{2}$$

such that the sum of all instance weights is $\sum_j w(j)N_j = N$. For $C(j) \geq 1$, $w(j)$ has the smallest value, $0 < \frac{N}{\sum_i C(i)N_i} < 1$, when $C(j) = 1$; and the largest value, $w(j) = \frac{C(j)\sum_i N_i}{\sum_i C(i)N_i} > 1$, when $C(j) = max_i C(i)$.

Similar to $p(j|t)$, $p_w(j|t)$ is defined as the ratio of the total weight of class j instances to the total weight in node t.

$$p_w(j|t) = \frac{W_j(t)}{\sum_i W_i(t)} = \frac{w(j)N_j(t)}{\sum_i w(i)N_i(t)}. \tag{3}$$

The standard greedy divide-and-conquer procedure for inducing minimum error trees can then be used without modification, except that $W_j(t)$ is used instead of $N_j(t)$ in the computation of the test selection criterion in the tree growing process and the error estimation in the pruning process. Thus, both processes are affected due to this change.

We modified C4.5 (Quinlan, 1993) to create C4.5CS. We only need to initialize the training instance weights to $w(j)$ since C4.5 has already employed $W_j(t)$ for the computation discussed above.[1]

This modification effectively converts the standard tree induction procedure that seeks to minimize *the number of errors*, regardless of cost, to a procedure that seeks to minimize *the number of errors with high weight/cost*. Note that minimizing the later does not guarantee that the total misclassification cost is minimized. This is because the number of low cost errors is usually increased as a result.

The advantage of this approach is that the whole process of tree growing and tree pruning is the same as that used to induce minimum error trees. This can

---

[1] C4.5 uses fractional weights for the treatment of missing values. See Quinlan (1993) for details.

be viewed as a generalization of the standard tree induction process where *only the initial instance weights determine the type of tree to be induced—minimum error trees or minimum high cost error trees.*

To classify a new instance, C4.5CS predicts the class which has the maximum weights at a leaf, as in C4.5.

Cost Matrix and C(j). In a classification task of I classes, the misclassification costs can be specified in a cost matrix of size $I \times I$. The row of the matrix indicates the predicted class, and the column indicates the actual class. The off-diagonal entries contain the costs of misclassifications; and on the diagonal lie the costs for correct classifications which are zero in this case since our main concern here is total misclassification costs of an induced tree.[2]

Let $cost(i, j)$ be the cost of misclassifying a class j instance as belonging to class i. In all cases, $cost(i, j) = 0.0$, for $i = j$. A cost matrix must be converted to a cost vector $C(j)$ in order to use Equation (2) for instance-weighting. In this paper, we employ the form of conversion suggested by Breiman *et al.* (1984):

$$C(j) = \sum_i^I cost(i, j). \tag{4}$$

In our experiments, without loss of generality, we impose a unity condition— at least one $cost(i, j) = 1.0$. The only reason to have this unity condition or normalization[3] is to allow us to measure the number of *high cost errors*, which is defined as the number of misclassification errors that have costs more than 1.0.

Note that the cost matrix to cost vector conversion is expected to work well with the cost-sensitive tree induction, as described in this section, when there are only two classes. But it might be inappropriate when there are more than two classes because it collapses $I \times I$ numbers to I. In order to investigate the potential problem due to this conversion, we explicitly divide the experimental datasets into two groups: two-class and multi-class. Any performance discrepancy between these two groups is due to this conversion.

3 Experiments

Four measures are used to evaluate the performance of the cost-sensitive tree induction algorithm in this paper. They are total misclassification costs (i.e., $\sum_l^{N'} cost$(predicted-class(l), actual-class(l)), where N' is the number of instances in the unseen test set), pruned tree size (i.e., total number of internal nodes and leaves), the number of high cost errors, and the total number of misclassification errors on unseen data. The first and the third are the most important measures. The aim of cost-sensitive classification is to minimize the number of high cost errors or misclassification costs, or both. Every thing being equal, a tree induction algorithm is better than the other if it induces smaller trees.

---

[2] In general, the costs of correct classifications can be non-zero. Minimizing the costs of correct classifications is a different issue outside the scope of this paper.

[3] Note that an arbitrary cost matrix can be normalized to become a cost matrix satisfying this unity condition.

We conduct experiments using twenty datasets obtained from the UCI repository of machine learning databases (Merz & Murphy, 1996) and two datasets with specified cost matrices (i.e., Heart_S and German) used in the Statlog project (Michie, Spiegelhalter & Taylor, 1994). The datasets are selected to cover a wide variety of different domains with respect to dataset size, the number of classes, the number of attributes, and types of attributes. They consist of twelve two-class datasets and ten multi-class datasets.

Ten 10-fold cross-validations are carried out in each dataset, except in the Waveform dataset where randomly generated training data size of 300 and test data size of 5000 are used in the 100 trials.

Random cost assignments with the unity condition are used in all datasets except the Heart_S and German datasets. In the later cases, the costs (i.e., $cost(1, 2) = 1.0$ and $cost(2, 1) = 5.0$) specified in Michie, Spiegelhalter & Taylor (1994) are used. In the former cases, a cost matrix is randomly generated at the beginning of each trial. Each non-diagonal entry in the cost matrix is assigned an integer randomly generated between 1 to 10.

We first compare C4.5CS with C4.5 to evaluate whether trees induced by C4.5CS are more cost sensitive than those produced by C4.5. Note that *the only difference between C4.5CS and C4.5 is the initial weight setting*. Any performance differences are due to this initial weight setting.

3.1 Can C4.5CS induce cost-sensitive trees effectively?

Given a training set and a cost matrix, C4.5CS induces a cost-sensitive tree which seeks to minimize the number of high cost errors and total misclassification costs. C4.5 produces a tree which seeks to minimize the total misclassification errors. Both trees are then tested using a separate test set, and the total misclassification costs are measured according to the given cost matrix.

Table 1 presents averages, over 100 trials, for the misclassification costs, the tree size, the number of high cost errors and the total errors for both C4.5CS and C4.5 in each dataset. The ratio (C4.5CS/C4.5) for each of these measures is also presented—a value less than 1 represents an improvement due to C4.5CS. The means of these ratios are given for the twelve two-class datasets as well as the ten multi-class datasets.

In terms of misclassification costs, C4.5CS achieves a mean reduction of 38% as compared to C4.5 in two-class datasets; but a mean reduction of only 2% in multi-class datasets.

In terms of tree size, C4.5CS produces trees 34% smaller than those produced by C4.5 in two-class datasets; and only 15% smaller in multi-class datasets. In only two datasets (Hypothyroid and Euthyroid), C4.5CS produces trees which are larger than those produced by C4.5. This is because the two datasets have very skewed class distribution (i.e., 95.2% and 90.7% of the total instances belong to one of the two classes in these two datasets, respectively). A high cost $C(j)$ assigned to the class which has small number of instances effectively reduces the class distribution skewness. This leads to larger trees as a result. Although the costs are randomly assigned without reference to the original class distribution,

Table 1. C4.5CS versus C4.5 in terms of misclassification cost, tree size, number of high cost errors and total number of errors.

Datasets	Cost			Tree Size			No. HC Errors			No. Errors*	
	C4.5CS	C4.5	ratio	C4.5CS	C4.5	ratio	C4.5CS	C4.5	ratio	C4.5CS	ratio
Echo	7.9	18.2	.44	6.0	10.8	.56	0.5	2.5	.22	5.4	1.15
Hepa	6.0	12.3	.48	9.5	17.0	.56	0.4	1.6	.27	3.9	1.15
Heart_S	10.9	17.1	.64	16.7	35.6	.47	1.0	2.8	.37	6.8	1.15
Heart	14.2	25.2	.56	18.2	39.5	.46	1.1	3.3	.34	8.7	1.32
Horse	16.4	21.8	.75	8.6	11.6	.74	1.1	2.9	.39	11.6	2.00
Credit	21.3	36.5	.58	10.5	33.2	.32	1.5	4.9	.31	13.7	1.34
Breast	9.9	14.4	.69	14.8	23.8	.62	1.0	2.0	.51	4.9	1.36
Diab.	35.8	69.6	.51	18.4	41.9	.44	2.0	9.4	.21	27.5	1.39
German	30.3	72.8	.42	2.2	149.3	.01	0.1	11.4	.01	29.9	1.10
Hypo	9.0	8.7	1.03	24.6	12.2	2.02	0.9	1.1	.81	4.0	1.74
Euthyr	20.7	24.2	.85	39.8	25.3	1.57	2.1	3.3	.64	10.1	1.60
Coding	942.2	2058.6	.46	302.7	2805.6	.11	22.2	278.2	.08	880.8	1.59
Mean			.62			.66			.35		1.41
Lympho	17.4	18.2	.96	19.0	27.4	.69	2.9	2.9	1.00	3.3	1.03
Glass	35.8	38.4	.93	39.2	45.5	.86	6.0	6.3	.95	6.9	.97
Wave	7119.0	7709.3	.92	42.7	51.0	.84	1177.9	1232.4	.96	1522.1	1.00
Soybean	33.8	30.4	1.11	91.1	96.4	.95	5.7	5.2	1.11	6.2	1.11
Anneal	35.4	35.7	.99	76.7	76.6	1.00	6.4	6.0	1.06	7.3	1.09
Vowel	115.1	111.8	1.03	175.2	187.0	.94	19.1	18.2	1.05	21.1	1.04
Splice	95.7	95.6	1.00	157.1	171.6	.92	16.2	15.3	1.06	22.7	1.22
Abalone	708.7	799.2	.89	402.1	579.2	.69	124.6	129.2	.96	168.4	1.04
Net(s)	507.9	514.2	.99	1650.4	2061.6	.80	86.0	84.2	1.02	99.6	1.06
Sat.	475.3	478.5	.99	472.4	561.2	.84	78.4	78.5	1.00	88.1	1.00
Mean			.98			.85			1.02		1.06

* the column on C4.5 is omitted because of lack of space.

reduction in skewness seems to have a larger effect than increase in skewness in these two datasets.

C4.5CS makes 65% fewer high cost errors than C4.5 in two-class datasets; but 2% more high cost errors in multi-class datasets. On the other hand, C4.5CS has 41% more errors than C4.5 in two-class datasets, but only 6% more errors in multi-class datasets.

Hypothyroid is the only two-class dataset in which C4.5CS has higher misclassification costs (by 3%) than C4.5. While C4.5CS is able to reduce the number of high cost errors by 19% in this highly skewed class distribution dataset, but the 74% increase in total errors outweighs this reduction which results a net increase in total misclassification costs.

3.2 Minimum expected cost criterion

A simple method to use a minimum error tree for cost-sensitive classifications is to employ the minimum expected cost criterion in selecting a predicted class during classification (Michie, Spiegelhalter & Taylor, 1994). It is interesting to find out how the proposed method compared to this simple method.

The expected misclassification cost for predicting class i with respect to the example x is given by:

$$EC_i(x) \propto \sum_j W_j(t(x))cost(i,j), \qquad (5)$$

where $t(x)$ is the leaf of the tree where instance x falls into, and $W_j(t)$ is the total weight of class j training instances in node t.

To classify a new example x using a minimum error tree and the minimum expected cost criterion, $EC_i(x)$ is computed for every class. The example x is assigned to class i with the smallest value for $EC_i(x)$. That is, $EC_i(x) < EC_{i'}(x)$ for all $i' \neq i$.

A comparison between C4.5CS_mc and C4.5_mc, both using the minimum expected cost criterion, is conducted here. The results in Table 2 show that it is still better to induce a cost-sensitive tree than a minimum error tree for cost-sensitive classifications in two-class datasets, even using the minimum expected cost criterion.

Table 2. Mean ratios for C4.5CS_mc against C4.5_mc.

	Two-class	Multi-class
Misclassification Cost ratio	.86	.99
Tree Size ratio	.66	.85
No. High Cost Errors ratio	.36	1.02
No. Errors ratio	1.57	1.07

3.3 Summary

We summarize the findings so far as follows.

- In terms of misclassification costs and the number of high cost errors, C4.5CS performs better than C4.5 in two-class datasets but only comparably in multi-class datasets.
- The relative poor performance of C4.5CS in multi-class datasets is due to the cost matrix to cost vector conversion.
- C4.5CS always makes fewer high cost errors than C4.5 in two-class datasets; but in datasets with highly skewed class distribution, C4.5CS might have higher total misclassification costs than C4.5.
- C4.5CS produces smaller trees than C4.5 because instance weighting effectively increases the skewness of the otherwise more balanced class distribution.
- Even using the minimum expected cost criterion, it is better to induce a cost-sensitive tree than to induce a minimum error tree for cost-sensitive classifications in two-class datasets.

4 Relation to Altered Priors

Breiman *et al.* (1984) discuss a method of incorporating variable misclassification costs via altered priors for cost-sensitive tree induction. Let priors, $\pi(j) = N_j/N$, and $C(j)$ as defined in Equation (4), then the altered priors are given by (Breiman *et al.*, 1984)

$$\pi'(j) = \frac{C(j)\pi(j)}{\sum_i C(i)\pi(i)} = \frac{C(j)N_j}{\sum_i C(i)N_i}.$$

In the instance-weighting method, every instance is weighted proportional to $C(j)$. The weight of a class j instance is computed as

$$w(j) = \frac{C(j)N}{\sum_i C(i)N_i} = \pi'(j)N/N_j = \frac{\pi'(j)}{\pi(j)}.$$

Thus, the instance weight is a ratio of the altered prior and the original prior. Both methods share the same idea of changing the class distribution according to the given misclassification costs, but one implementation is simpler and more effective than the other. Implementation using altered priors or by merely modifying instance weights will produce the same tree at the end of the tree growing process. But, the former would require an equivalent modification in the pruning process; otherwise, it will perform poorly. This is demonstrated by modifying C4.5 accordingly to yield C4.5(π'). Because instance weights are not altered, the tree induced by C4.5(π') will be pruned according to unit instance weights.

The mean ratios (C4.5CS/C4.5(π')) for misclassification cost and the number of high cost errors are .70 and .43 respectively. These figures are averaged over the twelve two-class datasets in which C4.5CS performs well. C4.5(π') is significantly worse than C4.5CS for the two important measures in cost-sensitive classifications. The poor result of C4.5(π') is due to the inconsistent use of instance weights from the tree growing process to the tree pruning process.

5 Conclusions

We have introduced an instance-weighting method to induce cost-sensitive trees, and demonstrated that it is a viable approach and simple to implement or adapt to an existing learning algorithm. It is a generalization of the standard tree induction process to include both minimum error trees and minimum high cost error trees. The instance-weighting method is simpler and more effective in implementation than a previous method based on altered priors.

Our empirical results show convincingly that the greedy divide-and-conquer procedure can effectively induce a truly cost-sensitive tree directly from the training data. This work refutes an earlier negative result (Pazzani *et al.*, 1994) with regard to cost-sensitive tree induction employing the greedy divide-and-conquer procedure in two-class datasets.

The algorithm incorporating the instance-weighting method is found to be better than the original algorithm in two-class datasets in terms of the number of high cost errors, total misclassification costs and tree size. The instance weighting which changes the class distribution directly contributes to this improved performance.

The current instance-weighting method has two weaknesses: (1) it requires the conversion of cost matrix to cost vector which hampers its performance in multi-class datasets, and (2) it might not perform well in terms of total misclassification costs in datasets with highly skewed class distribution. We have suggested a cost-sensitive version of boosting (Schapire *et al.*, 1997) to address these weaknesses, reported in Ting & Zheng (1998).

6 References

Breiman, L., J.H. Friedman, R.A. Olshen & C.J. Stone (1984), *Classification And Regression Trees*, Belmont, CA: Wadsworth.

Knoll, U., Nakhaeizadeh, G., & Tausend, B. (1994), Cost-Sensitive Pruning of Decision Trees, in *Proceedings of the Eighth European Conference on Machine Learning*, pp. 383-386, Springer-Verlag.

Merz, C.J. & Murphy, P.M. (1996), *UCI Repository of machine learning databases* [http://www.ics.uci. edu/mlearn/MLRepository.html]. University of California, Dept. of Information and Computer Science.

Michie, D., D.J. Spiegelhalter & C.C. Taylor (1994), *Machine Learning, Neural and Statistical Classification*, Ellis Horwood Limited.

Pazzani, M., C. Merz, P. Murphy, K. Ali, T. Hume & C. Brunk (1994), Reducing Misclassification Costs, in *Proceedings of the Eleventh International Conference on Machine Learning*, pp. 217-225, Morgan Kaufmann.

Quinlan, J.R. (1993), *C4.5: Program for machine learning*, Morgan Kaufmann.

Quinlan, J.R. (1996), Boosting, Bagging, and C4.5, in *Proceedings of the 13th National Conference on Artificial Intelligence*, pp. 725-730, AAAI Press.

Schapire, R.E., Y. Freund, P. Bartlett & W.S. Lee (1997), Boosting the margin: A new explanation for the effectiveness of voting methods, in *Proceedings of the Fourteenth International Conference on Machine Learning*, pp. 322-330, Morgan Kaufmann.

Turney, P.D. (1995), Cost-Sensitive Classification: Empirical Evaluation of a Hybrid Genetic Decision Tree Induction Algorithm, *Journal of Artificial Intelligence Research*, *2*, pp. 369-409.

Webb, G.I. (1996) Cost-Sensitive Specialization, in *Proceedings of the 1996 Pacific Rim International Conference on Artificial Intelligence*, pp. 23-34.

Ting, K.M. & Z. Zheng (1998), Boosting Trees for Cost-Sensitive Classifications, *Proceedings of the Tenth European Conference on Machine Learning*, Berlin: Springer-Verlag, pp. 190-195.

Model Switching for Bayesian Classification Trees with Soft Splits

Jörg Kindermann and Gerhard Paass

RWCP - Theoretical Foundation Lab
GMD – German National Research Center for Information Technology
D-52754 Sankt Augustin, Germany
kindermann@gmd.de   paass@gmd.de *

Abstract. Due to the high number of insolvencies in the credit business, automatic procedures for testing the credit-worthiness of enterprises become increasingly important. For this task we use classification trees with soft splits which assign the observations near the split boundary to both branches. Tree models involve an extra complication as the number of parameters varies as the tree grows and shrinks. Hence we adapt the reversible jump Markov Chain Monte Carlo procedure to this model which produces an ensemble of trees representing the posterior distribution. For a real-world credit-scoring application our algorithm yields lower classification errors than bootstrapped versions of regression trees (CART), neural networks, and adaptive splines (MARS). The predictive distribution allows to assess the certainty of credit decisions for new cases and guides the collection of additional information.

1 Introduction

During the last years *local* approaches are increasingly used for classification and regression tasks. They cover the input space $\mathcal{X}$ with a finite set of local regions $\mathcal{X}_\tau$ such that $\mathcal{X} = \bigcup_\tau \mathcal{X}_\tau$. Within each region the function $y = f(x)$ of interest is approximated by simple local functions $\hat{f}_\tau(x)$, e.g. a constant, a linear or quadratic polynomial. This is motivated by Taylor's theorem which states that if a local region is small enough any continuous function can be well approximated by a low order polynomial within it.

It is well known, that the mean square error can be decomposed into a systematic component (bias) and a random component (variance) [8]. For local learning the variance can be reduced by increasing the number of observations in a local region. On the other hand the bias is inflated if the size of the region grows, as then the data – especially near the border of the region – does no longer reflect the local characteristics of the underlying function. In addition the variance usually grows if the number of free parameters of the local function is increased. Hence the selection of local regions always involves a compromise.

Obviously the shape of regions should reflect the approximation properties of the local functions. A region can have a long extension in a direction, where the local function can approximate the real relation with little error. A new region should begin where the

---

* We thank Prof. Dr. Jörg Baetge, University of Münster for granting access to the dataset.

error gets larger than a certain threshold. There are two basic types of local procedures [7]:

- *Radial basis function* networks and *k-nearest neighbour* [13] models create local regions whose shape is globally uniform or is defined by the distribution of input values in the sample. Hence the shape is not determined according to the approximation error. For high input dimensions k the diameter of "local" regions containing a fraction of γ of the sample elements is approximately $\gamma^{1/k}$ of the regions containing all elements. Hence local regions in general have a large diameter even if they cover only a small fraction of sample values (curse of dimensionality).
- A *classification tree* [2, 3, 12] recursively partitions the input space into a number of disjunct regions $\mathcal{X}_\tau$ and separately trains a model $f_\tau(x)$ in each region. The regions are formed in such a way that the approximation error is minimised. However, as each region requires a number of observations to estimate the local function relatively few regions can be formed and the approximation error gets large near the boundaries.

In this paper we propose a tree based classification procedure which tries to combine the advantages of both types:

- Instead of recursively splitting each regions in two separate subregions we form an intermediate region between the new regions (soft split). Observations located in this intermediate region are assigned to both regions for training as well as for prediction. This increases the average number of observations in each final region. The bias is potentially reduced as a point near the boundary is predicted as the average of the predictions of adjacent regions.
- Not a single 'optimal' tree is determined in a greedy fashion, but using *Bayesian* statistics a large number of plausible trees is constructed. Each tree has a different set of local regions with different boundaries. As the prediction is determined as the average prediction of the single trees the biases near boundaries are potentially reduced.

The gradual change between the regions of a tree has been considered by several authors. Carter and Catlett [4] define upper and lower split points and use linear interpolation to smooth the "membership". Quinlan [12, p.75] discusses this setup and suggests a method for choosing cut-points based on the distribution of misclassified training cases. Ripley [13, p.239] suggests the use of a logistic function for "membership" and Friedman utilises splines [6] or a step function [7]. Jacobs and collaborators [10] proposed soft splits which are not perpendicular to the input axes but are induced by specific "gating models". For a review of these mixture-of-expert models see [14].

The procedure described in this paper for the first time applies the Bayesian paradigm to trees with soft splits along the coordinate axes. Bayesian statistics derives a probability measure on the model parameters, which characterises the plausibility that a model with this parameter has generated the data [1]. Tree models involve an extra complication as the number of parameters varies as the tree grows or shrinks. Hence we require a procedure which is able to switch between different model structures. We describe a Bayesian method for classification trees of varying size and implement the corresponding Markov Chain Monte Carlo procedure as a variant of [5].

We apply the procedure to a real world *credit-scoring* problem. In this setup it is vital to take into account the misclassification costs by a loss function. We compare the Bayesian approach with alternatives like neural networks, MARS [6], CART [2] and linear discriminant analysis as well as their bootstrapped versions [11]. Bayesian methods derive a predictive distribution for a new input. This may be used to assess the reliability of a classification in a real world situation.

In the next section we introduce the basic concepts of Bayesian classification and the Metropolis-Hastings algorithm which is used to obtain a representative set of models. Then an extension of the algorithm to switching between models of different dimensionality is described. Section 3 describes Bayesian classification trees with overlapping leaves and the generation of a Markov chain of trees. Section 4 describes a credit-scoring application and present the results for a set of over 6000 data records of balance sheet figures. The last section summarises the paper.

2 Bayesian Classification

2.1 Basic Concepts

Assume for each object we have features $x = (x_1, \ldots, x_k) \in \mathcal{X}$ and want to determine the class $y \in \{0, 1\}$ of the object. We assume a non-deterministic relation between x and y, given by a conditional distribution $p(y|x, w)$ with unknown parameters $w \in \mathcal{W}$. Suppose we have an independent random sample $(x^{(1)}, y^{(1)}), \ldots, (x^{(n)}, y^{(n)})$, where $y^{(i)}$ is distributed according to the 'true' $\mathring{p}(y|x^{(i)})$ conditional distribution. We denote the input data by $X := (x^{(1)}, \ldots, x^{(n)})$ and the output data by $y := (y^{(1)}, \ldots, y^{(n)})$.

Let $p(w)$ be our *prior* distribution of the model parameters describing the relative plausibility of parameter values *before* any data is available. For fixed data X and y $p(y|X, w) := \prod_{i=1}^{n} p(y^{(i)}|x^{(i)}, w)$ is the *likelihood* of w. Then the *Bayesian formula* yields the *posterior distribution*

$$p(w|y, X) = \frac{p(y|X, w)\, p(w)}{\int p(y|X, w)\, p(w)\, dw} \tag{1}$$

It describes the relative plausibility of different parameters w after the data X and y has been observed. Let q_1 be the probability that y has the class-value 1. For a fixed input x the 'parameter' q_1 is uncertain and has a probability distribution determined by the distribution of w. We can compute the probability $P(q_1 \leq \eta|x, y, X)$ that q_1 is smaller than some η as $\int_{\{w|p(y=1|x,w)\leq\eta\}} p(w|y, X)\, dw$. This means, that the class probability itself is uncertain, and the data supports different probability values to a varying extent. The expected 'average' probability that a new object with features x belongs to class 1 is

$$E(q_1|x, y, X) = \int p(y{=}1|x, w)\, p(w|y, X)\, dw \tag{2}$$

For classification we have to decide which class should be selected. More generally we have to take an action $a \in \mathcal{A}$, whose consequences depend on the class c of an object. In the case of credit-scoring a may be 'grant credit' or 'deny credit'. Let $L(a; c) \in \Re$ be the loss we incur, if action a is taken and c is the actual class of the object. The *expected loss* $E(L(a)|\boldsymbol{x}, \boldsymbol{y}, \boldsymbol{X})$ of a is

$$\int \sum_{y=0}^{1} L(a; y)\, p(y|\boldsymbol{x}, \boldsymbol{w})\, p(\boldsymbol{w}|\boldsymbol{y}, \boldsymbol{X})\, d\boldsymbol{w} = \sum_{y=0}^{1} L(a; y)\, E(q_y|\boldsymbol{x}, \boldsymbol{y}, \boldsymbol{X}) \qquad (3)$$

According to the Bayesian decision theory [1] it is optimal to select the action a with *minimal expected loss*. Note that only the mean value of q_c enters the decision, not its variance.

2.2 Markov Chain Monte Carlo Analysis

As (2) and (3) in general cannot be evaluated analytically, we have to perform a Markov chain Monte-Carlo (MCMC) analysis. This involves the construction of a Markov chain $\boldsymbol{w}(0), \boldsymbol{w}(1), \ldots$ designed to be distributed according to the posterior density $p(\boldsymbol{w}|\boldsymbol{y}, \boldsymbol{X})$. If the chain is currently at $\boldsymbol{w} = \boldsymbol{w}(t)$, the *Metropolis-Hastings algorithm* [15] requires a *proposal density* $q(\boldsymbol{w}, \tilde{\boldsymbol{w}})$, which is the conditional distribution of proposing a move from $\boldsymbol{w}$ to $\tilde{\boldsymbol{w}}$. The *acceptance probability* is defined as

$$p^{\mathrm{acc}}(\boldsymbol{w}, \tilde{\boldsymbol{w}}) = \min \left\{ 1, \frac{p(\tilde{\boldsymbol{w}}|\boldsymbol{y}, \boldsymbol{X})\, q(\tilde{\boldsymbol{w}}, \boldsymbol{w})}{p(\boldsymbol{w}|\boldsymbol{y}, \boldsymbol{X})\, q(\boldsymbol{w}, \tilde{\boldsymbol{w}})} \right\} \qquad (4)$$

With probability $p^{\mathrm{acc}}(\boldsymbol{w}, \tilde{\boldsymbol{w}})$ the candidate $\tilde{\boldsymbol{w}}$ is accepted and the chain moves to $\boldsymbol{w}(t + 1) = \tilde{\boldsymbol{w}}$. Otherwise the candidate is rejected and $\boldsymbol{w}(t + 1)$ takes the old value $\boldsymbol{w}$. For the actual transition probability $p(\boldsymbol{w}, \tilde{\boldsymbol{w}}) := q(\boldsymbol{w}, \tilde{\boldsymbol{w}})p^{\mathrm{acc}}(\boldsymbol{w}, \tilde{\boldsymbol{w}})$ the *detailed balance* condition holds for all $\boldsymbol{w}, \tilde{\boldsymbol{w}}$

$$p(\boldsymbol{w}|\boldsymbol{y}, \boldsymbol{X})\, p(\boldsymbol{w}, \tilde{\boldsymbol{w}}) = p(\tilde{\boldsymbol{w}}|\boldsymbol{y}, \boldsymbol{X})\, p(\tilde{\boldsymbol{w}}, \boldsymbol{w}) \qquad (5)$$

If the resulting Markov chain is aperiodic and irreducible (i.e. reaches all states with positive probability) then its distribution converges to an invariant stationary limit distribution, which is just the posterior distribution $p(\boldsymbol{w}|\boldsymbol{y}, X)$ [15].

For decision trees, where the number and interpretation of parameters varies, the approach cannot be used. Recently Green [9] has proposed an MCMC-scheme for varying dimension problems, termed *reversible jump MCMC*. When the current state is $\boldsymbol{w}$ and $p(\boldsymbol{w}|\boldsymbol{y}X)$ is the target probability measure (the posterior density) we consider a countable number of different moves m. Depending on the state $\boldsymbol{w}$ a move m and a destination $\tilde{\boldsymbol{w}}$ is proposed with a joint distribution $q_m(\boldsymbol{w}, \tilde{\boldsymbol{w}})$. $q_m(\boldsymbol{w}, \tilde{\boldsymbol{w}})$ may be a sub-probability measure, with probability $1 - \sum_m \int_{\tilde{\boldsymbol{w}}} q_m(\boldsymbol{w}, \tilde{\boldsymbol{w}})d\tilde{\boldsymbol{w}}$ no move is attempted.

For the case that $\boldsymbol{w}$ and $\tilde{\boldsymbol{w}}$ have the same dimension, the procedure reduces to the Metropolis-Hastings algorithm (4). Now suppose that starting from $\boldsymbol{w}$ a move of type m is proposed that yields a higher-dimensional $\tilde{\boldsymbol{w}}$. This can be implemented by drawing a vector $\boldsymbol{u}$ of continuous variables distributed according to a known density $p_m(\boldsymbol{u})$ independent of $\boldsymbol{w}$. It is required that the sum of the dimensions of $\boldsymbol{w}$ and $\boldsymbol{u}$ is equal to the dimension of $\tilde{\boldsymbol{w}}$. Then the new state $\tilde{\boldsymbol{w}}$ is defined by an invertible deterministic function $\tilde{\boldsymbol{w}} = h_m(\boldsymbol{w}, \boldsymbol{u})$. The reverse of the move can be accomplished by using the inverse transformation, so that the proposal is deterministic. Then we get the acceptance probability

$$p_m^{\mathrm{acc}}(w, \tilde{w}) = \min\left(1, \left|\frac{\partial h_m(u, w)}{\partial(u, w)}\right| * \frac{p(\tilde{w}|y, X)\, j_m(\tilde{w})}{p(w|y, X)\, j_m(w)\, p_m(u)}\right) \qquad (6)$$

Here $j_m(w)$ and $j_m(\tilde{w})$ are the probabilities of selecting move m or its inverse in states w and $\tilde{w}$ respectively. Green [9] shows that the detailed balance condition (5) holds and consequently the equilibrium distribution of the resulting Markov chain is the posterior distribution $p(w|y, X)$. Similar to the usual Metropolis-Hastings formula (4) the densities have to be known only up to a factor, which cancels out in (6).

3 Bayesian Classification Trees

3.1 Overlapping Regions

Tree models divide the predictor space $\mathcal{X}$ into rectangular regions $\mathcal{X}_\tau$ by recursive splits along the coordinate axes and assume that the conditional distribution of y within the terminal regions $\mathcal{X}_\tau$ is identical for all x. In this paper we recursively divide an existing region $\mathcal{X}_\tau$ into two new regions $\mathcal{X}_{\tau_1}$ and $\mathcal{X}_{\tau_2}$ which are not disjoint, but may have some overlap. We select a variable x_{s_τ} and define

$$\begin{aligned}
\mathcal{X}_{\tau_1} &= \{x \in \mathcal{X}_\tau | x_{s_\tau} \le \xi_\tau^+\} \\
\mathcal{X}_{\tau_2} &= \{x \in \mathcal{X}_\tau | x_{s_\tau} > \xi_\tau^-\}
\end{aligned} \qquad \text{where } \xi_\tau^- \le \xi_\tau^+ \qquad (7)$$

with *upper split point* ξ_τ^+ and *lower split point* ξ_τ^-. A recursive application of this procedure yields a binary tree structure. A Bayesian model has to specify, how the data is generated from the underlying model. If the tree consists of a single leaf $\mathcal{X}_\tau$ the dependent variable y is assumed to be binomially distributed with parameter $\theta_{\tau,1} := p(y=1|x \in \mathcal{X}_\tau)$. If the tree consists of two overlapping leaves $\mathcal{X}_{\tau_1}$ and $\mathcal{X}_{\tau_2}$, then in $\mathcal{X}_{\tau_1} \setminus \mathcal{X}_{\tau_2}$ the class variable y again is assumed to be binomially distributed with parameter θ_{τ_1} and in $\mathcal{X}_{\tau_2} \setminus \mathcal{X}_{\tau_1}$ y is assumed to be binomially distributed with parameter θ_{τ_2}. In $\mathcal{X}_{\tau_2} \cap \mathcal{X}_{\tau_1}$ it follows a binomial 'mixture' distribution with parameter $(\theta_{\tau_1} + \theta_{\tau_2})/2$. This scheme is recursively applied if a region $\mathcal{X}_\tau$ is covered by two subregions $\mathcal{X}_{\tau_1}$ and $\mathcal{X}_{\tau_2}$: The distribution in the overlap is just the mixture with weights 1/2 between the distributions within $\mathcal{X}_{\tau_1}$ and $\mathcal{X}_{\tau_2}$.

For prediction this has the interesting consequence, that a new observation x 'belongs' to more than one leaf and the predicted class probability is a mixture of the separate predictions of each leaf. If the two split points ξ_τ^- and ξ_τ^+ are identical for all τ, we get the usual binary trees as a special case. As an alternative, more complex distributions within the leaves can be considered, e.g. multinomial distributions or generalised linear models.

3.2 Prior and Posterior Distributions

Recall that each region $\mathcal{X}_\tau$ has various intersections with other regions $\mathcal{X}_\eta$, and that within these intersections the distribution is a weighted mixture of the binomial distributions with parameters θ_τ and θ_η and known weights. Consequently an observation

$(x^{(i)}, y^{(i)})$ is attributed to the different regions with varying weights. For a region $\mathcal{X}_\tau$ this uniquely determines the vector of counts $m_\tau = (m_{\tau,0}, m_{\tau,1})$, i.e. the number of y-values in each class.

As prior density $p(\theta)$ for the binomial parameter $\theta = ((1 - \theta), \theta)$ we use the Dirichlet density $\mathrm{Di}(\alpha)$ $p(\theta|\alpha) \propto \theta_0^{\alpha_0-1} \theta_1^{\alpha_1-1}$. If y has the counts m we get the likelihood $p(y|\theta) \propto \theta_0^{m_0} \theta_1^{m_1}$. Hence in each leaf we get posteriors of the form $p(\theta|m) \propto \theta_0^{m_0+\alpha_0-1} \theta_1^{m_1+\alpha_1-1}$ which again are Dirichlet densities $\mathrm{Di}(\alpha + m)$.

3.3 Comparing Splits with the Un-split Leaf

We want to assess the effect of splitting some leaf $\mathcal{X}_\tau$ containing n_τ observations into two subsets $\mathcal{X}_{\tau_1}$ and $\mathcal{X}_{\tau_2}$. We assume that within $\mathcal{X}_{\tau_i}$ the dependent variable is binomially distributed as $\mathrm{Bi}(\theta_{\tau_i}, n_{\tau_i})$. Hence we have to compare two hypotheses:

H_1: within each $\mathcal{X}_{\tau_i}$ the class variable y has been generated according to a binomial distribution $\mathrm{Bi}(\theta_\tau, n_{\tau_i})$ with a single but unknown parameter θ_τ.

H_2: within each $\mathcal{X}_{\tau_i}$ the class variable y has been generated according to a binomial distribution $\mathrm{Bi}(\theta_{\tau_i}, n_{\tau_i})$ with different unknown parameters θ_{τ_i}.

We assume that on $\mathcal{X}_\tau$ and $\mathcal{X}_{\tau_i}$ the prior is Dirichlet $p(\theta|\alpha_{\tau_i}) = \mathrm{Di}(\alpha_{\tau_i})$. As the posterior again is Dirichlet we get after some tedious algebra

$$\frac{p(H_1|y, X)}{p(H_2|y, X)} = \frac{p(y|X, H_1)p(H_1)}{p(y|X, H_2)p(H_2)} = \frac{p(H_1) \, R_{Di}(m_\tau, \alpha_\tau)}{p(H_2) \, R_{Di}(m_{\tau_1}, \alpha_{\tau_1}) \, R_{Di}(m_{\tau_2}, \alpha_{\tau_2})}$$

where $R_{Di}(m, \alpha) := \eta_{Di}(m + \alpha)/\eta_{Di}(\alpha)$, $\eta_{Di}(\alpha) = \Gamma(\alpha_0)\Gamma(\alpha_1)/\Gamma(\sum_c \alpha_c)$, and $p(H_i)$ is the prior probability of a hypothesis. This is the *Bayes factor* for comparing the models.

3.4 Possible Moves

To reduce the computational effort we make changes only at the bottom of the tree, as otherwise the calculation effort is too large.

GROW/PRUNE: Select a variable x_{s_τ} for splitting and split a leaf $\mathcal{X}_\tau$ into two new leaves $\mathcal{X}_{\tau_1}$ and $\mathcal{X}_{\tau_2}$, or collapse two leaves $\mathcal{X}_{\tau_1}$ and $\mathcal{X}_{\tau_2}$ into their common parent $\mathcal{X}_\tau$.

SHIFT: Move the split points ξ^+ and ξ^- of the parent of two leaves.

CHANGE: Split the parent of two leaves by another variable.

SHIFT does not change the number of parameters and is covered by the usual Metropolis-Hastings procedure. CHANGE is the combination of a GROW and a subsequent PRUNE. We demonstrate the algorithm for a GROW/PRUNE step. As the leaf probabilities θ_τ do not enter the model selection, the only parameters we have are the index i of the variables to be split and the split points ξ^+ and ξ^-.

We now have the task to define the different quantities in (6). The state w corresponds to a given tree, where w contains the continuous upper and lower split points for each nonterminal node. The m-th move is applicable only to two specific tree structures and involves the split of a specific leaf $\mathcal{X}_\tau$ of a tree or the pruning of children of $\mathcal{X}_\tau$ in the resulting tree. Note that for each different variable to be split we need a new move type. $j_m(w)$ is the probability of selecting move m if the current states is w. We define it according to the following lines:

- The split variable is randomly selected with equal probability for each variable.
- In the initial phase GROW/PRUNE, SHIFT and CHANGE are selected with probabilities $1/(3k)$, $1/3$ and $1/3$ respectively. This avoids that the tree grows too fast and a large number of split variables are not explored.
- Each eligible node (leaf to be split, or parent of two leaves to be pruned) is selected with identical probability.

Our prior distribution for the different tree shapes only takes into account the number N of nodes in the tree. It is proportional to $1/(1 + \beta \exp(\gamma N))$ with $\beta, \gamma > 0$ and penalises large trees. The variables used for splitting have equal prior probability to be selected.

As discussed by [3] it is advantageous to let the prior depend on the data X in some aspects. Assume $x_{(1)} \leq x_{(2)} \leq \ldots \leq x_{(l)}$ are the sorted observed values for some variable x_i in region $\mathcal{X}_\tau$. Then we first assume that both split points ξ^- and ξ^+ are located in the interval $(x_{(1)}, x_{(l)})$. In addition we currently suppose that the overlap covers a fixed proportion ρ of the interval $(x_{(1)}, x_{(l)})$. Therefore ξ^- is has a uniform prior over $(x_{(1)}, x_{max})$ with $x_{max} = x_{(1)} + (1 - \rho)(x_{(l)} - x_{(1)})$. ξ^+ is defined as $\xi^- + \rho(x_{(l)} - x_{(1)})$.

This allows a simple definition of the quantities in (8). The auxiliary variable u is defined as a univariate random variable with a uniform distribution $p_m(u)$ in $(x_{(1)}, x_{max})$. The map $h_m(u, w)$ is just the identity, which leaves w unchanged. Hence the Jacobian determinant $J_m(u, w) = 1$. Using these terms we may calculate the ratio of posteriors (8) defining the acceptance probability of a split.

3.5 Generating the Markov Chain

The procedure of generating the Markov chain involves the following steps

1. Randomly select a move m according to probability $j_m(w)$. In the case of GROW/PRUNE this involves the random decision whether two leaves are pruned or a split takes place, the random selection which variable is to be split, and the random selection of the leaf or parent node. In addition a lower and an upper split point has to be selected if SPLIT was chosen.
2. Calculate the ratio of posteriors (8).
3. Determine the acceptance probability by (6) and accept the new state or keep the old state.

The algorithm is iterated for some time until the number of nodes in the tree stabilises. Then the resulting tree is saved and a new tree is grown. This yields a set $w_1, \ldots, w_B$ of parameters distributed according to the posterior distribution $p(w|y, X)$ and defines

Table 1: β-error for different ensemble methods: Percentage of rejected solvent enterprises, if 8.75% of the insolvent enterprises were accepted as solvent.

Algorithm	Single Model	Sampling Method	Mean
LDA	69.54	bootstrap	49.23
MARS	48.08	bootstrap	39.90
CART	43.82	bootstrap	36.62
BayesTree	42.18	Bayes MCMC	33.72

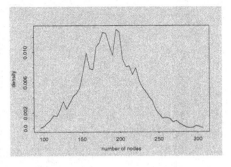

Fig.1 Distribution of tree sizes in an ensemble of Bayes trees.

a representative ensemble of models. We then may estimate, for instance, the expected probability that a new object with features x belongs to class c according to (2) by

$$E(q_c|\boldsymbol{x},\boldsymbol{y},\boldsymbol{X}) \approx \frac{1}{B}\sum_{i=1}^{B} p(y{=}c|\boldsymbol{x},\boldsymbol{w}_b) \qquad (8)$$

which converges to (2) by the Law of Large Numbers.

4 Results for Real World Data

We applied our procedure to a dataset containing 6667 records with 73 predictors. The predictors were indicators from balance sheet figures of enterprises. A fraction of 14% of the businesses were classified as 'not solvent' and the rest as 'solvent'. We divided the data randomly into a training set and a validation set. To compare the tree methods with the procedures analysed by [16] we determined a threshold on the validation set such that exactly 8.75% of the insolvent enterprises were wrongly accepted as solvent (α-error) and subsequently measured the percentage of solvent enterprises which were rejected (β-error). In [16] a β-error of 38% on the validation set is reported for a pruned MLP as the best result.

For bootstrapped[11] versions of the algorithms CART [2], LDA, MARS [6], and our Bayesian MCMC algorithm BayesTree, we computed ensembles of $B = 500$ models $\boldsymbol{w}_1, \ldots, \boldsymbol{w}_B$, using the data of the training set. The error percentages were determined from the validation set. The results of our experiments are shown in table 1. In the column 'single model' there is the β-error of a single model estimated by maximum likelihood without resampling. The column 'mean' reports the β-error when the mean of all 500 models is used for classification. The distribution of tree sizes for BayesTree is shown in figure 1.

For BayesTree the β-error on the validation set had a mean of about 33.7%. This shows that the tree procedures are able to beat MLPs in this classification task by about 5%. In addition the Bayesian trees have a small advantage over the bootstrap trees.

According to (3) the expected loss should be the decision criterion: only if the expected loss is negative (a profit) the loan should be granted. This defines a threshold

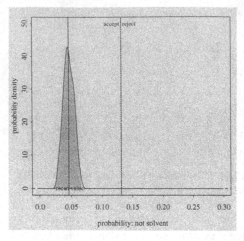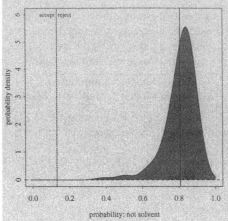

Fig.2 Posterior density of the probability q_{ns} "not solvent" for two previously unseen enterprises. In these cases the decision is clear cut.

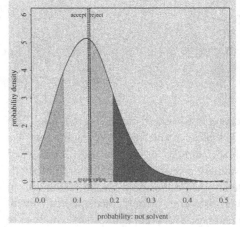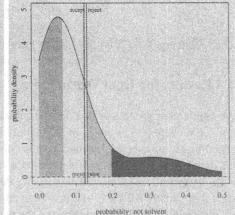

Fig.3 Posterior density of the probability q_{ns} "not solvent" for two previously unseen enterprises.

for the mean value of the predicted risk (probability of insolvency). For a plausible loss function in the figures 2-3 this threshold is depicted as a straight vertical line: If the expected probability of insolvency (vertical dotted line) is above the threshold, we can expect a net loss on the average and the credit application should be rejected.

Figure 2 shows predictive densities for other inputs x, which were determined by (8). In both cases the mean value of the posterior distribution is far away from the decision boundary, and both distributions show low variance. Therefore the left case readily can be accepted and the right case can be rejected. By (3) we may also calculate a distribution of plausible losses. Figure 3 shows two different predictive densities with expectations near the decision boundary. The distribution on the right side has a a larger uncertainty and hence a much higher chance that the true probability is further away from the decision boundary. This means that the collection of new information (e.g. an audit of the enterprise) has a high chance of revealing that the credit risk is much lower (or much higher) than the borderline. Hence the uncertainty of the credit risk can be used to select cases for a further investigation.

5 Summary

In this paper we developed a Bayesian classification procedure using an ensemble of models which is representative for the distribution of model parameters. The models are allowed to switch between different levels of complexity. This is controlled by a special Metropolis-Hastings algorithm which approximates the desired posterior distribution by the stationary distribution of a Markov chain.

We adapted this procedure to classification trees with overlapping regions. In a real-world credit-scoring task significantly improved results were obtained as compared to both single-model classification and bootstrap methods. The work on Bayes trees is still in progress. So far we use fixed percentages of leaf overlap. This can be generalised to adaptively determine the optimal percentage of overlap for each pair of split points in each leaf of the tree.

References

1. J.O. Berger. *Stat. Dec. Theory, Foundations, Concepts and Methods*. Springer, NY, 1980.
2. L. Breiman, J.H. Friedman, R. Olshen, and C.J. Stone. *Classif. and Regr. Trees*. Wadsworth Int. Group, Belmont, CA, 1984.
3. W. Buntine. Learning classification trees. *Statistics and Computing*, 2:63–73, 1992.
4. C. Carter and J. Catlett. Assessing credit card appl. using machine learning. *IEEE Expert*, 2(3):71–79, 1987.
5. H. Chipman, E. George, and R. McCulloch. Bayesian CART. TR, Dept. of Stat., Univ. of Texas,Austin, 1995.
6. J. H. Friedman. Multivariate adaptive regression splines. *Ann. of Stat.*, 19(1):1–67, 1991.
7. J.H. Friedman. Local learning based on recursive covering. TR, Stanford Uni, August 1996.
8. S. Geman, E. Bienenstock, and R. Doursat. Neural networks and the bias/variance dilemma. *Neural Computation 4, p.-58*, 1992.
9. P. J. Green. Reversible jump Markov chain Monte Carlo computation and Bayesian model determination. TR, Bristol Univ., 1995.
10. R.A. Jacobs, M.I. Jordan, S.J. Nowlan, and G.E. Hinton. Adaptive mixtures of local experts. *Neural Computation*, 3:79–87, 1991.
11. Gerhard Paaß. Assessing and improving neural network predictions by the bootstrap algorithm. In S. Hanson, J. Cowan, and C. Giles, editors, *NIPS-5*, pages 196–203. Morgan Kaufmann, San Mateo, CA, San Mateo, CA., 1993.
12. J.R. Quinlan. *C4.5: Prog. f. Machine Learning*. Morgan Kaufmann, San Mateo, CA, 1993.
13. B.D. Ripley. *Pattern Recog. and Neural Networks*. Cambridge Univ. Press, 1996.
14. Waterhouse S.R. *Classification and Regression using Mixtures of Experts*. PhD thesis, Cambridge Univ. Engineering Dept., October 1997.
15. L. Tierney. Markov chains for expl. post. distr. TR 560, School of Stat., UMinnesota, 1994.
16. J. Wallrafen. Kreditwürdigkeitsprüfung von Unternehmen mit neuronalen Klassifikationsverfahren. Master's thesis, University of Erlangen-Nürnberg, 1995.

Interactive Visualisation for Predictive Modelling with Decision Tree Induction

Tu Bao Ho, Trong Dung Nguyen

Japan Advanced Institute of Science and Technology
Tatsunokuchi, Ishikawa, 923-1292 JAPAN

Abstract. In this paper we describe system CABRO for decision tree induction (DTI) that contributes to the combination of machine learning, visualisation and model selection techniques. We first discuss some issues in data mining and briefly introduce R-measure for attribution selection problem in DTI. We then present the DTI interactive visualisation system CABRO, based on R-measure and a combination of several DTI techniques, in which we focus on solutions to two problems: (1) support for understanding of large decision trees, and (2) support for interactive learning and model selection.

1 Introduction

For the KDD predictive modelling task, *decision tree induction* (DTI) is certainly the most applicable technique due to its power and simplicity. The performance of a DTI system depends strongly on its methods to solve three key problems: *attribute selection, pruning*, and *discretisation*. For the problem of attribute selection, most measures used in DTI are based on either information theory such as information gain, gain-ratio [12], or statistics such as χ^2, gini-index [2]. In [5], a measure based on rough set theory, called *R-measure*, was introduced. In this paper we first briefly present R-measure (section 2), and lately by using tools for model selection we show experimentally that R-measure can be used effectively in KDD (subsection 3.1).

Though decision trees are a simple notion it is not easy to understand and analyse large decision trees generated from huge data sets. For example, the widely used program C4.5 [12] produces a decision tree of nearly 18,500 nodes with 2624 leaf nodes from the census bureau database given recently to the KDD community that consists of 199,523 instances described by 40 numeric and symbolic attributes (103 Mbytes). It is extremely difficult for the user to understand and use that big tree in its text form. In such cases, a graphic visualisation of discovered decision trees with different ways of accessing and viewing trees is of great support and recently it receives much attention from the KDD researcher and user. In [7] the authors developed an interactive-graphic environment for automatic generation of decision trees. In [13], the process of inducing bagged decision trees is visualised by CAT scan (classification aggregation tablet). System MineSet provides a 3D visualisation of decision trees [3]. The interactive visualisation system CABRO described in this paper, associated with a *tree visualiser*, presents an alternative efficient way that allows the user to manipulate graphically and interactively trees in the learning process (subsection 3.1).

There exist various available DTI methods for solving three main DTI key problems mentioned above. It raises in practice the problem of *model selection* that is how to choose the most appropriate DTI methods/models for a given application task. Currently, it is a matter of consensus that there are no universally superior models and methods for DTI. The key question of which DTI method is better than others for a given task has still no answer. Such an answer requires meta-knowledge and/or empirical comparative evaluations of models. Even when meta-knowledge is available, empirical evaluations are always necessary for model selection. Though multiple training-and-testing experiments on a large number of data sets, for empirical evaluations of datamining results, provide reliable evaluations they have not always been done well [14]. Another motivation of this work is to develop in CABRO an *automatic and interactive evaluation* tool based on a well designed benchmark, that supports the user to carry out experimental comparative evaluations of DTI methods/models in order to select the most appropriate ones for a given task (subsection 3.2).

Though this work is about DTI, its general principles can be applied to other KDD tasks, e.g., to clustering as done in clustering system OSHAM [6].

2 R-measure for attribute selection

Rough set theory introduced by Pawlak in early 1980s is a mathematical tool to deal with imprecise and incomplete information [10]. The *lower* and *upper* approximations of any $X \subseteq O$, regarding an equivalence relation E, are defined as

$$E_*(X) = \{o \in O : [o]_E \subseteq X\} \tag{1}$$

$$E^*(X) = \{o \in O : [o]_E \cap X \neq \emptyset\} \tag{2}$$

where $[o]_E$ denotes the equivalence class of objects which are indiscernible with o with respect to the equivalence relation E. A key concept in rough set theory is the *degree of dependency* of a set of attributes Q on a set of attributes P, denoted by $\mu_P(Q)$ $(0 \leq \mu_P(Q) \leq 1)$, defined as

$$\mu_P(Q) = \frac{card(\bigcup_{[o]_Q} P_*([o]_Q))}{card(O)} = \frac{card(\{o \in O : [o]_P \subseteq [o]_Q\})}{card(O)} \tag{3}$$

If $\mu_P(Q) = 1$ then Q totally depends on P; if $0 < \mu_P(Q) < 1$ then Q partially depends on P; if $\mu_P(Q) = 0$ then Q is independent of P. The measure of dependency is fundamental in rough set theory as based on it many basic notions are defined, such as reducts and minimal sets of attributes, attribute significance, etc.

The limitation of the deterministic model of rough sets when dealing with uncertain information has been recognised and studied, e.g., by probabilistic model [11] and the variable precision model [15]. However, the former cannot inherit all useful properties of the original rough set model, and the latter raises a new problem of specifying an appropriate threshold. R-measure, inspired by the attribute dependency measure $\mu_P(Q)$, is an alternative one to deal with uncertain information while preserving properties of the rough set model without requiring thresholds. In brief, R-measure measures the dependency of Q on P in maximizing the predicted membership of an instance in the family of equivalence classes generated by Q given its membership in the family of equivalence classes generated by P. It is initially formulated by

$$\mu'_P(Q) = \frac{1}{card(O)} \sum_{[o]_P} max_{[o]_Q} card([o]_Q \bigcap [o]_P) \tag{4}$$

Theorem *For every sets P and Q of attributes we have*

$$\frac{max_{[o]_Q} card([o]_Q)}{card(O)} \leq \mu'_P(Q) \leq 1 \tag{5}$$

An analysis based on the notion of impurity function provides a basis to go from μ' to $\tilde{\mu}$ for DTI in order to deal better with large data sets. We have the following general form of the measure for arbitrary attribute sets P and Q and called it *R-measure*

$$\tilde{\mu}_P(Q) = \frac{1}{card(O)} \sum_{[o]_P} max_{[o]_Q} \frac{card([o]_Q \bigcap [o]_P)^2}{card([o]_P)} \tag{6}$$

R-measure is applied to selecting attributes in DTI by considering Q as the class attribute and P a descriptive attribute. System CABRO provides the user a set of tools based on techniques to solve three main DTI problems: the gain-ratio [12], gini-index [2], χ^2 [8] and R-measure for attribute selection; the error-complexity [2], reduced-error and pessimistic error [9] for pruning; and the entropy-based and error-based discretisation [4] for discretisation. Generally, these techniques are independent and the user can combine them to obtain different DTI models.

3 An Interactive Visualisation System

KDD is an iterative cycle in which the system provides and receives interactively feedback to and from the user. To support the learning and understanding decision trees, CABRO uses a *Visual Interactive Model* (VIM) through a rich graphical environment. The VIM aims at combining "meaningful pictures and easy interactions to stimulate creativity and insight; promoting a process of 'generate and test', it facilitates a rapid cycle of learning" [1]. In CABRO, the VIM offers: (1) a *Tree Visualiser* that supports the understanding and analysing decision trees; (2) an *Interactive Mode* that supports the user participation in the model selection and the learning process. CABRO has been implemented in UNIX workstations under the X Window, and recently in MS Windows 95, particularly on super-power PCs with 384 MB of SDRAM.

CABRO supports the user to load a data set, to select and evaluate DTI models, to induce decision trees, to navigate and analyse generated trees with different views and operations, to match decision trees with unknown cases.

3.1 Tree Visualiser

The *Tree Visualiser* is a graphical interface that displays a tree in a graphical form of a set of nodes and connections. Its most important feature is *the transformation of a decision tree from a static form (text) to a dynamic form (graphic) on which a certain operations can be carried out.* The user can dynamically navigate through the tree and have different views on generated trees, switch among several view modes, choose alternatively parts of the tree or paths to one class to be focused on. The basic views and operations in the Tree Visualiser are:

– *View of the tree structure*: Initially, a tree is displayed with only the root node and its direct sub-nodes (top-left window, Figure 1). The tree then can be *collapsed* or *expanded* partially or fully from the root or from any decision node. It allows the user to manipulate even a large tree by expand it from the root node step by step, either level by level (breadth-first) or branch by branch (depth-first). The user can exploit different *multiple views* on parts of the tree, such as to view only a subtree of interest from a decision node, to collapse some nodes (denoted by a ⊡) and/or expand some other ones (denoted by a ⊟) in order to hide non-interest subtrees and to focus on interest subtrees, etc.

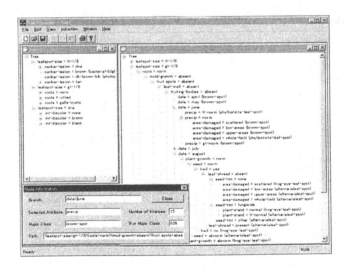

Fig. 1. CABRO's Tree Visualiser

– *View of decision/leaf nodes*: The user can click on a node to see its information: branching attribute and branched attribute-value, number of covered

cases, the major class, the percentage of major class, the path leading from the root to this decision/leaf node (dark color in boxes for class "brown-spot", Figure 2), etc.
- *View of a class on the tree*: The user can focus on observing decision paths to leaf nodes of a class. Only these leaf nodes are highlighted and proportions of cases bearing this class label are indicated approximately in decision nodes.

Figure 1 presents two different collapsed and expanded views of a tree.

3.2 Model Selection and Interactive Learning

Model Selection

There are three main criteria for selecting DTI models – size, accuracy and understandability of trees [8]. The understandability of trees is difficult to be quantified or measured and a tree visualiser will be of great support for the judgements of domain experts or users. The tree size and accuracy can be quantitatively evaluated, among them the accuracy is widely considered to be of great importance. The *k-fold stratified cross validation* has been recommended as a more reliable method for evaluating learning models, but it is time-consuming and not always be done well [14]. Doing carefully evaluations of discovered knowledge with good benchmarks has to become a principle in KDD.

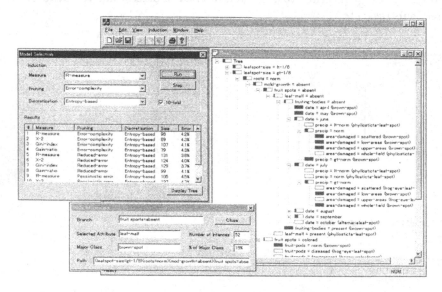

Fig. 2. Support for Model Selection

The CABRO's model selection tool, using the *k*-fold stratified cross validation (by default, *k* = 10), supports the user to select an appropriate DTI technique/model from the candidate ones by automatically generating and evaluating decision trees induced by the considered techniques/models. In the current version of CABRO, the user can try a new model composed by an attribute selection measure chosen from the gain-ratio, the gini-index, χ^2 and R-measure; a pruning technique from error-complexity, reduced-error and pessimistic error; and a discretisation technique from the entropy-based and error-based techniques (Figure 2). The open structure of program CABRO permits to add new DTI techniques to the set of component techniques. When a model candidate is considered, CABRO generates the corresponding decision tree and evaluates its performance as follows:

– The system carries out automatically a random shuffle of the data set then divides the data set into 10 mutually exclusive subsets (folds) of approximately equal size and the same proportions of labels as in the original data set.
– The system carries out automatically a run of 10-fold cross validation for the considered model, where one run is 10 times of applying the model to training data (the union of 9 subsets) for inducing a decision tree, and to testing data (the rest subset) for obtaining one estimation of the model predictive accuracy and tree size. It evaluates the final estimation of the model accuracy and tree size as the average of those obtained from 10 runs, and adds these into the "result" table (Figure 2).

This process is repeated for different model candidates with the same division of the original data set into 10 folds for the sake of a fair evaluation. For each model candidate, CABRO visualizes graphically the corresponding *pruned tree, its size, its prediction error rate*. CABRO offers the user a multiple view of these trials and facilitates the user to compare results of trials in order to make his/her final selection of techniques/models of interest.

Interactive Learning

In addition to the ability of interacting with the system by the Model Selection and Tree Visualiser tools, CABRO also provides the user the interaction during the generating-and-test process to obtain more appropriate results. An *Interactive Learning Mode* (ILM) allows the user participate actively in the DTI process. In fact, the user can execute a full automatic learning of decision trees without intervention by pressing the "run" button, or execute a step-by-step learning of decision trees by pressing the "step" button, or combine these two modes (Figure 2). The ILM provides currently two interactive functions:

– *interactively selecting an attribute* to branch decision nodes from several promising evaluated attributes. There are two reasons for doing that: (1) impurity functions are independent at each decision node on a tree then it is reasonable and better to evaluate the impurity of decision nodes by several measures and the selected attribute can be obtained by a plurality vote among them, and (2) it may happen that a considering measure finds some attributes whose values are slightly different from the best one, and it is not necessarily to select the attribute with biggest value to branch the node. By displaying this information (Figure 3) CABRO supports the user to combine his/her domain knowledge with the automatically evaluated attributes by system. This opportunity is meaningful, particularly at several first levels or at a branch of interest on the decision tree.

– *backtracking and regrow the tree*: while step-by-step generating a decision tree, the user can easily examine intermediate trees, backtracking to re-grow the tree at some node with respect to the induction scheme in changing parameters (e.g. the minimum size of a node or the expected accuracy of a leaf). Thus, the iteration can be done partially on the tree.

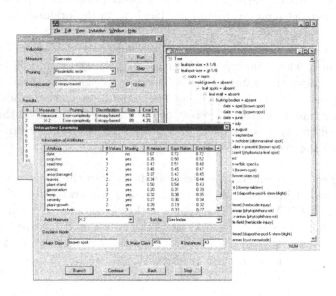

Fig. 3. Support for Interactive Learning

Illustration: Evaluation of R-measure

We have used the Model Selection tool to evaluate the performance of R-measure in comparison with three widely used attribute selection measures: the gain-ratio, the gini-index and χ^2. We carried out an experimental comparative evaluation on 18 data sets from the University California Irvine repository of databases for four selected models. These are formed by combining fixed methods of error-complexity pruning and entropy-based discretisation with gain-ratio (c), gini-index (g), χ^2 (χ) and R-measure (R).

Table 1 presents experimental results on size and error rates (both unpruned and pruned trees) of these four measures obtained automatically. As error rates of pruned trees are of most importance (columns 4 and 8), we indicate the lowest values on each by bold numbers. The other columns are the pruned tree sizes, error rates and sizes before pruning. It is worth noting that it will be very time-consuming and difficult to carry out precisely all of these experiments without such an automatic tool. This evaluation results show that R-measure is comparable to the best attribute selection measures in the current data mining literature.

	unpruned		pruned		unpruned		pruned	
	size	errors	size	errors	size	errors	size	errors
Vote, 16x300, symbolic					**Cancer, 9x700, symbolic**			
c	22.6±2.5	7.3±3.6	4.0±0.0	**5.0±2.8**	87.9±23.1	7.3±2.2	46.1±19.1	7.4±2.9
g	24.7±2.8	7.0±3.0	7.0±4.2	5.9±2.7	92.3±26.0	6.9±2.3	36.2±11.9	7.4±3.5
χ	24.7±2.8	7.0±3.0	7.0±4.2	5.9±2.7	92.3±26.0	6.9±2.0	36.2±11.9	7.4±3.5
R	25.0±3.0	7.5±3.4	5.8±2.9	5.7±2.7	94.5±26.4	7.0±2.2	37.3±11.2	**7.1±3.4**
Shuttle, 9x956, symbolic					**Promoters, 45x105, symbolic**			
c	88.4±10.9	0.2±0.1	53.4±15.8	**0.2±0.1**	18.2±3.3	25.5±9.8	9.8±4.3	24.5±7.5
g	144.8±6.6	0.2±0.1	114.2±12.2	**0.2±0.1**	19.0±4.0	23.6±12.7	9.4±3.7	**22.7±10.0**
χ	199.0±17.2	0.3±0.1	162.7±30.4	0.3±0.1	19.0±4.0	23.6±10.9	9.4±3.7	**22.7±10.0**
R	165.3±15.6	0.2±0.1	135.3±18.3	0.3±0.1	19.0±4.0	23.6±12.7	9.4±3.7	**22.7±10.0**
Solar Flare, 12x1286, symbolic					**Diabetes, 8x768, numeric**			
c	104.0±11.6	26.8±2.5	26.8±7.8	**25.3±1.5**	41.2±2.2	24.4±3.1	18.2±9.4	**25.3±2.6**
g	150.8±15.0	28.4±2.9	54.4±15.0	27.8±1.3	53.0±4.4	25.3±2.7	22.0±4.8	25.6±2.5
χ	168.6±24.6	28.3±2.2	45.8±18.1	26.6±2.0	47.6±5.1	25.3±2.7	13.6±6.2	25.5±2.5
R	155.0±19.4	26.9±1.8	44.6±31.1	25.5±1.0	74.2±8.6	24.7±2.6	27.8±19.8	**25.3±2.6**
Splice, 45x3189, numeric					**Glass, 9x214, numeric**			
c	529.8±68.0	10.2±1.5	245.8±36.8	**8.0±1.7**	21.0±3.2	33.2±8.6	17.3±5.5	**34.5±8.2**
g	565.8±72.0	10.4±2.4	214.6±39.8	8.4±1.8	35.2±4.4	33.2±7.7	22.3±6.9	36.8±6.8
χ	585.8±76.0	10.5±2.4	253.0±56.8	8.8±1.7	29.6±2.8	35.0±5.6	19.1±7.5	37.3±6.4
R	509.8±77.4	11.0±2.5	207.4±30.4	8.6±1.9	32.2±5.8	34.1±7.3	18.7±6.8	35.9±6.9
Waveform, 36x3195, symbolic					**Heart Disease, 13x270, mixed**			
c	1148.3±179.5	28.9±1.7	223.9±72.9	25.7±1.1	13.8±5.4	25.6±4.1	8.8±3.8	25.6±4.1
g	1320.5±193.9	27.8±1.3	244.5±69.5	**24.4±1.6**	33.0±4.0	27.4±4.7	25.8±2.6	25.6±5.6
χ	1355.7±185.0	28.4±1.6	340.6±191.6	26.8±1.3	26.6±9.7	27.4±4.7	9.0±3.2	26.3±4.9
R	1432.3±193.5	29.3±1.5	249.6±78.4	25.1±1.1	38.0±13.4	27.4±4.7	8.2±5.1	**25.2±4.6**
Vehicle, 18x846, numeric					**Hypothyroid, 25x3163, numeric**			
c	174.5±35.9	32.4±5.2	131.9±40.7	32.7±5.1	22.6±2.5	1.1±0.4	11.8±1.5	**0.9±0.4**
g	222.8±38.4	31.9±3.2	111.4±37.8	32.0±3.7	49.2±5.4	1.3±0.5	16.8±3.7	**0.9±0.4**
χ	216.2±40.4	30.2±3.9	111.4±47.4	31.9±3.2	54.8±5.0	1.3±0.5	10.6±0.6	**0.9±0.4**
R	218.2±39.6	31.6±3.2	101.5±28.7	**31.8±3.5**	57.8±6.0	1.4±0.4	18.2±4.9	**0.9±0.4**
Audiology, 70x226, symbolic					**Cars, 8x392, numeric**			
c	49.8±9.0	29.6±13.7	28.4±13.3	30.9±11.0	32.3±2.0	24.8±4.8	17.1±9.5	26.0±2.0
g	68.2±12.4	29.6±11.5	37.0±16.0	30.9±11.9	44.7±10.3	24.0±4.8	21.4±8.5	26.8±5.2
χ	93.9±22.3	44.3±8.9	66.9±14.9	45.2±8.7	41.8±8.8	23.8±5.0	17.4±9.1	26.5±5.2
R	72.1±10.3	28.3±10.9	41.3±13.4	**29.1±11.7**	44.6±12.5	24.2±5.1	21.8±12.8	**25.2±4.8**
Horse-colic, 28x368, numeric					**Pima-diabetes, 8x768, numeric**			
c	48.9±9.1	16.2±3.8	8.2±4.1	**14.3±5.1**	34.3±6.7	24.9±4.5	17.6±5.8	**23.4±3.6**
g	86.4±19.1	17.8±1.9	30.9±20.3	16.8±3.5	45.4±3.5	24.7±4.2	25.4±8.3	23.5±3.5
χ	92.0±25.8	18.1±2.3	22.0±22.4	17.0±3.3	40.0±4.2	24.7±4.2	18.5±9.0	23.5±3.5
R	115.6±22.7	17.0±1.7	15.8±13.7	15.9±4.2	65.1±8.5	24.7±4.2	30.6±17.4	23.9±3.2
Segmentation, 19x2310, numeric					**Iris, 4x150, numeric**			
c	327.4±48.2	6.3±1.5	236.4±46.5	6.2±1.6	4.3±0.5	4.0±3.2	4.0±0.0	3.3±3.3
g	341.3±30.9	5.9±1.7	257.5±81.2	**6.1±2.0**	4.3±0.5	3.3±3.3	4.0±0.0	**2.7±3.2**
χ	373.2±25.2	7.3±1.6	310.7±48.3	7.6±2.0	4.3±0.5	4.7±3.7	4.0±0.0	4.0±4.0
R	342.5±33.6	6.1±1.8	272.0±90.4	**6.1±2.1**	4.3±0.5	4.7±3.7	4.0±0.0	4.0±4.0

Table 1. Experimental comparative evaluation results

4 Conclusion

We have described the interactive visualisation system CABRO for DTI. The system employs several DTI well-known techniques selected from the KDD and machine learning literature, including our proposed R-measure for attribute selection. Implemented as an interactive-graphic environment, CABRO supports a creative combination of contributing techniques, in particular the tree visualisation, the model selection, the interactive learning which are certainly important principles of data mining and knowledge discovery. Using the model selection tool, we have carried out carefully a comparative evaluation that shows the high application potential of CABRO and R-measure.

References

1. Belton, V. and Elder, M.D.: Decision Support Systems: Learning from Visual Interactive Modelling, *Decision Support Systems*, 12, pp. 355–364 (1994).
2. Breiman, L., Friedman, J., Olshen, R. and Stone, C.: *Classification and Regression Trees*, Belmont, CA: Wadsworth (1984).
3. Brunk, C., Kelly, J. and Kohavi, R.: MineSet: An Integrated System for Data Mining, *Proceedings of Third International Conference on Knowledge Discovery and Data Mining*, pp. 135–138 (1997).
4. Fayyad, U.M. and Irani K.B.: On the Handling of Continuous-Valued Attributes in Decision Tree Generation, *Machine Learning*, pp. 87–102 (1992).
5. Ho, T.B., Nguyen, T.D. and Kimura, M.: Induction of Decision Trees Based on the Rough Set Theory, in *Data Science, Classification and Related Methods*, C. Hayashi et al. (Eds.), Springer, 215-222 (1997).
6. Ho, T.B.: Discovering and Using Knowledge From Unsupervised Data, *Journal Decision Support Systems*, Elsevier Science, Vol. 21, No. 1, 27–41 (1997).
7. Kervahut, T. and Potvin, J.Y.: An Interactive-Graphic Environment for Automatic Generation of Decision Trees, *Decision Support Systems*, Vol. 18, pp. 117–134 (1996).
8. Mingers, J.: An Empirical Comparison of Selection Measures for Decision Tree Induction, *Machine Learning*, 3, pp. 319–342 (1989).
9. Mingers, J.: An Empirical Comparison of Pruning Methods for Decision Tree Induction, *Machine Learning*, 4, pp. 227–243 (1989).
10. Pawlak, Z.: *Rough sets: Theoretical Aspects of Reasoning About Data*, Kluwer Academic Publishers (1991).
11. Pawlak, Z., Wong, S.K.M. and Ziarko, W.: Rough Sets, Probabilistic versus Deterministic Approach, *International Journal of Man-Machine Studies*, 29, pp. 81–95 (1988).
12. Quinlan, J.R.: *C4.5: Programs for Machine Learning*, Morgan Kaufmann (1993).
13. Rao, J.S., Potts, W.J.E.: Visualizing Bagged Decision Trees, *Proceedings of Third International Conference on Knowledge Discovery and Data Mining*, pp. 243–246 (1997).
14. Salzberg, S.L.: On Comparing Classifiers: Pitfalls to Avoid and a Recommended Approach, *Data Mining and Knowledge Discovery*, 1, 317–327 (1997).
15. Ziarko, W.: Variable Precision Rough Set Model, *Journal of Computer and System Sciences*, 46, pp. 39–59 (1993).

Discovery of Diagnostic Patterns from Protein Sequence Databases

Björn Olsson, Kim Laurio

Dept. of Computer Science, University of Skövde, Box 408, 54128, Skövde, Sweden
bjorne@ida.his.se, kim@ida.his.se

Abstract. We show how prior domain knowledge can be used in a system for mining databases of biological data. Our system performs automated discovery of diagnostic patterns from a database of protein sequences. Such patterns are used for classification of new sequences, and identification of biologically interesting positions in the proteins. The patterns have a simple syntax and can be translated into regular expressions, which can be used for rapid scanning of databases. Current pattern libraries are built semi-manually, since the correctness of the pattern depends on the incorporation of domain knowledge. Due to the dramatic growth of the databases it is desirable to automate this process. Our results show that the patterns derived by our fully automated system compete well with the semi-manually constructed patterns.

1 Introduction

In the past few years, there has been a dramatic increase in the amount of biological sequence data in public-domain databases. Since 1987, the number of protein sequences in the SWISSPROT database [2] has doubled every year, and the November 1997 release contains 68,830 entries. The December 1997 release of the EMBL database [7] of RNA and DNA sequences contains 1,917,868 sequence entries, and this database also doubles in size every year. This explosive growth of the amount of available sequence data will continue well into the 21st century. The Human Genome Project alone will contribute another estimated 60,000 to 80,000 protein sequences before the target date of completion in 2005. It can also be noted that the August 1995 release of the GenBank database [4] of DNA sequences, although containing 492,483 sequence records, only had sequences from 15,511 species [11]. Since the estimates of the number of extant species range from 5 to 50 million [8], the GenBank database only had sequences from at most 0.3% of the species. An average of 10 new species are added per day.

The fields of molecular biology and bioinformatics, although undergoing rapid development, still have problems in keeping up with the new data. An example is the problem of determining the 3D structure of proteins. The structure is known for less than 3% of all sequenced proteins [12], and the gap between the number of known sequences and solved structures is rapidly increasing [12] [13].

This paper addresses the construction and maintenance of a library of patterns for classification of protein sequences. Current pattern libraries, such as PROSITE [3], are built using semi-manual approaches, making it time-consuming to construct the initial patterns. Also, since new sequences are continuously added to the database, the patterns degrade over time. To maintain the discriminatory power of the patterns, they must frequently be inspected and updated.

Our work aims at a system for automatic discovery of biologically significant patterns, and automatic updates of the pattern library as new sequences are added to the database. Our method for pattern construction is based on information theory, but also makes extensive use of biological information to guide the construction process. Thus, we show an example of how knowledge discovery techniques can be amended by incorporating domain knowledge - in this case knowledge of typical amino acid frequencies found in protein sequence data.

The next chapter is a brief introduction to protein sequence analysis, and can be skipped by readers familiar with the area. The third chapter is an overview of our system, while chapter four discusses algorithms for constructing diagnostic patterns and shows how we extend and improve on current algorithms by using prior knowledge. The fifth chapter presents our results and conclusions.

2 Protein Sequences and Sequence Analysis

Genes are blueprints for the myriad of proteins which perform the important tasks within organisms. Through many generations, proteins have evolved which perform an impressive variety of tasks: acting as enzymes in biochemical reactions, performing transportation of nutrients, being sensors for taste and smell, being detectors of invading viruses in the immune system, and acting as switches turning genes on or off. Understanding the details of how proteins perform their function is one of the most important issues in molecular biology.

The building blocks of proteins are 20 different types of amino acids. The basic chemical structure of an amino acid is to contain a carboxyl group and an amino group, both attached to a central carbon atom. In addition, each type of amino acid has a unique side chain, which determines the specifics of its chemical properties. A protein is made up of a sequence of amino acids, joined together by peptide bonds. When an amino acid occurs in the sequence, it is called a residue. Many proteins consist of several hundred residues, and in some cases several thousand. The residue sequence is termed the primary structure of the protein. Before the protein becomes biologically functional in the cell, it undergoes a folding process, where the primary structure folds into a specific three-dimensional, tertiary structure (an example is shown in figure 4.

The central tenet in protein sequence analysis is that the amino acid sequence determines the tertiary structure, and that the tertiary structure determines the function of the protein [12]. Mutations are changes at sequence level, which may or may not have any significant effect on the folded conformation. Proteins with similar sequences are evolutionary related and have similar folds [6], whereas unrelated sequences generally produce different folds. Computational approaches in bioinformatics address many difficult problems by analysing the sequence, which can easily be handled by computer algorithms. One example of such a problem is to derive phylogenetic trees, showing the evolutionary relationships between proteins. Another problem is the one addressed in this paper: to derive patterns which can be used to classify new sequences according to family membership.

One of the most important basic techniques in sequence analysis is to derive alignments. As a very simple example of a sequence alignment, consider the following alignment of four variants of the word "sequence":

$$
\begin{array}{l}
\text{S E - Q U E N C E} \\
\text{S E - Q - E N C E} \\
\text{S E a Q U E N C E} \\
\text{S E - Q U E N S E}
\end{array}
$$

The types of changes occurring in the example also occur in protein sequences, i.e. deletion (U in SEQENCE), insertion (A in SEAQUENCE), and replacement (S in SEQUENSE). The alignment highlights the changes, and clearly shows the positions which are preserved. Algorithms for constructing alignments seek to minimize the mutational distance between the sequences. In the analysis

of a protein family, a multiple sequence alignment can be used to discover the
residue positions which are evolutionarily conserved in the family. Such positions
often correspond to important biological functionality of the protein.

Sequence analysis algorithms rely on public-domain databases, such as SWIS-
SPROT [2], which contains sequences and extensive documentation for over
70,000 proteins. PROSITE [3] is a database of patterns for 997 protein families.
The patterns can be seen as signatures, distinguishing family from non-family
sequences. The Pfam database [17] contains 527 protein families. Among other
things, Pfam contains an alignment of a subset of the sequences for each family.

3 Overview of Method

We aim to achieve an automated system for discovering and maintaining diagnostic protein sequence patterns. We are currently building a library of patterns
derived through a system which interfaces three public-domain databases. Figure 1 shows an overview of our method. Every step of the method can be fully
automated, making it possible to achieve large scale updates, so that the patterns
can be continuously refined to take new sequences into account.

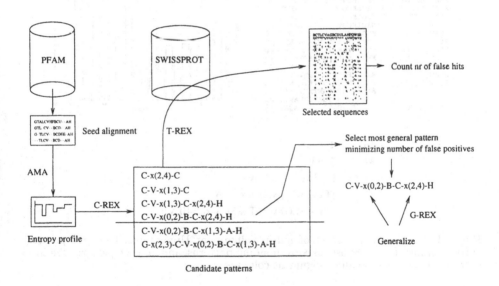

Fig. 1. Overview of the method.

When generating a pattern for a family, the system uses a multiple alignment from the Pfam database [18], aligning a subset of the sequences belonging
to the family. The alignment is analysed by AMA (Analysis of Multiple Alignments [10]), which generates an entropy profile. The profile can be used to detect
positions which are likely to be conserved in the family, and therefore good candidates as pattern elements. In estimating the entropy of columns, AMA takes into
account biological domain knowledge by using a Dirichlet mixture. It was shown

in [9] and [16] that use of this prior information improves the degree of generalisation in statistical models of small samples of protein sequence data. This is important since many Pfam alignments contain only a handful of sequences.

Using the entropy profile, C-REX (Creating REgular eXpressions) creates initial patterns by adding the most conserved columns, separated by wild-cards. More elements are added in the order of increasing entropy, and the gradually more specific patterns are tested by searching SWISSPROT. Since initial patterns match many false positives, C-REX adds elements until all false positives are excluded. In some cases, the pattern at this stage matches every family member, but in most cases it is too specific, and excludes some family members. Figure 2 illustrates the algorithm for extracting initial patterns. Low entropy columns correspond to promising pattern elements, and are used first. Column 12 is a conserved T-column with estimated entropy $\overline{p} \simeq 0.16$, and column 16 is a conserved A-column, having the second lowest estimated entropy ($\overline{p} \simeq 0.18$).

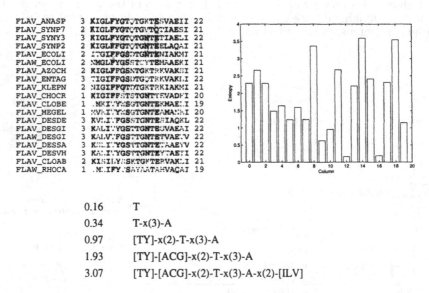

0.16	T
0.34	T-x(3)-A
0.97	[TY]-x(2)-T-x(3)-A
1.93	[TY]-[ACG]-x(2)-T-x(3)-A
3.07	[TY]-[ACG]-x(2)-T-x(3)-A-x(2)-[ILV]

Fig. 2. Upper left: Small portion of multiple alignment. Upper right: The corresponding entropy profile. Lower: Subset of corresponding patterns, and for each pattern, the total entropy of the corresponding alignment columns.

G-REX (Generalising REgular eXpressions) generalises the pattern, but only allows generalisations which still exclude all false positives. The result is a more sensitive pattern, with the specificity of the original pattern being preserved. We define sensitivity and specificity as

$$Sens = \frac{True_{pos}}{True_{pos} + False_{neg}} \qquad Spec = \frac{True_{pos}}{True_{pos} + False_{pos}} \qquad (1)$$

where $True_{pos}$ is the number of family sequences matched by the pattern, and $False_{neg}$ the number of family sequences not matched by the pattern, whereas

$False_{pos}$ is the number of non-family sequences matched by the pattern. This sensitivity measure is equal to the fraction of the known family sequences which are matched by the pattern, whereas specificity equals the probability that a sequence which is matched by the pattern really belongs to the family.

4 Construction of Sequence Patterns

An overview of algorithms for the construction of patterns is given in [5]. Briefly, the algorithms can be divided into two groups: those using "bottom-up" and "top-down" approaches. The essence of the bottom-up approach is to enumerate candidate patterns and count the number of occurrences of the candidate patterns that can be found in the sequences. The obvious limitation of this approach is that the size of the search space is exponential in the length of the patterns. In contrast, top-down approaches look for local similarities between sequences, and extract candidate patterns based on these similarities. This can be done in several ways, for example by searching for sufficiently long common substrings, or by first aligning the sequences to minimize the mismatches, and extract patterns from the alignment. Both the problem of finding the longest common substring, and that of finding the optimal alignment are NP-complete, and top-down algorithms therefore incorporate the use of heuristics.

Our algorithm is a top-down approach, and uses an alignment as starting point. Currently, we use Pfam's so called 'seed alignments' [18], which are hand-designed or automatically generated alignments of a subset of the family. Our algorithm makes no assumptions regarding the origin of the alignment, so that later versions of the system may include construction of the alignment.

4.1 Deriving an Entropy Profile Using Prior Knowledge

Central to our approach is the use of both information theory and Dirichlet mixture priors [16] in the alignment analysis. The entropy of each column of the alignment is estimated, and low-entropy columns used for building initial candidate patterns. The assumption is that low-entropy columns generally correspond to conserved positions in the protein, and that a pattern built from these columns will represent the most characteristic properties of the family. To estimate the entropy of columns we use the method developed in [10], based on the concept of entropy from Shannon's classical work [14]. The entropy of an alignment column can be estimated by

$$ent(\overrightarrow{p}) = -\sum_i p_i \, log \, p_i \tag{2}$$

where p_i is the estimated probability of observing symbol i in the column, so that a "flat" distribution over the symbol alphabet gives maximum entropy. The simplest way of estimating p_i is to use the observed frequency, but such a naive approach does not take into account the number of observations. This is a serious problem, since for small samples, there is a high risk that the observed frequencies do not correspond to the true distribution [16]. This problem is relevant in our case, since the input to our system is often an alignment of only 10 sequences or less, and we therefore use Dirichlet mixtures in the estimation of p_i. Dirichlet mixtures were shown in [9] to be close to the theoretical optimum for a prior, and have previously been used in other biosequence applications, such as hidden Markov models of protein families [1] and phylogenetic trees [15].

A Dirichlet mixture contains a number of components, representing typical amino acid distributions. The observed amino acid frequencies are combined with all components, using a weighting scheme where the the component which best matches the frequencies is given highest weight. This is done using pseudo-counts, which gradually shifts the emphasis from the mixture to the observed frequencies when more observations are added.

Given the count vector $\overrightarrow{n}$ of observations of the amino acids in a column, the estimated (posterior) probability of observing amino acid i in the column is

$$p_i = \sum_{j=1}^{l} Prob(\alpha_j | \overrightarrow{n}, \Theta) \times ((n_i + \alpha_{j,i})/(|\overrightarrow{n}| + |\alpha_j|)) \tag{3}$$

and is a sum over the components α_j of some Dirichlet mixture Θ. In the product, the first term implements the weighting scheme over the mixture components $\overrightarrow{\alpha}$, where the component which best matches the observed counts returns the highest weight. The second term of the product adds the pseudo-counts to the observed counts and normalises the sum. In our work we have used the nine-component Dirichlet mixture from [16].

4.2 Using an Entropy Profile to Build a Pattern

Given a multiple alignment of sequences from a protein family, AMA creates a profile of estimated entropy values. Each value is determined by equation 2, with p_i estimated according to equation 3. To build patterns from the profile, the low entropy columns are chosen, and corresponding pattern elements generated. The individual elements are combined into a complete pattern, which is meant to reflect the conserved positions in the sequences.

A *pattern* is a description of common syntactic features of a set of sequences [5]. A sequence is matched by the pattern if it contains the features described by the pattern. A pattern is diagnostic for a family if it matches every sequence in the family, and no other known sequences [5]. Many of the patterns in PROSITE are diagnostic, but the majority gives some false positives or negatives. It is potentially possible to improve on their diagnostic power by using an automated algorithm for their construction, since such an algorithm may be able to explore a much larger set of candidate patterns.

Patterns in the PROSITE syntax can be expressed on the form

$$E_1 - x(i_1, j_1) - E_2 - x(i_2, j_2) - ... - E_n$$

where each E_k is an element, and each $x(i_k, j_k)$ is a wild-card. An element specifies a single amino acid (e.g. L) or a set of amino acids (such as $[LIV]$). A wild-card specifies an arbitrary stretch of amino acids, the length of which must be at least i_k and at most j_k. For $i_k = j_k$ the shorter notation is $x(i_k)$, and $x(1)$ can be written x. Example patterns are shown in figure 4.

C-REX incrementally creates patterns of increasing complexity by adding elements from the alignment, in order of increasing entropy. An individual element is created simply by enumerating the observed symbols from the corresponding alignment column. To create a complete pattern from n elements, $n - 1$ wild-cards must be added to connect the elements. For a wild-card $x(i, j)$, the values of i and j are determined by counting the minimum and maximum number of residues occurring between the two columns in the alignment.

By testing the patterns generated by C-REX against SWISSPROT, we find the most general pattern with maximum specificity. Testing starts with the most general pattern, and stops if a pattern excludes all false positives. If no such pattern is found, the most general pattern among those with the minimal number of false positives is used during the subsequent generalisation phase.

4.3 Generalising a Pattern

A pattern minimizing the number of false positives is often too specific to match all family members. This because C-REX builds patterns using an alignment in which only a subset of the family is represented. Therefore, the generalisation program G-REX is used to find a more general pattern, matching all members of the family. G-REX currently uses three classes of operations for generalisation, where two operate on elements and one on wild-cards:

- An element can be generalised by adding one new symbol.
- An element can be excluded from the pattern.
- A wild-card region can be expanded by decreasing the lower bound on the length (or increasing the upper bound).

The generalisation phase currently involves only testing of randomly applied generalisations. A generalisation is tested by updating the pattern and testing the specificity and sensitivity. Unless both measures improve or stay the same, the generalisation is undone. This is repeated for a given number of trials, resulting in a gradually more general pattern. The current version, in other words, performs a crude form of search in the space of possible generalisations.

For each pattern there is in fact a very large number of possible generalisations. Consider a pattern of n elements, $E_1, .., E_n$. Let s_k denote the number of symbols in the element E_k. Since the cardinality of the alphabet is 20, there are 2^{20-s_k} possible generalisations of E_k. In addition, every wild-card $x(i_k, j_k)$ has $i_k + (j_{max} - j_k)$ possible generalisations, where j_{max} denotes an arbitrary upper bound on the j-values. For a pattern of n elements, there are

$$\sum_{k=1}^{n} 2^{20-s_k} * \sum_{k=1}^{n-1} i_k * (j_{max} - j_k) \tag{4}$$

possible generalisations. Our restricted operators for generalisation (e.g. only adding one symbol at a time) impose a partial ordering, and thus constrains the search. Also, since G-REX keeps any generalisation which does not degrade the results, the algorithm is a simple hill-climber. Although G-REX often finds patterns with improved sensitivity, it is clear from our results that the search performed by G-REX in the space of possible generalisations is sub-optimal, and that there is potential for improvement of the generalisation phase.

5 Results and Conclusions

We tested our method on 439 families represented in both Pfam and PROSITE. For each family, we derived one pattern using our method, and compared it with the corresponding PROSITE pattern. For families where PROSITE reports more than one pattern, we chose only the 'best' pattern. Figure 3 shows a comparison between our patterns and those in PROSITE. For 87% of families our pattern had equal or better specificity than the PROSITE pattern, which is certainly a satisfactory result. However, our patterns had equal or better sensitivity for only 25% of the families. Further work is therefore needed to improve our results on the sensitivity measure. In analysing the worst-performing patterns, we have discovered some errors in the PROSITE documentation, resulting in family

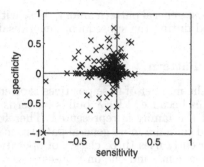

Fig. 3. Comparison of sensitivity and selectivity between our patterns and those in PROSITE, for 439 protein families. Positive values denote that our pattern was better than the PROSITE pattern.

members being treated as false positives by our system. However, no definitive conclusions can be drawn about the effect of the errors on the sensitivity.

Given the size of the search space, the current algorithm for searching generalisations is clearly inadequate. Currently, the sensitivity only improves from 0.883 to 0.906 (the average sensitivity of the Prosite patterns is 0.957). The hill-climbing done by G-REX will easily get trapped in local optima. We are currently investigating improved search algorithms for this purpose.

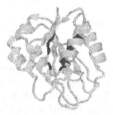

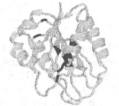

[LIV]-[LIVFY]-[FY]-x-[ST]-x(2)-[AGC]-x-T-x(3)-A-x(2)-[LIV]   [TY]-[ACG]-x-T-x(3)-A-x(33,40)-G-x(2)-[AT]-x(22,31)-[DG]-x(5)-[FY]-[AGS]-x(20,26)-G

Fig. 4. 3D structure of FLAV_ANASP, and comparison of the location of the residues corresponding to the PROSITE pattern (left) and our pattern. Although our pattern spans a longer subsequence, the residues matched by the pattern are located closely in 3D space, in the region involved in phosphate binding.

In examining our patterns, we noted that they are typically longer than those in PROSITE - modeling conserved alignment columns distributed over a larger part of the alignment (an example is shown in figure 4). By examining example 3D conformations from the PDB database, we hypothesise that our patterns include more of the structural constraints of the conformation. This is a possible reason that some of our patterns discriminate better than PROSITE patterns.

While local properties of an active site, modeled by PROSITE, may occur in an unrelated protein with another principal function, these properties would occur within another conformational context in the unrelated protein. Thus, our patterns model local details as well as global, conformational constraints.

As part of our future work, we aim to do a detailed analysis of patterns for a small number of families, to determine the exact differences between our patterns and PROSITE's. Such an analysis may provide further insight into what properties of the sequences our patterns model, which may result in improvements of the algorithm for pattern discovery and refinement. In addition, it may provide biologically interesting insight into the functionality of the proteins. It is conceivable that the patterns discovered by our system correspond to new discoveries of the proteins' functionality. This part of the analysis, may require laboratory experiments as a complement to statistical and computational modeling.

References

1. Krogh A., Brown B., Mian I.S., Sjölander K., and Haussler D. Hidden markov models in computational biology: Applications to protein modeling. *Journal of Molecular Biology*, 235:1501–31, 1994.
2. A. Bairoch and R. Apweiler. The SWISS-PROT protein sequence data bank and its supplement TREMBL. *Nucleic Acids Research*, 25:31–6, 1997.
3. A. Bairoch, P. Bucher, and K. Hofmann. The PROSITE database, its status in 1997. *Nucleic Acids Research*, 25:217–221, 1997.
4. D.A. Benson, M.S. Boguski, D.J. Lipman, J. Ostell, and B. Ouellette. GenBank. *Nucleic Acids Research*, 26(1):1–7, 1998.
5. A. Brāzma, I. Jonassen, I. Eidhammer, and D. Gilbert. Approaches to the automatic discovery of patterns in biosequences. Technical Report 113, Dept. of Informatics, Univ. of Bergen, 1993.
6. T.E. Creighton. Protein folding. In R.A. Meyers, editor, *Molecular Biology and Biotechnology: A Comprehensive Desk Reference*. VCH Publishers, 1995.
7. EMBL nucleotide sequence database: Release notes, release 53, December 1997.
8. L. Hunter. Molecular biology for computer scientists. In L. Hunter, editor, *Artificial Intelligence and Molecular Biology*. AAAI Press/MIT Press, 1993.
9. K. Karplus. Evaluating regularizers for estimating distributions of amino acids. In C. Rawlings, D. Clark, R. Altman, L. Hunter T. Lengauer, and S. Wodak, editors, *Proc. of ISMB95*. AAAI Press, 1995.
10. K. Laurio. Probabilistic modeling of protein families. Master's thesis, University of Skövde, Sweden, 1997.
11. NCBI News. NIH Publication No. 95-3272, September 1995.
12. B. Rost. Learning from evolution to predict protein structure. In *Biocomputing and Emergent Computation - Proceedings of BCEC97*. World Scientific, 1997.
13. B. Rost and R. Schneider. Pedestrian guide to analysing sequence databases. In K. Ashman, editor, *Core Technologies in Biochemistry*. Springer, 1997.
14. C. Shannon. A mathematical theory of communication. *Bell Systems Technical Journal*, 27, 1948.
15. K. Sjölander. Bayesian evolutionary tree estimation. In *Proceedings of the Computing in the Genome Era conference*, Washington DC, March 1997.
16. K. Sjölander, K. Karplus, M. Brown, R. Hughey, A. Krogh, I.S. Mian, and D. Haussler. Dirichlet mixtures: A method for improved detection of weak but significant protein sequence homology. *CABIOS*, 12(4):327–45, 1996.
17. E.L.L. Sonnhammer, S.R. Eddy, E. Birney, A. Bateman, and R. Durbin. Pfam: Multiple sequence alignments and hmm-profiles of protein domains. *Nucleic Acids Research*, in press, 1998.
18. E.L.L. Sonnhammer, S.R. Eddy, and R. Durbin. Pfam: A comprehensive database of protein domain families based on seed alignments. *Proteins*, 28:405–20, 1997.

The PSP Approach for Mining Sequential Patterns

F. Masseglia[2], F. Cathala[1,4], and P. Poncelet[1,3]

[1] LIM ESA CNRS 6077, Case 901, 163 Avenue de Luminy, 13288 Marseille Cedex 9,
France E-mail: {poncelet,cathala}@lim.univ-mrs.fr
[2] LIRMM UMR CNRS 5506, 161, Rue Ada, 34392 Montpellier Cedex 5, France,
E-mail: massegli@lirmm.fr
[3] IUT d'Aix-en-Provence
[4] Cemagref, division Aix-en-Provence, France

Abstract. In this paper, we present an approach, called PSP, for mining sequential patterns embedded in a database. Close to the problem of discovering association rules, mining sequential patterns requires handling time constraints. Originally introduced in [3], the issue is addressed by the GSP approach [10]. Our proposal resumes the general principles of GSP but it makes use of a different intermediary data structure which is proved to be more efficient than in GSP.

1 Introduction

Motivated by decision support problems, data mining, also known as knowledge discovery in databases, has been extensively addressed in the few past years (e.g. [5]). Among takled issues, the problem of mining association rules, initially introduced in [1], has recently received a great deal of attention [1, 2, 4, 5, 9, 11]. The problem of mining association rules is often referred to as the "market-basket" problem, because purchase transaction data collected by retail stores offers a typical application groundwork for discovering knowledge.

The concept of sequential pattern is introduced to capture typical behaviours over time, i.e. behaviours sufficiently repeated by individuals to be relevant for the decision maker [3].The GSP algorithm, proposed in [10], is intended for mining Generalized Sequential Pattern. It extends previous proposal by handling time constraints and taxonomies (*is-a* hierarchies).

In this paper we present an approach for discovering sequential patterns. It is widely inspired from the GSP algorithm, but it introduces some improvements which makes it possible to perform retrieval optimizations.

This paper is organized as follows. In section 2, the problem is stated and illustrated. An outline of GSP is given in section 3. Our proposal is detailed in section 4, and compared with GSP.

2 Mining maximal sequential pattern

This section widely resumes the formal description of the "market-basket" problem, introduced in [10].

First of all, we assume that we are given a database D of customers' transactions, each of which having the following characteristics: sequence-id or customer-id, transaction-time and the items involved in the transaction. Such a database is called a base of data sequences (Cf. Fig. 1).

Definition 1 Let $I = \{i_1, i_2, ..., i_m\}$ be a set of literals called *items*. An *itemset* is a non-empty set of items. A sequence s is a set of itemsets ordered according to their time-stamp. It is denoted by $< s_1 s_2...s_n >$ where s_j is an itemset. A *k-sequence* is a sequence of k-items (or of length k). A sequence $< s_1 s_2...s_n >$ is a sub-sequence of another sequence $< s'_1 s'_2...s'_m >$ if there exist integers $i_1 < i_2 < ... < i_n$ such that $s_1 \subseteq s'_{i_1}, s_2 \subseteq s'_{i_2}, ...s_n \subseteq s'_{i_n}$.

For aiding efficiently decision making, the aim is discarding non typical behaviours according to user's viewpoint. Performing such a task requires providing data sub-sequence s in the DB with a support value ($supp(s)$) giving its number of actual occurrences in the DB. In order to decide whether a sequence is frequent or not, a minimum support value (σ) is specified by user, and the sequence s is said frequent if the condition $supp(s) \geq \sigma$ holds.

From the problem statement presented so far, discovering sequential patterns resembles closely to mining association rules. However, elements of handled sequences are itemsets and not items, and a main difference is introduced with time concerns.

The user can decide that it does not matter if items were purchased separately as long as their occurrences enfold within a given time window, thus itemsets in the data sequence d could be grouped together with respect to the sliding window. Moreover when exhibiting from d, sub-sequences possibly matching with the supposed pattern, non adjacent itemsets in d could be picked up successively. Minimum and maximum time gaps are introduced to constrain such a construction. Window size and time constraints as well as the minimum support condition are parametrized by user as defined in [10].

Example 1 Let us consider the base D given in figure 1, reporting facts about a population merely reduced to four customers. Let us assume that the minimum support value is 50%, thus to be considered as frequent a sequence must be observed for at least two customers. The only frequent sequences, embedded in the DB are the following: $< (20)\ (90) >$, $< (30)\ (90) >$ and $< (30)\ (40, 70) >$. By introducing a sliding window of 2 days, a new frequent sequence $< (20\ 30)\ (90) >$ is discovered because it matches with the first transaction of C_4 while being detected for C_1, within a couple of transactions respecting the window size.

3 Related Work

This section is devoted for setting the groundwork of our proposal and not offering an overview of the whole domain. The interested reader could refer to [1, 2, 4, 5, 11] in which approaches for discovering association rules are presented and compared. In a different context, the issue of exhibiting sequences is addressed

Customer	Time	Items	Customer	Time	Items
C_1	01/01/1998	20,60	C_3	05/01/1998	30,50,70
C_1	02/02/1998	20	C_3	12/02/1998	10,20
C_1	04/02/1998	30			
C_1	18/02/1998	80,90			
C_2	11/01/1998	10	C_4	06/02/1998	20,30
C_2	12/01/1998	30	C_4	07/02/1998	40,70
C_2	29/01/1998	40,60,70	C_4	08/02/1998	90

Fig. 1. A data-sequence database example

in [3, 6, 10]. Since it is the basis of our approach, particular emphasis is placed on the GSP approach.

Basically, exhibiting frequent sequences requires firstly retrieving all data sequences satisfying the specified time constraints. These sequences are considered as candidates for being patterns. The support of candidate sequences is then computed by browsing the DB. Sequences for which the minimum support condition does not hold are discarded. The result is the set of frequent sequences. For building up candidate and frequent sequences, the GSP algorithm performs several iterative steps such as the kth step handles sets of k-sequences which could be candidate (the set is noted C_k) or frequent (in L_k). The latter set, called seed set, is used by the following step which, in turn, results in a new seed set encompassing longer sequences, and so on.

The first step aims to compute the support of each item in the database. When completed, frequent items (i.e. satisfying the minimum support) are discovered. They are considered as frequent 1-sequences (sequences having a single itemset, itself being a singleton). This initial seed set is the starting point of the second step. The set of candidate 2-sequences is built according to the following assumption: candidate 2-sequences could be any couple of frequent items, embedded in the same transaction or not. From this point, any step k is given a seed set of frequent $(k-1)$-sequences and it operates by performing the two following sub-steps:

- The first sub-step (join phase) addresses candidate generation. The main idea is to retrieve, among sequences in L_{k-1}, couples of sequences (s, s') such that discarding the first element of the former and the last element of the latter results in two sequences fully matching. When such a condition holds for a couple (s, s'), a new candidate sequence is built by appending the last item of s' to s.
- The second sub-step is called the prune phase. Its objective is yielding the set of frequent k-sequences L_k. L_k is achieved by discarding from C_k, sequences not satisfying the minimum support. For yielding such a result, it is necessary to count the number of actual occurrences matching with any possible candidate sequence.

Candidate sequences are organized within a *hash-tree* data-structure which can be accessed efficiently. These sequences are stored in the leaves of the tree while intermediary nodes contain hashtables. Each data-sequence d is hashed to find the candidates contained in d. When browsing a data sequence, time constraints must be managed. It is performed by navigating through the tree in a downward or upward way resulting in a set of possible candidates. For each candidate, GSP checks whether it is contained in the data-sequence. Because of the sliding window, minimum and maximum time gaps, it is necessary to switch during examination between forward and backward phases. Forward phases are performed for dealing progressively items. Let us notice that during this operation the min-gap condition applies in order to skip itemsets too close from their precedent. And while selecting items, sliding window is used for resizing transaction cutting. Backward phases are required as soon as the max-gap condition no longer holds.

4 The PSP approach

Our approach fully resumes the fundamental principles of GSP. Its originality is to use a different hierarchical structure than in GSP for organizing candidate sequences, in order to improve efficiency of retrievals.

The general algorithm [7] is similar than in GSP. At each step k, the DB is browsed for counting the support of current candidates (procedure CANDIDATE-VERIFICATION). Then the frequent sequence set L_k can be built. From this set, new candidates are exhibited for being dealt at the next step (procedure CANDIDATE-GENERATION). The algorithm stops when the longest frequent sequences, embedded in the DB are discovered thus the candidate generation procedure yields an empty set of new candidates. Support is a function giving for each candidate its counting value stored in the tree structure.

The tree structure, managed by the algorithms, is a *prefix-tree* close to the structure used in [8]. At the kth step, the tree has a depth of k. It captures all the candidate k-sequences in the following way. Any branch, from the root to a leaf stands for a candidate sequence, and considering a single branch, each node at depth l ($k \geq l$) captures the lth item of the sequence. Furthermore, along with an item, a terminal node provides the support of the sequence from the root to the considered leaf (included). Transaction cutting is captured by using labelled edges. More precisely, let us consider two nodes, one being the child of the other. If the items embodied in the nodes originally occurred during different transactions, the edge linking the nodes is labelled with a '-' otherwise it is labelled with a '+' (dashed link in figure 2).

Example 2 Let us assume that we are given the following set of frequent 2-sequences : $L_2 = \{< (10) (30) >, < (10) (40) >, < (30) (20) >, < (30\,40) >, < (40\,10) >\}$. It is organized according to our tree structure as depicted in figure 2. Each terminal node contains an item and a counting value. If we consider the node having the item **40**, its associated value 2 means that two occurrences of the sequence $\{< (10) (40) >\}$ have been detected so far.

Proposition 1 *Our structure requires less memory than the tree used in the GSP approach.*

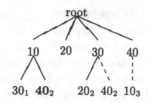

Fig. 2. Tree data structure

In GSP, due to the adopted tree structure, all candidates sequences are pre-served and fully stored in the leaves. We argue that our prefix-tree structure is less costly from a memory viewpoint because it organizes candidates according to their common elements. In fact, initial sub-sequences common to several candidates are stored only once.

Let us now detail how candidates and data-sequences are compared through the CANDIDATE-VERIFICATION algorithm. The data sequence is progressively browsed starting with its first item. Its time-stamp is preserved in the variable l_a. Then successive items in d are examined and the variable u_a is used for giving the time-stamp of the current item. Of course if $u_a - l_a = 0$, the couple of underlying items (and all possible items between them) appears in a single transaction. When u_a becomes different from l_a, this means that the new selected item belongs to a different transaction. However, we cannot consider that performed so far the algorithm has detected the first itemset of d because of the sliding window. Thus the examination must be continued until the selected item is too far from the very first item of d. The condition $u_a - l_a \geq ws$ does no longer hold. At this point, we are provided with a set of items (I_p). For each frequent item in I_p (it matches with a node at depth 1) the function FINDSEQUENCE is executed in order to retrieve all candidates supported by the first extracted itemset. The described process is then performed for exhibiting the second possible itemset. l_a is set to the time-stamp of the first itemset encountered and once again u_a is progressively incremented all along the examination. The process is repeated until the last itemset of the sequence has been dealt.

CANDIDATE VERIFICATION ALGORITHM
input: T the tree containing all candidate and frequent sequences, a data-sequence d and its sequence identifier *idseq*. The step k of the General Algorithm.
output: T the set of all candidate sequences contained in d.
$l_a = FirstItemSet(d).time();$
while ($l_a <= LastItemSet(d).time()$) **do**
   $u_a = l_a;$
   while (($u_a - l_a$) $< ws$) **do**
     $I_p = \{i_p \in d/i_p.time() \in [l_a, u_a]\};$
     for each $i_p \in I_p$ **do**
       if ($i_p \in root.Children$) **then**

```
        depth = 0;
        FindSequence(l_a, u_a, root.Children(i_p), i_p, d, idseq, depth);
     u_a = (u_a.succ()).time() ;
   l_a = (l_a.succ()).time();
```

The function FINDSEQUENCE is successively called by the previous algorithm for retrieving candidate sequences firstly beginning with a sub-set of the first item of d, then with the second, and so on. When a leaf is reached, the examined sub-sequence supports the candidate and its counting value must be incremented.

FIND SEQUENCE ALGORITHM
input: Two integers l_a, u_a standing for the itemset size, N, a node of T, i the item in d, the depth of the go down on the tree $(depth)$.
output: T updated with respect to constraint times.
if $(leaf(N)$ and $depth = k)$ **then**
  if $(idseq \neq N.idlast)$ **then**
    $N.idlast = idseq$; $N.cpt + +$;
else
  /* same transaction */
  $I_p = \{i_p \in d/i_p \; follows \; i \; and \; i_p.time() \in [l_a, u_a]\}$;
  for each $i_p \in I_p$ **do**
    if $(i_p \in N.Same)$ **then**
      $FindSequence(l_a, u_a, N.Same(i_p), i_p, d, idseq, depth + 1)$;
  /* other transaction */
  $l_b = (u_a.succ()).time()$; /*mingap constraint*/
  while $((l_b - u_a) < mingap)$ **do** $l_b = (l_b.succ()).time()$;
  while $(l_b \neq LastItem(d).time())$ **do**
    $u_b = l_b$;
    while $((u_b - l_b) < ws \; and \; (u_b - l_a) < maxgap)$ **do**
      $I_p = \{i_p \in d/i_p.time() \in [l_b, u_b]\}$;
      for each $i_p \in I_p$ **do**
        if $(i_p \in N.Other)$ **then**
        $FindSequence(l_b, u_b, N.Other(i_p), i_p, d, idseq, depth + 1)$;
      $u_b = (u_b.succ()).time()$;
    $l_b = (l_b.succ()).time()$;

When all the candidates to be examined are dealt, the tree is pruned in order to minimize required memory space. All leaves not satisfying the minimum support are removed. When such deletions complete, the tree no longer captures candidate sequences but instead frequent sequences.

Theorem 1 *For all data-sequence d and for all candidate sequence c in the tree T, if c is a sub-sequence of d then $c.support$ will be incremented by* CANDIDATE-VERIFICATION *and for all candidate sequence c' in T, if $c'.support$ is incremented by* CANDIDATE-VERIFICATION *then c' is a sub-sequence of d.*

Due to space limitation, we do not provide the proof of the theorems which could be found in [7].

The algorithm of candidate generation (defined in [7]) builds, step by step, the tree structure. At the beginning of step 2, the tree has a depth of 1. All nodes at depth 1 (frequent items) are provided with children supposed to capture all frequent items. This means that for each node, the created children are a copy of its brothers. When the kth step of the general algorithm is performed, the candidate generation operates on the tree of depth k and yields the tree of depth $k+1$. For each leaf in the tree, we must compute all its possible continuations of a single item. Exactly like at step 2, only frequent items can be valid continuations. Thus only items captured by nodes at depth 1 are considered. Moreover we refine this set of possible itemsets by discarding those which are not captured by a brother of the dealt leaf. The basic idea under such a selection is the following. Let us consider a frequent k-sequence s and assume that s extended with a frequent item i is still frequent. In such a case, $s' = < s_1 s_2 ... s_{k-1} \ i >$ must necessarily be exibited during the candidate verification phase. Thus s' is a frequent k-sequence and its only difference with s is its terminal item. Associated leaves, by construction of the tree, are brothers.

Theorem 2 *Given a database D, for each sequence of length k, the structures used in GSP and in our approach capture the very same set of candidate sequences.*

Experiments

The proposed approach is implemented on an Ultra Sparc with 256 MB main memory. For experimentation, we generate synthetic customer transactions using the data generation program of [2][1]. Due to space limitation, we do not provide detailed results which could be found in [7]. Figure 3 gives the execution times of our algorithm applied to two DB examples.

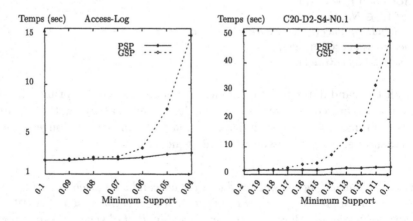

Fig. 3. Execution times

---

[1] Available at the following URL (*http://www.almaden.ibm.com/cs/quest*).

Discussion

Although our approach resumes GSP principles, we believe that the proposed prefix-structure is more efficient than the tree structure used in GSP. Before explaining why, let us have a comparative illustration.

Example 3 Figure 4 depicts the data structures used in our approach (left tree) and in GSP (right tree), managed at the very same step of the general algorithm. More precisely, from the frequent 2-sequences given in example 2, candidate 3-sequences are obtained. Thus we have C_3 =< (10) (40 10) > < (10) (30) (20) > < (10) (30 40) > < (40 10) (30) > < (40 10) (40) >. As stated in proposition 1, the number of items stored in our structure is significantly reduced compared with GSP.

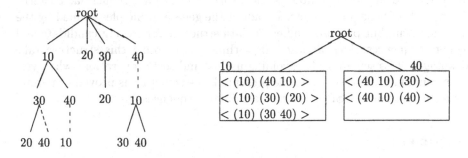

Fig. 4. Illustration of the prefix-tree and hash-tree structures

During the candidate verification phase in GSP, a navigation is performed through the tree until reaching a leaf storing several candidates. Then the algorithm operates a costly backtracking for examining each sequence stored in the leaf. In our approach, retrieving candidates means a mere navigation through the tree. Once a leaf is reached, the single operation to be performed is incrementing the support value.

In the tree structure of GSP, sequences grouped in terminal nodes share a common initial sub-sequence. Nevertheless, this feature is not used for optimizing retrievals. In fact, during the candidate verification phase, the GSP algorithm examines each sequence stored in the leaf from its first item to the last. In our approach, we make advantage of the proposed structure: all terminal nodes (at depth k) which are brothers stand for continuations of a common $(k-1)$-sequence. Thus it is costly and not necessary to examine this common sequence for all k-sequences extending it.

Moreover, the advantage of our tree-structure is increased by applying the following ideas. Let us imagine that a frequent k-sequence is extended to capture several $(k+1)$-candidates. Once the latter are proved to be unfrequent, they are of course pruned from the tree and the k-sequence is provided with a mark.

This mark avoids to attempt building possible continuations of the considered sequence during further steps. The mark is also used in order to avoid testing j-sequences $(2 < j < k)$.

Furthermore, at each step when a candidate k-sequence c is proved to be frequent, its possible sub-sequences of length l $(2 < l < k)$ ending with the k-1th item of c are examined. For each of which matching with a candidate l-sequence, the considered l-sequence is pruned from the tree. In fact, such sub-sequences are no longer relevant since longer sequences continuing them are discovered. Applying this principle reduces the number of stored candidates.

5   Conclusion

The presented approach addresses the problem of mining sequential patterns within a DB of behavioural facts. We adopt the general principles defined by the GSP algorithm but propose a different data structure for storing candidate and frequent sequences. The proposed algorithms for handling this structure take advantages of its semantics for avoiding useless and costly operations when verifying candidates. Furthermore, the presented tree structure is proved to require less memory than in GSP for storing candidate sequences.

References

1. R. Agrawal, T. Imielinski, and A. Swami. Mining Association Rules between Sets of Items in Large Databases. In *Proc. of the SIGMOD'93*, Washington, 1993.
2. R. Agrawal and R. Srikant. Fast Algorithms for Mining Generalized Association Rules. In *Proc. of the VLDB'94*, Santiago, Chile, September 1994.
3. R. Agrawal and R. Srikant. Mining Sequential Patterns. In *Proc. of the ICDE'95*, Tapei, Taiwan, March 1995.
4. S. Brin, R. Motwani, J.D. Ullman, and S. Tsur. Dynamic Itemset Counting and Implication Rules for Market Basket Data. In *Proc. of the SIGMOD'97*.
5. U.M. Fayad, G. Piatetsky-Shapiro, P. Smyth, and R. Uthurusamy, editors. *Advances in Knowledge Discovery and Data Mining*. AAAI Press, 1996.
6. H. Mannila, H. Toivonen, and A.I. Verkamo. Discovery of Frequent Episodes in Event Sequences. *Data Mining and Knowledge Discovery*, 1(3), 1997.
7. F. Masseglia. Le pré-calcul appliqué à l'extraction de motifs séquentiels en data mining. Technical report, LIRMM, France, June 1998.
8. A. Mueller. Fast Sequential and Parallel Algorithms for Association Rules Mining: A Comparison. Technical Report CS-TR-3515, Univ. Maryland-College, 1995.
9. A. Savasere, E. Omiecinski, and S. Navathe. An Efficient Algorithm for Mining Association Rules in Large Databases. In *Proc. of the VLDB'95*, Zurich, 1995.
10. R. Srikant and R. Agrawal. Mining Sequential Patterns: Generalizations and Performance Improvements. In *Proc. of the EDBT'96*, Avignon, France, Sept 1996.
11. H. Toivonen. Sampling Large Databases for Association Rules. In *Proc. of the VLDB'96*, September 1996.

Knowledge Discovery in Spatial Data by Means of ILP

Luboš Popelínský

Faculty of Informatics, Masaryk University Brno and
Faculty of Electrical Engineering, CTU Prague
Czech Republic
Email: popel@fi.muni.cz

Abstract. We show that inductive logic programming(ILP) is a powerful tool for spatial data mining. We further develop the direction started (or symbolised) by *GeoMiner* [9] and argue that the technique developed for database schema design in deductive object-oriented databases is fully usable for spatial mining and overcome, in expressive power, some other mining methods. An inductive query language, with richer semantics, is proposed and three kinds of inductive queries are described. Two of them are improved versions of *DBMiner* [8] rules. The third kind of rules, dependency rules, allow to compare two or more subsets. Then a description of *GWiM* mining system as well as results reached by the system are given. We conclude with discussion of weaknesses of the method. [1]

1 Knowledge Discovery in Spatial Data

Knowledge discovery in geographic data is, no doubts, challenging and very important. However, the classical KDD, either statistical or based on machine learning, are not convenient for the task. The spatial data have to be managed by means that respect(and exploit) their structural nature. Moreover, non-spatial data need to be used, too, e.g. to find a region with some non-spatial characteristics. Main tasks when mining geographic data [13] are, among others, understanding data, discovering relationship as well as (re)organising geographic databases. This paper addresses those three tasks. We show that inductive logic programming(ILP) is a powerful tool for spatial data mining.

2 Mining Knowledge by Means of ILP

Inductive Logic Programming (ILP) [14] is a research area in the intersection of machine learning and computational logic. The main goal is development of a

---

[1] The initial portion of this work was done during author's stay in LRI Université Paris-Sud thanks to French government scholarship. This work has been partially supported by Esprit LTR 20237 Inductive Logic Programming II ILP².

theory and algorithms for inductive reasoning in first-order logic. ILP aims to construct a theory covering given facts. Given a set of positive examples E^+, a set of negative examples E^-, we construct a logic program P such that $P \vdash E^+$ and $P \not\vdash E^-$. In case of noisy data we aim at a first-order logic formula that describes a significant majority of positive examples and may be a non-significant part of negative examples.

Since early 90'th there are attempts to exploit ILP in knowledge discovery in databases [4]. $CLAUDINE$ [2] can learn both data dependencies and integrity constraints in relational databases. A problem of mining association rules in multiple relations has been solved in [3]. Interactive system that provides support for inductive database design is presented in [1].

■

In [15] we addressed the possibilities of inductive logic programming (ILP) in restructuring object-oriented database schema. In deductive object-oriented databases, both classes and attributes as well as methods may be defined by rules. We showed that inductive logic programming can help in synthesis of those rules to support the database schema design and modification.

Exploiting that method we further develop the direction started(or symbolised) by $GeoMiner$ [9]. We argue that the technique developed for database schema design in deductive object-oriented databases is fully usable for spatial mining. $GWiM$ system is presented that outperforms in some aspects $GeoMiner$. Namely $GWiM$ can mine a richer class of knowledge, Horn clauses. Background knowledge used in $GeoMiner$ may be expressed only in the form of hierarchies. $GWiM$ accepts any background knowledge that is expressible in a subset of object-oriented F-logic [12].

In the Section 3. we demonstrate the method on the simple mining task. Then an inductive query language is described. A description of $GWiM$ mining system is given in Section 5. We conclude with discussion of results and mainly the weaknesses of the method. We propose solutions how to improve the mining method.

3 Example

We will demonstrate a data mining task on the database in Pic.1 . The $BRIDGE$ class consists of all road bridges over rivers. Each bridge has two attributes – Object1 (a road) and Object2 (a river). Each river (as well as roads and railways) inherits an attribute $Geometry$ (a sequence of (x,y) coordinates) from the class $LINEAR$. Objects of a class $RIVER$ has no more attributes but Named of the river. In a class $ROAD$, the attribute State says whether the road is under construction (state=0) or not. The Importance defines a kind of the road: 1 stands for highways, 2 for other traffic roads, and 3 for the rest(e.g. private ones).

Our goal is to find a description of the class $HIGHWAY\_BRIDGE$ in terms of other classes in the given database.

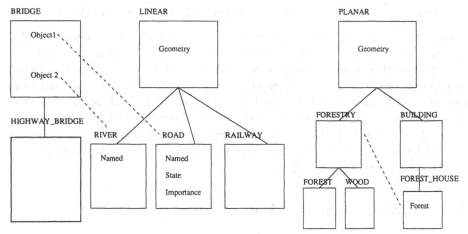

Pic. 1: Object-oriented database schema

That task is expressed in inductive query language (for a full description see Section 4) as

> **extract characteristic rule**
> **for** highway_bridge.

Let us have 2 rivers with object identifiers `river1`,`river2`, named Svratka and Svitava, and two roads (with object identifiers `road1`, `road2`) a highway D1 and a state road E7 that cross those rivers. E.g. an object `bridge1` can be expressed in first order logic(FOL) [2] as

```
bridge(bridge1) :- object1(bridge1,road1),
    object2(bridge1,river1).

road(road1) :- named(road1,'D1'),
    geometry(road1,[(375,500),(385,350), ... ]),
    state(road1,1),importance(road1,1).

river(river1) :- named(river1,'Svratka'),
    geometry(river1,[(0,40),(40,60),(77,76), ... ]).
```

All instances of the class *HIGHWAY_BRIDGE* are as positive examples. The rest of members of the class *BRIDGE* serves as negative examples. Then the expected results is as

```
highway_bridge(X):-object1(X,Y),importance(Y,1).
```

GWiM starts with a minimal language which consists of `object1`, `object2` attributes of the class *HIGHWAY_BRIDGE* itself. The best clause being found

---

[2] Actually, *GWiM* works with object-oriented F-logic. Here we prefer to use FOL what is an internal representation of *GWiM* system. More on translation from/to F-logic, see [15].

```
highway_bridge(X):-bridge(X),object1(X,Y),object2(X,Z).
```

is over-general as it covers all negative examples. In that case when no solution is found, the language is extended by adding attributes from neighbouring classes(either super/subclasses or referenced classes). If there is a referenced class, the most general superclass is added first. In our case, an attribute **geometry** of the class $LINEAR$ (both for $RIVER$ and $ROAD$) has been added. As it does not help, the language has been further enriched by attributes of classes $RIVER, ROAD$, i.e. **State, Importance** and **Named**. For this language, $GWiM$ has eventually found a logic formula that successfully discriminates between positive and negative examples.

4 Language for Spatial Data Mining

In this section we present three kinds of inductive queries. Two of them, that ask for characteristic and discriminate rules, are adaptation of $DBMiner$ [8] rules. The dependency rules add a new quality to the inductive query language. The general syntactic form, adapted from $DBMiner$ of the language is as follows.

> **extract** < KindOfRule > **rule for** < NameOfTarget >
> [**from** < ListOfClasses >] [< Constraints >]
> [**from point of view** < Explicit Domain Knowledge >] .

Semantics of those rule differs from that of $DBMiner$. Namely < Explicit Domain Knowledge > is a list of predicates and/or hierarchy of predicates. At least one of them has to appear in the answer to the query. Actually a clause **from point of view** enables to specify a criterion of interestingness [5]. The answer to those inductive queries is a first-order logic formula which characterises the subset of the database which is specified by the rule.

Characteristic Rule. Characteristic rules serve for a description of a class which exists in the database or for a description of a subset of a database. The example of that kind of rule has been shown in Section 3 . See 6.1, too.

Discriminate Rule. Discriminate rules find a difference between two classes which exist in the database, or between two subsets of the database. They allow to find a quantitative description of a class in contrast to another one.

> **extract discriminate rule**
> **for** < NameOfClass >
> [**where** < ConstraintOnClass >]
> **in contrast to** < ClassOfCounterExamples >
> [**where** < ConstraintOnCounterExamples >]
> [**from point of view** < DomainKnowledge >] .

Positive examples of the concept < NameOfTarget > are described by

> **for** < NameOfClass >
> **where** < ConstraintOfListOfClasses >

negative examples are described by

from < ListOfClasses >
in contrast to < ClassOfCounterExamples >
where < Constraint On Counterexamples >

E.g. forests have an area greater than 100 hectares. Woods serve as counterexamples there. For an example, see 6.2.

Dependency Rule. Dependency rules aim to find a dependency between different classes. In opposite to discriminate rules, dependency rules look for a qualitative characterisation of a difference between two classes.

extract dependency rule
for < NameOfClass >
from < ListOfClasses >
[**where** < ConstraintOnClasses >]
[**from point of view** < DomainKnowledge >] .

The objects are defined by the **from ... where ... from point of view ...** formula. The target predicate < NameOfTarget > is of arity equal to a number of classes in < ListOfClasses >. E.g. for forests and woods, an area of a forest is always greater than an area of a wood. See 6.3 for an example.

5 Description of *GWiM*

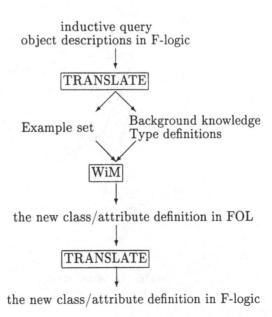

inductive query
object descriptions in F-logic
↓
TRANSLATE

Example set   Background knowledge
                Type definitions

WiM
↓
the new class/attribute definition in FOL
↓
TRANSLATE
↓
the new class/attribute definition in F-logic

Pic. 2: *GWiM* schema

GWiM is built upon the *WiM* ILP system. *WiM* [6, 11], a program for synthesis of closed Horn clauses further elaborates the approach of *MIS* [17] and *Markus* [7]. It works in top-down manner and uses shift of language bias. Moreover, a second-order schema, as a part of *WiM* truth maintenance system, can be defined which the learned program has to much. This schema definition can significantly increase an efficiency of the learning process because only the synthesised programs which match the schema are verified on the learning set.

6 Results

In this section we will demonstrate (in)capabilities of *GWiM*. The geographic data set contains descriptions of 31 roads, 4 rails, 7 forest/woods, and 59 buildings [3]. Geographic data are on the Pic.3. The thick lines are rivers. Learning sets that has been generated from those raw data by *GWiM* are in the following table.

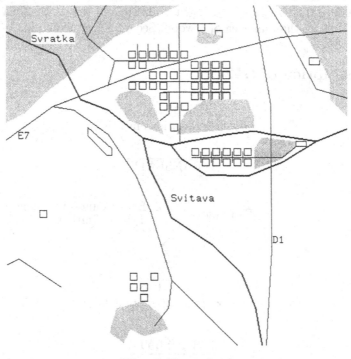

Pic. 3: Raw data

---

[3] See http://www.gmd.de/ml-archive/frames/datasets/ilprev/ilprev-frames.html for more information

	# positive	# negative
bridge	2	1
forest	3	4
forestOrWood	7	7

Tab.1: Summary of results

In following paragraph, particular mining tasks are described.

6.1 Bridge with Additional Domain Knowledge

Find a description of bridge in terms of attributes of classes *road*, *river*, using a predicate *common(X, Y)*. That predicate succeeds if geometries X and Y has a common point.

| extract characteristic rule |
| for bridge |
| from road, river |
| from point of view common. |

```
bridge(X,Y):-
    object1(X,Z),geometry(Z,G1),
    object2(Y,U),geometry(U,G2),
    common(G1,G2).
```

6.2 Discrimination of Forests and Woods

Find a difference between forests and woods from the point of view of area. *area* is the name of set of predicates like *area(Geometry, Area)*.

| extract discriminate rule |
| for forest |
| in contrast to wood |
| from point of view area. |

```
forest(F) :-
    geometry(F,GForest),
    area(GForest,Area),
    100 < Area.
```

6.3 Relation between Forests and Woods

Find a relation between forests and woods from the point of view of area. *area* is the name of set of predicates like *area(Geometry, Area)*.

| extract dependency rule |
| for forestOrWood |
| from forest, wood |
| from point of view area. |

```
forestOrWood(F,W) :-
    geometry(F,GF),area(GF,FA),
    geometry(W,GW), area(GW,WA),
    WA<GA.
```

7 Towards Discovery in Real Databases

The query language is quite powerful. It means that even quite complex queries can be formulated. However, the price that user has to pay for is sometimes too big. Namely an explicit domain knowledge has to be declared almost exactly (see examples above). To avoid that drawback, more meta-knowledge is needed, both on the particular database and on the spatial relations. We point out that the meta-knowledge can be easily expressed in F-logic and exploited in *GWiM* truth maintenance system.

Another fault concerns *GWiM*'s incapability to process large amount of data. However, even there is a way out. The general-to-specific learning method of *GWiM* consists of 2 phases. In the first step a promising clause is generated which is, in the second step, tested on the example set. Complexity of the generation step does not practicaly depend on cardinality of the example set. Moreover, in the testing step, it seems be straightforward to employ the database management system(DBMS) itself. Actually, we only need to know how many examples (both positive and negative) is (un)covered by the promising clause. It remains to implement a communication channel connecting an ILP system, with the DBMS. *WiM* can work in interactive mode [16]. There are oracles that allow to ask for examples an external device and even evaluate a given hypothesis on external data. A hypothesis is first translated into a (sequence of) SQL queries. The answers are then evaluate and the hypothesis is either specialised(if some positive examples are newly covered by the hypothesis and some negative examples are covered, too) or accepted as an answer to the particular inductive query.

We will demonstrate it again on the same example as in Section 3. Let us have 2 positive examples and 1 negative example and let the minimal success rate for a hypothesis to be accepted be set to 1 – all positive examples need to be covered and none of negative ones does. An initial portion of examples is randomly chosen from the database employing *random oracle*. Let we ask for just 1 positive example. The learned hypothesis

```
highway_bridge(X) :- bridge(X),object1(X,Y),object2(X,Z)
```

has to be verified using the full database. A *success rate oracle* is called that returns the percentage of correctly covered positive examples and correctly uncovered negative examples. The result is 2/3 as there is 1 negative example covered. Thus the hypothesis is over-general and need to be further specialised. The process continues until the limit for a minimal success rate is reached.

8 Conclusion

We have presented *GWiM* system for mining spatial data. The system outperforms in some aspects *GeoMiner*, namely it can mine a richer class of knowledge, Horn clauses. *GWiM*, too, accepts any background knowledge that is expressible in a subset of object-oriented F-logic i.e. richer than those one exploited by *GeoMiner*. It seems not to be hopeless to apply that approach in a warehouse technology [10]. The most serious problem is the computational complexity of the current implementation. A way how to solve it as been proposed in the previous section.

Acknowledgements

The main part of the work has been done during my stay at LRI Université Paris-Sud. Thanks are mainly due to Yves Kodratoff and I&A group members. I thank, too, database research team at LRI Universite Paris-Sud for their assistance. The first version of $GWiM$ has been implemented by Petr Lecián. Last but not least, I thank to Olga Štěpánková and members of Gerstner Laboratory at CTU Prague for fruitful discussions and to anonymous referees for their comments.

References

1. Blockeel H., De Raedt L.: Inductive Database Design. Accepted for Applied Artificial Intelligence, special issue on first order knowledge discovery in databases.
2. Dehaspe L., Van Laer W., De Raedt L.: Applications of a logical discovery engine. In: [18].
3. Dehaspe L., De Raedt L.: Mining Association Rules in Multiple Relations. In Proc. of ILP'97 pp.125-133, LNAI Springer-Verlag
4. Džeroski S., Lavrač: Inductive Learning in Deductive Databases. IEEE Trans. on Knowledge and Data Engineering, Vol 5. No. 6, December 1993.
5. Fayyad, U.M., Piatetski-Shapiro G., Smyth P.: From Data Mining to Knowledge Discovery: An Overview. In: Advances in Knowledge Discovery and Data Mining. AAAI Press/ The MIT Press, Menlo Park, California (1996) 1-34.
6. Flener P., Popelínský L. Štěpánková: ILP nad Automatic Programming: Towards three approaches. In: [18].
7. Grobelnik M.: Induction of Prolog programs with Markus. In Deville Y.(ed.) Proceedings of LOPSTR'93. Workshops in Computing Series, pages 57-63,Springer-Verlag, 1994.
8. Han et al.: DMQL: A Data Mining Query Language for Relational Databases. In: ACM-SIGMOD'96 Workshop on Data Mining
9. J. Han, K. Koperski, and N. Stefanovic: GeoMiner: A System Prototype for Spatial Data Mining, Proc. 1997 ACM-SIGMOD Int'l Conf. on Management of Data(SIGMOD'97), Tucson, Arizona, May1997(System prototype demonstration)
10. Kouba Z., Matoušek K., Mikšovský P., Štěpánková O. : On Updating the Data Warehouse from Multiple Data Sources. In: Proceedings of DEXA'98, Vienna 1998.
11. Lavrač N., Džeroski, Kazakov D., Štěpánková O.: ILPNET repositories on WWW: Inductive Logic Programming systems, datasets and bibliography. AI Communications Vol.9, No.4, 1996, pp. 157-206 .
12. Kifer M., Lausen G., Wu J.: Logical Foundations of Object-Oriented and Frame-Based Languages. TR 93/06, Dept. of Comp. Sci. SUNY at Stony Brook, NY, March 1994 (accepted to Journal of ACM).
13. Koperski K., Han J., Adhikary J.: Mining Knowledge in Geographical Data. To appear in Comm.of ACM 1998
14. Muggleton S., De Raedt L.: Inductive Logic Programming: Theory And Methods. J. Logic Programming 1994:19,20:629-679.
15. Popelínský L.: Inductive inference to support object-oriented analysis and design. In: Proc. of 3rd JCKBSE Conference, Smolenice 1998, IOS Press.
16. Popelínský L.: Interactive WiM: User Guide. 1998
17. Shapiro Y.: Algorithmic Program Debugging. MIT Press, 1983.
18. Wrobel S.(ed.): Proc. of 4th Workshop on Inductive Logic Programming ILP'94, Bad Honeff,Germany, 1994.

Querying Inductive Databases:
A Case Study on the MINE RULE Operator

Jean-François Boulicaut*, Mika Klemettinen, and Heikki Mannila

University of Helsinki, Department of Computer Science
P.O. Box 26, FIN–00014 University of Helsinki, Finland
e-mail:{boulicau,mklemett,mannila}@cs.helsinki.fi

Abstract. Knowledge discovery in databases (KDD) is a process that can include steps like forming the data set, data transformations, discovery of patterns, searching for exceptions to a pattern, zooming on a subset of the data, and postprocessing some patterns. We describe a comprehensive framework in which all these steps can be carried out by means of queries over an *inductive database*. An inductive database is a database that in addition to data also contains intensionally defined generalizations about the data. We formalize this concept: an inductive database consists of a normal database together with a subset of patterns from a class of patterns, and an evaluation function that tells how the patterns occur in the data. Then, looking for potential query languages built on top of SQL, we consider the research on the MINE RULE operator by Meo, Psaila and Ceri. It is a serious step towards an implementation framework for inductive databases, though it addresses only the association rule mining problem. Perspectives are then discussed.

1 Introduction

Data mining sets new challenges to database technology and new concepts and methods are needed for general purpose query languages [9]. A possible approach is to formulate a data mining task as locating interesting sentences from a given logic that are true in the database. Then the task of the user/analyst can be viewed as querying this set, the so-called *theory* of the database. Formally, given a language $\mathcal{L}$ of sentences (or patterns), the theory of the database $\mathbf{r}$ with respect to $\mathcal{L}$ and a selection predicate q is the set $Th(\mathbf{r}, \mathcal{L}, q) = \{\theta \in \mathcal{L} \mid q(\mathbf{r}, \theta)\}$. The predicate q indicates whether a sentence of the language is interesting. This definition is quite general: asserting $q(\mathbf{r}, \theta)$ might mean that θ is a property that holds, that almost holds, or that defines (in some way) an interesting subgroup of $\mathbf{r}$. This approach has been more or less explicitly used for various data mining tasks (see [12] for a survey and [13] for a detailed study of this setting).

Discovering knowledge from data can be seen as a process containing several steps: understanding the domain, preparing the data set, discovering patterns, postprocessing of discovered patterns, and putting the results into use [6]. This is an interactive and iterative process for which many related theories have to

---

* On sabbatical leave from INSA Lyon (F). This work is partly supported by AFFRST, Association Franco-Finlandaise pour la Recherche Scientifique et Technique.

be computed: different selection predicates and also classes of patterns might be used. Therefore, a general-purpose query language should enable the user to select subsets of data, but also to specify and select patterns. It should also support crossing the boundary between data and patterns, e.g., when exceptions to a pattern are to be analysed or for sophisticated postprocessing methods like rule covering [17]. This has motivated the concept of *inductive databases*, i.e., databases that contain inductive generalizations about the data, in addition to the usual data [9].

The contribution of this paper concerns a formalization of this concept of inductive database and a first approach for an implementation based on SQL servers. The formalization carries a twopart basic message: (i) an inductive database consists of a normal database associated to a subset of patterns from a class of patterns, and an evaluation function that tells how the patterns occur in the data; (ii) an inductive database can be queried (in principle) just by using a straightforward extension of relational algebra. This point of view is also considered in [3] although that paper has a different focus: it considers the add-value of this framework for KDD process modeling. The search for solutions based on SQL is motivated by the industrial perspective of relational database mining. A huge amount of work has already been done to provide efficient and portable implementations of SQL, and tightly-coupled architectures between SQL servers and data mining systems are being developed. As a starting point, we study the **MINE RULE** operator proposed by Meo, Psaila and Ceri [14, 15] and consider its connections with our framework.

The paper is organized as follows. In Section 2 we define the inductive database framework. Section 3 is an overview of the **MINE RULE** operator. Section 4 is a discussion of the adequacy of this proposal as an inductive database implementation framework. Section 5 is a short conclusion.

2 Inductive Databases

Our goal is to describe a data model that makes it possible to view the whole KDD process as querying a database structured according to the model. Thus the database has to contain both data and generalizations about that data. This motivates the following definition (simplified from the one in [11]).

Schema The *schema of an inductive database* is a pair $\mathcal{R} = (\mathbf{R}, (\mathcal{Q_R}, e, \mathcal{V}))$, where $\mathbf{R}$ is a database schema, $\mathcal{Q_R}$ is a collection of patterns, $\mathcal{V}$ is a set of *result values*, and e is the *evaluation function* that defines how patterns occur in the data. This function maps each pair $(\mathbf{r}, \theta_i)$ to an element of $\mathcal{V}$, where $\mathbf{r}$ is a database over $\mathbf{R}$ and θ_i is a pattern from $\mathcal{Q_R}$.

Instance An *instance* $(\mathbf{r}, s)$ of an inductive database over the schema $\mathcal{R}$ consists of a database $\mathbf{r}$ over the schema $\mathbf{R}$ and a subset $s \subseteq \mathcal{Q_R}$.

The simple association rule mining problem has received much attention since its introduction in [1]. The concept of inductive database is quite general and is not dedicated to this class of patterns. However, for didactic reasons, we use it in our examples.

s_0	e(r_0).f	e(r_0).c		s_1	e(r_1).f	e(r_1).c
$A \Rightarrow B$	0.25	0.33		$A \Rightarrow B$	0.33	0.33
$A \Rightarrow C$	0.50	0.66		$A \Rightarrow C$	0.66	0.66
$B \Rightarrow A$	0.25	0.50		$B \Rightarrow A$	0.33	1.00
$B \Rightarrow C$	0.50	1.00		$B \Rightarrow C$	0.33	1.00
$C \Rightarrow A$	0.50	0.66		$C \Rightarrow A$	0.66	1.00
$C \Rightarrow B$	0.50	0.66		$C \Rightarrow B$	0.33	0.50
$AB \Rightarrow C$	0.25	1.00		$AB \Rightarrow C$	0.33	1.00
$AC \Rightarrow B$	0.25	0.50		$AC \Rightarrow B$	0.33	0.50
$BC \Rightarrow A$	0.25	0.50		$BC \Rightarrow A$	0.33	1.00

s_2	e(r_2).f	e(r_2).c
$B \Rightarrow C$	0.50	1.00

Instance r_0

A	B	C
1	0	0
1	1	1
1	0	1
0	1	1

Table 1. Patterns in three instances of an inductive database.

Example 1 Given a schema $R = \{A_1, \ldots, A_n\}$ of attributes with domain $\{0, 1\}$, and a relation r over R, an *association rule* about r is an expression of the form $X \Rightarrow B$, where $X \subseteq R$ and $B \in R \setminus X$ [1]. Intuitively, if a row of the matrix r has a 1 in each column of X, then the row tends to have a 1 also in column B. This semantics is captured by *frequency* and *confidence* values. Given $W \subseteq \mathbf{R}$, $freq(W, \mathbf{r})$ denotes the fraction of rows of $\mathbf{r}$ that have a 1 in each column of W. The frequency of the rule $X \Rightarrow B$ in $\mathbf{r}$ is defined to be $freq(X \cup \{B\}, \mathbf{r})$ while its confidence is $freq(X \cup \{B\}, \mathbf{r})/freq(X, \mathbf{r})$. Typically, we are interested in association rules for which the frequency and the confidence are greater than given thresholds. However, we can define an inductive database such that $\mathcal{Q}_R$ contains all association rules, i.e., $\mathcal{Q}_R = \{X \Rightarrow B \mid X \subseteq R, B \in R \setminus X\}$. In this case, $\mathcal{V}$ is the set $[0, 1]^2$, and $e(\mathbf{r}, \theta) = (f(\mathbf{r}, \theta), c(\mathbf{r}, \theta))$, where $f(\mathbf{r}, \theta)$ and $c(\mathbf{r}, \theta)$ are the frequency and the confidence of the rule θ in the database $\mathbf{r}$. □

Queries A typical KDD process operates on both of the components of an inductive database. At each stage of manipulating the inductive database $(\mathbf{r}, s)$, the user can think that the value of $e(\mathbf{r}, \theta)$ is available for each pattern θ which is present in the set s. Obviously, if the pattern class is large, an implementation will not compute all the values of the evaluation function beforehand; rather, only those values $e(\mathbf{r}, \theta)$ that user's queries require to be computed should be computed. Mining association rules as defined in Example 1 is now considered as querying inductive database instances of schema $(R, (\mathcal{Q}_R, e, [0, 1]^2))$.

Example 2 Assume the dataset is the instance r_0 in Table 1 of the schema $R = \{A, B, C\}$. The inductive database $idb = (r_0, s_0)$ associates to r_0 the rules on the leftmost table of Table 1. We illustrate the selection on tuples (Q_1) and the selection on patterns (Q_2).

1. (Q_1) Select tuples from (r_0, s_0) for which the value for A is not 0. The result is a new instance (r_1, s_1) where the data part r_1 does not contain the tuple $(0, 1, 1)$, and the pattern part s_1 contains the rules in the middle table of Table 1, i.e., the rules of s_0 with updated frequency and confidence values.
2. (Q_2) Select rules from (r_0, s_0) that exceed the frequency and confidence thresholds 0.5 and 0.7, respectively. A new instance (r_0, s_2) is provided where s_2 contains the rules in the rightmost table of Table 1.

An important feature is that operations can be composed due to the *closure property*: an operation takes an instance of an inductive database and provides a new instance. For instance, the query $Q_2 \circ Q_1$ if applied to (r_0, s_0) gives (r_3, s_3), where r_3 is r_1 as defined above and s_3 is reduced to the association rule $C \Rightarrow A$ with frequency 0.66 and confidence 1. □

Query Languages Using the above definition for inductive databases it is easy to formulate query languages for them. For example, we can write relational algebra queries, where in addition to the normal operations we can also refer to the patterns and the value of the evaluation function on the patterns. To refer to the values of $e(\mathbf{r}, \theta)$ for any $\theta \in s$, we can think in terms of object-oriented databases: the evaluation function e is a method that encodes the behavior of the patterns in the data.

For the association rule example, it motivates the notations $e(\mathbf{r}).f$ and $e(\mathbf{r}).c$ when values for frequency and confidence are needed. Furthermore, it is useful to consider that other properties of patterns should be available; as for instance, the values for part of them, their lengths, etc. Following an abstract data type approach, we can consider operations that provide theses properties. Hence, continuing Example 1, we use *body*, *lbody* and *head* to denote respectively the value of the left-hand side, its length and the value of the right-hand side of an association rule. More generally, specifying an inductive database requires the definition of all these properties.

We now give a few queries by using, hopefully, self-explanatory notations for the simple extension of the relational algebra that fits to our need. Selection of tuple and patterns are respectively denoted by σ and τ. As it is clear from the context, the operation is also applied on inductive database instances, e.g., we write $\sigma_C((r, s))$ to denote $(\sigma_C(r), s)$.

Example 3 We now consider association rules in the concrete and popular context of the basket analysis problem. Assume data is available in an instance of the schema $R =$ (Tid, Item, Price, Date). Tid denotes the transaction identifier, Item the product purchased, Price its price and finally, Date the date for this transaction. By (r, s) we denote an inductive database for association rules between itemsets; s_0 denotes the intensionally defined collection of all these rules. Table 2(a) gives a dataset called r_0 in the sequel and one sample collection of patterns with their properties and answers in r_0. Notice that such a collection can typically be stored in a nested relation, e.g., an SQL3 table [10].

Consider the following process. First, the user decides to look at association rules derived from r_0, the dataset for the current month, and he/she wants to prune out all rules that have confidence under 30% or frequency under 5% or more than 7 items (phase 1 in Table 2(b)). Then, he/she decides to focus on the rules that hold for the data about the last discount day (say Date = 13) and to restrict to 5 the maximum amount of items in the rule (phase 2). Then, he/she wants to eliminate all the patterns that contain item D in their body. Finally, he/she tries to get association rules that imply expensive items (say Price ≥ 7). A lower threshold for frequency (say 1%) is considered for phase 4. □

Different types of KDD processes are easily described using the notion of inductive database. The key is the closure property, which makes the composition of queries possible [3].

Tid	Item	Price	Date
1	A	7	1
2	A	7	1
2	B	5	1
2	C	9	1
3	A	7	1
3	C	9	1
4	B	5	1
4	C	9	1

body	head	lbody	$e(r_0).f$	$e(r_0).c$
$\{A\}$	$\{B\}$	1	0.25	0.33
$\{A\}$	$\{C\}$	1	0.50	0.66
$\{A,B\}$	$\{C\}$	2	0.25	1
$\{A,C\}$	$\{B\}$	2	0.25	0.5

(a)

Phase	Query and conditions
1	$\tau_{F_1}((r_0, s_0)) = (r_0, s_1)$ $F_1 = e(r_0).f \geq 0.05 \wedge e(r_0).c \geq 0.3 \wedge$ $lbody \leq 6$
2	$\tau_{F_2}(\sigma_{C_1}((r_0, s_0))) = (r_1, s_2)$ $C_1 = (Date = 13)$ $F_2 = e(r_1).f \geq 0.05 \wedge e(r_1).c \geq 0.3 \wedge$ $lbody \leq 4$
3	$\tau_{F_3}((r_1, s_2)) = (r_1, s_3)$ $F_3 = D \not\subseteq body$
4	$\tau_{F_4}(\sigma_{C_2}((r_1, s_0))) = (r_2, s_4)$ $C_2 = (Price \geq 7)$ $F_4 = e(r_2).f \geq 0.01 \wedge e(r_2).c \geq 0.3 \wedge$ $lbody \leq 4 \wedge D \not\subseteq body$

(b)

Table 2. *Basket data as an inductive database (a) and a few queries (b).*

3 MINE RULE Operator

In the following, we provide an overview of the MINE RULE operator [14, 15] and then discuss how it can be related to our framework for inductive databases. MINE RULE is an SQL-like operator which captures most of the association rule mining tasks that have been formulated so far (simple or generalized association rules, association rules with item hierarchies, etc). Moreover, there are quite efficient evaluation techniques that ensure the possibility of solving these mining tasks. It is not possible here to consider all the aspects of such an operator. We introduce it by means of one typical example and refer to [14] for other examples and a complete definition of its syntax and operational semantics.

Given the dataset r_1 as defined in Table 2, phase 4 is defined by the MINE RULE statement in Table 3. The MINE RULE operator takes a relational database and produces an SQL3 table [10] in which each tuple denotes a mined rule.

Several possibilities exist to precisely define the input data. Basically, the whole potential of SQL can be used here. The input tables might themselves have been selected using the second WHERE clause. Rules are extracted from groups as defined by a GROUP BY clause (frequency is related to groups and if the clause is missing, any tuple is a group). The schema of the output table is determined by the SELECT clause that defines the structure of the rules (here, BODY, HEAD, SUPPORT and CONFIDENCE). Sizes of the two components of a rule can be bounded (4 and 1 in our example). The keyword DISTINCT specifies that duplicates are not allowed in these components.

Data is encoded such that one gets all possible couples of itemsets (extracted from the groups) for the body and the head of a rule. It is possible to express mining conditions (first WHERE clause) that limit the tuples involved in this en-

```
MINE RULE s₁ AS
SELECT DISTINCT
        1..6 Item AS BODY,
        1..1 Item AS HEAD,            SELECT * AS s₃
        SUPPORT, CONFIDENCE          FROM s₂
FROM r₀                              WHERE D NOT IN BODY
GROUP BY Tid
EXTRACTING RULES WITH
        SUPPORT: 0.05,
        CONFIDENCE: 0.03
        (Phase 1)                          (Phase 3)
```

```
MINE RULE s₂ AS                     MINE RULE s₄ AS
SELECT DISTINCT                     SELECT DISTINCT
        1..4 Item AS BODY,                  1..4 Item AS BODY,
        1..1 Item AS HEAD,                  1..1 Item AS HEAD,
        SUPPORT, CONFIDENCE                 SUPPORT, CONFIDENCE
FROM (SELECT * AS r₁                WHERE BODY.Item <> D
    FROM r₀                         FROM (SELECT * AS r₂
    WHERE Date = 13)                    FROM r₁
GROUP BY Tid                            WHERE Price >= 7)
EXTRACTING RULES WITH               GROUP BY Tid
        SUPPORT: 0.05,             EXTRACTING RULES WITH
        CONFIDENCE: 0.3                     SUPPORT: 0.01,
                                            CONFIDENCE: 0.3
        (Phase 2)                          (Phase 4)
```

Table 3. *Phases 1 to 4 of Table 2 using* **MINE RULE**.

coding. In our example, the mining condition indicates that **Item** in the body should not be D. An interesting feature is that mining conditions can be different for body and head, e.g., **BODY.price < 7 AND HEAD.price >= 7** indicates that one wants association rules with cheap products (less than 7) in the body and an expensive product in the head. It is possible to choose the types of the elements in the rules (e.g., **Price** instead of **Item**) as well as grouping attributes. This enables the specification of many different mining tasks over the same dataset. Another important feature of **MINE RULE** is the possibility to consider clusters. One can require that the body and the head of mined rules refer to clusters within the same group. Typically, it makes possible to look for association rule of items purchased at the same date if a **CLUSTER BY** clause on the **Date** attribute is used. In fact, most of the association rule mining tasks identified in the literature can be specified by means of a **MINE RULE** statement.

The architecture proposed in [15] has been designed on top of an SQL-server. It is a tightly-coupled architecture that provides a closure property: the user can materialize the selected dataset as well as the collection of association rules that hold in the dataset and satisfy its mining requirements. Data and patterns are then a collection of SQL3 tables. The phases of the simple scenario given in Table 2(b) are easily translated into **MINE RULE** queries as given in Table 3. Note that phase 3 is not achieved by means of a **MINE RULE** statement. Instead, we use a query over the materialization of s_2.

The mining algorithms that can not be expressed in terms of SQL queries are activated by the so-called **core** operator. The three main components of the architecture defined in [15] are:

- *Preprocessor.* After the interpretation of a **MINE RULE** statement, a preprocessor retrieves source data, evaluates the mining, grouping and cluster conditions and encodes the data that will appear in the rules: it produces a set of encoded tables that are stored in the database. These encoded tables are optimized in the sense that mining conditions have been already applied and that unfrequent items do not appear anymore.

- **core** *operator.* The **core** operator uses these encoded tables and performs the generation of the association rules using known algorithms, e.g., APRIORI [2]. It then provides encoded rules. Basically, from each pair of body and head, elements are extracted to form a rule that satisfy mining conditions and both frequency and confidence criteria.

- *Postprocessor.* At the end of the process, the post-processor decodes the rules and produces the relations containing the desired rules in a table that is also stored in the database.

4 Discussion

Consider an inductive database for association rules. An instance is made of a current dataset and a current collection of rules. As defined in the previous section, both can be materialized as SQL3 tables. Modifying the current dataset implies a new computation of the evaluation function for the current collection of rules. The only way to modify the current collection of rules is to apply selections or set-oriented operations on it. However, a fundamental feature of inductive databases is that these selections can refer to arbitrary rules, e.g., rules whose frequencies and confidences have not been computed beforehand. The challenge for implementing an inductive database is then to use available materializations and constraints in order to compute efficiently the desired rules.

Indeed, the architecture presented in [15] provides a basis for an implementation. Using it, it is possible to define the current dataset, and it is possible to select patterns that hold in it and that satisfy a selection condition like a frequency and/or a confidence threshold, or other mining conditions. Other typical operations (e.g., union of patterns) can be simulated by SQL3 queries over the output tables and a "degenerate" **MINE RULE** statement that would just recompute frequency and confidence values for the current collection of rules using the current dataset. Note that sophisticated postprocessing is often needed in order to reduce the number of rules and that it can also be considered as a query on the current collection of rules. For instance, [7] shows how to use OQL in order to perform "structural rule covering" and "rule covering" [17], two global filtering methods over a collection of association rules stored in a nested relation.

So, the **MINE RULE** architecture can be used to simulate the closure property we defined on inductive databases. This closure property is not cosmetic: it enables the description of complex mining processes as sequence of queries. This view is an essential basis for an efficient query compilation when replays occur, a frequent situation according to our experience. For instance, suppose that three steps in a scenario lead to the following composition: $\tau_{F_3}(\tau_{F_2}(\tau_{F_1}((r_0, s_0)))) = (r_0, s_1)$, where $F_1 = e(r_0).f \geq 0.05 \wedge e(r_0).c \geq 0.3$, $F_2 = lbody \leq 4$, and $F_3 = A \notin \{body \cup head\}$. Assume now that one decides to replay this sequence on a new dataset. The situation is that some selections are cheap (e.g., bounds on the number of items) while some are very expensive (e.g., bounds on frequency and confidence values). So it is possible to optimize such sequences by combining or modifying the sequence of selections.

From an object-oriented viewpoint, the specific property of inductive data-bases is that we use some very expensive methods that can lead to database scans. A framework for query optimization has been studied for this case [8] and can serve as a basis for optimization strategies. Note also the interesting work [16] that starts a systematic study of those constraints that can be used actively in order to speed up association rule mining.

Another major issue is to consider the genericity of the approach. There are two aspects: specifying a new inductive database (or some **MINE RULE** operator for other kind of rules) and implementing it. Indeed, an inductive database can easily be defined for other kind of patterns than association rules: episode rules, integrity constraints in databases, classifiers, etc. The feasibility of implement-ation in some general case is an open problem. The most challenging problem comes from the pattern selection and can be formulated as follows: given a data-set and a potentially infinite collection of patterns, how can we use the selection criteria in order to optimize the generation/evaluation of the relevant patterns.

Generic mining algorithms should also be defined. Interesting ideas come from recent generalizations of APRIORI. [4] generalizes it in the context of fre-quent atomsets. It provides an inductive logic programming tool that mines the so-called frequent Datalog queries [5]. [18] consider query flocks that are para-metrized Datalog (or SQL) queries for which filter condition is related to the number of parameters values. They propose an optimizing scheme that provides subqueries for eliminating parameter values at a cheaper price.

5 Conclusion

The concept of inductive database has been suggested in [9] as a basis for a long-term database perspective on data mining. We presented a formalization for inductive databases considering that the whole process of data mining can be viewed as a querying activity. It appears that without introducing any additional concepts, object-oriented and relational database terminology enable to carry out inductive database querying, though effort to query optimization techniques for expensive selections must be pursued. From the architectural point of view, there is clearly a challenge in identifying the border between mining systems and relational processing that should be given to SQL servers. The architecture proposed by Meo, Psaila and Ceri for the **MINE RULE** operator is a good starting point, but it is an open problem to extend it to other classes of patterns.

References

1. R. Agrawal, T. Imielinski, and A. Swami. Mining association rules between sets of items in large databases. In *SIGMOD'93*, pages 207 – 216. ACM, 1993.
2. R. Agrawal, H. Mannila, R. Srikant, H. Toivonen, and A. I. Verkamo. Fast discovery of association rules. In *Advances in Knowledge Discovery and Data Mining*, pages 307 – 328. AAAI Press, 1996.
3. J.-F. Boulicaut, M. Klemettinen, and H. Mannila. Modeling KDD processes within the inductive database framework. Technical Report C-1998-29, Department of Computer Science, P.O. Box 26, FIN-00014 University of Helsinki, Finland, June 1998. Submitted.
4. L. Dehaspe and L. D. Raedt. Mining association rules in multiple relations. In *ILP'97*, volume 1297 of *LNAI*, pages 125–132. Springer-Verlag, 1997.
5. L. Dehaspe and H. Toivonen. Frequent query discovery: a unifying ILP approach to association rule mining. Technical Report CW-258, Department of Computer Science, Katholieke Universiteit Leuven, Belgium, March 1998.
6. U. M. Fayyad, G. Piatetsky-Shapiro, P. Smyth, and R. Uthurusamy, editors. *Advances in Knowledge Discovery and Data Mining*. AAAI Press, 1996.
7. B. Goethals, J. V. den Bussche, and K. Vanhoof. Decision support queries for the interpretation of data mining results. Manuscript, University of Limburg (Belgium), available at http://www.luc.ac.be/~vdbuss, 1998.
8. J. M. Hellerstein. Optimization techniques for queries with expensive methods. *ACM Transaction on Database Systems*, 1998. To appear.
9. T. Imielinski and H. Mannila. A database perspective on knowledge discovery. *Communications of the ACM*, 39(11):58 – 64, Nov. 1996.
10. G. Lausen and G. Vossen. *Models and Languages of Object-Oriented Databases*. Addison-Wesley Publishing Company, 1997.
11. H. Mannila. Inductive databases and condensed representations for data mining. In *ILPS'97*, pages 21–30. MIT Press, 1997.
12. H. Mannila. Methods and problems in data mining. In *ICDT'97*, volume 1186 of *LNCS*, pages 41–55. Springer-Verlag, 1997.
13. H. Mannila and H. Toivonen. Levelwise search and borders of theories in knowledge discovery. *Data Mining and Knowledge Discovery*, 1(3):241 – 258, 1997.
14. R. Meo, G. Psaila, and S. Ceri. A new SQL-like operator for mining association rules. In *VLDB'96*, pages 122–133. Morgan Kaufmann, 1996.
15. R. Meo, G. Psaila, and S. Ceri. A tightly-coupled architecture for data mining. In *ICDE'98*, pages 316–322. IEEE Computer Society Press, 1998.
16. R. Ng, L. Lakshmanan, J. Han, and A. Pang. Exploratory mining and pruning optimizations of constrained associations rules. In *SIGMOD'98*, pages 13–24. ACM, 1998.
17. H. Toivonen, M. Klemettinen, P. Ronkainen, K. Hätönen, and H. Mannila. Pruning and grouping of discovered association rules. In *Workshop Notes of the ECML-95 Workshop on Statistics, Machine Learning, and Knowledge Discovery in Databases*, pages 47 – 52. MLnet, 1995.
18. D. Tsur, J. D. Ullman, S. Abiteboul, C. Clifton, R. Motwani, S. Nestorov, and A. Rozenthal. Query flocks: A generalization of association-rule mining. In *SIGMOD'98*, pages 1–12. ACM, 1998.

Classes of Four-Fold Table Quantifiers

Jan Rauch

Laboratory of Intelligent Systems, Faculty of Informatics and Statistics, University of
Economics, W. Churchill Sq. 4, 13067 Prague, Czech Republic rauch@vse.cz

Abstract. Four-fold table logical calculi are defined. Formulae of these
calculi correspond to patterns based on four-fold contingency tables of
two Boolean attributes. An FFT quantifier is a part of the formula, it
corresponds to an assertion concerning frequencies from four-fold table.
Several classes of FFT quantifiers are defined and studied. It is shown
that each particular class has interesting properties from the point of
view of KDD. Deduction rules concerning formulae of four-fold tables
calculi are demonstrated. It is shown that complex computation of statistical tests can be avoided by using tables of critical frequencies.

1 Introduction

Interesting patterns - assertions concerning analyzed database are the the core of
KDD process . Some of these assertions can be easily understood as formulae of a
suitable logical calculus. Names of relations and names of fields of the analyzed
database belong to basic symbols of such calculus. There are interesting and
useful features of these calculi, e.g., deduction rules [7].

There is a group of important patterns concerning two Boolean attributes
derived from the analyzed database. The patterns correspond to the relations of
the Boolean attributes. The patterns are evaluated on the basis of a four-fold
table Tab.1. Here φ and ψ are attributes, a is the number of objects (records
of the analyzed database) satisfying both φ and ψ, b is the number of objects
satisfying φ and not satisfying ψ, etc.

	ψ	$\neg\psi$
φ	a	b
$\neg\varphi$	c	d

Table 1. Four-fold table of φ and ψ

An example of a pattern based on the four-fold table is the *association rule*,
see [1]. Attributes φ and ψ with four-fold table $\langle a, b, c, d \rangle$ are associated by an
association rule with parameters *conf* and *sup* if and only if

$$\frac{a}{a+b} \geq conf \wedge \frac{a}{a+b+c+d} \geq sup .$$

Further examples are given, e.g., in [2], [8], [9].

Observational calculi are logical calculi formulae of which correspond to various assertions concerning analyzed data. They are defined and studied in [2], see also [7]. A special case of observational calculi is defined in section 2. It is a *Four-Fold Table Predicate Calculus*, further only FFTPC. The formulae of FFTPC are of the form $\varphi \sim \psi$, where φ and ψ are Boolean attributes. Symbol $\sim$ is an *FFT quantifier*. It expresses the relation of attributes φ and ψ.

The goal of this paper is to show that it is useful to understand the relations of two Boolean attributes as formulae of FFTPC. Several classes of FFT-quantifiers are defined in section 3, e.g., implicational or equivalence quantifiers. Deduction rules concerning the formulae of FFTPC are studied in section 4. Tables of critical frequencies are discussed in section 5. They can be used to avoid a complex computation when testing patterns of the form $\varphi \sim \psi$.

2 Four-fold Table Predicate Calculi

We have to define a language of FFTPC, its models and values of formulae.

Definition 1. The **type of FFTPC** is an integer positive number T.

Definition 2. A **language of the FFTPC of type** T is given by:

1. **Basic symbols**:
   Basic attributes $A_1, \ldots, A_T$, *propositional connectives* $\land$, $\lor$, $\neg$, and *FFT quantifier* $\sim$.
2. **Attributes:**
   - If φ is a basic attribute, then φ is an attribute.
   - If φ and ψ are attributes, then also $\varphi \land \psi$, $\varphi \lor \psi$ and $\neg\varphi$ are derived attributes.
   - If φ is a derived attribute, then φ is an attribute.
   - Usual conventions concerning parentheses are valid.
3. **Formulae:**
   If φ and ψ are attributes and $\sim$ is an FFT quantifier, then $\varphi \sim \psi$ is a formula.

Definition 3. A **model of the FFTPC of type** T is each $\{0, 1\}$-data matrix with T columns.

Definition 4. We consider each model M with n rows to be the result of an observation of n objects. The i-th observed object corresponds to the i-th row. We say that the i-th **object has the basic attribute** A_1 in M if value 1 is in the first column of the i-th row of M . We say that the i-th object has derived attribute $A_1 \land A_2$ in M if value 1 is both in the first and in the second column of the i-th row of M . Similarly for other basic and derived attributes.

Definition 5. **Frequency** $Fr(\varphi, M)$ **of an attribute** φ **in a model M** is the number of objects having attribute φ.

Definition 6. Associated function $F_\sim$ of the FFT quantifier $\sim$ is a $\{0,1\}$ - valued function defined for all quadruples $< a, b, c, d >$ of non-negative integer numbers such that $a + b + c + d > 0$. We usually write only $\sim (a, b, c, d)$ instead of $F_\sim(a, b, c, d)$.

Definition 7. Let $\varphi \sim \psi$ be a formula of an FFTPC Φ. Let M be a model Φ. Then **value** $Val(\varphi \sim \psi, M)$ **of the formula** $\varphi \sim \psi$ **in the model M** is defined as the value

$$F_\sim(Fr(\varphi \wedge \psi, M), Fr(\varphi \wedge \neg\psi, M), Fr(\neg\varphi \wedge \psi, M), Fr(\neg\varphi \wedge \neg\psi, M)) .$$

If $Val(\varphi \sim \psi, M) = 1$, then we say that $\varphi \sim \psi$ is *true in* M. If $Val(\varphi \sim \psi, M) = 0$, then $\varphi \sim \psi$ is *false in* M.

The quadruple $\langle a, b, c, d \rangle$, where $a = Fr(\varphi \wedge \psi, M)$, $b = Fr(\varphi \wedge \neg\psi, M)$, $c = Fr(\neg\varphi \wedge \psi, M)$ and $d = Fr(\neg\varphi \wedge \neg\psi, M)$, is called the four-fold table of the formula $\varphi \sim \psi$ in a model (data matrix) M. We shall write only FFT instead of four-fold table.

3 Classes of Quantifiers

Properties of a formula $\varphi \sim \psi$ depend on properties of its associated function $F_\sim(a, b, c, d)$. We define the function $F_\sim$ to make the pattern $\varphi \sim \psi$ interesting from the point of view of a database user. One of the interesting relations of attributes φ and ψ is the relation φ *implies* ψ. An important question is: "*Which quantifier expresses the relation of implication?*" A class of implicational quantifiers is defined in [2].

Definition 8. An FFT quantifier $\sim$ is implicational if

$$\sim (a, b, c, d) = 1 \ \wedge \ a' \geq a \ \wedge \ b' \leq b \ \text{ implies } \ \sim (a', b', c', d') = 1$$

for non-negative integers a, b, c, d, a', b', c', d' such that $a + b + c + d > 0$ and $a' + b' + c' + d' > 0$.

The condition $a' \geq a$ and $b' \leq b$ means that the four-fold table $\langle a', b', c', d' \rangle$ is "better from the point of view of implication" than the four-fold table $\langle a, b, c, d \rangle$ (i-better, see [2]). If $\langle a, b, c, d \rangle$ is an FFT of $\varphi \sim \psi$ in model M and $\langle a', b', c', d' \rangle$ is an FFT of $\varphi \sim \psi$ in model M', then the sentence "Better from the point of view of implication" means: In model M' are more objects satisfying both φ and ψ than in M , and in model M' are fewer objects satisfying φ and not satisfying ψ than in M. Thus it is reasonable to expect that if formula $\varphi \sim \psi$ is true in model M, then it is also true in model M'. This expectation is ensured for implicational quantifiers by definition 8.

Example 1. Quantifier $\Rightarrow_{p,s}$ of *founded implication* for $0 < p \leq 1$ and $s > 0$ is implicational, see [2]. It is $\Rightarrow_{p,s} (a, b, c, d) = 1$ if and only if $\frac{a}{a+b} \geq p \wedge a \geq s$.

Example 2. Quantifier $\Rightarrow^!_{p,\alpha,s}$ of *lower critical implication* for $0 < p < 1$, $0 < \alpha < 1$ and $s > 0$ is implicational, see [2]. It is

$$\Rightarrow^!_{p,\alpha,s} (a,b,c,d) = 1 \text{ if and only if } \sum_{i=a}^{a+b} \frac{(a+b)!}{i!(a+b-i)!} p^i (1-p)^{a+b-i} \leq \alpha \wedge a \geq s .$$

Let us note that the formula $\varphi \Rightarrow^!_{p,\alpha,s} \psi$ corresponds to the test (on the level α) of the null hypothesis $H_0 : P(\psi|\varphi) \leq p$ against the alternative one $H_1 : P(\psi|\varphi) > p$. Here $P(\psi|\varphi)$ is the conditional probability of the validity of ψ under the condition φ, see [2] for more details.

It is easy to prove for an implicational quantifier $\Rightarrow^*$ that the value $\Rightarrow^*$ (a,b,c,d) does not depend either on c or on d. Thus we shall write only $\Rightarrow^* (a,b)$ instead of $\Rightarrow^* (a,b,c,d)$ for each implicational quantifier $\Rightarrow^*$.

We call conditions like "$a' \geq a$ and $b' \leq b$" **truth preservation conditions**, see [8]. The condition $a' \geq a$ and $b' \leq b$ is **a truth preservation condition for implicational quantifiers** . Further classes of FFT quantifiers are defined in [8], some of them using truth preservation conditions.

Definition 9. An **FFT quantifier** $\sim$ **is double implicational** if

$$\sim (a,b,c,d) = 1 \wedge \ a' \geq a \ \wedge b' \ \leq b \ \wedge \ c' \leq c \ \text{ implies } \sim (a',b',c',d') = 1$$

for non-negative integers a, b, c, d, a', b', c', d' such that $a+b+c+d > 0$ and $a'+b'+c'+d' > 0$.

We can see a reason for such a definition in an analogy to propositional logic. If u and v are propositions and both $u \to v$ and $v \to u$ are true, then u is equivalent to v ($\to$ is a propositional connective of implication). Thus we can try to express the relation of equivalence of attributes φ and ψ using "double implicational" FFT-quantifier $\Leftrightarrow^*$ such that

$$\varphi \Leftrightarrow^* \psi \text{ if and only if } \varphi \Rightarrow^* \psi \wedge \psi \Rightarrow^* \varphi,$$

where $\Rightarrow^*$ is a suitable implicational quantifier. If we apply the truth preservation condition for implicational quantifier to $\varphi \Rightarrow^* \psi$, we obtain $a' \geq a \ \wedge \ b' \leq b$. If we apply it to $\psi \Rightarrow^* \varphi$, we obtain $a' \geq a \ \wedge \ c' \leq c$, ($c$ is here instead of b, see Tab.1). This leads to **the truth preservation condition for double implicational quantifiers** $a' \geq a \wedge b' \leq b \wedge c' \leq c$, see definition 9. Several FFT quantifiers are defined according to this idea in [3], an example follows.

Example 3. A quantifier $\Leftrightarrow_{p,s}$ of *founded double implication* for $0 < p \leq 1$ and $s > 0$ is double implicational, see [8]. It is $\Leftrightarrow_{p,s} (a,b,c,d) = 1$ if and only if $\frac{a}{a+b+c} \geq p \ \wedge \ a \geq s$.

It is proved in [8] that quantifier $\Leftrightarrow_{p,s}$ belongs to the class of Σ-double implicational quantifiers:

Definition 10. An **FFT quantifier** $\sim$ is Σ-**double implicational** if

$$\sim (a,b,c,d) = 1 \ \wedge \ a' \geq a \ \wedge \ b' + c' \leq b + c \ \text{ implies } \ \sim (a',b',c',d') = 1$$

for non-negative integers a, b, c, d, a', b', c', d' such that $a+b+c+d > 0$ and $a' + b' + c' + d' > 0$.

It is obvious that each Σ-double implicational quantifier is also double implicational. It follows from the definition that if a quantifier $\Leftrightarrow^*$ belongs to Σ-double implicational quantifiers, then the value $\Rightarrow^* (a,b,c,d)$ does not depend on d. Thus we shall write only $\Leftrightarrow^* (a,b,c)$ instead of $\Leftrightarrow^* (a,b,c,d)$ for Σ-double implicational quantifier $\Leftrightarrow^*$.

We have a similar situation for equivalence quantifiers. If u and v are propositions and both $u \rightarrow v$ and $\neg u \rightarrow \neg v$ are true, then u is equivalent to v. Thus we can try to express the relation of equivalence of attributes φ and ψ using an "equivalence" FFT-quantifier $\equiv^*$ such that

$$\varphi \equiv^* \psi \ \text{ if and only if } \ \varphi \Rightarrow^* \psi \wedge \neg \varphi \Rightarrow^* \neg \psi \, ,$$

where $\Rightarrow^*$ is a suitable implicational quantifier. If we apply the truth preservation condition for implicational quantifier to $\varphi \Rightarrow^* \psi$ we obtain $a' \geq a \ \wedge \ b' \leq b$, if we apply it to $\neg \varphi \Rightarrow^* \neg \psi$, we obtain $d' \geq d \ \wedge \ c' \leq c$, ($c$ is here instead of b and d instead of a, see Tab.1). This leads to the *truth preservation condition for equivalence quantifiers*: $a' \geq a \wedge b' \leq b \wedge c' \leq c \wedge d' \geq d$ and consequently to the definition of **equivalence quantifiers** [8] (associational quantifiers according to [2]). In [3] are defined several FFT quantifiers as equivalence quantifiers.

Example 4. A quantifier $\equiv_p$ of *p-equivalence* for $0 < p \leq 1$ is equivalence quantifier, see [8]. It is $\Leftrightarrow_{p,s} (a,b,c,d) = 1$ if and only if $\frac{a}{a+b+c} \geq p \wedge a \geq s$. The quantifier $\equiv_p$ is also a Σ-equivalence quantifier [8].

Several further classes of implicational quantifiers are defined and studied in [8], e.g., *pure double implicational, typical double implicational, pure equivalence,* and *typical Σ-equivalence*. Each of these classes of FFT quantifiers contains useful quantifiers. Some of them are implemented in the system PC-GUHA, see [6]. Some important features of FFT-quantifiers related to classes of FFT are discussed in the following sections.

4 Deduction rules

A deduction rule is the relation of the form

$$\frac{\alpha_1, \ldots, \alpha_n}{\beta} \, ,$$

where $\alpha_1, \ldots, \alpha_n, \beta$ are formulae. This **deduction rule is correct** if for each model M holds: if $\alpha_1, \ldots, \alpha_n$ are true in M, then also β is true in M. We are interested in correct deduction rules of the the the form $\frac{\varphi \sim \psi}{\varphi' \sim \psi'}$, where $\varphi \sim \psi$ and $\varphi' \sim \psi'$ are formulae of an FFTPC. Such deduction rules can be used, e.g., in the following ways:

- **To reduce the output of a data mining procedure:** If formula $\varphi \sim \psi$ is a part of a data mining procedure output (thus it is true in analyzed data) and if $\frac{\varphi \sim \psi}{\varphi' \sim \psi'}$ is a correct deduction rule, then it is not necessary to put $\varphi' \sim \psi'$ into the output. The used deduction rule must be clear enough from the point of view of the user of the data mining procedure. An example of a simple deduction rule is dereduction deduction rule $\frac{\varphi \Rightarrow^* \psi}{\varphi \Rightarrow^* \psi \vee \chi}$, which is correct for each implicational quantifier $\Rightarrow^*$ [2].
- **To decrease the number of actually tested formulae:** If formula $\varphi \sim \psi$ is true in an analyzed model (data matrix) and if $\frac{\varphi \sim \psi}{\varphi' \sim \psi'}$ is a correct deduction rule, then it is not necessary to test $\varphi' \sim \psi'$.

Let us note that correct deduction rules (not only in the form of $\frac{\varphi \sim \psi}{\varphi' \sim \psi'}$) are used in the GUHA procedure PC-ASSOC, see, e.g., [4] or [6]. Anyway, it is reasonable to ask when the deduction rule of the form $\frac{\varphi \sim \psi}{\varphi' \sim \psi'}$ is correct. Several results concerning this problem were achieved in [5]. We are going to show some of them. We need several notions.

Definition 11. Let φ be an attribute. Then an **associated propositional formula** $\pi(\varphi)$ to φ is the same string of symbols as φ, but the particular basic attributes are understood as the propositional variables.

Example 5. If $A_1 \wedge A_7$ is a derived attribute, then $\pi(A_1 \wedge A_7)$ is propositional formula $A_1 \wedge A_7$ with propositional variables A_1 and A_7.

Definition 12. Let $\sim$ be an FFT quantifier. Then

1. $\sim$ is **a-dependent** if there are non-negative integers a, a', b, c, d such that $\sim (a, b, c, d) \neq \sim (a', b, c, d)$. Analogously for **b-dependent**.
2. $\sim$ is **(b+c)-dependent** if there are non-negative integers a, b, c, d, b', c' such that $b + c \neq b' + c'$ and $\sim (a, b, c, d) \neq \sim (a, b', c', d)$. Analogously for **(a+d)-dependent**.

Definition 13. Interesting quantifiers:

1. An **implicational quantifier** $\Rightarrow^*$ **is interesting** if $\Rightarrow^*$ is both a-dependent and b-dependent, and if $\Rightarrow^* (0, 0) = 0$.
2. A Σ**-double implicational quantifier** $\Leftrightarrow^*$ **is interesting** if $\Leftrightarrow^*$ is both a-dependent and $(b + c)$-dependent, and if $\Leftrightarrow^* (0, 0, 0) = 0$.
3. A Σ**-equivalence quantifier** $\equiv^*$ **is interesting** if $\equiv^*$ is $(a + d)$-dependent and if $\equiv^* (0, b, c, 0) = 0$ for $b + c > 0$.

Theorem 14. *Correct deduction rules:*

1. *If $\Rightarrow^*$ is an interesting implicational quantifier, then deduction rule $\frac{\varphi \Rightarrow^* \psi}{\varphi' \Rightarrow^* \psi'}$ is correct if and only if at least one of the following conditions a), b) is satisfied (see also [7]):*

   a) *Both (i) and (ii) are tautologies:*

(i) $\pi(\varphi) \wedge \pi(\psi) \rightarrow \pi(\varphi') \wedge \pi(\psi')$,

(ii) $\pi(\varphi') \wedge \neg\pi(\psi') \rightarrow \pi(\varphi) \wedge \neg\pi(\psi)$.

b) $\pi(\varphi) \rightarrow \neg\pi(\psi)$ *is a tautology.*

2. *If* $\Leftrightarrow^*$ *is an interesting* Σ-*double implicational quantifier, then deduction rule* $\frac{\varphi \Leftrightarrow^* \psi}{\varphi' \Leftrightarrow^* \psi'}$ *is correct if and only if at least one of the following conditions a), b) is satisfied:*

a) *Both (i) and (ii) are tautologies:*

   (i) $\pi(\varphi) \wedge \pi(\psi) \rightarrow \pi(\varphi') \wedge \pi(\psi')$,

   (ii) $\pi(\varphi') \wedge \neg\pi(\psi') \vee \neg\pi(\varphi') \wedge \pi(\psi') \rightarrow \pi(\varphi) \wedge \neg\pi(\psi) \vee \neg\pi(\varphi) \wedge \pi(\psi)$.

b) *(i):* $\pi(\varphi) \rightarrow \neg\pi(\psi)$ *or (ii):* $\pi(\psi) \rightarrow \neg\pi(\varphi)$ *are tautologies.*

3. *If* $\equiv^*$ *is an interesting* Σ-*equivalence quantifier, then deduction rule* $\frac{\varphi \equiv^* \psi}{\varphi' \equiv^* \psi'}$ *is correct if and only if* $(\pi(\varphi) \wedge \pi(\psi) \vee \neg\pi(\varphi) \wedge \neg\pi(\psi)) \rightarrow (\pi(\varphi') \wedge \pi(\psi') \vee \neg\pi(\varphi') \wedge \neg\pi(\psi'))$ *is a tautology.*

Proof. Let us outline the proof of a theorem concerning correct deduction rules for implicational quantifiers, see point 1. We have to prove:

A): If 1.a is satisfied, then deduction rule $\frac{\varphi \Rightarrow^* \psi}{\varphi' \Rightarrow^* \psi'}$ is correct.

B): If 1.b is satisfied, then deduction rule $\frac{\varphi \Rightarrow^* \psi}{\varphi' \Rightarrow^* \psi'}$ is correct.

C): If neither 1.a nor 1.b are satisfied, then deduction rule $\frac{\varphi \Rightarrow^* \psi}{\varphi' \Rightarrow^* \psi'}$ is not correct.

We suppose: M is a model, $\varphi \Rightarrow^* \psi$ is a formula, and $\langle a, b, c, d \rangle$ is a contingency table of $\varphi \Rightarrow^* \psi$ in M, analogously for $\varphi' \Rightarrow^* \psi'$ and $\langle a', b', c', d' \rangle$.

A): Let $Val(\varphi \Rightarrow^* \psi, M) = 1$. It means $\Rightarrow^* (a, b) = 1$. The condition 1.a(i) implies $a \leq a'$, the condition 1.a(ii) implies $b' \leq b$. Thus it is also $\Rightarrow^* (a', b') = 1$, see the definition 8 of the implicational quantifier.

B): If $\pi(\varphi) \rightarrow \neg\pi(\psi)$ is a tautology, then it is $a = 0$ for each model M. The quantifier $\Rightarrow^*$ is an interesting implicational quantifier, thus $\Rightarrow^* (0, 0) = 0$. It implies $\Rightarrow^* (0, b) = 0$ for each b (see definition 13 of the interesting implicational quantifier). Thus $Val(\varphi \Rightarrow^* \psi, M) = 0$ for each model M. It means that the assertion: *If* $Val(\varphi \Rightarrow^* \psi, M) = 1$ *then* $Val(\varphi' \Rightarrow^* \psi', M) = 1$ is true.

C): We suppose that neither 1.a nor 1.b are satisfied. We have to find a model M such that $Val(\varphi \Rightarrow^* \psi, M) = 1$ and $Val(\varphi' \Rightarrow^* \psi', M) = 0$. If neither 1.a nor 1.b are satisfied, then **D)** or **E)** are satisfied:

D): Neither 1.a(i) nor 1.b are satisfied.

E): Neither 1.a(ii) nor 1.b are satisfied.

D): The implicational quantifier $\Rightarrow^*$ is a-dependent, thus there are A, B such that $\Rightarrow^* (A, B) = 1$. The condition 1.a(i) is not satisfied, thus there is an object o, such that o has the attribute $\varphi \wedge \psi$, and o has not the attribute $\varphi' \wedge \psi'$. Let M be a model with A objects o (a data matrix with A identical rows, each of them equal to a row corresponding to the row of o). It means $a = A$, $b = 0$ and also $a' = 0$, $b' \geq 0$. The quantifier $\Rightarrow^*$ is implicational and $\Rightarrow^* (A, B) = 1$, thus also $\Rightarrow^* (A, 0) = 1$. Further, $a' = 0$ and $\Rightarrow^* (0, 0) = 0$ ($\Rightarrow^*$ is interesting implicational), thus also $\Rightarrow^* (a', b') = 0$. It means that $Val(\varphi \Rightarrow^* \psi, M) = 1$ and $Val(\varphi' \Rightarrow^* \psi', M) = 0$.

E): The quantifier $\Rightarrow^*$ is *b-dependent*, thus there are non-negative integers A, B, B' such that $\Rightarrow^* (A, B) = 1$ and $\Rightarrow^* (A, B') = 0$. The condition 1.a(ii) is not satisfied, thus there is an object which has the attribute $\varphi' \wedge \neg \psi'$ and has not the attribute $\varphi \wedge \neg \psi$. Let us call it *object of type* **B**. The condition 1.b is not satisfied, thus there is an object which has both the attribute φ and the attribute ψ. Let us call it *object of type* **A**. Let M be a model with A objects of type **A** and B objects of type **B**. Values of attributes important for computing $Val(\varphi \Rightarrow^* \psi, M)$ and $Val(\varphi' \Rightarrow^* \psi', M)$ and consequences for contingency tables $\langle a, b, c, d \rangle$ and $\langle a', b', c', d' \rangle$ are in Tab. 2. Symbol " - " means that we do not know

line	attribute	A objects of type **A**	B objects of type **B**	consequence
1	$\varphi \wedge \psi$	**X**: T by definition	-	$a \geq A$
2	$\varphi' \wedge \psi'$	-	B, see **Y**	$a' \leq A$
3	$\varphi \wedge \neg \psi \ \vee \neg \varphi \wedge \psi$	F, see **X**	F by definition	$b = 0$
4	$\varphi' \wedge \neg \psi' \ \vee \neg \varphi' \wedge \psi'$	-	**Y**: T by definition	$b' \geq B$

Table 2. Values of attributes for case E

the corresponding value, **X**: and **Y**: are labels. Symbol T means that an object of a corresponding type has a corresponding attribute (symbol F means "has not"). It is $\Rightarrow^* (A, B) = 1$, $a \geq A$ and $b = 0$, thus also $\Rightarrow^* (a, b) = 1$. Further, it is $\Rightarrow^* (A, B') = 0$, $a' \leq A$ and $b' \geq B'$, thus $\Rightarrow^* (a, b') = 0$. This finishes the proof. $\square$

5 Tables of critical frequencies

Theorem 15. *Let $\Rightarrow^*$ be an implicational quantifier. Then there is a non-negative and non-decreasing function $Tb_{\Rightarrow^*}$ with value $Tb_{\Rightarrow^*}(a) \in \{0, 1, 2, \ldots\} \cup \{\infty\}$ such that it is*

$$\Rightarrow^* (a, b) = 1 \quad \text{if and only if } b < Tb_{\Rightarrow^*}(a)$$

for all integers $a \geq 0$ and $b \geq 0$.

Proof. We define $Tb_{\Rightarrow^*}(a) = \min\{e \mid \Rightarrow^* (a, e) = 0\}$, see the definition of implicational quantifiers. $\square$

We call function $Tb_{\Rightarrow^*}$ a *table of critical frequencies for implicational quantifier* $\Rightarrow^*$. It is used in the GUHA procedure PC-ASSOC [7]. It is important that the function $Tb_{\Rightarrow^*}$ makes it possible to use a simple test of inequality instead of a rather complex computation. E.g., we can use inequality $b < Tb_{\Rightarrow^*_{p,\alpha,s}}(a)$ instead of condition $\sum_{i=a}^{a+b} \frac{(a+b)!}{i!(a+b-i)!} p^i (1-p)^{a+b-i} \leq \alpha \wedge a \geq s$ for quantifier $\Rightarrow^*_{p,\alpha,s}$ of lower critical implication, see example 2. An other form of the table of critical frequencies for implicational quantifier is defined in [2]. Further tables of critical frequencies for Σ-double implicational quantifiers and for Σ-equivalence quantifiers are defined in [8].

6 Conclusions

We have defined several classes of FFT quantifiers. Deduction rules and tables of critical frequencies have been discussed as useful tools for dealing with some patterns in the KDD process. We have shown that properties of these tools are closely related to classes of FFT quantifiers.

There are further useful classes of FFT quantifiers, e.g., symmetrical quantifiers, a,d-symmetrical quantifiers, strong double implicational quantifiers, strong double equivalence quantifiers and F-quantifiers (with the same behaviour as Fisher's test), see [2], [5], [8].

This work is supported by grant 47160008 of the Ministry of Education and by grant 201/96/1445 of the Grant Agency of the Czech Republic.

References

1. Aggraval, R. et al: Fast Discovery of Association Rules. In Fayyad, U. M. et al.: Advances in Knowledge Discovery and Data Mining. AAAI Press / The MIT Press, 1996. 307–328
2. Hájek, P., Havránek T.: Mechanising Hypothesis Formation - Mathematical Foundations for a General Theory. Berlin - Heidelberg - New York, Springer-Verlag, 1978, 396 p.
3. Hájek, P. - Havránek, T., Chytil M.: Metoda GUHA. Praha, Academia, 1983, 314 p. (in Czech)
4. Hájek, P., Sochorová, A., Zvárová, J.: GUHA for personal computers. Computational Statistics & Data Analysis **19**, (1995) 149–153
5. Rauch, J.: Logical foundations of mechanizing hypotheses formation from databases (in Czech). Thesis, Mathematical Institute of Czechoslovak Academy of Sciences Prague, 1986, 133 p.
6. Rauch, J.: GUHA as a Data Mining Tool. In: Practical Aspects of Knowledge Management. Schweizer Informatiker Gesellshaft Basel, 1996
7. Rauch, J.: Logical Calculi for Knowledge Discovery in Databases. In Principles of Data Mining and Knowledge Discovery, (J. Komorowski and J. Zytkow, eds.), Springer Verlag, Berlin, 47-57, 1997.
8. Rauch, J.: Four-Fold Table Calculi. LISp, Technical Report LiSp9710 (in Czech), 1998
9. Zembowicz R. - Zytkow J.: From Contingency Tables to Various Forms of Knowledge in Databases. In Fayyad, U. M. et al.: Advances in Knowledge Discovery and Data Mining. AAAI Press/ The MIT Press, 1996. s. 329 - 349.

Detection of Interdependences in Attribute Selection

Javier Lorenzo, Mario Hernández and Juan Méndez

Dpto. de Informática y Sistemas
Univ. de Las Palmas de Gran Canaria
35017 Las Palmas, Spain
jlorenzo@dis.ulpgc.es

Abstract. A new measure for attribute selection, called GD, is proposed. The GD measure is based on Information Theory and allows to detect the interdependence between attributes. This measure is based on a quadratic form of the Mántaras distance and a matrix called Transinformation Matrix. In order to test the quality of the proposed measure, it is compared with other two feature selection methods, namely Mántaras distance and Relief algorithms. The comparison is done over 19 datasets along with three different induction algorithms.

1 Introduction

Knowledge Discovery in Databases and the part of Machine Learning dealing with learning from examples overlap in the algorithms and the problems addressed. In both areas induction algorithms have to deal with attributes or fields that are not relevant to the definition of a concept, so an important task is to filter those attributes to avoid the noise that they can introduce. The irrelevant or redundant attributes do not affect the ideal Bayesian classifier because the addition of new attributes never decreases the performance of the classifier. However, many practical classifiers decrease its performance when irrelevant or redundant attributes arise. To overcome this problem, different approaches have been proposed to select the more relevant attributes that define a concept (or class) [4]. Some works on attribute selection were the WINNOW algorithm proposed by Littlestone [16], the FOCUS algorithm proposed by Almuallim and Dietterich [3] and the Relief algorithm proposed by Kira and Rendell [11]. All these algorithms have a common feature, they do not include the performance of the classifier as a measure to guide the selection of the attributes. John et al. [10] propose the *wrapper* method that utilizes the performance of the classifier to carry out the selection of the attributes. There is much evidence that wrapper method give good results [1, 10]. However, due to the computational cost, the wrapper methods can only be applied in combination with classifiers of low complexity.

The method proposed in this work utilizes a measure based on Information Theory to guide the selection of the attributes. The use of Information Theory concepts in feature selection is not recent. Quinlan [21] proposed a measure called Gain Ratio that corresponds to the ratio between the mutual information and the entropy [24]. Another approach based on Information Theory is proposed by López de Mántaras [17], where a distance measure is defined and analyzed in its relationship with the Gain Ratio measure proposed by Quinlan. Wettschereck and Dieterich [23] demonstrated that the performance of the k-NN and Nearest-Hyperrectangle classifiers increases when the attributes are weighted by mutual information. Similar conclusions are presented by Daelemans [7], when the features used in the Exemplar-based Generalization algorithm are weighted with the mutual information in a problem of assignment of syllable boundaries in Dutch. Koller and Sahami [14] utilize the Kullback-Liebler distance as a "correlation" metric in an approximation to the Markov blankets for feature selection.

In the previous works the attributes are considered independent, they do not take into account the relation among them. In this work a measure called *GD*, between an attribute subset and the class is proposed. This measure, unlike the Gain Ratio, tries to get the possible interdependence among attributes and is based on a quadratic form of the distance proposed by López de Mántaras and a matrix called *Transinformation Matrix*.

The organization of the rest of this paper is as follows. The GD measure is defined Sect. 2, and a comparison with the Mántaras distance and Relief algorithm on several datasets is presented in Sect. 3. The selection of the attributes is carried out from a set of labeled samples. Each sample of the data set is composed of a n dimensional vector of attributes $X = \{X_1, X_2, \ldots, X_n\}$ and a label Y which indicates the class the sample belongs to.

2 GD Measure

López de Mántaras [17] proposes a distance measure between two partitions to select the attributes associated with the nodes of a decision tree. In each node, it is chosen the attribute that produces the partition closest to the correct partition of the samples subset in the examples.

The Mántaras distance has the following expression:

$$d_{LM}(P_A, P_B) = H(P_A/P_B) + H(P_B/P_A) \tag{1}$$

where $H(P_A/P_B)$ and $H(P_B/P_A)$ correspond to the entropy of a partition when the other is known. This measure fulfils the properties of a metric distance function. If we change the references to partitions by attributes and class in the definition of the Mántaras distance, we get the following expression

$$d_{LM}(X_i, Y) = H(X_i/Y) + H(Y/X_i) = H(X_i, Y) - I(X_i; Y) \tag{2}$$

where $H(X_i, Y)$ is the joint entropy of X_i and Y, and $I(X_i; Y)$ is the mutual information of X_i over Y.

Similar to the Gain Information proposed by Quinlan, the Mántaras distance can be considered an attribute selection measure because for each node of the tree the most relevant attribute is selected.

The use of Gain Ratio and the Mántaras distance has the drawback of operating over isolated attributes because they assume that attributes are independent and therefore these methods do not detect the interdependencies that could exist between attributes. A way to get into account the dependencies between attributes it is to compute the mutual information for each pair of attributes $I(X_i; X_j)$. These interdependencies of attributes can be represented with the aid of *Transinformation Matrix* T, a square matrix of dimension n (number of attributes) where each element *(i,j)* of the matrix is the mutual information between attributes *i-th* and *j-th*.

$$T = [I(X_i; X_j)]_{i,j=1,n}$$

Once the Transinformation matrix has been defined, it is necessary to find an expression for the GD measure that includes the Transinformation matrix and the distance (2). This expression must be defined in such a way that subsets of attributes with strong dependencies between attributes yields lower values than other ones without these strong dependencies. A solution come from the analogy to significance level between the Transinformation matrix and the covariance matrix (Σ) of two random variables. This analogy can be established because both matrices measure interrelation between variables. In the Mahalanobis distance [8], the covariance matrix is utilized to correct the effects of cross covariances between two components of a random variable. The expression of the Mahalanobis distance between two samples *(X,Y)* of a random variable is:

$$d_{Mahalanobis}(X,Y) = (X - Y)^t \Sigma^{-1}(X - Y) \tag{3}$$

Therefore the GD measure can be defined in a similar way to the Mahalanobis distance, using the Transinformation matrix instead of the covariance matrix and the distance (2) instead of the Euclidean distance. The GD measure $d_{GD}(X,Y)$ between the set of attributes X and the class Y is expressed as:

$$d_{GD}(X,Y) = D(X,Y)^t T^{-1} D(X,Y) \tag{4}$$

where $D(X,Y) = (d_{LM}(X_1,Y), d_{LM}(X_2,Y), \ldots, d_{LM}(X_n,Y))^T$, is a vector whose *i-th* element is the distance (2) between the attribute X_i and the class, and T is the Transinformation matrix of the set of attributes X. From the equation (2) we can observe that the elements of the $D(X,Y)$ vector are smaller as the information that the attribute gives about the class is greater. This statement can be proved from the expression of the mutual information [6], that is $I(X_i,Y) = I(Y,X_i) = H(Y) - H(Y/X_i)$ where $H(Y)$ is the entropy of Y and $H(Y/X_i)$ is the conditional entropy of Y when X_i is known.

Given a set of attributes and the associated Transinformation matrix, the GD measure fulfils the following properties:

1. $d_{GD}(X,Y) \geq 0, \forall X,Y$ and $d_{GD}(X,X) = 0$
2. $d_{GD}(X,Y) = d_{GD}(Y,X), \forall X,Y$

The demonstration of the two previous properties is trivial if we take into account the properties of the distance (2) and the properties of the Transinformation matrix [18]. The triangle inequality property has not been demonstrated for the GD measure yet, and so it can be considered as an semimetric distance function. The GD measure satisfies the monotonicity property that states that the measure increases with dimensionality. This property is easily probed using the expression 4 and the properties of the Transinformation matrix. Therefore, only subsets with the same cardinality can be compared between one another.

The use of GD measure for feature selection is based on the fact that the distances $d_{LM}(X_i, Y)$ decreases as the information of an attribute subset about the class increases. On the other hand, if an element of the Transinformation matrix is large (it indicates that the mutual dependence between two attributes is high) then the GD measure increases. Therefore it can be concluded that a low value of the GD measure between an attribute subset and the class indicates that the attributes give a lot of information about the class and that high dependencies do not exist between the attributes.

In the GD measure an important aspect is the singularity of the Transinformation matrix. It has been analytically demonstrated that the Transinformation matrix is non singular for dimension two and three. An analytical demonstration have not been found for greater dimensions yet, but all the matrices generated in the examples of Sect. 3 were found non-singular.

3 Results

In this section we compare the quality of the selected attributes by the GD measure with the selected attributes by other two methods. The other two methods chosen in the comparative are the Mántaras distance and the ReliefF algorithm. On the one hand, the Mántaras distance has been chosen because it has a conceptual resemblance with the GD measure. On the other hand, the ReliefF method has been chosen because it has been widely referenced in the bibliography [5, 22, 12]. The ReliefF method is a version of the Relief method due to Kononenko [15] that allows attributes with missing values and multiclass problems. The quality of each selected attribute subset was tested by means of the accuracy that three classifiers yields. As we are interested in comparing the selection methods, we do not make any optimization in the classifiers to avoid bias in the accuracy due to the optimizations. The classifiers are: the Naive Bayes classifier [8], a decision tree induced with the ID3 method [21] and the IB1 algorithm [2]. The implementation of the induction algorithms was carried out with the $\mathcal{MLC}++$ library [13] and the comparison was performed with 19 databases of the UCI Machine Learning Databases Repository [19]. The databases are the following ones: Breast Cancer Ljubljana (BC), Breast Cancer Wisconsin (BW), Credit Card (CR), Glass (GL), Glass2 (G2), Heart Disease (HD), Iris (IR), Led (LE), Liver Disorder (LD), Monks (M1,M2,M3), Parity5+5 (P5), Pima Indian Diabetes (PI), Post-operative (PO), Tic-Tac-Toe (TT), Voting (VO), Wine (WI), Zoo (ZO).

Table 1. Results on Naive Bayes classifier and branch-and-bound

	d_{GD}		$Relief F$			d_{LM}		
	# attr.	Acc.	# attr.	Acc.	Concl.	# attr.	Acc.	Concl.
BC	4	74.09±0.80	8	74.13±0.73	=	7	74.05±0.79	=
BW	10	96.30±0.22	7	96.74±0.23	<	10	96.30±0.22	=
CR	1	86.37±0.37	1	86.37±0.37	=	1	86.37±0.37	=
GL	8	48.08±1.04	8	48.08±1.04	=	3	49.18±1.10	=
G2	4	69.92±1.10	4	65.11±1.10	>	2	61.67±1.10	>
HD	8	85.04±0.62	11	85.45±0.65	=	12	85.15±0.62	=
IR	2	96.00±0.49	2	96.00±0.49	=	2	96.00±0.49	=
LE	7	74.99±0.44	7	74.99±0.44	=	7	74.99±0.44	=
LD	6	55.58±0.82	3	59.45±0.91	<	6	55.58±0.82	=
M1	1	75.00±0.60	3	75.00±0.60	=	3	75.00±0.60	=
M2	1	67.14±0.74	1	67.14±0.74	=	1	67.14±0.74	=
M3	2	97.22±0.23	2	97.22±0.23	=	4	97.22±0.23	=
P5	1	45.13±0.24	1	44.84±0.24	=	1	45.13±0.24	=
PI	6	75.67±0.46	2	76.60±0.50	<	4	75.70±0.47	=
PO	1	70.49±1.68	1	71.18±1.64	<	1	69.47±1.67	>
TT	6	72.12±0.43	6	73.00±0.43	<	6	73.02±0.44	<
VO	1	95.63±0.28	1	95.63±0.28	=	1	95.63±0.28	=
WI	6	97.53±0.34	13	97.43±0.34	=	12	97.59±0.35	=
ZO	7	93.65±0.74	8	93.75±0.73	=	8	93.75±0.73	=

All the previous databases have less than 10% of samples with missing values that were removed. With respect to the continuous attributes, they were discretized with the simple equal width discretization method with 10 intervals. The process we follow to test the quality of the attributes selected with the GD measure was the following. For all datasets, we selected the best attribute subset according to each of the three methods compared. Then we estimate the accuracy that each classifier yields with the selected attributes. The accuracy was estimated taking the mean of ten runs of a 10 k-fold cross validation.

Due to the monotonicity property we implement the branch-and-bound method [20] to search the subset with minimum value of GD measure. For the ReliefF algorithm we sort the attributes in decreasing order of relevance and take in each case the number of attributes we were considering. With the Mántaras distance we do the same but sorting the attributes in increasing value of the distance. The best results obtained for each classifier are shown in Tables 1, 2 and 3.

To assess the results, two paired t statistical tests with a confidence level of 90% were accomplished. Under the null hypothesis of the first statistical test, the subsets selected by the two methods yield the same accuracy. If the null hypothesis of this first statistical test is rejected, another statistical test is accomplished in which the null hypothesis is that the subset selected by the GD measure yields lower or equal to the another method.

Table 2. Results on ID3 classifier and branch-and-bound

	d_{GD}		$Relief F$			d_{LM}		
	# attr.	Acc.	# attr.	Acc.	Concl.	# attr.	Acc.	Concl.
BC	4	75.77±0.70	1	72.50±0.80	>	4	75.05±0.77	=
BW	2	95.32±0.23	3	95.46±0.23	=	10	94.72±0.29	>
CR	1	86.37±0.37	1	86.37±0.37	=	1	86.37±0.37	=
GL	6	69.72±0.96	6	69.72±0.96	=	8	69.27±0.98	=
G2	5	82.56±0.96	3	83.42±0.95	=	6	88.20±0.81	<
HD	4	79.07±0.71	5	81.41±0.72	<	8	78.96±0.75	=
IR	2	95.93±0.49	2	95.93±0.49	=	2	95.93±0.49	=
LE	7	73.44±0.42	7	73.44±0.42	=	7	73.44±0.42	=
LD	4	64.37±0.78	4	64.37±0.78	=	5	63.51±0.75	=
M1	5	99.93±0.07	3	100.0±0.00	=	5	99.93±0.07	=
M2	5	77.80±0.69	5	77.80±0.69	=	5	77.80±0.69	=
M3	5	100.0±0.00	6	100.0±0.00	=	5	100.0±0.00	=
P5	8	99.96±0.04	5	100.0±0.00	=	8	99.96±0.04	=
PI	8	70.65±0.49	8	70.65±0.49	=	8	70.65±0.49	=
PO	4	70.56±1.62	1	71.18±1.64	=	1	69.47±1.67	=
TT	9	85.46±0.33	9	85.46±0.33	=	9	85.46±0.33	=
VO	1	95.63±0.28	1	95.63±0.28	=	1	95.63±0.28	=
WI	3	94.61±0.49	5	95.28±0.53	=	3	94.61±0.49	=
ZO	9	96.42±0.59	8	96.03±0.60	=	8	96.03±0.60	=

The conclusions obtained from these statistical tests appear in Tables 1, 2, 3 under the column labeled "Concl.".

If we compare the accuracy of the three classifiers (Naive Bayes, ID3 and IB1) with the three selection methods (GD measure, ReliefF and Mántaras distance) on the 19 databases we get 114 results.

In 9 (7.9%) of the 114 cases, the set of attributes selected by the GD measure yields better accuracy than the two other methods. In 90 (78.9%) of the 114 cases, the set of attributes selected by the GD measure yields a accuracy that is equal to the two other methods. Considering the comparative with the two methods separatively we get that with respect to the ReliefF method in 4 (7%) of the cases the set of attributes selected by the GD measure is better than the selected by ReliefF and in 43 (75.4%) is equal. On the other hand, with respect to the Mántaras distance in 5 (8.8%) of the cases the results obtained by the GD measure improve the results of the Mántaras distance, and in 47 (82.4%) cases the results are equals.

After the previous global evaluation of the results, we are going to focus on two databases where the ability of the GD measure for filtering irrelevant and redundant attributes is stated. The BW database has a completely irrelevant attribute that is the identifier of each sample. This attribute has been the last selected attribute by ReliefF and the GD measure whereas the Mántaras distance selects it firstly. In the CRX database, the attributes A4 and A5 are

Table 3. Results on IB1 classifier and branch-and-bound

	d_{GD}		ReliefF			d_{LM}		
	# attr.	Acc.	# attr.	Acc.	Concl.	# attr.	Acc.	Concl.
BC	6	73.53±0.73	8	74.03±0.72	=	7	74.08±0.75	=
BW	9	95.81±0.23	5	96.38±0.21	<	7	95.90±0.23	=
CR	11	83.49±0.43	9	82.92±0.40	=	1	82.31±1.23	=
GL	6	76.53±0.89	6	76.53±0.89	=	9	68.59±0.99	>
G2	5	87.85±0.73	5	87.85±0.73	=	4	86.68±0.83	=
HD	11	80.78±0.69	5	79.30±0.73	=	8	76.52±0.71	>
IR	4	95.73±0.50	4	95.73±0.50	=	4	95.73±0.50	=
LE	7	64.81±0.66	7	64.81±0.66	=	7	64.81±0.66	=
LD	5	66.01±0.81	5	66.01±0.81	=	5	66.01±0.81	=
M1	5	99.79±0.12	3	100.0±0.00	<	5	99.79±0.12	=
M2	5	67.01±0.70	5	67.01±0.70	=	5	67.01±0.70	=
M3	5	99.66±0.15	2	96.94±0.28	>	5	99.66±0.15	=
P5	8	99.92±0.05	5	100.0±0.00	=	8	99.92±0.05	=
PI	8	70.63±0.44	8	70.63±0.44	=	8	70.63±0.44	=
PO	1	50.08±2.37	2	56.52±1.69	<	1	54.76±2.74	<
TT	9	80.77±0.38	8	81.98±0.37	<	8	81.94±0.37	<
VO	14	93.98±0.33	10	93.77±0.33	=	10	93.84±0.39	=
WI	11	97.54±0.37	11	96.69±0.41	>	9	98.26±0.32	<
ZO	11	97.71±0.44	10	97.03±0.48	=	13	97.51±0.48	=

completely correlated and one of them has been removed in some distributions of this database. This correlation between attributes A4 and A5 is detected by the GD measure and selects the A5 attribute in last position, however ReliefF and the Mántaras distance do not take into account the correlation between the attributes and they select both of them before other attributes.

In Table 2, it can be noticed that the attribute selection do not improve significantly the performance of the induced decision tree, in 89.5% of cases using ID3 we get the same accuracy with the three methods. However, the attribute selection can reduce the size of the induced tree. To assess this statement, we accomplish two statistical tests similar to the used with the accuracy but now making reference to the number of nodes of the generated decision trees. Focusing on the 34 cases of databases of Table 2 whose accuracies are not statistically different, we observe that in 5 (14.7%) cases the trees induced with the attribute set obtained with the GD measure has less nodes than the obtained with the attributes selected by the other two methods, and in 22 (64.7%) the number of nodes is equal.

With the Naive Bayes classifier, when the GD measure yields the same accuracy that the other methods the cardinality of the selected attribute sets is smaller. So the computational cost of the induced classifier will be lower, giving the same accuracy. On the contrary, the GD measure and Mántaras distance use more attribute than ReliefF to yield the same accuracy. This fact is due to the nature of the ReliefF algorithm that is very similar to the schema of the IB1 classifier.

4 Conclusions

From the above results in the datasets, we conclude that the GD measure does not improve the performance of the ReliefF algorithm significatively. Although the number of selected attributes is smaller and so the induced classifier will have a lower computational cost. Also, we have found that the proposed measure detects irrelevant and redudant attributes where the other two methods fail.

On the other hand, the results obtained with the GD measure improve the results obtained with the Mántaras distance and with less attributes, so we can conclude that the use of the Transinformation matrix improve the performance of the Mántaras distance.

The smaller cardinality of the selected attribute sets is due to the nature of the GD measure that allows to detect the dependencies between attributes. So, redundant attributes are rejected and a reduction of the cardinality of the selected sets is achieved.

As future works we are interested in testing the performance of the GD measure with other discretization methods as the proposed by Fayyad and Irani [9]. Another important point to test is the strength of the measure with datasets with missing values. Finally, it is interesting to find a method that permits to establish the dimension of the attribute subset from the GD measure automatically.

Acknowledgements

This work was supported by the Spanish Ministry of Education under project TAP95-0288. We want to thank Prof. López de Mántaras for his helpful suggestions on the experiments of this work.

References

1. D. W. Aha and R. L. Bankert. Feature selection for case-based classification of cloud types: An empirical comparison. In *Proc. of the 1994 AAAI Workshop on Case-Based Reasoning*, pages 106–112. AAAI Press, 1994.
2. D. W. Aha, Dennis Kibler, and M. K. Albert. Instance-based learning algorithms. *Machine Learning*, 6:37–66, 1991.
3. H. Almuallim and T.G. Dietterich. Learning with many irrelevant features. In *Proc. of the Ninth National Conference on Artificial Intelligence*, pages 547–552. AAAI Press, 1991.
4. A. L. Blum and P. Langley. Selection of relevant features and examples in machine learning. *Artificial Intelligence*, 97:245–271, 1997.
5. R. Caruana and D. Freitag. Greedy attribute selection. In *Proc. of the 11th International Machine Learning Conference*, pages 28–36, New Brunswick, NJ, 1994. Morgan Kaufmann.

6. T. M. Cover and J. A. Thomas. *Elements of Information Theory*. John Wiley & Sons Inc., 1991.

7. Walter Daelemans and Antal van den Bosch. Generalization performance of back-propagation learning on a syllabification task. In *Proc. of the Third Twente Workshop on Language Technology*, pages 27–38, 1992.

8. R. Duda and P. Hart. *Pattern Classification and Scene Analysis*. John Willey and Sons, 1973.

9. U. M. Fayyad and K. B. Irani. Multi-interval discretization of continuous-valued attributes for classification learning. In *Proc. of the 13th Int. Joint Conference of Artificial Intelligence*, pages 1022–1027, 1993.

10. G. H. John, R. Kohavi, and K. Pfleger. Irrelevant features and the subset selection problem. In W. William and Haym Hirsh, editors, *Procs. of the Eleventh International Conference on Machine Learning*, pages 121–129. Morgan Kaufmann, San Francisco, CA, 1994.

11. K. Kira and L. A. Rendell. The feature selection problem: Traditional methods and a new algorithm. In *Proc. of the 10th National Conf. on Artificial Intelligence*, pages 129–134, 1992.

12. R. Kohavi and G. H. John. Wrappers for feature subset selection. *Artificial Intelligence*, 97(1-2):273–324, December 1997.

13. R. Kohavi, D. Sommerfield, and J. Dougherty. Data mining using MLC++: A machine learning library in C++. In *Tools with Artificial Intelligence*, pages 234–245. IEEE Computer Society Press, 1996. Received the best paper award.

14. D. Koller and M. Sahami. Toward optimal feature selection. In *Proc. of the 13th Int. Conf. on Machine Learning*, pages 284–292. Morgan Kaufmann, 1996.

15. I. Kononenko. Estimating attributes: Analysis and extensions of relief. In F. Bergadano and L. de Raedt, editors, *Machine Learning: ECML-94*, pages 171–182, Berlin, 1994. Springer.

16. N. Littlestone. Learning quickly when irrelevant attributes abound: A new linear-threshold algorithm. *Machine Learning*, 2:285–318, 1988.

17. R. Lopez de Mántaras. A distance-based attribute selection measure for decision tree induction. *Machine Learning*, 6:81–92, 1991.

18. J. Lorenzo, M. Hernández, and J. Méndez. GD: A Measure based on Information Theory for Attribute Selection. In Helder Coelho, editor, *Proc. of the 6th Ibero-American Conference on Artificial Intelligence*, Lectures Notes in Artificial Intelligence, Springer Verlag, 1998.

19. C. J. Merz and P.M. Murphy. *UCI Repository of machine learning databases*. Irvine, CA: University of California, Department of Information and Computer Science., 1996.

20. P.M. Narendra and K. Fukunaga. A branch and bound algorithm for feature selection. *IEEE Trans. on Computers*, 26:917–922, 1977.

21. J. R. Quinlan. Induction of decision trees. *Machine Learning*, 1:81–106, 1986.

22. D. Wettschereck and D. W. Aha. Weighting features. In *Proc. of the First Int. Conference on Case-Based Reasoning*, pages 347–358, 1995.

23. D. Wettschereck and T. G. Dieterich. An experimental comparison of the nearest-neighbor and nearest-hyperrectangle algorithms. *Machine Learning*, 19:5–27, 1995.

24. A. P. White and W. Z. Liu. Bias in information-based measures in decision tree induction. *Machine Learning*, 15:321–329, 1994.

Postponing the Evaluation of Attributes with a High Number of Boundary Points

Tapio Elomaa[1] and Juho Rousu[2]

[1] Joint Research Centre, European Commission, elomaa@cs.helsinki.fi
[2] VTT Biotechnology and Food Research, juho.rousu@vtt.fi

Abstract. The efficiency of the otherwise expedient decision tree learning can be impaired in processing data-mining-sized data if superlinear-time processing is required in attribute selection. An example of such a technique is optimal multisplitting of numerical attributes. Its efficiency is hit hard even by a single troublesome attribute in the domain.

Analysis shows that there is a direct connection between the ratio of the numbers of boundary points and training examples and the maximum goodness score of a numerical attribute. Class distribution information from preprocessing can be applied to obtain tighter bounds for an attribute's relevance in class prediction. These analytical bounds, however, are too loose for practical purposes.

We experiment with heuristic methods which postpone the evaluation of attributes that have a high number of boundary points. The results show that substantial time savings can be obtained in the most critical data sets without having to give up on the accuracy of the resulting classifier.

1 Introduction

Identifying and eliminating either irrelevant attributes [4, 13] or untrustworthy training examples [3, 12, 17] prior to classifier construction are techniques used to aid and enhance the induction process (for a comprehensive survey see [1]). Such cleaning methods can be heavier than the actual process of building a classifier. Moreover, irreversible decisions to remove attributes or examples are taken. In this paper we explore efficient ways of enhancing the induction process by overlooking some attributes at some stages, but without losing the possibility to use them later if they turn out to be beneficial then.

Inductive process that is based on univariate partitioning of the given data set—e.g., top-down induction of decision trees—is inherently myopic to interrelations between attributes. Its stronghold is the extreme efficiency on mid-sized data sets. However, when large databases are processed even this advantage may vanish; in particular, if the attribute selection entails processing that requires superlinear time in the number of examples or some other characteristic figure.

Evaluating nominal attributes is efficient. Numerical attribute domains, on the other hand, need to be discretized, which may be time consuming if the domain at hand has a very high number of candidate cut points. Even a linear-time method like *binarization* can require substantial amount of time. This presents a particular problem for learning algorithms that have to manipulate numerical attributes exhaustively; e.g., optimal [8, 11] or greedy [10] multisplitters in decision tree learning. The inconvenience for all attribute selection strategies alike is that the time consumption of attribute selection is dominated by the attributes that require the heaviest evaluation. Hence, even a single difficult attribute can ruin the efficiency of an otherwise manageable domain.

This paper studies how *boundary points* [9] can be utilized to determine the relevance of an attribute in univariate induction. It is shown that an attribute with many boundary points is not relevant for class prediction. As evaluating such an attribute is also time consuming, postponing its evaluation should turn out beneficial in the resulting classifiers quality and speed of classifier construction. We do not want to trade accuracy for efficiency or simplicity, but strive to maintain the prediction ability of the resulting decision tree while speeding up the classifier construction by simple and efficient dynamic data processing.

During the iterative top-down induction of a decision tree the number of boundary points that have to be taken into account in one dimension decreases, since the recursive partitioning of the data removes possible cut points—and boundary points as well. Also, the number of available training examples decreases during tree construction as the training set gets partitioned into smaller and smaller subsets. Due to this dynamics, we do not definitely disregard an attribute, which at some point has a too high number of boundary points, but keep it for further evaluation in the changed situation.

2 Preliminaries

All numerical dimension of data represented as attribute value assignments share as a common characteristic figure the *number of instances*, n. Another characteristic figure is the *number of different values*, V, for the attribute. Numerical attributes can have a very large, even infinite, domain. As a third figure numerical dimensions have the *number of boundary points*, $B - 1$. Intuitively, boundary points are such values of a numerical value range that partitioning the data with those values as thresholds will not needlessly separate two instances of the same class to different subsets of the partition. Such a partitioning will not obviously harm the prediction of the example class labels.

The basic relationships of these three figures are $B \leq V \leq n$, but it is the common (mis)conception that $B \ll V \ll n$ in real-world data. Recently the relationship of these figures have been studied in detail [8] for a large collection of the most commonly used machine learning data sets from the UCI data repository [16]. It turns out that most typically the number of boundary points in a numerical dimension is at least half of the total number of existing values in the data. The claim $V \ll n$ is better grounded, and $B \ll n$ even more so.

The minimum preprocessing in handling a numerical attribute is to sort the training data by its value. The data cannot be partitioned in this dimension so that two examples with equal values for the underlying attribute would belong to different subsets. Therefore, we can consider a categorized version of the data, where all examples with an equal value constitute a *bin* of examples. There are as many bins as distinct values for the attribute, V.

Fayyad and Irani's [9] analysis of the binarization technique proved that for the information gain function [18] only *boundary points* need to be considered as potential cut points, because optimal binary splits always fall on them due to the convexity of the function. Codrington and Brodley [5] present further studies of the convexity properties of many common attribute evaluation functions.

Definition 1. Let a sequence S of examples be sorted by the value of a numerical attribute A. The set of *boundary points* is defined as follows: A value $T \in \text{Dom}(A)$ is a boundary point if and only if there exists a pair of examples $s_1, s_2 \in S$, having different classes, such that $\text{val}_A(s_1) = T < \text{val}_A(s_2)$; and there does not exist another example $s \in S$ such that $\text{val}_A(s_1) < \text{val}_A(s) < \text{val}_A(s_2)$.

In the original definition a boundary point was taken to be a value that is strictly in between the values $\text{val}_A(s_1)$ and $\text{val}_A(s_2)$ [9]. The above definition leads to partitions with the same subsets. Let us now define a *block* of examples. It is a concept that facilitates the discovery of all boundary points of a data set.

Definition 2. Let the example set S be ordered by the value of a numerical attribute A. Let C be the class attribute. A *block* of examples is a *maximal-length* sequence of consecutive examples $s_1, \ldots, s_b \subseteq S$ such that

1. $\text{val}_C(s_1) = \ldots = \text{val}_C(s_b)$ and there does not exist an example $s \in S$ such that $\text{val}_A(s_1) \leq \text{val}_A(s) \leq \text{val}_A(s_b)$ and $\text{val}_C(s) \neq \text{val}_C(s_1)$, or
2. $\text{val}_A(s_1) = \ldots = \text{val}_A(s_b)$ and there exists s_i, $i \in \{2, \ldots, b\}$, such that $\text{val}_C(s_i) \neq \text{val}_C(s_1)$.

Blocks of type (1) are *uniform* ones and those of type (2) are *mixed* ones. Boundary points of a set are exactly the borders of blocks, which makes finding them simple. Blocks are obtained from bins by merging only adjacent class uniform bins with the same class label into a block. Mixed bins are never merged into a block with another bin.

In decision tree learning the number of boundary points in a numerical dimension depends on the phase of tree construction: it is the highest at the root level, when the data has not yet been partitioned, reduces through some splits defined by other attributes, until finally, at the level of the last decision nodes, it reaches a linear correlation with the decision tree's accuracy on the training data (if the numerical attribute in question is to be chosen to the tree).

A *well-behaved* function always has an optimal multisplit on boundary points [8]. All the most commonly used attribute evaluation functions are well-behaved. By using a well-behaved function we may concentrate on boundary points independent of whether the partition arity is limited *a priori* or not. If a well-behaved evaluation function also has the so-called *cumulativity* property, the general optimal partitioning algorithm of Fulton *et al.* [11] can be adapted to operate in time that is quadratic in the number of blocks instead of bins.

3 Boundary points as an indication of attribute relevance

Let us study the well-behaved evaluation function *average class entropy*, ACE. For a partition $\uplus_i S_i$ of the data set S, ACE is defined to be

$$ACE(\uplus_i S_i) = (1/|S|) \sum_i |S_i| H(S_i) = (1/n) \sum_i |S_i| H(S_i),$$

where H is the entropy function: $H(S) = -\sum_{j=1}^m P(C_j, S) \log_2 P(C_j, S)$, in which m denotes the number of classes and $P(C, S)$ stands for the proportion of examples in S that have class C.

Let us bound the minimum value of average class entropy in the following situation. We are partitioning a numerical attribute's value range into ℓ intervals; there are n training examples and the domain in question contains B blocks.

Since ACE is a well-behaved function, its optimal ℓ-partition is defined by $\ell - 1$ boundary points. Hence, there are $B - \ell$ further boundary points within the partition subsets. It pays to maximize the number of examples belonging to partition subsets that have zero entropy, i.e., such examples that belong to class uniform intervals. To that end, intervals into which the unused boundary points fall, have to be as short as possible. That is obtained if each example in such a subset alone constitutes an uniform block, then there is a boundary point in between every pair of consecutive examples. We are approximating the minimum value of ACE, so we can freely assume there to be only two classes.

Let us now settle the question into how many subsets should the extra boundary points be distributed. As the above motivation shows $|S_i| H(S_i)/b_i$ minimizes when $b_i = |S_i| - 1$. It can be easily verified that the function $|S_i| H(S_i)/b_i = H(S_i)|S_i|/(|S_i| - 1)$ decreases monotonically when $|S_i|$ increases and, hence, it holds that $\sum_{i=1}^\ell |S_i| H(S_i)/b_i \geq |\bigcup_{i=1}^\ell S_i| H(\bigcup_{i=1}^\ell S_i)/(\sum_{i=1}^\ell b_i)$ for any set of subsets $S_1, \ldots, S_\ell$ which contain $b_i = |S_i| - 1$ boundary points each. Therefore, packing the extra boundaries into a single interval will lead to a smaller ACE value than segregating the boundary points.

The above construction gives the idealized minimum value of ACE: No other partition subset, except the one into which all unused boundary points have been packed, contributes to the impurity of the partition. Hence, the average class entropy of the partition is $ACE(\uplus_{i=1}^\ell S_i) \geq (B - \ell)/n$. In other words, the lowest obtainable average class entropy of a partition depends directly on the ratio B/n.

Due to the heavily idealized assumptions underlying the above calculations, we do not expect this lower bound to be very tight. Nevertheless, it shows that there is a direct correlation between the B/n ratio and an attribute's relevance for class prediction in univariate induction. The way to apply the bound is straightforward: if the ratio $(B - \ell)/n$ shows that by partitioning the data along this dimension cannot lead to a better choice of an attribute than the current best choice, then we can leave this attribute unevaluated (at this point).

The above calculated minimum value for ACE serves as the basis for an upper bound of the highest obtainable value of the *information gain* function [18]. It is defined as $IG(\uplus_i S_i) = H(S) - ACE(\uplus_i S_i)$. $H(S)$—the entropy of the data set S prior to partitioning it—is constant with respect to the dimensions of the data. Therefore, IG's maximum value coincides with ACE's minimum value and its relevance assignment can, by the same rationale, be bound by the ratio B/n.

Many other evaluation functions use IG as their building block, which means that from the above analysis of ACE we can obtain bounds for the values of these functions as well. Such functions include, e.g., *balanced gain* [8,14], *gain ratio* [19,20], and *normalized distance* measure [15]. Also, the *gini index* (of diversity) [2] has a very similar formula as IG, and ought to be easy to analyze. In this paper we, however, only consider balanced gain, $BG_{\log}$, which is defined as $BG_{\log}(\uplus_{i=1}^{k} S_i) = IG(\uplus_{i=1}^{k} S_i)/\log_2 k$. It has turned out to be a function with, in most cases, superior performance than information gain and gain ratio functions. In addition, it has other desirable properties [8].

4 Utilizing information from preprocessing

No matter which partitioning strategy is used to handle numerical attributes, preprocessing of the data is required. At least the examples have to be sorted. Identification of candidate cut points requires a scan over the data set. Hence, the direct approximation of attribute relevance on the basis of the number of boundary points presented in the preceding section requires time that has a linear dependency on the number of examples n. However, from the preprocessing stage we can also extract, at the low cost of $O(mB)$, the class distributions of blocks. In practice, this preprocessing time has been observed to be negligible with respect to the time required by actual evaluation of candidate partitions [8]. These distributions give another possibility to bound (sometimes more tightly) the relevance of an attribute on the basis of boundary points.

For the function ACE it is quite easy to show—using basic information theoretical results—that its optimal (least) value is obtained by the partition that is defined by all the boundary points of the data.

Theorem 3 (Log Sum Inequality [6]). *Given non-negative $a_i, b_i, i = 1, \ldots, k$,*

$$\sum_{i=1}^{k} a_i \log(a_i/b_i) \geq \left(\sum_{i=1}^{k} a_i\right) \log\left(\sum_{i=1}^{k} a_i / \sum_{i=1}^{k} b_i\right)$$

with equality iff a_i/b_i is constant, $i = 1, \ldots, k$.

Let us substitute into the Log Sum Inequality the non-negative fractions $a_i = n_{i,j}/n$ and $b_i = n_i/n$, where $0 \leq n_{i,j} \leq n_i \leq n$, $i = 1, \ldots, k$; we get

$$\sum_{i=1}^{k} (n_{i,j}/n) \log(n_{i,j}/n_i) \geq (n_j/n) \log(n_j/n).$$

Negating both sides and summing over $j = 1, \ldots, m$ we get

$$-\sum_{i=1}^{k} (n_i/n) \sum_{j=1}^{m} (n_{i,j}/n_i) \log(n_{i,j}/n_i) \leq -\sum_{j=1}^{m} (n_j/n) \log(n_j/n).$$

Bringing the notation in accord with the earlier one, we have $n = |S|$, $n_i = |S_i|$, $n_j/n = P(C_j, S)$, and $n_{i,j}/n_i = P(C_j, S_i)$, which maintain the non-negativity of a_i and b_i. Taking, furthermore, the logarithms to have base 2, the above inequality can be rewritten as

$$(1/|S|) \sum_i |S_i| H(S_i) \leq H(S) \Leftrightarrow ACE(\biguplus_i S_i) \leq ACE(S).$$

In other words, any partition $\biguplus_i S_i$, $i = 2, \ldots, B$, of a data set S will have at most the same average class entropy as the whole data set.

ACE is convex in between any two consecutive boundary points [5, 9] and any further partitioning of the data on a boundary point reduces the average class entropy of the partition. Hence, the minimum ACE value over a data set is always obtained by the B-partition that has as its subsets all the blocks of the data. Let us denote the value of ACE in such a case by $\sigma_B = (1/n) \sum_{i=1}^{B} |S_i| H(S_i)$. The value of this partition serves as an approximation of a numerical attribute's utility in class prediction: $ACE(\biguplus_i S_i) \geq \sigma_B$, for any partition $\biguplus_i S_i$, $i = 2, \ldots, B$, of the data set S. Clearly, this lower bound can be computed in linear time.

The value of $H(S)$ can, of course, be computed at the same single pass through the data and it is constant for all attributes. $H(S) - \sigma_B$ is a lower bound for information gain of any partition of S. Incidentally, this explains why the information gain function is so eager to favor higher arity partitions of numerical attribute domains and nominal attributes with many potential values [19]. Furthermore, we can use this value to obtain an upper bound for the balanced gain. Observe that $BG_{\log}$ does not (necessarily) obtain its maximum value when all blocks of the data constitute a partition subset of their own since the denominator $\log_2 k$ biases against unnecessary splitting.

It is common to set an upper bound k for the arity of the partition. Obviously, the above-derived approximations are not very tight if $k \ll B$. We cannot use partitions of arity k as our approximation, since enumerating them requires $O(B^2)$ time.

5   Empirical evaluation

This section presents the results of comparative experiments in which C4.5 algorithm [20] changed to multisplit numerical attributes optimally using the balanced gain function and equipped with four different postponing strategies:

- **Analytic.** We combine the two analytically derived bounds and compare the best observed $BG_{\log}$ score with the value $(H(S) - \sigma_{\max})/\log_2 k$, where $\sigma_{\max} = \max\{(B - \ell)/n, \sigma_B\}$.
- **Heuristic1**. This heuristic postpones the evaluation of an attribute if $B/n > t$. As threshold t we try values .5, .2, and .1.
- **Heuristic2**. This heuristic orders the numerical attributes by the number of boundary points and postpones the evaluation $(1 - t)100\%$ of them, those that have the highest number of boundary points. We test values $t = \{.9, .7, .5\}$.
- **Heuristic3**. The final heuristic postpones the evaluation of those numerical attributes that have $B_{\min}/B > t$, where $B_{\min}$ is the least boundary point count among the attributes. Threshold values .9, .7, and .5 are attempted.

Into our comparison we have chosen 15 data sets mainly from the UCI repository with such properties that they contain numerical attributes, have attributes

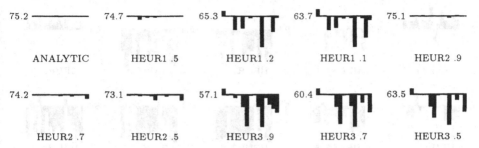

Fig. 1. The average accuracies of the postponing strategies in the 5x2cv test. The average accuracy of not postponing the evaluation of any attributes is 75.2%. The bars represent the relative gain or loss with respect to not postponing attribute evaluation.

with a high number of boundary points, or are large. Most of the domains are well-known; we do not describe them here, for a comprehensive description of their characteristic figures see, e.g., [8]. The domains are Abalone, Adult, Australian, Auto imports, German, Glass, Letter recognition, Mole, Page blocks, Satellite, Segmentation, Shuttle, Vehicle, Waveform, and Yeast.

As the test strategy we use two-fold cross validation testing repeated five times, 5x2cv; it has been observed to be a reliable statistical test in experiments that involve comparison of more than two learning algorithms [7].

The average prediction accuracies obtained using the strategies in the 5x2cv test are depicted in Fig. 1. The most salient observation to be made from these results is that we cannot claim Heuristic3 nor Heuristic1 with thresholds .2 and .1 to maintain the overall level of prediction accuracy that exists when the evaluation of attributes is not delayed. Heuristic2, on the other hand, maintains the overall accuracy even when 50% of attributes are left unevaluated at each attribute selection step. The strategy Analytic does not change the prediction accuracy significantly but, as can be observed from the representation in Fig. 2, that is mainly due to it not postponing the evaluation of attributes near the root level of the tree; only when the number of remaining boundary points approaches that of the partition arity limit, the analytical bounds start to have an effect. The analytically derived bounds are not tight enough to gain speed-up in practice.

The utility of the heuristic methods is ultimately decided on the time saving that is obtained through using them. In particular, on the domains that contain singular malignant attributes that cause the optimal multisplitting algorithm to use excessive amounts of time. The reference time is that of not postponing the evaluation of attributes. The overall performance is summarized by the *geometric mean* of these results.

Fig. 2 shows the average time consumptions of the postponing strategies. We can observe that Heuristic1 with threshold .5—which still maintains the overall prediction accuracy well—cannot bring time savings, except for one domain: Abalone. It is, however, important to notice that for all time critical domains, except Waveform, the tighter thresholds maintain (or even increase) accuracy and bring speed-ups; they are substantial whenever there are individual malig-

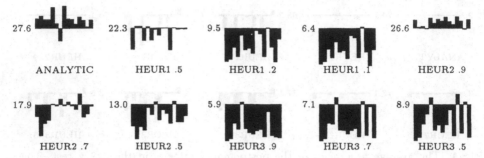

Fig. 2. The geometric mean times of the postponing strategies in the 5x2cv test. The mean time required when not postponing the evaluation of attributes is 23.0 seconds. The bars represent relative speed-up or slow-down on individual domains.

nant attributes in the domain—e.g., Abalone and Adult—but less impressive in other cases—e.g., Page blocks and Shuttle:

From Fig. 2 we can see that the speed-up of Heuristic2 depends on the strictness of the threshold: with parameter value .9 no time savings are obtained, but the lower values bring better results. Again the best results are obtained for the most critical domains. A small accuracy-efficiency tradeoff exists also for this heuristic (cf. Fig. 1). Heuristic3 gains a lot of speed for the decision tree construction, but—with these threshold values—the loss of accuracy is intolerable.

Altogether, all three heuristics do well in getting rid of singular malignant attributes, which are not useful in induction in any case. The achieved speed-up depends on the domain and on the strictness of the threshold. Unfortunately, in other cases the heuristics can work against the accuracy of the result by postponing the evaluation of an important attribute, forcing the learning algorithm to make a less profitable choise. Heuristic 2 appears very safe in this respect.

6   Conclusions and further work

We presented an analysis on the relationship of a numerical attribute's relevance to class prediction and the number of boundary points in the data dimension determined by the attribute. The analytic bounds are not tight enough to screen out malignant attributes, but suggest efficient heuristics that can be used to enhance univariate decision tree induction by postponing the evaluation of attributes that are very likely to have a low relevance and would require substantial amount of time for evaluation. The empirical evaluation confirms the benefits that can be obtained in case of removing malignant attributes, but also show that some heuristics can work against the accuracy of the resulting decision tree.

The most obvious direction for further work is to continue the analysis of the multisplitting of numerical attributes to obtain tighter and more practical bounds for the utility of an attribute in class prediction. In case of the bound that utilizes information from the preprocessing, the most urgent need would be to close the gap between the arity of the lower bound, B, and that of the partition under consideration, ℓ. That gap is the reason for this bound's looseness.

Further heuristics that take the number of boundary points into account are easy to figure out, as well as enhancements to the heuristics studied in this paper. For instance, turning off the postponing in case of small domains or when the tree construction has proceeded to a certain stage would both probably enhance the efficiency of the heuristics.

References

1. Blum, A., Langley, P.: Selection of relevant features and examples in machine learning. Artif. Intell. **97** (1997) 245–271
2. Breiman, L., Friedman, J., Olshen, R., Stone, C.: Classification and Regression Trees. Wadsworth (1984)
3. Brodley, C., Friedl, M.: Identifying and eliminating mislabeled training instances. In: Proc. 13th Natl. Conf. on Artificial Intelligence. AAAI Press (1996) 799–805
4. Caruana, R., Freitag, D.: Greedy attribute selection. In: Machine Learning: Proc. 11th Intl. Conf. Morgan Kaufmann (1994) 28–36
5. Codrington, C., Brodley, C.: On the qualitative behavior of impurity-based splitting rules I: The minima-free property. Tech. Rep. 97-5. Purdue Univ., School of Electrical and Computer Engineering, 1997
6. Cover, T., Thomas, J.: Elements of Information Theory. Wiley & Sons (1991)
7. Dietterich, T.: Approximate statistical tests for comparing supervised classification learning algorithms. Neural Comput. (to appear)
8. Elomaa, T., Rousu, J.: General and efficient multisplitting of numerical attributes. Mach. Learn. (to appear)
9. Fayyad, U., Irani, K.: On the handling of continuous-valued attributes in decision tree generation. Mach. Learn. **8** (1992) 87–102
10. Fayyad, U., Irani, K.: Multi-interval discretization of continuous-valued attributes for classification learning. In: Proc. 13th Intl. Joint Conf. on Artificial Intelligence. Morgan Kaufmann (1993) 1022–1027
11. Fulton, T., Kasif, S., Salzberg, S.: Efficient algorithms for finding multi-way splits for decision trees. In: Machine Learning: Proc. 12th Intl. Conf. Morgan Kaufmann (1995) 244–251
12. John, G.: Robust decision trees: Removing outliers from data. In: Proc. 1st Intl. Conf. on Knowledge Discovery and Data Mining. AAAI Press (1995) 174–179
13. Kohavi, R., John, G.: Wrappers for feature subset selection. Artif. Intell. **97** (1997) 273–324
14. Kononenko, I., Bratko, I., Roškar, E.: Experiments in automatic learning of medical diagnostic rules. Tech. Rep. Josef Stefan Institute (1984)
15. López de Màntaras, R.: A distance-based attribute selection measure for decision tree induction. Mach. Learn. **6** (1991) 81–92
16. Merz, C., Murphy, P.: UCI repository of machine learning databases. http://www.ics.uci.edu/~mlearn/MLRepository.html.
17. Oates, T., Jensen, D.: Large datasets lead to overly complex models: an explanation and a solution. In: Proc. 4th Intl. Conf. on Knowledge Discovery and Data Mining. AAAI Press (to appear)
18. Quinlan, R.: Learning efficient classification procedures and their application to chess end games. In: Michalski, R., Carbonell, J., Mitchell, T. (eds.): Machine Learning: An Artificial Intelligence Approach. Tioga (1983) 391–411
19. Quinlan, R.: Induction of decision trees. Mach. Learn. **1** (1986) 81–106
20. Quinlan, R.: C4.5: Programs for Machine Learning. Morgan Kaufmann (1993)

A Hybrid Approach to Feature Selection

Moussa Boussouf

IRIN, Université de Nantes, 2 rue de la Houssiniére,
BP 92208 - 44322, Nantes Cedex 03, France.
boussouf@irin.univ-nantes.fr

Abstract. The irrelevant and redundant features may degrade the learner speed (due to the high dimensionality) and reduce both the accuracy and comprehensibility of induced model. To cope with these problems, many methods have been proposed to select a subset of pertinent features. In order to evaluate these subsets, two main approaches are generally distinguished: (1) filter approach: which considers only data i.e. algorithm-independent; (2) wrapper approach: which takes into account both data and a given learning algorithm i.e. algorithm-dependent.
In this paper, we address the problem of subset selection using α–RST (a generalized rough sets theory). We propose an algorithm to find a set of α–reducts which are non deterministic reducts. To select the best one among them, we also propose a *Hybrid Approach* by putting filter and wrapper together to overcome the disadvantages of each approach. Our study shows that generally the highest-accuracy-subset is not the best one as regards to the filter criteria. The highest accuracy subset is found by the new approach with minimum cost.

1   Introduction

In supervised machine learning, an induction algorithm deals with a set of training instances where each instance is described by a vector of feature values and a class label. The induction task consists creating a model of data (training set). This model can be used to predict the label of new instances. The irrelevant and redundant features may reduce predictive accuracy, degrade the learner speed (due to the high dimensionality) and reduce the comprehensibility of the induced model. So, doing away with these features or selecting relevant ones became necessary.

The difficulties which were faced during the feature selection prodecss can be explained as follows: for N features, there are 2^N possible subsets, evaluating them is an impracticable process. The optimal selection can only be done by testing all possible sets of M features chosen from N, i.e. by applying the criterion $\binom{N}{M} = \frac{N!}{M! + (N-M)!}$ times. If there are M relevant features, the total number of times is $\sum_{i=0}^{M} \binom{N}{i} = O(N^M)$. This is prohibitive when N and/or M is large.

To deal with the problem of feature selection, many methods have been proposed. In general, they can be classified into two categories: (1) the filter approach, which serves as a filter to sieve the irrelevant and/or redundant features without taking into account the induction algorithm [1][5][10]; and (2) the wrapper approach , which uses the induction algorithm itself as a black box in the phase of attributes selection to select a good features subset which improve the performance, i.e. the accuracy of the induction algorithm [4][8][11][16]. Although the wrapper approach has significantly improved the accuracy of well known algorithms, like C4.5 and Naive-Bayes, its generalization is limited for many reasons i.e.: (1) the former's computational cost, which results from calling the induction algorithm for each feature subset considered; (2) dealing with large datasets being impracticable. Using the wrapper approach to evaluate random generated subsets LVW, Liu and Setenio in [11] concluded that it is not commendable to use LVW in the applications where time is a critical factor. On the other hand, the main critics of filter approach are: (1) it totally ignores the effects of selected feature subset on the performance of the induction algorithm [4]; (2) various heuristics tend to overestimate the multi-valued attributes [9]. In order to cope with the above problems, the two main approaches were extended considering probability foundations: a probabilistic filter approach [10] and a probabilistic wrapper approach [11] [6].

In the rough sets theory [13][14], many reducts can be found. Their number depends on the indiscernibility of examples and cannot be known beforehand. Consequently, the evaluation and selection of the best reduct is still a serious problem, especially when the number of reducts is large.

In this paper, we use the generalized rough sets theory, called α–RST, which is proposed by Quafafou in [15] as the theoretical framework. We propose a new attribute selection process, called *Hybrid Approach*. This new approach combines the two above approaches. It inherits the advantages and eliminates the disadvantages of both filter and wrapper approach.

The remainder of this paper is organized as follows: section 2 presents the feature selection in the rough sets framework. It introduces the new definitions of the generalized concepts, which are necessary for our investigation. Section 3 presents our reducts algorithm. In order to evaluate the generated reducts, section 4 is an examination of two filters. Section 5 presents our experimental results with filter approach, wrapper approach and with the new hybrid approach. We conclude in section 6.

2 Feature subsets selection in rough sets theory

In the rough sets theory [13][14], the most important and fundamental notions are the need to discover *redundancy*, *dependency* between features, *reduction* of features and definition of the *core*, which is a set of attributes which contains all indispensable features. The feature subset selection can be viewed as finding reducts. In this context, different works have been developed to deal with the problem of subset selection. Moderzejewski in [12] proposes a heuristic feature selector algorithm, called PRESET. It consists ordering attributes to obtain an optimal preset decision tree (according to absolute significance of attribute measure). Kohavi and Frasca in [7] have shown that, in some situations, the *useful* subset does not necessarily contain all the features in the *core* and may be different from a reduct. Using α–RST, we have proposed in [16] an algorithm based on wrapper approach to solve this problem. We have shown that we can obtain lower size reducts with higher accuracy than those obtained by classic rough sets concepts.

Before presenting the algorithm which finds α–reducts, we will present an overview of the necessary concepts of α–RST.

Generalized information system In rough sets theory, an information system has a data table form. Formally, an information system S is a 4-tuple $S = (U, Q, V, f)$, *where* U : *is a finite set of objects.* Q : **is** *a finite set of attributes.* $V = \cup V_q$, *where* V_q *is a domain of attribute q. f is an information function assigning a value of attribute for every object and every attribute, i.e. $f : U \times Q \mapsto V$, such that for every $x \in U$ and for every $q \in Q$ $f(x, q) \in V_q$.*

To deal with quantitative attributes, a preprocessing discretization phase is necessary to transform continuous attributes into qualitative terms (nominal value). This process may influence the results of systems using rough sets theory [17]. In order to take into account uncertainty inherent to both data and preprocessing, Quafafou in [15] has proposed a new information system. The information function f being defined as follows:
$f : U \times Q \to V \times [0, 1]$ *such that for every $x \in U$ and for every $q \in Q$ $f(x, q) \in (V_q, [0, 1])$.*

Each attribute q of each object x is described by a pair of a nominal value and a cardinal value. The cardinal value represents the degree of possibility, $\pi \in [0, 1]$, that the attribute q may have the value V_q for the object x (Table 1).

Definition 1. α–Indiscernibility relation : *Let R be a subset of Q, α a given similarity threshold. The α–indiscernibility relation denoted by $IND(R, \alpha)$ is defined as*

$$IND(R, \alpha) = \{(x, y) \in U \times U \mid f(x, q) = f(y, q) \ \forall q \in R, \ and \ \Im(\pi_x, \pi_y) \geq \alpha\}$$

If $(x, y) \in IND(R, \alpha)$, then x and y are α–indiscernible with respect to R, that means that they have the same value of attributes and that their similarity degree, computed by the function $\Im$, is greater than α. Consequently, the equivalence class of an obejct x, denoted $[x]_{IND(R, \alpha)}$, is defined by the set $\{y \in U \mid (x, y) \in IND(R, \alpha)\}$. The opposite of this relation is called α–*discernibility* relation, denoted $DIS(R, \alpha)$.

Definition 2. α–Dependency: *Let P and R be two subsets of attributes, such that $R \subseteq P$ and $\alpha \in [0, 1]$. R α–depends on P if and only if $\exists \beta \in [0, 1]$ such that: $P \overset{\beta}{\to} R \Leftrightarrow \forall B \in U/IND(P, \alpha) \ \exists B\prime \in U/IND(R, \alpha) \ deg(B \subseteq B\prime) \geq \beta$*

The α–dependency can be seen as partial dependency between values of R and P, i.e. R partially explains P.

Definition 3. α–reducts : *Let P and R be two subsets of attributes, such that $R \subseteq P$. R is an α–reduct of P if and only if $\exists \beta \in [0,1]$ such that (i) $P \xrightarrow{\beta} R$ and $R \xrightarrow{\beta} P$ and (ii) R is minimal. R is minimal means there is no subset T of R which is an α–reduct of P.*

3 α–Reducts Algorithm

In this section we show how to find α–reducts using α–discernibility relation. Firstly, we calculate the α–discernibility–list, denoted αDL, of all minimal α–discernible subsets which contain the class label. Each element of this list contains a subset of features which discern a pair of examples. To deal with redundancy, all non minimal subsets are deleted. Secondly, we construct the minimal α–reducts–list, denoted αRL, from minimal α–discernible–list.

α–Reducts Algorithm

```
Input      GIS : Generalized Information System of N examples;
           Q : All Features includes Class;
           C : Class;
           α : similarity threshold;
Output     αRL := { {} } : α-Reducts-List;
           αDL =: {} : α-Discernibility-List;
for i := 1 to N+1
    for j := i+1 to N
        TempSubset := α-DIS(Q,α,GIS[i],GIS[j]);
        /* the set of features which discern GIS[i] and GIS[j] */
        if C ⊂ TempSubset
            if ∄ E ∈ α DL such that E ⊆ TempSubset
                add(TempSubset - { C }, αDL);
            endif
        endif
    endfor
endfor /*end construction of minimal α-Discernibility-List */
if card(αDL) ≤ 1 αRL := αDL
else for each element EDL of αDL
        for each element ERL of αRL
            for each feature F of EDL
                ERL := ERL ∪F;
            endfor
        endfor
        Delete all not minimal elements of αRL;
    endfor
endif
```

The example bellow (Table 1) illustrates the presented concepts. For each example, the first value expresses the nominal value of an attribute, the second represents the degree of possibility that this attribute may have this value.
$U = \{e1, e2, ..., e8\}$,
$Q = \{W, X, Y, Z, C\}$
$\alpha\text{-}DIS(Q, 0, e1, e2) = \{W, X, Y, C\}$;
$\alpha\text{-}DIS(Q, 0, e1, e3) = \{W, X, Y, Z, C\}$.

	W	X	Y	Z	C
e1	5 1.0	1 0.6	3 0.6	2 0.7	2
e2	4 1.0	4 0.8	4 1.0	2 1.0	0
e3	3 0.9	2 1.0	2 1.0	0 1.0	1
e4	5 0.7	3 0.6	4 0.7	1 0.6	1
e5	3 0.6	4 1.0	3 0.8	1 0.8	2
e6	4 0.6	1 1.0	3 1.0	0 1.0	0
e7	3 1.0	3 1.0	4 0.8	1 1.0	1
e8	5 0.7	3 0.7	4 0.9	2 0.7	2

Table 1. Example of 8 elements

Where $\alpha=0$, the reader can verify that:
α–discernibility–list: $\alpha DL = \{\{X, Y\}, \{W, X\}, \{Z\}\}$.
α–reducts–list : $\alpha RL = \{\{X, Z\}, \{W, Y, Z\}\}$.

The strong characteristics of α–Reducts Algorithm are: (1) The parameter α influences and controls the granularity and the number of reducts, i.e.: when *alpha* increases, the size of reducts decreases and the number of reducts generally increases; (2) we obtain the classical reducts (corresponding to classical framework of rough sets) when $\alpha=0$; (3) the best reduct with highest accuracy is obtained when $\alpha > 0$ i.e. using α–RST concepts [16]; (4) theoretically, the algorithm can find $\binom{N}{\lfloor N/2 \rfloor}$ reducts.

4 Evaluating α–Reducts

As described above, α–reducts algorithm can generate many reducts. Selecting the best one is still a serious problem, especially when the number of α–reducts is high. Consequently the application of the wrapper method is impracticable. We focus our study on examining two filter algorithms which evaluate a given subset entirely. Other heuristic measures are summarized in [9].

Almuallim and Dietterich MIG: In order to improve FOCUS algorithm, Almuallim and Dietterich in [1] proposed tree heuristics for the MIN–FEATURES bias. The Mutual–Information–Greedy algorithm use the entropy measure to evaluate a subset entirely. This algorithm searches the minimum-size attribute subset sufficient to maintain consistency on the training data. Generally, databases are not consistent even when all attributes are present, i.e. a subset cannot be more consistent than its superset. Caruana and Freitag in [2] solved this problem to apply FOCUS in CAP by returning the smallest subset of attributes that contains the same inconsistency compared with all attributes.
Liu and Setiono inconsistency measure: Liu and Setiono in [10] proposed a measure to evaluate selected features. The inconsistency rate of data described by a selected subset is checked against a prespecified threshold. The one which has the lowest value is chosen for further tests using a learning algorithm.

To apply the filter measures described above, the subset which has minimum value must be returned.

5 Experiment Results

In order to evaluate candidate strong feature subsets generated by α-reducts algorithm, we ran experiments on 7 real-world datasets taken from the UCI Irvine repository, their characteristics are summarized in Table 2. Original data are transformed using Fayad and Irani method [3].

Datasets	Exam.	Att.	Cla.	%Num.
Iris	150	4	3	100
Pima	768	8	2	100
Australian	690	14	2	43
Glass	214	9	6	100
Heart	270	13	2	46
Vehicle	746	18	4	100
Wave	600	21	3	100

Table 2. Datasets considered: the number of examples and attributes, class cardinality and the percentage of numeric features

To estimate the accuracy for feature subsets we used 5-fold cross validation. The algorithm ALPHA is used as an inducer algorithm.

We applied the above filter on generated reduct. The best subset, the one which has the lowest value is chosen for further tests using the learning algorithm. We also applied the wrapper model around all reducts.

5.1 Filter *or* wrapper

In our experiments we found that the best subset selected by Liu&Setanio filter is generally different from the subset selected by Almualim&Dietrich filter. Table 3 shows that the reduct chosen by the two filters improves slightly the accuracy of ALPHA (with all features) for Pima, Australian and Heart. The accuracy falls for Vehicle, Wave and significantly for Glass. On the other hand, the reduct selected by wrapper method improves the accuracy of ALPHA in all databases except for Glass. The improvements are significant for Heart, Vehicle and Wave.

Datasets	α	N. Red.	ALPHA	Filter/ALPHA		Wrapper/	Size of
				L&S	A&D	ALPHA	best Red
Iris	0.2	1	96.00	96.00	96.00	96.00	3
Pima	1.0	3	75.39	75.78	75.78	75.78	7
Australian	0.8	6	81.44	82.90	82.32	**83.04**	12
Glass	1.0	**10**	**61.68**	56.34	56.34	**59.91**	5
Heart	0.9	**51**	83.33	84.81	84.81	**85.56**	7
Vehicle	0.9	**288**	68.44	67.73	68.91	**70.33**	10
Wave	0.5	**4349**	74.00	69.67	72.67	**77.50***	11
Mean			77.18	76.18	76.69	78.44	

Table 3. Similarity threshold, number of α-reducts; the accuracy of ALPHA, the accuracies of ALPHA using Liu and Setiono filter, Almualim and Dietrich filter, wrapper model and size of best reduct. *: Due to the former's computational cost, we ran wrapper method around 1600 reducts.

The accuracy of the reducts chosen by the wrapper method is superior to that of the filter method, especially when the number of reducts is higher than one. In the Wave database the difference with L&S filter equals 4.83% and with A&D filter equals 7.83% .

In order to capture the best reduct which improves significantly the accuracy, and which is not obtained by the filter method, we have considered filtering a few reducts and execute the induction algorithm around them, which is the topic of the next section.

5.2 The Hybrid Approach: filter *and* wrapper

As described above, the main disadvantage of the wrapper approach is the former's computational cost. For example running inducer algorithm on 4349 subsets of Wave database takes a lot of time. However, the various filters do not obtain relevant results. We propose a new *Hybrid Approach*, it combines the two above approaches, which were based on tree phases: (1) α–reducts computation, (2) filtration of α–reducts to focus our attention on only a few reducts, (3) use of the wrapper method to select the best one among the filtered ones. This new approach inherits the advantages and eliminates the disadvantages of both filter and wrapper approach. We define a threshold of allowable filter rate γ. The learning algorithm is applied only on each reduct in which the filter criterion rate is lower than γ.

Hybrid algorithm

Input   GIS : Generalized Information System (training data);
           α : similarity threshold;
           γ : allowable filter criterion rate;
Output Hsfs : Hybrid strong feature subset;
MaxAcc=0;
CandidateHsfs := αReducts(GIS,α) /*Calling α–Reducts algorithm*/
while NotEmpty(CandidateHsfs) **do**
      Current := select(CandidateHsfs);
      CandidateHsfs := CandidateHsfs - Current;
      if filter(Current) $\leq \gamma$
        Acc=IAlgo(GIS,α); /*Calling Inducer Algorithm*/
        if Acc > MaxAcc
          Hsfs := current;
          MaxAcc := Acc;
        endif
      endif
endwhile

We apply the hybrid approach on databases which have many reducts. Experimentally, the allowable filter rate value depends on the original datasets inconsistency. The inconsistency of Glass, Heart, Vehicle and Wave, according to L&S

measure criterion are: 11.21%, 0.74%, 3.31% and 0.0% respectively. In addition to the advantages of α–reducts algorithm mentioned in the 3rd section, all generated reducts when $\alpha=0$ have the same inconsistency value, and they are equal to inconsistency value of original datasets (with all attributs).

For the remainder of the experiments, we put the allowable filter rate equal to: 10%, 2%, 6% and 0.5% for the above databases respectively (we put other adjusted value for A&D filter).

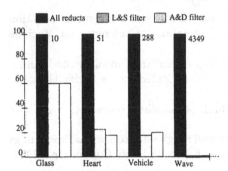

Datasets	Hybryd/ALPHA
Glass	59.91
Heart	85.56
Vehicle	70.33
Wave	77.50

Table 4. The accuracy of reducts selected by the hybrid approach

Figure 1. Pourcentage of filtred reducts using L&S and A&D filter.

Figure 1 shows the percentage of filtered reducts. The induction algorithm used around 6 reducts among 10 for Glass. It is only used to evaluate 22% and 17% of subsets for Heart and Vehicle using L&S inconsistency measure. The best subset found by the wrapper approach is captured in the mentioned interval. It is found with minimum cost (very early) comparing with the wrapper approach. The very interesting result is obtained in Wave database. Among 4349 reducts, we only evaluated 33 reducts (0.76%). It is the 5th best reduct according to L&S filter. It improves the accuracy of ALPHA by 3.5%. In addition, its accuracy is greater than the L&S filter by 7.83%.

6 Conclusion

In this paper we have studied the problem of feature selection using the generalized rough sets theory, α–RST. We have proposed an algorithm to find non deterministic reducts. We have developed the wrapper approach and some filter measures which evaluate a subset entirely. Assuming that (α–)rough sets theory can generate many (α–)reducts, our experiments show that the accuracy of the best reduct using a filter method is lower than the best one using the wrapper approach. The hybrid approach proposed in this paper overcomes the bias of filter approach, by proposing many probable best reducts and speeds up the wrapper approach, by wrapping only around the filtered ones. It inherits the performance of the wrapper approach by guaranteeing the selection of the best reduct with respect to an induction algorithm.

References

1. Almuallim, H., Dietterich, T.G.: Learning boolean concepts in the presence of many irrelevant features. Artificial Intelligence, **69(1-2)** (November 1994) 279–305
2. Caruana, R., Freitag, D.: Greedy attribute selection. Proceedings of the Eleventh International Conference. M. Kaufman Publ. in Cohen&Hirsh eds, Machine learning Inc. (1994) 28–36
3. Fayyad U.M., Irani K.B.: Multi-interval Discretization of Continuous-attributes for classification learning IJCAI'93, (1993) 1022–1027
4. John, G. H., Kohavi, R., Pfleger, K.: Irrelevant features and the subset selection Problem. In Proceedings of the Eleventh International Conference on Machine Learning, (1994) 121–129
5. Kira, K., Rendell, L.A.: The feature selection problem: traditional methods and a new algorithm. In Proceedings of the 9th National Conference on Artificial Intelligence, (1992) 129–134
6. Kohavi, R.: Feature subset selection as search probabilistic estimates. AAAI Fall Symposium on Relevance, (1994) 122–126
7. Kohavi, R., Frasca, B.: Useful feature subset and rough sets reducts. In Proceedings of the Third International Workshop on Rough Sets and Soft Computing, (1994) 310–317
8. Kohavi, R., Sommerfield, D.: Feature subset selection using the wrapper method: over-fitting and dynamic search space topology. In proceeding of the First International Conference on Knowledge Discovery and Data Mining, (1994) 192–197
9. Kononenko, I.: On biases of multi-valued attributes. In proceeding oh the 14th international joint conference on artificial intelligence, in C.S.mellish ed. (1995) 1034–1040.
10. Liu, H., Setiono, R.: A probabilistic approach for feature selection: A filter solution. In 13th International Conference on Machine Learning (ICML'96), (1996) 319–327
11. Liu, H., Setiono, R.: Feature selection and classification - a probabilistic wrapper approach. In Proceedings of the 9th International Conference on Industrial and Engineering Applications of AI and ES, (1996) 419–425
12. Modrzejewski, M.: Feature selection using rough sets theory. In Proceedings of the European Conference on Machine Learning, (1993) 213–226
13. Pawlak, Z.: Rough Sets: Theoretical Aspects of Reasoning About Data. Kluwer Academic Publishers, Dordrecht, The Netherlands (1991)
14. Pawlak, Z.: Rough Sets: present state and the future. Foundations of Computing and Decision Sciences, **18(3-4)**, (1993) 157–166.
15. Quafafou, M.: α-RST: A generalization of rough sets theory. In Proceedings in the Fifth International Workshop on Rough Sets and Soft Computing, RSSC'97. (1997)
16. Quafafou, M., Boussouf, M.: Induction of Strong Feature Subsets. In 1st European Symposium on Principles of Data Mining and Knowledge Discovery PKDD'97, (1997) 384–392
17. Slowinsky K., Slowinsky R.: Sensitivity analysis of rough classification. International journal of Man-Machine studies, **32** (1990) 693–705

Discretization and Grouping:
Preprocessing Steps for Data Mining

Petr Berka[1] and Ivan Bruha[2]

[1] Laboratory of Intelligent Systems
Prague University of Economic
W. Churchill Sq. 4, Prague CZ–13067, Czech Republic
email: berka@vse.cz

[2] Department of Computer Science and Systems, McMaster University
Hamilton, Ont., Canada L8S4K1
email: bruha@mcmaster.ca

Abstract. Unlike on-line discretization performed by a number of machine learning (ML) algorithms for building decision trees or decision rules, we propose off-line algorithms for discretizing numerical attributes and grouping values of nominal attributes. The number of resulting intervals obtained by discretization depends only on the data; the number of groups corresponds to the number of classes. Since both discretization and grouping is done with respect to the goal classes, the algorithms are suitable only for classification/prediction tasks.

As a side effect of the off-line processing, the number of objects in the datasets and number of attributes may be reduced.

It should be also mentioned that although the original idea of the discretization procedure is proposed to the KEX system, the algorithms show good performance together with other machine learning algorithms.

1 Introduction

The Knowledge Discovery in Databases (KDD) process can involve a significant iteration and may contain loops among data selection, data preprocessing, data transformation, data mining, and interpretation of mined patterns. The most complex steps in this process are data preprocessing and data transformation. The result of these steps should be data in the form suitable for the data mining algorithms used[1]. Thus, the necessary preprocessing and transformation operations are e.g. "merging" data to create singe data matrix from a number of related data tables, creating new attributes, excluding unnecessary attributes, discretization or grouping.

We present here algorithms for the last two mentioned operations: "off-line" discretization of numerical attributes and "off-line" grouping values of nominal attributes. Such transformations can help in better understanding the data that

---

[1] If we insist on *interpretability* of the discovered knowledge, we should prefer symbolic machine learning algorithms.

enter into the data mining step. Both algorithms are class-sensitive, so they can be used only for classification/prediction tasks.

The described algorithms were developed within the KEX framework [2] but can be used as a preprocessing tool for other ML algorithms as well.

2 Discretization

The task of discretization of numerical variables is well known to statisticians. Different approaches are used such as discretization into a given number of categories using equidistant cutpoints, or discretization based on mean and standard deviation. All these approaches are "class-blind", since they do not take into account that objects belong to different classes. Hence they can be used if the data mining algorithms perform unsupervised learning[2]. If the task is classification/prediction the information about the class label can be used during discretization.

In the TDIDT family, the algorithms for discretization are based mostly on binarization within a subset of training data created during tree generation [6]. Well known algorithm by Fayyad and Irani extended this idea to multi-interval discretization [8]. KnowledgeSeeker, a commercial system of the TDIDT family, looks for "best" k-way split of each variable using F statistics for numerical attributes and χ^2 statistic for nominal attributes; so the system performs both discretization and grouping [4].

Discretization in the set covering algorithm CN4 (a large extension of CN2) is based on entropy or Laplacian estimate [5].

All these systems discretize numerical attributes "on-line", during learning. The algorithms described in the paper preprocess the data "off-line" before starting the machine learning step.

3 Discretization and grouping for KEX

3.1 A survey of the system

KEX performs symbolic empirical multiple concept learning from examples, where the induced concept description is represented as weighted decision rules in the form

$$Ant \implies C \ (weight)$$

where Ant is a combination (conjunction) of attribute-value pairs,

C is a single category (class),

$weight$ from the interval $[0, 1]$ expresses the uncertainty of the rule.

KEX [2] works in an iterative way, in each iteration testing and expanding an implication $Ant \implies C$. This process starts with an "empty rule" weighted

---

[2] This case is carried out when the data mining task is to find some interesting groups of objects with similar characteristics or to find associations.

with the relative frequency of the class C and stops after testing all implications created according to the user defined criteria. During testing, the validity (conditional probability $P(C|Ant)$) of an implication is computed[3] . If this validity significantly differs from the composed weight (value obtained when composing weights of all subrules of the implication $Ant \implies C$), then this implication is added to the knowledge base. The weight of this new rule is computed from the validity and from the composed weight using inverse composing function. For composing weights we use a pseudobayesian (PROSPECTOR-like) combination function

$$x \oplus y = \frac{x * y}{x * y + (1 - x) * (1 - y)}.$$

During expanding, new implications are created by adding single categories to Ant.

3.2 Algorithm for discretization

We treat each numerical attribute separately. The basic idea is to create intervals for which the *aposteriori* distribution of classes $P(C|interval)$ significantly differs from the *apriori* distribution of classes $P(C)$ in the whole training data. This can be achieved by simply merging such values, for which most objects belong to the same class. Within the KEX knowledge acquisition approach, this will lead to rules of the form

$$interval \implies C,$$

but this approach can be used for other learning algorithms, too.

The number of resulting intervals is "controlled" by giving a threshold for minimal number of objects within one interval; less frequent intervals are labeled as "UNKNOWN" in the step **3.1** (the algorithm is shown in Figure 1).

3.3 Algorithm for grouping

Grouping values of a nominal attribute becomes important if the number of these values is too large (e.g. hundreds of ZIP codes or profession codes). To deal with each value separately can bring problems both during computation (e.g. branching a node) and interpretation.

The grouping algorithm for KEX is based on the same idea as the discretization described above. Again, we create groups of values such, that the aposteriori distribution $P(C|group)$ significantly differs from the apriori distribution $P(C)$. The main difference to the discretization algorithm is that we create single group for each value of class attribute and an additional group labeled "UNKNOWN"; so the number of groups is fixed. The grouping algorithm is shown in Figure 2.

---

[3] The validity $P(C|Ant)$ is computed from the data as $\frac{||Ant \cap C||}{||Ant||}$.

MAIN LOOP:
1 create ordered list of values of the attribute;
2 for each value do
    2.1 compute frequencies of occurrence of objects with respect to each class;
    2.2 assign the class label to every value using procedure ASSIGN;
enddo
3 create the intervals from values using procedure INTERVAL;

ASSIGN:
  if for the given value all objects belong to same class, then assign the value to
    that class
  else if for the given value the distribution of objects with respect to class mem-
    bership significantly differs (according to χ^2 or relative frequency criterion)
    from frequencies of goal classes, then assign that value to the most frequent
    class
  else assign the value to the class "UNKNOWN";

INTERVAL:
3.1 if a sequence of values belongs to the same class, then create the interval
    $INT_i = [LBound_i, UBound_i]$ from these values;
3.2 if the interval INT_i belongs to the class "UNKNOWN" then
  if its neighbouring intervals INT_{i-1}, INT_{i+1} belong to the same class then create
    the interval by joining $INT_{i-1} \cup INT_i \cup INT_{i+1}$
  else create the interval either by joining $INT_{i-1} \cup INT_i$ or by joining $INT_i \cup$
    INT_{i+1} according to given criterion (For χ^2 test join the intervals according
    to the higher value of χ^2, for frequency criterion join the intervals according
    to higher relative frequency of the majority class.);
3.3 create continuous coverage of the attribute by assigning $LBound_i :=$
    $(LBound_i + UBound_{i-1})/2$ and $UBound_{i-1} := LBound_i$;

Fig. 1. Algorithm for discretization

MAIN LOOP:
1 for each value do
    1.1 compute frequencies of occurrence of objects with respect to each class;
    1.2 assign the class label to every value using procedure ASSIGN;
enddo
2 create the groups from values using procedure GROUP;

ASSIGN:
  if for the given value all objects belong to same class, then assign the value to
    that class
  else if for the given value the distribution of objects with respect to class mem-
    bership significantly differs (according to χ^2 or relative frequency criterion))
    from frequencies of goal classes, then assign that value to the most frequent
    class
  else assign the value to the class "UNKNOWN";

GROUP:
3.1 create groups for values with the same class label;

Fig. 2. Algorithm for grouping

3.4 Evaluation of the algorithms

During discretization/grouping of an attribute, we can loose some information hidden in the data. We can measure this loss by the number of contradictions before and after the preprocessing. Contradiction here means a situation when objects described by same attribute values belong to different classes. Any learning algorithm will classify such objects as objects belonging to the same (usually the majority) class and objects belonging to other classes will be classified wrongly. We can count such errors and thus estimate the maximal possible accuracy as:

$$1 - \frac{\text{no. of errors}}{\text{no. of objects}}$$

As a side effect of the off-line processing, the number of objects in the datasets and number of attributes may be reduced. This reduction can give us some information about regular patterns in the data.

Another useful information is the number of intervals or groups. If the preprocessing results in a single interval/group or in one interval/group with very high frequency in the data, we can ignore the corresponding attribute in the subsequent machine learning step.

4 Empirical results

We have tested our algorithm on different datasets taken from the UCI Machine Learning Repository [10]. The results are summarized in Table 1. This table gives for the used data sets[4] the number of (different) objects and the maximal possible accuracy both before and after discretization. We present also the results of classification accuracy for different systems to show that there is no significant difference between KEX (system, that motivates the discretization algorithm) and other systems (CN4 ordered mode, CN4 unordered mode, and C4.5).

data	accuracy in data	#.diff. objects	classification accuracy KEX	CN4 ord.	CN4 unord.	C4.5
credit (orig.)	100%	125	-	97%	81%	83%
credit (disc.)	100%	117	97%	95%	88%	76%
iris (orig.)	100%	147	-	99%	97%	98%
iris (disc.)	98%	35	95%	98%	95%	96%
diab. (orig.)	100%	768	-	96%	79%	90%
diab. (disc.)	95%	538	85%	84%	81%	75%
aust. (orig.)	100%	690	-	100%	87%	91%
aust. (disc.)	99%	663	87%	92%	89%	89%

Table 1. Discretization of some UCI data

---

[4] *Credit* stands for Japanese credit data, *iris* stands for Iris data, *diab* for Pima Indian diabetes data, and *aust* for Australian credit data.

We used our discretization/grouping algorithm also to preprocess a more complex data [3]. The KDD Sisyphus data is an excerpt from a Swiss Life data warehouse system MASY [9]. These data consist of several relations describing relationship between Swiss Life partners, insurance contracts and components of insurance tariffs. The goal of KDD on this data is to find concept description for given class (TaskA, TaskB). After creating single data matrix for each task we run the discretization and grouping algorithms for the TaskA and TaskB data. The results (in terms of maximal possible accuracy before and after this preprocessing) are shown in table 2. Discretization and grouping helped us also to find unimportant attributes; lines `Taskx` (`disc.+red.`) in the table show the accuracy and number of objects after removing such attributes.

data	accuracy in data	#.diff. objects	#. attributes
TaskA (orig.)	100%	17267	46
TaskA (disc.)	98%	13138	46
TaskA (disc.+red.)	98%	12773	43
TaskB (orig.)	100%	12945	83
TaskB (disc.)	100%	12945	83
TaskB (disc.+red.)	100%	12945	75

Table 2. Discretization and grouping of KDD Sisyphus data

5 Conclusion

Unlike on-line discretization performed by a number of ML algorithms during building decision trees or decision rules, we propose off-line algorithms for discretizing numerical attributes and grouping values of nominal attributes. The number of resulting intervals obtained during discretization depends only on the data; the number of groups corresponds to the number of classes. Since both discretization and grouping is done with respect to the goal classes, the algorithms are suitable only for classification/prediction tasks.

The obtained intervals/groups can be interpreted as potential knowledge. The results of the off-line discretization and grouping can also help during further preprocessing of the data. If we obtain single interval, we can conclude that the discretized attribute is irrelevant for the classification task. We can draw the same conclusion also if after discretization or grouping almost all objects fall into one interval/group.

It should be also mentioned that although the original idea of the discretization procedure is related to the KEX, the algorithms show good performance together with other machine learning algorithms.

References

1. Berka,P. - Bruha,I.: Various discretization procedures of numerical attributes: Empirical comparisons. In: (Kodratoff, Nakhaeizadeh, Taylor eds.) Proc. MLNet Familiarization Workshop on Statistics, Machine Learning and Knowledge Discovery in Databases, Herakleion, 1995, p.136-141.
2. Berka,P. - Ivánek,J.: Automated Knowledge Acquisition for PROSPECTOR-like Expert Systems. In. (Bergadano, deRaedt eds.) Proc. ECML'94, Springer 1994.
3. Berka,P. - Sochorová,M. - Rauch,J.: Using GUHA and KEX for Knowledge DIscovery in Databases; the KDD Sisyphus Experience. In Proc: Poster Session ECML'98, TU Chemnitz 1998.
4. Biggs,D. - de Ville,B - Suen,E.: A method of choosing multiway partitions for classification and decision trees. Journal of Applied Statistics, Vol. 18, No. 1, 1991, 49-62.
5. Bruha,I. - Kočková,S.: A covering learning algorithm for cost-sensitive and noisy environments. In: Proc. of ECML'93 Workshop on Learning Robots, 1993.
6. Catlett,J.: On changing continuous attributes into ordered discrete attributes. In: Y. Kodratoff, ed.: Machine Learning - EWSL-91, Springer-Verlag, 1991, 164-178.
7. Clark,P. - Niblett,T.: The CN2 induction algorithm. Machine Learning, 3 (1989), 261-283
8. Fayyad,U.M. - Irani,K.B.: Multi-Interval Discretization of Continuous-Valued Attributes for Classifiacation Learning. In: Proc. IJCAI'93, 1993.
9. Kietz,J.U. - Reimer,U. - Staudt,M.: Mining Insurance Data at Swiss Life. In: Proc. 23rd VLDB Conference, Athens, 1997.
10. Merz,C.J. - Murphy,P.M.: UCI Repository of Machine Learning Databases. Irvine, University of California, Dept. of Information and Computer Science, 1997.

Fuzzy Spatial OQL for Fuzzy Knowledge Discovery in Databases

Nara Martini Bigolin* and Christophe Marsala

LIP6, Université Pierre et Marie Curie,
4 place Jussieu, 75252 Paris cedex 05, FRANCE.
email: {Nara.Martini-Bigolin, Christophe.Marsala}@lip6.fr

Abstract. In this paper, we introduce a fuzzy spatial object query language, called FuSOQL, to select, process and mine data from Spatial Object-Oriented Databases (SOODB). Fuzzy set theory is introduced in this extension of OQL to handle spatial data. Afterwards, the knowledge discovery process is applied to the selected data. In our case, this data mining is done by means of a fuzzy decision tree based technique. An experiment on a region of France is conducted with this algorithm to discover classification rules related to houses and urban area.

Keywords: Data mining, knowledge discovery in databases, spatial object-oriented databases, fuzzy decision tree.

1 Introduction

Knowledge discovery in databases (KDD) [7] has been used to extract implicit information from vast amounts of data. Recently, this technology has attracted the interest of researchers in several fields such as databases, statistics, machine learning, data visualization and information theory.

Researchers in Geographic Information Systems (GIS) [8] have also shown interest in knowledge discovery in spatial databases, called *Spatial Data Mining*, which has been defined as *the extraction of interesting spatial patterns and features, general relationships between spatial and non-spatial data, and their general data characteristics not explicitly stored in spatial databases* [14]. This technology is becoming more and more important because a tremendous amount of spatial and non-spatial data have been collected and stored in large spatial databases using automatic data collection tools. The main challenge of Spatial Data Mining has been the relevant data selection to discover knowledge. Thus, new data selection methods have to be studied. Usually, these methods have been developed as extensions of query languages. The more significant query languages to mine spatial data have been developed to discover knowledge from relational databases [6], [10], [12]. However, the development of query languages to access Spatial Object-Oriented Databases (SOODB) is still an open research area with large potential.

---

* Supported by the CNPq - Brazil.

In this paper, an object query language (OQL) extension to select and process data from a SOODB is presented. Fuzzy set theory is introduced in this language to handle spatial data. Afterwards, the knowledge discovery process can be applied with the selected data. For instance, in our case, this process is a fuzzy decision tree based technique.

This paper is composed as follows: in Section 2, query languages are introduced. In Section 3, our approach based on the extension of a query language to discover knowledge from an SOODB, is presented. An application of this approach is given in Section 4. Finally, we conclude and present some directions for future works.

2 Query languages

The first standard query language to access a relational database is SQL [11]. Its basic structures consists of **select**, **from** and **where** clauses. Typical query has the form: **SELECT** A_1, A_2,...,A_n **FROM** r_1, r_2,...,r_n **WHERE** P. where each A_i represents an *attribute* of a database, each r_i is a data collection (a *relation* in this case), and P is a *selection predicate* (condition).

Severals extensions of SQL were developed to handle complex data such as object structure (Object Query Language (OQL) [4]), spatial data (Spatial SQL [5]. Others extensions of SQL integrating operations to process data have been proposed. For instance, a Fuzzy Query Language (Fsql) [2] processes fuzzy data, and a Data Mining Query Language (DMQL) [9] discovers knowledge.

2.1 Object Query Language

An OQL [4] is an extension of the standard query language SQL to query an OODB. An OODB is composed by a set of *objects*. An object is associated with an *object-identifier* and a *value*. A value possesses a type either *atomic* (string,...) or *structured*. The structure can be a *collection* (a list, a set,...) or a *tuple* (a set of typed attributes). Objects are grouped into *classes* which are organized in *hierarchies*. The object's behavior is determined by a set of methods. The instances of a class are defined as a set of *objects*. Each object is associated with a *name* that references it in the database.

In an ODL, the statement of the **select** clause can be composed by, for instance, a set of objects, structures,... The statement of the **from** clause is composed by *expression paths* associated with a name. An expression path describes a path in the hierarchies beginning from this name. The statement of the **where** clause is a condition on the objects to select. The answer to a query is a set of objects or a set of values for these objects.

2.2 Spatial Query Language

A spatial query language [5] handles spatial data which are stored, for instance, in a geographical database. Such a database is composed of non-spatial and spatial data. Non-spatial data are information describing objects such as: name, population of town etc... Spatial data specify the localization of the non-spatial data. It is generally represented by three spatial primitives: points, lines and area. A point represents (the geometric aspect of) an object for which only its location in space, but not its extent, is relevant.

For example, a city can be a point in a large geographic area (a large scale map). A region is the abstraction for something having an extent in 2d-space, e.g. a country, a lake, a national park or a house in small scale map (Figure 1a). A line is the basic abstraction for facilities for moving through space, or connections in space (roads, rivers, cables for phone, electricity, etc) [13].

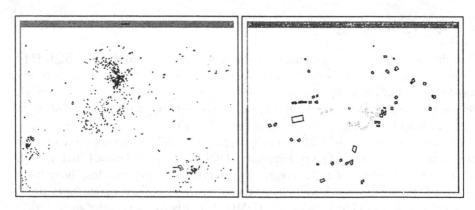

1a. A region of France (1:125000)   **1b.** Result of a query (1:31860)

Figure1. Geographical data

Non-spatial data can be handled with a classic query language, but the characteristics of spatial data require specific operations that can process and handle graphically spatial data. In a spatial query, these operations are represented by methods in the **where** clause. The **select** clause can be done by means of the graphical interface.

2.3   Fuzzy Query Language

A Fuzzy Query Language [2] is based on fuzzy set theory. In classical theory, given a set $\mathcal{X}$ and a set $U \subseteq \mathcal{X}$, each element $x \in \mathcal{X}$ either belongs to U or does not belong to U. It can be summarized as follows: given a set $\mathcal{X}$ and a set $U \subseteq \mathcal{X}$, let μ_U be the *characteristic function* such that: $\mu_U : \mathcal{X} \longrightarrow \{0, 1\}$, and $\forall x \in \mathcal{X}$, if $x \in U$ then $\mu_U(x) = 1$, otherwise $\mu_U(x) = 0$. In *fuzzy set theory* [17], the *membership degree* of an element x can vary from 0 to 1. The membership function μ_U of the *fuzzy set U* is defined as: $\mu_U : \mathcal{X} \longrightarrow [0, 1]$.

Given a numerical attribute U that takes numerical values in $\mathcal{X}$, a *fuzzy partition* can be defined on $\mathcal{X}$ by means of a set of fuzzy sets of $\mathcal{X}$. For instance, in Figure 2, the numerical attribute *distance* and its fuzzy values (*near, far, very far*) forming a fuzzy partition of its universe $\mathbb{R}^+$ are represented.

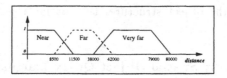

Figure2. Fuzzy values for the distance

The **where** clause of a fuzzy query is composed by fuzzy values. The answer to this kind of query is a fuzzy set of elements defined by these fuzzy values.

2.4 Data Mining Query Language

Data mining query language is used to discover knowledge in databases. This kind of languages has been introduced by [9] for relational databases. Their language is an extension of the classical SQL to mine a relational database. It is based on four major primitives: the set of data relevant to data mining, the kind of rules to discover, the background knowledge and the justification of the interestingness of the knowledge (*cf.* [9]). In addition to the **select**, **from** and **where** part, a data mining query is composed by a clause that defines the kind of rules to discover and the data mining algorithm to be used.

3 Fuzzy Spatial Object Query Language and Data Mining

To discover knowledge from an SOODB, both the object-oriented nature of the data and their spatial specificity need to be taken into account simultaneously. However, no data mining techniques that can handle these two data properties exist yet.

We propose a *Fuzzy Spatial Object Query Language* (FuSOQL) that is an object query language (OQL) extension to select and process data from a SOODB. Fuzzy set theory is introduced in this langage to handle spatial data. Afterwards, a data mining process is applied to the selected data to discover knowledge. A *Fuzzy Spatial Object Query* has the form:

> **DATAMINING** <*Data mining algorithm*>
> **WITH**
> > **SELECT** A_1, A_2,...,A_n
> > **FROM** o_1, o_2,...,o_n
> > **WHERE** P

In the clause **DATAMINING**, the statement <*Data mining algorithm*> is the algorithm that has been chosen to mine the selected data. The other part of the query is a traditional **select** clause extended to spatial objects stored in object structure. The *condition P* of the clause is composed by: graphical methods of the graphical interfaces to visualize spatial data; spatial methods to compute informations from spatial data; and fuzzy methods to process numerical values of spatial data. These methods make use of background knowledge such as the semantics linked to the object structure, the spatial object topology and the expert knowledge.

3.1 FuSOQL : Fuzzy Spatial Object Query Language

The data selection is made through a fuzzy spatial query $Q : SOODB \longrightarrow SO$. This query is run on the $SOODB$ to extract a subset of spatial objects SO relevant to the data mining task. Afterwards, a process is done on every spatial data stored in an object structure. This process is a function $\sigma : SO \longrightarrow TS$ which transforms a set of spatial objects SO into a training set TS. Such processing functions can be of two kinds: mathematical functions or fuzzy set theory based functions.

Mathematical functions. The transformation of a spatial object $O_S \in SO$ into a data set $D \subseteq TS$ is performed thanks to a set $\mathcal{S}$ of *compute* operations C. We have $\mathcal{S} = \{C \mid C : SO \longrightarrow \mathcal{X}_C\}$ where $\mathcal{X}_C$ is the set of values computed by the function C.

For instance, a *line* l is composed by a set of points $\{p_{l_1}, ..., p_{l_n}\}$ and the Euclidean distance is the function $C : SO \longrightarrow \mathbb{R}$ defined as $C(l) = ||p_{l_1} - p_{l_n}||$.

Fuzzy set theory based functions. For a given *fuzzy* operation f, if $\mathcal{X}_f$ is a set of continuous values (*ie.* $\mathcal{X}_f \subseteq \mathbb{R}$), a transformation $T_{\mathcal{X}_f}$ of these values into fuzzy values can be done according to a fuzzy partition of $\mathcal{X}_f$ into m fuzzy sets $U_1, ..., U_m$. Thus, we have $T_{\mathcal{X}_f} : \mathcal{X}_f \longrightarrow [0.1]^m$.

For instance, the Euclidean distance $||p_1 - p_2||$ between two points is a real value from $\mathbb{R}^+$. Given the set {*near, far, very far*} of fuzzy sets describing the distance (see Figure 2), the real value $||p_1 - p_2||$ is converted into a set of three membership degrees to each fuzzy set: $\mu_{near}(||p_1 - p_2||)$, $\mu_{far}(||p_1 - p_2||)$ and $\mu_{very\ far}(||p_1 - p_2||)$.

3.2 Data mining: Fuzzy decision trees

The statement of the DATAMINING clause transforms a training set into a set of rules. Given a training set TS and a particular attribute $A_d \in \mathcal{A}$ (the decision), provided by the expert, the data mining step is a *mining* operation $\Theta : TS \times \mathcal{A} \longrightarrow RB$. This operation generates a set $RB = \{R_1, ..., R_N\}$ of rules $R_i : Pr_i \longrightarrow Co_i$. The premise Pr_i of a rule R_i is a conjunction of tests $A_k = a_{k_j}$ on values a_{k_j} of attributes $A_k \in \mathcal{A} - \{A_d\}$. The conclusion Co_i of a rule is a value d_i for A_d.

In our application, the DATAMINING clause is performed thanks to the *fuzzy decision trees* data mining technique [3, 15]. Each node in a decision tree is associated with a test on the values of an attribute, all edges from a node are labeled with values of the attribute belonging to a partition of its universe, and each leaf of the tree is associated with a value of the class. Edges can also be labeled by fuzzy values that lead to the generalization of decision trees into *fuzzy decision trees* [3]. Fuzzy decision trees handle fuzzy values either during their construction or when classifying new cases. The use of fuzzy set theory enhances the understandability of decision trees when considering numerical attributes. An example of a fuzzy decision tree is given in Figure 4. A decision tree can be constructed from a set of examples (the *training set*). Each example is a case completely known, associated with a pair [description, class] where the *description* is a set of pairs [attribute, value] which is the available knowledge. Moreover, a fuzzy decision tree is equivalent to a fuzzy rule base $RB = \{R_1, ..., R_N\}$. A path of the tree is equivalent to an IF...THEN rule $R : Pr \longrightarrow Co$. Where the premise Pr is composed by tests on values of attributes, and the conclusion Co is the value of the decision that labels the leaf of the path.

4 Application

An application of our method is presented in this section. Its aim is to find a set of classification rules related to the description of houses and their localization in an *urban* or in a *non-urban* area.

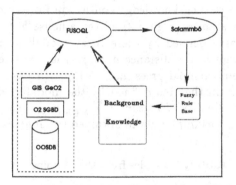

Figure3. System architecture

The system architecture used in this application is shown in Figure 3. The FuSOQL is developed on top of the O_2 DBMS [1] using the GIS GeO_2 component [16]. The queries are performed using background knowledge as detailed in Section 3. The Salammbô system of [15] is used to generate a fuzzy decision tree from the answer to the Fuzzy Spatial OQL. The SOODB and the GIS were provided by the French "Institut Géographique National" (IGN).

4.1 Query

The used fuzzy spatial object query is:

        DATAMINING Fuzzy Decision Tree
        WITH
            SELECT x.house
            FROM x in Database1

WHERE x.house→inArea(CoordPtMin, CoordPtMax);

The clause **DATAMINING** is based on the algorithm to build fuzzy decision trees. It extracts a set of fuzzy rules, given as a fuzzy decision tree, from the data selected by means of the clause **select**. In the *condition* of this clause, the method *inArea(CoordPtMin, CoordPtMax)* determines whether an object *house* is in the area defined by the two points *CoordPtMin* and *CoordPtMax*.

This area has been defined by the user with the graphical interface system. A point has been selected with the mouse. It is associated with the center of the area and **CoordPtMin** and **CoordPtMax** are the boundaries of this area, computed from this selected point.

4.2 Fuzzy spatial object query

First of all, the result of the **select** clause is the data set $\mathcal{H}$ of all houses pertaining to the given area (see Figure 1b). Each object from $\mathcal{H}$ is associated with additional information to make up an example of a training set. This information is computed by means of knowledge related to the application. For instance, such knowledge is represented as the mathematical function $d(p_1, p_2)$ which computes the Euclidean distance between the two points p_1 and p_2.

A particular kind of such knowledge consists in fuzzy modalities on the numerical universe of distances (Figure 2). Given a house h, the number of houses in the three fuzzy area defined by these fuzzy modalities is valued. For each house h' different from h, the distance $d(p_h, p_{h'})$ is evaluated. This distance is transformed into membership degrees $\mu_{near}(h')$, $\mu_{far}(h')$ and $\mu_{very\ far}(h')$. Thus, the number of houses in the area defined by the modality *near* is given by the fuzzy measure of cardinality: $Nr\ near = \sum_{h' \in \mathcal{H}} \mu_{near}(h')$ And so on, for the other modalities. Some examples of the obtained training set are shown Table 1.

Table1. Examples from the Training set

House	Nr near	Nr far	Nr very far	Urban
h1	0.1	4.2	5.7	No
h2	2.0	2.0	6.0	No
h3	3.3	3.8	7.9	No
h4	16.3	15.7	12.0	Yes
h5	11.0	24.2	9.7	Yes
h6	7.7	20.2	16.1	Yes

4.3 Data Mining

The statement of the **DATAMINING** clause is the algorithm to construct fuzzy decision trees implemented in the system Salammbô [15]. A fuzzy decision tree, that can be considered as a set of classification rules, is constructed from the training set obtained in the last section (*cf* Figure 4). It enables us to decide wether a house is urban or not.

As mentioned, the Salammbô system generates automatically a fuzzy decision tree and determines fuzzy modalities for the universe of values of each numerical attribute. The obtained fuzzy modalities on the number of houses in area are given in Figure 2. These fuzzy modalities will label the premises of the induced classification rules.

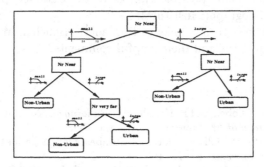

Figure4. Fuzzy decision tree

4.4 Validation of the fuzzy rule base

This set of rules, induced from houses belonging to a zone around a particular town, has been tested with other houses pertaining to a zone around another town. The selection clause and the processing step 4.2 were resumed with another center for a zone to generate a set (the *test set*) to check the fuzzy rule base obtained in step 4.3.

In our application, the studied region (Figure 1a) is composed of three towns T_1, T_2 and T_3. A training set was generated from a zone around the town T_1 (Figure 1b) and a test set was generated from a zone around the two other towns. The average error rate when classifying houses around towns T_2 and T_3 with the obtained fuzzy decision tree is 10.1%. In other words, given 413 houses from the new zone, 371 houses are perfectly classified as *urban* or *non-urban* with the induced set of fuzzy rules.

5 Conclusion

In this paper, we propose a fuzzy spatial object query language, called Fu-SOQL, which selects and processes data from Spatial Object-Oriented Databases (SOODB). This language is based on the introduction of mathematical and fuzzy set theory based functions to process and mine a SOODB. After a spatial object query and a mathematical and fuzzy preprocessing, we apply a fuzzy decision tree based technique to discover knowledge. This introduction of a preprocessing step and a fuzzy decision tree technique enables us to handle spatial data related to a geographical region. Our algorithm has been applied and validated on a region of France to discover characterization rules related to houses and urban area.

In future work, new experiments will be conducted to discover another kind of knowledge. Moreover, we plan to automate the process of building the queries used to construct the training set.

Acknowledgments

This work has been made possible thanks to the database provided by IGN (French National Geographic Institute).

The authors express their thanks to Bernadette Bouchon-Meunier and Anne Doucet for their guidance and their helpful comments.

References

1. F. Bancilhon, C. Delobel, and P. Kanellakis. *Building an Object-Oriented Databases Systems: The story of O2*. Morgan Kaufmann, 1992.
2. P. Bosc and O. Pivert. Sqlf : A relational databases language for fuzzy query. *IEEE Trans. on Fuzzy Systems*, 3:1–17, 1995.
3. B. Bouchon-Meunier, C. Marsala, and M. Ramdani. Learning from imperfect data. In H. P. D. Dubois and R. R. Yager, editors, *Fuzzy Information Engineering: a Guided Tour of Applications*, pages 139–148. John Wileys and Sons, 1997.
4. R. Cattell. Odmg-93 - le standard des bases de donnees objet. ITP France, Paris, France, 1995.
5. M. Egenhofer. Spatial sql: A query and presentation language. *IEEE Transactions on Knowledge and Data Engineering*, 6(1):86–95, 1994.
6. M. Ester, H.-P. Kriegel, and J. Sander. Spatial data mining: A database approach. *Proc. 5th Symp. on Spatial Databases, Berlin, Germany*, 1997.
7. U. Fayyad, G. Piatetsky-Shapiro, and P. Smyth. From data mining to discovery knowledge in databases. *AI Magazine*, 3(17):37–54, 1996.
8. A. Fotheringham and S. P. Rogerson. *Spatial analysis and GIS : applications in GIS*. London Washington, 1993.
9. J. Han, Y. Fu, W. Wang, K. Koperski, and O. Zaiane. DMQL: A data mining query language for relational databases. In *Proceedings of SIGMOD'96 Workshop on Research Issues on Data Mining and Knowledge Discovery (DMKD'96)*, Montreal, Canada, June 1996.
10. J. Han, K. Koperski, and N. Stefanovic. Geominer: A system prototype for spatial data mining. *Proc. 1997 ACM-SIGMOD Int'l Conf. on Management of Data(SIGMOD'97), Tucson, Arizona*, May 1997.
11. ISO. Database language sql. ISO/IEC 9075, 1992.
12. K. Koperski, J. Han, and J. Adhikary. Mining knowledge in geographic data. *Comm. ACM (to appear)*, 1998.
13. R. Laurini and D. Thompson. Fundamentals of spatial information systems. Academic Press., 1992.
14. W. Lu, J. Han, and B. C. Ooi. Discovery of general knowledge in large spatial databases. *Proc. of 1993 Far East Workshop on Geographic Information Systems-(FEGIS'93), Singapore*, pages 275–289, June 1993.
15. C. Marsala. *Apprentissage inductif en présence de données imprécises : construction et utilisation d'arbres de décision flous*. Thèse de doctorat, Université Pierre et Marie Curie, Paris, France, Janvier 1998. Rapport LIP6 n° 1998/014.
16. L. Raynal and G. Schorter. Geo2. Technical report, COGIT - IGN, 1995.
17. L. A. Zadeh. Fuzzy sets. *Information and Control*, 8:338–353, 1965.

Extended Functional Dependencies as a Basis for Linguistic Summaries

Patrick Bosc[1], Ludovic Liétard[2], and Olivier Pivert[1]

[1] IRISA/ENSSAT Technopole ANTICIPA BP 447 22305 Lannion Cedex France
{bosc|pivert}@enssat.fr
[2] IRISA/IUT Rue Edouard Branly BP 150 22302 Lannion Cedex France
ludovic.lietard@iut-lannion.fr

Abstract. This paper is concerned with knowledge discovery in databases and linguistic summaries of data. The summaries proposed here allow for a qualitative description of data (instead of the quantitative description given by a probabilistic approach) and they involve linguistic terms to obtain a wider coverage than Boolean summaries. They are based on extended functional dependencies and are situated in the framework of the relational model of data. Such summaries express a meta-knowledge about the database content according to the pattern "for any tuple t in relation R: the more A, the more B" (for instance: the *taller* the player, the *higher* his score in the NBA championship) where A and B are two linguistic terms. In addition, an algorithm to implement the discovery process (which takes advantage of properties of extended functional dependencies) is given. This algorithm is iterative and each tuple is successively considered in order to refine the set of valid summaries.

1 Introduction

Knowledge discovery in databases aims at extracting knowledge from information contained in a database. Many items may be the subject of discovery and among them are linguistic summaries of data [1, 2]. Such summaries are statements of the natural language (such as "*young* people are *well-paid*") and represent properties about the database current content. The objective of this paper is to propose linguistic summaries of data which offer a qualitative description of data and no longer a quantitative one as that given by a probabilistic approach. We also present an algorithm implementing the knowledge discovery process. In this algorithm, tuples are successively accessed in order to refine the set of valid summaries.

The linguistic summaries discussed later are based on extended functional dependencies [3] and are situated in the context of the relational model of data. Intuitively, the extended functional dependency (age, [20, 25]) → (salary, [5000, 7000]) means that an age between 20 and 25 imposes a salary between 5000 and 7000. One may point out that this property is too demanding, since a single tuple where age = 24 and salary = 7500 is enough to make it false. In addition, this extension is not linguistic and sharp boundaries (here [20, 25] and [5000, 7000]) may be challenged. Obviously, these aspects are due to the Boolean requirements regarding age and salary (i.e., all or nothing membership functions). Consequently, we consider fuzzy subsets [4] of attribute domains which are more appropriate to express some flexibility. More precisely, we will consider linguistic terms in the summaries which will have a fuzzy set-based interpretation [5]. As an example, when defining the fuzzy sets *young* and *well paid* on the attributes age and salary, the previous extended functional dependency is turned into (age, *young*) → (salary, *well paid*) which means that "*young* people are *well paid*". This type of pattern (extended functional dependencies with graduality) allows for defining linguistic summaries of data. It is worth mentioning that a clear semantics of such a statement calls on establishing a connection between the degrees attached to young and well-paid. This is achieved through extended (fuzzy) implications which generalize the regular one in use in the expression of functional dependencies (FDs).

The paper is organized as follows: section 2 is devoted to fuzzy sets and extended implications; section 3 introduces previous propositions to define linguistic summaries. Section 4 introduces linguistic summaries defined as extended FDs and their properties, and proposes the discovery algorithm.

2 Fuzzy Sets and Extended Implications

Fuzzy sets were proposed by Zadeh [4] in order to define sets having non sharp boundaries. A fuzzy set F on the universe X (a fuzzy subset of X) is defined by a function μ_F which associates a membership degree in [0,1] to each element x of X. When $\mu_F(x) = 0$, x does not belong at all to F and the closer to 1 $\mu_F(x)$, the more x belongs to F.

Set operations have been extended to fuzzy sets according to the following definitions where A and B stand for two fuzzy sets defined over the universe X: i) $\forall$ x $\in$ X, $\mu_{A \cap B}(x) = op_1(\mu_A(x), \mu_B(x))$, where op_1 is a triangular norm (associative, commutative, monotonic operator such that $op_1(a, 1) = a$), ii) $\forall$ x $\in$ X, $\mu_{A \cup B}(x) = op_2(\mu_A(x), \mu_B(x))$, where op_2 is a triangular co-norm (associative, commutative, monotonic operator such that $op_2(a, 0) = a$). Among the pairs norm/co-norm of operators op_1/op_2, let us mention: $op_1(x,y) = min(x,y)$; $op_2(x,y) = max(x,y)$ which will be assumed later.

The implication operator has also been extended and two main families can be distinguished [6]. The extension based on the following definition of the Boolean implication: $(A \Rightarrow B) \Leftrightarrow$ (B is at least as true as A) leads to Rescher-Gaines implication ($a \Rightarrow_{R-G} b = 1$ if $a \leq b$ and 0 otherwise) which will be used later on.

3 Linguistic Summaries: Previous Approaches

A linguistic summary of data describes the content of the database. Dubois and Prade [1] propose a summary given by a fuzzy set describing the frequency of events knowing a similarity relation over attribute values. Yager and Rasmussen's proposal [2] is more qualitative and the authors propose to summarize a relation R by a sentence of the type "*Q* are *S*" where *Q* is a linguistic quantifier [7] and *S* a property whose satisfaction is gradual. Both *Q* and *S* are defined as fuzzy sets. A summary is associated with a degree T (in [0, 1]) which indicates its validity. When *Q* defines a proportion such as *about half* (resp. a number such as *at most 3*) it is defined by a fuzzy subset of [0,1] (resp. of the naturals) and T is given by:

$$T = \mu_Q(\sum_{t \in R} \mu_S(t)/n) \qquad (resp. \ T = \mu_Q(\sum_{t \in R} \mu_S(t)))$$

where n is the number of tuples in relation R.

Example 1. The fuzzy quantifier *about half* and *S* the fuzzy set *young* are given by Fig. 1.

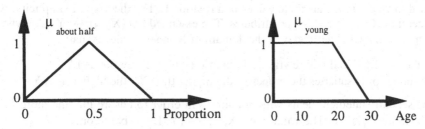

Fig. 1. A definition for *about half* and *young*.

The following relation EMP describes employees:

EMP	Name	Age	Salary	Firm	Country
	Durand	25	6 000	Comp. Inc.	France
	Dupond	25	7 000	Comp. Inc.	France
	James	18	5 000	Softw. Inc.	UK
	Peter	33	17 000	Softw. Inc.	UK
	Walker	45	28 000	Softw. Inc.	UK
	Müller	50	17 000	Netw. Inc.	Germany

The summary "*about half* are *young*" is valid at degree $\mu_Q((0.5+0.5+1)/6) = 2/3$ ♦

It is important to notice that two relations R and R' may lead to a same summary with the same value T even if they convey very different situations (it is just necessary that $\mu_Q(\sum_{t \in R} \mu_S(t)/n) = \mu_Q(\sum_{t \in R'} \mu_S(t)/n)$).

4 Summaries as Extended Functional Dependencies

4.1 Extended Functional Dependencies

A functional dependency (FD) over a relation R(U) is a property denoted $X \rightarrow Y$ (X, $Y \subseteq U$) defined as:

$$\forall\ t, t' \in R,\ (t.X = t'.X) \Rightarrow (t.Y = t'.Y).$$

Example 2. The FD Firm $\rightarrow$ Country holds in relation EMP of Example 1 ♦

FDs share a number of properties among which augmentation ($X \rightarrow Y$ and $Z \subseteq U$ $\Rightarrow XZ \rightarrow Y$), decomposition ($X \rightarrow Y \Rightarrow \forall\ Z \subseteq Y, X \rightarrow Z$) and union ($X \rightarrow Y$ and

$X \to Z \Rightarrow X \to YZ$). These three properties will play a key role in our algorithm aiming at the discovery of linguistic summaries of data (see section 5).

An extension of FDs has been proposed [3] where fuzzy sets (or linguistic labels) are used to characterize attribute values in a relation R. For the sake of simplicity, we consider that X and Y are single attributes. The extended FD $(X, L_i) \to (Y, L'_j)$, where L_i (resp. L'_j) is a label defined over the domain of X (resp. Y) means that:

- $\forall$ t, t' $\in$ R, if t.X and t'.X rewrite as L_i then t.Y and t'.Y rewrite as L'_j,
- each tuple t of R satisfies the property "the higher $\mu_{L_i}(t.X)$, the higher $\mu_{L'_j}(t.Y)$".

The second statement deals with graduality in order to ensure that the more L_i is t.X, the more L'_j is t.Y. The validity of $(X, L_i) \to (Y, L'_j)$ is based on:

$$(X, L_i) \to (Y, L'_j) \text{ holds} \Leftrightarrow \forall t \in R, \mu_{L_i}(t.X) \Rightarrow_{R\text{-}G} \mu_{L'_j}(t.Y),$$

where $\Rightarrow_{R\text{-}G}$ is Rescher-Gaines implication. In other words, $(X, L_i) \to (Y, L'_j) \Leftrightarrow$ $(\min_{t \in R} [\mu_{L_i}(t.X) \Rightarrow_{R\text{-}G} \mu_{L'_j}(t.Y)] = 1) \Leftrightarrow \forall t \in R, \mu_{L_i}(t.X) \leq \mu_{L'_j}(t.Y)$.

Example 3. When considering the relation EMP of Example 1, the usual FD Age $\to$ Salary does not hold (due to the first two tuples). However, we may consider the linguistic labels *old*, *high* and *low* defined by the fuzzy sets of Fig. 2 and *young* defined in Fig. 1.

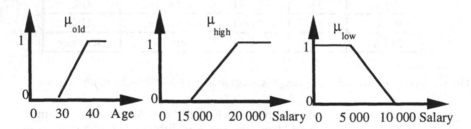

Fig. 2. The linguistic labels *old, high* and *low*

Then, relation EMP can be rewritten (from a conceptual point of view) as:

EMP	Name	Age	Salary	Firm	Country
	Durand	*Young* (0.5)	*Low* (0.8)	Comp. Inc.	France
	Dupond	*Young* (0.5)	*Low* (0.6)	Comp. Inc.	France
	James	*Young* (1)	*Low* (1)	Softw. Inc.	UK
	Peter	*Old* (0.3)	*High* (0.4)	Softw. Inc.	UK
	Walker	*Old* (1)	*High* (1)	Softw. Inc.	UK
	Müller	*Old* (1)	*High* (0.4)	Netw. Inc.	Germany

Each value of Age and Salary is replaced by its label along with the associated membership degree. In this case, the extended FD (age, *young*) $\to$ (salary, *low*) holds in EMP, which means that the *younger* an employee, the *lower* his salary. On the other hand, the extended FD (age, *old*) → (salary, *high*) does not hold♦

4.2 Linguistic Summaries

Let us consider a relation R defined over n attributes A_1, A_2, ..., A_n. Each A_i has its domain partitioned into k fuzzy sets $L_{i,k}$ which intersect at degree 0.5 (cf. next example).

Example 4. The domain [0, 50] of Age (A_1) is partitioned into 6 fuzzy sets (k = 6): *around 0* ($L_{1,1}$), *around 10* ($L_{1,2}$), *around 20* ($L_{1,3}$), *around 30* ($L_{1,4}$), *around 40* ($L_{1,5}$) and *around 50* ($L_{1,6}$) as described in Fig. 3. Such a partitioning has the advantage of covering the entire domain. In this context, a linguistic summary which involves two different attributes A_i and A_j is expressed by an extended FD (A_i, $L_{i,u}$) → (A_j, $L_{j,v}$) where u (resp. v) indicates the label associated with A_i (resp. A_j.) (cf. Example 3).

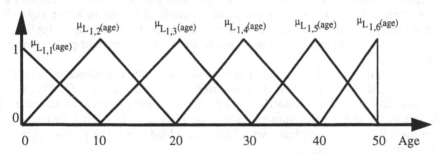

Fig. 3. Labels for the attribute Age♦

The general form of an extended FD is:

$$(A\sigma(1), L\sigma(1),f(1)), ..., (A\sigma(p), L\sigma(p),f(p)) \rightarrow$$
$$(A_{\sigma(p+1)}, L_{\sigma(p+1),f(p+1)}), ..., (A_{\sigma(q)}, L_{\sigma(q),f(q)}) \tag{1}$$

where σ (resp. f) is a permutation of q values among {1, ..., n} (resp. an application from {1, ..., q} to {1, ..., k}) which characterize attributes (resp. the chosen labels). Without loss of generality we will consider that: 1) an attribute cannot appear several times in left or right part (otherwise the summary is not meaningful) and 2) an attribute cannot appear both in left and right parts. To simplify the notations, in the following, expression (1) will be denoted :

$$(A_1, L_1), ..., (A_p, L_p) \rightarrow (A_{p+1}, L_{p+1}), ..., (A_q, L_q).$$

The validity of this summary over R is given by:

$$\min_{t \in R} [\min(\mu_{L1}(t.A_1), ..., \mu_{Lp}(t.A_p)) \Rightarrow_{R-G} \min(\mu_{Lp+1}(t.A_{p+1}), ..., \mu_{Lq}(t.A_q))],$$

and the summary is valid iff:

$\forall$ t in R, $\min(\mu_{L1}(t.A_1), ..., \mu_{Lp}(t.A_p)) \leq \min(\mu_{Lp+1}(t.A_{p+1}), ..., \mu_{Lq}(t.A_q))$.

This means that each tuple t in R satisfies the property "t is at least as (L_{p+1} and ... and L_q) as it is (L_1 and ... and L_p)".

It is possible to show that these summaries satisfy the following properties:

- **Augmentation.** The left part of a summary is denoted by LP and its right part by RP. If the summary LP → RP is valid then: $\forall$ j the summary [LP, (A_j, L_j)] → RP is valid.

- **Decomposition.** If LP → RP is valid then $\forall$ RP' $\subseteq$ RP, LP → RP' is valid.

- **Union.** We consider two valid summaries LP → RP1 and LP → RP2 with the same left part, but different right parts RP1 and RP2. The property of union states that the summary LP → [RP1, RP2] is valid.

4.3 The Discovery Algorithm

The algorithm intended for the discovery of summaries can be limited to extended FDs with a single attribute in the right part. This is justified by the fact that any valid summary can be decomposed into such summaries (property of decomposition) and is the composition of summaries having a single attribute in their right parts (property of union).

The algorithm is based on an iteration over tuples t of the considered relation (R). It computes the minimal set S of summaries which are valid on R. This set is minimal in the sense that summaries in S have a minimum number of attributes in their left parts. Other valid summaries can be obtained by a left extension of a summary in S (i.e., new attributes with labels are added to the left part according to the property of augmentation).

At the beginning of the algorithm, the set S is empty. Tuples t of relation R are successively processed. The invariant of the loop is: "from S, it is possible to obtain any summary valid on already processed tuples". The progression consists in constructing the set S_t made of summaries which are valid for t and to merge S and S_t in order to obtain a new set S. These two aspects are dealt with in sections 4.3.1 and 4.3.2 and the resulting algorithm is given in 4.3.3.

4.3.1 Principle for the Determination of S_t

For a given tuple t, S_t is made of summaries which are valid on {t} and whose left part involves a single attribute. This is sufficient since: i) any summary which is valid on {t} is the left extension of one of such summaries (next property), ii) the left extension of any such summary is valid on {t} (property of augmentation).

Property. $(A_1, L_1), ..., (A_p, L_p) \rightarrow (A_{p+1}, L_{p+1})$ is valid on t $\Rightarrow$ $\exists$ i ($1 \leq i \leq p$) such that $(A_i, L_i) \rightarrow (A_{p+1}, L_{p+1})$ is valid on t.

4.3.2 Merging S and S_t

This merge delivers the new set S. When S is empty (it is the case at the beginning of the algorithm), set S_t is delivered (S = S_t). If S is not empty, the merge necessitates to compute the set S' made of summaries compatible with S and S_t. The construction of S' needs to access each summary r of S_t: $(A_i, L_{i,u}) \rightarrow (A_j, L_{j,v})$ and to compare r with summaries in S having $(A_j, L_{j,v})$ as a right part (which are acceptable summaries). Three exclusive cases must be investigated:

case 1: if there is no acceptable summary in S, the next summary in S_t is processed.

case 2: if $(r \in S)$ then $S' = S' \cup \{r\}$.

case 3: acceptable summaries which are already a left extension of r are added to S'. Moreover, since any left extension of r is valid for t, and any left extension of an acceptable summary is valid for already processed tuples, it is possible to extend the ones by the others. Consequently, the left part of r is extended using each left part of acceptable summaries (as many extensions as acceptable summaries). The extension is performed only when the acceptable summary does not already refer to A_i (otherwise no extension is possible because the obtained summary would refer to A_i twice and would not be meaningful). The obtained summaries are added to S'.

However, some redundancy may result from the introduction in S' of summaries which are left extensions of summaries already in S' (cf. next example).

Example 5. $S_t = \{(A_1, L_{1,u}) \rightarrow (A_3, L_{3,w}); (A_2, L_{2,v}) \rightarrow (A_3, L_{3,w})\}$, $S = \{(A_2, L_{2,v}) \rightarrow (A_3, L_{3,w})\}$ and $S' = \varnothing$. After an access to $(A_1, L_{1,u}) \rightarrow (A_3, L_{3,w})$, $S' = \{(A_1, L_{1,u}), (A_2, L_{2,v}) \rightarrow (A_3, L_{3,w})\}$ (case 3). After an access to $(A_2, L_{2,v}) \rightarrow (A_3, L_{3,w})$, $S' = \{(A_1, L_{1,u}), (A_2, L_{2,v}) \rightarrow (A_3, L_{3,w}); (A_2, L_{2,v}) \rightarrow (A_3, L_{3,w})\}$ (case 2). The first summary in S' is redundant because it is the extension of the second one ◆

4.3.3 The Algorithm

At the beginning of the algorithm, the first tuple t of R is accessed and $S = S_t$. In addition if S is empty after the process of a tuple, the algorithm is stopped and the result is empty (since no summary is valid for already processed tuples, no summary can be expected to be valid on R). We obtain the algorithm:

```
begin
    first tuple t in R is accessed;
    S := determination_of_valid_summaries(t);
    for each remaining tuple t in R do
        St := determination_of_valid_summaries(t);
        S' := ∅;
        for any summary r: (Ai, Li,u) → (Aj, Lj,v) in St do
            if (r ∈ S) then S' := S' ∪ {r};                      /* case 2 */
            else for each summary LP → (Aj, Lj,v) in S do        /* case 3 */
                if ((Ai, Li,u) ∈ LP) then S' := S' ∪ {LP → (Aj, Lj,v)}
                elsif there is no k such that (Ai, Li,k) ∈ LP then
                    S' := S' ∪ {LP, (Ai, Li,u) → (Aj, Lj,v)} endif
            enddo
            endif
        enddo
```

```
        S := remove_redundancy(S');
        if S = ∅ then stop endif;
    enddo
end
```

determination_of_valid_summaries(t). This function determines the summaries of the type $(A_i, L_{i,u}) \rightarrow (A_j, L_{j,v})$ which are valid on t. They are characterized by $\mu_{L_{i,u}}(t.A_i) \le \mu_{L_{j,v}}(t.A_j)$.

remove_redundancy(S'). This function delivers non redundant summaries from S'. A summary is delivered if it is not the left extension of a summary already in S'.

In terms of data accesses, the complexity of this algorithm is linear (each tuple is accessed once). Concerning the function determination_of_valid_summaries(t), it is possible to show that its complexity in the worst case (in terms of implication values to compute) is $(n*k)^2$ where n is the number of attributes and k the number of labels for each attribute. In practise n is less than 20 and k is around 5. The complexity of the computation of S' appears very tricky and its study is beyond the scope of this paper.

Example 6. We consider a relation PLAY which describes professional basket-ball players. The labels are *young*, *tall* and *high* (this last label applies to the number of points scored by the player during a given period).

Player	(age, *young*)	(score, *high*)	(height, *tall*)
Paul	0.9	0.8	0.5
Peter	0.7	0.7	0.9

The algorithm accesses the tuple describing Paul: $S_t = S = \{(\text{score}, high) \rightarrow (\text{age}, young)$; (height, *tall*) → (age, *young*); (height, *tall*) → (score, *high*)}. The tuple describing Peter is then accessed: S_t is {(age, *young*) → (score, *high*); (age, *young*) → (height, *tall*); (score, *high*) → (age, *young*); (score, *high*) → (height, *tall*)}. The merging of S and S_t delivers the new set S = {(age, *young*), (height, *tall*) → (score, *high*); (score, *high*) → (age, *young*)}. Relation PLAY satisfies "the *younger* and the *taller* a player, the *higher* his score" and "the *higher* the score, the *younger* the player" ♦

5 Conclusion

This paper has introduced a new type of summary for knowledge discovery in databases. These summaries offer a qualitative description of the database content and are based on extended FDs. They are situated in the framework of the relational model of data and follow the pattern: "∀ t in R, the more A it is, the more B it is" where A and B are conjunctions of linguistic labels (*young, well paid, ...*) defined by fuzzy sets. In this approach, the properties of augmentation, union and decomposition valid on FDs still hold on extended FDs.

The proposed algorithm takes advantage of these properties and assumes that attribute domains are partitioned by fuzzy sets corresponding to linguistic labels. It delivers a minimal set of valid summaries of the form (A_1, L_1), ..., $(A_p, L_p) \rightarrow (A_{p+1}, L_{p+1})$, ..., (A_q, L_q) which means that each tuple t in R satisfies the property "t is at least as $(L_{p+1}$ and ... and $L_q)$ as it is $(L_1$ and ... and $L_p)$".

In the near future, we aim at experimenting the proposed algorithm with user-defined linguistic labels.

References

1. D. Dubois, H. Prade (1993). On data summarization with fuzzy sets. *Proceedings of the 5th IFSA Congress*, Seoul (Korea), 465-468.
2. D. Rasmussen and R.R. Yager (1996). Summary SQL - A flexible fuzzy query language. *Proceedings of the Flexible Query-Answering Systems Workshop (FQAS'96)*, Roskilde (Denmark), 1-18.
3. P. Bosc, L. Liétard and O. Pivert (1997). Gradualité, Imprécision et Dépendances Fonctionnelles. In *13ème Journées Bases de Données Avancées*, Grenoble (France), 391-413.
4. L.A. Zadeh (1965). Fuzzy sets. *Information and Control*, 8, 338-353.
5. L.A Zadeh (1981). Test-score semantics for natural languages and meaning representation via PRUF. In *Empirical semantics*, (B.B. Rieger ed.), Brockmeyer, Bochum, 1, 281-349.
6. D. Dubois, H. Prade (1985). A review of fuzzy set aggregation connectives. *Information Sciences*, 36, 85-121.
7. L.A. Zadeh (1983). A computational approach to fuzzy quantifiers in natural languages. *Computer Mathematics with Applications*, 9, 149-183.

A Comparison of Batch and Incremental Supervised Learning Algorithms

Leonardo Carbonara[1], and Alastair Borrowman[2]

[1] Database Marketing Team, British Telecom,
PP411.7, 120 Holborn, London EC1N 2TE, UK
leonardo.carbonara@bt.com
[2] Department of Computing Science, University of Aberdeen,
King's College, Aberdeen AB24 3UE
abj@csd.abdn.ac.uk

Abstract. This paper presents both a theoretical discussion and an experimental comparison of batch and incremental learning in an attempt to individuate some of the respective advantages and disadvantages of the two approaches when learning from frequently updated databases. The paper claims that incremental learning might be more suitable for this purpose, although a number of issues remain to be resolved.

1 Introduction

An important problem in KDD is deriving data models from frequently updated databases. Real-world databases, such as those held by credit card or telecommunications companies are constantly being enriched with new information, while old data is discarded. Although supervised learning algorithms have been used extensively to infer classification models from data, a number of issues still remain to be resolved to make them cope effectively with rapidly changing data. These algorithms can be divided into two distinct categories: incremental algorithms are able to build and refine a model in a step-by-step basis by incorporating new training cases into the model as they become available, whereas non-incremental algorithms work in batch mode. Incremental learning systems include Utgoff's (1989) ID5R and his more recent ITI (Utgoff, 1994), and Kalles & Morris's (1996) TDIDT. Among the most renown non-incremental learning algorithms are Michalski's (1980) AQ and Quinlan's (1993) C4.5.

Similarly to incremental learning systems, theory revision systems take as input an approximately correct model of a domain, usually expressed as a set of rules, and a set of training instances, and by means of a predefined set of refinement operators revise the rules to make them consistent with the training set. Although these systems cannot be considered pure learning algorithms as they assume that an initial model is provided, they share nevertheless with incremental learning algorithms the ability to incorporate new data into an existing model. Hence, for the purpose of this paper they will be treated as incremental learning systems. Theory revision systems include Ginsberg's (1988) SEEK2, EITHER (Ourston & Mooney, 1991), PTR (Koppel, *et al.*, 1994), and Carbonara & Sleeman's (1996) STALKER.

The most appealing property of non-incremental learning algorithms is possibly their ability to achieve high classification accuracy, due to the fact that processing a batch of instances help them improve generalisation and avoid over-fitting. Incremental learning, on the other hand, is desirable because knowledge revision is typically much less expensive than knowledge creation.

This paper presents a comparison of batch and incremental learning in an attempt to individuate some of the advantages and disadvantages of these approaches when learning from frequently updated databases. The paper is organised as follows. Section 2 discusses some of the properties of the batch and incremental learning systems. Section 3 presents some experimental results comparing the performance of a batch learning system, C4.5, an incremental learning system, ITI, and a theory revision system, STALKER. Section 4 summarises the results and gives some conclusions.

2 Batch vs. Incremental Learning

It is commonly thought that batch algorithms achieve higher classification rates than incremental learners, as, in general, batch learners seem to be less prone to problems such as over-fitting. In fact, they can exploit their "global view" of the data to generate more robust classifiers. Incremental algorithms, on the other hand, follow a more 'myopic' approach as they attempt to incorporate each single instance into the model. However, in the context of rapidly changing domains there are three major problems that can be identified with the batch approach:

1. *Abrupt transition between successive models.* When inferring a classification model from data, the learning algorithm selects the attributes to be included in the model using some heuristic, e.g., Quinlan's *information gain* (Quinlan, 1986). This heuristic often depends on the distribution of the possible values of the attributes across the instances. Since, when new cases are added to the initial database, this distribution might change, the new model derived from the updated database can be based on different attributes from those used in the original model. Hence, there is no clear and explicit relationship between two successive models, and it becomes difficult to keep track of the evolution of the model over time. Some methods that are being investigated to overcome this problem include feature selection, discretization, and boosting.

2. *Inconsistency over data.* The fact that the subsequent models produced by a batch algorithm are unrelated also means that cases which were correctly classified by an earlier model may be mis-classified by a subsequent model, and vice versa. In other words, there is no assurance whatsoever that, moving from one model to another, any kind of consistency over the data will be maintained. As we shall see below, consistency is not always a desirable property. However,

there must be some way to monitor and control the inconsistencies introduced so that the user is informed of the reasons why inconsistency is achieved on a number of cases.

3. *Time inefficiency*: when dealing with very large collections of data which are constantly being updated, generating a new model from scratch every time new instances are received is a very inefficient way to revise the model. Sampling is a possible solution to this problem, although in the case of very skewed data interesting concepts which have little statistical support may not be identified.

Incremental learning inherently solves the first two problems identified above:

1. *Smooth transition between successive models.* Since the new model is not generated from scratch using the now-augmented set of instances, but is a revision of the initial model, there is a clear relationship between the two models. By analysing the changes implemented it is possible to know exactly how the initial model was modified to produce the revised model.

2. *Consistency over data.* The incremental approach also assures that the changes in the model are truly incremental, i.e., the classification performance of the revised model is unaltered on the cases contained in the initial data set.

Whether the incremental approach can also solve the third problem, i.e., the time inefficiency of the batch approach, needs to be investigated further. Batch algorithms such as C4.5 work in linear time in the number of cases processed. Incremental learners usually require more computational effort to incorporate each instance into an existing model. However, it is not necessary that the sum of the incremental costs be less than the batch cost, as every time the incremental algorithms only work on the updates. Hence, if the model needs to be updated frequently, the incremental approach should be less expensive.

It has already be pointed out that the second property possessed by incremental learning, i.e. the ability to make changes to the model which are consistent with the previously seen instances may not always be desirable. This is the case when the concepts of interest depend on some *hidden context* that changes over time. Changes in the hidden context can induce more or less radical changes in the target concepts, producing what is generally known as *concept drift* (Schlimmer & Granger, 1986). Widmer & Kubat (1996) showed that incremental learners can be adapted to successfully detect, and react to, concept drift. Although it is not the purpose of this paper to investigate learning in the presence of concept drift, this is another reason why incremental learning may prove superior to the batch approach in rapidly changing domains.

In this section some of the properties of incremental and batch learners have been presented and discussed. The main advantage of batch algorithms seems to be their superior classification power, while the incremental approach appears to be preferable when it is likely that new data will become available after the initial classifier has been built. Since this is a common occurrence in practical applications of machine learning, where the continual collection of data is the norm, it is evident that incremental learners able to achieve high classification accuracy would constitute an appealing alternative to batch learners. In the next section, the results of some experiments are presented which attempt to understand the proportion of the gap, if any, between the classification power of current batch and incremental algorithms.

3. Some experiments comparing batch and incremental learning systems

In this section the results of some experiments comparing the classification accuracy of the batch learning algorithm C4.5, the incremental learning algorithm ITI, and the theory revision system STALKER will be presented. C4.5 and ITI are two state-of-the art decision tree induction algorithms. STALKER has been shown to perform at comparable levels with other well known theory revision systems on a number of benchmark domains (Carbonara & Sleeman, 1996). Moreover, it uses an incremental algorithm to refine each incorrectly solved instance, its approach therefore being closer to pure incremental learners than other batch theory revision systems.

C4.5 probably does not need any introduction as it is one of the most widely used algorithm for batch induction of decision trees. C4.5 produces an initial decision tree using the *information gain* metric to select the test at each decision node. The tree is then pruned to prevent overfitting. The final tree can also be converted into a collection of simplified rules.

ITI (Utgoff, 1994) produces models of the data in the form of binary decision trees, that is each test at a decision node can be answered *true* or *false*. ITI can be used both in batch and incremental mode.

Theory revision is the task of automatically refining a domain theory usually expressed as a set of rules to make it consistent with a given set of training instances. The theory revision system STALKER (Carbonara & Sleeman, 1996) generates a set of alternative refinements to correct each incorrectly solved training case. These alternative corrections are tested against all the previously seen instances to select the one that achieves the highest classification accuracy. The best refinement is implemented and the process repeated for the next training instance. Since testing each alternative correction is computationally expensive, STALKER overcomes this problem by converting rules and instances into a *Truth Maintenance System* (TMS), which is then used to efficiently test the refinements.

In the next subsection the method used to compare the three algorithms is described. The results of experiments with four domains from the UCI repository of machine learning databases are then presented.

3.1. The evaluation method

As already noticed, STALKER is not a pure incremental learning system as it needs to be given as input an initial set of rules to be refined. Hence, to compare its performance with the two other systems the following method has been used. An initial ruleset was produced with C4.5 using a subset of the training instances. This set of rules was then refined by STALKER using the remaining training instances. The classification accuracy of the resulting ruleset was then compared to that of the ruleset produced by C4.5 using all the training instances. ITI was tested in a similar way, by generating an initial tree using the system in batch mode and then adding the remaining instances to the tree. However, the same results would have been obtained by generating the final tree from all the instances in batch mode, as ITI's tree transposition operator ensures that the incremental algorithm generates the same tree as it would have been produced with the batch algorithm. The ratio of batch and incremental instances was different in each subset to enable the investigation of the relationship between the accuracy of the final data model produced and the number of instances used to build the initial batch model. The ratio, or step, between the number of batch and incremental instances was decided upon based on the total number of training instances. A ratio was chosen which produced 4 or 5 subsets for each dataset considered. The results presented were averaged over ten independent trials.

The three systems were tested on four datasets from the UCI Repository of Machine Learning Databases (Merz & Murphy, 1996). A brief description of the domains and the results of the experiments follow.

Tables 1 to 4 show the classification accuracy results for the experiments carried out with the above domains. The figures reported are:

- **Initial KB** is the accuracy achieved by the ruleset produced by C4.5 with the 'batch' subset of training data which was used as the initial theory for the STALKER experiments;
- **STALKER** is the accuracy achieved by STALKER using the 'incremental' subset of training data to refine the Initial KB;
- **C4.5** is the classification performance of C4.5 on the full set of training data (this explains why the curve is a straight line);
- **ITI Batch** represents the accuracy of the initial tree generated by ITI from the 'batch' data;
- **ITI Incremental** is the accuracy of the final tree obtained by ITI by incorporating into the initial tree the remaining 'incremental' training instances. As ITI is always able to accommodate all the training instances, this is also a straight line.

Table 1. Classification accuracy for the Breast Cancer domain

Training Data					
Data Split	Initial Training Data	ITI Batch	STALKER	ITI Incremental	C4.5 - 600 cases
100/500	92.40	93.58	96.50	100	97.95
200/400	93.90	95.04	97.43	100	97.95
300/300	94.07	96.70	97.93	100	97.95
400/200	94.85	97.99	98.05	100	97.95
500/100	95.60	99.17	99.20	100	97.95
Test Data					
Data Split	Initial Test Data	ITI Batch	STALKER	ITI Incremental	C4.5 - 600 cases
100/500	93.23	93.23	94.34	95.05	95.96

200/400	94.34	93.43	95.95	95.05	95.96
300/300	94.24	94.04	95.65	95.05	95.96
400/200	94.54	93.03	95.85	95.05	95.96
500/100	94.54	93.83	95.85	95.05	95.96

Table 2. Classification accuracy for the Splice domain

Training Data					
Data Split	Initial Training Data	ITI Batch	STALKER	ITI Incremental	C4.5 - 900 cases
150/750	77.72	82.368	93.48	100	95.04
300/600	83.15	90.268	94.37	100	95.04
450/450	86.51	93.102	96.40	100	95.04
600/300	88.47	95.289	95.97	100	95.04
750/150	90.20	97.881	98.67	100	95.04
Test Data					
Data Split	Initial Test Data	ITI Batch	STALKER	ITI Incremental	C4.5 - 900 cases
150/750	76.70	78.60	86.60	91.30	92.80
300/600	85.30	87.20	91.00	91.30	92.80
450/450	88.70	87.20	92.10	91.30	92.80
600/300	91.80	88.20	94.20	91.30	92.80
750/150	92.10	90.50	93.50	91.30	92.80

Table 3. Classification accuracy for the Adult domain

Training Data					
Data Split	Initial Training Data	ITI Batch	STALKER	ITI Incremental	C4.5 - 1000 cases
200/800	79.33	74.77	87.03	100	87.39
400/600	80.77	79.43	92.00	100	87.39
600/400	81.65	83.13	93.55	100	87.39
800/200	82.40	86.20	94.60	100	87.39
Test Data					
Data Split	Initial Test Data	ITI Batch	STALKER	ITI Incremental	C4.5 - 1000 cases
200/800	79.32	79.62	81.80	81.44	83.22
400/600	80.80	80.62	80.88	81.44	83.22
600/400	81.36	81.30	82.20	81.44	83.22
800/200	82.12	81.38	82.24	81.44	83.22

Table 4. Classification accuracy for the Diabetes domain

Training Data					
Data Split	Initial Training Data	ITI Batch	STALKER	ITI Incremental	C4.5 - 600 cases
100/500	70.76	72.90	75.80	100	81.97
200/400	72.35	78.23	79.90	100	81.97

300/300	73.50	84.47	81.63	100	81.97
400/200	75.40	90.33	86.15	100	81.97
500/100	73.20	94.77	86.90	100	81.97
Test Data					
Data Split	Initial Test Data	ITI Batch	STALKER	ITI Incremental	C4.5 - 600 cases
100/500	66.90	66.90	69.52	67.98	72.44
200/400	69.23	67.56	72.26	67.98	72.44
300/300	71.01	69.35	72.14	67.98	72.44
400/200	73.33	67.62	73.15	67.98	72.44
500/100	71.37	67.86	73.45	67.98	72.44

As can be seen from the tables above the three systems seem to achieve comparable levels of accuracy on all the domains considered. Perhaps the only domain where there is a noticeable difference is the Diabetes domain, ITI performing significantly worse than C4.5 and STALKER.

STALKER is particularly sensitive to the accuracy of the initial KB which it is given to revise. This is somehow consistent with the *minor tweaking* assumption under which most theory revision systems work, i.e. the supposition that the initial KB is 'approximately' correct, and only needs minor tweaking rather than a major overhaul. This makes theory revision systems prefer 'minimal' refinements, i.e. corrections that are considered to be the least radical according to some metric (e.g., syntactical complexity). It is possible that this bias towards minimal revisions prevents such systems from making the more drastic changes that may be needed to refine very inaccurate theories. However, it must be noticed that, starting with an accurate KB, in two domains (Splice and Diabetes) STALKER outperforms the other two systems. In the Adult domain, on the other hand, a superior performance to C4.5 on the training data is not matched by a similar result on the test data, perhaps indicating over-fitting.

Some other possible cases of over-fitting can be seen in the test results for Diabetes experiments where for the 300/300 split and the 400/200 split, respectively, ITI's and C4.5's initial trees are more accurate than the corresponding final trees.

ITI has the desirable feature that trees built incrementally are always the same as the batch trees generated from the same data. This is achieved by means of its tree restructuring operators. However, this implies that extra work must be done to reshape the incrementally built trees which can affect the system's time performance. In fact, in the above experiments the time taken by ITI to incrementally revise the initial trees is consistently higher than the time taken by C4.5 to build the final batch trees. (Note that both C4.5 and ITI are implemented in C, and were tested on the same machine.) Another appealing characteristic of ITI's is that it always accommodates all training instance. This, however, can cause the trees generated by ITI to be exceedingly complex, which in turn can lead to over-fitting. In fact, ITI's test results are always slightly less accurate than those for the other two systems. To overcome this problem pruning could be used to eliminate subtrees that overfit the data. Utgoff (1994) explains that no pruning technique was used in ITI to retain the property that the same tree will be found for the same set of instances, independent of the order in which they are presented. Nevertheless, he suggests that a pruning method could be incorporated if, instead of actually discarding unwanted subtrees, one could mark nodes as 'virtually pruned'. Thus subtrees could be marked in and out of existence without the expense of destroying or reconstructing anything. When one arrives at a virtually pruned decision node, one treats it as a leaf, returning the corresponding class.

We shall conclude this section with some notes on the time performance of the algorithms compared. A direct comparison of timings was not possible as the systems were developed with different programming languages (C4.5 and ITI are written in C, while STALKER is implemented in Common Lisp). Hence, we shall limit this discussion to the computational complexity of the three algorithms. C4.5 is linear in the number of training instances processed. In the incremental learner ITI, the incremental cost is, in general, proportional to the number of nodes in the decision tree. The tree generally grows to its approximate final size early in the training, with the rest of the training serving to improve the selection of the test at each node. Of concern is whether the incremental training cost continues to grow even after the size of the tree has more or less stabilised. Experimental results on a number of domains with both symbolic and numeric variables (Utgoff, 1994) seem to suggest that ITI's training cost appears to be effectively independent of the number of training instances seen. In theory, however, this is not the case when numeric variables are involved. For each numeric variable at each node, a sorted list of the values observed is maintained, which is used to select the best test for that node. Hence, more training instances means a greater cost to maintain each such list. In the theory revision system STALKER, training time is split between generation of alternative refinements and testing of revised KBs against previously processed training instances. Refinement generation is a potentially exponential process when dealing with long rule chains, although in most cases takes a negligible amount of time. Testing of refined KBs with the Truth Maintenance System is in theory cubic in the number of cases, although experiments in a number of domains seem to suggest that the process is in fact quadratic in the number of cases represented in the TMS (Carbonara, 1996). In conclusion, it seems that C4.5 is more efficient than the other two incremental algorithms. However, as pointed out in Section 2, when dealing with frequently updated very large databases the cost of incrementally updating an initial model should be less than building the model from scratch every time.

4. Conclusions

This paper presented a comparison of incremental and batch learning algorithms. In the literature, batch learning is often praised for its ability to achieve high classification accuracy, but it is considered to be inefficient when applied to frequently updated, large databases. Not only should incremental learning obviate this shortcoming, but, as shown by the results of an experimental comparison, can also achieve comparable levels of accuracy to batch learning. Moreover, incremental learners also possess some other interesting properties, such as the ability to monitor changes in the data model and to detect concept drift, which are particularly desirable when dealing with rapidly changing domains.

Acknowledgments

The work presented in this paper was supported by the Data Mining Research Project and was carried out at the BT Labs, Ipswich. The authors wish to thank Gavin Meggs for his useful comments on an earlier version of this paper.

References

Carbonara, L. and Sleeman, D. (1996). Improving the Efficiency of Knowledge Base Refinement. In *Proceedings of the 13th International Conference on Machine Learning* (pp. 78-86), Bari, Italy: Morgan Kauffman.

Clark, P. & Nibblet, T. (1989). The CN2 induction algorithm. *Machine Learning*, 3, 261-283.

Ginsberg, A. (1988). Automatic Refinement of Expert System Knowledge Bases. Morgan Kaufmann, San Mateo, California.

Kalles, D. & Morris, T. (1996). Efficient Incremental Induction of Decision Trees. *Machine Learning*, 24, 231-242.

Koppel, M., Feldman, R., & Segre, A.M. (1994). Bias-Driven Revision of Logical Domain Theories. *Journal of Artificial Intelligence Research*, 1, 159-208.

Michalski, R.S. & Chilauski, R.L. (1980). Learning by being told and learning from examples: An experimental comparison of the two methods of knowledge acquisition in the context of developing an expert system for soybean disease diagnosis. *Policy Analysis and Information Systems*, 4, 125-160.

Merz, C.J., & Murphy, P.M. (1996). UCI Repository of machine learning databases [http://www.ics.uci.edu/~mlearn/MLRepository.html]. Irvine, CA: University of California, Department of Information and Computer Science.

Ourston, D. and Mooney, R. (1991). Changing the Rules: A comprehensive approach to Theory Refinement. In *Proceedings of the 8th National Conference on Artificial Intelligence* (pp. 815-820), Cambridge, MA: MIT Press.

Quinlan, J.R. (1986). Induction of Decision Trees. *Machine Learning 1*, 81-106.

Quinlan, J.R. (1993). C4.5: Programs for machine learning. San Mateo, California: Morgan Kauffman.

Schlimmer, J.C. & Granger, R.H. (1986). Incremental Learning from Noisy Data. *Machine Learning*, 1, 317-354.

Utgoff, P.E. (1989). Incremental Induction of decision trees. *Machine Learning, 4*, 161-186.

Utgoff, P.E. (1994). An Improved Algorithm for Incremental Induction of Decision Trees. In *Proceedings of the 11th International Conference on Machine Learning*, New Brunswick, NJ, Morgan Kauffman.

Widmer, G. & Kubat, M. (1996). Learning in the Presence of concept Drift and Hidden Contexts. *Machine Learning*, 23, 69-101.

Knowledge Discovery with Qualitative Influences and Synergies

Jesús Cerquides, Ramon López de Màntaras

Artificial Intelligence Research Institute, IIIA
Spanish Council for Scientific Research, CSIC
08193, Bellaterra, Barcelona, Spain
{cerquide,mantaras}@iiia.csic.es

Abstract We review some approaches to qualitative uncertainty and propose a new one based on the idea of Absolute Order of Magnitude. We show that our ideas can be useful for Knowledge Discovery by introducing a derivation of the Naive-Bayes classifier based on them: the Qualitative Bayes Classifier. This classification method keeps Naive-Bayes accuracy while gaining interpretability, so we think it can be useful for the Data Mining step of the Knowledge Discovery process.

1 Introduction

Comprehensibility is a key characteristic for algorithm results to be useful in Knowledge Discovery in Databases tasks.

Bayesian reasoning has been usually criticized as hard to explain and understand, but achieves high performance rates with simple constructs, as happens for instance with the Naive-Bayes classifier[5].

Some approaches to increasing Bayesian reasoning comprehensibility appear in [3, 6, 12, 14, 15]. The main idea in all these approaches was to attach linguistic labels as "probable" or "very unlikely" to numerical probabilities, that is to absolutes degrees of belief. Bayesian reasoning works primarily with changes in probability values, and these approaches do not seem to give any interpretation of such changes, giving as result hardly understandable explanations. It has been accepted that, unlike physical parameters, absolute probabilities do not seem to have values (except the endpoints) that are universally interesting [13].

This problem was noticed also by Elsaesser, that in [1] proposed the use of a version of Polya's "shaded inductive patterns" [10] for linguistic explanation of Bayesian inference. Elsaesser uses Oden's model [8] to create the linguistic labels related to changes in probability. Elsaesser explanations are comprehensible, but we have no security that reasoning with the information given by these explanations really bring us to coherent conclusions, this is because explanation and reasoning are performed at different levels, and we are not allowed to use a previous explanation in a future case.

Another approach is the one followed by Neufeld [7], Wellman [13] and Parsons [9], using ideas from the field of qualitative uncertainty. The idea behind their work is finding whether a fact A is favoured, unfavoured or not altered by another fact B. Quoting Parsons:

Whereas in probabilistic networks the main goal is to establish probabilities of hypotheses when particular observations are made in qualitative systems the main aim is to establish how values change.

Our approach can be viewed as a refinement of qualitative probabilistic networks (QPNs) showing that slightly modified, Elsaesser explanations can be used not just for explanatory purposes but also for reasoning and prediction achieving results similar to those of non-qualitative probabilistic reasoning, while keeping intact its interpretability.

Next section briefly introduces qualitative probabilistic networks, concretely Wellman and Neufeld approaches. Section 3 introduces our qualitative approach to influences and synergies, making use of the absolute orders of magnitude model. Section 4 describes our proposal to use the qualitative influences and synergies in a Qualitative Bayesian classifier. Finally, Section 5 describes an empirical comparative study based on 15 datasets and analyses the results obtained with the aim of showing the good performance of our approach in terms of classification accuracy.

2 Introduction to Qualitative Probabilistic Networks

Two main approaches have been done to the concept of QPN. We will shortly review both here.

2.1 Wellman approach

For Wellman, a QPN is a pair $G = (V, Q)$, where V is the set of variables or vertices of the graph and Q is a set of qualitative relationships among the variables. He introduces two main concepts for modelling QPNs as are *qualitative influences* and *qualitative synergies*.

Wellman qualitative influences. Qualitative influences can be thought of as qualitative relations describing the sign (direction) of the relationship between a pair of variables. A variable can influence another positively (+), negatively (-), or in no way (0). We should also consider the possibility that the sign of the influence is unknown to us (?). If we use δ to denote one of $\{+,-,0,?\}$ we say a qualitative influence of a on b in direction δ holds in the graph $G = (V, Q)$ if $(a, b, \delta) \in Q$. For formally introducing the probabilistic semantic of this concept the way Wellman does, we need to previously define the set of predecessors that influence a variable in a network.

$$pred_G(b) = \{a|(a, b, \delta) \in Q, for some\ \delta \in \{+, -, ?\}\} \tag{1}$$

Now we can assign probabilistic meaning to influences. We say that an influence edge $(a, b, +) \in Q$ is satisfied in a concrete domain if for all $x \in pred_G(b) - \{a\}$ such that x is consistent with both a and $\neg a$, we have

$$Pr(b|a, x) \geq Pr(b|\neg a, x) \tag{2}$$

The meaning of this expression can be stated as: under any circumstances (x) that are known to affect b, the presence of a makes b more likely than its absence.

Parallel definitions can be done for $(a, b, -)$, $(a, b, 0)$ and $(a, b, ?)$, replacing $\geq$ by $\leq$, $=$, and "no condition at all" ($(a, b, ?)$ always holds) respectively.

Wellman qualitative synergies. Qualitative synergies describe the qualitative interaction among influences. The idea behind them is that two variables synergically influence a third if their joint influence is greater than separate, statistically independent, influences. The formalisation of this idea can be seen in [13], and will be skipped here.

2.2 Neufeld approach

Neufeld formalises the idea of qualitative influence by means of the concept of favouring. He says a favours b if $Prob(b|a) > Prob(a)$. He includes four types of edges in what he calls inference graphs:

- *Defeasible links.* Given a, b is more likely to happen.
$$a \to b \text{ if } 1 > Prob(b|a) > Prob(b) \tag{3}$$

- *Logical links.* Given a, b will surely happen.
$$a \Rightarrow b \text{ if } 1 = Prob(b|a) > Prob(b) \tag{4}$$

- *Negative defeasible links.* Given a, b is less likely to happen.
$$a \nrightarrow b \text{ if } 1 > Prob(\neg b|a) > Prob(\neg b) \tag{5}$$

- *Negative logical links.* Given a, b will not happen.
$$a \nRightarrow b \text{ if } 1 = Prob(\neg b|a) > Prob(\neg b) \tag{6}$$

Once introduced these concepts Neufeld uses them to do common sense reasoning. For more details on his approach to qualitative uncertainty see [7].

3 Influences and synergies revisited

Neufeld and Wellman ideas are useful for common sense reasoning, planning under uncertainty and when qualitative differential equations are not applicable. Our idea is to adapt them in order to make them useful for classification and characterization of sets.

The qualitative model used by both approaches is the signs model, composed of three categories +,-,0 and ? for representing the unknown. More sophisticated models have risen from the field of qualitative reasoning. One of these models is the absolute orders of magnitude model [11], that considers a finer partition of the real line than the one given by the signs, allowing also distinctions in quantities of the same sign. This model qualifies quantities into seven classes, from *Negative Large* to *Positive Large*, including *Zero*. Quantities of the same sign are divided into three classes(*Large*, *Medium* and *Small*) that are very natural in human reasoning. We have discretized influences into this new model, in a way coherent with Neufeld works. Neufeld states a $favours$ b if $Prob(b|a) > Prob(b)$ that is, if $\frac{Prob(b|a)}{Prob(b)} > 1$. This quotient was also used by Elaesser, in his work trying to explain bayesian reasoning, to denote the shift in belief that a produces in b. We will define influence of a in b as:

$$Influence(a, b) = \frac{Prob(b|a)}{Prob(b)} \tag{7}$$

We note that:

$$Influence(a, b) = Influence(b, a) \tag{8}$$

Once we have a definition for influence, we make use of the absolut order of magnitudes model to make influences comprehensible. By discretizing influences into the seven classes seen in Figure 1, we perform a process similar to that of Elsaesser assigning linguistic labels as "much more likely", "a little less likely", and so on. The boundary values established in Figure 1 were selected over a set of alternatives because they performed better than the rest in the classification experiments described in Section 5.

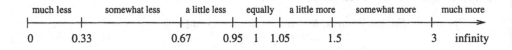

Figure 1. Influence discretization scale

We have given an expression for influences and a scale for their discretization. What about synergies?. Synergies can be seen as the difference in influence between two facts that happen together with respect to these two facts happening separately. We can give the following expression for synergies of two variables:

$$Synergy(\{a_1, a_2\}, b) = \frac{Influence(a_1 \cap a_2, b)}{Influence(a_1, b) * Influence(a_2, b)} \tag{9}$$

4 An application of qualitative influences and synergies: The Qualitative Bayesian Classifier

In this section we will show that qualitative influences and synergies can be used for reasoning and, more concretely, for classification tasks, giving high classification rates. We will use them to get a qualitative version of a well known classification method, the Bayesian classifier.

The Naive-Bayes classifier [5] is a classification method based on Bayesian reasoning. Given a test example **e** from a probabilistic viewpoint we must choose the class i that maximizes $P(C = i|\mathbf{E} = \mathbf{e})$. Developing this conditional probability according to the Bayes rule we have:

$$P(C = i|\mathbf{E} = \mathbf{e}) = P(C = i) * \frac{P(\mathbf{E} = \mathbf{e}|C = i)}{P(\mathbf{E} = \mathbf{e})} \tag{10}$$

If the attributes are independent given the class, it holds:

$$P(\mathbf{E} = \mathbf{e}|C = i) = \prod_{j=1}^{N} P(E_j = e_j|C = i) \tag{11}$$

where N is the number of features of the example. Since $P(\mathbf{E} = \mathbf{e})$ is independent of the class, Naive-Bayes tells us to choose the class which maximizes:

$$P(C = i) * \prod_{j=1}^{N} P(E_j = e_j|C = i) \tag{12}$$

An interpretation of this formula can be that $P(C = i)$ is our initial belief in the fact that i is the class of our example, and each one of the factors $P(E_j = e_j|C = i)$ can be seen as shifts that modify this belief. We will adapt these shifts in belief to coincide with our previously defined influences.

Returning to Equation 10, and assuming statistical independence between the attributes, we are allowed to develop the denominator the same way we have done with the numerator:

$$P(\mathbf{E} = \mathbf{e}) = \prod_{j=1}^{N} P(E_j = e_j) \tag{13}$$

and substituting in 10 we have:

$$P(C = i|\mathbf{E} = \mathbf{e}) = P(C = i) * \frac{\prod_{j=1}^{N} P(E_j = e_j|C = i)}{\prod_{j=1}^{N} P(E_j = e_j)} \tag{14}$$

that in terms of influences can be expressed as

$$P(C = i|\mathbf{E} = \mathbf{e}) = P(C = i) * \prod_{j=1}^{N} Influence(E_j = e_j, C = i) \tag{15}$$

Now we can apply this rule with qualitative influences and analyze the differences in accuracy between applying the Naive-Bayes classifier where shifts in belief vary continuously from 0 to 1 and our qualitative influences framework, where shifts only can have the seven values we have previously seen.

Before doing this, we want to introduce the idea of synergy in our classifier, because we have made two independence assumptions and synergy can improve the performance when the classification problem at hand does not fulfill this assumptions, because synergies precisely try to express interattribute dependencies with respect to the class. Our first idea was to calculate all the synergies between all pairs of variables and apply them. The problem with this approach is that it is not an approximation of the Bayes formula, and hence is not theoretically well founded and empirically does not perform correctly. In fact, applying synergies that way made accuracy get worse. The reason is that synergies can be seen as corrections of the approximation to the probabilities given by influences. It is not correct to apply a synergy correction for two variables E_i and E_j and also apply it to E_j and E_k, because we are correcting E_j influence twice. That is why we will follow the next schema:

We first classify the set of synergies that affect to our example into Large, Medium and Small synergies, no matter if they are positive or negative. Then we try to apply as many Large synergies as possible. Once this has been done we repeat the same process for medium and finally for small synergies.

Algorithmically, it can be expressed as shown in Figure 2. The operations in the algorithm are calculated by using a representative for each interval. We tested two approaches, one taking as representative a value in the center of each interval and the other taking the value of the class that is nearer to equality. Using the discretization values of 1, our first method will give as representative of "much less" 0.165, as representative of "somewhat less" 0.5 and so on, while for the same values, the second method will choose 0.33 as representative of "much less", 0.67 for "somewhat less" and so on. The second approach performed better empirically, consequently it is the one we will use from now on.

When our Qualitative Bayesian Classifier (QBC) is restricted to influences we call it First Order QBC (FOQBC), when synergies of two variables are applied we call it Second Order QBC (SOQBC). The development for order greater than second is not trivial because different developments of the greater order approximations are possible.

```
program SOQBC;
    foreach class i
                                    N
        ClassProb[i] = P(C=i) *   ∏  Influence(Ej = ej, C = i)
                                   j=1
        InfluencesCorrected[i] = ∅;
        ApplySynergies(LargeSynergies(class i));
        ApplySynergies(MediumSynergies(class i));
        ApplySynergies(SmallSynergies(class i));
    end
    Select the class i with highest ClassProb[i];
end
procedure ApplySynergies(SynergySet)
    While SynergySet ≠ ∅
        Randomly choose a Synergy (namely {Ej = ej, Ek = ek})
                and delete it from SynergySet
        if ({Ej = ej, Ek = ek}∩ InfluencesCorrected) = ∅
           ClassProb[i] = ClassProb[i] * Synergy({Ej = ej, Ek = ek},C=i)
           InflCorrected[i] = InflCorrected[i] ∪{Ej = ej, Ek = ek}
```

Figure2. Synergies application strategy

5   Empirical comparison

We have evaluated the classification accuracy for First and Second Order QBC and compared it with the Naive-Bayes classifier, as well as with other widely used machine learning algorithms. Our experiment consists in evaluating the average accuracy of each classifier, as well as its standard deviation for 15 datasets from the Irvine repository. Some information regarding these datasets can be seen in 1 For each dataset and classification method we performed 50 runs, keeping the 70% of the dataset as training set and the remaining 30% as test set. We included our algorithms in the $\mathcal{MLC}++$ [4] library, and used the facilities this library provides for machine learning experimentation. We compared the First and Second Order QBC with the well known machine learning algorithms CN2, Naive-Bayes classifier, IBL, and ID3. The results are summarized in Table 2.

Furthermore, in table 3 we show how many times each classification algorithm ranked in the position indicated by the column identifier. In this table "1" means the algorithm ranked once in the position specified by the column under which it appears, "22" that it ranked twice , "333" that it ranked three times and so on.

Dataset	Attributes	Instances	Classes	Missing
BREAST-CANCER	9	286	2	none
BREAST	10	699	2	16
CRX	15	690	2	few
GLASS2	10	214	2	none
HEART	13	270	2	none
HYPOTHYROID	25	3162	2	some
IRIS	4	150	3	none
MONK1	6	432	2	none
MONK2	6	432	2	none
MONK3	6	432	2	5%
PARITY 5+5	10	100	2	none
SOYBEAN-LARGE	35	316	19	some
SOYBEAN-SMALL	35	47	4	none
VOTES	16	435	2	few
WAVEFORM-21	21	5000	3	none

Table1. Datasets information

Dataset	CN2	Bayes	IBL	ID3	FOQBC	SOQBC
BREAST-CANCER	73.82 ± 0.39	69.56 ± 0.5	**77.01 ± 0.54**	74.04 ± 0.52	69.98 ± 0.52	71.69 ± 0.49
BREAST	95.88 ± 0.15	**97.5 ± 0.11**	97.09 ± 0.11	96.2 ± 0.15	97.42 ± 0.11	97.35 ± 0.11
CRX	86.86 ± 0.29	86.51 ± 0.21	87.17 ± 0.23	86.97 ± 0.23	86.22 ± 0.2	**87.75 ± 0.19**
GLASS2	78.92 ± 0.79	77.89 ± 0.75	**83.28 ± 0.59**	80.89 ± 0.83	76.72 ± 0.76	76.96 ± 0.73
HEART	79.70 ± 0.62	82.11 ± 0.42	79.90 ± 0.49	80.76 ± 0.52	81.34 ± 0.48	**82.25 ± 0.5**
HYPOTHYROID	98.9 ± 0.04	98.43 ± 0.05	97.7 ± 0.05	**98.94 ± 0.03**	98.56 ± 0.05	98.44 ± 0.05
IRIS	96.24 ± 0.42	94.99 ± 0.35	96.52 ± 0.33	**96.80 ± 0.37**	94.69 ± 0.4	94.92 ± 0.36
MONK1	**91.63 ± 0.95**	74.67 ± 0.61	81.68 ± 0.61	83.76 ± 0.47	71.66 ± 0.66	88.73 ± 0.62
MONK2	**72.77 ± 0.59**	57.41 ± 0.53	70.01 ± 0.51	69.2 ± 0.73	60.94 ± 0.47	61.37 ± 0.54
MONK3	90.04 ± 0.63	**92.25 ± 0.36**	85.83 ± 0.53	91.60 ± 0.39	91.82 ± 0.51	91.46 ± 0.4
PARITY 5+5	64.26 ± 0.71	50.45 ± 0.76	**65.43 ± 0.7**	64.14 ± 0.75	51.71 ± 0.64	50.67 ± 0.66
SOYBEAN-LARGE	89.52 ± 0.28	90.66 ± 0.22	**92.59 ± 0.2**	91.44 ± 0.25	88.04 ± 0.2	86.33 ± 0.39
SOYBEAN-SMALL	90.93 ± 1.36	**99.14 ± 0.77**	98.55 ± 0.81	93.76 ± 1.11	99.01 ± 0.78	99.02 ± 0.77
VOTES	94.89 ± 0.2	89.74 ± 0.25	93.99 ± 0.23	**95.09 ± 0.18**	88.17 ± 0.28	91.61 ± 0.26
WAVEFORM-21	74.33 ± 0.43	82.81 ± 0.35	82.16 ± 0.41	78.31 ± 0.39	79.98 ± 0.4	**83.07 ± 0.4**

Table2. Average accuracies and their standard deviations

	First	Second	Third	Fourth	Fifth	Sixth
ID3	333	333	55555	1	333	
IBL	4444	333	22	333	1	22
SOQBC	333	22	1	55555	333	1
CN2	22	333	333	22	1	4444
BAYES	333	22	1	22	4444	333
FOQBC		22	333	22	333	55555

Table3. Ranking table

5.1 Result analysis and justification

Table 3 shows that the SOQBC has an accuracy in the level of the best classifiers being the best one in 3 out of 15 times, so it can be considered as a valuable alternative to these methods. Our method has an accuracy at least as good as the one provided by Naive-Bayes and offers the advantage of a common classification-explanation space. That is, we are not keeping two separate representations, one for reasoning and the other for explanation. That allows the user to actually *apply* the discovered knowledge in his own decisions with a greater confidence, because we have shown that reasoning with it gives acceptable accuracy results.

On the other hand, we consider the FOQBC results good enough considering the simplicity of the classifier induced. Its results are not too far from the ones given by continuous Bayes (surprisingly four times FOQBC outperforms Bayes as shown in Table 2). This can be seen as a confirmation of the idea exposed by Friedman in [2]:

> *Good probability estimates are not necessary for good classification; similarly, low classification rates does not imply that the corresponding class probabilities are being estimated (even remotely) accurately.*

FOQBC makes a extremely inexact estimation of the probabilities, but has classification results only slightly worse than the ones given by more complex classifiers. Our intuition is that the difference in performance between FOQBC and Naive-Bayes will increase when the number of examples in the dataset increases but we have not tested it yet.

6 Conclusions

We have introduced qualitative influences and synergies based on the absolute orders of magnitude model. We have developed a competitive learning algorithm (SOQBC) based on these ideas, that offers a good balance between the accuracy of its predictions and its understandability. These facts make us believe that both the ideas of qualitative influences and synergies and the classifier can be useful to the Knowledge Discovery community.

7 Acknowledgements

This work has been partially supported by UBILAB (Union Bank of Switzerland) and by the Spanish CICYT project SMASH, TIC96-1038-C04001. Jesús Cerquides research is supported by a doctoral scholarship of the CIRIT (Generalitat de Catalunya). We wish to thank Carina Gibert, Monica Sánchez and Núria Piera for carefully revising the preliminary versions of this paper.

References

1. Christopher Elsaesser. Explanation of probabilistic inference. In L. N. Kanal, T. S. Levitt, and J. F. Lemmer, editors, *Uncertainty in Artificial Intelligence 3*, pages 387–400. Elsevier Science Publishers B.V. (North-Holland), 1989.
2. Jerome H. Friedman. On Bias, Variance, 0/1-Loss, and the Curse-of-Dimensionality. *Data Mining and Knowledge Discovery*, 1:55–77, 1997.
3. Edgard M. Johnson. Numerical encoding of qualitative expressions of uncertainty. Technical Report 250, Army Research Institute for the Behavioural and Social Sciences, Arlington, Virginia, 1973.
4. R. Kohavi, G. John, R. Long, D. Manley, and K. Pfleger. MLC++: A machine learning library in C++. In *Tools with Artificial Intelligence*, pages 740–743. IEEE Computer Society Press, 1994.
5. Pat Langley, Wayne Iba, and Kevin Thompson. An Analysis of Bayesian Classifiers. In *Proceedings of the Tenth National Conference on Artificial Intelligence*, pages 223–228. AAAI Press and MIT Press, 1992.
6. S. Lichtenstein and J. R. Newman. Empirical scaling of common verbal phrases associated with numerical probabilities. *Psychon. Sci.*, 9(10), 1967.
7. Eric Neufeld. A probabilistic commonsense reasoner. *International Journal of Intelligent Systems*, 5:565–594, 1990.
8. G. C. Oden. Integration of fuzzy logical information. *Journal of Experimental Psychology: Human Perception and Performance*, 3(4):565–575, 1977.
9. Simon Parsons. Further results in qualitative uncertainty. *International Journal of Uncertainty, Fuzziness and Knowledge-Based Systems*, 3(2):187–210, 1995.
10. George Polya. *Mathemathics and Plausible Reasoning, Vol II: Patterns of Plausible Inference*. Princeton, New Jersey: Princenton University Press, 1954.
11. L. Trave and N. Piera. The orders of magnitude models as qualitative algebras. In *11th IJCAI*, Detroit, 1989.
12. T. S. Wallsten, D. V. Budescu, A. Rapoport, R. Zwick, and B. Forsyth. Measuring the vague meanings of probability terms. Technical Report 173, The L. L. Thurstone Psychometrich Laboratory, Chapel Hill, N.C., 1985.
13. Michael P. Wellman. Fundamental concepts of qualitative networks. *Artificial Intelligence*, 44:257–303, 1990.
14. Alf C. Zimmer. Verbal vs. numerical processing of subjective probabilities. In R. W. Scholz, editor, *Decision Making Under Uncertainty*, pages 159–182. Elsevier Science Publishers B.V. (North-Holland), 1983.
15. Alf C. Zimmer. The estimation of subjective probabilities via categorical judgments of uncertainty. In *Proceedings of the Workshop on Uncertainty and Probability in Artificial Intelligence*, pages 217–224. UCLA, 1985.

Language Support for Temporal Data Mining

Xiaodong Chen [1] and Ilias Petrounias [2]

[1] Department of Computing & Mathematics, Manchester Metropolitan University
John Dalton Building, Manchester M1 5GD, UK
X.Chen@doc.mmu.ac.uk
[2] Department of Computation, UMIST, P.O. Box 88, Manchester M60 1QD, UK
ilias@sna.co.umist.ac.uk

Abstract. Time is an important aspect of all real world phenomena. Any systems, approaches or techniques that are concerned with information need to take into account the temporal aspect of data. Data mining refers to a set of techniques for discovering previously unknown information from existing data in large databases and therefore, the information discovered will be of limited value if its temporal aspects, i.e. validity, periodicity, are not considered. This paper presents a generic definition of temporal patterns and a framework for discovering them. A query language for the mining of such patterns is presented in detail. As an instance of generic patterns, temporal association rules are used as examples of the proposed approach.

1. Introduction

Data mining has been regarded as a field, which potentially offers additional knowledge for a particular application domain. In real world applications, the knowledge that is used in order to aid decision making is always time-varying. Most existing data mining approaches, however, take a static view of an application domain so that the discovered knowledge is considered to be valid indefinitely on the time line. Temporal features of the knowledge are not taken into account in the mining models or processes, despite the fact that the time that something happened is also known and recorded (e.g. the date and time that a point-of-sale transaction took place, or a patient's temperature was taken). If data mining is to be used as a vehicle for better decision making, the existing approaches will in most cases lead into not very significant or interesting results. Consider, for example, a possible association - concerning a supermarket's transactions- between butter and bread (i.e. people who buy butter also buy bread). If someone looks at all the supermarket transactions that are available, let's say for the past ten years, that association might be -with a certain possibility- true. If, however, the highest concentration of people who bought butter and bread can be found up to five years ago, then the discovery of the association is not significant for the present and the future of the supermarket organisation.

Similarly, if someone looks at the rule "over a year 50% of people buy umbrellas" this might be true. However, if the periodic pattern *"during autumn 85% of people buy umbrellas"* is true, then it is certainly more interesting to a company making or selling umbrellas, since it also tells them when and how often the highest concentration of people buying umbrellas can be found. In fact, if one takes into account time components, there is a lot of time-related knowledge which may be discovered from databases in real world applications. For example, in stock market databases, we may find that *"over the last 6 months some stocks rose by 5% when the financial index rose by 10%"*. In retail applications, one may also be interested in a rule which states that *"during the summer customers who buy bread and butter, also buy milk"*, while in the medical domain, it may be discovered that "some patients experience nausea for about an hour followed by headache *after each meal"*. It has been recognised recently ([8], [11]) that such temporal patterns or rules should be investigated and discovered from temporal databases since they can provide accurate information about an evolving business domain, rather than a static one. In this paper, temporal data mining is referred to as a set of techniques for extracting temporal knowledge hiding in temporal databases. The discovered temporal knowledge by temporal data mining can initiate business process change and redevelopment activities in order for an organisation to adopt to changes within its operating area.

The work presented in this paper is focused on the design of a temporal discovery language, which is a part of a framework for temporal data mining [2]. Since the process of knowledge discovery consists of several interactive and iterative stages [4], powerful languages should be used to express different ad hoc data mining tasks [6]. Because SQL has been used almost exclusively as a query language due to the extensive use of relational DBMSs in organisations, it is practically reasonable to develop SQL-like data mining languages ([5], [7]). Following this idea, an SQL-like temporal query and mining language is proposed in the paper, aiming to supply users with the ability to express any temporal data mining problem addressed within the framework. The rest of the paper is organised as follows. As an essential issue within the framework for temporal data mining, temporal mining problems are firstly addressed in section 2, based on the definition of temporal patterns. A temporal query and mining language (TQML) is presented in section 3. Implementation issues are discussed in section 4. Conclusions and future work are presented in section 5.

2. Temporal Data Mining Problems

There are many temporal aspects which can be associated with patterns to depict temporal features of discovered knowledge. The major concerns in this paper are the valid period and the periodicity of patterns. The valid period shows the time interval during which the pattern is valid, while the periodicity conveys when and how often a pattern is repeated. The notion of periodicity [10] is an important temporal feature in the real world. A series of repeated occurrences of a certain type of event at regular intervals is described as a periodic event, which exists in many temporal applications. Both the valid period and the periodicity can be specified by calendar time expressions, which are composed of calendar units in a specific calendar and may represent different time features such as a calendar interval, an arbitrary contiguous time interval, a periodic time, and a limited periodic time. The following is an example of the limited periodic expression:

Weeks·Days(2)·Hours(12:13) starts_from Years(1993)·Months(5)
and finishes_by Years(1996)·Months(8)

In this expression, "Weeks", "Days", "Hours", "Years", and "Months" are calendar units in the Gregorian calendar. "Weeks·Days(2)·Hours(12:13)" is a *periodic expression*, describing *a periodic time* which consists of a series of periodic intervals (lunchtime) on the repeated cycles (week). "starts_from Years(1993) ·Months(5) and Years(1996)·Months(8)" is an *interval expression*, describing a specific contiguous time framework (May 1993 to August 1996). The whole expression represents "the lunch time of every Monday during the period between May 1993 and August 1996".

According to the discrete, linear model of time, an instant can be represented by a chronon, which is a non-decomposable time interval of some fixed, minimal duration, in which an event takes place. Time line is a totally ordered set of chronons and an interval may be represented by a set of contiguous chronons. We use $\Phi(TimeExp)$ to denote the interpretation of a time expression. The interpretation of a periodic expression, $\Phi(PeriodicExp)$, is a set of periodic intervals. The interpretation of an interval expression, $\Phi(IntervalExp)$, is a contiguous time interval. The interpretation, $\Phi(Periodic° IntervalExp)$, of a limited periodic expression, consisting of a periodic expression and a interval expression, is also a set of periodic intervals, such that :

$\Phi(PeriodicExp° IntervalExp) =$

$\{ p \mid \exists \, p' \in \Phi(PeriodicExp), p = p' \cap \Phi(IntervalExp) \text{ and } p \neq \varnothing \}$

Definition 1: A *temporal pattern* is a triplet <*Patt, PeriodicExp, IntervalExp*>, where *Patt* is a general pattern which may be a trend, a classification rule, an association, a causal relationship, etc., *PeriodicExp* is a periodic time expression or a special symbol *p_null* with $\Phi(p\_null)$ being $\{T\}$, and *IntervalExp* is a general interval expression or a special symbol *i_null* with $\Phi(i\_null)$ being T. It expresses that *Patt* holds during each interval in $\Phi(PeriodicExp ° IntervalExp)$. T is the time domain.

For any temporal pattern of the form < Patt, *PeriodicExp, IntervalExp* >, if *PeriodicExp* is *p_null* and *IntervalExp* is not *i_null*, the expression represents a pattern that refers to an absolute time interval $\Phi(IntervalExp)$; if *PeriodicExp* is not *p_null* and *IntervalExp* is *i_null*, it represents a periodic pattern without any time limitation; if neither *PeriodicExp* is *p_null* nor *IntervalExp* is *i_null*, it represents a periodic pattern which is valid during the time interval $\Phi(IntervalExp)$; otherwise, it represents a non-temporal pattern. The following are some examples of temporal patterns that refer to absolute time intervals or periodic times:

- < "(Emp,=),(Rank,<)$\Rightarrow$(Salary,$\leq$)", *p_null*, starts_from Years(1992)·Months(3) and finishes_by Years(1993) ·Months(7) >: describes the fact that during the period between March 1992 and July 1993, if an employee's rank increases then his/her salary does not decrease.

- < "HikingBoots $\Rightarrow$ Outerwear", Years·Months(4:6), starts_from Years(1990) and finishes_by Years(1995)] > : shows that every Spring, between 1990 and 1995, shoppers who buy hiking boots, also want outerwear at the same time;

- <"nausea→headache",Days·Hours(6:8),*i_null*>:indicates that patients with a certain disease feel nausea, followed by headaches from 6 to 8 o'clock every morning.

The above examples express a trend appearing during a specific period, a periodic association happening within a relevant period, and a periodic causal relationship, respectively.

Definition 2: Given a set *D* of time-stamped data over a time domain *T*, we use *D*(p) to denote a subset of *D*, which contains all data with timestamps (whatever they may be: user-defined, valid, decision or transaction time according to the temporal databases literature [10]) belonging to time interval p. We define:

- <*Patt, PeriodicExp, IntervalExp*> holds during interval p, p ∈ Φ(*PeriodicExp ° IntervalExp*), if *Patt* satisfies all relevant thresholds in *D*(p).
- <*Patt, PeriodicExp, IntervalExp*> satisfies all relevant thresholds with respect to the frequency *f* % in the dataset *D* if <*Patt, PeriodicExp, IntervalExp*> holds during no less than *f* % of intervals in Φ(*PeriodicExp ° IntervalExp*).

In the above definition, the relevant thresholds are given in terms of the forms of interested patterns. The notion of frequency is introduced for measuring the proportion of intervals, during which *Patt* satisfies all relevant thresholds, when compared to the intervals in Φ(*PeriodicExp ° IntervalExp*). It is required that the frequency of any discovered temporal pattern < *Patt, PeriodicExp, IntervalExp* > should not be smaller than the user-specified minimum frequency which is a fraction within [0,1]. In case that |Φ(*PeriodicExp ° IntervalExp*)| = 1, Φ(*PeriodicExp ° IntervalExp*) just includes a single interval, so that any non-zero minimum frequency has the same meaning, that is, *Patt* must satisfy all the relevant thresholds during this single interval. Ideally, people might expect that all possibly hidden patterns of a certain type could be discovered without any known temporal features of patterns.

Definition 3 (General Mining Problem): Given a time-stamped dataset *D* over a time domain *T*, the problem of mining temporal patterns is to discover all patterns of the form <*Patt, PeriodicExp,IntervalExp* > in *D* that satisfy all the user-specified thresholds with respect to the user-specified minimum frequency *min_f* %.

From a practical point of view, however, people might ask for something with some known temporal features: the mining of all patterns of a certain type during a specific time interval, the mining of all patterns of a certain type with a specific periodicity or the mining of all patterns of a certain type with a specific periodicity during a specific time interval. Additionally they might also be interested in looking for temporal features of a specific pattern: finding all contiguous time intervals during which a specific pattern holds, finding all periodicities of a specific pattern during a specific time interval or finding all limited periodicities of a specific pattern.

3. Temporal Query and Mining Language (TQML)

To a greater or lesser extent, data mining is application-dependent and user-dependent, and knowledge discovery is the process of interactively and iteratively querying patterns. It is important that KDD systems supply users with flexible and powerful descriptive languages to express data mining tasks. Other languages have been proposed in the literature in order to aid the mining task [5], [7]. The second one of those is only intended to discover association rules, while both of them do not offer any support for discovering temporal patterns and/or features. Here we focus on the requirements for querying a database for the mining of temporal patterns and present TQML which offers the ability -in an SQL-like format- to achieve this task.

The structure of TQML is briefly defined as follows in the BNF grammar:
1) <TQML> ::=
2) Mine <Pattern-Form-Descriptor> (ALL | <specific-pattern>)
3) With Periodicity (ALL | OMISSION | <periodic-expression>)
4) During Interval (ALL | T_DOMAIN | <interval-expression>)
5) [Having Thresholds <threshold-expression-list>]
6) [Shown As <display-form>]
7) In
8) Select <relevant-attribute-list> [, <time-attribute>]
9) From <relation-list>
10) [Where <condition-expression>]
11) [Group By <group-attribute-list> [Having <condition-expression>]]

A mining task in TQML consists of the mining target part (lines 2-6) and the data query part (lines 8-11). In the above definition, <pattern-form-descriptor> points out the form of patterns which users may be interested in and it may be "Trend", "Classification", "Association", "Causality", etc. The option that follows that indicates whether all of the possible patterns should be found or the temporal features of a specific pattern should be extracted. The periodicity of patterns can be expressed by With-Periodicity (option), where "ALL" expresses that all possible periodic patterns or the periodicities of the specific pattern are expected, "OMMISION" shows that the periodicity of patterns is not of interest, and <periodic-expression> gives the periodicity of the expected patterns. The During-Interval(option) can be used for describing the valid period of patterns, where "ALL" expresses that all contiguous time intervals during which patterns (periodic or non-periodic) may exist are expected to be extracted, "T_DOMAIN" makes the assumption that the expected patterns are valid indefinitely, and <interval-expression> indicates the specific time period that users are interested in. Thresholds relevant to different forms of expected patterns can be stated in the Having-Threshold clause and presentation demands can be stated in the Shown-As clause. Note that the granularity of the time interval should be considered as one of criteria if people want to extract the contiguous time intervals during which a specific pattern exists. The data relevant to the data mining task can be stated in the Select-From-Where-Group clause. The Select subclause indicates attributes which are relevant to the mining task. The attribute in <relevant-attribute-list> may be an attribute that exists in the tables appearing in the From clause, an aggregate function (such as Max, Sum, etc.), or a set function which forms an attribute of a nested relation. Each attribute in <relevant-attribute-list> may also be followed by a descriptor, which is relevant to a specific mining model for certain types of patterns that the mining users are interested in. The <time-attribute> indicates the time dimension that users are concerned with in the database, such as transaction-time, valid-time, decision-time or user-defined-time, as defined in the temporal databases literature [9]. The From-Where clause has the same syntax and semantics as SQL92, constituting a basic query to collect the set of relevant data. The Where subclause can also contain time-related conditions. The selected data may also be grouped by <group-attribute-list>, being presented in the form that mining algorithms expect. The Having clause can be used to filter groups which users want to consider.

3.1 An Example: Mining Temporal Association Rules

The problem of finding association rules was introduced in [1]. Given a set of transactions, where each transaction is a set of items, an association rule is an expression of the form $X \Rightarrow Y$, where X and Y are sets of items, and indicates that the presence of X in a transaction will imply the presence of Y in the same transaction. Consider a supermarket database where the set of items purchased by a customer is stored as a transaction. An example of an association rule is: "60% of transactions that contain bread and butter also contain milk; 30% of all transactions contain both of these items." Here, 60% is called the confidence of the rule and 30% the support of the rule. The meaning of this rule is that customers that purchase bread and butter also buy milk. The problem of mining association rules is the attempt to find all association rules satisfying the user-specified minimum support and minimum confidence. This problem has been extended for discovering temporal association rules in [3].

Let $I = \{i_1, i_2, \dots, i_l\}$ be a set of literals which are called items. A set of items $X \subset I$ is called an itemset. Let D be a set of time-stamped transactions. Each time-stamped transaction S is a triplet <tid, itemset, timestamp>, where S.tid is the transaction identifier, S.itemset is a set of items, such that S.itemset $\subseteq I$, and S.timestamp is an instant which the transaction S is stamped with, such that S.timestamp $\in T$. We say a transaction S contains an itemset X if $X \subseteq$ S.itemset.

Definition 4: *A temporal association rule is a triplet <AssoRule, PeriodicExp,IntervalExp>*, where *AssoRule* is an implication of the form $X \Rightarrow Y$ such that $X \subset I$, $Y \subset I$ and $X \cap Y = \emptyset$, *PeriodicExp* is a periodic expression and *IntervalExp* is an interval expression. We define:

1) The rule has confidence $c\%$ during interval p_i, $p_i \in \Phi(PeriodicExp \circ IntervalExp)$, if not less than $c\%$ of transactions in $D(p_i)$ that contain X also contain Y.

2) The rule has support $s\%$ during interval p_i, $p_i \in \Phi(PeriodicExp \circ IntervalExp)$, if no less than $s\%$ of transactions in $D(p_i)$ contain $X \cup Y$.

3) The rule has confidence $c\%$ and support $s\%$ with respect to the frequency $f\%$ in the transaction set D (or saying the database D) if it has confidence $c\%$ and support $s\%$ during not less than $f\%$ of intervals in $\Phi(PeriodicExp \circ IntervalExp)$.

Depending on user's interest, the mining problem may be finding all possible associations with a specific periodicity, or finding all possible periodicities of a specific association. In any case, the potential temporal association, $<X \Rightarrow Y$, *TimeExp>*, must satisfy the user-specified minimum support *min_s %* and confidence *min_c %* with respect to the user-specified minimum frequency *min_f %*.

The discussion about mining algorithms for temporal association rules is beyond the scope of this paper. Here, we only take the problem of mining temporal association rules as an example, in order to demonstrate the use of the temporal discovery language. Consider a Sales database containing two relations Items and Purchase as shown in Figure 1.

Example 1: Find all periodic association rules that convey purchase patterns every summer (assuming that summer starts from the sixth month of each year) between July 1990 and June 1996, with the thresholds of support, confidence and frequency being 0.6, 0.75 and 0.8, respectively. Here, we are only concerned with items whose retail prices are not less than £10 and transactions in which the number of purchased items is greater than 3:

Mine Association_Rules (ALL)
   With Periodicity(Years·Months(6:8))
   During Interval(starts_from Years(1990)·Months(7)
          and finishes_by Years(1996)·Months(6))
   Having Thresholds support = 0.6, confidence = 0.75, frequency = 0.8.
In
   Select *trans-no: TID, Set(item-name): ItemSet, trans-time: TimeStamp*
   From purchase, items
   Where purchase.item-no = items.item-no and items.retail-price ≥ £10
   Group By purchase.trans-no Having Count(*) > 3

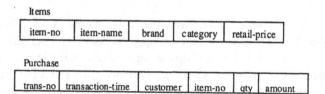

Fig. 1. Relation Schemes in Sales Database

Example 2: Find all periodicities of the association, "H*iking Boots⇒Outerwear*", with the thresholds of support, confidence and frequency being 085, 0.90 and 0.75, respectively:

Mine Association_Rules ("HikingBoots⇒Outerwear")
   With Periodicity(ALL)
   During Interval(T_DOMAIN)
   Having Thresholds support = 0.85, confidence = 0.90, frequency = 0.75.
In
   Select *trans-no: TID, Set(item-name): ItemSet, trans-time: TimeStamp*
   From purchase, items
   Where purchase.item-no = items.item-no
   Group By purchase.trans-no.

In the above examples, the "Select-From-Where-Group" part expresses a basic data query demand. The result of the data query is a nested relation, forming the data set relevant to this mining task. "TID" and ItemSet are descriptors which indicate the "trans-no" and "Set(item-name)" as the "tid" and "itemset", respectively, in the mining model for temporal associations. The "trans-time" in the database is chosen as the time-stamp.

4. Implementation Issues

There are various challenging works involved in the implementation of the temporal query and mining language. As space is limited, only three major issues are discussed below.

Query Generation: The first step in extracting interesting knowledge hidden in databases is querying the data relevant to the potential knowledge. Although the essential data for date mining is specified in the data query part, the mining target should also be considered in order to generate the actual query (expressed in a TSQL2-like intermediate language) for only necessary data. Consider example 1 in section 3, for instance, the temporal aspects in the mining target implicitly show that only those transactions that happened during June to August of every year between July 1990 and June 1996 will make contribution to the mining task.

Time Support: This is a key issue for supporting the processing of temporal aspects in data mining. Time support is required over the entire course of temporal data mining. Time support mechanisms are used to interpret any time aspects in the mining task in TQML while generating relevant temporal query demands and constructing internal representations for temporal mining models, and to evaluate periodicities and interval comparison operations when accessing data and searching for patterns. Currently, some commercial DBMSs provide support for dates and time. However, they usually support conventional calendar units, such as Hours, Days, Weeks, Months and Years, in the Gregorian calendar. A calendar knowledge base is needed for time support mechanisms. The definitions of all relevant calendars are maintained and managed in this knowledge base.

Search Performance: The performance of search algorithms for temporal patterns is another crucial issue in temporal data mining. In many cases, where only specific temporal features are interesting, the search performance is reasonable. However, the performance of search algorithms attempting to identify all possible temporal patterns (especially, periodic patterns) may be worse than the performance of one that does not take into account the time component. Special techniques for different mining problems and models need to be used for improving the search performance.

5. Conclusions and Future Work

With the large amount of temporal knowledge stored in databases and the growth of temporal database research, more and more attention is being paid to temporal data mining due to the value of temporal data. We argue that the temporal aspects of potential patterns hidden in temporal databases are important since they can provide companies or organisations with accurate and evolving information for decision making. Until now little work involves the discovery of temporal patterns with temporal features. This paper presented a temporal discovery language with support for mining temporal patterns. Temporal patterns have been defined in this paper by associating general patterns with temporal features which are represented by calendar time expressions. Two different aspects of temporal features of patterns are identified in this paper: the valid period and periodicity of patterns. The presented mining language is an effective tool for expressing different kinds of temporal data mining tasks addressed within a framework for temporal mining.

Current work is concentrating on the implementation of the temporal discovery language and the extension of calendar support beyond that of the Gregorian calendar. Also work is being carried out in order to enhance the language so that it can be used both as a fully fledged temporal and data mining language. Finally, we are focusing on the effects of changes of business rules on temporal patterns.

References

1. Agrawal, R., Imielinski, T., and Swami, A., 1993, *"Mining Associations between Sets of Items in Massive Databases"*, Proceedings of the ACM SIGMOD International conference on Management of Data, Washington D.C., May 1993.
2. Chen, X. and Petrounias, I., 1998, "An Architecture for Temporal Data Mining", IEE Digest (The IEE Colloquium on Knowledge Discovery and Data Mining), No.98/310, PP.8/1-8/4, London, UK, May 1998.
3. Chen, X., Petrounias, I., and Heathfield, H., 1998, "Discovering Temporal Association Rules in Temporal Databases", in the Proceedings of the International Workshop on Issues and Applications of Database Technology (IADT'98), Berlin, Germany, July 1998.
4. Fayyad, U, Piatetsky-Shapiro, G., Smyth, P., Uthurusamy, R., 1996, *"Advances in Knowledge Discovery and Data Mining"*, The AAAI Press/The MIT Press, 1996.
5. Han, J., Fu, Y., Koperski, K., Wang W., and Zaiane, O., 1996, "DMQL: A Data Mining Query Language for Relational Databases", 1996 SIGMOD Workshop on Research Issues on Data Mining and Knowledge Discovery (DMKD'96), Montreal, Canada, June 1996.
6. Imielinski, T., and Mannila H., 1996, "A Database Perspective on Knowledge Discovery", CACM, Vol.39, No.11, Nov. 1996.
7. Meo, R., Psaile, G., and Ceri, S., 1996, *"A New SQL-like Operator for Mining Association Rules"*, Proceedings of the 22nd International Conference on Very Large Data Bases (VLDB'96), Bombay, India, 1996.
8. Saraee, M., and Theodoulidis, B., 1995, *"Knowledge Discovery in Temporal Databases"*, Proceedings of IEE Colloquium on Knowledge Discovery in Databases, pp. 1-4, 1995.
9. Tansel, A., et al, 1994, *"Temporal Databases: Theory, Design, and Implementation"*, Benjamin/Cummings, Redwood City, CA, 1994.
10. Tuzhilin, A. and Clifford, J., 1995, *"On Periodicity in Temporal Databases"*, Information Systems, Vol.20, No.8, PP.619-639,1995.
11. Weiss, S. and Indurkhya, N., 1998, *"Predictive Data Mining"*, Morgan Kaufmann Publishers, Inc., San Francisco, USA, 1998.

Resampling in an Indefinite Database to Approximate Functional Dependencies

Ethan Collopy and Mark Levene
Email:{ecollopy, mlevene}@cs.ucl.ac.uk

Department of Computer Science
University College London
Gower Street, London WC1E 6BT, U.K.

Abstract. Functional Dependency satisfaction, where the value of one attribute uniquely determines another, may be approximated by Numerical Dependencies (NDs), wherein an attribute set determines at most k attribute sets. Hence, we use NDs to "mine" a relation to see how well a given FD set is approximated. We motivate NDs by examining their use with indefinite information in relations. The family of all possible ND sets which may approximate an FD set forms a complete lattice. Using this, a proximity metric is presented and used to assess the distance of each resulting ND set to a given FD set.

Searching for a definite relation extracted from an indefinite relation which satisfies a given set of FDs, known as the consistency problem, has been shown to be NP-complete. We propose a novel application of the bootstrap, a computer intensive resampling technique, to determine a suitable number of definite relations upon which to apply a heuristic based hill-climbing algorithm which attempts to minimise the distance between the best ND set and the given FD set. The novelty is that we repeatedly apply the bootstrap to an indefinite relation with an increasing sample size until an approximate fixpoint is reached at which point we assume that the sample size is then representative of the indefinite relation. We compare the bootstrap with its predecessor, the jackknife, and conclude that both are applicable with the bootstrap providing additional flexibility. This work highlights the utility of computer intensive resampling within a dependency data mining context.

Key Words - Functional Dependency, Numerical Dependency, Data Mining, Indefinite Relation, Resampling, Bootstrap

1 Introduction

Numerical Dependencies (NDs)[1] are generalisations of Functional Dependencies (FDs) which allow an attribute set to uniquely determine up to k different attribute set values, noting that $k = 1$ in the case of FDs. Indefinite information representation in relations has been shown to be a useful facility for incomplete specifications in design and planning applications [2]. We define *indefinite cells* as cells containing one or more values which represent a set of possibilities denoting the current limit of knowledge in the database. A definite relation extracted from one containing indefinite information is a relation with the same schema and definite cells, which are invariant throughout, but with each indefinite cell, say C, replaced with a definite cell containing one value from C. Associated with an indefinite relation may be a set of integrity constraints. There may be cases, highlighted below, where the traditional FD is too strict and a *weaker* integrity constraint, such as an ND, is required. Table 1 shows how we might want to represent indefinite information in a teaching relation $PLAN$(Lecturer,Course). Irrespective of whatever courses Mark and Robin decide to teach no definite relation extracted from $PLAN$ will satisfy the FD $Lecturer \rightarrow Course$ though all satisfy the ND $Lecturer \rightarrow^2 Course$, representing that a Lecturer can teach up to two courses in a year. For an FD $X \rightarrow Y$, the set of all possible NDs, $X \rightarrow^k Y$, which may approximate this allow k to range from 1 up to the maximum active domain size (ADS) combination in Y. All of these possibilities are shown to form a complete lattice which is then used as the base for a metric on ND sets which we use to gain a value between 0 and 1 for the proximity of a relation to FD set satisfaction.

Table 1. An indefinite relation $PLAN$

Lecturer	Course
Mark	{B11a,C320}
Robin	B11a
{Robin,Mark}	B151

Given a set of FDs F and an indefinite relation r (a relation with one or more indefinite cells) we tackle the problem of attempting to find a definite relation extracted from r which satisfies F. This is widely known as the *consistency problem*, shown to be NP-Complete in general, and of polynomial time complexity in the case where indefinite information is only allowed in attributes which are present in the right hand side of FDs (referred to as a *good* database) or when the FDs have a singleton right hand side and attributes of at most arity two are allowed in the left hand side [2]. Within our algorithm we use the chase process [3], a heuristic designed to modify a database to satisfy constraints, extended in [4] for numerical dependencies and indefinite information, and used in a hill-climbing fashion. Henceforth, we refer to definite relations as *possible worlds*.

We use the bootstrap procedure [5], a computationally intensive statistical resampling procedure that requires no assumptions on the distribution of the possible worlds. We initially take a sample S of n observed possible worlds. Based upon this sample we perform a number of bootstrap replications. Each bootstrap replication, of size n, samples from S with replacement. In this way the bootstrap can be used to provide a guide to the distribution of ND satisfaction in the possible worlds. The key assumption we make in this case is that our sample of observed possible worlds is representative of the indefinite relation. We repeat the bootstrap with an increasing sample size of observed possible worlds. After each bootstrap iteration we calculate the mean and standard error. The number of observed possible worlds (sample size) is increased until the bootstrap procedure converges to an approximate fixpoint, defined as the state where the change in variance is sufficiently small. In this sense the convergence of the bootstrap mean value tells us, with a high probability, that increasing the sample size further will not provide us with any additional information concerning the distribution of data within the indefinite relation. Our results have shown this convergence always occurs at a sample size that is an upper bound on the number actually used by the chase hill-climbing procedure. This is a novel application of sampling within databases, not previously used within the limits of our experience.

We also experimented with the jackknife resampling technique for comparison purposes. The jackknife creates n resamples from an original sample of size n where each resample is of size $n - 1$ with a single possible world left out of each resample. Given the restricted choice of points within the jackknife resamples the returned variance is smaller, on average, than that obtained from the bootstrap and it reaches a fixpoint with a fewer number of worlds. As anticipated, the difference between the bootstrap and the jackknife is minimal. The jackknife was shown to approximate the bootstrap in [5] though we conclude that the bootstrap is generally superior in its role of parameter estimation, providing a better but not excessive parameter for a suitable sampling size as well as being more flexible. We conducted simulations to test the viability of our approach. These are described extensively in [4] and indicate that our use of the bootstrap for parameter setting is a useful tool.

The rest of the paper is organised as follows. In Section 2 we introduce the concepts of indefinite information and numerical dependency, which is central to the process of approximating the distance to FD sets, as well as the background on the lattice of NDs and the proximity metric. Section 3 introduces the framework for the bootstrap and in Section 4 we describe and analyse the bootstrap and jackknife algorithms. Finally, in Section 5 we give our concluding remarks.

2 Relational Database Background

Definition 1 (Relation schema and indefinite relations). Let $\mathcal{U}$ be a countable set of attributes and $\mathcal{D}$ be a countable set of domain values. A *relation schema* R is a finite set of attributes in $\mathcal{U}$. An *(indefinite) tuple* t over R is a total mapping from R into $\mathcal{P}(\mathcal{D})$ such that $\forall A \in R$, $t(A) \in \mathcal{P}(\mathcal{D})$. A tuple t over R is *definite* if $\forall A \in R$, $\mid t(A) \mid = 1$, i.e. $t(A)$ is a singleton, where $\mid t(A) \mid$ denotes the cardinality of $t(A)$.

A *indefinite relation* r over R is a finite (possibly empty) set of indefinite tuples over R. A relation over R is *definite* if all of its tuples are definite. The set of all possible worlds which may be formed from r is precisely the set of all combinations of replacing each indefinite cell with one of its values. From now on we let R *be a relation schema,* r *be a relation over* R *and* $t \in r$ *be an indefinite tuple.* Letters from the beginning of the alphabet such as A, B denote singleton attribute sets {A},{B} in R. We generalise the concept of an FD by a *numerical dependency*.

Definition 2 (Numerical dependency). A *numerical dependency* over R (or simply an ND) is a statement of the form X $\to^k$ Y, where X, Y $\subseteq$ R and $k \geq 1$. X $\to^k$ Y is satisfied when for each unique attribute set value in X there are at most k different attribute set values in Y. A set of NDs N is *satisfied* in s, denoted by $s \models N$, whenever $\forall$ X $\to^k$ Y $\in$ N, $s \models$ X $\to^k$ Y.

From now on we let N *be a set of NDs over* R, F *a set of FDs over* R, and X $\to^k$ Y *be a single ND over* R, with $k \geq 1$. When $k = 1$, X $\to^1$ Y is an FD, written as X $\to$ Y. A set of FDs F is *weakly* satisfied (or simply satisfied whenever no ambiguity arises) in a relation r, denoted by $r \approx$ F, whenever r has a possible world s such that $s \models$ F. If $r \approx$ F we say that r is *consistent* with respect to F; otherwise if $r \not\approx$ F then we say that r is *inconsistent* with respect to F (or simply r is inconsistent). We define a set of NDs N to be weakly satisfied in a relation r in the same way as for FDs; similarly we define a relation r to be consistent with respect to a set of NDs if $r \approx$ N and otherwise to be inconsistent. We note that if $r \approx$ X $\to^k$ Y then it is also the case that $r \approx$ X $\to^{k+1}$ Y, i.e. the smaller k the *more functional* the ND. We consider, without loss of generality, only FDs and NDs with singleton right hand sides.

Definition 3 (The consistency problem). Given a set of FDs F and a relation r, possibly containing indefinite cells, the *consistency problem* is the problem of deciding whether $r \approx$ F.

Definition 4 (More functional set of NDs). A set of NDs N_1 over R is *more functional* than a set of NDs N_2 over R, denoted by $N_2 \sqsubseteq N_1$, whenever X $\to^{k_2}$ A $\in N_2$ if and only if X $\to^{k_1}$ A $\in N_1$ and $k_1 \leq k_2$.

The set-theoretic relation, more functional than, is a partial order in the sets of NDs. Assume that we are considering only sets of NDs which are more functional than a given set of NDs, N over R, each of the form X $\to^k$ Y, for some $k \geq 1$. Then the family of sets of NDs that are more functional than N form a lattice whose bottom element is N and whose top element is the set of FDs induced by N, i.e. $\{X \to Y \mid X \to^k Y \in N\}$. The *least upper bound*, *lub*, of N_1 and N_2 is the set of NDs $\{X \to^{min(k_1,k_2)} Y \mid X \to^{k_1} Y \in N_1$ and X $\to^{k_2} Y \in N_2\}$, where $min(k_1, k_2)$ is the minimum of k_1 and k_2, and the *greatest lower bound*, *glb*, is defined similarly using maximum. We call the lattice, whose top element is the set of FDs F over R and whose bottom element is the set of NDs $\{X \to^m Y \mid X \to Y \in F\}$, $\mathcal{L}_m(F)$ (or simply $\mathcal{L}_m$ if F is understood from context), with $m \geq 1$. Therefore, we can *approximate* a set of FDs F by a set of NDs N such that $N \sqsubseteq$ F. The *closer* N is to F in $\mathcal{L}_m$ the better the approximation is. From now on we let $\mathcal{L}_m$ *be the lattice of NDs whose top element is* F and assume that $\mid r \mid = m + 1$, with $m \geq 1$. A set of NDs N over R is the *best approximation* of a set of FDs F over R with respect to a relation r over R, with $\mid r \mid = m + 1$ (or simply the best approximation of F if r is understood from context), if $r \approx$ N and there does not exist a set of NDs, $N' \in \mathcal{L}_m$ such that $N \prec N'$ and $r \approx N'$.

We introduce a measure for calculating the proximity of two ND sets using their position within the lattice. We show in [4] that this measure is a metric. We define the *size* of a set of NDs N to be the number of attributes appearing in N including repetitions and define a *step*, either up or down, to be exactly minus or plus one, respectively, to a single branch of one ND within an ND set. Furthermore, we say that N_2 is *covered by* N_1, denoted by $N_2 \prec N_1$, where $N_1, N_2 \in \mathcal{L}_m$, if $N_1 \neq N_2$, $N_2 \sqsubseteq N_1$ and $\forall N' \in \mathcal{L}_m$ such that $N_2 \sqsubseteq N' \sqsubseteq N_1$ we have $N' = N_2$. In our simulations one of the ND sets is always the given FD set F in which case the metric tells us the proximity between the ND set and F. We define *distance* to be the sum of *steps* taken in the lattice. We define the bottom of the lattice to be the set of NDs with each branching factor equivalent to the domain size of the attribute on the right hand side of each ND.

Proposition 5. The maximum distance between any two points in the lattice to their *lub* is always equivalent to the distance from the bottom to the top of the lattice.

Proof. By induction, presented in [4]. □

Definition 6 (Proximity of two ND sets). Given two sets of NDs N_1 and N_2 we define the metric as follows:

$$p(N_1, N_2) = \frac{\Sigma_{i=1,2} \text{ Distance from } N_i \text{ to } lub\{N_1, N_2\}}{\text{Max distance between any two ND sets to their } lub \text{ in the lattice}}$$

Fig. 1. Average Number of Worlds given as upper bounds by the Bootstrap and Jackknife techniques

Fig. 2. Lattice of NDs for a relation of 2 FDs (not specified) and an ADS of 4 for each dependency

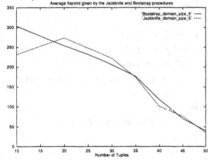

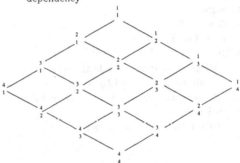

3   Incorporating the Bootstrap and the Jackknife

The bootstrap [5] is a data driven simulation method for non-parametric statistical inference. Given that the number of possible worlds of an indefinite relation increases exponentially in the size of the relation it is impossible to examine all possible worlds for the best solution. The complete population distribution is unknown; otherwise we would know exactly how many definite relations to generate to have a specific probability of finding the closest ND set to the given FD set. This suggests applying a bootstrap procedure to a sample of definite instances to approximate the population distribution based on the sample distribution [5]. We use the bootstrap procedure to tell us how many worlds we need to consider so that we have a high confidence that generating additional worlds will not improve our solution. Algorithm 1 presents this procedure and Algorithm 2 presents a corresponding procedure using the jackknife.

Definition 7 (The Bootstrap Sample). Given an indefinite relation r over schema R we uniformly randomly extract n possible worlds. Each of these worlds will satisfy a set of NDs (which may contain FDs). These n possible worlds are referred to as the original sample or *observed possible worlds* and are written as $\tilde{p} = (r_1, r_2, \ldots, r_n)$. A bootstrap sample is $\tilde{p}^\star = (r_1^\star, r_2^\star, \ldots, r_n^\star)$ where for all $i = 1, 2 \ldots, n$ each $r_i^\star$ is randomly selected with replacement from the n observed possible worlds in $\tilde{p}$.

We denote the q NDs which may hold in r by $X_i \to^{k_i} Y_i$ where $1 \le i \le q$ and refer to the branching factor k which holds for ND $X_i \to^k Y_i$ in r as $br_{X_i Y_i}(r)$. When we refer to the sample mean of a set of possible worlds we are implying the sample mean of the sets of NDs of the possible worlds.

Definition 8 (The Bootstrap Sample Mean). Given a bootstrap sample $\tilde{p}^\star = (r_1^\star, r_2^\star, \ldots, r_n^\star)$, we calculate the mean $\bar{s}(\cdot)$, or any other statistic of interest, in exactly the same way as we would have for the original sample of ND sets, each containing m NDs, $\bar{s}(\tilde{p}^\star) = \{K_j \mid 1 \le j \le m\}$ where $K_j = \sum_{i=1}^{n} \frac{br_{X_j Y_j}(r_i^\star)}{n}$

Definition 9 (The Bootstrap Mean of all Values). Given a set of B bootstrap samples $\tilde{p}_b^\star$, we calculate the mean $\bar{s}(\cdot)$, or any other statistic of interest, in exactly the same way as we would have for the original sample, $\bar{s}(\tilde{p}_b^\star) = \Sigma_{i=1}^{B} \bar{s}(\tilde{p}_i^\star)/B$.

Algorithm 1 (BOOTSTRAP(nd_bg, B)).
```
1.begin
2.ND_m := ∅ ;
3.n := | nd_bg |;
4.for  1 to B do
5.   ND_s := Uniform Randomly select n
          ND sets from nd_bg with replacement;
6.   Insert the mean of ND_s into ND_m;
7.end for
8.return the mean of ND_m;
9.end.
```

Algorithm 2 (JACKKNIFE(nd_bg)).
```
1.begin
2.ND_m := ∅;
3.n := | nd_bg |;
4.for  j := 1 to n do
5.   ND_s := nd_bg - nd_j;
6.   Insert the mean of ND_s into
        ND_m;
7.end for
8.return the mean of ND_m;
9.end.
```

The Bootstrap Replication Size (BRS), B in Algorithm 1, is the number of times a bootstrap sample of size n is created from the observed possible worlds and evaluated on a parameter of interest. We denote the B bootstrap samples by $\tilde{p}_b^\star = (\tilde{p}_1^\star, \tilde{p}_2^\star, \ldots, \tilde{p}_B^\star)$. [5] tackles how large the BRS should be. Given a BRS B, [5] refers to the *ideal bootstrap estimate* which takes B equal to infinity. This is not true for indefinite relations where the ideal limit is the number of possible worlds in the relation. [5] show the amount of computation time it takes for increased BRS sizes increases linearly. We show that this is also the case for increasing the BRS for indefinite relations, exemplified in [4].

Definition 10 (The Bootstrap Standard Error for Indefinite Relations). The sample standard error in the values for B bootstrapped values is:

$$\hat{se}_B = \{\frac{1}{B}\Sigma_{i=1}^{B}(\bar{s}(\tilde{p}^\star) - \bar{s}(\tilde{p}_b^\star))\}^{1/2}$$

We now describe the methods of our Bootstrap application, detailed in Algorithm 3. We start with a small initial sample size and a Bootstrap Replication Size B. Having created B bootstrap samples we will have a bootstrap mean of all values in the form of an ND set. From this value we can use the bootstrap to calculate its standard deviation. From this we can empirically infer the width of the interval in which a certain percentage of the relations occur, either using standard confidence intervals or by creating the confidence intervals empirically using an ordering of the bootstrap resamples. We increase the sample size on each iteration by a fixed amount, δ, until we reach a point where the mean value of the NDs in the ND set stabilises. The convergence to stability is controlled by the accuracy to t significant digits, with $t = 3$ providing a sufficient accuracy in our simulations. This convergence provides a parameter whereupon anything higher is unlikely to have much additional change in variance and this is also verified by the convergence of the empirical confidence intervals. It is unlikely, even for an ND set with just one dependency, for the fixpoint to be reached randomly, and running our simulations in batches of 500 implied that any outlying fixpoint values would have a negligible impact on the final results obtained.

Algorithm 3 (WORLD_LIMIT (r, F, B)).

```
1.  begin
2.    n := initial(r); % sample size
3.    N̂₀ := Highest ND set satisfiable in r using chase ;
4.    N̂₁ := ∅; j := 1;
5.    while N̂ⱼ, N̂ⱼ₋₁ are not approximate fixpoint do
6.      ND_bag := n ND sets from n possible worlds;
7.      N̂ⱼ := BOOTSTRAP(ND_bag, n, B);
8.      n := n + δ; j := j + 1; % Increase the sample size by δ
9.    end while
10.   return n;
11. end.
```

We also examined the variance of the observed possible worlds, for a range of original sample sizes, as the bootstrap replication size was scaled from 20 up to 50,000 to decide on a suitable BRS. As this was increased we noted that above 1000 there was negligible change in the variance. For the purposes of our experiment setting B at 100 gave suitable results above which there was negligible change.

4 Applying Resampling to the Consistency Problem

Algorithm 3, WORLD_LIMIT(r,F,B), describes our novel use of the bootstrap procedure. Details of the simulations we conducted for different FD sets and indefinite relations are discussed in [4]. Our procedure relies on the assumption that different sample sizes are required proportional to the variance within an indefinite relation in the different ND sets which may be satisfied in possible worlds. The number of dependencies in the given FD set also influences the results obtained from our use of the bootstrap. We use the BOOTSTRAP algorithm in exactly the same manner as a standard bootstrap procedure despite that we potentially have all possible worlds within the indefinite relation. Based on this we conducted experiments whereby the bootstrap resamples were obtained not from the original sample but from the indefinite relation. The variance of resampling from the relation was much higher than resampling from the sample and in such cases the upper bound was much higher. Therefore, based on our results, we conjecture that it is suitable to use just one original sample from the indefinite relation within each iteration of WORLD_LIMIT.

In Figure 4 we see that, for both FD set $F_1 = \{A \rightarrow B, A \rightarrow C, A \rightarrow D\}$ and $F_2 = \{A \rightarrow B, B \rightarrow C, C \rightarrow D\}$, as the number of tuples increases there is a

Fig. 3. Efron's empirical percentile confidence limits shown to converge for the distance measure of ND sets

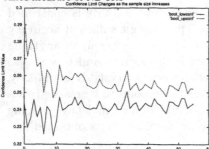

Fig. 4. Average Number of Worlds required by the chase and hill-climbing approach

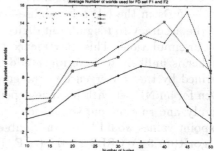

slight peak, after which further increases in the number of tuples results in a fall in the average number of worlds required. This is due to every relation within a batch having a fixed domain size d and a maximum indefinite cell arity, reaching a point where it is likely that any further increases in the tuple size will lead to the satisfaction of the numerical dependency set with each branch determining up to d branches and so fewer worlds are required before any attempts to apply the chase returns an undefined relation implying that nothing better can be found. The peaks in Figure 4 were reflected in the values of α returned by our bootstrap technique. In our application of the bootstrap, as the relation size of a random relation is increased and the domain size is held constant, the sampling will also reach a point where the variance in the samples amongst the randomly generated possible worlds is reduced due to most possible worlds satisfying the NDs each with a branching factor close to their domain size.

The question of why the bootstrap provides an upper bound remains. The chase and hill-climbing algorithm exits if the chase heuristic returns an undefined relation for the current highest found ND set N_T in the lattice. This implies that the indefinite relation is unable to satisfy any ND sets above N_T. Given that this generally occurs before reaching the limit α (provided by the bootstrap) it seems reasonable to propose that the variance across the possible worlds of an indefinite relation, in terms of ND set satisfaction, is a naive statistic and our hill-climbing and chase heuristic method is sufficient to reach a *good* approximation before examing α initial points. The correspondence between the heuristic and the changing upper limit, due to changing variance of ND set satisfaction in indefinite relations, is to be expected and its usefulness is highlighted in this work.

4.1 Differences between resampling methods

The strategy of the jackknife is to remove a single data point from each resample. This allows the creation of n jackknife resamples from an original sample of size n. The bootstrap provides additional flexibility in that the sample is made up of any values uniformly and randomly selected with replacement from the original and, additionally, is not limited to n resamples. In our process the number of worlds required is increased until a fixpoint is reached. Using the jackknife as the worlds reach a large number q we are constrained to q resamples, each of size $q - 1$. Under the bootstrap application we have a fixed number of resamples which, in the majority of cases, will increase to a sample size that is smaller than the q required by the jackknife. We found that the results were very similar for both the bootstrap and jackknife, highlighted in Figure 1, despite our use of the bootstrap conducting fewer replications than the jackknife at large sample sizes. Figure 1 also presents the falling limit of the fixpoint as the domain size is held constant but the tuple size increases, due to a reduction in variance within possible worlds as the relation size grows, highlighted in Figure 3 where the empirical confidence limits for the bootstrap process are shown to converge for the distance measure of an ND set.

5 Conclusion

We have described how the representation of indefinite information lends itself to utilising ND sets. In addition to this we note that NDs suitably approximate FDs in a data mining context. In many dependency data mining applications, which range from data summarisation to learning within decision trees [6], we may wish to obtain a numerical value, between 0 and 1, denoting how close a set of FDs are to being satisfied; the metric presented in this paper achieves this. In [2] we are shown how indefinite information may be used to represent a possible schedule. Our approach allows us to discover an approximation to an *ideal* relation, that which satisfies a set of FDs. NDs are a useful tool in this context and schedule representation within relational databases is enhanced with their use. The consistency problem for relations with indefinite information is widely known to be *NP-complete*. Therefore we cannot expect to develop a polynomial time based solution unless $P = NP$ or the database is restricted as in [2]. Our approach does however introduce an interesting new technique based on sampling, incorporating the bootstrap to provide useful approximations for problems such as the consistency problem. Simulations imply that the bootstrap provides a suitable upper bound. We are also planning to explore resampling within the temporal database domain, another area where there is a combinatorial explosion of data points.

References

1. J. Grant and J. Minker. Inferences for numerical dependencies. *Theoretical Computer Science*, 41:271–287, 1985.
2. K. Vadaparty and S. Naqvi. Using constraints for efficient query processing in nondeterministic databases. *IEEE Transactions on Knowledge and Data Engineering*, 7(6):850 – 864, 1995.
3. H. Mannila and K-J. Räihä. *The Design of Relational Databases*. Addison–Wesley, 1992.
4. E. Collopy and M. Levene. Using numerical dependencies and the bootstrap for the consistency problem. Technical Report RN/98/2, University College London, U.K., 1998.
5. B. Efron and R. Tibshirani. Bootstrap methods for standerd errors, confidence intervals, and other measures of statistical accuracy. *Statistical Science*, 1(1):54 – 77, 1986.
6. G. Piatetsky-Shapiro and C. J. Matheus. Measuring data dependencies in large databases. In *Proceedings of the Workshop on Knowledge Discovery in Databases*, pages 162–173, Washington DC, 1993.

Knowledge Discovery from Client-Server Databases

Neil Dewhurst and Simon Lavington

Department of Computer Science, University of Essex, Wivenhoe Park, Colchester
CO4 4SQ, UK
neil@essex.ac.uk, lavington@essex.ac.uk
WWW home page:
http://cswww.essex.ac.uk/Research/SystemsArchitecture/DataMining/Welcome.html

Abstract. The subject of this paper is the *implementation* of knowledge discovery in databases. Specifically, we assess the requirements for interfacing tools to client-server database systems in view of the architecture of those systems and of "knowledge discovery processes". We introduce the concept of a *query frontier* of an *exploratory process*, and propose a strategy based on optimizing the current query frontier rather than individual knowledge discovery algorithms. This approach has the advantage of enhanced genericity and interoperability. We demonstrate a small set of query primitives, and show how one example tool, the well-known decision tree induction algorithm C4.5, can be rewritten to function in this environment.

1 Introduction

Relational databases are the current dominant database technology in industry, and many organizations have collected large amounts of data in so-called *data warehouses* expressly for the purpose of decision support and data mining. In general the data must be queried in place: the question then arises of how knowledge discovery algorithms can be integrated with relational databases.

We will describe the architecture of a system being implemented at Essex University to address this problem. Essentially our proposal is that the client software should be in two halves, a "bottom half" which optimizes query transmission to the server, and a knowledge discovery algorithm which is implemented so as to give maximum scope for optimization. We believe it is possible to provide these services in a way which is to some extent *generic*, in the sense that it is independent of exactly which algorithm or tool is being implemented.

Most of the existing literature, including much of the work on scalable knowledge discovery algorithms [6], assumes that the database to be explored is stored in local main memory. But it is quite common to find a client accessing a server-resident database over a network, and the efficiency of algorithms as reported in published papers often depends on programming techniques that cannot be ported to this environment.

This is true, to take a particular example, of the well-known decision tree algorithm C4.5 [7], whose run-time efficiency is achieved by manipulating manipulating pointers into arrays of records. This technique cannot be applied to data stored in a relational database.

Moreover, knowledge discovery as it is practised in the real world is an iterative, multi-strategy process [1], and individually-optimized algorithms inevitably have limited interoperability. There is therefore a case for investigating methods of data access optimization whose benefits can be shared between multiple algorithms.

1.1 Framework: the concept of an "exploratory process"

We will abstract away from the details of the particular model or visualization tools being used, and assume only that there exists some *exploratory process* which acts as a source of queries and a consumer of result sets. The process has this general form: some set of initial queries is scheduled, after which the following two steps are repeated an unpredictable number of times:

- request a result set, optionally specifying that it should be one of a given subset of the outstanding queries
- schedule zero or more new queries

The intuition here is that the client can only examine one query result at a time, but can produce multiple queries simultaneously when an advance in the exploratory process opens up several new avenues at once. (Consider branching in a decision tree, or the task of filling in the probabilities in a Bayesian network.)

The result is that at any one time there is a set of outstanding queries, which we call the *query frontier*. Our approach to optimizing knowledge discovery is essentially to optimize the query frontier by combining individual queries into larger queries, a simple kind of multiple query optimization.

To exploit this kind of query optimization fully, knowledge discovery tools must be implemented so that queries are scheduled as soon as they become known. Later in this paper we describe our implementation of C4.5 as an example.

1.2 Client-server requirements

We assume that our principal aim is to minimise running times (as distinct from, for example, minimising network traffic). With that in mind, these are the requirements our system needs to satisfy.

Firstly, we need to ensure that work is divided between the server and client roughly according to their capacities, and that they are working simultaneously as much as possible. If either of these is not the case, there is an obvious waste of resources.

Secondly, since the server and network are both *shared* resources, they are subject to variable loading. Our query optimization should adjust dynamically to increased load on the server by transferring more processing to the client, and to a busy network by fetching less data from the server (which probably implies doing more processing on the server).

2 Related work

The idea exploited in this paper, of optimizing database access by answering queries from the results of larger superqueries, is related to the materialization of selected views as described in [4]. For the view materialization problem, the set of queries to be optimized is known in advance, and the problem is to select among them: for knowledge discovery, the set of queries generally only emerges at runtime, so the superqueries must be generated dynamically.

The use of client-side caching to speed up processing for general database queries has a long history [8], [5]. Generally the idea is to cache query result sets on the client, indexed by some structure that supports *query matching* so it can be quickly determined whether a new query can be answered from the cache. The key concept is query *inclusion* - query q_1 includes query q_2 if q_2 can be answered by applying some further unspecified operation to q_1's result set.

A similar approach was used by [10] to implement a knowledge-base management system on top of an object-oriented database. They also address, as we do, the problem of balancing the work done by the server and client.

The BrAID system [9], which interfaces a logic-based AI system to a database, includes a subsystem that caches result sets and can reason with them.

3 Implementation of database queries

We summarize here some relevant background. A relational database query is expressed in SQL. Typically there is no client-side caching, so once the query has been parsed, it is processed entirely on the server. The philosophy is that there should be a simple division of labour between server and client: the server implements database operations, and the client implements a user interface. As [5] point out, this means that if the client is a reasonably powerful modern workstation, it tends to be under-utilised.

The parsed form of the SQL query is a tree of objects corresponding to physical database operations, called *iterators* [3]. An individual iterator might for example implement a table scan, a hash join, or a sort with consolidation. Each iterator is an object in the OOP sense of the word, implementing the same three methods: open(), fetch(), and close(). open() initialises the operation (this includes, but is not limited to, calling open on the iterator's children); fetch() retrieves the next row of the operation's result set; close() terminates the operation.

The time taken to perform a query may therefore be split into two phases, an *open phase* during which the client is idle, and a *fetch phase* during which rows are transferred from server to client, and both machines are working.

4 Primitive queries

Our technique for query optimization assumes that the queries emitted by the exploratory process are restricted in form. Specifically, we assume that the set of possible queries can be embedded in a larger set of queries which is a *semilattice* under the operation of query inclusion. Informally, this means that for any pair of queries q_1 and q_2, there is a unique "simplest" query Q which includes both q_1 and q_2. We denote Q by $SUP(q_1, q_2)$. This property extends to any finite set of queries.

The larger set of queries, that is a semilattice, we refer to as the set of *primitives* of the exploratory process.

Our current implementation limits the primitives to one of three forms: the *select* primitive, the *count by group* primitive and the *ordered count by group* primitive. See Figure 1. (The select primitive, not shown, is a version of the count-by-group query without the GROUP BY clause.) These queries can be used as the basis for a wide range of knowledge discovery tasks [2]. They also provide good opportunities for splitting processing between client and server, because the count by group and ordered count by group primitives require either sorting or hashing large datasets using disks for temporary storage: both are expensive operations.

The ordered count-by-group primitive is used with databases that contain continuous (floating-point) data. Knowledge discovery tools typically handle continuous data by *discretizing* it, and the first step of a discretization algorithm is usually to sort the data. Our strategy is therefore to use the server to filter and sort the data, then use a client-side operator to calculate the discretized intervals as the sorted data streams off the network.

We will assume for the rest of this paper that the database contains only discrete values - in this case only the select and count-by-group primitives will be used.

From Figure 1 we can see that a count by group query has three parameters: a list of column names **a**, another list of (different) column names **b**, and a list of data values **v**. A typical query can therefore be denoted by CBG(**a,b,v**).

Definition 1. *The SUP of two count-by-group queries CBG(**a,b,v**) and CBG(**a′,b′,v′**) is CBG(**a⋆,b⋆,v⋆**) where*
$$\mathbf{b}^\star = [b_i : b_i = b'_i \wedge v_i = v'_i]$$
$$\mathbf{v}^\star = [v_i : b_i \in \mathbf{b}^\star]$$
$$\mathbf{a}^\star = \mathbf{a} \cup \mathbf{a}' \cup (\mathbf{b} - \mathbf{b}') \cup (\mathbf{b}' - \mathbf{b})$$
The extension to select queries is straightforward. The SUP of two select queries is another select: the SUP of a select and a count-by-group is a count-by-group.

Example 1. Let A1, A2, A3 be attribute names.
The SUP of CBG([A1], [A2,A3], [2,3]) with CBG([A6], [A2,A3], [2,5])
is CBG([A1,A3,A6], [A2], [2]).

If q_1 and q_2 are count-by-group primitives and q_1 includes q_2, then q_2's result can be derived from q_1 by applying a combined projection, selection and aggregation operator, usually called *consolidation* in the OLAP literature.

```
SELECT a1, a2 .., am, COUNT(*)        SELECT a*, a1, a2, .., am, COUNT(*)
FROM table                           FROM table
WHERE b1=v1 AND b2=v2 ...            WHERE b1=v1 AND b2=v2 ...
GROUP BY a1, a2, .., am              GROUP BY a*, a1, a2, .., am
COUNT BY GROUP                       ORDER BY a*
                                     ORDERED COUNT BY GROUP
```

Fig. 1. primitives for knowledge discovery

4.1 Optimization of the query frontier

The optimization of the query frontier is based on the following idea. Given two queries q_1 and q_2, let Q be SUP(q_1, q_2). We consider two possible joint query plans for this pair of queries: either we can execute both queries on the server, or we can execute Q=SUP(q_1, q_2) on the server and derive q_1 and q_2 from Q by consolidation on the client. We thus have a pair of competing *physical query plans*. It is easy to generalize this to the case where there is a set of n queries, $q_1 \cdot\cdot q_n$.

We consider two possible plans: to execute all the queries individually, or to derive each of the q_i from their SUP. The first plan has two open phases and (in general) a shorter fetch phase, compared to a single open phase plus a longer fetch. It is not obvious which of the plans will execute more quickly. We use a cost model, specific to a given client and server, to estimate for a given set of queries which of the two possible plans is the best.

4.2 Dynamic cost estimation

For cost estimation we use a pair of cost functions, denoted c_o and c_f, which estimate respectively the cost of the open phase and the fetch phase of the server query. We use two functions so the system can react flexibly to variable loading on the server, and varying network bandwidth. The estimated costs for a query plan are multiplied by a pair of factors reflecting the discrepancy between predicted and actual performance of previously executed query plans. At the start of a session both factors are set to one.

4.3 Implementation of the query frontier

The query frontier is optimized by partitioning it greedily and dynamically into disjoint subsets. At each turn one partition is selected, and its SUP is scheduled. Each subset of the frontier has a number associated with it, its *benefit*, which is an estimate of the advantage of scheduling that SUP query over scheduling its subqueries individually. (The benefit is calculated using the cost functions c_o and c_f.)

When the exploratory process schedules a new query q, the process is as follows. The query manager considers inserting q into each subset of the frontier, and calculates the effect on that frontier's benefit: q is then inserted into the subset whose benefit it most improves. If it does not improve any of the subsets, it is inserted into a new subset on its own, with benefit zero.

4.4 Scheduling server queries

Each successive query's open phase is scheduled at the start of the preceding query's fetch phase, the aim being to ensure that both client and server are working continuously. See Figure 2 for an illustration.

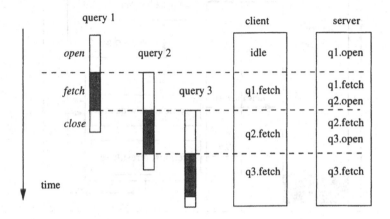

Fig. 2. query scheduling strategy

4.5 Client-side memory management

Client-side memory management is the responsibility of a separate software module, which manages both the main memory (where result sets are stored while they are created) and a persistent result-set cache on disk. When a dataset is cached, a new partition in the query frontier is created with a fixed root to represent it. The idea is that new queries from the exploratory process can be answered either by querying the server, or from cache if the data is available there. Client-only queries against the cache are implemented similarly to server queries, the difference being that rows are streamed off the disk rather than from the server.

5 Software architecture

The design of the query optimizer has some implications for the structure of the knowledge discovery tools that interface to it. Specifically, tools must be implemented using *callbacks*. The idea is that each query sent to the optimizer has an ID attached to it, a number which uniquely identifies it to the application. When the result set is ready, it is passed to a result-set handler function, together with that ID. The initialization function initializes the model and schedules one

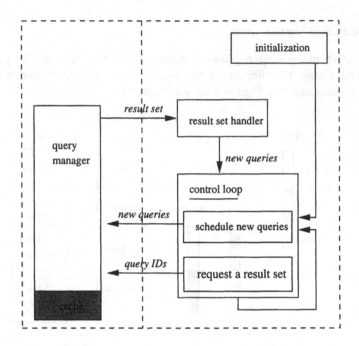

Fig. 3. skeleton "top half" architecture

or more initial queries. Control is then transferred to the control loop, which repeatedly requests a result set from the query manager, which replies to the result set handler. The result-set handler may pass one or more new queries to the control loop for scheduling.

The control loop should if possible avoid requesting a *specific* result set, to give the query manager maximum latitude for optimization. (Refer to the discussion of the query frontier in Section 1.1.) We will illustrate how this is done using the decision tree induction algorithm C4.5 [7].

5.1   Implementation example: C4.5

C4.5 as originally implemented builds the decision tree in strict depth-first order, and completes the tree before postpruning it. Our implementation removes both these constraints. The order in which the nodes are expanded depends on the order in which result sets are returned, which is left entirely to the query manager. Pruning of a node begins as soon as the whole subtree below the node has been finalized, and while other parts of the tree are still being built.

If (as we have assumed) the database contains only discrete data, C4.5 requires database access for three purposes:

- to calculate the "purity" of a node, in order to evaluate the stopping criterion (prepruning)
- to calculate the information gain for each candidate attribute at a given node (splitting)
- to calculate the revised error rate during postpruning (postpruning).

Each of these actions requires one or more count-by-group queries. Details of the calculations performed can be found in the Quinlan book [7]. We will use the following notation: PREPRUNE(N) denotes the query required for prepruning at node N; SPLIT(N,A) denotes the query needed to calculate the information gain of attribute A at node N; and POSTPRUNE(L) denotes the query needed at leaf node L during postpruning. The query ID that identifies a query encodes its type, a node number, and an optional attribute number.

In addition to these, we make use of a pseudoquery NOTIFY to allow a child node to "signal" its parent. This is implemented by calling the result-set handler recursively.

Each node of the decision tree is assigned a *state*. The node begins in state CALC-STOP, and proceeds through states CALC-SPLIT, WAIT, PRUNE-WAIT and several iterations of CALC-BRANCH, until it ends in state FINAL. The process terminates when the root node is in state FINAL.

The initialization step creates a single node (the root node, N_0) in state CALC-PRUNE, and schedules an initial query STOP(N_0). The action taken by the result-set handler when a result set is received for node N is then dependent on the state of N.

- **CALC-STOP**: The purity of the node is calculated, and the stopping criterion evaluated. If the criterion is satisfied, the node state is set to FINAL, and its parent node is notified.
- **CALC-SPLIT**: The incoming result set is for query SPLIT(N, A): the information gain for attribute A is calculated and stored. If all the attriibutes have been evaluated, the best split is chosen, a set of child nodes in state CALC-STOP is created, and STOP(N_i) is scheduled for each child N_i. The node state is set to WAIT.
- **WAIT**: The node remains in this state until a NOTIFY message has been received from each child. The node can then begin postpruning. One of the options considered is to replace the node with the root of its largest (in the sense of covering most cases) subtree, N_0 say. Each child in the tree below N_0 is moved to state CALC-BRANCH, and query POSTPRUNE(L) is scheduled for each leaf node L. The node state is set to PRUNE-WAIT.
- **PRUNE-WAIT**: The node receives a NOTIFY message from its largest child when the revised error estimates are done. Depending on the result, the node is either postpruned or not. Its parent is notified, and the node state is set to FINAL.
- **CALC-BRANCH**: If N is a leaf node, the incoming result set is used to calculate an estimated error rate for the node. Its parent is then sent a NOTIFY. A non-leaf node will decrement a count of its child nodes each

time a NOTIFY is received: when the count reaches zero the revised error rate for that node is calculated, and a NOTIFY sent to its parent.

6 Summary

We have described an architecture for the generic optimization of exploratory processes, based on the use of primitive queries which have a certain algebraic structure. Processing is split between client and server by the use of SUP queries, which are overlapped to ensure that client and server work in parallel. The problem of varying loads on the server and the network is addressed by using dynamically adjustable cost functions to choose between query plans. All the client-server issues identified at the outset have therefore been addressed in a way that allows efficient integration between knowledge discovery tools and database servers.

7 Acknowledgement

The research described in this paper was supported by the Engineering and Physical Sciences Research Council, grant number GR/L/16002.

References

1. Brachman, R.J., Anand,T: The Process of Knowledge Discovery in Databases: A Human-Centred Approach. In Usama M. Fayyad et al eds, Advances in Knowledge Discovery and Data Mining, AAAI Press (1996) 37–58
2. Freitas, A.A., Lavington, S.H.: Mining Very Large Databases with Parallel Processing. Kluwer Academic Publishers (1997)
3. Graefe, G. Query Evaluation Techniques for Large Databases. ACM Computing Surveys 25/2 (June 1993) 73–170
4. Harinarayan, V., Rajaraman, A., Ullman, J.D.: Implementing Data Cubes Efficiently. Proc. ACM SIGMOD Conference (1996) 205–216
5. Keller, A.M., Basu, J: A Predicate-Based Caching Scheme for Client-Server Database Architectures. The VLDB Journal 5 (1996) 35–47
6. Provost, F.J., Kolluri, V.: A Survey of Methods for Scaling Up Inductive Learning Algorithms. Proc. 3rd International Conference on Knowledge Discovery and Data Mining (1997)
7. Quinlan, J.R.: Programs for Machine Learning. Morgan Kaufman Publishers (1993)
8. Roussopoulos, N.: Materialized Views and Data Warehouses. Proc. 4th KRDB Workshop, Athens, Greece (1997) 12.1-12.6
9. Sheth, A.P., O'Hare, A.B.: The Architecture of BrAID: A System for Bridging AI/DB Systems Proc. 7th In. Conf. on Data Engineering (1991) 570–581
10. Thomas, J., Mitschang, B., Mattos, N., DeBloch, S.: Enhancing Knowledge Processing in Client/Server Environments. Proc. 2nd International Conference on Information and Knowledge Management (1993) 324–334

Discovery of Common Subsequences
in Cognitive Evoked Potentials

Arthur Flexer[1] and Herbert Bauer[2]

[1] The Austrian Research Institute for Artificial Intelligence
Schottengasse 3, A-1010 Vienna, Austria
`arthur@ai.univie.ac.at`
[2] Department of Psychology, University of Vienna
Liebiggasse 5, A-1010 Vienna, Austria

Abstract. This work is about developing a new method for the analysis of evoked potentials of cognitive activities that combines methods from statistics and sequence alignment to tackle the following two problems: the visualization of high dimensional sequential data and the unsupervised discovery of patterns within this multivariate set of real valued time series data. The sequences of the original high dimensional vectors are transformed to discrete sequences by vector quantization plus Sammon mapping of the codebook. Instead of having to conduct a time-consuming search for common subsequences in the set of multivariate sequential data a multiple sequence alignment procedure can be applied to the set of one-dimensional discrete symbolic time series. The methods are described in detail and the results are shown to be significantly better than those obtained for two sets of randomized artificial data.

1 Introduction

This work is part of the development of a new method for the analysis of evoked potentials (EP) of cognitive activities that combines methods from statistics and sequence alignment to tackle the following two problems: the visualization of high dimensional sequential data and the unsupervised discovery of patterns within this multivariate real valued set of time series data.

A cognitive EP is the electro cortical potential measurable in the electro encephalogram (EEG) during a cognitive task (spatial imagination). Since an EP is measured via a number of electrodes it is a multi dimensional time series. Our approach to visualize this high dimensional sequential set of data is to replace the sequence of the original vectors by a sequence of prototypical codebook vectors obtained from a clustering procedure. Additionally, a dimensionality reduction technique is applied to obtain an ordered one-dimensional representation of the high dimensional codebook vectors that allows for the depiction of the original sequence as a one-dimensional time series.

The fact that cognitive activities do not elicit one specific EP waveform time locked to the onset of the recording prohibits the conventional approach of simply computing the arithmetic average of all EPs at each sample point. Only subsequences of the whole EPs that do not occur at fixed time after the onset of the recording can be expected to be due to the cognitive task. Searching for such subsequences in the set of real valued multivariate sequential data is computationally prohibitive. Instead we can use the set of univariate discrete time series, the trajectories across codebook vectors, and apply a multiple sequence alignment procedure [1] that has originally been designed for molecular biology.

Other already existing data mining approaches to processing of sequential patterns are not applicable to our problem for the following reasons: Template based approaches require a query pattern [6] or frequent episode [8] to be defined before the search is started. No such sequential patterns can be formulated for cognitive EPs since only very vague knowledge about the subsequences to be discovered exists. Additionally, these template based approaches are designed for univariate and often symbolic sequences. [7] describes a method to cluster whole sequences of complex composite objects which is not suited for finding subsequences of multivariate real valued data.

Our work is structured in the following way: First we describe the EP data plus two sets of artificial data, which we need to ensure statistical significance of our results. Then all applied methods (clustering, dimensionality reduction, sequence comparison) are presented and optimal parameters are found via computer experiments. Finally, the results of the completed algorithm are described. The results are confirmed via an analysis of variance and discussed.

2 The data

The data stems from 21 EP trials from one person recorded during a spatial imagination task. After appropriate preprocessing (essentially limiting the signals to frequencies below $8Hz$ and eliminating the DC-like trend by subtracting a linear fit), each EP trial consists of 2125 samples, each being a 22 dimensional real valued vector. One complete 22-channel EP trial (duration is 8.5 seconds) is depicted in Fig. 1(a).

To verify that our procedure yields different results for real human EEG and for unstructured random input and thereby ensuring statistical significance, we produced two kinds of artificial data sets. To produce *time-shuffled EEG* we took a concatenation of the 21 unfiltered EP trials of length 2125 described above and submitted it to a random permutation of the samples in time. 21×2125 times the positions of 2 of the 21×2125 samples were exchanged. The procedure produced 21 EP sequences with destroyed temporal but intact spatial structure. After preprocessing identical to that applied to the real EPs, the time-shuffled EEG data was divided into 21 sequences of length 2125. It should be noted that this procedure also changes the frequency properties of the EPs, i.e. it intensifies higher frequencies and diminishes lower ones, which makes time-shuffled EEG look more random.

To have another set of data that resembles the frequency spectrum of the real EP data more closely, *random Gaussian EEG* was produced by computing 21 sequences of dimension 22 and length 2125 of random Gaussian data and subjecting it to an FFT (Fast Fourier Transform). The power spectrum of the Gaussian random data was changed so that it resembled the characteristics of the real EEG instead of those of white noise Gaussian random data by directly changing the real and imaginary parts of the FFT-ed signal appropriately and then retransforming it back to the time domain. In doing so we were able to produce artificial EPs which showed the same limitation to frequencies below $8Hz$ with an emphasis of very slow parts around $1Hz$ as real EPs and which are therefore hard to distingiush from real EPs even by a human expert.

To compensate for different amplitude ranges across channels and between real and artificial EEG, all signals in all the dimensions are being standardized separately to zero mean and unit variance.

3 Dimensionality reduction and visualization

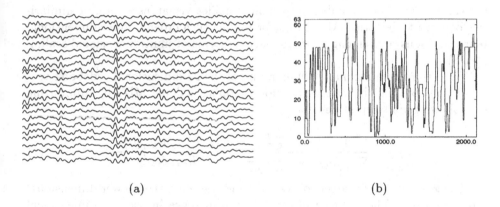

(a)   (b)

Fig. 1. (a) Example of a complete 8.5 second 22-channel EP recording. (b) The corresponding trajectory across codebook vectors depicted as ordered codebook numbers (y-axis) as a function of time (x-axis).

The EP time series are vector quantized together by using all the EP vectors at all the sample points as input vectors to a clustering algorithm disregarding their ordering in time. Then the sequence of the original vectors x is replaced by the sequence of the prototypical codebook vectors $\hat{x}$. There is a double benefit of this step: it is part of the visualization scheme and the sequences of $\hat{x}$ serve as input to the sequence alignment procedure.

K-means clustering (see e.g. [3, p.201]) is used for vector quantization using the sum of squared differences $d(x, \hat{x}) = \sum_{i=0}^{k-1} \mid x_i - \hat{x}_i \mid^2$ as measure of distance, where both x and $\hat{x}$ are of dimension k. Since observation of the sum of distances $d(x, \hat{x})$ with growing size of codebooks did not indicate an optimal codebook size, we pragmatically decided to use 64 codebook vectors based on the following consideration: We vector quantized the EP data with increasing numbers of codebook vectors. We then took the original EPs and substituted at each sample point the original real valued vector x_l with the appropriate codebook vector $\hat{x}_i$ (i.e. where $d(x_l, \hat{x}_i) < d(x_l, \hat{x}_s)$ for all s). We then visually inspected both the original EP time series and the coarser codebook time series as series of topographical patterns (surface plots of the 22 values at a single point in time) and checked, whether the important features of the topographies still were existent in the coarser codebook approximation. "Important" features are positive and negative peaks and their development in time. Instead of a set of 22-dimensional time series, we now have sequences of discrete symbols, where each symbol is drawn from the alphabet of the 64 codebook vectors $\hat{x}$.

The sequences of codebook vectors can be visualized in a graph where the x-axis stands for time and the y-axis for the number of the codebook vector. Since in the course of time, the trajectory moves only between codebook vectors that are close to each other in the 22 dimensional vector space, this neighbourhood should also be reflected by an appropriate ordering of the numbers of the codebook vectors. Such an ordered numbering results in smooth curves of the time vs. codebook number graphs and enables visual inspection of similarities between trajectories. Algorithms for finding such ordered lower dimensional representations are, amongst others, various forms of multidimensional scaling (MDS).

We performed a Sammon [10] mapping of the 22-dimensional codebook vectors to one output dimension. Sammon mapping is doing MDS by minimizing the following via steepest descent:

$$\frac{1}{\sum_{i=0}^{c-1}\sum_{j<i} d(\hat{x}_i, \hat{x}_j)} \sum_{i=0}^{c-1}\sum_{j<i} \frac{\left(d(\hat{x}_i, \hat{x}_j) - \dot{d}(y_i, y_j)\right)^2}{d(\hat{x}_i, \hat{x}_j)} \tag{1}$$

The $\hat{x}$ are the $c=64$ codebook vectors and the y are their lower dimensional representations. The distance $\dot{d}(y_i, y_j)$ is the distance in the one-dimensional output space that corresponds to the distance $d(\hat{x}_i, \hat{x}_j)$ in the 22-dimensional input space. This combined technique of K-means clustering plus Sammon mapping of the codebook is described in [4]. An example for a trajectory across an ordered set of codebook vectors is given in Fig. 1(b). Note that the ordering of the numbers of the codebook vectors is needed only for visualization and is not necessary for the subsequent sequence alignment.

4 Unsupervised discovery of patterns in sequences

4.1 Computation of distance matrix

We have 21 sequences made of 64 different items (corresponding to 64 codebook vectors) of length 2125, each for the real, the time-shuffled and the artificial EP data. When running the sequence alignment algorithm, we will need distances between single elements of our sequences. For the 64 codebook vectors, we can calculate a 64×64 distance matrix D which serves as a lookup table for these comparisons. This avoids the repeated computation of distances between the original multivariate vectors which would be computationally intractable.

When running the k-means clustering algorithm as well as when computing trajectories across clusters centers, we used the sum of squared differences $d(x, \hat{x})$ as a measure of distance between an input vector x and a codebook vector $\hat{x}$. By using a codebook vector $\hat{x}(S_i)$ as representative of its partition S_i ($S_i = \{x_l | d(x_l, \hat{x}_i) < d(x_l, \hat{x}_s)$ for all $s\}$), the mean of all $| x_l \in S_i |$ points of S_i is chosen as representative of S_i. We decided to use the more accurate average of all $n_i \times n_j$ possible distances, $d'(S_i, S_j) = \frac{1}{n_i n_j} \sum_{x_l \in S_i, x_m \in S_j} d(x_l, x_m)$, for computation of the distance matrix D. This measure of distance additionally takes into account the variances of the partitions. Contrary to the earlier tasks, the singular computation of the 64×64 distance matrix allows using the computationally more expensive distance function.

4.2 Fixed segment algorithm

We chose a so-called *fixed length segment* approach for sequence comparison. Given two sequences A and B of length m and n, all possible overlapping segments having a particular window length W from A are compared to all segments from B. This requires of the order $m \times n$ comparisons to be made. For each pair of elements the score taken from our 64×64 distance matrix D is recorded and summed up for the segmental comparison. The distance between two segments of length W from two sequences A and B is therefore:

$$D_{align}(s_a, s_b, W) = \sum_{i=0}^{W-1} d'(A_{s_a+i}, B_{s_b+i}) \tag{2}$$

The indices s_a and s_b are the starting points of the segments in the sequences A and B and A_{s_a+i} and B_{s_b+i} are the codebook vectors or the corresponding partitions respectively. Successive application of this pairwise methods allows for the alignment of more than two sequences. Such a *fixed segment* approach that is explicitly designed for *multiple sequence alignment* is given by [1]. It computes a multiple alignment by iteratively comparing sequences to the multiple alignment obtained so far, keeping always just the L best segments as an intermediate result. The succession of sequences is chosen at random. It starts with first evaluating all possible segment pairs of the first two sequences, keeping the best L of them. The intermediate L two-way alignment segments are compared against all segments of the third sequence, again keeping only the L best three-way alignments (each is a set of three segments, every segment from one of the sequences). This procedure continues until all sequences have been aligned. When a segment is compared to an intermediate "more"-way (let us say p-way) segment, the resulting score is computed as the sum of the p pairwise comparisons of the segments in the intermediate solution with the new segment that is to be aligned. The number of all such crosswise comparisons within the final overall alignment is given by $P = (1 + 2 + \ldots + (p - 1)) = \sum_{i=1}^{p-1} i$. The number of all element-wise comparisons within the final overall alignment is given by WP, and its average per element, the average element-wise within alignment distance, by:

$$\bar{D}_{align} = \frac{1}{WP} \sum_{i=1}^{p-1} \sum_{j=i+1}^{p-1} D_{align}(s_i, s_j, W) \tag{3}$$

Desired is a set of starting points s_i for which $\bar{D}_{align}$ is minimal. This approach guarantees that the obtained multiple alignments contain segments that are subsequences of all the original sequences. The number of single element-wise comparisons is $LW(m + 1 - W)P$, where m=2125, the length of the p=21 sequences. For a given L and m, this function is proportional to p^2, in contrast with m^p comparisons in "brute force" searching where not just the L best but all possible alignments are considered.

4.3 Finding optimal parameters

The number of alignments, L, that are being kept as intermediate results during sequence comparison, has to be sufficiently large to avoid the omission of good alignments that are weak in the first few sequences but strong in the later ones. It should also be small enough to allow for tractable computation time.

The following experiments have been conducted with the real EP data: The window length W was set to 125 (half a second of EP), L was varied from 100 to 1000 and 10000. For each of these three settings, five runs of the fixed segment algorithm have been computed. To compare the results, the average element-wise within alignment distances $\bar{D}_{align}$ (see Equ. 3) of the best scoring alignments for each of fifteen runs were computed. The results are (mean $\pm$ std.dev.) 3.99$\pm$.033 for L=100, 3.97 $\pm$ .017 for L=1000 and 3.96 $\pm$ .022 for L=10000. The mean of the distribution of values of the distance matrix D is 6.67$\pm$2.78. Comparing this to the results of our experiment, it can be seen that keeping 1000 or even 10000 alignments yields only an insignificant improvement above storing just 100.

The window length W should not be too short, since EP subsequences shorter than 0.25 seconds are of little significance in terms of their psychophysiological interpretation. If the window is made too big, only poorly matched segments can be found, since so-called gaps are not allowed (see Sec. 6).

The following experiments have been conducted with the real EP data: The number of best scoring elements that are being kept, L, was set to 1000, the window length W was varied from 31 to 62, 125 and 187 (corresponding to $0.125, 0.25, 0.5$ and 0.75 seconds). For each of the four settings, five runs of the fixed segment algorithm have been computed. To compare the different results, again the average element-wise within alignment distance $\bar{D}_{align}$ (see Equ. 3) of the best scoring alignments for each of the twenty runs were computed. The results are (mean $\pm$ std.dev.) 3.10 $\pm$ .035 for W=31, 3.46 $\pm$ .012 for W=62, 3.97 $\pm$ .020 for W=125 and 4.28 $\pm$ .041 for W=187.

If all of our sequences really did contain very similar subsegments of a certain length w, the following behaviour could be expected for values of $\bar{D}_{align}$: For $W \leq w$, $\bar{D}_{align}$ would always be approximately at the same low level (indicating good alignments), since subsegments shorter than w should be detected with the same high performance as subsegments of the full length w. $\bar{D}_{align}$ should increase steadily for $W > w$ because ever longer parts of subsequences which are not similar across all sequences become part of the alignment. Computations with sufficiently high values W should asymptotically reach the average of the distance array (6.67 in the case of our real EP data).

The $\bar{D}_{align}$ values of our experiments do not show the behaviour described above. Instead of staying at a low level beginning at the smallest window length $W=31$, they rather increase at a steady pace from $W=31$ to $W=187$. We decided to use a window length of $W=125$ which is sufficiently long enough to allow for psychophysiological interpretation of the results but short enough to yield alignments of still satisfactory quality.

5 Results and comparison with artificial EPs

After having found optimal parameters, the following experiments have been conducted with our real EP data as well as with the time-shuffled and random Gaussian data. The number of best scoring elements that are being kept, L, was set to 100, the window length W to 125 (half a second of EP). For each of the three settings, five runs of the fixed segment algorithm have been computed. To compare the results for real and artificial EPs, the average element-wise within alignment distance $\bar{D}_{align}$ (see Equ. 3) of the best scoring alignments for each of the fifteen runs has been computed. The means and standard deviations for each of the three settings are given in Tab. 1.

type of EP	real EP	time-shuffled EP	random Gaussian EP
mean ± std.dev.	$3.97 \pm .020$	$4.38 \pm .010$	$6.33 \pm .017$

Table 1. Results of the 3×5 experiments to compare real and artificial EEG.

A one-way analysis of variance (ANOVA) for the variable "type of EP" (real EP, time-shuffled EP, random Gaussian EP) yielded an value $F=29070 > 18=F_{99}(df=2$ and 4). This indicates that the null hypothesis that the means of the three EP groups are equal is extremely unlikely, in fact its probability is very close to zero. Additional Duncan t-Tests allow us to rank the result for real EP as being significantly better than the result for time-shuffled EP, which is again significantly better than the result for random Gaussian EP, both with a probability of 99%. In Fig. 2, an alignment plus its average is depicted as a trajectory across ordered codebook centers. Since an average alignment corresponds to a time series of 22-dimensional codebook vectors, it can be depicted as a series of topographical patterns (surface plots of the 22 values at a single point in time) and thereby transformed back to its multivariate real valued representation. This series of topographical patterns is now accessible to interpretation for the psychophysiologist.

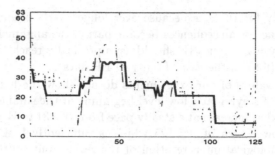

Fig. 2. An example of a best scoring alignment plus its average (the thick line).

6 Discussion

The analysis of cognitive evoked potentials is a largely unsolved problem in psychophysiological research. Classical methods are designed for univariate time series of simpler motoric or sensoric EPs only and can therefore not really cope with the harder problem of analysing cognitive EPs. Nevertheless they are still state of the art.

The transformation of the multivariate real valued EPs to sequences of discrete symbols achieved by using vector quantization plus a dimensionality reduction technique makes a wealth of algorithms for sequence alignment applicable to our problem. This enables psychophysiologists to look at their cognitive EP data by discovering subsequences of fixed length that are, with a certain variance, similar across all EP trials in their multivariate timely appearance.

One of the issues that need some further investigation is the self-consistency of the algorithm. Since our method of sequence comparison is a stochastic algorithm, repeated runs on the same set of data do not necessarily produce the same output alignment. Although the very similar values for $\bar{D}_{align}$ in Tab. 1 for each of the three sets of five runs seem to indicate similar solutions, this still needs some thorough consideration.

If the variance of the obtained alignments would be recognized as being too large for a successful psychophysiological interpretation, this could be due to the fact that so-called gaps are not allowed. When discrete symbolic sequences are compared element-wise three basic things can happen (see e.g. [11]): a *match* if two elements are identical, a *substitution* if they are different and so-called *deletions* or *insertions*, where an element in one subsequence is too different too match or substitute it and it is therefore deleted (inserted if you see it the other way round) which results in a gap in one of the subsequences. Future work could aim for subsequences showing considerable variation on the time axis, therefore needing algorithms that are able to deal with gaps. Since only subsequences and not the whole sequences are to be aligned, a so-called *local multiple sequence alignment* method is needed. Existing global approaches (see e.g. [2] or [12]) would have to be extended to the local case. Hidden Markov Models (see e.g. [9]) are another promising candidate to solve this problem.

Our general approach to the visualization of high dimensional sequential data and the unsupervised discovery of patterns within multivariate sets of time series data is of course not restricted to the problem presented in this work. The methods described can either be applied to multivariate real valued data by using the full approach including the transformation to sequences of discrete symbols through vector quantization plus Sammon mapping or, if already symbolic sequences are available, the fixed segment algorithm alone can be applied.

Acknowledgements: The EEG recordings have been made by R. Gstättner, Dept. of Psychology, University of Vienna. Parts of this work were done within the BIOMED-2 BMH4-CT97-2040 project SIESTA, funded by the EC DG XII. The Austrian Research Institute for Artificial Intelligence is supported by the Austrian Federal Ministry of Science and Transport. The author was supported by a doctoral grant of the Austrian Academy of Sciences.

References

1. Bacon D.J., Anderson W.F.: Multiple Sequence Alignment, Journal of Molecular Biology, 191, 153-161, 1986.
2. Barton G.J.: Protein Multiple Sequence Alignment and Flexible Pattern Matching, Methods in Enzymology, Vol. 183, pp.403-428, 1990.
3. Duda R.O., Hart P.E.: Pattern Classification and Scene Analysis, John Wiley & Sons, N.Y., 1973.
4. Flexer A.: Limitations of Self-Organizing Maps for Vector Quantization and Multidimensional Scaling, in Mozer M.C., et al.(eds.), Advances in Neural Information Processing Systems 9, MIT Press/Bradford Books, pp.445-451, 1997.
5. Heckerman D., Mannila H., Pregibon D., Uthurusamy R.(eds.): KDD-97: Proceedings Third International Conference on Knowledge Discovery & Data Mining, AAAI Press, Menlo Park, 1997.
6. Keogh E., Smyth P.: A Probabilistic Approach to Fast Pattern Matching in Time Series Databases, in [5], pp.24-30.
7. Ketterlin A.: Clustering Sequences of Complex Objects, in [5], pp.215-218, 1997.
8. Mannila H., Toivonen H., Verkamo A.I.: Discovery of Frequent Episodes in Event Sequences, Data Mining and Knowledge Discovery, Volume 1, Issue 3, 1997.
9. Rabiner L.R., Juang B.H.: An Introduction To Hidden Markov Models, IEEE ASSP Magazine, 3(1):4-16, 1986.
10. Sammon J.W.: A Nonlinear Mapping for Data Structure Analysis, IEEE Transactions on Comp., Vol. C-18, No. 5, p.401-409, 1969.
11. Sankoff D., Kruskal J.B.(eds.): Time warps, string edits, and macromolecules: the theory and practice of sequence comparison, Addison-Wesley, Reading, MA, 1983.
12. Taylor W.R.: Multiple Protein Sequence Alignment: Algorithms and Gap Insertion, Methods in Enzymology, Vol. 266, pp.343-367, 1996.

Improving the Discovery of Association Rules with Intensity of Implication

Sylvie Guillaume[1], Fabrice Guillet[1] and Jacques Philippé[1,2]

[1] IRIN, Equipe SIC, IRESTE - Rue Christian-Pauc - La Chantrerie,
44306 Nantes Cedex 3 – France
{sguillau, fguillet, jphilipp}@ireste.fr
[2] PERFORMANSE - 3 rue Racine,
44000 Nantes - France

Abstract. In this paper, we propose a way to improve the rule-learning step in a Knowledge Discovery in Databases (KDD) process. Our purpose is to make possible the discovery of relevant rules in a large database.
To achieve this goal, we merge :

- a quality index proposed by *R. Gras* : *intensity of implication*,
- together with a specific algorithm written by *Agrawal et al*.

The algorithm itself is efficient in a large database but delivers a prohibitively large set of knowledge.
Intensity of implication is a new measurement of the quality of association rules. Hence, we analyze it in detail and compare it with conditional probability index. We show that it is possible to significantly improve the relevance of association rules supplied by the algorithm proposed by *Agrawal et al*, by using the quality index : *intensity of implication*.
An improved algorithm has been implemented, and has been tested both at the experimental level and on a real-life database.

1 Introduction

This study fits within the framework of KDD : how to extract knowledge from a database in the form of association rules [1], [2].
On large databases two main practical limits arise : algorithms are little efficient and they deliver a prohibitively large set of knowledge. So, relevant rules are not easy to highlight and the task of the end-user is heavy.
These two problems come from the fact that :

- the *complexity* of knowledge discovery grows exponentially with the number of attributes in the database; so algorithms may rapidly become inefficient.
- the *number of discovered rules* may be far larger than the number of examples, thus it may be impossible to exploit discovered knowledge in large databases.

To push back those two limits and work with large databases, we propose to improve an algorithm, published by *Agrawal et al.*, that is efficient on large databases. This improvement is made by coupling it with a new index to measure the relevance of the rules : *intensity of implication.*

With this association we expect the following properties :

- With the. algorithm proposed by Agrawal et al., discovery of association rules may run in reasonable time on large databases.
- Due to the properties of intensity of implication, the number of discovered rules may be reduced to the most relevant rules.

In this paper, we will show how intensity of implication can be used in order to find more relevant rules than rules discovered with conditional probability. Indeed, intensity of implication measures the relevance of a rule : the probability that a rule results from random phenomena. Therefore the efficiency of algorithm is improved, while the processing of large data volumes is more accessible.

2 Agrawal's Algorithm (A)

Agrawal [3], [4], [5] provides an efficient algorithm, called (A), for finding association rules between items in a database.

An association rule is an expression $X \rightarrow Y$ where X and Y are sets of items describing objects in the database. The intuitive meaning of such a rule is that objects in the database which are covered by Y tend to contain objects covered by X. Furthermore, rules are *statistical* : they can have negative examples.

Rules must meet the following requirements :

1. a sufficient number of objects must verify the rule (*support* also called *frequency*).
2. the number of objects which contradict the rule must be small (*confidence* also called *reliability*).

Formal Presentation. Let $D = \{d_0, d_1, ..., d_p\}$ be a set of p literals, each literal d_i is a binary attribute called an *item*[1]. Let E be a set of objects[2], and each element e of E is described by an itemset X, where X is a part of D.

To say that "object e is described by the itemset $X = \{d_0, d_1, d_3\}$", means "e shows all items of X and none of the others" or "e is described by the conjunction $d_0 \wedge d_1 \wedge \overline{d_2} \wedge d_3 \wedge d_4 \wedge .. \wedge d_p$". The description X may also be seen as a p-uple $(x_0, x_1, ..., x_p)$ where $x_i = 1$ if $d_i \in X$ and $x_i = 0$ otherwise.

An *association rule* is an implication of the form $X \rightarrow Y$, between disjoined itemsets $(X \cap Y = \varnothing)$. $X \rightarrow Y$ means that "all objects that show the items of X show the items of Y, as well". This rule being of statistical nature, it is understood that some negative examples may exist.

The statistical feature of a rule $X \rightarrow Y$ is characterized by two indexes :

1. the *support* $T(X \rightarrow Y)$ (or coverage rate) and
2. the *confidence* $P(X \rightarrow Y)$ (or conditional probability).

---

[1] or variable in Data Analysis, feature in Machine Learning, attribute in Cognitive Science, field in Databases ...

[2] examples in Machine Learning, transactions in Databases, observations ...

Let (f,g) be two functions between parts of D and E. Let f(e)=X be the itemset describing object e, and let g(X)={e∈E / X⊆f(e) } be the part of all objects covered by itemset X (subset of all objects showing at least all the items in X), then the two indexes are defined by :

$$T(X{\rightarrow}Y)=t(X{\cup}Y)=\ |g(X{\cup}Y)|/|g(X)| \tag{1}$$

$$P(X{\rightarrow}Y)=Proba(Y/X)=\ |g(X{\cup}Y)|/|E| \tag{2}$$

Given two thresholds α and β in [0, 1], algorithm (A) uses the following criteria to select a convenient statistical rule X→Y : T(X→Y) ≥α and P(X→Y)≥β. When T(X→Y) ≥α, we say that itemset X∪Y is *α-frequent*, and when P(X→Y)≥β, we say that association rule X→Y is *β-convenient*.

Comments. The efficiency of algorithm (A) follows from the two previous indexes (1), (2) :
- The support limits the combinatorial explosion, because only α-frequent itemsets are retained: the itemsets that covers at least α% of objects. Thus, algorithm (A) selects a restricted subset of 2^D, the set of all parts of D.
- The confidence improves the reliability of the discovered rules set, because only the β-convenient rules are kept : the rules with few negative examples, rules X→Y where at least β% of objects covered by X are also covered by Y.

3 Toward Intensity of Implication

3.1 Limits of Conditional Probability

The previous section shows that algorithm (A) is based upon the conditional probability (confidence) to select the convenient rules. But, the conditional probability of a rule X→Y is invariable when the size of g(Y) or E varies and insensitive to cardinal dilatation [6]. Nevertheless, X→Y is more likely to happen when the size of g(Y) increases or when the size of E decreases; and furthermore this implication will be more meaningful when the size of the all sets grows in the same proportion.

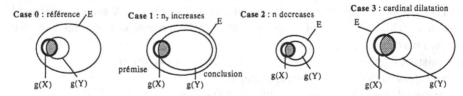

Fig. 1. Three cases with constant conditional probability

Fig. 1 shows that in case 1, when g(Y), the number of objects covered by conclusion Y is close to the size of E, it is not surprising that most of the objects covered by premise

X, are included in g(Y). In case 2, when the size of g(X) and the size of g(Y) are close to that of E, it is not surprising that g(X) and g(Y) share many objects. And to finish case 3, a more important sample will allow to be more confident in the statistical implication X→Y.

It could be interesting for this algorithm to find a new index which would vary according to the size of g(Y) and E. This would improve the quality of the discovered rules. *Intensity of implication* fulfils this goal.

3.2 Intensity of Implication

Let $A=g(X)$, $B=g(Y)$, $n=|E|$, $n_a=|A|$, $n_b=|B|$, $n_{a\bar{b}} = |A \cap \bar{B}|$; n is the number of objects, n_a and n_b are the number of objects covered by premise X and conclusion Y, and $n_{a\bar{b}}$ the number of negative examples (exceptions) of the rule X→Y.

One property of intensity of implication proposed by R. Gras [7], [8], [9] is that it evolves with the sizes n, n_a, n_b, $n_{a\bar{b}}$. Its meaning is to measure the *statistical surprise* of having so *few negative examples* on a rule as compared with a random draw.

Definition. Let X→Y be the observed rule; premise X and conclusion Y in 2^D are associated with sets of objects $A=g(X)$ and $B=g(Y)$ in E. Let U and V be two sets randomly chosen with the same cardinality as A and B : $|U|=|A|= n_a$ and $|V|=|B|= n_b$ (see Fig. 2).

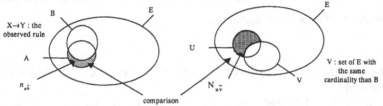

comparison

Fig. 2. U and V vary at random in E

Let $N_{u\bar{v}}=|U \cap \bar{V}|$ be the random variable measuring the number of random negative examples, and $n_{a\bar{b}}=|A \cap \bar{B}|$ the number of negative examples observed on the rule.

We shall compare $n_{a\bar{b}}$ with $N_{u\bar{v}}$, assuming that U and V are independent. If $n_{a\bar{b}}$ is unusually small as compared with $N_{u\bar{v}}$ the one we would expect at random, we will accept the statistical implication X→Y.

The quality of implication is even better if the number of negative examples is smaller than the expected one, in other words, if the quantity Proba($N_{u\bar{v}} \leq n_{a\bar{b}}$) is small. The observed "smallness" of $n_{a\bar{b}}$ is taken as a basic character of statistical implication X→Y.

Intensity of implication is then defined by function φ : $\varphi(X \rightarrow Y) = 1 - \text{Proba}(N_{uv}^- \le n_{ab}^-)$. The random variable $N_{uv}^- = |U \cap \bar{V}|$ follows the hypergeometric law [10], thus intensity of implication $\varphi(X \rightarrow Y)$ is defined by :

$$\varphi(X \rightarrow Y) = 1 - \sum_{k=\max(0,n_a-n_b)}^{n_{ab}^-} \frac{C_{n_a^-}^{n_b^- - k} \times C_{n_a}^k}{C_n^{n_b^-}} \qquad (3)$$

Sensitivity to Cardinal

Fig. 3 shows the variation of intensity of implication $\varphi(X \rightarrow Y)$ with the number n_b of conclusion, with the number n of objects, and by dilatation of n when $\frac{n_a}{n}$, $\frac{n_b}{n}$ and $\frac{n_{ab}^-}{n}$ remain constant; meanwhile conditional probability (convenience) $\frac{n_{ab}^-}{n_a}$ stay constant.

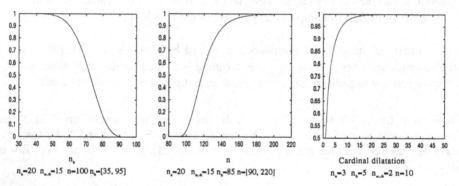

n_a-20 n_a.A-15 n-100 n_b-[35, 95]   n_a-20 n_a.A-15 n_b-85 n-[90, 220]   n_a-3 n_b-5 n_a.A-2 n-10

Fig. 3. Sensitivity of intensity of implication

Property of Symmetry. Intensity of implication is symmetric : $\varphi(Y \rightarrow X) = \varphi(X \rightarrow Y)$.
Demonstration :
We have $\varphi(Y \rightarrow X) = 1 - \text{Proba}(N_{uv}^- \le n_{ab}^-)$ and $N_{uv}^- = n_b - (n_a - N_{uv}^-)$ and $n_{ab}^- = n_b - (n_a - n_{ab}^-)$,
thus $\text{Proba}(N_{uv}^- \le n_{ab}^-) = \text{Proba}(n_b - n_a + N_{u\bar{v}} \le n_b - n_a + n_{ab}^-) = \text{Proba}(N_{uv}^- \le n_{ab}^-)$,
therefore : $\varphi(Y \rightarrow X) = \varphi(X \rightarrow Y)$
This symmetry of intensity of implication leads to use an other information to know the nature of the implication between X and Y : Y→X or X→Y. In this paper we choose conditional probability. In another knowledge discovery system : FIABLE [11], [12], [13] intensity of implication is also associated with conditional probability.

Behavior on Logical Rules. When no negative example occurs on rule X→Y, $n_{ab}^- = 0$, and

$$\varphi(X \rightarrow Y) = 1 - \frac{C_{n_a}^{n_b^-}}{C_n^{n_b^-}} = 1 - \frac{C_{n_b}^{n_a}}{C_n^{n_a}} \qquad (4)$$

Hence, while conditional probability still equals 1, intensity of implication is more selective and may reject some logical rules.

- the second one involves both large premise and conclusion (g(X) and g(Y) close to E) (see case 2 of Fig. 1); then sharing a lot of objects is also highly probable.

Case 1			Case 2		
Rules	**P(X→Y)**	**φ(X→Y)**	**Rules**	**P(X→Y)**	**φ(X→Y)**
{c,d}→{a}	0.86	0.59	{a}→{c}	0.80	0.63
{d,g}→{a}	0.83	0.48	{c}→{a}	0.80	0.63
{e,g}→{a}	0.87	0.69	{d}→{a}	0.88	0.78
{d,g}→{c}	0.83	0.48	{e}→{a}	0.81	0.60
{a,c,d}→{g}	0.83	0.48	{c}→{g}	0.80	0.63
{c,e,g}→{a}	0.83	0.48	{g}→{c}	0.80	0.63
{a,c,e}→{g}	0.83	0.48	{a,g}→{c}	0.84	0.79

Fig. 5. Discarded rules

With this example, we have seen that the intensity of implication has discarded the statistical rules which could be accidental.

Second Example. This example has 39 objects described by 21 items and studies the correlation between food and birds' shapes of beaks.
The following figure shows a part of learning set:

NAME	SHAPE	SIZE	THICKNESS	FOOD
Eagle	hooked	small	medium	animal
Snipe	straight	long	thin	worm
Crossbill	hooked	medium	medium	seed
Buzzard	hooked	small	thick	Animal and insect

Fig. 6. A part of learning set

The two algorithms produce the following number of rules, with a minimal support α varying from 0.01 to 0.20 and a minimal confidence $\beta=0.80$:

Support α	Number of statistical rules			Number of logical rules		
	$\beta=0.80$	$\beta=0.80$, φ	Rejected by φ	$\beta=1$	$\beta=1$, φ=0.8	Rejected by φ
0.20	52	52	0%	333	333	0%
0.10	53	53	0%	1586	1586	0%
0.01	53	53	0%	1848	1784	3.4%

Fig. 7. Number of discovered rules

First we can observe a prohibitive number of rules and a majority of logical rules. A deeper study shows that there are a lot of redundant rules, resulting from strong relationships between data and also because there are not many objects in the learning set.

After discarding redundant rules with the algorithm proposed by [14], only 43 rules are kept (initially, there were 1848 rules). Among these rules, 20 are considered as excellent rules (intensity of implication close to 1); 4 are considered as bad rules (intensity of implication below 0.8) and 19 are considered as good rules (intensity of implication between 0.8 and 1).

The non-redundant logical rules have values for intensity of implication varying from 0.63 to 1, while the conditional probability stays constant and equal to 1. Thus, this new index can measure the quality of this kind of rules where there is no counter-example.

The following figure shows examples of logical rules for each these three categories:

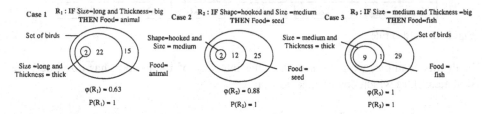

Fig. 8. Examples of logical rules

The first rule R_1 (see case 1 of Fig. 8) is regarded as a bad rule for intensity of implication while it is valuable for conditional probability. In fact, there are only two birds which own a long and large beak among the birds feeding on animals : this is not sufficient to infer rule R_1 because there are a lot of birds eating animals and there is an important probability of having such a small set included in the big one.

The second rule R_2 (see case 2 of Fig. 8) is regarded as a good rule for intensity of implication. In contrast of the previous rule, the small set of birds also composed of two objects is included in a smaller set. The chance of having this support is low and we can think that there is an implication between these two itemsets.

The last rule R_3 (see case 3 of Fig. 8) is regarded as an excellent rule. There is no doubt on the implication when we have two medium sets close to the learning set and when these two sets share a lot of objects.

Intensity of implication can measure the quality of logical rules while conditional probability cannot. This new index allows to discard rules which have a high probability of being accidental.

4.3 Study on a Real Case

Now, we are going to study the algorithm on two medical significant databases. One with 2178 transactions described by 75 items, and another with 1161 transactions and 103 items. Preliminary results, considering only the number of delivered rules, are presented in Fig. 9 :

DataBase	Support α	Number of statistical rules			Number of logical rules		
		β=0.80	β=0.80, ϕ	Rejected by ϕ	β=1	β=1, ϕ=0.8	Rejected by ϕ
Base 1	0.10	349	266	23.8%	4	4	0%
	0.01	21530	19812	8%	2758	2758	0%
Base 2	0.10	7760	6783	12.6%	2114	1560	26.2%

Fig. 9. Results in the two cases

Results are different for the two data sets. The first one (where there are essentially statistical rules) is close to the first experimental example. Meanwhile, the second one (where there is a lot of logical rules) is close to the second experimental example.
These differences are due to the structure of the databases. The first has a strong logical structure of implication between items that explain the large set of delivered logical rules. In the second, some items are owned by nearly all the objects, and the intensity of implication is more selective.

5 Conclusion

From the previous comments and examples, the integration of intensity of implication into algorithm (A) proposed by Agrawal *et al.* allows :
- the possibility of working on large databases in a reasonable amount of time,
- to obtain *better* rules : intensity of implication measures finer and more *relevant* phenomena than conditional probability and is also *noise-resistant*. This point is very important for improving quality of discovered rules by knowledge discovery algorithms in databases

These real-case results are still to be complete by an in-depth analysis of the discovered rules.
Nevertheless, it is obvious that in those two cases the number of discovered rules is far too large to be understood by an end-user. As the rules are saved in the database, they can be manipulated by SQL requests. This is helpful for the end-user who wants to select and explore discovered knowledge; but this is clearly insufficient. An extension of our work is to add to the algorithm a browsing interface and to couple to the algorithm a redundancy elimination.

References

1. Matheus C.J., Chan P.K., Piatetsky-shapiro G.: Systems for Knowledge Discovery in Databases, IEEE Trans. Knowl. Data Eng., vol. 5, n°6, (1993)
2. Frawley W. J., Piatetsky-Shapiro G., Matheus J.: Knowledge Discovery in Databases : an overview, in Knowledge Discovery in Databases, Cambridge, MA : AAAI/MIT (1991) pp. 1-27

3. Agrawal R., Imielinski T., and Swami A.: Mining Association Rules between Sets of Items in Large Databases. In Proceedings, ACM SIG-MOD Conference on Management of Data, 207-216. Washington, D.C. (1993)

4. Agrawal R. And Srikant R.: Fast Algorithms for Mining Association Rules. IBM Research Report RJ9839, IBM Almaden Research Center, San Jose, Calif. (1994)

5. Agrawal R., Mannila H., Srikant R., Toivonen H. et Inkeri Verkamo A.: Fast Discovery of Association Rules, Advances in Knowledge Discovery and Data Mining, AAAI Press, The MIT Press (1996)

6. Guillaume S., Guillet F., Philippé J.: Contribution of the integration of intensity of implication into the algorithm proposed by Agrawal, EMCSR'98, Vienna, vol. 2, pp. 805-810, April (1998)

7. Gras R.: Contribution à l'Étude Expérimentale et à l'Analyse de Certaines Acquisitions Cognitives et de Certains Objectifs Didactiques en Mathématiques, Thèse d'État, Université de Rennes 1 (1979)

8. Gras R., Larher A.: L'Implication Statistique, une Nouvelle Méthode d'Analyse de Données, Mathématiques, Informatique et Sciences Humaines n°120 (1993)

9. Gras R., Ag. Almouloud S., Bailleuil M., Larher A., Polo M., Ratsimba-Rajohn H., Totohasina A.: L'Implication Statistique, Nouvelle Méthode Exploratoire de Données. Application à la Didactique, Travaux et Thèses, édition La Pensée Sauvage (1996)

10. Anderson T.W.: An Introduction to Multivariate Statistical Analysis, Series in Probability and Mathematical Statistics, John Wiley and Son (1984) reviewed edition

11. Fleury L., Masson Y., Gras R., Briand H., Philippe J.: A Statistical Measure of Rule Strenght for Machine Learning, 2^d World Conference on the Fundamentals of Artificial Intelligence, WOCFAI, Paris (1995)

12. Fleury L., Briand H., Philippe J., Djeraba C.: Rules Evaluations for Knowledge Discovery in Database, 6th International Conference and Workshop on Database and Expert Systems Applications, DEXA, London (1995)

13. Fleury L., Masson Y.: The Intensity of Implication, a Measurement for Machine Learning, The 8th Int. Conf. On Industrail and Engineering Applications of Artificial Intelligence and Expert Systems, IEA/AEI, Melbourne (1995)

14. Lehn R., Guillet F., Briand H.: Eliminating redundant knowledge in an association rule-based system : An algorithm, EMCSR'98, Vienna, vol. 2, pp. 793-798, April (1998)

Generalization Lattices

Howard J. Hamilton, Robert J. Hilderman,
Liangchun Li, and Dee Jay Randall

Department of Computer Science
University of Regina
Regina, Saskatchewan, Canada S4S 0A2
{hamilton,hilder,lil,randal}@cs.uregina.ca

Abstract. Generalization lattices encode domain knowledge relevant to generalization. They provide a convenient framework for data visualization during user-guided exploration and for automated guidance during independent exploration. To reduce the size of a generalization lattice for an individual attribute, we define six types of pruning. Then we consider the generalization space defined by the cross product of lattices for several attributes. To increase the relevance of the data exploration results, we define five additional types of pruning. An interactive, web-based system for visualizing the generalization space allows the user to interactively guide the data exploration process.

1 Introduction

Generalization is fundamental to knowledge discovery and data mining. To provide a high-level view of the generalization operations permitted on data, various researchers have proposed similar structures, here called *generalization lattices* (*GLs*), but variously called *type hierarchies* [12, 9], *concept generalization graphs* [10], *domain generalization graphs* [6], *dependency lattices* [7], and *attribute lattices* [3]. A generalization lattice is an effective form of knowledge representation for encoding prior domain knowledge relevant to generalization.

In simple form, a generalization lattice shows the relationships between domains of values. Each generalization operation can be regarded as a mapping from one domain to a smaller domain. If a lattice is defined on the domains $D_1 = \{A, B, C\}, D_2 = \{A, BorC\}, D_3 = \{AorB, C\}, D_4 = \{AorBorC\}$, then D_1 is the most specific domain, with 3 possible values, D_2 and D_3 are domains of intermediate generality with two possible values each and no ordering defined between them, and D_4 is the most general domain, with one possible value. In the GL, an arc from node D_i to node D_j indicates that any value in domain D_i maps to a value in domain D_j. Mitchell's version space method is an example of a learning method based on a GL. Godin, Missaoui, and Alaoui's work on incremental concept formation is based on Galois lattices, a type of GL used in discrete mathematics [5]. Bournaud and Ganascia investigated the automatic creation of a GL from a set of objects described by conceptual graphs[1].

In data mining, GLs are used to conceptualize the process of generalizing data as a transformation of values from one domain to values of another, smaller domain. The original data, as retrieved from a database or other source, is considered the most specific representation of the data. Applying an operation to the data that maps any of several values in one domain to a single value in a smaller domain corresponds to traversing an arc in the GL from one node to a higher node. Many generalizations are possible, but for data mining, it is efficient and effective to limit the nodes to those representing generalized encodings of the domain that are of interest to the users of the knowledge discovery system. A GL is appropriate for this task because the possible generalizations form a partial order rather than a strict hierarchy (e.g., days can be generalized to weeks or months, but weeks cannot be generalized to months). A GL also allows a user to guide the generalization process by defining the domains of values to be considered in the data exploration process. Placing a node for a domain in a GL documents an inductive bias, namely that the partition of the original data values represented by that domain is at a level of granularity that the user finds interesting.

This work was motivated by the need to automate the data exploration process for cases where many ways of generalization may be be appropriate. For example, given a database with a time-related attribute, summaries can be created according to a GL containing the *hour of day, part of day, day, day of week, day of month, week, week in month, week in quarter, month, year*, and many others. Our system not only creates all these summaries, but also ranks them to help identify any anomalies, such as a disproportionate percentage of sales activity in the first week of a month. Furthermore, all attributes of interest can have arbitrarily complex GLs and our system will consider all resulting combinations. These features enable a database analyst to analyze the database from many different perspectives.

The remainder of this paper is organized as follows. In Section 2, we formally define GLs, and present an example GL for calendar attributes. In Section 3, we describe a semi-automated method for data exploration which uses pruning to identify the nodes of a GL that are distinct for a particular set of data. Six types of pruning are defined: reachability, preliminary manual, data-range, previous-discard, pregeneralization manual, and post-generalization. In Section 4, we consider the generalization space defined by the cross product of GLs associated with a set of attributes. We define five additional types of pruning and several measures for ranking the interestingness of the nodes in the generalization space. We also describe an interactive, web-based system for visualizing the generalization space that allows the user to interactively guide the exploration process and view the results. In § 5, we present conclusions.

2   Generalization Lattices

Given the domain of an attribute represented by a set $S = \{s_1, s_2, \ldots, s_n\}$, S can be partitioned in many different ways. For example, $D_1 = \{\{s_1\}, \{s_2\}, \ldots, \{s_n\}\}$, $D_2 = \{\{s_1\}, \{s_2, \ldots, s_n\}\}$, etc. Let D be the set of partitions of set S, and $\preceq$ be a nonempty binary relation (called a *generalization relation*) defined on D, such that $D_i \preceq D_j$ if for every $d_i \in D_i$ there exists $d_j \in D_j$ such that $d_i \subseteq d_j$. The generalization relation $\preceq$ is a partial order relation and $\langle D, \preceq \rangle$ defines a partial order set from which we can construct a lattice called a *generalization lattice* $\langle D, E \rangle$ as follows. First, the nodes of the graph are elements of D. And second, there is a directed arc from D_i to D_j (denoted by $E(D_i, D_j)$) iff $D_i \neq D_j$, $D_i \preceq D_j$, and there is no $D_k \in D$ such that $D_i \preceq D_k$ and $D_k \preceq D_j$. The partial order set $\langle D, \preceq \rangle$ is transitively closed and is a lattice.

Let $D_g = \{S\}$ and $D_d = \{\{s_1\}, \{s_2\}, \dots, \{s_n\}\}$. For any $D_i \in D$ we have $D_d \preceq D_i$ and $D_i \preceq D_g$, where D_d and D_g are called the bottom and top of D, respectively. We call the nodes (elements of D) *domains*, where the bottom is the *most specific level of generality* and the top is the *most general level*. There is a trivial GL where the bottom is mapped directly to the top (i.e., D_d is mapped to D_g). For each node D_i in $\langle D, E \rangle$, we define *descendants*(D_i) to be all nodes D_j such that $D_i \preceq D_j$ and *ancestors*(D_i) to be all nodes D_k such that $D_k \preceq D_i$.

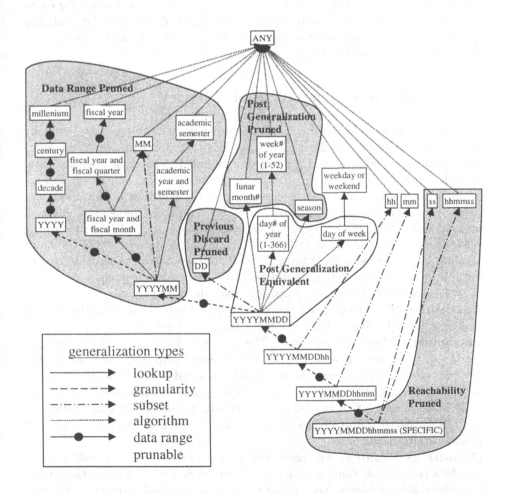

Fig. 1. Calendar GL with shading indicating pruning

We now describe an example GL for a calendar attribute, as shown in Figure 1, adapted from [11]. (The shading is explained in Sec. 3.) All attributes related to the time of an event's occurrence are combined into a *calendar attribute*, which contains subattributes such as year, month, etc. This GL is larger than the example GLs given in previous reports ([10], [3], [6], [7]), but the additional complexity is required to illustrate our method. In Figure 1, the node labelled *YYYYMMDDhhmmss* represents the most specific domain considered (i.e., the finest granularity of our calendar domain is one second). Every other node represents a generalization of this domain, and the arcs connecting the nodes represent generalization relations. To handle data containing calendar values specified to finer granularity (e.g., microseconds), more specific nodes could be added to the GL. A GL is specified for each attribute to be generalized.

Specification of a generalization relation is done using one of four techniques [11]: (1) granularity generalization for dropping in sequence the least significant subattribute, e.g., first drop *ss* and then *mm*; (2) subset generalization for dropping any combination of subattributes; (3) lookup generalization for explicitly specifying the mapping of values between the more specific and more general domains; and (4) algorithmic specification for all other cases.

3 Adaptation of Generalization Lattices

To guide the user quickly to the most interesting results, a GL can be manually and automatically pruned during the knowledge discovery process. Two automatic pruning techniques are: (1) based on a superficial examination of the data, the GL is pruned prior to generalization according to three heuristics, and (2) during generalization, if a step results in either no reduction in the number of values, or a complete reduction to one value, special processing is used. After all pruning is complete, the resulting GL can be displayed to guide the user to the generalizations of interest. In tasks involving multiple attributes, the method's first five steps can be applied independently to each attribute with a GL (see Sec. 4). In such cases, pruning would be particularly advantageous.

A GL for an attribute can be pruned in six steps, as follows.
Reachability Pruning: Once the user has specified how to map the data to a node in the GL, all nodes not reachable from this node are pruned.
Preliminary Manual Pruning: The user can hide any interior node regarded as uninteresting, and it is not subsequently displayed. To preserve the integrity of the GL for generalization, some hidden nodes are retained and used in the generalization process. The GL must not become disconnected. Any hidden node adjacent to "ANY" can be pruned and its incoming arcs can be directed to "ANY". Nodes with children may be pruned only if those children are still reachable afterwards.
Data-Range Pruning: Any node that does not correspond to a distinction in the data is removed. Some arcs in the GL represent monotonic functions mapping their domain (parent node data) to their range (child node data). Given a set of values A and some monotonic arc $E : A \rightarrow A_g$, we let $m = min(A)$,

$M = max(A)$, $E : m \to g$, and $E : M \to G$. Because E is monotonic, $\forall a \in A, E : a \to a_g, g \le a_g \le G$. For example, the range of data for a calendar attribute is determined by identifying its minimum and maximum values. These two values are generalized along all monotonic arcs, i.e., those permitting data range pruning. If these two values generalize to the same value at any node in the GL, then all occurring values for the calendar attribute generalize to this value, as described above. This node and all its descendants can be pruned, i.e., conceptually joined with the "ANY" node. Granularity generalizations are inherently monotonic, while algorithmic generalizations may or may not be.

Previous-Discard Pruning: Any node that is indistinguishable from another node except for information that data-range pruning has shown to be irrelevant is removed. This method is convenient for granularity and subset generalizations. If we are considering pruning node B, which is a generalization of node A, we look at what information is discarded when data is generalized from node A to node B. If we have already chosen to prune a node C that contains either exactly the subattributes or a superset of the subattributes that we are discarding when generalizing from node A to node B, then we should prune node B. Previous analysis has shown that at node C, the data will contain only a single value; thus, the information in node C does not distinguish any values. We do not automatically prune children of node B.

Pregeneralization-Manual Pruning: Again, the user is allowed to prune nodes from the GL. At this point, the time-consuming work of actually generalizing the data has not yet been done. Pruning nodes at this point may substantially reduce the time and space required to generalize the values.

Post-Generalization Pruning: The original data is now generalized step by step according to the GL, with each node corresponding to the data at that specified level of granularity and each arc corresponding to one transformation of the data. After each generalization step, we consider the number of values in the generalized data. If only one distinct value remains after the generalization step, then the corresponding node and any other interior node reachable from it can be pruned. Otherwise, if the number of values is the same before and after the step, then the data have been transformed by a one-to-one mapping rather than by a true generalizing, and we prune by conceptually joining the two nodes. This conceptual joining of nodes is transitive.

Example: We illustrate pruning for a calendar attribute. The input data are 8132 login times, collected over a one week period in January 1998: Jan 18 1998 00:26, Jan 18 1998 00:55, Jan 18 1998 01:21, ..., Jan 24 1998 23:48}. Times are not recorded to seconds.

Given this data and the (unshaded) GL shown in Figure 1, generalization and pruning proceeds as follows. First, the user identifies the initial node as *YYYYMMDDhhmm*. Reachability pruning (step 1) removes nodes *YYYYMMDDhhmmss*, *hhmmss*, and *ss*. We assume no preliminary manual pruning (step 2). For data range pruning (step 3), the minimum and maximum date values in the data are found to be **Jan 18 1998 00:26** and **Jan 25 1998 23:48**, respectively. These two dates are generalized by following all arcs allowing data range pruning (most arcs on the lower left of Figure 1). Both values generalize to the same value at *YYYYMM*. Node *YYYYMM* and all its children are pruned (the nodes in the upper left side of Figure 1). Previous-discard pruning (step 4), *DD* is pruned because *YYYYMM* has been pruned and generalization from *YYYYM-MDD* to *DD* is based on discarding *YYYYMM*. We assume no pregeneralization manual pruning (step 5). Finally, the data are generalized, guided by the pruned GL. After each generalization step, the result is checked for further pruning. For example, when the data are generalized from *YYYYMMDD* to *day# of year*, the number of values remains constant, indicating that results corresponding to only one of these nodes should be shown to the user. Thus, these nodes can be composed. Similarly, *YYYYMMDD* is also composed with *day of week*, and *weekday name*. When the data is generalized to *season, lunar month*, or *week# of year*, only one value remains; thus, all of these nodes are pruned.

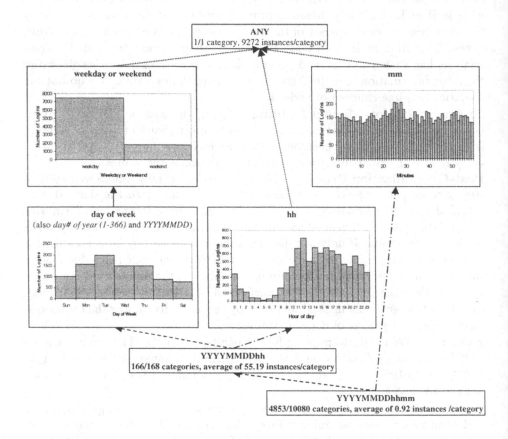

Fig. 2. Final Calendar GL

In Figure 2, we show the nodes remaining after pruning, enhanced where feasible with 2-D plots of the results. Each node gives a summary at a distinct level of temporal generality, e.g., the plot for node *hh* shows the number-of-logins vs hour-of-the-day. In our current implementation, each node is simply shown as a colored sphere, and the user must select it to obtain the detailed summary information shown in Figure 2.

4   Multi-Attribute Generalization

Given a set of attributes, each with an associated GL, we consider the generalization space formed by all combinations that include one node from each GL. Each combination represents a separate attribute-oriented induction task, where values for each attribute are independently generalized to the level of generality corresponding to the specified node in that attribute's lattice. In a naive implementation, each combination requires a complete pass over all input data, although by taking advantage of relationships in the GL, smaller intermediate results can be reused [10]. The size of the generalization space depends only on the number of nodes in the associated GLs; it does not depend on the number of tuples in the input relation. For m attributes, a database of n tuples, and an $O(n)$ generalization algorithm, creating all possible summaries requires $O(n \prod_{i=1}^{m} |D^i|)$ time, where $|D^i|$ is the number of nodes in GL D^i. We have implemented practical serial and parallel algorithms for traversing the generalization state space where m is small (≤ 5) and n is large ($> 1,000,000$) [6, 8].

Our approach to interactive data exploration includes visualizing the generalization space. A sample display from our web-based implementation is shown in Figure 3 for a data exploration task containing three attributes. GLs for three attributes are shown in the lower left, the generalization space is shown in the upper left, a plot of the interestingness versus the number of tuples in the generalized relation is shown in the lower right, and a generalized relation (i.e., summary in textual form) corresponding to one combination of nodes is shown in the upper right. The display of the generalization space is generated from a 3-D VRML (virtual reality modelling language) description, while the two lower panes are generated by Java applets.

Originally, the three GLs contained 4, 8, and 6 nodes; thus, the generalization space contained $4 \times 8 \times 6 = 192$ nodes, including the original relation. Manual pruning removed 1 node from the first GL and 2 nodes from the second GL, leaving $3 \times 6 \times 6 = 108$ nodes in the generalization space shown in Figure 3.

To identify summaries that a user might find most interesting, two measures are used to rank their interestingness: (1) *variance* compares the distribution defined by the tuples in a summary to that of a uniform distribution of the tuples, and (2) the *relative entropy measure* (Kullback-Leibler (KL) distance), which is also used for comparing data distributions in unstructured textual databases [4], compares the distribution defined by the structured tuples in a summary to that of a uniform distribution of the tuples. In Figure 3, more interesting nodes in the generalization space (upper left) are indicated by darker colors, while more interesting nodes in the scatterplot (lower right) are positioned to the right.

To reduce the number of summaries generated during data exploration, it is possible to prune the generalization space based on the interestingness measures.

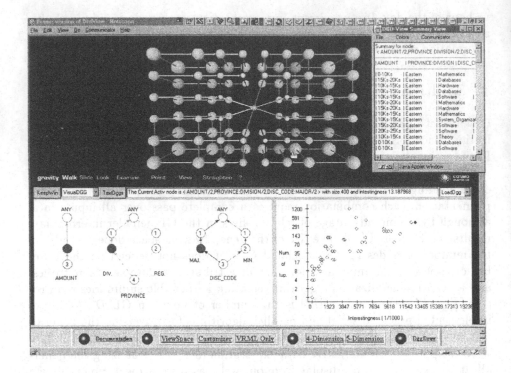

Fig. 3. GSS Display

We define five pruning heuristics as follows.

Ancestor Pruning: If a summary is a direct descendant of some other summary, but has higher interest, then the ancestor can be eliminated.

Descendant Pruning: If a summary is a direct descendant of a summary that has higher interest, then the descendant can be eliminated.

Interestingness Threshold Pruning: All summaries whose degree of interest is less than some user-specified interestingness threshold are deleted.

Table Threshold Pruning: All summaries containing more tuples than some user-specified table threshold are deleted, regardless of their degree of interest. This threshold is commonly used in attribute-oriented induction [2].

Attribute Threshold Pruning: All summaries containing an attribute where the number of distinct values for the attribute is greater than some user-specified attribute threshold, are deleted, regardless of their degree of interest. This threshold is also used extensively in attribute-oriented induction.

5   Conclusion

Generalization lattices allow users to specify the levels of granularity to consider when generalizing a dataset. We showed how pruning heuristics could be used to reduce the size of general-purpose generalization lattices for a specific set of data. We also showed how the number of combinations in the generalization space could be further pruned by a user, based on a chosen measure of interestingness or other attributes of the generalized relation. Our visual display gives a view of the overall space of possible generalizations. The user can interactively examine specific results and adjust the pruning heuristics.

Acknowledgement: We thank the reviewers for comments. This research was supported by the Natural Sciences and Engineering Research Council of Canada and the Institute for Robotics and Intelligent Systems.

References

1. I. Bournaud and J.-G. Ganascia. Accounting for domain knowledge in the construction of a generalization space. In *Proceedings of the Third International Conference on Conceptual Structures*, pages 446–459. Springer-Verlag, August 1997.
2. Y. Cai, N. Cercone, and J. Han. Attribute-oriented induction in relational databases. In G. Piatetsky-Shapiro and W. Frawley, editors, *Knowledge Discovery in Databases*, pages 213–228, Cambridge, MA, 1991. AAAI/MIT Press.
3. S. Chaudhuri and U. Dayal. OLAP and data warehousing. Technical report, AAAI, Newport Beach, CA, August 1997. Tutorial notes.
4. R. Feldman and I. Dagan. Knowledge discovery in textual databases (KDT). In *Proceedings of the First International Conference on Knowledge Discovery and Data Mining (KDD'95)*, pages 112–117, Montreal, August 1995.
5. R. Godin, R. Missaoui, and H. Alaoui. Incremental concept formation algorithms based on Galois (concept) lattices. *Computational Intelligence*, 11(2):246–267, 1995.
6. H.J. Hamilton, R.J. Hilderman, and N. Cercone. Attribute-oriented induction using domain generalization graphs. In *Proceedings of the Eighth IEEE International Conference on Tools with Artificial Intelligence (ICTAI'96)*, pages 246–253, Toulouse, France, November 1996.
7. V. Harinarayan, A. Rajaraman, and J.D. Ullman. Implementing data cubes efficiently. In *Proceedings of the ACM SIGMOD International Conference on Management of Data (SIGMOD'96)*, pages 205–216, May 1996.
8. R.J. Hilderman, H.J. Hamilton, R.J. Kowalchuk, and N. Cercone. Parallel knowledge discovery using domain generalization graphs. In J. Komorowski and J. Zytkow, editors, *Proceedings of the First European Conference on the Principles of Data Mining and Knowledge Discovery (PKDD'96)*, pages 25–35, Trondheim, Norway, June 1997.
9. G.M. Mineau and R. Godin. Automatic structuring of knowledge bases by conceptual clustering. *IEEE Transactions on Knowledge and Data Engineering*, 7(5):824–829, October 1995.
10. W. Pang, R.J. Hilderman, H.J. Hamilton, and S.D. Goodwin. Data mining with concept generalization graphs. In *Proceedings of the Ninth Annual Florida AI Research Symposium*, pages 390–394, Key West, Florida, May 1996.
11. D.J. Randall, H.J. Hamilton, and R.J. Hilderman. Generalization for calendar attributes using domain generalization graphs. In *Fifth International Workshop on Temporal Representation and Reasoning (TIME'98)*, pages 177–184, Sanibel Island, Florida, May 1998.
12. J.F. Sowa. *Conceptual Structures*. Addison-Wesley, Reading, MA, 1984.

Overcoming Fragmentation in Decision Trees Through Attribute Value Grouping

K. M. Ho and P. D. Scott

Department of Computer Science,
University of Essex,
Colchester, CO4 3SQ, UK
hokokx@essex.ac.uk and scotp@essex.ac.uk

Abstract. In this paper we investigate several methods for producing smaller decision trees by reducing fragmentation through the use of methods that lower the mean branching factor. All the methods considered achieve this goal by grouping the values that each attribute may take. We show how such grouping may be carried out by using either top-down iterative splitting or bottom-up iterative merging. Such methods may be applied either globally at the onset of tree construction or locally whenever a new node is considered. We also compare two approaches to assessing the quality of such attribute value groupings: information gain ratio, as employed in C4.5, and a combination of χ^2 and Cramer's V. The results of a comparative study of eight methods show that a top-down global method, using χ^2 and Cramer's V, produces consistently smaller tree sizes without loss of accuracy or computation time. These findings may be of considerable practical importance in data mining since it is widely recognised that smaller trees are much easier to understand.

1 Introduction

Decision tree induction ([1],[13]) has become firmly established as one of the most widely used data-mining techniques. Unfortunately experience with real world data sets has shown that existing methods may construct very large decision trees, that may be of limited practical utility. Any method for reducing the size of decision trees without sacrificing classification accuracy would be of considerable practical importance in mining large real world data sets.

In this paper we introduce and compare a number of techniques for restricting the size of decision trees by reducing their average branching factors. We begin, in Section 2, with a review of the origins of over-complexity in decision trees and existing methods for simplifying them. In particular we examine the problem of unnecessary fragmentation of the sample space that arises through forming distinct subtrees for every value of a nominal attribute. In the following section we examine several different approaches to grouping attribute values to reduce such fragmentation. Section 4 presents a series of experimental comparisons of eight alternative methods for grouping the values of nominal attributes. Seven of these are novel, while the eighth is the method provided as an option in C4.5 [13]. We conclude that a top-down global method is the most effective technique for reducing fragmentation in decision trees.

2 Controlling Decision Tree Size

One important advantage of using decision tree techniques is that this form of classification function can be easily understood, provided that the tree produced is reasonably small. In recent years, because of the rapidly rising interest in data mining, these techniques have been used with ever larger sets of training data. Unfortunately large training sets may lead to large decision trees containing many thousands of nodes. Oates and Jensen [11] have presented evidence that tree size often increases linearly with training set size. Large trees may prove excellent classifiers but they are so difficult to comprehend that they provide little useable information about the patterns that exist in the data. Developing methods of producing smaller decision trees without sacrificing classification accuracy is therefore an important research problem whose solution will have widespread practical application.

The size of a decision tree, defined as the number of nodes it contains, will depend on both the maximum depth and the mean branching factor of its nodes. It follows that if we are to develop decision tree construction techniques that produce smaller trees we must use one or both of two possible approaches:

1. Restrict the maximum depth of the tree and its subtrees.
2. Restrict the branching factor of the non-terminal nodes.

Each of these approaches could be applied either *a priori* or *a posteriori*. An *a priori* restriction is applied to constrain or eliminate a portion of the tree before it has been built, whereas an *a posteriori* restriction is used to remove a portion of the tree that has already been constructed. Depth restriction is often known as *pruning*.

2.1 Overfitting and Pruning

One important cause of excessive decision tree size is overfitting. It manifests itself in decision tree construction as excessively deep trees. It can be limited by restricting the depth to which the tree is allowed to grow, but the use of stopping criterion, sometimes called *pre-pruning*, may be ineffective in detecting when the procedure has begun to model characteristics peculiar to the sample [4]. Consequently the majority of researchers (e.g. [13]) favour some form of *post-pruning* in which apparently useless subtrees are removed from a complete decision tree. Breslow and Aha [2] have provided a comprehensive review of a wide range of pruning techniques.

In principle therefore, effective pruning is a technique for reducing tree size, without sacrificing classification accuracy, by eliminating those parts of the original tree that arise through overfitting. In practice, pruning is used extensively even at a small cost in accuracy because of the greater accessibility of smaller trees.

2.2 Fragmentation and Attribute Value Grouping

Overfitting leads to decision trees that are too deep. In contrast, a *fragmentation* occurs when a decision tree is too broad: that is, when nodes have more branches than would be necessary to produce the best possible classification accuracy. The following simple example shows how fragmentation is likely to arise frequently with the majority of decision tree construction procedures.

Suppose a decision tree program attempts to build a tree to recognise some class, C, using a training set made up of feature vectors of nominal attributes $A_1, A_2, ..A_k$. Suppose also that the class C is in fact defined thus:

$$C = V_{2,1} \land (V_{5,2} \lor V_{5,4}) \land V_{8,3}$$

where $V_{i,j}$ denotes that attribute A_i takes its jth value. When a typical decision tree program selects an attribute to construct a new node it will create a separate branch for each of the possible values for that attribute. Thus, assuming as an example that each attribute has four possible values, if the program selects attributes in the order A_5, A_2, A_8 it will construct a tree like that shown on the left of Figure 1. The entire subtree associated with $V_{5,2}$ is repeated

$V_{5,1} \cdots$ NO
$V_{5,2}$
$\qquad V_{2,1}$
$\qquad\qquad V_{8,1} \cdots$ NO
$\qquad\qquad V_{8,2} \cdots$ NO
$\qquad\qquad V_{8,3} \cdots$ YES
$\qquad\qquad V_{8,4} \cdots$ NO
$\qquad V_{2,2} \cdots$ NO
$\qquad V_{2,3} \cdots$ NO
$\qquad V_{2,4} \cdots$ NO
$V_{5,3} \cdots$ NO
$V_{5,4}$
$\qquad V_{2,1}$
$\qquad\qquad V_{8,1} \cdots$ NO
$\qquad\qquad V_{8,2} \cdots$ NO
$\qquad\qquad V_{8,3} \cdots$ YES
$\qquad\qquad V_{8,4} \cdots$ NO
$\qquad V_{2,2} \cdots$ NO
$\qquad V_{2,3} \cdots$ NO
$\qquad V_{2,4} \cdots$ NO

$V_{5,1}$ or $V_{5,3} \cdots$ NO
$V_{5,2}$ or $V_{5,4}$
$\qquad V_{2,1}$
$\qquad\qquad V_{8,1}$ or $V_{8,2}$ or $V_{8,4} \cdots$ NO
$\qquad\qquad V_{8,3} \cdots$ YES
$\qquad V_{2,2}$ or $V_{2,3}$ or $V_{2,4} \cdots$ NO

Fig. 1. Alternative decision trees for an example discussed in the text. Left: Without attribute value grouping. Right: With attribute value grouping

in node $V_{5,4}$. This immediately suggests that a much simpler tree could be constructed if the values of attributes could be grouped and then branches created for each group of values rather than for each value. Such a tree is shown on the right of Figure 1.

It is immediately obvious both that the tree without attribute value grouping is considerably larger and exhibits significant fragmentation in that it partitions the example space into 16 regions. In contrast the tree incorporating attribute grouping would produce identical classifications but only divides the example space into 4 regions. Clearly such fragmentation can have a major effect on tree size. In addition it may impair the classification accuracy of the resultant decision tree because the set of training examples must be distributed across more subtrees and hence will provide proportionally less reliable evidence for each.

Pruning will not help to solve this problem: removing any part of the larger tree will seriously affect its classification accuracy. The obvious remedy would be for the program to consider all possible groupings of an attribute's values when searching for the best attribute for a new node, and hence avoid producing more branches than necessary. Unfortunately the number of possible groupings rises very rapidly with the number of values an attribute can take, and hence exhaustive consideration of all groupings is often infeasible.

One solution to this difficulty is to restrict the number of groups. The original CLS program [8] always divided the attribute values into two groups; one containing only the best value and the other containing all the rest. Both CART [1] and Assistant-86 [3] also produce binary trees but permit several values in each group. Fayyad and Irani [6] have produced evidence that such binary groupings are likely to lead to smaller trees than k-way trees, but Kononenko [10] has produced a counter example to the stronger version of this hypothesis. Quinlan has adopted a different approach in C4.5 [13]. If the $-s$ option is selected then the program will search for the best grouping of an attribute's values using a form of agglomerative hierarchical clustering [5]. Such methods are essentially bottom-up hill-climbing procedures in which groups are repeatedly merged. C4.5 continues the process until any further merging would lead to significant degradation of gain ratio.

3 Approaches to Attribute Value Grouping

The development of attribute value grouping procedures to combat fragmentation appears to have attracted much less interest than the problem of devising pruning methods to combat overfitting. There is therefore considerable scope for research work whose goal is to develop alternative grouping procedures and establish how effective they are in decision tree construction.

3.1 Local or Global Groupings

All of the methods referred to in the previous section perform attribute grouping *locally*. They search for the best groupings of each attribute's values every time they select the best attribute for a proposed new node. Although such local groupings can be more finely tuned to the local region of the example space, this approach suffers from two disadvantages: it is potentially costly since the grouping operation is performed many times, and many of the groupings will be based on small samples and hence may not reflect the characteristics of the parent population. We therefore decided to investigate the possibility of developing procedures that carried out attribute value grouping *globally*. Such procedures partition each attribute's values once only, before tree construction begins, using the entire training sample.

Those methods that form only two groups of attribute values are not suitable for global grouping, since they would not be able to form three or more groups under any circumstances. This problem does not arise when they are applied locally since the same attribute may be subject to several successive groupings. Our investigations have therefore concentrated on methods that can partition a k-valued attribute into any number up to k groups.

3.2 Bottom-Up or Top-Down Grouping

As we noted above, C4.5 includes an option that evokes attribute value grouping using a hill-climbing bottom-up method applied locally. This suggests the possibility of a top-down approach that carries out repeated splitting. One such procedure would operate as follows:

1. Create an $m \times n$ table, where m is the number of class labels and n is the number of possible values of the attribute. Let cell$[i, j]$ of the table contain the number of training examples in class i that had the jth attribute value.
2. Identify the modal class for each column and form groups of columns that share the same modal class. There will be at most m such column groups.
3. Apply binary splitting repeatedly to each of these column groups until a point is reached at which either no more splitting is possible or no split satisfies some criterion function (discussed below).

3.3 Group Formation Criteria

Top down methods require a criterion to determine whether splitting a group is worthwhile; bottom-up methods need one to decide whether a pair of groups should be merged. In either case we require a function which will allow us to compare the quality of the representation with and without a particular grouping transformation.

The $-s$ option of C4.5 [13] uses the information gain ratio both to select the best grouping and to determine the point at which merging should stop. In earlier work, Quinlan [12] experimented with χ^2 as a stopping criterion for tree construction but abandoned it because of uneven results. We have had similar experiences using χ^2 as a grouping criterion: we encountered difficulties in setting thresholds that were appropriate for both large and small sets of training data.

This difficulty is not particularly surprising. The χ^2 test measures the statistical significance of an association between two variables, not its strength. Even the weakest association will appear significant in a large enough data set. We therefore experimented with Cramer's V, a standard statistical measure of the strength of association between two nominal variables [7], defined as:

$$Cramer'sV = \sqrt{\frac{\chi^2}{N(L-1)}} \qquad (1)$$

where L is the smaller of the number of rows and columns in 2-way table plotting values of one variable against those of the other.

Our initial experiments with Cramer's V also led to uneven results. This again is unsurprising. Cramer's V tells us whether a relationship is weak or strong if present but not whether there is sufficient evidence to conclude it exists. We therefore decided to use a criterion based on both χ^2 and Cramer's V: the former establishes that an apparent association exists while the latter determines if it is strong enough to be of any interest. As the results reported below show, this combination proved very satisfactory when we used a threshold of $p = 0.01$ for the χ^2 test, and 0.1 for Cramer's V.

	Data Sets	Cases	Classes	2	3	4-5	6-10	11-20	> 20
ad	adult	32562	2	2	1	1	5	3	1
b5	bhps5000	10265	2	3	15	16	59	17	0
b8	bhps8000	10265	2	3	16	16	58	17	0
sm	bhpssmoker	10265	2	6	17	13	57	17	0
bc	breast-cancer	286	2	3	2	0	2	2	0
bs	balance-scale	625	3	0	0	4	0	0	0
dna	DNA-nominal	3186	3	0	0	60	0	0	0
sp	splice	3190	3	0	0	0	60	0	0
car	car	1728	4	0	3	3	0	0	0
nur	nursery	12961	5	1	4	3	0	0	0
soy	soybean-large	683	19	15	14	5	1	0	0

Table 1. Characteristics of the data sets used in evaluations. The columns labelled with numbers indicate the number of values the nominal attributes could take.

3.4 Eight Procedures for Grouping Attribute Values

In this section we have seen that grouping procedures can be used locally or globally, can use a top-down or bottom-up strategy, and can employ either information gain ratio or χ^2 plus Cramer's V as the grouping criterion. Taken together the various combinations define eight distinct methods for attribute grouping. We will use a simple notation to name these in which TD-CC-G denotes a globally applied top-down method using χ^2 plus Cramer's V as its grouping criterion, while BU-IG-L denotes a locally applied bottom-up method using information gain ratio as grouping criterion.

4 An Experimental Comparison

In order to compare all eight attribute value grouping procedures we compared their performance on eleven data sets. Eight of these are well known and were taken from the UCI Repository. Because we wanted to investigate how the grouping procedures would perform using data sets that had a large number of nominal attributes, we created three more data sets using data from the 1991 wave of BHPS [1] , a large social science survey carried out annually in the UK. In $b5$ and $b8$ the variable to be predicted is income below 5K and below 8K respectively; in sm it indicates whether or not the respondent smokes. All continuous attributes are pre-discretized into categorical groups, therefore, all procedures receive the data as nominal (or discretized) attributes.

We used C4.5 (Release 8 [13],[14]) without the $-s$ attribute grouping option to provide a control, while setting the $-s$ flag provided the BU-IG-L method. The remaining seven methods were implemented by modifying the C4.5 code with different grouping procedures. The code to run the experiments and the generation of training and test datasets were taken from the MLC++ library [9].

Table 2 shows the mean classification accuracies obtained for all nine programs with each data set, while Table 3 shows the mean size of the trees constructed. Limitations of space

	C4.5	Local							
	k-way	BU-IG-L		BU-CC-L		TD-IG-L		TD-CC-L	
	accuracy	accuracy	ratio	accuracy	ratio	accuracy	ratio	accuracy	ratio
ad	86.02 ± 0.33	86.24 ± 0.22	1.00	86.18 ± 0.29	1.00	83.08 ± 0.56	0.97	82.90 ± 0.53	0.96
b5	83.51 ± 0.31	80.87 ± 0.46	0.97	82.38 ± 0.35	0.99	79.13 ± 0.52	0.95	81.39 ± 0.16	0.97
b8	85.06 ± 0.38	82.53 ± 0.27	0.97	83.60 ± 0.69	0.98	77.94 ± 3.60	0.92	83.11 ± 0.58	0.98
sm	72.60 ± 0.47	67.63 ± 0.48	0.93	71.96 ± 0.44	0.99	67.88 ± 1.74	0.93	71.64 ± 0.25	0.99
bc	71.00 ± 2.25	68.20 ± 2.38	0.96	70.65 ± 2.83	1.00	65.75 ± 2.92	0.93	71.00 ± 2.91	1.00
bs	65.12 ± 0.60	76.80 ± 1.36	1.18	65.12 ± 0.60	1.00	69.28 ± 3.00	1.06	77.92 ± 1.18	1.20
dna	93.72 ± 0.72	93.70 ± 0.91	1.00	92.72 ± 0.91	0.99	93.44 ± 0.58	1.00	93.75 ± 0.56	1.00
sp	93.95 ± 0.34	93.92 ± 0.34	1.00	94.01 ± 0.06	1.00	94.20 ± 0.55	1.00	93.73 ± 0.24	1.00
car	90.34 ± 0.31	97.05 ± 0.49	1.07	95.78 ± 0.49	1.06	90.05 ± 2.65	1.00	95.25 ± 0.40	1.05
nur	96.45 ± 0.18	99.41 ± 0.05	1.03	99.54 ± 0.07	1.03	90.17 ± 2.13	0.93	98.07 ± 0.10	1.02
soy	88.28 ± 1.98	89.17 ± 1.17	1.01	89.46 ± 1.55	1.01	82.13 ± 2.50	0.93	89.16 ± 1.39	1.01
ave	84.19	85.05	1.01	84.67	1.00	81.19	0.97	85.27	1.02
	C4.5	Global							
	k-way	BU-IG-G		BU-CC-G		TD-IG-G		TD-CC-G	
	accuracy	accuracy	ratio	accuracy	ratio	accuracy	ratio	accuracy	ratio
ad	86.02 ± 0.33	81.64 ± 0.81	0.95	86.08 ± 0.32	1.00	84.08 ± 0.28	0.98	85.32 ± 0.30	0.99
b5	83.51 ± 0.31	83.02 ± 0.30	0.99	82.37 ± 0.36	0.99	77.60 ± 1.76	0.93	83.42 ± 0.22	1.00
b8	85.06 ± 0.38	68.50 ± 4.28	0.81	83.60 ± 0.69	0.98	79.60 ± 0.42	0.94	84.68 ± 0.76	1.00
sm	72.60 ± 0.47	72.31 ± 0.17	1.00	71.96 ± 0.44	0.99	69.93 ± 0.66	0.96	73.89 ± 0.36	1.02
bc	71.00 ± 2.25	72.04 ± 1.76	1.01	71.34 ± 2.65	1.00	72.75 ± 2.43	1.02	70.29 ± 1.79	0.99
bs	65.12 ± 0.60	67.36 ± 1.88	1.03	68.32 ± 1.80	1.05	74.24 ± 2.01	1.14	77.76 ± 2.11	1.19
dna	93.72 ± 0.72	94.22 ± 0.55	1.01	94.38 ± 0.36	1.01	93.88 ± 0.58	1.00	94.54 ± 0.60	1.01
sp	93.95 ± 0.34	93.92 ± 0.34	1.00	94.04 ± 0.37	1.00	93.67 ± 0.51	1.00	94.80 ± 0.35	1.01
car	90.34 ± 0.31	85.82 ± 0.42	0.95	94.44 ± 0.77	1.05	87.10 ± 1.71	0.96	92.42 ± 0.89	1.02
nur	96.45 ± 0.18	86.92 ± 0.17	0.90	97.64 ± 0.12	1.01	92.32 ± 0.30	0.96	97.90 ± 0.12	1.02
soy	88.28 ± 1.98	89.90 ± 1.42	1.02	88.28 ± 1.98	1.00	88.72 ± 1.90	1.00	88.87 ± 2.06	1.01
ave	84.19	81.42	0.97	84.77	1.01	83.08	0.99	85.81	1.02

Table 2. Classification accuracies of decision trees produced using alternative methods for grouping attribute values. The columns labelled *accuracy* are the mean and standard deviation for 5 cross-validation runs. The columns labelled *ratio* are the ratio of the respective accuracies over the control, $k - way$ method.

preclude the inclusion of timing data, but as might be expected, the local methods were generally slower.

---

[1] BHPS data may be obtained from Data Archive, University of Essex, Colchester, CO4 3SQ, UK.

5   Discussion

As can be seen, the four local methods were not consistently more accurate than the control, $k - way$, but three of the four global methods were generally less accurate. The exception was TD-CC-G whose accuracy was very close to that of the control for all data sets except bs for which it performed significantly better. On the other hand the global methods usually produced considerably smaller trees than either local methods or the control. Indeed in three of the four cases they appeared to be grouping too much with a consequent loss of accuracy.

	C4.5	Local							
	k-way	BU-IG-L		BU-CC-L		TD-IG-L		TD-CC-L	
	nodes	nodes	ratio	nodes	ratio	nodes	ratio	nodes	ratio
ad	548 ± 49	706 ± 12	1.29	553 ± 20	1.01	112 ± 22	0.20	99 ± 17	0.18
b5	1051 ± 49	1204 ± 48	1.15	1133 ± 137	1.08	949 ± 60	0.90	849 ± 33	0.81
b8	789 ± 69	1144 ± 29	1.45	1123 ± 20	1.42	542 ± 270	0.69	850 ± 50	1.08
sm	1790 ± 73	2294 ± 67	1.28	1968 ± 199	1.10	676 ± 115	0.38	996 ± 25	0.56
bc	11 ± 4	29 ± 5	2.64	22 ± 3	2.00	27 ± 5	2.45	24 ± 2	2.18
bs	35 ± 2	63 ± 4	1.80	83 ± 8	2.37	55 ± 7	1.57	63 ± 4	1.80
dna	162 ± 4	121 ± 1	0.75	153 ± 4	0.94	145 ± 9	0.90	139 ± 6	0.86
sp	314 ± 5	170 ± 4	0.54	189 ± 10	0.60	152 ± 3	0.48	118 ± 3	0.38
car	152 ± 2	103 ± 3	0.68	103 ± 1	0.68	84 ± 5	0.55	70 ± 2	0.46
nur	466 ± 11	310 ± 4	0.67	291 ± 1	0.62	241 ± 17	0.52	207 ± 3	0.44
soy	86 ± 1	89 ± 4	1.03	98 ± 3	1.14	90 ± 3	1.05	81 ± 1	0.94
ave	491	567	1.21	520	1.18	279	0.88	318	0.88
	C4.5	Global							
	k-way	BU-IG-G		BU-CC-G		TD-IG-G		TD-CC-G	
	nodes	nodes	ratio	nodes	ratio	nodes	ratio	nodes	ratio
ad	548 ± 49	25 ± 1	0.05	238 ± 3	0.43	33 ± 2	0.06	100 ± 4	0.18
b5	1051 ± 49	259 ± 10	0.25	1180 ± 33	1.12	896 ± 31	0.85	978 ± 55	0.93
b8	789 ± 69	190 ± 13	0.24	943 ± 6	1.20	966 ± 70	1.22	691 ± 27	0.88
sm	1790 ± 73	1067 ± 59	0.60	1663 ± 123	0.93	2090 ± 63	1.17	167 ± 27	0.09
bc	11 ± 4	10 ± 2	0.91	10 ± 2	0.91	6 ± 0	0.55	6 ± 0	0.55
bs	35 ± 2	12 ± 0	0.34	47 ± 1	1.34	14 ± 1	0.40	36 ± 5	1.03
dna	162 ± 4	114 ± 3	0.70	134 ± 2	0.83	121 ± 2	0.75	117 ± 12	0.72
sp	314 ± 5	170 ± 4	0.54	183 ± 3	0.58	143 ± 3	0.46	140 ± 5	0.45
car	152 ± 2	23 ± 1	0.15	56 ± 1	0.37	30 ± 2	0.20	38 ± 3	0.25
nur	466 ± 11	30 ± 1	0.06	318 ± 15	0.68	80 ± 2	0.17	249 ± 12	0.53
soy	86 ± 1	69 ± 1	0.80	86 ± 1	1.00	91 ± 1	1.06	89 ± 1	1.03
ave	491	179	0.42	442	0.85	406	0.63	237	0.60

Table 3. Number of nodes in classification trees produced using alternative methods for grouping attribute values. The columns labelled *nodes* indicate the mean and standard deviation for 5 cross-validation runs. The columns labelled *ratio* indicate the ratio of the respective number of nodes over the control, $k - way$ method.

Again the exception was TD-CC-G, which was, rather surprisingly, not only more accurate but also more consistent in producing small trees. In some cases the local methods actually produced trees that were significantly larger than those generated by the control method.

The story concerning bottom-up and top-down methods is more muddled. Similarly neither Information Gain Ratio nor χ^2 plus Cramer's V showed a consistent advantage over the other.

Nevertheless it is possible to draw at least one firm and useful conclusion from these results. Of all those tested, TD-CC-G would appear to be the best method for reducing fragmentation in decision tree construction. It achieves the higher-end of the predictive accuracy compared while producing markedly smaller tree sizes. Fortunately it also required less computation time than any other method for all but one of the data sets.

Acknowledgements

We are grateful to the ESRC's programme on the ALCD for supporting part of the work reported in this paper under grant number H519255030.

References

1. L. Breiman, J. H. Friedman, R. A. Olshen, and C. J. Stone. *Classification and Regression Trees.* Wadsworth, Pacific Grove, CA., 1984.
2. L. A. Breslow and D. W. Aha. Simplifying Decision Trees: A Survey. *Knowledge Engineering Review*, 12:1–40, 1997.
3. B. Cestnik, I. Konoenko, and I. Bratko. A knowledge elicitation tool for sophisticated users. In I. Bratko and N. Lavrac, editors, *Progress in Machine Learning*. Sigma Press, Wilmslow, England, 1987.
4. P. R. Cohen and D. Jensen. Overfitting Explained. In *Proc. Sixth International Workshop on Artificial Intelligence and Statistics*, pages 115–122, FL, 1997. Ft. Lauderdale.
5. B. S. Everitt. *Cluster Analysis.* Heinemann, London, 2nd edition, 1980.
6. U. M. Fayyad and K. B. Irani. The attribute selection problem in decision tree generation. In *Proc. Tenth National Conference on Artificial Intelligence*, pages 104–110, San Jose, CA., 1992. AAAI Press.
7. J. Healey. *Statistics: A Tool For Social Research.* Wadsworth, Belmont, CA., 1990.
8. E. Hunt, J. Martin, and P. Stone. *Experiments in Induction.* Academic Press, New York, 1966.
9. R. Kohavi, G. John, D. Manley, and K. Pfleger. MLC++: Amachine learning library in C++. In *Tools with Artificial Intelligence*, pages 740–743. IEEE Computer Society Press, 1994.
10. I. Kononenko. A counter example to the stronger version of the binary tree hypothesis. In *ECML-95 Workshop on Statistics and Machine Learning in KDD*, Crete, 1995.
11. T. Oates and D. Jensen. The Effects of Training Set Size on Decision Tree Complexity. In *The Preliminary Papers of the Sixth International Workshop on Artificial Intelligence and Statistics*, pages 379–390, 1997.
12. J. R. Quinlan. The effect of noise on concept learning. In R.S.Michalski, J.G.Carbonell, and T.M. Mitchell, editors, *Machine Learning: An Artificial Intelligence Approach. Volume II.* Morgan Kaufman Publ. Inc., Los Altos, CA, 1986.
13. J. R. Quinlan. *Programs for Machine Learning.* Morgan Kaufman Publ. Inc., Los Altos, CA, 1993.
14. J. R. Quinlan. Improved use of continuous attributes in c4.5. *Journal of Artificial Intelligence Research*, 4:77–90, 1996.

Data Mining at a Major Bank: Lessons from a Large Marketing Application

Petra Hunziker, Andreas Maier, Alex Nippe, Markus Tresch, Douglas Weers, and Peter Zemp

Credit Suisse
P.O. Box, CH–8070 Zurich
Switzerland

e-mail contact: peter.zemp@credit–suisse.ch

Abstract. This paper summarizes experiences and results of productively using knowledge discovery and data mining technology in a large retail bank. We present data mining as part of a greater effort to develop and deploy an integrated IT-infrastructure for loyalty based customer management, combining data warehousing, and campaign management together with data mining technology. We have completed a first campaign where potential customers were selected using the new built data warehouse together with data mining. Because of the better insight we have used a decision tree as selection method.

1 Introduction

Recent developments of technology, like for example storage management or the Internet, have made it very easy and cheap to collect tera bytes of data and make them on-line accessible in very large databases. However, these valuable assets are still not comprehensively and systematically exploited as part of daily business processes.

The growing competition, the increased speed of business changes and developments of new businesses has dramatically shown the need for knowledge about data and domain-spanning quantitative data analysis. Today, understanding a small detail in data or understanding data faster can make a difference and improve productivity.

This paper summarizes experiences and results at Credit Suisse, a large Swiss retail bank, in developing and deploying knowledge discovery and data mining technology, applications, and solutions. We intentionally don't consider the technology stand-alone (i.e., for the sake of its beauty), but present it as part of a greater effort to develop and deploy in a very short time an integrated IT-infrastructure based on data mining. Notice that we furthermore don't present theoretical experiences with data mining technology, but experiences in actually using it as part of a productive system.

From a business point of view, the general goal of the project is to establish loyalty based customer management (LBM), that is,

- to strengthen customer acquisition by direct marketing and establish multi-channel contacts,
- to improve customer development by cross selling and up selling of products, and
- to increase customer retention by behaviour management.

The paper is organized as follows: In Section 2, we present the project architecture and show how data mining fits as one piece of technology into a whole system for marketing campaign management. In Section 3, we discuss experiences in integrating data mining in business processes. Chapter 4 draws conclusions for the future.

1.1 LBM Project and Architecture

From a technical point of view, the goal of the LBM project is to set up an IT infrastructure bringing together data warehousing, data mining, campaign management and online analytical processing (OLAP) technologies. In a first release, the infrastructure will be able to run direct marketing campaigns. The difference to traditional marketing campaigns is that data mining is used for customer selection to find likely targets [2].

The LBM technical architecture is shown in Figure 1. Its major components are operational and external data sources (feeder systems), a comprehensive data staging system (extraction, transformation, cleansing, and integration), the central data repository (warehouse), and the data mining, campaign management, and OLAP systems with their own data stores. It is important to see that the project works only if all pieces - warehouse, mining and campaign - work together.

Logically, the data flow is driven by the target campaign to be launched. Hence, the first step is to define the campaign (1) and identify the data required (2). Data from several operational systems is loaded, including customer, product, transaction, and business structure data, as well as customer profitability data. External data complements the repository with information about credit worthiness.

Getting consistent and high quality data is important, therefore data used by all LBM parts is extracted from operational and external sources (3) and feed into the repository (4). Usually, this extraction will be a repetitive, incremental process. A major task of the cleansing is to create a subject-oriented customer view, which requires de-duplication and merge of data records from the same customer. Cleansing creates added value, for example, information about who shares the same household, which is not contained in the operational systems.

Now the data mining model is built (5) and customer data records are scored. The campaign management system selects data records based on these scores (6) to run the campaign (7). The result and evaluation of the campaign flows back

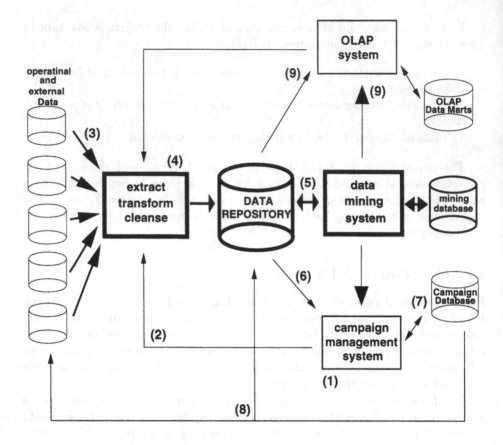

Fig. 1. The overall LBM system architecture

into the data repository and operational systems (8). Alternatively, an OLAP system supports ad-hoc and prepared data analysis and reporting (9) based on scored data.

Notice that this architecture is highly dynamic. The launch of a new campaign or the request of a new analysis may require inclusion of new feeder systems and hence the extension of the data repository.

The LBM infrastructure was set up in a record time of only two months. We defined a pilot campaign as driving force for the system development. In addition to the modeling process the whole environment had to be set up. The infrastructure is based on a Sun Microsystems Enterprise Server 10000 symmetric parallel processor running an 8 CPU license of the data mining suite Darwin from Thinking Machines Corporation. An Oracle 8 relational database is used as the data repository. The campaign management software is Vantage from Prime Response.

2 Data Mining Experiences and Results

The following steps can be distinguished in the mining process:

- data extraction
- construction of target variables
- data set building
- simple statistics, distributions
- initial modeling
- refined modeling.

The first four steps are a major part of the work and can take up to 80% of the whole time used for mining. It is important that one has a lot of different cross checks to be sure about the quality and correctness of the data. The different items are now explained in more detail.

The data is extracted from several tables of the warehouse using SQL statements and joining them into one big flat file to be used by the mining tool. Depending on the business requirements, aggregations of variables are computed. Data preparation turned out to be particularly cumbersome and time consuming, due to the lack of tool support to deal with the 100 GB warehouse data.

The target variable is constructed from the extracted fields. The target typically indicates whether a customer owns a certain product or not (yet). The purpose of data mining is to find a model, predicting potential customers of a product, depending on the information on customers actually having the product.

Four data sets have to be constructed to build the model: three balanced data sets for training, testing and evaluating the model, and one unbalanced set for the validation process. Balancing data sets means having the same number of records for each target value. This is necessary since there is a large discrepancy between targets (customers owning the product) and non–targets (customers not owning the product). The amount of targets can be as low as only 1% of the records. Nevertheless, all balanced data sets must still have reasonable size (more than 10'000 records) to guarantee statistical significance, which obviously requires a huge amount of data.

The analysis starts with simple statistics of single variables (e.g., mean, std. deviation). Analysis is then extended to pairs of variables, in order to detect correlation. One of the variables is typically the target field. There is a tradeoff in the use of variables appearing with a high correlation to the target variable. On the one hand, they are suited for building the mining model. On the other hand, an information leaker might be found that need to be excluded, because it is likely to produce bad models. The only way to solve this problem is a first interaction with business people, discussing the meaning of the high correlation.

Then the modeling process starts. A straightforward way is to build a decision tree with all non information leaking variables. The data mining suite DARWIN uses a parallelized implementation of the CART algorithm [1].

Decision trees have the advantage (in contract for example to artificial neural networks) of being able to show understandable rules as well as getting a quick overview of the quality of the model. Evaluation is required on how well the model selects target fields and how many of them are selected. Good rules show almost no error in classifying the target and are at the same time applicable to a large number of records. An optimum of lift, coverage and error rate has to be chosen. Notice however, that maximum lift decides which model to use and not minimal global error. We used the false positive assessment method in addition.

Decision tree building and evaluation can well be parallelized, which is a big advantage. There are quick turnover times such that multiple alternatives mining models can be built and assessed.

Then, choosing different input parameters and fields refines the model. For example, only a subrange of a field may be used as input to the tree building, due to noisy data or outliers. Other data transformations, for example from continuos into some few discrete values or introducing derived variables, have a high influence on the quality of the data mining.

Subsequent pruning of the decision tree is quite standard. However, the traditional cost complexity pruning method didn't show convincing improvements, because it simply considers the global error rate of a subtree. Alternatively, we are using lift based pruning. This method determines the lift of each node and step–by–step cuts the subtrees of the node with the highest lift. With this method, those rules are optimized that really predict the target. As usual, models are verified with validation data sets.

Due to lack of time, the good understanding of the data needed and the necessity of tractability and explanation of proposed decisions to business experts, no neural network model was deployed to production so far. As soon as one gets more experience with our data and with business requirements we will start using in addition other methods (like neural networks or nearest neighbour) in production models.

During the model building process we have developed around 50 to 60 models. The time consuming factor was not the computing time but the time we needed to understand the results and to discuss the next steps with business experts. Such discussions are crucial because metadata knowledge is often not written down or even available in the warehouse.

For our first campaign we used a data sample of about 1.1×10^6 records (corresponding to about the same number of customers) and around 150 fields. The density of the target was about 13%. After splitting the data into the different sets we obtained a training set of about 80'000 records (40'000 targets). From this roughly 40 field where excluded during data cleaning or we found out during the discussions with business experts that they where information leakers.

In the end we had around 8'000 false positives, these means customers who do not have the product but for which the model predicts that they have the profile of a potential customer.

In the future, mining agents will take over real-time relationship discovery and scoring of data and will produce (email) messages for the customer advisor. For this purpose, mining models will be turned into C++ code, compiled, and deployed to the computers of the customer advisor's desk. Hence, data mining tools need to be open. It must be possible to export scripts and program code, and deploy it to other machines.

For our first campaigns we loaded back the scores into the data warehouse. The scores are based on the accuracy of the model. Finally the campaign was started using the scored records of the customers.

3 Conclusion and Outlook

Time seems to be right for data mining. The technology is available, namely affordable parallel computers, cheap storage technology, and fast pattern finding algorithms. The data is available in huge enterprise–wide data warehouses. The business need is there, as a consequence of increasing competition.

Data mining is not a stand-alone technology, but can be an important piece in many business processes. Hence, a real challenge is to make it work together with other components, like the warehouse, OLAP, and campaign management system. Managing all these dependencies and interfaces, in a short time of only two months, was a real challenge. A large effort was required to extract the data from the warehouse and turn it in a format to be used by the data mining.

Permanent interaction with business case leaders is important. It is crucial that the business supports the idea. They must understand what data mining can do for them and what it can't (the right expectations). The results of the data mining have to be explained to business. In depth discussions and presentation using visualization of the results is a good approach.

One relies on close contacts to the people that acquired the data in the past. Input and feedback from data owners is crucial. They must explain the data and comment for meaningful relationships and information leakers. The data sets we analyzed had hundreds of poorly documented variables from different OLTP systems. Data mining can not be done without a business question in mind. However, the combination of exploratory and confirmative knowledge discovery turned out to be very promising. Whereas business users provide a hypothesis to be confirmed by data mining, data miners can complement by newly discovered relationships. The support of iterative knowledge discovery (model building, model assessment, model refinement, ...) by the data mining tool is crucial.

Data mining tools of today are still too much of a bare-bone technology. More efforts should be made to integrate the technology in a comprehensive knowledge discovery method [3], providing better guidelines to miners.

In this paper, we focused on application of data mining for marketing campaigns, which is one of the most useful and promising applications [4]. However, due to the growing competition in retail banking, at Credit Suisse we see many more potential application areas, like for example risk management, credit fraud detection, or cross–selling of all–finance products [5] (mortgages together with life insurance).

Acknowledgements

We are grateful to M.Beddows and P. Ossadnik for elucidating discussions.

References

1. Breimann L., Friedman J.H., Olshen R.A. and Stone C.J.: Classification and Regression Trees. Monterey, CA, Wadsworth (1984)
2. Berry M. and Linoff G.: Data Mining Techniques for Marketing, Sales and Customer Support. John Wiley & Sons (1997)
3. Fayyad U., Piatetsky–Shapiro G, Smyth P., Uthurusamy R., editors: Advances in Knowledge Discovery and Data Mining. AAAI/MIT Press (1996)
4. Foley J. and Russell J.D.: Mining Your Own Business. Information Week, March 16 (1998)
5. Kietz J.-U., Reimer U. and Staudt M.: Mining Insurance Data at Swiss Life. Proc. 23rd VLDB Conference, Athens, Greece (1997)

PolyAnalyst Data Analysis Technique and Its Specialization for Processing Data Organized as a Set of Attribute Values

Mikhail V. Kiselev[1], Sergei M. Ananyan[2], Sergei B. Arseniev[1]

[1]Megaputer Intelligence Ltd., 38 B.Tatarskaya, Moscow 113184, Russia
megaputer@glas.apc.org
[2]IUCF, Indiana University, 2401 Sampson Lane, Bloomington, IN 47405
sananyan@indiana.edu

Abtract. The data analysis techniques of the PolyAnalyst data mining system [2] are based on the automated synthesis of functional programs treated as the multi-dimensional non-linear regression models. This approach provides the system with two valuable properties: 1) it can discover in data the hidden relations that might be of a great variety of forms, 2) it can explore arbitrarily complexly structured data if the corresponding data access primitives are provided. The paper contains a formal description of the final version of the basic PolyAnalyst mechanisms, which are utilized in the general case, as well as in a particular case of data organized as a set of attribute values (SAV), which is the most common format for data explored by KDD methods.

1 Introduction

A great variety of methods proposed for the automated discovery of numerical relations in data can be ordered with respect to some measure of generality of the functional relations found or, alternatively, measure of their computational complexity. On the one pole are the fast algorithms discovering very narrow classes of relations, such as, for example, the linear regression. On the opposite pole are the methods based on an extensive search in wide sets of all possible relations. The latter methods are able to discover and formalize complex non-linear dependencies but the price to pay for their generality is a very large computational time. As examples of this kind of systems one can mention FAHRENHEIT [7], ARE [5], or 49er [6]. These systems construct more involved formulae that express the relations in data by combining simpler formulae using the functional composition mechanism, and eventually finding a sufficiently accurate form for the relation. Probably the most extreme position in this row is occupied at present by the PolyAnalyst data mining system [2; 3; 4], whose main module formulates and tests hypotheses about the sought relation in the form of programs automatically written in a simple internal functional language (henceforth this main module of the system will be referred to as simply

PolyAnalyst). The internal programming language has a sufficient expressive power to formalize any relation which can be expressed in an algorithmic form if a necessary set of functional primitives is provided.

Since the search for the best regression model in a set of functional programs is a very difficult problem, the logical structure of the PolyAnalyst system is quite complex. The system includes the following components, which are described in detail in the present paper:
- internal programming language;
- mechanism preventing creation of trivial and equivalent programs;
- program evaluation module;
- strategy of search in space of functional programs.

PolyAnalyst implements a very general mechanism for generating and testing the regression models. For example, this mechanism can work with data that have an arbitrary structure because the programs generated by PolyAnalyst access the explored data via the special data access primitives, which can provide an access to specific elements of vectors, matrices, lists, and other arbitrarily complex data structures. However, in the case when the database records are represented as sets of scalar values, some of the PolyAnalyst algorithms can be implemented much simpler. An exact definition of this data format and the corresponding modification of the PolyAnalyst techniques specialized for the exploration of data represented as sets of scalar values, are the subject of the last section of the paper.

2 PolyAnalyst internal programming language

We start the description by considering the PolyAnalyst internal programming language, which is used for formulating hypotheses about the relations in data. This language is a functional programming language in the sense defined in [1]. Similar to any other programming language, the PolyAnalyst internal language includes three principal components: data types, functional primitives, and control structures, which can also be considered as the methods for constructing more complex programs from the simpler programs.

The data types of the PolyAnalyst internal language form the two classes: universal data types, which are defined for all application domains, and user-defined domain-specific data types. The former class includes only two data types, namely, *boolean*, denoted as $\mathbf{L}$, and *numerical* (real number), denoted as $\mathbf{N}$. The $\mathbf{N}$ type is the only data type containing an infinite number of values. All other data types, including $\mathbf{L}$ and all user-defined types, involve finite sets of values. To clarify the term "user-defined data types" it is necessary to explain our understanding of the concept of the structure of the explored data. We consider the records of the analyzed database as sets of mappings from some sets to other sets. Say, the data represented as a two-dimensional matrix of numerical values can be considered as a mapping from the direct product of the sets of the vertical and horizontal positions to $\mathbf{N}$: $PosX \times PosY \rightarrow \mathbf{N}$. Generally speaking, any data structure can be thought of as a mapping from some sets of keys determining the access to individual values, to the sets of these values, so that such an approach does not limit our ability to work with arbitrarily complexly organized data.

In our formalism the properties of every data type are determined by two characteristics. The first characteristic describes the ordering properties, namely, whether the relation "greater than" or the operator "next" are defined for the data of this type. The second characteristic is called enumerability. It determines whether the instruction "For each value from the data type X perform the following actions ..." makes sense for the considered data type.

The functional primitives of the PolyAnalyst internal language are at the same time the simplest programs of this language, so that prior to describing them it is necessary to explain how the programs synthesized by the system are represented. A program P is considered as an object having a certain set (possibly empty) of inputs **in**(P) and one output. Every input $\alpha \in$ **in**(P) is marked by its data type DT(α) and also by some other attributes to be discussed below. The data type of the program output is denoted as DT(P). Every input α of the program can be assigned some value $p(\alpha)$ in accordance with its data type. The set of all possible mappings from the set of inputs **in**(P) to the set of their values will be denoted as *EVIN*(P). For every $p \in EVIN$(P) the value P(p) returned by the program can be computed as a result of the sequence of operations determined by its internal structure. If the program contains the so called data access primitives (see below) then a database record for which the program is evaluated should be specified. In that case the output value of the program depends on the database record number i explicitly: P(p, i).

The functional primitives which can be included in the programs created by PolyAnalyst, are also broken into two classes: universal and user-defined primitives. The first class includes various operations defined on the universal data types **L** and **N**. These are the boolean operations AND, OR, and NOT, which are represented as primitives with two (AND, OR) or one (NOT) inputs of the type **L** and an output of the type **L**. As a generalization of the numerical relational operators a ternary primitive *inr* with the prototype *inr*:**L**(x:**N**, y:**N**, z:**N**) is used. The value of this primitive is the value of the proposition $y \le x < y + z$. In addition to these primitives the universal primitives include a so called TF-commutator *if*:**N**(b:**L**, x:**N**, y:**N**). If $b = 1$ then the value of this primitive is x otherwise it is y. The user-defined primitives are divided to primitives generated automatically for defined data types, data access primitives, and special primitives. For example, for each data type T a primitive expressing the equality relation with the prototype **L**(T, T) and the TF-commutator with the prototype T(**L**, T, T) are created automatically. The primitives implementing the "greater than" relation and the "next" operation are produced if the respective data types are described as ordered. The prototypes and the bodies of the data access primitives are determined by the structure of the analyzed database records. For example, if the records are organized as two-dimensional matrices containing the values of the type D, then PolyAnalyst creates a primitive with the prototype $D(PosX, PosY)$ where $PosX$ and $PosY$ are the data types representing the horizontal and vertical positions in the matrix. And finally, the subgroup of special primitives includes the primitives corresponding to the operations specific for the explored application domain. For example, the calculation of the sine function might be required only in a narrow class of the application areas. Therefore a primitive implementing the calculation of sine should be defined explicitly by its body and prototype when necessary.

As it has been mentioned before, the functional primitives are considered as the simplest programs. In order to create more complex programs from the simpler programs, several production methods (or control structures) are used. The PolyAnalyst internal language has two basic types of the production methods: functional composition and iteration/recursion.

1. **Functional composition**. A program created using the functional composition is defined by the quadruplet $P_{FC} = <P_{up}, \Pi_{down}, A \subset in(P_{up}), m: A \xrightarrow{m} \Pi_{down}>$, where Π_{down} is a set of programs (it must be non-empty) and $DT(m(\alpha)) = DT(\alpha)$. A new program P_{FC} has the following syntactic characteristics: $DT(P_{FC}) = DT(P_{up})$, $in(P_{FC}) = \bigcup_{P \in \Pi_{down}} in(P) \cup in(P_{up}) \backslash A$. The semantics of this construction is quite obvious.

To determine the value of P_{FC} for given input values the values returned by the programs comprising Π_{down} are calculated. Then every input α of P_{up}, which belongs to A, is assigned the value of $m(\alpha)$ and P_{up} is evaluated. Its output value becomes the output value of P_{FC}.

2. **Iteration/recursion**. In contrast with a simple and clear functional composition, the production method dedicated to creating iterative and recursive constructions is very complex. Due to the space limitation, we provide here only its formal definition without supplying any additional comments or examples concerning this production method. The most general form of this construction is expressed by the following twelve components: $P_{iter} = <P_{pred}, P_{ord}, P_{cond}, \Pi_{act}, \Omega, A_{pred} \subset in(P_{pred}), A_{ord} \subset in(P_{ord}), A_{iter} \subset in(P_{cond}) \cup \bigcup_{P \in \Pi_{act}} in(P), m_{pred}: A_{pred} \xrightarrow{m_{pred}} \Omega, m_{ord}: A_{ord} \xrightarrow{m_{ord}} \Omega, m_{iter}: A_{iter} \xrightarrow{m_{iter}} \Omega \cup \Pi_{act}, out \in \Omega \cup \Pi_{act}>$, where P_{xxx} are programs, Π_{act} is a set of programs, and Ω is a set of loop variables. From the syntactic point of view, the loop variables are the objects which have a single attribute - their data type (this type should be enumerable). The iterative/recursive construction is syntactically correct if the following additional conditions hold: $DT(P_{pred}) = DT(P_{cond}) = \mathbf{L}$, $DT(P_{ord}) = \mathbf{N}$, $DT(m_{xxx}(\alpha)) = DT(\alpha)$ for all m_{xxx}. A special pseudo-program without inputs denoted as $\mathfrak{I}$ may be substituted in place of some components of the considered construction. The output value of this pseudo-program always equals to 1. For example, if $\Omega = \varnothing$, then P_{pred} and P_{ord} should be $\mathfrak{I}$. The prototype of P_{iter} is defined as $DT(P_{iter}) = DT(out)$, $in(P_{iter}) = \bigcup_{P \in \Pi_t} in(P) \cup (in(P_{pred}) \backslash A_{pred}) \cup$

$(in(P_{ord}) \backslash A_{ord}) \cup (in(P_{cond}) \backslash A_{iter})$. The semantics of this construction is determined by the following algorithm for its evaluation. (Note that the mappings m_{xxx} describe the method of passing the values to the inputs of programs included in the construction.)

1. If $\Omega \neq \varnothing$, create a list **LOOPVAR** of all combinations of the possible loop variable values for which the value of P_{pred} equals to 1. The method of passing the values of the loop variables to the inputs of P_{pred} is determined by the mapping m_{pred}.

2. If $\Omega \neq \emptyset$, sort the list **LOOPVAR** in the order of ascending values returned by P_{ord} for the combinations of the loop variable values from **LOOPVAR**. The **LOOPVAR** list can be considered as a matrix $LV[i,\omega]$, where i is the variable value combination number, and ω is the loop variable.

3. $i \leftarrow 1$.

4. Calculate the values of all the programs from the set Π_{act}. The values of their inputs are determined by the following rule. If $m_{iter}(\alpha) \in \Omega$, then the value of the input α equals to $LV[1,m_{iter}(\alpha)]$, otherwise it is equal to the value of the respective input of P_{iter}.

5. Evaluate P_{cond}.

6. If $\Omega \neq \emptyset$ and $i =$ <number of rows of LV>, or the value of P_{cond} equals to 0, stop the computation. Take the value of *out* as the value of the whole construction P_{iter}.

7. $i \leftarrow i + 1$.

8. Calculate the values of all programs from the set Π_{act}. The values of their inputs are taken from the loop variables, the outputs of the programs that belong to Π_{act}, or from the inputs of P_{iter} in accordance with the mapping m_{iter}. For example, if $m_{iter}(\alpha) = \omega \in \Omega$, then $LV[i,\omega]$ should be taken as the value of α.

9. Go to step 5.

Passing the values between the components of this production is depicted schematically in Fig. 2. In addition to the described general form, the iteration/recursion production method has several special forms which are not considered here.

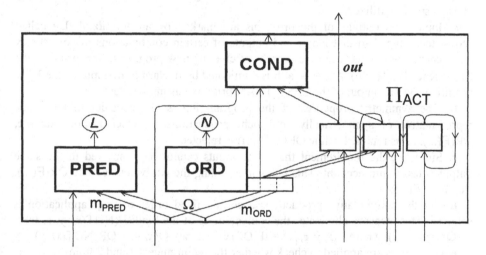

Fig. 1 Iteration/recursion production method.

Although the two discussed production methods are sufficient to provide the PolyAnalyst internal language with the expressive power of a universal programming language, an important special case of the functional composition was selected as a third production method. This mechanism is used for representing numerical dependencies. It is based on the inclusion of the programs returning numerical values in the form of rational expressions (i.e. polynomial divided by polynomial). The reasons for singling out this form of numerical relations, as well as the details of the implementation of this production method are described in [3] and will not be discussed in the present paper.

3 Prevention of building trivial and equivalent programs

Applying the production methods to the existing programs we obtain new programs. However, one cannot guarantee that the new programs will be "good" programs from the semantic point of view. The synthesized programs should satisfy the following three requirements to be considered as semantically correct:

1. *Dependence on all inputs.* This requirement is applicable if $\mathbf{in}(P) \neq \varnothing$.

$\forall \alpha \in \mathbf{in}(P) \exists p, q \in EVIN(P): P(p) \neq P(q) \wedge \forall \beta \in \mathbf{in}(P) \setminus \{\alpha\}: p(\beta) = q(\beta)$.

2. *Dependence on a database record.* This requirement is applicable to the programs containing data access primitives. $\exists p \in EVIN(P) \exists i \exists j: P(p, i) \neq P(p, j)$.

3. *Inequivalence to existing programs.* For all existing programs Q for which there exists an isomorphism $f: \mathbf{in}(P) \xrightarrow{\ f\ } \mathbf{in}(Q)$ such that $DT(f(\alpha)) = DT(\alpha)$ and for all such isomorphisms: $\exists p \in EVIN(P): P(p) \neq Q(f[p])$, where *f[p]* is defined by the equality $f[p](\alpha) \overset{def}{=} p(f^{-1}(\alpha))$.

In order to sift out the programs not obeying these conditions the following mechanisms are utilized:

a. Inputs and outputs of the programs are marked by an additional flag called "consistency type" so that inputs and outputs of certain combinations of consistency types cannot be connected in the process of creating new programs. For example, the equivalence NOT(a<b) $\Leftrightarrow$ a=b $\vee$ a>b is eliminated by declaring the input of the NOT primitive and the output of the LESS_THAN primitive as inconsistent.

b. The symmetry properties of the program inputs are considered. Only one representative of symmetrically equivalent productions is selected. For example, OR(P(...), ...) is retained, while OR(...,P(...)) is rejected.

c. Similarly, the requirement that some inputs cannot be connected to the same output is taken into account. This helps in avoiding the equivalencies like OR(P(...), P(...)) $\Leftrightarrow$ P(...).

d. For the commutative productions a certain fixed order of their application is selected. This measure eliminates the equivalencies of the kind: P(NOT*(x)*, y, z, w) = IF(Q*(x, y)*, z, w), where P(x, y, z, w) = IF(OR*(x, y)*, z, w), Q(x, y) = OR(NOT*(x)*, y).

e. Direct tests are applied to check whether the requirements 1 and 2 hold.

f. For each constructed program PolyAnalyst calculates a special value called the input-output signature, which depends on the values of its inputs and the respective returned values. The procedure of calculating this signature guarantees that the programs equivalent in the sense defined in requirement 3 have the same signature values. The procedures with equal signatures are tested for satisfying the requirement 3.

4 Evaluation of the constructed programs

As it has been mentioned, the created programs are considered as solutions of some problem. For example, if the problem of the discovery of a numerical relation is being solved, then the programs constructed by PolyAnalyst are treated as regression functions and are evaluated in terms of standard error of the respective regression models. Strictly speaking, not every program is considered as a potential solution: the programs, which involve no data access primitives, and even some classes of programs including such primitives serve only as components for other programs. The module performing the evaluation of programs can realize an arbitrary functional $Ev[P]$, which should be minimized. This feature provides the system with a great flexibility: the ability to solve a wide class of KDD and optimization problems. It should be noted that each program P represents in general a set of mappings from a set of database records to DT(P), parametrized by the values of its inputs. Therefore for an individual program P the problem of finding the best values for its inputs must be solved. Depending on the functional $Ev[P]$ and the form of the program P, the methods of combinatorics, numerical optimization, or other approaches may be used to solve this problem.

5 GT-search

The last but not least part of the PolyAnalyst system is a module that chooses the production methods, and components for building new programs. The generation of new programs is performed by two processes. The first process, with a lower priority, implements the full search in the space of programs in the order of increasing complexity (which approximately equals the number of primitives constituting the program). The other process, which has a higher priority, creates new programs using the so called generalizing transformations (GT) [3]. The application of GT to an existing program yields a new program called a GT-derivative. The program P' is called a GT-derivative of the program P (that is denoted as $P \overset{GT}{\succ} P'$) iff:

1. There exists an isomorphism $f: \text{in}(P) \overset{f}{\longrightarrow} I \subset \text{in}(P')$ such that $DT(f(\alpha)) = DT(\alpha)$;

2. There exists an isomorphism $F: EVIN(P) \overset{F}{\longrightarrow} E \subset EVIN(P')$ such that $q = F(p)$ $\Rightarrow q(f(\alpha)) = p(\alpha)$ and

$\forall \alpha \in \text{in}(P') \setminus I \forall p, q \in E: p(\alpha) = q(\alpha) \wedge \forall p \in E: P'(p) = P(F^{-1}(p))$.

For any program there exists a large number of classes of transformations of the program structure, which lead to the creation of a GT-derivative of this program. The success of the utilization of the GT-search for navigating in the space of programs is based on an obvious fact that $P \overset{GT}{\succ} P' \Rightarrow Ev[P'] \leq Ev[P]$. This property makes it possible to organize a GT-based search in the space of programs in the following way.

When the process of the full search finds a program for which $Ev[P]$ is sufficiently small, this program becomes a parent for a generation of programs created from this program with the help of GT. If one of these programs demonstrates a significant decrease of Ev, this program in turn is taken as a starting point for building new programs with the help of GT and so on. By utilizing this approach the system can build rather complex programs over a reasonable period of time. This description of the GT-search concludes the discussion of the internal PolyAnalyst mechanisms employed in a general case. The next section is devoted to discussing a special case when the data has a "set of attribute values" (SAV) structure.

6 Specialization of PolyAnalyst mechanisms for the case of data represented as a set of attribute values (SAV)

First of all, let us furnish a precise definition of the SAV data format. From the point of view of PolyAnalyst a data format is defined completely by specifying the data access primitives, a set of possible data types, and a set of the user-defined primitives. The term "set of attribute values" implies that each considered database record constitutes a set of scalar values of different types. Therefore for every position of the data record a data access primitive with no inputs is generated. The data type of the output of this primitive matches the data type of the attribute value in the respective position. Also an additional data type is introduced for every position of the record, which contains unordered non-numerical values. Beside the access primitives, the only class of the user-defined primitives which can be introduced for a domain of that kind is the class of equality primitives for additional data types. It can be easily shown that this set of data types and functional primitives leaves very few possibilities for employing the iteration/recursion production method for building new programs. For this reason, and also because the functional composition method is much easier to implement, it is reasonable to use in the SAV application domains only the functional composition method. Furthermore, in this case the majority of programs are generated utilizing an important subclass of the functional composition method, namely the production of rational expressions.

Beside the internal language, the other component of the PolyAnalyst system, which is influenced greatly by the assumption of the SAV data organization, is the GT-search mechanism. Since in this case the **rational** production method plays a very important role, the following two kinds of generalizing transformations applicable to rationals are used most often:

1. Let us denote the rational expression subjected to GT as $P = A/B$ where A and B are polynomials. If Q is a program returning a numerical value, while C and D are polynomials, then as it can be readily seen, the program $R = \dfrac{Q*A+C}{Q*B+D}$ is a GT-derivative of P.

2. If we multiply any term in A or B by a construction $IF(Q, a, b)$, where Q is a program returning a boolean value, while a and b are inputs of the type N, then the

new rational expression will be a GT-derivative of P. This is true because if $a = b = 1$ then IF(Q, a, b) $\equiv 1$.

It should be noted that the basic commercially available version of PolyAnalyst utilizes only these two classes of GT.

7 Conclusion

The history of successful utilization of PolyAnalyst in various fields including banking, marketing, manufacturing, and many other fields proves the efficiency of applying the automated program synthesis techniques to KDD problems. The universality of the described approach is achieved due to the absence of any inherent limitations on the structure of analyzed data, as well as on the procedure of evaluating the built programs in accordance with arbitrary criteria implemented in the PolyAnalyst's program evaluation module. The GT search and the mechanisms suppressing the generation of trivial and equivalent programs solve, or at least soften the problem of combinatorial growth of the number of the generated programs. The assumption of the SAV data structure allows one to make important simplifications, which increase the performance of the system even further.

References

1. Backus, J. (1978) Can programming be liberated from the von Neumann style? *Commun. ACM*, v.21, pp 613-541.
2. Kiselev, M.V. (1994) PolyAnalyst - a machine discovery system inferring functional programs, In: *Proceedings of AAAI Workshop on Knowledge Discovery in Databases'94*, Seattle, pp. 237-249.
3. Kiselev, M.V., Arseniev, S.B. (1996) Discovery of numerical dependencies in form of rational expressions, in; *Proceedings of ISMIS'96 (Ninth International Symposium on Methodologies for Intelligent Systems) poster session*, Zakopane, Poland, pp. 134-145.
4. Kiselev, M.V., Ananyan, S. M., and Arseniev, S. B. (1997) Regression-Based Classification Methods and Their Comparison with Decision Tree Algorithms, In: *Proceedings of 1st European Symposium on Principles of Data Mining and Knowledge Discovery*, Trondheim, Norway, Springer, pp 134-144.
5. Shen Wei-Min (1990) Functional Transformations in AI Discovery Systems, *Artif.Intell.*, v.41, pp 257-272.
6. Zembowicz, R., Zytkow, J. M. (1992) Discovery of Equations: Experimental Evaluation of Convergence, In: *Proceedings of AAAI-92*, AAAI Press, Menlo Park, CA, pp 70-75.
7. Zytkow J.M., Zhu J. (1991) Application of Empirical Discovery in Knowledge Acquisition, In: *Proceedings of Machine Learning - EWSL-91*, pp 101-117.

Representative Association Rules and Minimum Condition Maximum Consequence Association Rules

Marzena Kryszkiewicz

Institute of Computer Science, Warsaw University of Technology
Nowowiejska 15/19, 00-665 Warsaw, Poland
mkr@ii.pw.edu.pl

Abstract. Discovering association rules (*AR*) among items in a large database is an important database mining problem. The number of association rules may be large. To alleviate this problem, we introduced in [1] a notion of representative association rules (*RR*). *RR* is a least set of rules that covers all association rules. The association rules, which are not representative ones, may be generated by means of a cover operator without accessing a database. On the other hand, a subset of association rules that allows to predict as much as possible from minimum facts is usually of interest to analysts. This kind of rules we will call minimum condition maximum consequence rules (*MMR*). In this paper, we investigate the relationship between *RR* and *MMR*. We prove that *MMR* is a subset of *RR* and it may be extracted from *RR*.

1 Introduction

Discovering association rules (*AR*) among items in large databases is recognized as an important database mining problem. The problem was introduced in [2] for sales transaction database. The association rules identify sets of items that are purchased together with other sets of items. For example, an association rule may state that 90% of customers who buy butter and bread buy also milk. Several extensions of the notion of an association rule were offered in the literature (see e.g. [3-4]). One of such extensions is a generalized rule that can be discovered from a taxonomic database [3]. Applications for association rules range from decision support to telecommunications alarm diagnosis and prediction [5-6].

The number of association rules is usually large. A user should not be presented with all of them, but rather with these which are original, novel, interesting. There were proposed several definitions of what is an interesting association rule (see e.g. [3,7]). In particular, pruning out uninteresting rules which exploits the information in taxonomies seems to be quite useful (resulting in the rule number reduction amounting to 60% [3]). The interestingness of a rule is usually expressed by some quantitative measure.

In the paper we consider two other approaches to extracting interesting rules from a database. In the first approach, rules are regarded as interesting if they allow to predict as much as possible from minimum facts (see e.g. [8]). Association rules of this kind will be called minimum condition maximum consequence rules (MMR). The second approach, introduced in [1], consists in looking for a least set of association rules that allows to deduce all other association rules without accessing a database. Such a basic set of association rules is called a set of representative association rules (RR). An efficient *FastGenAllRepresentatives* algorithm of computing representative rules was proposed in [9].

In this paper, we investigate the relationship between RR and MMR. We prove that MMR is a subset of RR. We also show how to extract MMR from RR instead of extracting it from the whole set of association rules.

2 Association Rules

The definition of a class of regularities called *association rules* and the problem of their discovering were introduced in [2]. Here, we describe this problem after [2,10]. Let $I = \{i_1, i_2, ..., i_m\}$ be a set of distinct literals, called *items*. In general, any set of items is called an *itemset*. Let D be a set of transactions, where each transaction T is a set of items such that $T \subseteq I$. An *association rule* is an expression of the form $X \Rightarrow Y$, where $\varnothing \neq X, Y \subset I$ and $X \cap Y = \varnothing$. X is called the antecedent and Y is called the consequent of the rule.

Statistical significance of an itemset X is called *support* and is denoted by $sup(X)$. $Sup(X)$ is defined as the number of transactions in D that contain X. Statistical significance (*support*) of a rule $X \Rightarrow Y$ is denoted by $sup(X \Rightarrow Y)$ and defined as $sup(X \cup Y)$. Additionally, an association rule is characterized by *confidence*, which expresses its strength. The confidence of an association rule $X \Rightarrow Y$ is denoted by $conf(X \Rightarrow Y)$ and defined as the ratio $sup(X \cup Y) / sup(X)$.

The problem of mining association rules is to generate all rules that have support greater than some user specified minimum support $s \geq 0$ and confidence not less than a user specified minimum confidence $c > 0$. In the sequel, the set of all association rules whose support is greater than s and confidence is not less than c will be denoted by $AR(s,c)$. If s and c are understood then $AR(s,c)$ will be denoted by AR.

3 Cover Operator

A notion of a *cover operator* was introduced in [1] for deriving a set of association rules from a given association rule without accessing a database. The *cover C* of the rule $X \Rightarrow Y$, $Y \neq \varnothing$, is defined as follows:

$$C(X \Rightarrow Y) = \{X \cup Z \Rightarrow V | Z, V \subseteq Y \text{ and } Z \cap V = \varnothing \text{ and } V \neq \varnothing\}.$$

Each rule in $C(X \Rightarrow Y)$ consists of a subset of items occurring in the rule $X \Rightarrow Y$. The antecedent of any rule r covered by $X \Rightarrow Y$ contains X and perhaps some items from Y, whereas r's consequent is a non-empty subset of the remaining items in Y. It was proved in [1] that each rule r in the cover $C(r')$, where r' is an association rule having support s and confidence c, belongs in $AR(s,c)$. Hence, if r belongs in $AR(s,c)$ then every rule r' in $C(r)$ also belongs in $AR(s,c)$. The number of different rules in the cover of the association rule $X \Rightarrow Y$ is equal to $3^m - 2^m$, where $m = |Y|$ (see [1]).

Example 3.1 Let $T_1 = \{A,B,C,D,E\}$, $T_2 = \{A,B,C,D,E,F\}$, $T_3 = \{A,B,C,D,E,H,I\}$, $T_4 = \{A,B,E\}$ and $T_5 = \{B,C,D,E,H,I\}$ are the only transactions in the database D. Let $r: (B \Rightarrow CDE)$. Fig. 1 contains all rules belonging in the cover $C(r)$ along with their support and confidence in D. The support of r is equal to 4 and its confidence is equal to 80%. The support and confidence of all other rules in $C(r)$ are not less than the support and confidence of r. $\qquad\square$

#	Rule r' in $C(r)$	Support of r'	Confidence of r'
1.	$B \Rightarrow CDE$	4	80%
2.	$B \Rightarrow CD$	4	80%
3.	$B \Rightarrow CE$	4	80%
4.	$B \Rightarrow DE$	4	80%
5.	$B \Rightarrow C$	4	80%
6.	$B \Rightarrow D$	4	80%
7.	$B \Rightarrow E$	5	100%
8.	$BC \Rightarrow DE$	4	100%
9.	$BC \Rightarrow D$	4	100%
19.	$BC \Rightarrow E$	4	100%
11.	$BD \Rightarrow CE$	4	100%
12.	$BD \Rightarrow C$	4	100%
13.	$BD \Rightarrow E$	4	100%
14.	$BE \Rightarrow CD$	4	80%
15.	$BE \Rightarrow C$	4	80%
16.	$BE \Rightarrow D$	4	80%
17.	$BCD \Rightarrow E$	4	100%
18.	$BCE \Rightarrow D$	4	100%
19.	$BDE \Rightarrow C$	4	100%

Fig. 1. The cover of the rule $r: (B \Rightarrow CDE)$

Below, we present a simple property, which will be used further in the paper.

Property 3.1 Let $r: (X \Rightarrow Y)$ and $r': (X' \Rightarrow Y')$ be association rules.

$$r \in C(r') \text{ iff } X \cup Y \subseteq X' \cup Y' \text{ and } X \supseteq X'.$$

4 Representative Association Rules

In this section we describe a notion of representative association rules which was introduced in [1]. Informally speaking, a set of all representative association rules is a least set of rules that covers all association rules by means of the cover operator.

A set of *representative association rules* wrt. minimum support s and minimum confidence c will be denoted by $RR(s,c)$ and defined as follows:

$$RR(s,c) = \{r \in AR(s,c) | \neg \exists r' \in AR(s,c), r' \neq r \text{ and } r \in C(r')\}.$$

If s and c are understood then $RR(s,c)$ will be denoted by RR. Each rule in RR is called a *representative association rule*. By the definition of RR no representative association rule may belong in the cover of another association rule.

Property 4.1

$$RR(s,c) = \{(X \Rightarrow Y) \in AR(s,c) | \ \neg\exists(X' \Rightarrow Y') \in AR, (X=X' \wedge X \cup Y \subset X' \cup Y') \vee$$
$$(X \supset X' \wedge X \cup Y = X' \cup Y')\}.$$

Proof: $RR = \{r: (X \Rightarrow Y) \in AR | \ \neg\exists r': (X' \Rightarrow Y') \in AR, r' \neq r \wedge X \supseteq X' \wedge X \cup Y \subseteq X' \cup Y'\} = \{(X \Rightarrow Y) \in AR | \quad \neg\exists(X' \Rightarrow Y') \in AR, \quad (X=X' \wedge X \cup Y \subset X' \cup Y') \quad \vee (X \supset X' \wedge X \cup Y \subseteq X' \cup Y')\}.$

Let $(X \Rightarrow Y)$ be an association rule. One can notice that:

$$\exists(X' \Rightarrow Y') \in AR, (X \supset X' \wedge X \cup Y \subseteq X' \cup Y') \tag{1}$$

is true iff the expression:

$$\exists(X'' \Rightarrow Y'') \in AR, (X \supset X'' \wedge X \cup Y = X'' \cup Y'') \tag{2}$$

is true. The proof of implication: (1) if (2) is trivial, so it will be omitted. Now, we will prove that (2) follows from (1). Let $(X' \Rightarrow Y')$ be an association rule such that $(X \supset X' \wedge X \cup Y \subseteq X' \cup Y')$. Let $X''=X'$ and $Y''=(X \backslash X') \cup Y$. Then, $X \supset X''$ and $X \cup Y = X'' \cup Y''$. Additionally, $(X'' \Rightarrow Y'') \in C(X' \Rightarrow Y')$ because $X'' \cup Y'' \subseteq X' \cup Y'$ and $X''=X'$. Thus, $X'' \Rightarrow Y''$ is an association rule as a rule belonging to the cover of an association rule. Applying the equivalence of the expressions (1) and (2), we obtain: $RR = \{(X \Rightarrow Y) \in AR | \quad \neg\exists(X' \Rightarrow Y') \in AR, \quad (X=X' \wedge X \cup Y \subset X' \cup Y') \quad \vee (X \supset X' \wedge X \cup Y = X' \cup Y')\}.$ □

Property 4.1 tells us that an association rule r is representative one if there is no longer rule that has the same antecedent as r and is built from a superset of all items occurring in r, and if there is no rule the antecedent of which is a proper subset of the antecedent of r and which is built from all items occurring in r.

Example 4.1 Given minimum support $s = 2$ and minimum confidence $c = 80\%$, the following representative rules would be found for the database D from Example 3.1:

$$RR(2,80\%) = \{AC \Rightarrow BDE, AD \Rightarrow BCE, B \Rightarrow CDE, C \Rightarrow BDE, D \Rightarrow BCE, E \Rightarrow BCD,$$
$$A \Rightarrow BE, B \Rightarrow AE, E \Rightarrow AB\}.$$

There are 9 representative association rules in $RR(2,80\%)$, whereas the number of all association rules in $AR(2,80\%)$ is 93. Hence, $RR(2,80\%)$ constitute 9.68% of all association rules. □

5 Minimum Condition Maximum Consequence Association Rules

In the classification problems, rules with minimum conditions seem to be very useful. Here we extend the problem for generation of rules not only with minimum antecedents but also with maximum consequents. Formally, a set of *minimum condition maximum consequence association rules* wrt. minimum support s and minimum confidence c will be denoted by $MMR(s,c)$ and defined as follows:

$$MMR(s,c) = \{r: (X \Rightarrow Y) \in AR(s,c)|\ \neg\exists r': (X' \Rightarrow Y') \in AR(s,c), r' \neq r \text{ and}$$
$$X' \subseteq X \text{ and } Y' \supseteq Y\}.$$

If s and c are understood then $MMR(s,c)$ will be denoted by MMR. Below we prove a property stating that the minimum condition maximum consequence rules constitute a subset of the representative association rules.

Property 5.1

$$MMR(s,c) \subseteq RR(s,c).$$

Proof: $MMR = \{r: (X \Rightarrow Y) \in AR|\ \neg\exists r': (X' \Rightarrow Y') \in AR, r' \neq r \wedge X' \subseteq X \wedge Y' \supseteq Y\} = \{r: (X \Rightarrow Y) \in AR|\quad \forall r': (X' \Rightarrow Y') \in AR,\quad r' = r\quad \vee\quad \neg(X' \subseteq X) \vee \neg(Y' \supseteq Y)\} = \{r: (X \Rightarrow Y) \in AR|\ \forall r': (X' \Rightarrow Y') \in AR, r' = r \vee \neg(X' \subseteq X) \vee ((X' \subseteq X) \wedge \neg(Y' \supseteq Y))\}.$

$RR = \{r \in AR|\ \neg\exists r' \in AR, r' \neq r \wedge r \in C(r')\} = \{r: (X \Rightarrow Y) \in AR|\ \forall r': (X' \Rightarrow Y') \in AR, r' = r \vee \neg(X' \subseteq X) \vee \neg(X \cup Y \subseteq X' \cup Y')\} = \{r: (X \Rightarrow Y) \in AR|\ \forall r': (X' \Rightarrow Y') \in AR, r' = r \vee \neg(X' \subseteq X) \vee ((X' \subseteq X) \wedge \neg(X \cup Y \subseteq X' \cup Y'))\}.$

Let us note that $((X' \subseteq X) \wedge \neg(Y' \supseteq Y))$ implies $((X' \subseteq X) \wedge \neg(X \cup Y \subseteq X' \cup Y'))$. Hence, $RR = \{\{r: (X \Rightarrow Y) \in AR|\quad \forall r': (X' \Rightarrow Y') \in AR,\quad r' = r\quad \vee\quad \neg(X' \subseteq X)\quad \vee\quad ((X' \subseteq X) \wedge \neg(X \cup Y \subseteq X' \cup Y')) \vee ((X' \subseteq X) \wedge \neg(Y' \supseteq Y))\}.$

The obtained formulae expressing MMR and RR allow us to conclude that MMR is a subset of RR. $\qquad\square$

In the next property we prove that it is sufficient to know only the representative association rules to compute the minimum condition maximum consequence rules.

Property 5.2

$$MMR(s,c) = \{r: (X \Rightarrow Y) \in RR(s,c)|\ \neg\exists r': (X' \Rightarrow Y') \in RR(s,c), r' \neq r \text{ and}$$
$$X' \subseteq X \text{ and } Y' \supseteq Y\}.$$

Proof: By Property 5.1, MMR are contained in RR. So, $MMR = \{r: (X \Rightarrow Y) \in RR|\ \neg\exists r': (X' \Rightarrow Y') \in AR, r' \neq r \wedge X' \subseteq X \wedge Y' \supseteq Y\}.$

Let $r: (X \Rightarrow Y) \in AR$. It can be noticed that the expression:

$$\exists r': (X' \Rightarrow Y') \in AR, r' \neq r \wedge X' \subseteq X \wedge Y' \supseteq Y \tag{3}$$

is equivalent to the expression:

$$\exists r'': (X'' \Rightarrow Y'') \in RR, r'' \neq r \wedge X'' \subseteq X \wedge Y'' \supseteq Y. \tag{4}$$

Let $r': (X' \Rightarrow Y')$ be an association rule such that $r' \neq r$ and $X' \subseteq X$ and $Y' \supseteq Y$. Each association rule belongs in the cover of some representative rule, so there is some $r'': (X'' \Rightarrow Y'')$ in RR, such that $r' \in C(r'')$. Hence, $X'' \subseteq X' \subseteq X$ and $Y'' \supseteq Y' \supseteq Y$ and thus, (3) implies (4). The inverse implication is trivial (any representative rule is association one). Applying the equivalence of the expressions (3) and (4), we obtain: $MMR = \{r: (X \Rightarrow Y) \in RR|\ \neg\exists r': (X' \Rightarrow Y') \in RR, r' \neq r \wedge X' \subseteq X \wedge Y' \supseteq Y\}. \qquad\square$

The efficient computation of MMR may be performed as follows:

1. Compute the representative association rules (e.g. by applying the efficient algorithm *FastGenAllRepresentatives* [9]; see also Appendix).
2. Compute the minimum condition maximum consequence rules from the representative association rules according to Property 5.2.

Example 5.1 Given minimum support $s = 2$ and minimum confidence $c = 80\%$, the following minimum condition maximum consequence association rules would be found for the database D from Example 3.1:

$$MMR(2,80\%) = \{B{\Rightarrow}CDE, C{\Rightarrow}BDE, D{\Rightarrow}BCE, E{\Rightarrow}BCD, A{\Rightarrow}BE, B{\Rightarrow}AE, E{\Rightarrow}AB\}.$$

There are 7 minimum condition maximum consequence association rules in $MMR(2,80\%)$, whereas the number of rules in $AR(2,80\%)$ is 93 and the number of rules in $RR(2,80\%)$ is 9 (see Example 4.1). The representative rules $AC{\Rightarrow}BDE$ and $AD{\Rightarrow}BCE$ are not minimum condition maximum consequence rules. The former rule is redundant wrt. the representative rule $C{\Rightarrow}BDE$ and the latter one is redundant wrt. the representative rule $D{\Rightarrow}BCE$. Hence, $MMR(2,80\%)$ constitutes 7.53% of $AR(2,80\%)$ and 77.78% of the representative association rules $RR(2,80\%)$. ☐

6 Conclusion

In this paper, we have investigated the relationship between representative rules and minimum condition maximum consequence rules. *RR* constitute the minimal set of rules that allow to derive all association rules without accessing a database. *MMR* are rules that allow to predict as much as possible from minimum facts. We proved that *MMR* is a subset of *RR*. We have also shown how to extract *MMR* from *RR* instead of extracting it from the whole set of association rules.

References

1. Kryszkiewicz, M.: Representative Association Rules. In: Proc. of PAKDD '98. Melbourne, Australia. Lecture Notes in Artificial Intelligence 1394. Research and Development in Knowledge Discovery and Data Mining. Springer-Verlag (1998) 198-209
2. Agraval, R., Imielinski, T., Swami, A.: Mining Associations Rules between Sets of Items in Large Databases. In: Proc. of the ACM SIGMOD Conference on Management of Data. Washington, D.C. (1993) 207-216
3. Srikant, R., Agraval, R.: Mining Generalized Association Rules. In: Proc. of the 21st VLDB Conference. Zurich, Swizerland (1995) 407-419
4. Meo, R., Psaila, G., Ceri, S.: A New SQL-like Operator for Mining Association Rules. In: Proc. of the 22nd VLDB Conference. Mumbai (Bombay), India (1996)
5. Communications of the ACM, November 1996, Vol. 39. No 11. (1996)
6. Fayyad, U.M., Piatetsky-Shapiro, G., Smyth, P., Uthurusamy, R. (eds.): Advances in Knowledge Discovery and Data Mining. AAAI, Menlo Park, California (1996)
7. Piatetsky-Shapiro, G.: Discovery, Analysis and Presentation of Strong Rules. In: Piatetsky-Shapiro, G., Frawley, W. (eds.): Knowledge Discovery in Databases. AAAI/MIT Press, Menlo Park, CA (1991) 229-248

8. Washio, T., Matsuura, H., Motoda, H., Mining Association Rules for Estimation and Prediction. In: Proc. of PAKDD '98. Melbourne, Australia. Lecture Notes in Artificial Intelligence 1394. Research and Development in Knowledge Discovery and Data Mining. Springer-Verlag (1998) 417-419

9. Kryszkiewicz, M., Fast Discovery of Representative Association Rules. To appear in Proc. of RSCTC '98. Rough Sets and Current Trends in Computing. Springer-Verlag. Warsaw, Poland (1998) 214-221

10. Agraval, R., Mannila, H., Srikant, R., Toivonen, H., Verkamo, A.I.: Fast Discovery of Association Rules. In: [6] (1996) 307-328

11. Savasere, A, Omiecinski, E., Navathe, S.: An Efficient Algorithm for Mining Association Rules in Large Databases. In: Proc. of the 21st VLDB Conference. Zurich, Swizerland (1995) 432-444

Appendix: Generation of Representative Association Rules

The process of generating representative association rules was described in [1,9]. In general, the process may be decomposed into two subprocesses:
1. Generate all itemsets whose support exceeds the minimum support s. The itemsets of this property are called *frequent (large)*.
2. From each frequent itemset generate representative association rules whose confidence is not less than the minimum confidence c. Let Z be a frequent itemset and $\varnothing \neq X \subset Z$. Then any rule $X \Rightarrow Z\backslash X$ is association one if $sup(Z)/sup(X) \geq c$. The association rule $X \Rightarrow Z\backslash X$ is representative if there is no association rule $(X \Rightarrow Z'\backslash X)$, where $Z \subset Z'$, and there is no association rule $(X' \Rightarrow Z\backslash X')$ such that $X \supset X'$ (see Property 4.1).

Several efficient solutions to the first subproblem were proposed (see [3,10-11]). We will remind briefly the main idea of the *Apriori* algorithm [10] computing frequent itemsets. Next, we will present the efficient algorithm [9] of computing representative association rules from the found frequent itemsets.

In the sequel, we will apply the following simple notions:

The number of items in an itemset will be called the *length of the itemset*. An itemset of the length k will be referred to as a *k-itemset*. Similarly, the *length of an association rule* $X \Rightarrow Y$ will be defined as the total number of items in the rule's antecedent and consequent ($|X \cup Y|$). An association rule of the length k will be referred to as a *k-rule*. An association k-rule will be called *shorter* than, *longer* than or *of the same length* as an association m-rule if $k < m$, $k > m$, or $k = m$, respectively.

Computing Frequent Itemsets

The *Apriori* algorithm exploits the following properties of frequent and non-frequent itemsets: All subsets of a frequent itemset are frequent and all supersets of a non-frequent itemset are non-frequent. The following notation is used in the *Apriori* algorithm: C_k - set of candidate k-itemsets; F_k - set of frequent k-itemsets. The items in itemsets are assumed to be ordered lexicographically. Associated with each itemset is a *count* field to store the support for this itemset.

```
Algorithm Apriori
  F₁ = {frequent 1-itemsets};
  for (k = 2; Fₖ₋₁ ≠ ∅; k++) do begin
  Cₖ = AprioriGen(Fₖ₋₁);
  forall transactions T ∈ D do
    forall candidates Z ∈ Cₖ do
      if Z ⊆ T then
        Z.count++;
  Fₖ = {Z ∈ Cₖ | Z.count > s};
  endfor;
return ∪ₖ Fₖ;
```

First, the support of all 1-itemsets is determined during one pass over the database D. All non-frequent 1-itemsets are discarded. Then the loop "for" starts. In general, some k-th iteration of the loop consists of the following operations:
1. The *AprioriGen* function is called to generate the candidate k-itemsets C_k from the frequent $(k-1)$-itemsets F_{k-1}.
2. Supports for the candidate k-itemsets are determined by a pass over the database.
3. The candidate k-itemsets that do not exceed the minimum support are discarded; the remaining k-itemsets F_k are found frequent.

```
function AprioriGen(frequent (k-1)-itemsets Fₖ₋₁);
  insert into Cₖ
  select (Z[1], Z[2], ... , Z[k-1], Y[k-1]) from Fₖ₋₁ Z, Fₖ₋₁ Y
  where Z[1]=Y[1] ∧ ... ∧ Z[k-2]=Y[k-2] ∧ Z[k-1]<Y[k-1];
  delete all itemsets Z ∈ Cₖ such that some (k-1)-subset of Z
  is not in Fₖ₋₁;
return Cₖ;
```

Computing Representative Association Rules

The *FastGenAllRepresentatives* algorithm generates representative association rules from frequent itemsets. In order to justify the correctness of the algorithm we will apply Property 4.1 and the following observation: no rule $X \Rightarrow Z\backslash X$ is representative if there is a proper superset Z' of Z having the same support as Z. The observation may be justified as follows:

If $X \Rightarrow Z\backslash X$ is not an association rule then it is not representative. However, if $X \Rightarrow Z\backslash X$ is an association rule and there is $Z' \supset Z$ such $sup(Z)= sup(Z')$ then $X \Rightarrow Z'\backslash X$ has the same support and confidence as $X \Rightarrow Z\backslash X$. Hence, $X \Rightarrow Z'\backslash X$ is also an association rule. Additionally, $X \Rightarrow Z\backslash X$ belongs in the cover of $X \Rightarrow Z'\backslash X$, so $X \Rightarrow Z\backslash X$ is not representative.

```
procedure FastGenAllRepresentatives(all frequent itemsets F);
  forall Z ∈ Fₖ,k ≥ 2, do begin
    maxSup = max({sup(Z')| Z⊂Z'∈Fₖ₊₁} ∪ {0});
```

```
if Z.sup ≠ maxSup then begin
  A₁ = {{Z[1]}, {Z[2]}, ... , {Z[k]}};  //create 1-antecedents
  /* Loop1 */
  for (i = 1; (Aᵢ ≠ ∅) and (i < k); i++) do begin
    forall X ∈ Aᵢ do begin
      find Y∈Fᵢ such that Y = X;
      XCount = Y.count;
      /* Is X ⇒ Z\X an association rule? */
      if (Z.count/XCount ≥ c) then begin
/*Isn't any longer assoc. rule X⇒Z'\X that covers X⇒Z\X?*/
        if (maxSup/XCount < c) then          // see Property 4.1
          print(X, "⇒", Z\X, " with support: ", Z.count,
                " and confidence: ", Z.count / XCount);
        /* Antecedents of association rules are not extended */
        Aᵢ = Aᵢ \ {X};
      endif;
    endfor;
    Aᵢ₊₁ = AprioriGen(Aᵢ);                  // compute i+1-antecedents
  endfor;
 endif;
endfor;
endproc;
```

The *FastGenAllRepresentatives* algorithm computes representative association rules from each k-itemset, $k \geq 2$, in F. Let Z be a considered itemset in F_k. Only k-rules are generated from Z. First, *maxSup* is determined as a maximum from the supports of these itemsets in F_{k+1} which are supersets of Z. If there is no superset of Z in F_{k+1} then *maxSup*=0. Let us note that the supports of other proper supersets of Z, which do not belong in F_{k+1}, are not greater than *maxSup*. Clearly, *maxSup*>s or *maxSup*=0. If $sup(Z)$ is the same as *maxSup* then no representative rule can be generated from Z. Otherwise, single-item antecedents of candidate k-rules are created. Loop1 starts. In general, the i-th iteration of Loop1 looks as follows:

Each candidate $X \Rightarrow Z\backslash X$, where $X \subset Z$ belongs in i-itemsets A_i, is considered. Z is frequent, so X, which is a subset of Z, is also frequent. In order to check if $X \Rightarrow Z\backslash X$ is an association rule its confidence: $sup(Z)/sup(X)$ has to be determined. $sup(Z)=Z.count$, while $sup(X)$ is computed as $sup(Y)$ of a frequent itemset Y in F_i such that $Y=X$. Only association rules that satisfy Property 4.1 are representative. Checking whether there is a longer association rule $X \Rightarrow Z'\backslash X$ that covers $X \Rightarrow Z\backslash X$ is performed explicitly in the algorithm. If *maxSup/XCount* $\geq c$ then there is such a longer rule. Otherwise, $X \Rightarrow Z\backslash X$ is a representative rule. Checking if there is another association rule $X' \Rightarrow Z\backslash X'$, $X \supset X'$, that covers $X \Rightarrow Z\backslash X$ is not necessary since no candidate rules, whose antecedents are proper supersets of antecedents of some association rules, are considered in the algorithm. This feature is obtained by removing the itemsets from i-itemsets A_i that are antecedents of association rules and by applying the *AprioriGen* function in order to generate A_{i+1} antecedents from the remaining itemsets in A_i.

Discovery of Decision Rules from Databases: An Evolutionary Approach

Wojciech Kwedlo and Marek Krętowski

Institute of Computer Science
Technical University of Białystok
Wiejska 45a, 15-351 Białystok, Poland
e-mail: {wkwedlo,mkret}@ii.pb.bialystok.pl

Abstract. Decision rules are a natural form of representing knowledge. Their extraction from databases requires the capability for effective search large solution spaces. This paper shows, how we can deal with this problem using evolutionary algorithms (EAs). We propose an EA-based system called EDRL, which for each class label sequentially generates a disjunctive set of decision rules in propositional form. EDRL uses an EA to search for one rule at a time; then, all the positive examples covered by the rule are removed from the learning set and the search is repeated on the remaining examples. Our version of EA differs from standard genetic algorithm. In addition to the well-known uniform crossover it employs two non-standard genetic operators, which we call changing condition and insertion. Currently EDRL requires prior discretization of all continuous-valued attributes. A discretization technique based on the minimization of class entropy is used. The performance of EDRL is evaluated by comparing its classification accuracy with that of C4.5 learning algorithm on six datasets from UCI repository.

1 Introduction

Knowledge Discovery in Databases (KDD) is the process of identifying valid, potentially useful and understandable regularities in data [5]. The two main goals of KDD are *prediction* i.e. the use of available data to predict unknown values of some variables and *description* i.e. the search for some interesting patterns and their presentation in easy to understand way.

One of the most well-known data mining techniques used in KDD process is extraction of decision rules. During the last two decades many methods e.g. AQ-family [12], CN2 [2] or C4.5 [15] were proposed. The advantages of the rule-based approach include natural representation and ease of integration of learned rules with background knowledge.

In the paper we present a new system called EDRL (EDRL, for Evolutionary Decision Rule Learner), which searches for decision rules using an evolutionary algorithm (EA). EAs [11] are stochastic search techniques, which have been inspired by the process of biological evolution. They have been applied to many optimization problems. The success of EAs is attributed to their ability to avoid local optima, which is their main advantage over greedy search methods. Several

EA-based systems, which learn decision rules in either propositional (e.g. GABIL [3], GIL [10], GA-MINER [7]) or first order (e.g. REGAL [8, 14], SIAO1 [1]) form have been proposed.

There are two key issues in our approach. The first one is the use of two non-standard genetic operators, which we call changing condition operator and insertion operator. The second issue is the application of entropy-based discretization [6, 4], which allows us to effectively deal with continuous-valued features.

The reminder of the paper is organized as follows. In the next section we present basic definitions and outline the rule induction scheme used by EDRL. Section 3 describes a heuristic based on entropy minimization, which is used to discretize the continuous-valued attributes. Section 4 presents the details of our EA including representation of rules, the fitness function and genetic operators. Preliminary experimental results are given in Section 5. The last section contains our conclusions and possible directions of future research.

2 Learning decision rules

Let us assume that we have a learning set $E = \{e_1, e_2, \ldots, e_M\}$ consisting of M examples. Each example $e \in E$ is described by N attributes (features) $\{A_1, A_2, \ldots, A_N\}$ and labelled by a class $c(e) \in C$. The domain of a nominal (discrete-valued) attribute A_i is a finite set $V(A_i)$ while the domain of a continuous-valued attribute A_j is an interval $V(A_j) = [l_j, u_j]$. For each class $c_k \in C$ by $E^+(c_k) = \{e \in E : c(e) = c_k\}$ we denote the set of *positive examples* and by $E^-(c_k) = E - E^+(c_k)$ the set of *negative examples*. A *classification rule* R takes the form $t_1 \wedge t_2 \wedge \ldots \wedge t_r \rightarrow c_k$, where $c_k \in C$ and the left-hand side is a conjunction of $r(r \leq N)$ conditions $t_1, t_2, \ldots, t_r$. Each condition t_j concerns one attribute A_{k_j}. It is assumed that $k_j \neq k_i$ for $j \neq i$. If A_{k_j} is a continuous-valued attribute than t_j takes one of three forms: $A_{k_j} > a$, $A_{k_j} \leq b$ or $a < A_{k_j} \leq b$, where $a, b \in V(A_{k_j})$. Otherwise (A_{k_j} is nominal) the condition takes the form $A_{k_j} = v$, where $v \in V(A_{k_j})$.

EDRL builds separately for each class $c_k \in C$ the set of disjunctive decision rules $RS(c_k)$ covering all (or near all) positive examples from $E^+(c_k)$. This aim is achieved by repeating for each c_k the following procedure (also called *sequential covering*): First "the best" or "almost best" classification rule is found using some global search method (an EA in our case). Next all the positive examples covered by the rule are removed and the search process is iterated on the remaining learning examples. The criterion expressing the performance of a rule (in terminology of EAs called the *fitness function*) prefers rules consisting of few conditions, which cover many positive examples and very few negative ones. The sequential covering is stopped when either all the positive examples are covered or the EA is unable (after three consecutive trials) to find a decision rule covering more then τ percent of all the positive examples from $E^+(c_k)$, where τ is a user-supplied parameter called *rule sensitivity threshold*.

It is important to notice that, when learning decision rules for a class c_k it is not necessary to distinguish between all the classes $c_1, c_2, \ldots, c_K$. Instead we merge all the classes different from c_k creating a class c_k^- . Then we run discretization algorithm and finally we generate decision rules.

3 Discretization of continuous-valued attributes

As it was mentioned before, each continuous-valued attribute A_j requires prior *discretization*. In this section we briefly explain the method we use (for a more detailed description the reader is referred to [6]) The aim of discretization is to find a partition of the domain $V(A_j) = [l_j, u_j]$ into d_j subintervals $[a_j^0, a_j^1)$, $[a_j^1, a_j^2), \ldots, [a_j^{d_j-1}, a_j^{d_j}]$. Any original value of the attribute A_j is then replaced by the number of the interval to which it belongs.

EDRL employs a supervised top-down greedy heuristic based on entropy reduction. Given a subset of examples $S \subseteq E$ its *class information entropy* H(S) is defined by:

$$H(S) = - \sum_{c_k \in C} p(S, c_k) \log p(S, c_k), \qquad (1)$$

where $0 \leq p(S, c_k) \leq 1$ is the proportion of examples with class c_k in S. The partitioning of the domain of A_j is performed as follows : First the initial interval $I = [l_j, u_j)$ is divided into two subintervals $I_1 = [l_j, a)$ and $I_2 = [a, u_j)$ in such way that this partition maximizes the information gain [15]:

$$Gain(A_j, I, a) = H(S) - \frac{|S_1|}{|S|} H(S_1) - \frac{|S_2|}{|S|} H(S_2), \qquad (2)$$

where $S, S_1, S_2 \subseteq E$ denote sets of examples for which the value of A_j belongs to the intervals I, I_1 and I_2 respectively. This procedure is then recursively applied to both subintervals I_1 and I_2. The recursive partitioning is performed only when the condition proposed by Fayyad and Irani [6] based on the Minimal Description Length Principle is met:

$$Gain(A_j, I, a) \geq \frac{log_2(|S| - 1)}{|S|} + \frac{\Delta(A_j, I, a)}{|S|}, \qquad (3)$$

where $\Delta(A_j, I, a) = \log_2(3^n - 1) - [nH(S) - n_1 H(S_1) - n_2 H(S_2)]$, and n, n_1, n_2 denote the number of class labels presented in S, S_1, S_2 respectively.

Dougherty *et al.* in a large experimental study [4], compared the above method with three others. The results indicated that an entropy-based discretization outperformed its competitors, namely equal interval binning, equal frequency binning, and 1R discretizer.

4 Searching for decision rules with EA

Our version of evolutionary algorithm follows the general description presented in [11]. In this section we present the following application-specific issues: representation, the evolutionary operators, the termination condition and the fitness function. We assume that all continuous-valued features have already been discretized.

4.1 Representation

Given the class label c_k any decision rule can be represented as a fixed-length string $S = \langle f_1, f_2, \ldots f_N, \omega_1, \omega_2, \ldots, \omega_N \rangle$ where f_i is a binary flag and $\omega_i \in V(A_i)$ is the value of attribute A_i encoded as an integer number. The flag f_i is set if and only if the condition $A_i = \omega_i$ is present in conjunction on the left-hand side of rule. The rule represented by string S can be expressed as follows:

$$(A_{j_1} = \omega_{j_1}) \wedge (A_{j_2} = \omega_{j_2}) \wedge \cdots \wedge (A_{j_L} = \omega_{j_L}) \rightarrow c_k \tag{4}$$

where L is the length of the rule and $j_1, j_2, \ldots, j_L \in \{j : f_j = 1\}$. One can see that if the flag f_i is not set the value of ω_i is irrelevant.

4.2 The Fitness function and the infeasibility criterion

Consider a string S encoding a decision rule, which covers POS positive examples and NEG negative ones. Its fitness is defined by the equation:

$$f(S) = \frac{POS^\alpha}{L+1} PE(x), \tag{5}$$

where

$$x = \frac{NEG}{POS + NEG)} - \beta,$$

L is the number of conditions constituting the left-hand side of the rule, α and β ($0 \leq \beta \leq 1$) are two users-supplied parameters, $PE(x)$ is the function which significantly degrades the fitness of the rule when the proportion of the number of covered negative examples to the total number of covered examples is greater than β. In all the experiments $PE(x)$ was given by

$$PE(x) = \frac{1}{1 + \exp(\gamma_1(x - \gamma_2))}, \tag{6}$$

where $\gamma_1 = 30$ and $\gamma_2 = 0.05$ (see Fig. 1), although other forms (e.g. threshold function) might also be used.

The value of β should be chosen carefully. β excessively close to 0 allows the generated rules to cover very few negative examples. Such rules are likely be too specialized and *overfit* the data. They will classify perfectly the examples from the learning set but their accuracy will by very poor when tested on previously unseen examples. On the other hand, excessively high value of β will increase the classification error by making the rules cover many negative examples.

When $PE(x)$ is too small (we have chosen $PE(x) < 0.05$) the rule is regarded as the *infeasible* one. It is rejected and the string S is re-initialized, as described in the next subsection.

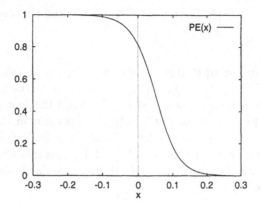

Fig. 1. The plot of $PE(x)$ ($\gamma_1 = 30$ and $\gamma_2 = 0.05$).

4.3 Initialization, termination condition and selection

Each string in the population is initialized using a randomly chosen positive example e from $E^+(c_k)$. Let us assume that $i_1, i_2, ..., i_r$ denote the numbers of non-missing features describing e and $\omega_{i_1}, \omega_{i_2}, ..., \omega_{i_r}$ denote the values of these attributes. A new string S is created in such way that it represents the decision rule $(A_{i_1} = \omega_{i_1}) \wedge (A_{i_2} = \omega_{i_2}) \wedge ... \wedge (A_{i_r} = \omega_{i_r}) \rightarrow c_k$. This method assures that the rule represented by S covers at least one positive example and if the learning set is consistent it does not cover any negative ones.

The algorithm terminates if the fitness of the best string in the population does not improve during N_{TERM} generations where N_{TERM} is the user-supplied parameter.

As a selection operator we use proportional elitist selection with linear scaling [9].

4.4 Genetic operators

The search in EAs is performed by genetic operators. They alter the population changing some individuals. Early implementations of EAs used the same operators and representation for every problem they were applied to. For instance a Standard Genetic Algorithm (SGA) [9, 11] represents individuals as binary strings and uses two genetic operators: crossover and mutation. The SGA was successfully applied to many problems, however many researchers e.g. Michalewicz in [11] report that it can be outperformed by the algorithm with carefully designed problem-dependent genetic operators and representation. Michalewicz and others argue that the use of problem-aware operators allows the EA to exploit the knowledge about the problem, which improves the performance. The weakness of domain-specific EA is that it can be applied only to the task it was designed for, while SGA can be used to solve any optimization problem.

Changing condition operator. This unary operator takes as an argument a single string $S = \langle f_1, f_2, \ldots f_N, \omega_1, \omega_2, \ldots, \omega_N \rangle$. It works as follows: First we choose a random number i where $1 \leq i \leq N$. Then the flag f_i is tested. If it is set i.e. the condition concerning attribute A_i is present in the rule represented by S we reset f_i and drop this condition from the rule. If f_i is not set we set f_i and replace ω_i with randomly chosen $\omega_i' \subseteq V(A_i)$ thus introducing the condition $A_i = \omega_i'$ to the rule. This operator is similar to standard mutation operator of genetic algorithms [9].

Insertion operator. The aim of this unary operator is to modify a classification rule R in such manner that it will cover a randomly chosen positive example e currently uncovered by R. This can be achieved by removing from R all logical conditions $A_i = \omega_i$ which return false when the rule is tested on the example e. The removal is done by resetting the corresponding flag f_i. As a result the string $S = \langle f_1, f_2, \ldots f_N, \omega_1, \omega_2, \ldots, \omega_N \rangle$ representing the classification rule R is replaced by $S' = \langle f_1', f_2', \ldots f_N', \omega_1, \omega_2, \ldots, \omega_N \rangle$ where

$$f_i' = \begin{cases} 0 \ if \ f_i = 1 \text{ and the condition } A_i = \omega_i \text{ is not satisfied by example } e \\ f_i \quad \text{otherwise} \end{cases}$$

$$(7)$$

Because the string modified by this operator will cover at least one new positive example there is a chance that its fitness (5) will increase. Of course it may decrease if the new string covers some new negative examples.

Crossover operator. We use a modification of the uniform crossover [11]. This binary operator requires two arguments $s_1 = \langle f_1, f_2, \ldots, f_N, \omega_1, \omega_2, \ldots, \omega_N \rangle$ and $s_2 = \langle g_1, g_2, \ldots, g_N, v_1, v_2, \ldots, v_N \rangle$. For each $i = 1, 2, \ldots, N$ it exchanges f_i with g_i and ω_i with v_i with the probability 0.5.

5 Preliminary experimental results

In this section some initial experimental results are presented. We have tested EDRL on 6 datasets from UCI Repository [13]. Table 1 describes these datasets. Table 2 shows the classification accuracies obtained by EDRL and C4.5 (Rel 8) learning algorithm. The results concerning C4.5 were taken from [16]. In both cases the accuracies were estimated by running ten times the complete tenfold crossvalidation. The mean of ten runs and the standard error of this mean are presented. As a reference we show the accuracy of the majority classifier[1]

---

[1] The majority classifier assigns an unknown example to the most frequent class in the learning set.

The values of the parameter β of the fitness function are also given; in all the experiments we used $\alpha = 2.0$ and the rule sensitivity threshold $\tau = 3\%$. Table 3 shows the number of rules and the total number of conditions obtained when the rules were extracted from the complete datasets.

Dataset	Features	Examples	Classes
australian	15 (9 nominal)	690	2
diabetes	8	768	2
german	20 (13 nominal)	1000	2
glass	9	214	7
hepatitis	19 (13 nominal)	155	2
iris	4	150	3

Table 1. Description of the datasets used in the experiments.

Dataset	Majority	C4.5	EDRL	β
australian	55.5	85.3 ± 0.2	86.1 ± 0.4	0.05
diabetes	65.1	74.6 ± 0.3	77.9 ± 0.3	0.2
german	70.0	71.6 ± 0.3	70.1 ± 0.8	0.2
glass	35.5	67.5 ± 0.8	66.7 ± 1.0	0.3
hepatitis	79.4	79.6 ± 0.6	81.2 ± 1.8	0.1
iris	33.3	95.2 ± 0.2	96.0 ± 0.0	0.05

Table 2. Classification accuracies of our method and C4.5 (Rel 8) algorithm.

6 Conclusions and future work

In the paper we proposed an rule learning EA-based system EDRL and conducted its experimental evaluation. The preliminary experimental results merely entitle us to conclude, that the classification accuracy of the current version of EDRL is comparable to that of C4.5. A real improvement was observed only for diabetes dataset. However we believe that the performance of our system can be further improved.

Several directions of future research exist. Currently all the continuous-valued features are discretized *globally* [4] prior to extraction of rules. Each feature is discretized independently from the others. We are working on the modification of EDRL, which will enable it to perform simultaneous search for all attribute thresholds during the induction of rules.

Dataset	Number of rules	Number of conditions
australian	5	15
diabetes	8	21
german	8	36
glass	9	19
hepatitis	12	50
iris	5	7

Table 3. Number of rules and conditions obtained.

Another idea is the extension of the rule representation form to VL_1 [12] language, in which a test can contain comparison to multiple values (internal disjunction). This could be especially beneficial for datasets with nominal attributes with large domains.

We also intend to replace the current strategy of dealing with infeasible rules by a more sophisticated method e.g. repair algorithm [11].

Acknowledgments The authors are grateful to Prof. Leon Bobrowski for his support and useful comments. This work was partially supported by the grant 8T11E00811 from State Committee for Scientific Research (KBN), Poland and by the grant W/II/1/97 from Technical University of Białystok.

References

1. Augier, S., Venturini, G., Kodratoff, Y.: Learning first order logic rules with a genetic algorithm. In: *Proc. of The First International Conference on Knowledge Discovery and Data Mining KDD-95*, AAAI Press (1995) 21-26.
2. Clark, P., Niblett, T.: The CN2 induction algorithm. *Machine Learning* 3 (1989) 261-283.
3. De Jong, K.A., Spears, W.M., Gordon, D.F.: Using genetic algorithm for concept learning. *Machine Learning* 13 (1993) 168-182.
4. Dougherty, J., Kohavi, R., Sahami, M.: Supervised and unsupervised discretization of continuous features. In: *Machine Learning: Proc of 12th International Conference*. Morgan Kaufmann (1995) 194-202.
5. Fayyad, U.M., Piatetsky-Shapiro, G., Smyth, P., Uthurusamy, R. (eds.): *Advances in Knowledge Discovery and Data Mining*. AAAI Press (1996).
6. Fayyad, U.M., Irani, K.B.: Multi-interval discretization of continuous-valued attributes for classification learning. In *Proc. of 13th Int. Joint Conference om Artificial Intelligence*. Morgan Kaufmann (1993) 1022-1027.
7. Flockhart, I.W., Radcliffe, N.J.: A Genetic Algorithm-Based Approach to Data Mining. In: *Proc. of The Second International Conference on Knowledge Discovery and Data Mining KDD-96*, AAAI Press (1996) 299-302.
8. Giordana, A., Neri, F.: Search-intensive concept induction. *Evolutionary Computation* 3(4) (1995) 375-416.

9. Goldberg, D.: *Genetic Algorithms in Search, Optimization and Machine Learning*. Addison-Wesley (1989).
10. Janikow, C.: A knowledge intensive genetic algorithm for supervised learning. *Machine Learning* 13 (1993) 192-228.
11. Michalewicz, Z.: *Genetic Algorithms + Data Structures = Evolution Programs*. 3rd edn. Springer-Verlag (1996).
12. Michalski, R.S., Mozetic, I., Hong, J., Lavrac, N., : The multi-purpose incremental learning system AQ15 and its testing application to three medical domains. In: *Proc. of the 5th National Conference on Artificial Intelligence* (1986) 1041-1045.
13. Murphy, P.M., Aha, D.W.: *UCI repository of machine-learning databases*, available on-line: http://www.ics.uci.edu/pub/machine-learning-databases.
14. Neri, F., Saitta, L.: Exploring the power of genetic search in learning symbolic classifiers. *IEEE Transaction on Pattern Analysis and Machine Intelligence* 18 (1996) 1135-1142.
15. Quinlan, J.R.: *C4.5: Programs for Machine Learning*. Morgan Kaufmann (1993).
16. Quinlan, J.R.: Improved use of continuous attributes in C4.5. *Journal of Artificial Intelligence Research* 4 (1996) 77-90.

Using Loglinear Clustering for Subcategorization Identification*

Nuno Miguel Marques (nmm@di.fct.unl.pt)**[1], Gabriel Pereira Lopes
(gpl@di.fct.unl.pt)[1], and Carlos Agra Coelho (coelho@isa.utl.pt)[2]

[1] Dep. Informática - FCT/UNL
[2] Dep. Matemática - ISA/UTL

Abstract. In this paper we will describe a process for mining syntactical verbal subcategorization, i.e. the information about the kind of phrases or clauses a verb goes with. We will use a large text corpus having almost 10,000,000 tagged words as our resource material. Loglinear modeling is used to analyze and automatically identify the subcategorization dependencies. An unsupervised clustering algorithm is used to accurately determine verbal subcategorization frames. In this paper we just tackle verbal subcategorization of noun phrases and prepositional phrases. A sample of 81 Portuguese verbs was used for evaluation purposes 97% precision and 99% recall for noun phrases and 92% precision and 100% recall for prepositional phrases was obtained.

1 Introduction

Recent experiments led us to find that loglinear models can be used for clustering verbs and other words with similar subcategorization requirements [MLC98]. We will show how it is possible to extract subcategorization information from a tagged corpus by co-occurrence counting of certain part-of-speech tags in the corpus. Relative positional information of those tags will be taken into account. In this paper we will elaborate on verbal subcategorization but the same approach is also feasible for other syntactic categories. The only grammatical information supplied to our system was originated in a hand tagged corpus containing about 5000 words that was used to train a neural network tagger [ML96]. Then a larger corpus with almost 10,000,000 words was automatically tagged using this trained tagger. This larger tagged corpus was used for clustering purposes. It should be stressed that the used tags are word tags not phrase tags.

Other authors have also worked on subcategorization extraction. Michael Brent [Bre93] proposed an approach where each subcategorization frame could be extracted by using a small set of highly specific and discriminating cues (mainly pronouns and proper nouns). According to [Man93], these cues represented 3% of the interesting information for subcategorization information. More recently,

* Work supported by JNICT Projects CORPUS (PLUS/C/LIN/805/93) and DIXIT (2/2.1/TIT/1670/95)
** Work supported by PhD scholarship JNICT-PRAXIS XXI/BD/2909/94

Manning [Man93] and Briscoe and Carroll [BC97] instead of using Brent's cues used a part-of-speech tagger and a parser (a simple finite state parser by Manning and a wide coverage partial parser by Briscoe and Carroll) for counting phrases. The main problem with each of these approaches is the grammatical knowledge they require. Only previously known grammatical subcategorization patterns can be extracted and this can bias the analysis because verbs with unusual patterns will be systematically ignored.

Ushioda et all. [UEGW96] parses (using regular expression grammar rules) all sentences of a corpus containing a given verb. The frequency of use of a given rule after a verb was used to build a contingency table for that verb[Agr90]. By using a loglinear model for supervised statistical learning [Fra96], Ushioda et. all built a system that classifies the verbs according to the selection of the subcategorization frame. However supervision requires a corpus tagged with subcategorization information and even for English this is a problem since there is no annotated corpora carrying such information.

In this paper we show that unsupervised clustering, using loglinear models, can be applied to subcategorization extraction from automatically tagged corpora. Moreover, as we will discuss prior parsing of corpora is not mandatory. In the next section we will describe how loglinear independence models, [Agr90] can be applied to determine clusters of verbs subcategorizing the same type of phrase or clause. Then we will describe two distinct experiments that empirically evaluate the validity of the proposed methodology. Acquired clusters will be analysed and confronted with the information supplied by a Portuguese standard dictionary and by two subcategorization dictionaries. Finally conclusions will be drawn.

2 Independence Loglinear Model

Let's assume we have a set of counts for m features over any verb (v). In this paper we will use both the total number of verbal forms followed by a part-of-speech $(f(POS|v))$[1] and the total number of verb forms in the corpus $(f(v))$. Based on these counts we can also determine the total number of verbs not followed by that part-of-speech $(f(\overline{POS}|v))$.

In the table bellow we present the frequencies of the pair article-noun (second column), article-absence of noun (third column) and absence of article (fourth column), for verbs *afirmar* (to assert) and *encontrar* (to meet).

	(art, n)	$(art, \bar{n})$	$\overline{art}$	$\lambda^{\widehat{X}}$
$v_{afirmar}$	514	379	7290	0
$v_{encontrar}$	413	320	6092	-0.1815
$\lambda^{\widehat{Y}}$	0	-0.2823	2.670	$\hat{\lambda} = 6.225$

---

[1] As part-of-speech (POS) we will use article (art) or preposition a (to or at, denoted $prep(a)$).

1100 verbs and only informs about the prepositional subcategorization. [Bus94] presents the main subcategorization classes for 2000 verbs.

In the reported experiment for transitive verbs we have used the features $\overline{art}$ and art already described in previous section. In the Prepositional phrase experiments we have used the counts for Portuguese preposition a (to or at). This experiment will be denoted by features $prep(a)$ (counted by $f(prep(a)|v)$) and $\overline{(prep(a))}$ (counted by $f(v) - f(prep(a)|v)$). This preposition has two very interesting features: it is ambiguous between article, demonstrative pronoun, personal pronoun and preposition, so we are testing how does our approach support noise inserted by the part-of-speech tagger. Second it is one of the most frequent prepositions in Portuguese. So, we don't have to worry about scarce data.

3.2 The art, $\overline{art}$ Experiment

One of the most used verbal classifications distinguishes between transitive and intransitive verbs. It is assumed that a transitive verb subcategorizes a noun phrase. So, we have measured the frequency of articles appearing immediately after the verb (denoted by feature art). In order to know how frequent a verb is we have also measured the frequency of non articles occurring just after the considered verbs (denoted by feature $\overline{art}$). Table 1 synthesizes the acquired results after applying our algorithm to the selected list of verbs. In this table, second row, headed by tr, regards the verbs that are classified in clusters where the first element is a transitive verb. But we notice that there are 2 intransitive verbs classified as transitive. Row three refers to verbs that are classified as both transitive and intransitive in the consulted dictionaries. Verbs that were reported by rows 2 and 3 give rise to 22 clusters. Row 4 is related to verbs classified as intransitive in the consulted dictionaries. For these verbs we notice that 3 transitive verbs are clustered with intransitive verbs. Verbs that were both identified as transitive or intransitive, have been considered transitive just for our precision recall/evaluation[3]. Since the total number of transitive verbs in our sample was of 73 we have a 90% (73/81) global precision baseline over the dictionary and 88% over the corpus.

Inspecting the acquired clusters, we find that our reference dictionary is incomplete — verb ser (to be) is only classified there as intransitive. However this verb has a transitive nature in certain occurrences:

Este é o terceiro dia do ano *(this is* **the third day of the year***)*.

Two transitive verbs are clustered with verb ser. The counts presented in table 1 have been corrected assuming that verb ser is in class $tr+intr$. The remaining three intransitive verbs clustered as transitive belong to the same cluster. This cluster has six verbs three transitive and three intransitive. It is

---

[3] As usual, precision is the percentage of correctly classified verbs (correctly classified verbs/total verbs) and recall is the percentage of classified verbs that were correct (correctly classified verbs/total of verbs classified).

	tr	tr+intr	intr	TtD	TtC	clusters	PrcD	PrcC
tr	33	4	2	74	225854	22	95%	97%
tr+intr	12	21	2					
intr	3	0	4	7	25631	2	57%	93%
TtD	73	8	81	—		24		
TtC	220786	30699	—	251485	189076			
RclD	96%	50%	—				91%	—
RclC	99%	77%					—	97%

Table 1. Number of verbs in each type of cluster for the noun phrase experiment. Columns represent the dictionary data and rows the acquired clusters as evaluated by their first element. *C* stands for frequencies in the corpus, *D* for frequencies in the dictionary. *Tt* stands for total, *Prc* stands for precision and *Rcl* stands for recall. Columns and rows headed by *tr* represent transitive verbs, headed by *intr* intransitive verbs. *clusters* presents the total number of clusters.

headed by verb *vir* (to come, or to reveal). There is an explanation: Portuguese preposition *a* was wrongly tagged as An article, as in:

> *o caso veio* **a** *público (the case was revealed* **to** *the public)*

Moreover, some forms of verb *vir* are identical to forms of verb *ver* (to see). Since verb *ver* is transitive, some articles are due to this yet unsolved lexical ambiguity. Another problem with some intransitive verbs is due to the exchange of positions between the verb and its subject - the verb appears before its subject:

> *veio* **a velhice** *e chegou a vez dela* (she had grown old and her time has elapsed)

The remaining two intransitive verbs clustered as transitive were *caber* (to fit) and *funcionar* (to work, in the sense that something works). Most of the articles appearing conjointly with *caber* were due to wrong tagging of noun *cabo* as a verb in the Portuguese expression *levar a cabo* (to perform). In this expression noun *cabo* is usually followed by article (*levar a cabo a operação* — to perform the action). In some other cases preposition *a* was wrongly tagged as an article.

3.3 The *prep(a)*, $\overline{prep(a)}$ Experiment

Previous experiment was repeated for the same list of verbs using Portuguese preposition *a* to cluster our data. We used features *prep(a)* and $\overline{prep(a)}$. Results are shown in table 2. Again the second row, headed by *PP(a)*, regards the verbs that subcategorize phrases headed by preposition *a*. There are 16 verbs that don't subcategorize *PP(a)* but were incorrectly clustered as if they did. Row three regards verbs that don't subcategorize *PP(a)*. According to our data no errors were detected for these verbs. A 53% precision baseline over dictionary and corpus could be achieved by tagging all clusters as *dont* (the verb doesn't subcategorize prep(a)).

	PP(a)	dont	TtD	TtC	clusters	PrcD	PrcC
PP(a)	38	16	54	128323	17	70%	92%
dont	0	27	27	123162	4	100%	100%
TtD	38	43	81	—	21	—	—
TtC	118540	132945	—	251485	183794		
RclD	100%	63%	—			80%	—
RclC	100%	93%				—	96%

Table 2. Number of verbs in each type of cluster for the prepositional phrase experiment. *C* stands for frequencies in the corpus, *D* for frequencies in the dictionary. *Tt* stands for total while *Prc* stand for precision and *Rcl* stands for recall.

Just by looking at this table we found, that while identifying subcategorization in the presence of the preposition is fairly easy (there was no errors, and a 100% recall was achieved), identifying the absence of it is more difficult. Confirming this is the number of clusters needed to describe each pattern. We find much more distinct patterns in verbs with the preposition than in verbs without it. The algorithm needed 17 clusters in the first case and only 4 in the latter. These results conform with what could be expected: Verbs that don't subcategorize the preposition, co-occur less with it. This way, occurrences of the preposition are mainly due to chance, or to the presence of some complement.

There are 3 main causes of errors for clusters regarding verbs that subcategorize *PP(a)*: verb complements (mainly time and space locatives), tagger errors and low frequency errors. Tagger errors further subdivide into two types: verb tagging errors and argument tagging errors. Complements are a common cause of error. Some verbs just tend to co-occur too frequently with time complements. Example: verb *assinar* (to sign) occurs frequently with a date in our corpus, and is clustered as subcategorizing *PP(a)*.

As it was previously mentioned, Portuguese preposition *a* is ambiguous with the article *a*. In some cases the article (much more frequent than the preposition), is tagged as preposition *a*. This way, verbs subcategorizing a noun phrase, could be grouped in a *PP(a)* cluster. Fortunately, the tagger is extremely accurate in tagging prepositions, and so, few errors are due to this problem. The same does not occur with article *a*, example: verb *integrar* (to integrate), in the expression *integrar a força* ... (to integrate the [military] force), the article *a* is systematically tagged as a preposition. This error will probability be ameliorated in future versions of the tagger.

Incorrect identification of verbs is another cause for error. Nouns, tagged as verbs, could be counted as the verbal forms with which they are ambiguous. Example: town named *Caminha* was wrongly tagged as verb *caminhar* (to walk). Verb *caminhar* is not generally followed by preposition *a*, but name *Caminha* is usually followed by such preposition. This way, *caminhar* was wrongly grouped in a *PP(a)* cluster.

Low frequency errors refer to rare subcategorization frames of frequent verbs. So, occasional presence of the selected feature tends to cluster a less frequent non subcategorizing verb with a much more frequent subcategorizing one. Example:

in the cluster headed by *acrescentar* (to add), having seven verbs, the five less frequent ones have only one or two occurrences of feature (*prep(a)*). As a result these verbs have all been clustered as subcategorizing *PP(a)* verbs.

4 Conclusions

In related work, only Brent [Bre93], presents results specific for the subcategorization of noun phrases. A total of 66 verbs are identified having noun phrase arguments. Of these 63 were correct. Other 127 verbs had been manually identified as having a noun phrase argument. So this means a 49% recall and 95% precision. Brent used 5 subcategorization frames and obtained 96% precision and 76% recall. Other presented results in literature have smaller precision, but use a much richer subcategorization set. For instance Briscoe and Carroll ([BC97]) report 81% precision and 80% recall using more than two hundred subcategorization frames. Although comparisons are difficult (we are working in a different language, and we are evaluating our data by comparison with a dictionary, not manually, as Brent did), our acquired precision/recall results seem encouraging.

We think the algorithm that we have just presented is a good way to determine word subcategorization. The main drawback we have found was on low frequency verbs but this can be overcome by automatically looking for extra text having those verbs. Despite this we still expect to find some low frequency words due to Zipfs law. The best way to handle these verbs is probably by using a partial parser and model based fault finding but this is a complementary research problem. A small change in our algorithm may also be effective on low frequency verbs. First we should determine and evaluate the basic clusters for the most frequent verbs. Then a probability threshold P should be established, lets say at 95%. At that value the G^2 statistic could be used in hypothesis testing. A new verb should be considered tagged as belonging to all the clusters where the independence hypothesis couldn't reject it. We intend to evaluate this change to the algorithm for low frequency words soon.

We also intend to extend our algorithm in order to support a better search through our cluster space. For that we intend to insert cluster merging and cluster splitting operators, similarly to Fisher's Cobweb [Fis87]. Regarding the number of used features we are also presently researching for the effects of adding new dimensions to our contingency tables. One of the advantages of doing this by using loglinear models is the possibility of inserting interaction terms among the several features in our model. This way we will no longer need to assume statistical independence among our features[Fra96].

The best behavior of our algorithm was achieved when we counted for the presence of a certain unigram, bigram or trigram and its complement (that is the frequency of the verb minus the frequency of the feature) after the verb. We empirically found that the increase in the number of features tends to increase the used number of clusters. Similarly, if we don't use the complement of the features we have found that recall values were worst.

Additionally to the subcategorization frame, we have for each considered verb its expected value given by the loglinear model. By using this value we are providing frequencies that, although influenced by the verb subcategorization frame, are still particular to each verb. Our results, if we take into consideration verb relative frequencies in the corpus, are outstanding: 97% of all occurrences of transitive verbs are correctly identified, having a recall of 99%. In the prepositional phrase experience, 92% of precision was achieved without missing any verb that subcategorizes a prepositional phrase headed by the preposition under study. Moreover our approach has the additional advantage that almost no linguistic information is needed by our algorithm and so, it can be used as a tool for extracting subcategorization frames.

References

[Agr90]   Alan Agresti. *Categorical Data Analysis*. John Wiley and Sons, 1990.

[BC97]   Ted Briscoe and John Carroll. Automatic extraction of subcategorization from corpora. In *Proceedings of the 5th Conference on Applied Natural Language Processing (ANLP'97)*, 1997.

[Bre93]   Michael R. Brent. From grammar to lexicon: Unsupervised learning of lexical syntax. *Computacional Linguistics*, 19(2):245–262, 1993.

[Bus94]   Winfried Busse. *Dicionário Sintáctico de Verbos Portugueses*. Livraria Almedina, 1994.

[Fis87]   D. H. Fisher. Knowledge acquisition via incremental conceptual clustering. *Machine Learning*, 2:139–172, 1987.

[Fra96]   Alexander Franz. *Automatic Ambiguity Resolution in Natural Language Processing*, volume 1171 of *LNAI Series*. Springer, 1996.

[Hea88]   M. J. R. Healy. *GLIM: An Introduction*. Clarendon Press, Oxford, 1988.

[LMR94]   José Gabriel Lopes, Nuno Cavalheiro Marques, and Vitor Ramos Rocio. Polaris, a POrtuguese Lexicon Acquisition and Retrieval Interactive System. In *Proceedings of the conference on Pratical Applications of PROLOG*, 1994.

[Man93]   Cristopher Manning. Automatic acquisition of a large subcategorization dictionary from corpora. In *Proceedings of the 31st Annual Meeting of ACL*, pages 235–242, 1993.

[ML96]   Nuno C. Marques and José Gabriel Lopes. A neural network approach to part-of-speech tagging. In *Proceedings of the Second Workshop on Computational Processing of Written and Spoken Portuguese*, pages 1–9, Curitiba, Brazil, October 21-22 1996.

[MLC98]   N.M.C. Marques, J.G.P. Lopes, and C. A. Coelho. Learning verbal transitivity using loglinear models. In *Lecture Notes in AI (LNAI): Proceedings of the 10th European Conference on Machine Learning*. Springer Verlag, Berlin, April 1998.

[UEGW96] A. Ushioda, D. Evans, T. Gibson, and A. Waibel. Estimation of verb subcategorization frame frequencies based on syntactic and multidimensional statistical analysis. In H. Bunt and M. Tomita, editors, *Recent Advances in Parsing Technology*. Kluwer Academic Publishers, 1996.

[VC92]   Helena Ventura and Maunela Caseiro. *Dicionário Prático de Verbos Seguidos de Preposições*. Fim de Século Edições, LDA., 2 edition, 1992.

Exploratory Attributes Search for Time-Series Data: An Experimental System for Agricultural Application

Kazunori MATSUMOTO

System Integration Technology Center,
TOSHIBA,
3-22 Katamachi, Fuchu, Tokyo, 183-8512, Japan
E-mail: kazunori@sitc.toshiba.co.jp

Abstract. This paper reports an experimental agricultural datamining system which purposes to find weather patterns influencing yield of rice. Necessary data for this system are separately maintained in various databases. We then show how this system integrate them into one database with an assistance of support databases. Next we discuss the attribute selection problem for the data in the integrated database. Our method first exploratory search for a candidate set of attributes. In this case, the support databases is used to avoid a searching space explosion. Once the candidate set is identified, we apply a greedy search in the set to find the most useful subset of attributes.

1 Introduction

Agriculture is an information-intensive industry from an essential point of view. So many factors such as soil, fertilizer, temperature, precipitation, sunray, etc. are all affect harvest, so that information about them is carefully investigated by expert persons in deciding agricultural activities. We thus expect to build up an intelligent computerized agricultural information system [7] to assist the experts and to help an improvement on agricultural technologies. Towards this purpose, we firstly need to provide a system which can reveal hidden relations among agricultural factors. Although traditional statistical methods have already applied to this field, we expect recent datamining technologies [1] to bring still more fruitful results. For example, an expert can easily understand IF - THEN style rules extracted by the typical datamining methods, then he may give further investigation around the rules. In this paper we reports an experimental agricultural datamining system whose purpose is to find weather patterns determining yield of rice. Necessary data for this datamining are maintained in separated databases. We then need to integrate them into one database. Since each database is built independently, their integration cannot achieve in direct way. We show how they are integrated by using support databases which store additional agricultural information.

Most datamining methods [1,6] run with a set of training data which is specified as a set of tuples of attribute values with class information. Then we must identify the set of attributes, and transform data in the integrated database with the attributes. This attribute selection problem is actively studied [3,4,5], however, previous works mostly concern the method of removing unimportant attributes from the initially given ones. We show the usual attribute selection is not adequate for our purpose.

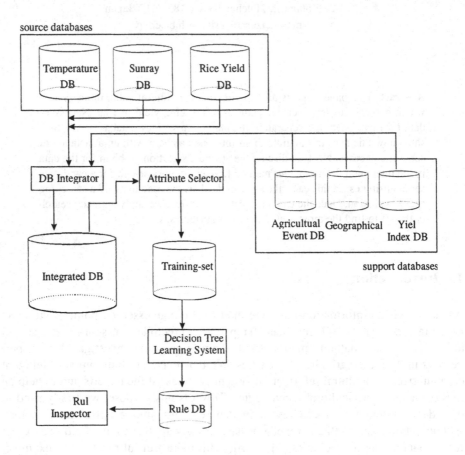

Fig. 1 Outline of the experimental system

2   Outline of the system

According to the general flow shown in Fig.1, the system arranges databases and analyze them by using datamining techniques. The raw data necessary for the datamining phase are separately maintained in the left above three source databases.

The DB Integrator makes the Integrated DB which stores all necessary information in an unified form. In this case, the DB Integrator uses the support databases to bridge the gap among source databases. The Attribute Selector searches in the Integrated DB for an adequate set of attributes with an assistance of the support databases. Data in the Integrated DB are re-expressed in terms of the attributes and are stored in the Training-set DB. The Decision tree learning system datamines the training-set DB and extracted classification rules which are stored in the rule DB. The Inspector with the Rule DB re-analyze the training-set DB and the Integrated DB to proceed further examination of the rules.

3   Making the Training-set database

As we seen in the outline, the training-set DB is built via the Integrated DB. In this chapter, we explain how the Training-set database is made with the support databases.

3.1   Integrating the source databases

In this experiment, we use the following three source databases. Before integration, they are separately arranged by using the support databases.

Rice Yield DB
This database records, in tabular form,   yearly yield of rice by the kilogram per ten are (kg/10a) for each prefecture in Japan. The schema is given as:
<Prefecture Name,   Year,   Yield>. Fig.2 graphically shows a part, Hokkaido which is the northmost prefecture in Japan, of this databases.   From this graph, we see the yield tend to increase in general with sudden oscillation. The general increasing tendency is mainly brought by the progress of agricultural technologies in the long period. On the other hand, sudden rises and falls mostly due to the natural conditions, especially weather is one of the most affective factors.   For the purpose of our experiment, we need to remove the contribution of the technological improvement from the graph. In case of rice, the Japanese Agricultural Ministry publishes the yield index every year, which are stored in the Yield Index DB. Before the integration, we rewrite the Yield value in theYield DB with the index.

Temperature DB and Sunray DB
We use these two weather databases in this experiment. These values are observed at several weather stations in each prefecture, and their daily averages are recorded in each databases. The both databases are in tabular form and their schema is common as: <Weather Station Name, Year, Value of Jan.1, ..., Value of Dec.31>.

The join operation [8] provides a standard way of integrating several databases in tabular forms into a new tabular form database. This operation combines two tuples when they match on the join columns. In case of our experiment, we need to resolve the difference of Prefecture Name and Weather Station Name before applying the join operation. The Geographical DB is used for this purpose.

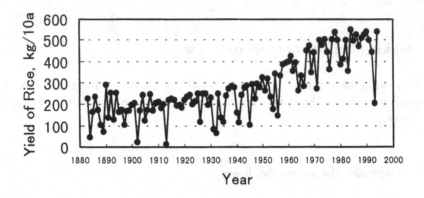

Fig. 2 Yearly yield at Hokkaido Prefecture

Geographical DB(support database)

This database stores the geographical information about the weather stations. The data schema is: <Weather Stations Name, Prefecture Name, Altitude,Longitude, Latitude>. With this information, we can get all weather station names for a given prefecture. Then, temperature (sunray) data for a prefecture X can be calculated as the average of the values at all weather stations in X (Fig.3).   In this case, a station of which altitude considerably different from others is ignored. Outliers can also be removed in this step by ignoring extreme values. Similarly, a data lack at a station can be compensate with other station's value.

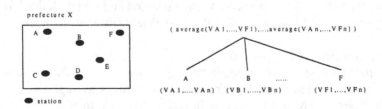

Fig. 3 Prefecture Data is Calculated from Station Data

Finally, we can integrate above three source databases into the integrated DB, whose schema is: <Prefecture Name, Year, Arranged Yield, Temperature of Jan.1, ..., Temperature of Dec.31, Sunray of Jan.1, ..., Sunray of Dec.31>.

3.3 Exploratory Search for Attributes

Most datamining tools assume a set of training data is specified as a set of tuples of attribute values with class information. A typical datamining is a process to build good rules in terms of attributes or attribute values, which correctly classifies most of the training data. It is reported [3,4,5] that inadequately selected attributes cause a searching space explosion and cause decreasing the extracted rule quality. Then, defining a set of suitable attributes is an important issue. Most studies concerning this issue formalize it as the attribute subset selection problem, which identifies unrelevant (or unimportant) attributes from given initial set of attributes.

A direct application of the subset selection approach to our case regards every time points as the initial attributes, then remove unrelevant time points from the initial set. This direct method is not enough for our case because of the following reasons:

(1) This is unaware of a data behavior on an time interval. In case of rice growing, existing agricultural knowledge says that weather patterns on a relatively long interval are important rather than momentary patterns.

(2) Date of agricultural activities or events, such as seeding, harvesting, are changed year by year (Fig.4). A direct comparison of different years has few agricultural meaning.

Then, we successively enumerate a time intervals, as a candidate for an attribute, by focusing on the meaningful date specified in the Agricultural Event DB, then check its importance in exploratory manner. In this case, we introduce heuristics to avoid generating too many intervals. First, we can immediately exclude portions which are obviously unrelated to rice growing. It starts at the day of seeding (SD, for short), usually at the middle of April, and ends at the day of harvesting (HD, for short), usually at the end of September, then it is enough to focus on this interval [SD,HD]. Second, since all of SD,TD,ED,and HD are used as milestones in planning agricultural activities, we restrict at least one boundary of an interval must be one of these date. Third, from agricultural commonsense, an interval length can be set greater than two weeks.

According to above the heuristics and the following criterion, we search for a set of useful intervals.

Criterion: We say an interval is useful, if the class difference of the training data can be well explained by their difference on the interval.

In this experiment, the class difference of two training data is defined as the difference of their class values, and the difference of two training data is defined as the difference of their average value on the interval. According to these definitions, we exploratory investigate the data for searching useful intervals. Currently, the main work of this stage is various kinds of visual inspection of data with an assistance of statistical information.

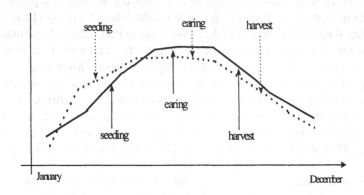

Fig. 4 Agricultural Events Differ Year by Year

The left side of Fig. 5 shows an example of visual investigation on the interval [SD,TD]. The X-axis is the training data difference and the Y-axis is the class difference. The right side of the figure shows the similar investigation on the interval [ED, ED+3weeks]. In this case, we conclude [ED,ED+3weeks] is useful, on the other hand [SD,TD] is regarded as not useful. Continuing this investigation, we finally select 8 intervals (4 is for temperature data, and others are for sunray data)as the attributes set.

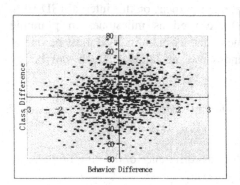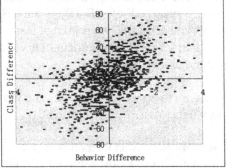

Fig. 5   Class difference and data difference on intervals

4 Mining the training-set database

Once the training-set database has been prepared, we datamine it with the decision tree learning system. Currently we use the C4.5 [6], which is one of the most successful datamining tool. Due to the limitation of the C4.5, we replace the continuous class values by discrete values of 'good' and 'bad'. By an direct application with the training-set DB, we can extract a set of rules, which have 20.9% of estimated error rate. This is not satisfactory result. Here each element of the current attribute set is checked its usefulness by the visual exploration, however, usefulness of their combination is not yet verified. We then use greedy attribute selection over the current set of attributes. That is, we repeatedly run the C4.5 with every subset of the current attribute set, and select the best performed one. Since the exploratory selection stage focuses sufficiently small attributes, computational cost of the greedy selection can be ignored. Fig. 6 shows the results of the greedy selection. The X-axis shows subset rank in order of goodness. The Y-axis is the estimated error rate with the subset. We finally get a set of rules with 14.2 % estimated error rate, which is 6.2% improvement over the first application.

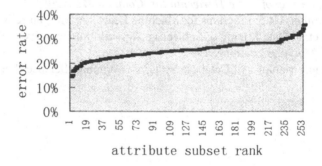

Fig.6 error rate for each attribute subset

5 Conclusion

We report an experimental agricultural datamining system. From a database perspective, method for integration of all necessary data from separately maintained various databases is an important issue. Recent studies on dataware house [2] provide applicable technologies, however, further improvement is inevitable for our purpose.
We plan to combine other datamining technologies into this experimental system to get more fruitful results.

Acknowledgment
The author would like to thank to Dr. Hiroshi SEINO of National Institute of Agro-Environmental Sciences for providing essential data and giving many suggestive advice.

References

[1] M.S. Chen, J. Han, and P.S. Yu, Data Mining: An Overview from a Database Perspective, IEEE Trans. on Knowledge and Data Engineering, Vol.8, No.6, 1996.

[2] R. Kimball, The Data Warehouse Toolkit, John wiley & Sons,1996

[3] K. Kira, and L.A. Rendell, The Feature Selection Problem: Traditional Methods and a New Algorithm, *Proc. of The Ninth National Conf. on AI*, 1992.

[4] R.Kohavi and D.Sommerfield, Feature Subset Selection using the Wrapper Model:
Overfitting and Dynamic Search Space Topology, First Int. Conf. on KDD, 1995.

[5] H. Liu, and R. Setiono, A Probabilistic Approach to Feature Selection - A Filter Solution , *Proc. of The Thirteenth Int. Conf. on ML*, 1996.

[6] J. R. Quinlan, C4.5: Programs for Machine Learning, Morgan Kaufmann, 1993.

[7] R.B. Rao et.al, Data Mining of Subjective Agricultural Data, Proc. of the Tenth Int. Conf. Machine Learning, 1993.

[8] J.F. Ullman, Principles of Database Systems, Computer Science Press, 1982.

A Procedure to Compute Prototypes for Data Mining in Non-structured Domains

J. Méndez, M. Hernández, and J. Lorenzo

Dpto. de Informática y Sistemas, Universidad de Las Palmas de Gran Canaria, 35017 Las Palmas, Spain. [jmendez, mhernandez,jlorenzo]@dis.ulpgc.es

Key words: learning, data mining, knowledge discovery, symbolic clustering.

Abstract. This paper describes a technique for associating a set of symbols with an event in the context of knowledge discovery in database or data mining. The set of symbols is related to the keywords in a database which is used as an implicit knowledge source. The aim of this approach is to discover the significant keyword groups which best represent the event. A significant contribution of this work is a procedure which obtains the representative prototype of a group of symbolic data. It can be used for both, unsupervised learning to describe classes, and supervised learning to compute prototypes. The procedure involves defining an objective function and the subsequent hypothesis-exploring system and obtaining an advantageous procedure regarding computational costs.

1 Introduction

Knowledge Discovery in Database and Data Mining involve a set of techniques used in an automated approach to exhaustively explore and bring to the surface complex relationships in very large datasets [4]. Data mining aims at finding useful regularities in large datasets. The interest in the field is motivated by the growth of computerized data collections and by the high potential value of patterns discovered in those collections [7]. Clustering is a technique used in a large number of data mining applications in different domains [9] [6] because it deals with two important issues: machine learning to generate abstractions and statistics to deals with data noise. Both, clustering and supervised learning, can need a procedure to compute class prototypes. This paper describes a technique for finding some symbolic description of an event. The symbolic description is established through labeled or attributed groups present in keywords of the database. The technique may be applied to the interpretation of any characteristic or event related with a database as long as an appropriate search engine exists. A similar approach is described by Guigó and Temple[10] applied to protein databases.

Biosequences Databases is a field where Data Mining tools play important and enabling roles [14] [13]. In most protein databases each entry contains, addicionality to its name and amino acid sequence, a set of annotated data which may be keywords associated with the functionality of protein characteristics. Likewise it may be accompanied by other data of diverse scientific interest. The information considered for each protein entry is a 3-tuple [*name,keywords,sequence*]. The sequence is useful for locating the patterns in it. Different tools may be used for this task. Some of them are general purpose and have relative low performance, others include specific search engines for matching in protein sequences and DNA, as, for example BLAST [12].

Most dataset used in Machine Learning are attribute based. Each attribute can be a numeric value or a symbol take from a discrete set. Attribute based datasets are structured domains in which an attribute can be considered as a dimension in a continuous or discrete space. In this paper non-structured domain of samples are considered, that is only as set of symbols without other organization or algebraic class. Samples in a non-structured domain have not fixed cardinality or length. In the work of Guigó and Temple[10] a logical combination of keywords is given as a result. Let k be a boolean expression of keywords in the database and $F(k)$ the set of proteins that are matched by a query in the database. Let p be a protein pattern or motif, and $H(p)$ the set of proteins that are matched by a search engine in the database. Guigó and Temple consider k to be a possible explanation of the p pattern if the similarity or correlation between $F(k)$ and $H(p)$ is maximum. That is, $s(F(k), H(p))$ must be maximized, where $s(A, B)$ is a similarity measure between A and B sets, expressed using the set cardinalities $|A|$ and $|B|$ as:

$$s(A, B) = \frac{|A \cap B|}{\sqrt{|A||B|}} \tag{1}$$

The approach used in this paper is very different. Rather than determine a boolean expression of keywords, *it involves inducing which types or classes, and its prototypes M, are derived from $H(p)$ by means of a process of symbolic clustering appropriate to the nature of the data considered*. Rather than obtain a *or-of-and* expression of keywords, it obtains a *set-of-set* of keywords. Prior to the process of symbolic clustering, the keywords for each protein in $H(p)$ is obtained based on the information contained in the database and selecting some keyword types. Annotated databases as SWISS-PROT [1] includes a lot of attributes which must be selected. The resulting data from this process include a protein dataset with its selected keywords. It is referred to as the items I set. The proposed procedure can be used in all applications which mach with:[*item-name, keywords, other-data*].

Clustering is a useful tool for analyzing data because it is an inductive method which can discover certain regularities in the experimental data. It is possible to discover natural types or data clusters which are derived from the use of distance or similarity measures from the data themselves [11][3]. The set of samples is made up of the set of items $I = \{I_i; i = 1, \ldots, n\}$ associated with the set of proteins obtained by the search engine. Each item I_i includes the set of symbols associated with the database keywords in $U = \{s_j; j = 1, \ldots, m\}$. Each item may be expressed as: $I_i = \{s_j, u_{ij}; j = 1, \ldots, m\}$ where $s_j \in U$. The value $u_{ij} \in \{0, 1\}$ is the membership degree of s_j in the item I_i. This value may also be defined as: $u_{ij} = |I_i \cap \{s_j\}|$. The addressed problem involves determining the groups of items

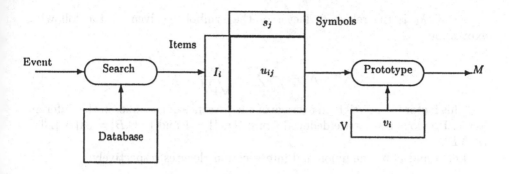

Fig. 1. Prototototype Computation from the data obtained after a search in a Database

that best represent the natural classes of the total I set. The characterization of these groups is determined through their respective prototypes or means.

2 Computing Prototypes

This section is concerning with the problem of how to determine the symbol set contained in M so that it is most similar to a non null set of items I. Specifically, it establishes a measure of similarity as an objective function expressed as:

$$f(M) = \frac{1}{n_v} \sum_{i=1}^{n} v_i s(I_i, M) = \frac{1}{n_v} \sum_{i=1}^{n} v_i \frac{|M \cap I_i|}{\sqrt{|M||I_i|}} \qquad (2)$$

where n_v it is given for:

$$n_v = \sum_{i=1}^{n} v_i > 0 \qquad (3)$$

The term $v_i \in \{0,1\}$ is the degree with which item I_i participates in the group which is used for computing the prototype. To carry out the computation different hypothetical solutions will be considered. Let X be a hypothesis about M that does not include a symbol s_k and X' a new hypothesis obtained by including this symbol, that is $X \xrightarrow{s_k} X'$.

$$X' = X \cup \{s_k\} \qquad X \cap \{s_k\} = \emptyset \qquad (4)$$

The objective function value of X' can be obtained recursively from that of X as follows:

$$f(X') = \frac{\sqrt{|X|} f(X) + \lambda_k}{\sqrt{|X| + 1}} \qquad (5)$$

where λ_k is the relevance factor of the symbol s_k given by the following expression:

$$\lambda_k = \frac{1}{n_v} \sum_{i=1}^{n} v_i \frac{u_{ik}}{\sqrt{|I_i|}} \tag{6}$$

This factor is the weighted average of the presence of a symbol in the different items. Previous results are deduced from: $|\{s_k\}| = 1$ and $|A \cup B| = |A| + |B| - |A \cap B|$.

Let S and P be the union and intersecction closures respectively:

$$S = \bigcup_{\forall i, v_i > 0} I_i \qquad P = \bigcap_{\forall i, v_i > 0} I_i \tag{7}$$

Let R be the complement of P into S, that is: $P \cup R = S$ and $P \cap R = \emptyset$, it is also expresed as : $R = S - P$. Let $h = |R|$ be its cardinality.

Theorem 1 *If a symbol s_k does not belong to the S union, then it does not belong to the prototype M.*

Proof: If $s_k \notin S$, in such case $s_k \notin I_i$, and for it $u_{ik} = 0$, verifying itself as $\lambda_k = 0$. For the hypotheses X and X' it stands that:

$$f(X') - f(X) = \frac{\sqrt{|X|} f(X)}{\sqrt{|X| + 1}} - f(X) < 0 \tag{8}$$

It generates a decreasing of the objective function value, and therefore such symbols are never found in the prototype M for which this value should be maximum.

Theorem 2 *If a symbol s_k belongs to the intersection P, then it belongs to the prototype M.*

Proof: If $s_k \in P$, in such case $s_k \in I_i$, and for it $u_{ik} = 1$, verifying itself as:

$$\lambda_k = \sigma = \frac{1}{n_v} \sum_{i=1}^{n} \frac{v_i}{\sqrt{|I_i|}} \tag{9}$$

The relevance of a symbol that participates in P is the greatest possible designated σ. For the hypotheses X and X' it is given that:

$$f(X') - f(X) =$$
$$\frac{1}{n_v} \sum_{i=1}^{n} \frac{v_i}{\sqrt{|I_i|}} \left(\frac{|X \cap I_i| + 1}{\sqrt{|X| + 1}} - \frac{|X \cap I_i|}{\sqrt{|X|}} \right) > 0 \tag{10}$$

This result is positive due to: $|X \cap I_i| \leq |X|$. It generates a increasing of the objective function value, and therefore such symbols must be found in the prototype M for which this value should be maximum. From all the previous results, we may deduce the following general conclusion:

Corollary 1 *M does not include any symbol that is not contained in S and therefore $M \subseteq S$, and in the same way, M includes all the symbols that are contained in P and therefore $P \subseteq M$. Thus, the M prototype contains the intersection P and is contained in the union S, that is: $P \subseteq M \subseteq S$.*

Given the graph $G =< N, L >$ compound of a set of nodes N and links L, each node is made up of the symbols contained in P and a combination of the contained in R, so the items as well as the closure sets are included in the N. The number of graph nodes is given by: $n_G = 2^h$. The set of nodes $N = \{N_0, \cdots, N_{2^h-1}\}$ is made up of all the combinations of possible symbols. It is verified that: $N_0 = P$ and $N_{2^h-1} = S$. Each link is determined by the inclusion or union with a symbol belonging to R. In the set of links, $L = \{l_{ij}\}$, l_{ij} represents a directed link between the node N_i and N_j, so if $l_{ij} = s_k$ then $N_j = N_i \cup \{s_k\}$. Each hypothesis of the solution corresponds to a N_i node, having associated a value of objective function $f(N_i)$. The process of finding the solution to the problem becomes a search for the graph node which has the maximum value in the objective function. Given that the number of nodes in the graph is 2^h, this problem seems **NP** class.

The node N_b has a distance $\Delta(N_b, N_a)$ from another node N_a, if it is verified that: $N_a \subset N_b$ and $|N_b| = |N_a| + \Delta(N_b, N_a)$. The objective function value of N_b can be expressed recursively from the value of that of N_a in the following way, where: $\sum_a^b \lambda$ is the sum of the relevance factor of all the symbols of difference between both nodes.

$$f(N_b) = \frac{\sqrt{|N_a|} f(N_a) + \sum_a^b \lambda}{\sqrt{|N_a| + \Delta(N_b, N_a)}} \tag{11}$$

Given that all the nodes can be derived from the one associated with P, the objective function of a N_i node can be expressed as:

$$f(N_i) = \frac{\sqrt{|P|} f(P) + \sum_P^{N_i} \lambda}{\sqrt{|P| + \Delta(P, N_i)}} = \frac{|P|\sigma + \sum_P^{N_i} \lambda}{\sqrt{|P| + \Delta(P, N_i)}} \tag{12}$$

Let $\{\xi_1, \ldots, \xi_h\}$ the set of maximal relevance factors obtained by sorting the relevance factor, λ_i, in such way that: $\xi_1 = \max(\lambda_i)$ and $\xi_h = \min(\lambda_i)$. The relevant symbols $\{w_1, \ldots, w_h\}$ are the results of sorting in R the symbols based on the relevance factor in decreasing order. Let, η_i, be the factor of maximum cumulative relevance:

$$\eta_0 = 0 \tag{13}$$

$$\eta_i = \eta_{i-1} + \xi_i = \xi_1 + \cdots + \xi_i \tag{14}$$

Theorem 3 *The highest value of the objective function from among all the nodes that have a distance $i \geq 0$ from the node N_0 is given as:*

$$f_i = \frac{|P|\sigma + \eta_i}{\sqrt{|P| + i}} \tag{15}$$

Table 1. False Positive and True Negative samples. All errors are contained in class3 and class7 which are the most spread classes.

Sample	Own Class	Most Similar Class
seasnake	class3	class4
slug	class7	class6
tortoise	class3	class2
worm	class7	class6

Proof: The number of nodes found at a distance i of N_0 is $\binom{h}{i}$. For all of them the denominator of the objective function is the same, obtaining the highest possible value choosing that which have the highest numerator value, that is, the sum of values of maximum relevance. A recursive expresion can be used also to compute f_i:

$$f_0 = \sigma\sqrt{|P|} \qquad C_0 = |P| \tag{16}$$

$$f_{i+1} = \frac{\sqrt{C_i}f_i + \xi_{i+1}}{\sqrt{C_{i+1}}} \qquad C_{i+1} = C_i + 1 \tag{17}$$

Theorem 4 *The highest value of the objective function of the nodes contained in G is contained in the set $F = \{f_0, f_1, \cdots, f_h\}$.*

Proof: From the fact that the highest value of the graph found among the distances $i = 0, 1, 2, \ldots, h$. In such a way that $f_0 = f(P)$ and $f_h = f(S)$.

If f_T is the highest value of the contents in F, then the solution of the M prototype is given as:

$$M = \begin{cases} P & \text{if } T = 0 \\ P \cup \{w_1, \cdots, w_T\} & \text{otherwise} \end{cases} \tag{18}$$

It must be emphasized that the set of operations carried out for obtaining this solution is polinomially expressable on h, m and n, so the problem seems to be in the **P** class.

3 Computing Prototypes with dependent Symbols

In the previous section non-structured applications where all symbols are independent have been considered. Many real applications are well structured attribute based, in this case different values in an atttribute are dependent symbols which can be considered as mutually exclusive. Previous procedure can be extended to deal with dependent symbols. Let s_j and s_k be two boolean related symbols, that is: $s_j = \bar{s}_k$, eg. in UCI Zoo dataset [5] [aquatic, no-aquatic]. In this case is verified that:

$$u_{ij} + u_{ik} = 1 \tag{19}$$

So is verified that:

$$\lambda_j + \lambda_k = \sigma \tag{20}$$

In a general case, given a set of exclusive symbols $B = \{b_1, \ldots, b_l\}$ (eg. in UCI Soybean dataset attribute area-damage =[scatterd, low-areas, upper-areas, whole-field]) it is verified that:

$$\sum_{i=1}^{l} \lambda(b_i) = \sigma \tag{21}$$

To compute prototypes it must be included an additional exclusion rule of a symbol if any other in the exclusive set is already included. Let B a set of mutually exclusive symbols, if b_t is the symbol with maximal relevance in B, then b_t symbol *can* be include in the prototype M and the others in B *must* be excluded.

Some experimental attribute based datasets can include unknow samples. Some approaches can be used to deal with unknow samples [8]. One of them is based in to assign unknow data to all possible symbols in this attribute. In this case is verified that:

$$\sum_{i=1}^{l} \lambda(b_i) \geq \sigma \tag{22}$$

Other approach is based on not assigning unknow data to any possible symbols in this attribute. In this case is verified that:

$$\sum_{i=1}^{l} \lambda(b_i) \leq \sigma \tag{23}$$

4   An Example

A practical case of prototype computation is presented using the UCI Zoo dataset [5]. This is an attribute based dataset with a small number of attributes, and so it is not the natural domain to apply the described procedure. However it can be applied to this type of domains including the concept of dependent symbols. In this case a dataset with 16 attributes is used to code 101 samples grouped in 7 predefined classes. Each sample corresponds to an animal which is classified into a zoological class. All attributes, except legs attribute, are boolean. In this paper this last attribute is considered as boolean with [legs, no-legs] values. The goal in this problem is to find a prototype for each class which minimizes missclassifications. A simple approach is to compute the prototype which maximizes the average similarity with all samples contained in that class. Four missclassifications in a dataset of 101 samples are obtained which are included in Table 1. Table 2 shows the average similarity $f(M)$ for each class, the relative relevance λ_k/σ and the attribute values of missclassified samples. Relative relevance can play an important role to introduce fuzzy related concept [2].

References

1. Bairoch A. and Apweiler R. The SWISS-PROT protein sequence data bank and its supplement TrEMBL. *Nucleic Acids Res.*, (25):31–36, 1997.
2. Zadeh L. A. Fuzzy sets. *Information and Control*, 8:338–352, 1965.
3. Jain A.K. and Dubes R.C. *Algorithms for Clustering Data*. Printice Hall, 1988.
4. Moxon B. Defining data mining. *DBMS online*, August 1996. http://www.dbmsmag.com/9608d53.html.
5. Merz C.J. and Murphy P. UCI repository of machibe learning databases. Technical report, Departament of Information and Computer Science, University of California, Irvine, CA, 1996. http://www.ics.uci.edu/mlearn/MLRepository.html.
6. Mannila H. Methods and problems in data mining. In *Proc. Int. Conf. on Database Theory*. Springer-Verlag, January 1997.
7. Toivonen H. Discovery of frecuent patterns in large data collections. Technical Report A-1996-5, Dept. of Computer Science, University of Helssinki, Finlad, 1996.
8. Quinlan J.R. Induction of decision trees. *Machine Learning*, 1:81–106, 1986.
9. Decker K.M. and Focardi S. Technology overview: A report on data mining. Technical Report CSCS TR-95-02, Swiss Scientific Computer Center, May 1995.
10. Guigó R. and Temple F.S. Inferring correlation between database queries: Analysis of protein sequence patterns. *IEEE PAMI*, 25(10):1030–1041, 1988.
11. Duda R.O., , and Hart P. *Pattern Classification and Scene Analysis*. Wiley and Sons, 1973.
12. Altschul S.F., Gish W., Miller W., Myers E.W., and Lipman D.J. Basic local alignment search tool. *J. Mol. Biol.*, (215):403–410, 1990.
13. Fayyad U.M., Haussler D., and Stolorz P. KDD for science data analysis; issues and examples. In *Proc. Second Int. Conf. on Knowledge Discovery and Data Minig*. AAAI Press, August 1996.
14. Fayyad U.M., Piatetsjy-Shapiro G., and Smyth P. *Advances in Knowledge Discovery and Data Mining*. AAAI/MIT Press, 1996.

404

Table 2. Mean similarity of each class, relative relevance λ_k/σ of symbols included in each class and missclassified items [seasnake, slug, tortoise, worm]. For all classes is verified that $\sigma = 0.25$. An contradictory case is realted to tortoise sample, which being included in the class3, is most similar with class2 having the airbone attribute. This can not be considered as a error because tortoise have 12 matched attributes with class3 and 13 with class2, and not all animals in class2 have airbone attribute as relative relevance shows.

attribute	class1	class2	class3	class4	class5	class6	class7	seas.	slug	tort.	worm
$f(M)$	0.907	0.912	0.875	0.951	0.953	0.922	0.887				
airborne		0.80				0.75					
aquatic				1.00	1.00		0.60	1			
backbone	1.00	1.00	1.00	1.00	1.00			1		1	
breathes	1.00	1.00	0.80		1.00	1.00			1	1	1
catsize	0.78									1	
domestic											
eggs		1.00	0.80	1.00	1.00	1.00	0.90		1	1	1
feathers		1.00									
fins				1.00							
hair	0.95					0.50					
legs	0.92	1.00			1.00	1.00	0.60			1	
milk	1.00										
predator	0.54		0.80	0.69	0.75		0.80	1			
tail	0.85	1.00	1.00	1.00				1		1	
toothed	0.98		0.80	1.00	1.00			1			
venomous								1			
no-airborne	0.95		1.00	1.00	1.00		1.00	1	1	1	1
no-aquatic	0.85	0.70	0.80			1.00		1	1		1
no-backbone					1.00	1.00		1			1
no-breathes				1.00			0.70	1			
no-catsize		0.70	0.80	0.69	1.00	1.00	0.90	1	1		1
no-domestic	0.80	0.84	1.00	0.92	1.00	0.88	1.00	1	1	1	1
no-eggs	0.98							1			
no-feathers	1.00		1.00	1.00	1.00	1.00	1.00	1	1	1	1
no-fins	0.90	1.00	1.00		1.00	1.00	1.00	1	1	1	1
no-hair		1.00	1.00	1.00	1.00		1.00	1	1	1	1
no-legs			0.60	1.00				1	1		1
no-milk		1.00	1.00	1.00	1.00	1.00	1.00	1	1	1	1
no-predator		0.55				0.88		1	1		1
no-tail					0.75	1.00	0.90	1			1
no-toothed		1.00				1.00	1.00	1	1	1	1
no-venomous	1.00	1.00	0.60	0.92	0.75	0.75	0.80		1	1	1

From the Data Mine to the Knowledge Mill: Applying the Principles of Lexical Analysis to the Data Mining and Knowledge Discovery Process

Jean Moscarola and Richard Bolden

Jean Moscarola is Professor of Management and Business Administration at the University of Savoie, France; and Richard Bolden (MA) works for Le Sphinx Développement, France.

Please contact: Richard Bolden
Le Sphinx Développement, 7 rue Blaise Pascal, 74600 Seynod, France.
Tel: 04 50 69 82 98   Fax: 04 50 69 82 78
Email: rbolden@lesphinx-developpement.fr

Abstract. This paper argues that the traditional approach to datamining is dominated by quantitative tools which assume knowledge to be inherent in the data: the data miners task simply being to find it. We propose, however, that true knowledge arises from an interaction between the information and the user.

The notion of user interaction in datamining demands a modified approach. An environment must be developed in which the user is encouraged to participate in an interactive learning cycle, where knowledge is progressively extracted from the data. The combined techniques of lexical approximation, hyper-text navigation and quantitative statistics can form the foundation stones of this "knowledge mill" by permitting a progressive entry into the information and the identification of trends not readily visible via other techniques. Such practices are no longer the exclusive domain of large corporations with in-house databases, but open to anyone wishing to explore internal or external data sets.

Introduction: the "Data Mine"

The notion of datamining arises from the duel effects of needs and opportunities: the need to follow and adapt to rapid changes in science, technology, markets, etc. and the opportunity offered by the existence of increasingly advanced, accessible and well documented information systems. Nowadays, the most recent discoveries may be found on bibliographic databases and the strategies of competitors revealed by examination of patent deposits, the Internet or other sources. Likewise, organisations with extensive in-house data sets of their own are finding them to contain important indicators of consumer behaviour and market trends. Information is becoming a strategic advantage [1,2] and hence also is the extent to which relevant and useful knowledge can be extracted from such resources [3,4].

A variety of methods and tools exist to guide the "data miner" in their quest of drawing useful knowledge from the voluminous data banks now available, but the investment, infrastructure and training often required tend to exclude smaller players from the game. Likewise, there is a tendency to focus on large-scale "number-crunching" activities in preference to the more ambiguous, yet rich domain of text analysis.

This paper presents the methods of statistical analysis applied to lexical approximation and hyper-text navigation as a solution to the general problem of making datamining accessible to the masses, and more importantly, of tapping into the knowledge which would otherwise remain buried within poorly structured text bases. Via these techniques the user is drawn into an interactive learning cycle, not only greatly facilitating the task of finding relevant information but also offering tools for the processing and extraction of knowledge not readily available by other means.

Who uses Datamining ?

Datamining has progressed a long-way since its origins in artificial intelligence (a domain largely closed to those outside the disciplines of I.T. and statistics). We now find comparatively user friendly applications which run on desktop PCs, although, where one wishes to use multiple search algorithms more advanced hardware and a great deal of external help and training are still required [5].

No matter what the system, however, the financial investment is nearly always high. The initial outlay on the soft and hardware itself is only the beginning. Consultants and training will often be required and an appropriate infrastructure established. Packages such as Darwin, for example, require at least three staff: one who creates the models, one who specifies the business rules and one who understands the database [6]. Likewise, the majority of large-scale datamining applications are designed for use on in-house data sets: sales records, client information, etc. This implies the need for additional personnel and investment in establishing and maintaining a comprehensive database. The susceptibility of datamining to "dirty data" also calls for extensive "data cleansing" operations. Aaron Zornes, an executive of the META Group, states that 60-80% of the datamining investment is usually in data preparation [6].

Such factors, thus, make it no surprise that large-scale datamining tends to be restricted to major corporations with clear productivity-oriented objectives. We hear many case studies of datamining in the banking and commercial sectors, focussing on topics such as: market segmentation, customer loyalty, fraud detection and marketing [7] but few in other sectors, such as health-care and education, where the data is available but not the money or personnel.

Extending the Domain of Datamining

We see a number of ways in which the datamining process could be extended to meet the needs of different users. Tools should:
- match the investment potential of small or non-profit orientated users;
- permit access to external data sources such as the Internet, CD-ROM and commercially and publicly available databases;
- require a minimum of data preparation, even for unstructured/deteriorated sources;
- draw on the immense knowledge contained within open-ended text;
- be easy to use and produce results which are intuitive to interpret;
- encourage user involvement such that knowledge can be constructed interactively, driven by needs rather than a computerized algorithm;
- offer a greater capacity for hypothesis formulation and testing.

Such tools would offer an intermediate level of datamining, falling somewhere between the full-scale corporate model and the heterogeneous mix of data management, processing and analysis software often promoted under the guise of "datamining".

Lexical Analysis: A Cross Between Quantitative and Qualitative Analysis

When exploring external data sets we face two distinct problems: (a) how do we find the information sources? and (b) how do we extract knowledge from them? By permitting the almost instant access to increasingly large information sources, the motors and engines of research (such as those found on the Internet) contribute strongly to solution of the first problem, but aggravate the second.

Traditional analysis is no longer viable in this context. Quantitative tools are seriously handicapped by their dependency on clean, well structured data and the inability to deal appropriately with open-ended text; whilst quantitative approaches (content analysis, trees and nodes, etc.) are far too labour intensive to be applied haphazardly to texts from relatively unknown sources.

Lexical analysis offers a middle-ground between quantitative and qualitative analysis, being rapidly applicable to texts of all types, and giving a far more flexible interface between the tasks of data acquisition, analysis and interpretation. This approach is typified by the calculation of "word lexicons": lists of words and their corresponding frequencies in the corpus. By viewing the most common or distinctive terms in a text one can rapidly determine the overall subject matter without the need for an in-depth reading.

The power of lexical analysis is greatly enhanced by the use of word dictionaries and hyper-text navigation. Dictionaries permit the suppression, highlighting, or grouping of terms; whilst hyper-text navigation offers a useful means for selective reading of text directed by the marked word lexicon.

What's more, lexical analysis can be applied to poorly maintained or unstructured data. Whilst it remains be true that if you wish to perform detailed, accurate analysis, some data preparation is necessary; for the preliminary exploration of a data set very little work needs to be done. In this manner you can select data almost at random and use the results of your lexical analysis to decide whether or not to continue.

User Involvement in the Datamining Process

Algorithmic datamining approaches (neural networks, decision trees, clustering, fuzzy logic, etc.) use the computer's processing power to search for patterns in the data. They are not hypothesis-lead, rather they browse through large volumes of information in search of trends. This may be a good means of identifying unanticipated results, but is less useful when wishing to find the response to a pre-defined query. Likewise, these practices are only really applicable to very large data sets (preferably of gigabyte dimensions) otherwise there is the possibility of error.

Social scientists, for example, are wary of results which have not been hypothesis-driven. The concept of statistical probability implies that of every 100 analyses on unrelated data, five will come out significant (a 5% probability threshold). It requires the informed judgement of the analyst to decide an appropriate significance level and which results to accept or discard. Where results are outputted cold from the machine, interpretation may be difficult, however, where the researcher has been involved throughout, the task is much easier.

Lexical analysis brings the user into an interactive learning loop where the preliminary hypotheses of the researcher are refined in accordance to the word lexicon and selective viewing of text. From this, new search terms, classifications and divisions may be determined with which to return to the data set. Rapidly, the investigation is narrowed to the most important or interesting aspects of the data, or abandoned to enable the individual to move on to the next text to analyze.

From the Data to the Overview

The ultimate aims of textual data mining, however, are greater than simply providing a peep-hole through which we can view relevant information. We wish to move beyond the raw text to gain a global understanding, to identify major themes and to distinguish systematic developments, trends and changes from the mass of information; in brief, we hope to pass from a preoccupation with detail to the "big picture". Such a level of knowledge is becoming essential for effective strategic reflection and one of the huge "prizes" of textual data mining.

Simply reading the text is no longer sufficient at this stage for a number of reasons:

- The quantity of information to take into consideration is too large when wishing to follow developments over a long period or from a large data set.
- The most relevant knowledge is often drawn from interactions between multiple considerations, thus complicating reading and synthesis.

- The most important effects may arise from the propagation of apparently insignificant trends or from a large body of information, which may well be missed even by the most attentive of readers.

Added to those of lexical approximation, the techniques of statistical analysis of the lexicon and textual data analysis greatly increase the potential for the researcher to draw important knowledge from computerized information sources. They enable the treatment of large bodies of information which not only would otherwise be unusable due to time restrictions, but also in which a key part of the content would escape identification from standard investigation. From the scientific analysis of textual and numerical data, the statistical approach allows one to identify and highlight structures and findings unobservable via other approaches.

Typical Lexical Analysis Procedures

The principle of lexical analysis is simple: it consists of applying quantitative analysis to the graphical forms present in a text; a "graphical form" being a continuous character string containing no separating character. Studying the statistical distribution of these forms enables the production of summaries and the identification of "significant" trends.

Stage 1: Preparing data for analysis

A number of key steps are involved when preparing a text for lexical analysis:
1. *Find the records*: the first step clearly is that of accessing the data set. Such sources may include the Internet, CD-ROM, databases, etc.
2. *Prepare the corpus*: once records have been located they need to be prepared for import by the lexical analysis software. This may simply involve saving the file in ASCII text format, and inserting markers and annotations as desired.
3. *Import the data*: structured, semi-structured and unstructured data can be opened. Variable names, types and missing values will be coded automatically. The user's task is simply to monitor the process to ensure it has been performed as intended.

Stage 2: Using the lexicon

Once the data file is established the process of lexical analysis can begin. Steps depend upon the ultimate aims of the research, however, some typical ones include:
1. *Compute the word lexicon*: lexical analysis is driven by the word lexicon. This is an automatically calculated list of graphical forms present in the corpus. It may be presented in a variety of ways, but the most common and useful is in descending order of frequency.
2. *Reduce the word lexicon*: in free text many of the most frequent terms are of little interest. These may include "tool words" (those terms vital for the construction of language but which convey little meaning) and numbers/codes. Deletion of such elements (via dictionaries and automated searches) will instantly give clearer of the specific content of the text.

3. *Mark lexicon words*: marking terms manually or via dictionaries enables further manipulation of the lexicon and provides a basis for hyper-text navigation.
4. *Group equivalent terms*: the inherent ambiguity of language can be reduced by grouping equivalent terms. This may be done automatically (by word stem), via dictionaries, or manually on-screen.
5. *Hyper-text navigation*: skim through the text selectively viewing only relevant entries (those containing marked words; those matching a specified profile; etc.).
6. *Word environment*: move beyond hyper-text navigation to display words in context and calculate "relative lexicons" (those words found before or after the chosen element).
7. *Search for expressions*: whilst individual words give a certain level of understanding, nothing speaks as loudly as expressions. A search for repeated word strings permits the extension of all the previous analyses to an expressions list.
8. *Lexical statistics*: calculation of indicators such as response banality and richness offers a new way of looking at text.
9. *Generate an index*: the word or expressions list could be used to calculate an index, permitting rapid identification of relevant observations.

Stage 3: Lexical cross-analysis

Where the power of lexical analysis becomes really clear, however, is its potential to combine the domains of quantitative and qualitative analysis. Open text variables can be crossed with closed response variables and quantitative statistics applied to the outcomes. Calculation of new variables from open text permits the application of analyses not readily available. Techniques may include:
1. *Lexical table*: a table crossing lexicon words (or expressions) with value labels of a closed response variable.
2. *Specific words table*: a search for the most distinctive terms for each modality of a closed response variable.
3. *Contextual summary*: lexical indicators calculated for each modality of a closed response variable.
4. *Cross analysis*: the recoding of open text to a closed response variable permits application of standard statistical techniques (Chi^2, t-test, etc.).
5. *Data visualisation*: techniques such as "factor mapping" permit a new, graphic representation of data originating from texts.

Example: Analysis of a Bibliographic Database

Here is an example of how lexical analysis could be applied to the exploration of a bibliographic database.

Data preparation and import

The Social Research Methodology database[i] is a CD-ROM directory containing details of over 34,000 publications in the domain of the social and behavioral sciences. A search was run to find entries classed under the category of "behavioral research" and the 278 corresponding records exported to an ASCII text file.

The text file was then opened directly by the analysis software[ii], simply by indicating which marker characters should be used (fields were preceded by a carriage return and followed by a colon). Variable names and types were identified automatically, with 18 different fields being detected (many of these differing according to whether the entry was a book or journal article). Fields available for nearly all entries were "Title", "Author", "Abstract" and "Date of publication". Missing values were recorded where fields were not present.

Variable modification

In order to permit simultaneous examination of all relevant text, fields containing similar information were combined; thus a new variable was calculated in which the fields "Title" and "Abstract" were merged. A second modification reduced the open-ended numerical variable "Date of publication" to a closed scaled variable in which dates were restricted to five comparable categories.

Generating the word lexicon

Once the data was ready the word lexicon was calculated. The list was generated automatically and reduced to eliminate "tool words", words containing a number and words of fewer than three letters.

Prior to lexicon reduction the 10 most frequent words were as follows: of (682), the (525), and (495), in (297), research (293), on (232), a (190), to (168), behavioral (161), for (152). The corpus consisted of 10137 words and the lexicon of 2070 different words.

After lexicon reduction the most frequent terms became: research (293), behavioral (161), analysis (126), behavior (78), data (71), methods (69), social (50), test (44) models (43), theory (40). The valid corpus was reduced by 40% (to 6383) simply by ignoring the 100 most ambiguous terms (reduced lexicon = 1915 words). From the reduced lexicon, key issues are easy to identify: "behavior", "research", "analysis", "methods", etc.

Identifying repeated expressions

Whilst isolated words give a certain insight into the meaning of a text, expressions can give a greater "feel" for the data. An automatic search for repeated segments of text was performed, searching for strings with between 2-10 words; a minimum frequency of three and ignoring "tool words". This identified 169 distinct expressions, the most common of which included: "behavioral research", "research methods", "data analysis" and "behavioral sciences". By generating a new variable in which terms from expressions were linked, we permitted the analysis of a combined word and expressions lexicon.

Looking for specific words over time

By performing a lexical cross analysis of the words and expressions in the new text variable with the recoded date variable we were able to identify trends over time. A Specific words table listed terms in order of decreasing distinctiveness over time.

Incorporating the 10 most distinctive words per category into a cross analysis permitted generation of a "factor map", a visual presentation of the key terms by date (Fig. 1).

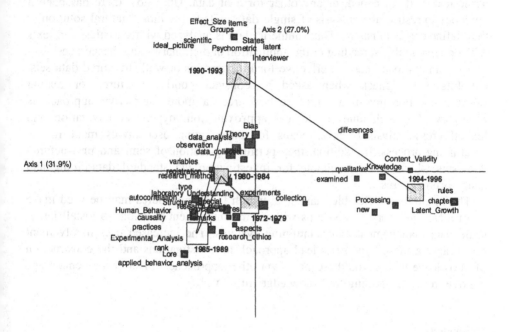

Fig. 1. Factor map of specific words by publication date.

Factor maps are intuitive to interpret: the proximity of points corresponding to the strength of relationship. We can thus conclude that throughout the 1970s and 1980s the field of behavioral research remained relatively unchanged. There was a primary focus upon experimental, quantitative approaches, combined with theoretical considerations regarding ethics, causality and research methodology. In contrast, however, throughout the 1990s there have been rapid changes. The early part of the decade (1990-1993) saw a move to consideration of psychometrics, groups, interviews, effect size, etc.; whilst the mid-part (1994-1996) brought out issues regarding qualitative analysis, content validity and latent growth.

Summary

By viewing findings in this context, the full power of lexical analysis becomes evident. We have moved from the raw text to a totally new environment in which statistical trends, not readily available in the raw data, come to light: from the "data mine" to the "knowledge mill"!

Conclusion: the "Knowledge Mill"

The task of extracting knowledge from the datamining process requires one to address the more general question of how to derive meaningful information from numerical, textual, coded, or any other form of data. Until now there has been a tendency to restrict the analysis of single data units to the most "natural solution" - that defined by data nature. Thus, numeric data is analyzed with statistics, and texts with content analysis, reading or the application of dictionaries and thesauruses.

Such an approach may be effective for homogenous or well structured data sets, but hits a bottleneck when asked to consider poorly structured or textual information. For investigation of such sources a more interactive approach is necessary. The techniques of lexical approximation, hyper-text navigation and lexical cross-analysis offer a means for encouraging user involvement in the datamining process. In addition, they permit exploration of semi and unstructured data sets which are not suitable for investigation via standard datamining and analysis procedures.

The intuitive and flexible manner in which these procedures may be used make them ideal tools for organisations without the investment potential to install large-scale data management and datamining systems. The increased user involvement encourages a more hypothesis-lead approach to investigations and the construction of knowledge which would escape us via other approaches. In short they encourage a move from "datamining" to "knowledge milling".

References

1. Jakobiak, F. Exemples commentés de veille technologique. Organisation (1991).
2. Rouach D. La veille technologique. Puf (1996).
3. Lesca, H. and Belkatir, M. Pertinence: un instrument pour évaluer le besoin de veille stratégie de l'entreprise. Eyrolles (1991).
4. Dou H. Veille technologique et compétitivité. Dunod (1995).
5. Darling, C. Datamining for the masses. Datamation (1998).
6. Freeman, E. Datamining unearths dollars from data. Datamation (1998).
7. McCarthy, V. Strike it rich! Datamation (1998).

---

[i] The SRM database is distributed by Scolari, Sage Publications Software.

[ii] The analysis software used in this example was the *SphinxSurvey (Lexica Edition)* package, developed by Le Sphinx Développement and distributed by Scolari, Sage Publications Software.

Preprocessing of Missing Values Using Robust Association Rules

Arnaud Ragel

ragel@info.unicaen.fr
GREYC - CNRS UPRESA 6072 - Université de Caen
14032 Caen cedex - France

Abstract. Many of analysis tasks have to deal with missing values and have developed specific and internal treatments to guess them. In this paper we present an external method for this problem to improve performances of completion and especially declarativity and interactions with the user. Such qualities will allow to use it for the data cleaning step of the KDD[1] process[6]. The core of this method, called MVC (Missing Values Completion), is the RAR[2] algorithm that we have proposed in [14]. This algorithm extends the concept of association rules[1] for databases with multiple missing values. It allows MVC to be an efficient preprocessing method: in our experiments with the c4.5[12] decision tree program, MVC has permitted to divide, up to two, the error rate in classification, independently of a significant gain of declarativity.

keywords: Association rules, Missing Values, Preprocessing, Decision Trees.

1 Introduction

The missing values problem is an old one for analysis tasks[8] [11]. The waste of data which can result from casewise deletion of missing values, obliges to propose alternatives approaches. A current one is to try to determine these values [9]. However, techniques to guess the missing values must be efficient, otherwise the completion introduces noise. With the emergence of KDD for industrial databases, where missing values are inevitable, this problem has become a priority task [6] also requiring declarativity and interactivity during treatments. At the present time, treatments are often specific and internal to the methods, and do not offer such qualities. Consequently the missing values problem is still a challenging task of the KDD research agenda [6].

We have proposed in [14] the RAR algorithm to correct the weakness of usual association rules algorithms[2] in mining databases with multiple missing values. The efficiency of this algorithm to extract quickly all the associations contained in such a database, allows to use it for the missing values problem. That is what

---

[1] Knowledge Discovery in Databases
[2] Robust Association Rules

we propose in this paper with the MVC (Missing Values Completion) method. It uses the association rules to fill the missing values, independently of any analysis tasks, during a preprocessing, declarative and interactive process with the user. MVC is interesting for its declarative concept and also for its performances which allow to use it to replace the ad-hoc missing values processing of analysis tasks: for example, the error rate of the classification software c4.5[12] has been divided up to two in our experiments using MVC rather its own missing values processing.

In this paper, we focus on the missing values problem for decision trees but we will see that MVC can be interesting for any analysis task. Section 2 briefly reviews usual approaches to deal with missing values in decision trees and points out problems. In Sect. 3 we present the RAR algorithm[14] and show in Sect. 4 its interest for the missing values problem in MVC. In Sect. 5 we present experiments using MVC for classification tasks with the decision tree program c4.5[12] and conclude in Sect. 6, on the possibility with MVC to control the noise introduced during the completion step.

2 Usual Missing Values Treatments

As deleting data with missing values may cause a huge waste of data, missing values are often filled. Because of no standard and independent method to deal with missing values, many of programs have developed specific and internal treatments. This is the case for decision trees for which missing values are an important problem[9], [13].

A current approach is to fill the missing values with the most common values in the datasets constructed for the classification task. There are also some variants, like in c4.5[12], where a missing value is filled with several weighted values. Critics of such approaches are that the treatment is not easy to understand, especially with c4.5, and that as the value is chosen in datasets constructed for the analysis task, and not to decide the missing value, completion may be wrong [9], [13]: the subdatasets are constructed to be homogeneous for the class attribute and not for the attributes with missing values.

Another technique, proposed by Breiman et al. in [3], is to use a surrogate split to decide the missing value for an attribute. The surrogate attribute is the one with the highest correlation with the original attribute. If this method uses more information than the precedent ones, its efficacy depends on the possibility to find correlation between two attributes. Looking for more associations have been proposed by Quinlan and Shapiro in [10] where they use a decision tree approach to decide the missing values for an attribute. If S is the training set and A an attribute with missing values, the method considers the subset S', of S, with only cases where the attribute A is known. In S' the original class is regarded as another attribute while the value of attribute A becomes the class to be determined. A classification tree is built using S' for predicting the value of attribute A from the other attributes and the class. Then, this tree can be used to fill the missing values. Unfortunately it has been shown that difficulties arise if the same case has missing values on more than one attribute[9]: during the construction of a tree to predict A, if a missing value is tested for an attribute B another tree must be constructed to predict B and so on. So this method cannot be used practically. More recently, in 1996, K. Lakshminarayan et. al proposed in [7] a similar approach where they use machine learning techniques (Autoclass[5] and c4.5[12]) to fill missing values. They avoid the problem of multiple missing values on a same data using the internal missing values treatment of c4.5 or of Autoclass. Consequently the machine learning approaches (Decision tree and Clustering) can be used only to decide missing values for only one attribute.

With this brief overview of missing values treatment for decision trees, which can be extended to other analysis methods, we see that the main difficulty is to find declarative associations between data in presence of multiple missing values. In the next section, we present a method which can be used for this task.

3 The Robust Association Rules Algorithm

The RAR algorithm, that we have proposed in [14], corrects a weakness of usual association rules algorithms: a lot of relevant rules are lost by these algorithms when missing values are embedded in databases. We briefly recall principles of association rules and we point out the main characteristics of the RAR algorithm.

An association rule[1] is an expression of the form $X \longrightarrow Y$, where X and Y are sets of items, and is evaluated by a support and a confidence. Its support is the percentage of data that contains both X and Y. Its confidence is the percentage of data that contains Y among those containing X. For example, the rule *fins=y and tail=y $\longrightarrow$ hairs=n* with a support of 13% and a confidence of 92% states that 13% of animals have fins, tail and no hairs and that 92% of animals with fins and tail have no hairs. The problem of mining rules is to find all rules that satisfy a user-specified minimum support and minimum confidence. Fast algorithms[2] [15] are used successfully to mine such rules in very large transaction databases. In such databases, the missing values problem do not exist in practically. In order to use the association rules concept in relational tables, where missing values are inevitable, we have proposed the RAR algorithm.

In order to avoid the collapse of fast association rules algorithms when a database has missing values, a key point of RAR is to discover rules in valid databases rather than in whole databases. A valid database (vdb) is defined for an itemset X as the largest database without missing values for this itemset.

For example, the first left dataset in the Fig. 1 is a vdb for the itemsets {X2}, {X3} and {X2, X3} because there is no missing value for X2 and X3. The second one is the vdb for itemsets {X1}, {X1,X2}, {X1,X3}, {X1,X2,X3} and the third one is a vdb for {X4}, {X2,X4}, {X3,X4}, {X2,X3,X4}.

We have implemented the RAR algorithm on the basis of the fast association rules algorithms [2] to assure an efficient computation time. Without this compatibility, the RAR algorithm would not be useful in practice and would not have permitted a deep exploration. The RAR algorithm has required a modifi-

Id	X1	X2	X3	X4
1	?	a	a	c
2	a	a	b	?
3	a	b	c	c
4	a	b	d	c
5	?	b	e	d
6	b	b	f	?
7	b	c	g	d
8	b	c	h	d

VDB 1

Id	X1	X2	X3	X4
1	Disabled			
2	a	a	b	?
3	a	b	c	c
4	a	b	d	c
5	Disabled			
6	b	b	f	?
7	b	c	g	d
8	b	c	h	d

VDB 2

Id	X1	X2	X3	X4
1	?	a	a	c
2	Disabled			
3	a	b	c	c
4	a	b	d	c
5	?	b	e	d
6	Disabled			
7	b	c	g	d
8	b	c	h	d

VDB 3

Fig. 1. RAR approach for dealing with missing values

cation of support and confidence definitions that we detail in [14].

This approach gives good results because missing values are temporarily ignored, without deleting data: if data are not all used together to compute one rule, they are all used to compute the ruleset. For example, in the Fig. 1, data 1 is not used to evaluate support of $\{X1, X3\}$ but it is used to evaluate support of $\{X2, X4\}$. We can see also that this approach works directly on the data and does not require any completion of missing values.

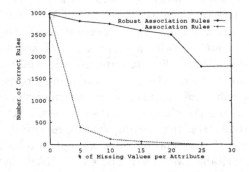

Fig. 2. Robust Association Rules Performances

Figure 2 depicts the results of an experiment comparing performances between the RAR algorithm and the main fast algorithm[2]: **a reference ruleset** is constructed from a database, 2000 data and 8 attributes, with no missing values. Then missing values are randomly introduced with a rate of 5% at first and 30% to finish with an increment of 5% on each attribute of this database. The number of correct rules, i.e include in **the reference ruleset**, retrieved with the two different approaches are shown by the curves in Fig 2. We see that the number of retrieved rules is clearly larger with RAR, especially when the number of missing values increases.

4   Interest of RAR for Missing Values

The efficiency of RAR, to find all the association rules quickly in a database with missing values, allows us to propose the method MVC. This method works as in the Fig 3, where it first extracts rules and then uses them to fill missing values, with a possible interaction with the user.

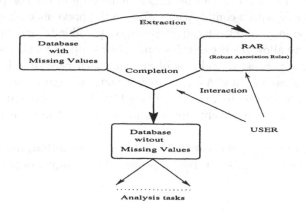

Fig. 3. The MVC Process

As we do not know which values will be missing, the first step of MVC consists of searching for all the rules above the thresholds given by the user. RAR enabled this strategy and we know that it is better, for computational time, than searching rules only when a missing value is encounted. The constructed ruleset is then used in the second step of MVC (the completion step).

For the completion, the rules matching a data and concluding on a attribute which is missing are used to decide its value. Two situations are possible:

1- All the matching rules indicate the same conclusion, then it is used.

2- Several matching rules conclude on different values. In this case the confidence measure and the number of rules concluding on a same value are used to solve the conflict automatically. Of course, the user can intervene. This approach is simple but, in our experiments, there is always a clear preference, in number of rules, for one value rather than the others.

We show below an example of completion for a data from the Zoo database[3]. In this example, *fins* and *hairs* are missing. The conclusions of the matched rules will be used to fill them:

aquatic=y, tail=y, hairs=?, legs=0, fins=?

with use of *aquatic=y, and, legs=0 → fins=y (sup[4]: 17%, conf[5]: 97%)*

---

[3] UCI Machine Learning Repository, http://www.ics.uci.edu/ mlearn/MLRepository.html

[4] support

[5] confidence

becomes: aquatic=y, tail=y, hairs=?, legs=0, fins=y

with use of *fins=y and tail=y* $\longrightarrow$ *hairs=n (sup: 13%, conf: 92%)*

becomes: aquatic=y, tail=y, hairs=n, legs=0, fins=y

Let us notice that recursion is permitted in MVC only with rules which have a high confidence (above 95%) to avoid series of wrong completion.

With this intuitive treatment the user can easily intervene in the completion process: he can visualize the ruleset, remove, change or add new rules. Furthermore the confidence of a rule can be a good indication of the correctness of the treatment: the rule with a confidence of 97%, in the previous example, indicates that 3% of noise may be introduced. It is always possible to find matched rules, to complete, if we allow the use of rules with a low support and a low confidence. This point can appear as a weakness of our approach because a low confidence may implicate noise in data. As a matter of fact, this critic can apply to any method which completes the missing values, like the ones presented in Sect. 2. But, as they cannot give a value like confidence to measure the noise, it does not point out.

In the next section we show with several experiments that, moreover to propose a preprocessing and declarative approach, MVC improves performances of analysis tasks.

5 Results

For this study, we use one of the most used decision tree programs, c4.5[12], which can handle missing values by sending them to each subset, with a weight proportional to the known values in the subset. For scientific exactness, to compare with the automatical missing values treatment of c4.5, MVC has been used without interaction with the user.

5.1 Introduction of multiple missing values

The aim of this experiment is to study the effect of missing values for a classification task, and to compare the ability of treatments (MVC and the internal method of c4.5) to correct the problem. To have a reference result, c4.5 is first run on an original database with no or few missing values. Then missing values are randomly introduced in the database and c4.5 is run twice. Firstly, using its own treatment to deal with missing values and secondly using MVC to preprocess the missing values. Then results are compared.

Two databases, coming from the UCI Machine Learning Repository has been used. The Vote database which has 435 data and 17 attributes and the Credit Card database which have 690 data and 15 attributes[6].

Tab. 1 gives the results of this experiment. We can see that classification error rate using MVC is lower: it can be divided up to two. Another result is

---

[6] some with missing values

Table 1. Average Results over ten trials with multiple missing values

Number of MV	Use of MVC	Unpruned Tree			Pruned Tree			
		Size Tree	Errors (Train)	Errors (Test)	Size Tree	Errors (Train)	Errors (Test)	Errors (Predic.)
Vote Database								
(Reference Result)		29.2	1.9%	4.8%	16	2.6%	4.4%	5.7%
5%	no	42.4	2.5%	7.8%	13.9	4.2%	6.7%	7.6%
10%	no	57.7	3.2%	9.2%	10.6	7.1%	8.3%	9.8%
15%	no	51.1	4.1%	8.0%	8.8	9.1%	10.1%	11.8%
20%	no	64.6	4.6%	9.7%	11.2	10.8%	12.9%	14.4%
5%	yes	35.5	2.5%	8.0%	6.1	4.6%	5.5%	6.5%
10%	yes	30.7	2.6%	6.2%	6.1	4.3%	5.3%	6.2%
15%	yes	37.6	2.6%	7.6%	8.8	4.5%	6.0%	6.7%
20%	yes	46.6	2.6%	8.5%	10.0	4.9%	6.7%	7.4%
Credit Card Database								
(Reference Result)		162.4	7.4%	16.5%	21.9	11.2%	13.2%	14.4%
5%	no	200.8	7.8%	16.8%	13.2	12.4%	13.5%	16.1%
10%	no	190.4	8.8%	17.9%	14.9	13.2%	13.8%	17.4%
15%	no	182.5	9.1%	18.0%	11.4	14.3%	15.1%	19.0%
20%	no	206.8	8.9%	16.8%	15.2	15.9%	17.8%	21.6%
5%	yes	141.5	7.4%	16.5%	23.3	11.3%	14.6%	14.9%
10%	yes	134.1	6.5%	13.9%	39.9	9.6%	13.8%	14.6%
15%	yes	155.1	6.3%	15.8%	22.1	11.0%	13.9%	14.3%
20%	yes	145.6	5.6%	13.9%	15.4	10.0%	12.0%	12.4%

that the more we introduce missing values in the credit card database the better are the results. Such a result may be explained by the fact that some unexpected values for data (e.g noise) may be set to unknown with this experiment and then are filled by MVC with typical ones.

MVC has completed all the missing values with an average value of correct completion of 97.3% for *Vote* and of 96.26% for *Credit Card*. Let us notice that we cannot have such information with c4.5 because of its internal and multiple completion approach.

5.2 Real world applications

In this experiment we use 2 databases, from real world, with missing values at origin:

1. OERTC database: This database is used, for classification tasks, in collaboration with the lymphome group of the O.E.R.T.C (European Organization of Research and Treatment of Cancer). We have used the H7 protocol which has 832 cases (1988-1993) and 27 attributes. Eleven of them have missing values with the following proportions: 52%, 43%, 88%, 84%, 39%, 8%, 6%, 7%, 2%, 6% and 6.5%.

2. Auto insurance database: it comes from the UCI Machine Learning Repository and has 205 cases with 25 attributes[7]. Six of them have missing values with the following proportions: 20%, 0.97%, 1.95%, 1.95%, 0.97%, 0.97%, 1.95%.

Tab. 2 gives the results. In the OERTC database results are significatively increased using MVC. An interesting point is that MVC has made to emerge an attribute not used otherwise. With it, qualities of the tree seem to be better (a predicted error of 6.8%). In the Auto database, results are the same but, the low rates of missing values and the few cases, cannot really decide if MVC could be useful. However MVC has completed missing values with an unique value, contrary to c4.5, which is better for the understanding.

Table 2. Average Results over ten trials on real world applications with c4.5

Database		Unpruned Tree			Pruned Tree			
	Use of MVC	Size of Tree	Errors (Train)	Errors (Test)	Size (of Tree)	Errors (Train)	Errors (Test)	Errors (Predic.)
OERTC	no	91.4	4.4%	8.5%	41.3	6.2%	7.3%	10.0%
	yes	89.7	2.2%	5.6%	40.4	3.5%	6.5%	6.8%
Autos	no	152.1	4.0%	16.6%	88.3	8.3%	19.5%	30.0%
	yes	149.2	4.3%	16.0%	83.4	8.3%	18.5%	29.9%

5.3 Conclusion on Results

Results seem to be noticeably improved in classification when there are many missing values. Otherwise, results are at least as good with the preprocessing. Unlike c4.5 approach, another advantage is that the completion is made with only one value which allows the user to understand and react about it.

6 Conclusion

Contrary to previous approaches reviewed in Sect. 2, the ability of RAR to discover associations in missing values databases has permitted to propose an efficient association technique. This method, MVC, uses RAR to guess the missing values in databases. Such an approach leads to a significant gain of performances: the error rate in classification, with c4.5[12], can be divided up to two, if MVC is used rather than the classical missing values treatment of c4.5. But the main advantage of MVC is to be a preprocessing method, independent of any analysis tasks, which offers a more understandable treatment of the missing values and a possible interaction with the user. Such qualities, rarely available as far as we

---

[7] numeric attributes have been discretized for this experiment

know for the missing values problem, may enable MVC to become a tool for the data cleaning step of the KDD process [6].

At the present time, we are working on several points to improve use of rules in MVC. One of them, is a definition of a new rule score, specially designed for the completion problem. A second one is on an adjustment of threshold completion: first experiments, using the noise measure given by the confidence of rules, seem to indicate that it is better to stop completion rather than introducing to much noise.

References

1. R. Agrawal, T. Imielinski, and A. Swami. Mining association rules between sets of items in large databases. In Proc. of the ACM SIGMOD Conference on Management of Data, Washington, D.C., p 207-216, May 1993.
2. R. Agrawal, H. Mannila, R. Srikant, H. Toivonen and A. I. Verkamo. Fast Discovery of Association Rules. In Advances in Knowledge Discovery and Data Mining, Chapter 12, AAAI/MIT Press, 1996.
3. L. Breiman, J.H Friedman, R.A Olshen, C.J Stone. Classification and Regression Trees, Wadsworth Int'l Group, Belmont, CA, The Wadsworth Statistics/Probability Series, 1984.
4. G. Celeux. Le traitement des données manquantes dans le logiciel SICLA. Technical reports number 102. INRIA, France, December 1988.
5. P. Cheeseman, J. Kelly, M. Self, J. Stutz, W. Taylor and D. Freeman. Bayesian Classification. In Proc. of American Association of Artificial Intelligence(AAAI), 607-611, San Mateo, CA, 1988.
6. U.M Fayyad, G. Piatetsky-Shapiro, and P. Smyth. From data mining to knowledge discovery: An overview. In Advances in Knowledge Discovery and Data Mining, pages 1-36, AAAI/MIT Press, 1996.
7. K. Lakshminarayan, S.A Harp, R. Goldman and T. Samad. Imputation of missing data using machine learning techniques. Proc. of the Second International Conference on Knowledge Discovery and Data Mining (KDD-96), AAAI/MIT Press, 1996.
8. R.J.A Little, D.B Rubin. Statistical Analysis with Missing Data. John Wiley and Sons, N.Y., 1987.
9. W.Z Liu, A.P White, S.G Thompson and M.A Bramer. Techniques for Dealing with Missing Values in Classification. In Second Int'l Symposium on Intelligent Data Analysis, London, 1997.
10. J.R Quinlan. Induction of decision trees. Machine learning, 1, p. 81-106, 1986.
11. J.R Quinlan. Unknown Attribute Values in Induction, in Segre A.M.(ed.), Proc. of the Sixth Int'l Workshop on Machine Learning, Morgan Kaufmann, Los Altos, CA, p. 164-168, 1989.
12. J.R Quinlan. C4.5: Programs for Machine Learning, Morgan Kaufmann, San Mateo, CA, 1993.
13. A. Ragel: Traitement des valeurs manquantes dans les arbres de décision. Technical reports, Les cahiers du GREYC. University of Caen, France, 1997.
14. A. Ragel and B. Crémilleux. Treatment of Missing Values for Association Rules. In Proc. of The Second Pacific-Asia Conference on Knowledge Discovery and Data Mining (PAKDD-98), p. 258-270, Melbourne, Australia, 1998.
15. H. Toivonen. Sampling large databases for association rules. In Proc. of the 22nd Int'l Conference on Very Large Databases (VLDB'96), p. 134-145, India, 1996

Similarity-Driven Sampling for Data Mining

Thomas Reinartz

Daimler-Benz AG, Research & Technology, FT3/KL
P.O. Box 2360, 89013 Ulm, Germany
e-mail: reinartz@dbag.ulm.daimlerbenz.com

Abstract. Industrial databases often contain millions of tuples but most data mining algorithms suffer from limited applicability to only small sets of examples. In this paper, we propose to utilize data reduction before data mining to overcome this deficit. We specifically present a novel similarity-driven sampling approach which applies two preparation steps, sorting and stratification, and reuses an improved variant of leader clustering. We experimentally evaluate similarity-driven sampling in comparison to statistical sampling techniques in different classification domains using C4.5 and instance-based learning as data mining algorithms. Experimental results show that similarity-driven sampling often outperforms statistical sampling techniques in terms of error rates using smaller samples.

1 Introduction

Industrial databases often contain millions of tuples but most data mining algorithms suffer from limited applicability to only small sets of examples. In principle, two main alternatives exist. First, scaling up data mining algorithms makes their applications to larger data sets more feasible. Second, data reduction techniques lead to smaller data sets, and if we then apply data mining algorithms to these smaller data sets, data mining becomes more feasible. In this approach, we have to ensure that reduced data sets still contain enough information to reveal appropriate results.

In this paper, we consider data reduction techniques. We specifically present a novel similarity-driven sampling approach which reduces the number of tuples rather than decreasing the number of attributes or values. In the next section, we outline leader sampling as the core approach in similarity-driven sampling and propose two data preparation steps, sorting and stratification, as well as automatic estimation and adaptation strategies for similarity thresholds to overcome negative properties of leader sampling. Thereafter, we experimentally evaluate similarity-driven sampling in comparison to statistical sampling techniques in different classification domains. Finally, we discuss related efforts and outline issues for future work.

2 Similarity-Driven Sampling

Existing efforts towards data reduction for data mining utilize statistical sampling techniques or apply clustering and prototyping approaches (e.g., windowing (Quinlan, 1993) and IBL2 (Aha et al., 1991)). In this paper, we propose to unify clustering and prototyping. The key idea is to generate subsets of sufficiently similar tuples and to select representative prototypes within each subset. Then, we reduce the original data set to the smaller set of prototypes.

2.1 Leader Sampling

The core approach in similarity-driven sampling reuses an improved variant of leader clustering (Hartigan, 1975). Leader clustering simultaneously generates partitions of data and selects leaders within each cluster by a single pass through the data. We propose to follow up leader clustering for data reduction by selecting leaders as representative prototypes without explicitly creating corresponding clusters. The resulting strategy, called leader sampling (LeaSam), works as follows. LeaSam selects the first tuple as the first prototype of the first cluster. For each following tuple, leader sampling considers similarities between this tuple and already selected prototypes. If the similarity between the tuple and the most similar prototype exceeds a pre-defined threshold δ, LeaSam proceeds with the next tuple. Otherwise, leader sampling adds the current tuple to the sample. In this paper, we assume an Euclidian like weighted cumulated similarity measure.

Besides an appropriate similarity measure, leader sampling mainly suffers from the following three drawbacks. First, prototype selection in leader sampling depends on the order of tuples. Second, execution time of leader sampling increases if the set of currently selected prototypes becomes large. Finally, leader sampling relies on appropriate settings of similarity threshold δ. In the following, we define two preparation steps, sorting and stratification, to overcome the first two drawbacks. Then, we develop automatic estimation and adaptation strategies for similarity thresholds.

2.2 Sorting

Sorting ensures a fixed well-defined order of tuples. Therefore, we define the following order relation between tuples which considers attribute values in order of attribute relevance. If the most important attribute value in tuple t is larger than the corresponding value in tuple $\tilde{t}$, then sorting places t after $\tilde{t}$ in the sorted table. If both values coincide, sorting recursively proceeds with the next important attribute in the same way. If two tuples are completely identical, their relation remains the same. For comparisons between continuous attribute values, we use the regular numeric order, whereas for symbolic attributes, we employ the lexicographic order. Note, leader sampling still depends on the new fixed well-defined order of tuples, but now LeaSam always selects the same sample independent of the original order of tuples.

2.3 Stratification

Stratification separates tuples into smaller subsets according to attribute values and again considers values in order of attribute relevance. For continuous attributes, a stratum contains tuples with values in the same interval, whereas for symbolic attributes, a stratum includes tuples with the same value. Note, for continuous attributes, stratification involves discretization approaches to generate intervals (e.g., Dougherty et al., 1995). In the current implementation, we discretize into equal-frequency intervals.

Stratification generates a strata tree. At each level, stratification separates tuples according to single attribute values. Stratification recursively iterates separation according to the next important attribute until a stratum contains less than a pre-defined maximum number of tuples, or no more attributes are available. Stratification returns all leaves of the resulting strata tree.

In terms of leader sampling, stratification is advantageous for two reasons. First, stratification separates tuples into smaller subsets. If we then apply LeaSam within each stratum separately, leader sampling becomes more efficient in terms of running time. Second, each stratum contains locally similar tuples, and the more attributes stratification takes into account, the higher are cumulated similarities within a stratum. Hence, leader sampling is likely to consider the most similar prototypes for each tuple without processing the entire data set.

2.4 Similarity Thresholds

In order to develop estimation and adaptation strategies for similarity thresholds in leader sampling, we relate different δ values and resulting samples to hierarchical clustering. For example, we assume $\delta < \delta' < \delta''$ and data illustrated in figure 1 (black and white bullets). If we apply LeaSam with δ and tuple 1 is the first tuple, leader sampling selects only the first tuple. This prototype represents all tuples within the dotted circle with radius $1 - \delta$. In terms of hierarchical clustering, this prototype represents the root cluster. For threshold δ', leader sampling selects an additional prototype. The final sample contains two tuples, and the corresponding clustering structure refines the initial clustering. If we now increase δ again, leader sampling generates a third sample which again corresponds to a more fine-grained clustering structure.

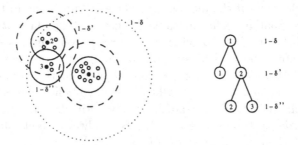

Fig. 1. Increasing similarity threshold values $\delta < \delta' < \delta''$ and resulting samples in leader sampling (left) correspond to refinements in hierarchical clustering (right).

In summary, increasing similarity thresholds correspond to more fine-grained clustering structures. In similarity-driven sampling, we attempt to callibrate δ until prototypes represent subsets of tuples at an appropriate level. Appropriateness of specific levels in hierarchical clustering depends on homogeneity within clusters and heterogeneity between clusters. The general goal is to construct clusterings such that homogeneity within clusters is higher than heterogeneity between clusters. We use minimum similarities between tuples within clusters as a measure of homogeneity and maximum similarities between tuples within different clusters as a measure of heterogeneity.

If we consider each subset of tuples represented by the same prototype in leader sampling as a single cluster, homogeneity depends on similarity threshold δ. High threshold values correspond to high homogeneity. Vice versa, we callibrate δ such that homogeneities within subsets of tuples represented by the same prototype approximately match true homogeneities at the most appropriate level in hierarchical clustering.

Occurring similarities between tuples and their prototypes yield estimates for true homogeneities. Hence, we adapt δ according to observed similarity values in leader sampling. For this reason, we keep minimum, average, and maximum similarities as aggregated information. If similarity-driven sampling adapts δ to the minimum of observed similarities, homogeneity within clusters is low, but heterogeneity between clusters is high. In this case, similarity-driven sampling only selects a few prototypes within a few clusters. If similarity-driven sampling applies the maximum strategy, homogeneity within clusters is high, but heterogeneity between clusters is low. Then, similarity-driven sampling selects more prototypes that represent small homogeneous clusters. The average strategy results in a compromise between homogeneity and heterogeneity.

2.5 Working Sets

In general, it is advisory to adapt similarity threshold values during sampling. If we fix δ, similarity-driven sampling only draws representatives at a single level in the corresponding hierarchical clustering. If we vary δ, it is possible to select representatives at different levels of granularity and to seek for the most appropriate value by moving up and down in the corresponding hierarchical clustering.

In order to reveal appropriate estimations of homogeneities within clusters and dynamically adapt δ, we propose to select intermediate working sets. We apply leader sampling to each working set and use occurring similarities to estimate the current similarity threshold. After each working set, we decide whether to adapt δ to a different value. Since similarity-driven sampling utilizes sorting in advance, we suggest to apply systematic sampling to generate intermediate working sets.

2.6 Algorithm SIMSAM

Now, we integrate sorting, stratification, and leader sampling with automatic estimation and adaptation of similarity thresholds into an algorithm for similarity-driven sampling (SimSam). SimSam starts sampling with sorting and stratifying the original input data. Within each stratum, similarity-driven sampling utilizes leader sampling on intermediate working sets with varying start positions. As soon as SimSam completes processing a working sample, it compares the last and the current sample size. If sampling does not make progress, i.e., the sample size does not increase, SimSam updates similarity threshold δ according to a pre-specified adaptation strategy. SimSam iterates leader sampling on working sets until either SimSam already processed all tuples in the current stratum, or if similarity-driven sampling does not make progress for a pre-defined number of iterations.

3 Experimental Evaluation

In this section, we experimentally evaluate similarity-driven sampling in comparison to statistical sampling techniques in different classification domains.

3.1 Experimental Procedure

In order to validate benefits of sorting and stratification as well as appropriateness of similarity-driven sampling, we conduct an experimental study on eight different data sets from the UCI repository (Murphy & Aha, 1994). Table 1 outlines characteristics of these data sets and data mining results. For each data set, we first separate the original data set into training and test set. The training set is a random sample which contains approximately 80% of the entire data, and the test set includes remaining tuples. We start data mining by applications of two different classification algorithms to the entire training set. In this study, we compare C4.5 (Quinlan, 1993) and inducer IB in $\mathcal{MLC}++$ (Kohavi et al., 1996). We apply both algorithms with default settings, and for C4.5, we only consider accuracies of pruned decision trees.

Table 1. Data Characteristics

Name	Training Set Size	Test Set Size	Number of Attributes	Error in %		Time in Sec.	
				C4.5	IB	C4.5	IB
Abalone	3342	835	9	79.4	82.0	10.7	106.5
Balance	500	125	5	30.4	16.0	0.1	3.5
Breast	560	139	11	6.5	5.8	0.2	5.1
Car	1383	345	7	8.7	7.3	0.1	13.0
Credit	552	138	16	16.7	21.0	0.4	6.0
German	800	200	21	26.0	25.5	1.1	22.8
Pima	615	153	9	30.7	30.7	0.6	4.8
Tic-Tac-Toe	767	191	10	10.5	0.0	0.1	6.7

Then, we apply different sampling approaches to each training set and use resulting samples for data mining. We examine six different sampling approaches: Simple random sampling with replacement (R), stratified simple random sampling with replacement (RS), systematic sampling (S), systematic sampling with sorting (SS), leader sampling (L), and similarity-driven sampling with maximum adaptation (SM). First, we apply leader sampling with varying similarity thresholds between $\delta = 0.9$ and $\delta = 0.99$. LeaSam determines its sample size according to the specified threshold. Similarly, SimSam chooses as many prototypes as it regards as necessary according to the selected adaptation strategy. For random and systematic sampling, we modify sample sizes within the range of sample sizes of leader and similarity-driven sampling.

For all non-deterministic sampling approaches, we repeat sampling and data mining ten times and present average results. In all experiments, we compute attribute relevance weights according to information gain ratio as if we select the first attribute at top of a decision tree (Quinlan, 1993).

3.2 Experimental Results

Table 2 summarizes experimental results. For each data set, for each sampling approach, and for each data mining algorithm, we show error rate differences in comparison to learning on the entire training set, relative reduced training set size in comparison to the original training set, as well as relative execution time of sampling and data mining in comparison to data mining on the entire training set. Note, each entry in table 2 refers to best results in terms of error rate for samples which contain less than 50% of the original data.

Negative error rate differences indicate that data mining on samples yields more accurate classifiers than learning on the original training set, whereas positive differences depict worse results. For execution time, values below 100 mean that sampling and data mining on resulting samples is faster than data mining on original training sets, whereas values above 100 indicate that sampling and data mining take more time than data mining without reducing the training set.

For each data set and for each data mining algorithm, bold entries refer to best results among different sampling approaches if we consider each aspect separately. For comparisons between sampling approaches, we consider a sampling approach as more appropriate than another sampling approach, if the former yields lower (or equal) error rates on smaller (or equally sized) samples than the latter. If the former approach results in lower error rates but uses larger samples than the latter (or vice versa), we regard these approaches as not comparable.

Detailed analyses of all results (including results not presented here) are beyond the scope of this paper. In summary, we stress the following conclusions:

- Stratification is useful as an enhancement to simple random sampling in some domains. In the majority of domains, both sampling approaches are not comparable.
- Sorting is generally beneficial in combination with systematic sampling. Only in two domains with applications of C4.5, pure systematic sampling outperforms systematic sampling with sorting.

Table 2. Experimental Results

Data	Sample	C4.5						IB					
		R	RS	S	SS	L	SM	R	RS	S	SS	L	SM
Abalone	Error Diff.	-0.3	-0.5	-0.6	-2.9	4.3	-1.9	-2.3	-2.2	-2.1	-4.0	2.9	-3.1
	Size in %	19.7	21.0	6.3	20.0	35.2	32.3	37.2	14.2	14.3	4.2	35.2	32.3
	Time in %	20.9	24.3	9.3	25.3	158.9	45.8	40.2	16.7	15.8	5.6	48.2	36.9
Balance	Error Diff.	5.0	4.4	5.4	2.4	5.3	2.4	13.2	12.6	11.7	7.2	19.4	8.8
	Size in %	45.6	43.2	33.4	11.2	27.0	19.6	45.6	46.6	33.4	33.4	42.4	45.6
	Time in %	200.0	200.0	200.0	200.0	500.0	300.0	51.4	54.3	57.1	42.9	65.7	57.1
Breast	Error Diff.	0.0	0.0	1.5	1.4	-0.9	2.1	-0.8	-0.8	0.0	-0.8	-0.3	-1.5
	Size in %	40.7	34.6	33.4	33.4	44.3	24.1	47.0	33.8	33.4	33.4	37.0	24.1
	Time in %	150.0	175.0	150.0	150.0	500.0	250.0	52.9	41.2	39.2	41.2	52.9	35.3
Car	Error Diff.	4.2	4.6	4.7	5.5	4.5	4.9	8.1	7.2	7.7	7.2	5.7	6.0
	Size in %	34.3	35.6	33.3	33.3	34.3	32.6	34.3	35.6	33.3	33.3	34.3	32.6
	Time in %	200.0	200.0	200.0	300.0	2200.0	500.0	34.6	38.5	18.5	40.0	53.8	35.4
Credit	Error Diff.	1.7	1.6	0.3	-1.5	0.5	0.0	-1.2	-0.6	-0.3	-5.8	1.5	2.2
	Size in %	26.8	48.7	33.3	16.7	47.6	6.2	48.6	7.2	33.3	6.0	47.6	5.3
	Time in %	50.0	100.0	75.0	75.0	350.0	125.0	55.0	13.3	40.0	13.3	70.0	16.7
German	Error Diff.	4.0	4.1	3.3	-4.0	15.9	0.5	5.8	5.4	5.5	2.5	12.0	11.5
	Size in %	18.2	33.8	33.2	20.0	30.1	13.5	32.2	32.0	33.4	10.0	30.1	14.5
	Time in %	54.5	81.8	72.7	54.5	290.9	127.3	36.0	36.0	42.1	14.5	46.9	22.8
Pima	Error Diff.	-2.1	-1.9	-1.0	-6.5	4.3	-3.2	-1.2	0.5	0.7	-1.9	8.6	-1.3
	Size in %	40.2	41.6	20.0	20.0	40.2	14.8	5.5	22.1	4.7	1.1	40.2	14.8
	Time in %	50.0	66.7	33.3	33.3	166.7	66.7	10.4	29.2	10.4	8.3	58.3	25.0
Tic-Tac-Toe	Error Diff.	10.9	9.0	10.8	12.5	11.3	7.8	6.8	5.2	6.1	5.8	5.0	2.6
	Size in %	31.8	43.3	33.4	33.4	28.8	41.6	42.6	43.3	33.4	33.4	28.8	42.2
	Time in %	100.0	200.0	100.0	200.0	900.0	500.0	46.3	46.3	37.3	37.3	43.3	49.3

- If experiments of leader sampling and similarity-driven sampling are comparable, SIMSAM always produces better results than LEASAM. We also notice that similarity-driven sampling is faster than leader sampling in all domains, except on tic-tac-toe if we apply instance-based learning.
- Although about 50% of experimental results are not comparable if we relate statistical sampling techniques to similarity-driven sampling, we recognize

that SIMSAM always outperforms simple random sampling as well as systematic sampling in domains where comparisons are reasonable.

All in all, these results indicate that both preparation steps, sorting and stratification, are useful enhancements and that similarity-driven sampling is an appropriate alternative to statistical sampling techniques.

4 Related Work

The origin of all efforts to learn on subsets of tuples is Quinlan's windowing approach in ID3. Wirth and Catlett (1988) showed that costs of using windowing in ID3 are almost always significantly increase running time or do not lead to improvements. Catlett (1991) considered windowing in C4.5 which uses stratification as SIMSAM but only according to the class attribute. Experimental results indicate that windowing increases accuracy for noisy domains with continuous attributes. In general, effects of windowing are not significant but it slows down induction.

John and Langley (1996) discuss static versus dynamic sampling for data mining. Dynamic sampling uses the PCE (probably close enough) criterion, and a sample meets this criterion if the probability is low that data mining on the entire data set achieves higher accuracy. For naive bayes, their comparison showed only minor differences between static and dynamic sampling.

Toivonen (1996) and Zaki et al. (1997) examine applications of random sampling for finding association rules. They both report that sampling speeds up computation of large itemsets by reducing I/O costs. Zaki et al. only consider computation of large itemsets and demonstrate that up to 80% of true large itemsets can be found on a random sample. Toivonen uses itemsets produced on a sample as hypotheses that are tested on the entire database.

Ester et al. (1995) describe sampling on representatives for data mining with CLARANS (Clustering Large Applications based on Randomized Search). They use R^*-trees to determine center points for each data page in a spatial database, and then run their clustering algorithm on the set of center points. In terms of efficiency, focusing on representatives gains a significant speed-up. In terms of effectiveness, their sampling approach is slightly worse than clustering the entire database.

5 Conclusion

In this paper, we introduced similarity-driven sampling for data mining. In summary, similarity-driven sampling often outperforms statistical sampling techniques in terms of error rates using smaller samples if we train C4.5 and instance-based learning on reduced data sets and estimate their accuracy on separate test sets. Systematic sampling with sorting also yields astonishing good results.

We propose several technical enhancements for future work. For example, SIMSAM's performance will benefit from more sophisticated discretization approaches in stratification. We also plan alternative uses of different similarity measures. Future work also includes efforts to re-implement similarity-driven sampling such that SIMSAM utilizes direct access to databases.

The experimental study also raises more basic research questions. Differences in success between statistical sampling techniques and more intelligent sampling approaches are less significant than generally expected. The best sampling approach depends on both data characteristics and the selected data mining algorithm. The ultimate goal is to provide a set of sampling approaches accompanied by guidelines which context requires which data reduction approach.

References

Aha, D.W., Kibler, D., & Albert, M.K. (1991). Instance-Based Learning Algorithms. *Machine Learning*, 6, p. 37-66.

Catlett, J. (1991). *Megainduction: Machine Learning on Very Large Data-bases*. Ph.D. Thesis, University of Sydney, Australia.

Dougherty, J., Kohavi, R., & Sahami, M. (1995). Supervised and Unsupervised Discretization of Continuous Features. in: Prieditis, A., & Russell, S. (eds.). *Proceedings of the 12th International Conference on Machine Learning*. July, 9-12, Tahoe City, CA. Menlo Park, CA: Morgan Kaufmann, pp. 194-202.

Ester, M., Kriegel, H.-P., & Xu, X. (1995). Knowledge Discovery in Large Spatial Databases: Focusing Techniques for Efficient Class Identification. in: Egenhofer, M.J., & Herring, J.R. (eds.) *Proceedings of the 4th International Symposium on Spatial Databases*. August, 6-9, Portland, Maine. New York, NY: Springer, pp. 67-82.

Hartigan, J.A. (1975). *Clustering Algorithms*. New York, NY: John Wiley & Sons, Inc.

John, G.H., & Langley, P. (1996). Static Versus Dynamic Sampling for Data Mining. in: Simoudis, E., Han, J., & Fayyad, U. (eds.) *Proceedings of the 2nd International Conference on Knowledge Discovery and Data Mining*. August, 2-4, Portland, Oregon. Menlo Park, CA: AAAI Press, pp. 367-370.

Kohavi, R., Sommerfield, D., & Dougherty, J. (1996). *Data Mining Using MLC++: A Machine Learning Library in C++*. http://robotics.stanford.edu/~ronnyk.

Murphy, P.M., & Aha, D. (1994). *UCI Repository of Machine Learning Databases*. ftp://ics.uci.edu/pub/machine-learning-databases.

Quinlan, J.R. (1993). *C4.5: Programs for Machine Learning*. San Mateo, CA: Morgan Kaufmann.

Toivonen, H. (1996). Sampling Large Databases for Finding Association Rules. in: Vijayaraman, T.M., Buchmann, A.P., Mohan, C., & Sarda, N.L. (eds.) *Proceedings of the 22nd International Conference on Very Large Databases*. September, 3-6, Mumbai, India. San Mateo, CA: Morgan Kaufmann, pp. 134-145.

Wirth, J., & Catlett, J. (1988). Experiments on the Costs and Benefits of Windowing in ID3. in: Laird, J. (ed.) *Proceedings of the 5th International Conference on Machine Learning*. June, 12-14, University of Michigan, Ann Arbor. San Mateo, CA: Morgan Kaufmann, pp. 87-99.

Zaki, M.J., Parthasarathy, S., Li, W., & Ogihara, M. (1997). Evaluation of Sampling for Data Mining of Association Rules. in: Scheuermann, P. (ed.) *Proceedings of the 7th Workshop on Research Issues in Data Engineering*. April, 7-8, Birmingham, England. Los Alamitos, CA: IEEE Computer Society Press.

Modeling the Business Process by Mining Multiple Databases

Arun P. Sanjeev[1] and Jan M. Żytkow[2]

[1] Office of Institutional Research, Wichita State Univ., Wichita, KS 67260, U.S.A.
[2] Computer Science Department, UNC Charlotte, Charlotte, N.C. 28223, U.S.A.
also Institute of Computer Science, Polish Academy of Sciences
sanjeev@cs.twsu.edu, zytkow@uncc.edu

Abstract. Institutional databases can be instrumental in understanding a business process, but additional databases are also needed to broaden the empirical perspective on the investigation. We present a few data mining principles by which a business process can be analyzed in quantitative details and new process components can be postulated. Sequential and parallel process decomposition can apply, guided by human understanding of the investigated process and the results of data mining. In a repeated cycle, human operators formulate open questions, use queries to get relevant data, use quests that invoke automated search, and interpret the discovered knowledge. As an example we use mining for knowledge about student enrollment, which is an essential part of the university educational process. The target of discovery has been quantitative knowledge useful in understanding the university enrollment. Many discoveries have been made. The particularly surprising findings have been presented to the university administrators and affected the institutional policies.

1 Business process analysis

Critical to the successful functioning of any business is understanding of the business process. Databases have been routinely developed to store detailed information about business processes. By design, data capture the key information about events that add up to the entire process. For instance, university databases keep track of student enrollment, grades, financial aid and other key information recorded each semester or each year.

Knowledge discovered in data can improve process understanding. In addition to the known elements of the process, which have been used in database design, further knowledge can be discovered by empirical analysis. We can use a discovery mechanism that mines a database in search of knowledge that can be used to justify a particular hidden structure within the process. For instance, it may turn out that students in different groups finish their degrees in different proportion or that they take drastically different numbers of credit hours.

In this paper we focus on knowledge automatically derived from data, in distinction to expert knowledge. We outline a discovery process that results in knowledge which aids the business process understanding. The discovery process is driven by two factors. The first is the apparent structure of the business process and the way it is represented by database schemas and attributes. The second factor is the data and empirical knowledge they provide. The first is used to plan data preparation and design the search for knowledge. The knowledge discovered from data can reveal the process structure and can also suggest further data preparation and further data mining.

Quests generate knowledge while queries prepare data. Automated search for knowledge can use discovery systems such as EXPLORA Klösgen, 1992; KDW:

Piatetsky-Shapiro and Matheus, 1991; 49er: Zytkow & Zembowicz, 1993; KDD-R: Ziarko & Shan, 1994; Rosetta: Ohrn, Komorowski, Skowron, Synak, 1998. A discovery system requires a well defined search problem, which we call a quest. It also requires data, which are typically a specific subset of all data available, and are obtained in response to a query. Queries can be supported by a DBMS, but when data come from several databases, data miners must use their own query execution programs. An extended KDD process can be described by a sequence of quests and queries.

Database design knowledge includes temporal relations between attributes. When data describe a business process, the temporal order of events captured by different records and attributes is clear most of the time. Since an effect cannot precede the cause, questions about possible causal relations are constrained within the temporal relation between attributes. The sophisticated search for causes, performed by systems such as TETRAD (Spirtes, Glymour & Scheines, 1993) can be substantially reduced. A typical question we will ask is "which among the temporarily prior attributes are good predictors of attributes that describe the results of the business process?"

Vital characteristics of a process include throughput, output and duration. No doubt that the output and throughput are the most important effects of each business process. But it is also important to know how long is the process active. This is needed to develop process effectiveness metrics and also to decide for how long should the data be kept in active records. The quest for knowledge about process output, throughput and duration will guide our data mining effort. In practical applications, a business process consists of many elementary "customer processes" added together. For instance, the university "production of credit hours" is the sum of the enrollment histories of individual students. Contingency tables can aggregate individual customer processes into different summaries of the business process.

For a given cohort of students, the total throughput can be described by the total number of credit hours. A more detailed knowledge on credit hour acquisition can be provided by the histogram of the attribute "credit hours". Still more detailed are contingency tables that relate credit hour production with other attributes.

Throughput in the next business cycle can be predicted from the regularities discovered in the past data. For instance, there can be a regularity on the total process output in the function of time. It may be revealed by data mining that a more accurate prediction may be obtained by splitting the process into several subprocesses.

Process can be split into parallel components. Each of the parallel subprocesses uses a part of the input and contributes part of the output or throughput. The inputs and outputs of parallel subprocesses add up to the input and output of the entire process, in analog to the Kirchoff Law for processes of current flow in the electric circuits.

Process can be decomposed sequentially. Process P can be divided into subprocess P_1 followed by P_2, when the output of process P_1 is the input to process P_2. The sequential approach can be also used when we seek explanation of the input to the business process P by processes that are sequentially prior to P and supply parts of P's input. Those data come from various sources, external to the business process database.

Parallel decomposition can be guided by regularities between input and output/throughput attributes. Let C be an attribute which describes the throughput of process P. Let V_C be the range of values of C. The histogram of C is the mapping $h : V_C \longrightarrow N$, where for each $c \in V_C, h(c) = n(n \in N)$ is the number of occurrences of c in the data about P. We can use the histogram of C as a measure of efficiency of the process P, but when the values of C are numbers, we can integrate the histogram to obtain the summary throughput $T_P = \sum_{c \in C}(c \times h(c))$.

Consider a regularity in the form of a statistical contingency table that captures the relationship between an attribute A that describes the input of P and the throughput

C. For instance, A can represent the grades received by the students in high school, while C can represent the number of credit hours taken in college. For each value $a \in V_A$ and each $c \in V_C$, $p(a, c)$ is the probability of the value combination (a, c) derived from data. Using the distribution of inputs given by the histogram $h(a), a \in V_A$ we can compute the throughput histogram, by converting probabilities $p(a, c)$ into conditional probabilities of c for each a, $p(c|a)$, and using the latter in the following way:

$$h(c) = \sum_{a \in A} p(c|a) \times h(a), \forall c \in V_C. \tag{1}$$

When the histograms of A and C and the contingency table have been derived from the same data, the equation (1) is an identity. But when, for a similar process Q, only the histogram of the input A is known, the probability distributions $p(c|a)$ derived from P for each a and equation (1) can provide valuable predictions for the output of Q.

When probability profiles (vectors) $p(c|x), x \in V_A$, differ for different values of C, it makes sense to think about process P as a combination of parallel processes P_a for each value $a \in V_A$. We can further decompose each P_a in different ways either in parallel or in sequence. Parallel decomposition is particularly useful when:

1. differences between probability profiles are big;
2. attribute A can be controlled by the business process manager;
3. the histograms of A undergo big variations for inputs made at different time;
4. we expect that process P goes on differently for different P_a.

Let Q be a new cycle of the business process represented by $p(a, c)$. Let $h_Q(a)$ be the histogram of the input A for Q. Let $I_P = \sum_{a \in A} h_P(a)$ be the total of input units for P, and $I_Q = \sum_{a \in A} h_Q(a)$ be the total of input units for Q. For a stable process P, using the total throughput T_P of P, the throughput of Q can be predicted as $T_Q = T_P \times (I_Q/I_P)$. The decomposition of P into processes $P_a, a \in A$ leads to the prediction of $T_Q = \sum_{c \in C}(c \times \sum_{a \in A} p(c|a) \times h_Q(a))$. When the conditions 1-3 above are satisfied, the difference between both predictions can be large, justifying the decomposition into parallel processes.

Sequential analysis is useful when some attributes describe stages of a process. Often, in addition to the input and output attributes, other attributes describe intermediate stages. Suppose that B is an attribute that allows us to decompose process P sequentially into P_1 and P_2, and use B as a measure of effectiveness of P_1. This is particularly useful, when the subprocess P_1 applies only to some inputs while some other inputs can be used as a control group, so that the effectiveness of P_1 can be compared with the control group. We will discuss remedial classes and financial aid and their effectiveness as examples of P_1.

Sequential analysis is also important when it leads to knowledge useful in predicting process input. For instance, the number of new students depends on the number of high school graduates, on the cost of study per credit hour, and so on. Regularities on new students enrollment derived from past data lead to predictions about new students who will enroll in the future.

Since the attributes that can provide predictions of new input to the business process are typically not available in the business process database **B**, other databases must be searched for relevant information. A relevant database **D** must include at least one attribute A_1 that provides information temporarily prior to the input A_2 of **B** and at least one attribute J that can be used to join **B** and **D**. Aggregation of data in one or both databases may be required to reach the same granularity of the values of A_1 and A_2. Further, the join'ed datatable **B+D** must yield a regularity between A_1 and A_2. In this way a regularity can be found between high school graduation and college freshmen enrollment. Since high school graduation figures are known in May, such a regularity provides predictions of college enrollment in August. The information from tables (1) and (3) (see the next section) is joined with data in (5) by the use of attribute "county". Enrollment data must be aggregated to provide the count of students who are residents of each county.

2 An example of process analysis: university enrollment

Understanding the factors in enrollment decline and increase is critical for universities, as often the resources available to the university depend on the number of credit hours the students enroll. Many specific steps to increase enrollment may not be productive because student enrollment is a complex phenomenon, especially in metropolitan institutions where the student population is diverse in age, ethnic origin and socio-economic status.

Student databases kept at every university can be instrumental in understanding the enrollment. We have applied the process analysis methodology to a university database exploration and step after step expanded our understanding of the university enrollment process. The initial discovery goals have been simple but their subsequent refinement led to sophisticated knowledge that surprised us and influenced university administrators. Within the limits of this paper we only describe a few steps and a few results that illustrate the business process analysis driven by knowledge discovered in data. Our previous research on enrollment has been reported by Sanjeev & Żytkow (1996).

The data came from several sources. Consider a student database that consists of the following files (tables) 1-4 and (5):
  (1) Grade Tape for each academic term (Mainframe, Sequential File)
  (2) Student History File (Mainframe, VSAM file)
  (3) Student Transcript file (Mainframe, VSAM file)
  (4) Student Financial Assistance (Mainframe, DB2 database)
  (5) High School Graduates; Kansas State Board of Education

We used temporal precedence to group the attributes into three categories. **Category 1** describes students prior to their university enrollment. It includes *demographics:* age at first term, ethnicity, sex, and so forth, as well as *high school information*: the graduation year, high school name, high school grade point average (HSGPA), rank in the graduating class, the results on standardized tests (COMPACT) and so on. All these attributes come from the tables (1) and (5).

The attributes in **Category 2** describe events in the course of studies: hours of remedial education in the first term (REMHR), performance in basic skills classes during the first term, cumulative grade point average (CUMGPA), number of academic terms skipped, maximum number of academic terms skipped in a row, number of times changed major, number of times placed on probation, and academic dismissal. All these attributes come from the tables (2), (3), and (4).

Category 3, also referred to as goal attributes, captures the global characteristics of a business process that describe output, throughput and duration. In our example we use academic degrees received (DEGREE) as direct measure of a successful output. Bachelor degrees are awarded after completing approximately 120 credit hours. But all credit hours taken by a student contribute to the total credit hours, which is the determinant of university's budget. Thus the total number of credit hours taken (CURRHRS) measures process throughput. Process duration can be measured in the number of academic terms enrolled (NTERM) by the students. All these attributes come from table (3).

Query-1 prepared the initial data table. In our walk-through example we use attributes in all three categories. We analyze a homogeneous yet large group of students, containing first-time, full-time freshmen with no previous college experience, from the Fall 1986. The choice of the year 1986 provides sufficient time for the students to receive a bachelor's degree by the time we conducted our study, even after a number of stop-outs.

Table 1. Counts for HSGPA vs{CURRHRS, NTERM, DEGREE}; COMPACT vs CURRHRS

CURRHRS (a)

120 +	0	11	102	92	73
90-119	0	13	67	26	32
60-89	0	6	54	25	25
30-59	0	34	100	32	22
1-29	4	164	243	60	29
0	0	14	17	5	3
HSGPA	F	D	C	B	A

$\chi^2 = 229, Q = 1.7 \cdot 10^{-32}, V = 0.19$

CURRHRS (b)

120 +	40	78	59	108	5
90-119	40	44	24	38	3
60-89	26	32	28	29	0
30-59	57	68	43	36	0
1-29	262	196	65	56	1
0	38	8	4	2	0
COMPACT	missing	< 19	≤ 22	≤ 29	> 29

$\chi^2 = 221, Q = 6 \cdot 10^{-34}, V = 0.2$

NTERM (c)

12 +	0	10	41	26	8
9-11	0	16	107	70	42
6-8	0	17	98	47	67
3-5	1	42	110	31	31
1-2	3	158	228	69	36
HSGPA	F	D	C	B	A

$\chi^2 = 168, Q = 3 \cdot 10^{-23}, V = 0.2$

DEGREE (d)

Bachelor's	0	15	128	97	91
Associate	0	2	14	8	13
No-degree	4	226	443	139	81
HSGPA	F	D	C	B	A

$\chi^2 = 157, Q = 1.5 \cdot 10^{-28}, V = 0.25$

many attributes averaged over the student body. Since we considered records for individual students we have been able to derive further interesting conclusions.

Among the measures of high school performance and academic ability, our results indicate that composite ACT score is a better predictor than either high school grade point average (HSGPA) or the ranking in the graduating class. This can be seen by comparing Tables 1-a and -b. Table 1-b shows a regularity which is slightly more significant ($Q : 10^{-34} vs 10^{-32}$) and stronger (V:0.20 vs 0.19).

Analogous patterns of approximately the same strength and significance relate COMPACT and HSGPA with the remaining two goal variables. The corresponding tables cannot be reproduced due to the space limit.

In conclusion, parallel decomposition of the process by the ACT scores is very useful, and may lead to further findings, when different subprocesses are analyzed in detail. We will see that happen in the case of remedial instruction. Since the values of ACT and HSGPA are closely related, it does not make sense to create separate parallel processes for HSGPA.

A sequential analysis problem: does financial aid help retention? Financial aid belongs to Category 2, the events that occur during the study process. It is available in the form of grants, loans and scholarships. The task of **Query-2** has been to utilize the financial aid data. By joining the source table (4) with the table obtained as a result of query-1 we augmented that table with 64 attributes (eight types of financial aid awarded to the students in each of the 8 fiscal years 1987-94).

Quest-2 confronted the new aid attributes with with our goal attributes (Category 3). The results were surprising. No evidence has been found that financial aid causes students to enroll in more terms, take more credit hours and receive degrees. For instance, the patterns for financial aid received in the first fiscal year represented very high probabilities of random fluctuation $Q = 0.88$ (for terms enrolled), $Q = 0.24$ (for credit hours taken) and $Q = 0.36$ (for degrees received). None would pass even the least demanding threshold of significance.

These negative results stimulated us to use **query-3** and **query-4** to select the subgroups of students at two extremes of the spectrum: those needing remedial instruction and those who had received high school grade 'A'/'B'. In each of two subgroups we tried **quest-3** and **quest-4** analogous to query-2.

In the quest-3 (remedial needing students) we sought the possible impact on Category 3 variables of financial aid received in the first fiscal year, that is, when the remedial instruction has been provided. The results were negative: the patterns among the amount of financial aids received and the goal variables had the following high

Table 2. Actual Tables for DEGREE vs REMHR (a) all students (b) remedial needing

DEGREE (a)

Bachelor's	302	0	27	10	1	7
Associate	32	0	3	3	1	0
No-degree	735	2	119	82	10	47
REMHR	0	2	3	5	6	

$\chi^2 = 31.2, Q = 0.0, V = 0.106$

DEGREE (b)

Bachelor's	19	4	1	0	4
Associate	2	1	1	0	0
No-degree	174	39	36	4	21
REMHR	0	3	5	6	8

$\chi^2 = 5.06, Q = 0.89, V = 0.091$

probabilities of random fluctuation: $Q = 0.11$ (for terms enrolled), $Q = 0.22$ (for credit hours taken) and $Q = 0.86$ (for degrees received). In response to quest-4, in the group of students receiving high school grade 'A'/'B', the corresponding probabilities were $Q = 0.99$ (for terms enrolled), $Q = 0.99$ (for credit hours taken) and $Q = 0.94$ (for degrees received). These findings indicate that financial aid received by students in the first year was not helpful in their retention.

Using **query-5** we created an attribute which provides the total dollar amount of aid received in all fiscal years 1987 – 1994. Now, with **quest-5** we sought the impact of this variable on the goal attributes in Category 3. Finally, a positive influence of financial aid has been detected (Sanjeev & Zytkow, 1996), but the results are due to the fact that in order to receive financial aid the student must be enrolled. We could not demonstrate that financial aid plays the role of seed money by increasing the enrollment to years when it hasn't been received.

It is useful to combine data from different datasets. Within one database the join operation can be performed on keys such as social security number, while the joins across different databases may require group values and be preceded by aggregation.

An example of sequential analysis: remedial instruction: One of the independent variables in Category 2, used in query-1 has been REMHR (total number of remedial hours taken in the first term). An intriguing regularity has been returned by the search (Table 2-a): *"Students who took remedial hours in their first term are less likely to receive a degree".* The percentage of students receiving a degree decreased from 31% for REMHR=0 to 13% for REMHR=8. This is a disturbing result, since the purpose of remedial classes is to prepare students for the regular classes.

Query-6: Select students needing remedial instruction. After brief analysis we realized that Table 2-a is misleading. Remedial instruction is intended only for the academically under-prepared students, while students who do not need remedial instruction are not the right control group to be compared with. In order to obtain relevant data we had to identify students for whom remedial education had been intended and analyze the success only for those students. After discussing with several administrators, the need for remedial instruction was defined as: (query-6:) a composite ACT score of less than 20 and either having high school grade of 'C'/'D'/'F' or graduating in the bottom 30% of the class. Those students for whom the remedial instruction was intended but did not take it, played the role of the control group.

Quest-6: For data selected by query-6 search for regularities between REMHR and process performance attributes. Use attributes in Category 1 to make subsets of data. 49er's results were again surprising because no evidence has been found that remedial instruction helps the academically under-prepared students to enroll in more terms, take more credit hours and receive degrees.

Table 2-b indicates that taking remedial classes does not improve the chances for a student to persist to a degree. For instance, those students who did not take any remedial classes, but needed them according to our criteria, received bachelor's and associate degrees at about the same percentage (10.8% vs 9.9%) when compared to those who took from 3 to as much as 8 hours of remedial class. A similar table indicated no relationship ($Q = 0.98$) between hours of remedial classes taken and terms enrolled.

Finally, let us briefly discuss how **external data can be used to predict part of the input.** Table (5) provides the number of high school graduates by county.

Knowing the fraction of that number who enroll at WSU, we can predict in June, a part of university enrollment in August. **Query-7** joined tables (1) and (5) by the year, but prior to that it aggregated each table (1) for the corresponding years by the county, counting the numbers of students per county. Now, **quest-7** has determined the percentage of students who transfer from high school to WSU. That number, recently at about 20% can be used to predict new enrollment.

3 Impact of findings on the business process

In 1995-97 the results of our enrollment research have been presented to senior university administrators such as *Associate to the President, Vice President of Academic Affairs, Associate Vice Presidents, Director of Budget, and Deans*. Many of them chaired or were part of executive purpose committees like *Strategic Plan Task Force, Academic Affairs Management Group, and University Retention Management Committee*.

Starting in the Spring 1997, for the fourth consecutive enrollment period, WSU's enrollment has increased. It is the most consistent increase in the 1990s. While business decisions are not always based entirely on empirical evidence, such evidence certainly helps to make well-informed decisions. We discuss here some of the strategic decisions, and outline how our findings have formed their underlying empirical foundation.

"WSU will recruit and retain high quality students from a variety of ethnic and socioeconomic backgrounds" is the second out of the five stated *Goals and Objectives* in the draft *Strategic Plan for Wichita State University*. This strategic plan, outlined in 1997, is currently being presented to the various university constituencies, such as the faculty senate, for review and acceptance.

In 1995 and 1996, our research uncovered that academic results in high school are the best predictor of persistence and superior performance in college. Tables 1 show regularities between composite ACT and average grade in high school (HSGPA) as predictors and the college performance attributes: cumulative credit hours taken (CURRHRS), academic terms enrolled (NTERM), and degrees received (DEGREE).

The eighth year graduation rate measure has been included as WSU's performance indicator. A strategic planning process called VISION 2020, initiated by the State of Kansas, requires the universities to formulate a set of performance indicators and report the results (Chambers & Sanjeev, 1997). The first of the core indicators concerns *undergraduate student retention and graduation rates*. The report mandated by the Regents asked for graduation rate measures after four, five, and six years. But WSU's students take usually longer than six years to graduate: they tend to stop-out for several academic terms during their college careers and enroll in less than 15 hrs in one semester. This phenomenon has been a conclusion from our studies in 1995 and 1996. It can be partially observed in Table 1-c. It shows that a significant percentage of students enroll above 11 terms. In addition many students stop out for few semesters. As a result, among the six Regents universities in Kansas, WSU is the only institution in which the graduation rate is also measured at the end of the eighth year.

Our negative results increased the awareness of the cost of remedial education. The upcoming replacement of open admission by entry requirements is pushing aside the question of reforming the remedial education, but university administrators are increasingly focusing on the effectiveness of remedial classes. Most recently, in the Fall 1997, a cost study has been conducted on remedial education programs. *Can those costs be justified in the absence of empirically provable success?* is currently discussed by the administrators.

4 Process networks vs. Bayesian networks

While Bayesian networks (Buntine, 1996; Heckerman, 1996; Spirtes *et al.* 1993) emphasize the relationships between attributes, the business process networks captures the relations between states of affairs at different time. They resemble the physical approach to causality: the state of a system at time T_1 along with the domain regularities causes the state at time T_2. This is a more foundational understanding of causes.

In distinction to Bayesian networks that relate entire data through probabilistic relations between attributes, a subprocess often involves only a slice of data. For instance, remedial classes are taken by only some students. One part of a process can be decomposed differently than another part and the corresponding subsets of records can hold different regularities. For instance, a causal relation between attributes may differ or not exist in a subset of data characterized by a subset of attribute values.

5 Conclusions

We have introduced a number of knowledge discovery techniques useful in analyzing a business process. Business processes can be divided into parallel components when it improves the predictive power. Processes can be analyzed sequentially, to find out how the preceding process influences the next in sequence.

We also demonstrated how queries that seek data can be combined with quests that seek knowledge. In a KDD process, queries are instrumental to quests. In addition to explicit queries, the search process "asks" many queries internally.

The data that we used as a walk-through example have been obtained from a large student database, augmented with statistics kept by the State of Kansas. Both have been explored by 49er. In this paper we discuss a few examples of practically important findings that have influenced the University policies.

References

Bhattacharyya, G.K., and Johnson, R.A. 1986. *Statistical Concepts and Methods.* Wiley: New York.

Buntine, W. 1996. Graphical Models for Discovering Knowledge, in Fayyad, Piatetsky-Shapiro, Smyth & Uthurusamy eds. *Advances in Knowledge Discovery and Data Mining*, AAAI Press, p.59-82.

Chambers, S. & Sanjeev, A., 1997. Reflecting Metropolitan-Based Missions in Performance Indicator Reporting, Metropolitan Universities, Vol. 8, No. 3, p. 135-152.

Druzdzel, M., and Glymour, C. 1994. Application of the *TETRAD II* Program to the Study of Student Retention in U.S. Colleges. In Proc. of the AAAI-94 KDD Workshop, p. 419-430.

Heckerman, D. 1996. Bayesian Networks for Knowledge Discovery, in Fayyad, Piatetsky-Shapiro, Smyth & Uthurusamy eds. *Advances in Knowledge Discovery and Data Mining*, AAAI Press, p.59-82.

Klösgen, W. 1992. Patterns for Knowledge Discovery in Databases. In Proc. of the ML-92 Workshop on Machine Discovery, 1-10. National Institute for Aviation Research, Wichita, KS: Żytkow J. ed.

Ohrn, A.; Komorowski, J.; Skowron, A. & Synak, P. 1998. The Design and Implementation of a Knowledge Discovery Toolkit Based on Rough Sets - The ROSETTA System, To appear in *Rough Sets in Knowledge Discovery*, L. Polkowski and A. Skowron (eds.), Physica Verlag, 24 pages.

Piatetsky-Shapiro, G. and Matheus, C. 1991. Knowledge Discovery Workbench. In Proc. of AAAI-91 KDD Workshop, 11-24. Piatetsky-Shapiro, G. ed.

Sanjeev, A., & Zytkow, J., 1996. A Study of Enrollment and Retention in a University Database, Journal of the Mid-America Association of Educational Opportunity Program Personnel, Vol. VIII, No. 1, Fall, p. 24-41.

Spirtes, P.; Glymour, C.; and Scheines, R. 1993. *Causality, Statistics and Search.*

Ziarko, W. & Shan, N. 1994. KDD-R: A Comprehensive System for Knowledge Discovery in Databases Using Rough Sets, in T.Y.Lin & A.M. Wildberger eds. Proc. of Intern. Workshop on Rough Sets and Soft Computing, pp. 164-73.

Żytkow, J.; and Zembowicz, R. 1993. Database Exploration in Search of Regularities. Journal of Intelligent Information Systems 2:39-81.

Data Transformation and Rough Sets

Jaroslaw Stepaniuk   Marcin Maj

Institute of Computer Science
Bialystok University of Technology Wiejska 45A,·
15-351 Bialystok, Poland
e-mail: {jstepan, mmaj}@ii.pb.bialystok.pl

Abstract. Knowledge discovery and data mining systems have to face several difficulties, in particular related to the huge amount of input data. This problem is especially related to inductive logic programming systems, which employ algorithms that are computationally complex. Learning time can be reduced by feeding the ILP algorithm only a well-chosen portion of the original input data. Such transformation of the input data should throw away unimportant clauses but leave ones that are potentially necessary to obtain proper results. In this paper two approaches to data reduction problem are proposed. Both are based on rough set theory. Rough set techniques serve as data reduction tools to reduce the size of input data fed to more time-expensive (search-intensive) ILP techniques. First approach transforms input clauses into decision table form, then uses reducts to select only meaningful data. Second approach introduces a special kind of approximation space. When properly used, iterated lower and upper approximations of target concept have the ability to preferably select facts that are more relevant to the problem, at the same time throwing out the facts that are totally unimportant.

1 Introduction

Knowledge discovery in databases (KDD) is concerned with identifying interesting patterns and describing them in a concise and meaningful manner. Rough set methodology for knowledge discovery was introduced by Pawlak [8]. It provides a powerful tool for knowledge discovery from incomplete data. A number of algorithms and systems have been developed based on rough set theory which may induce a set of decision rules from a given decision table, and may use induced decision rules to classify future examples. Most of them are attempting to find and select the best minimal set of decision rules that use only a minimal subset of attributes (called reduct) from the given data table.

Rough set based systems, such as KDD-R [14], PRIMEROSE [13] and ROSETTA [7] have been applied to KDD problems. The patterns discovered by the above systems are expressed in attribute-value languages which have the expressive power of propositional logic. These languages sometimes do not allow for proper representation of complex structured objects and relations among objects or their components. The background knowledge that can be used in the discovery process is of a restricted form and other relations from the database cannot be used in the discovery process. Using clausal logic has some advantages over propositional logic. Clausal logic provides a uniform and very expressive means of representation. The background knowledge and the examples, as well as the induced patterns, can all be represented as formulas in a clausal language. Unlike propositional learning systems, the first order approaches do not require that the relevant data be composed into single relation but, rather can take into account data, which is organized in several database relations with various connections existing among them.

In this paper we consider two directions in applications of rough set methods to discovery of interesting patterns expressed in a clausal language.

The first direction is based on translation of data represented in clausal language to decision table [8] format and next processing using rough set methods based on the notion of reduct. Our approach is based on the iterative checking whether a new attribute adds to the information.

The second direction concerns reduction of the size of the data in clausal language and is related to results described in [4, 5]. The discovery process is performed only on well-chosen portions of data which correspond to approximations in the rough set theory. Our approach is based on iteration of approximation operators.

2 Approximation Spaces and Rough Sets

In this section we recall general definition of approximation space [10, 11, 12] which can be used for example for the tolerance based rough set model.

An approximation space is a system $AS = (U, I, v)$, where U is a non-empty set of objects, $I: U \to P(U)$ is an uncertainty function ($P(U)$ denotes the set of all subsets of U) and $v: P(U) \times P(U) \to [0,1]$ is a rough inclusion function. An uncertainty function defines for every object $x \in U$ objects related to x. The rough inclusion function defines the value of inclusion between two subsets of U. Definitions of the lower and the upper approximations can be written as follows:

$$LOW(AS, X) = \{x \in U: v(I(x), X) = 1\} \text{ and } UPP(AS, X) = \{x \in U: v(I(x), X) > 0\}.$$

We recall some notions of the rough set theory in the case of generalized approximation spaces [12].

Let $AS = (U, I, v)$ be an approximation space and let $\{X_1, ..., X_r\}$ be a classification of objects (i.e. $X_1, ..., X_r \subseteq U$, $\bigcup_{i=1}^{r} X_i = U$ and $X_i \cap X_j = \varnothing$ for $i \neq j$, where $i, j = 1, ..., r$).

The positive region of the classification $\{X_1, ..., X_r\}$ with respect to approximation space AS is defined as

$$POS(AS, \{X_1, ..., X_r\}) = \bigcup_{i=1}^{r} LOW(AS, X_i).$$

The quality of approximation of the classification $\{X_1,...,X_r\}$ in the approximation space AS is defined as follows:

$$\gamma(AS,\{X_1,...,X_r\}) = \frac{card(POS(AS,\{X_1,...,X_r\}))}{card(U)}.$$

This coefficient expresses the ratio of the number of all AS-correctly classified objects to the number of all objects in the data table.

It is always desirable to reduce the amount of information required to predict an outcome. A reduced number of attributes results in a large number of objects in class of objects similar to a given object, making the results more meaningful. If we can remove some of the condition attributes without affecting the degree of dependency between the subset of condition attributes and the decision, the remaining attributes will be termed a reduct [8].

To explain in more detail the notion of reduct, let $(U, A \cup \{d\})$ be a decision table with condition attributes A and a decision attribute d. Let for every subset $B \subseteq A$ approximation space AS_B is defined.

A subset $B \subseteq A$ is a relative reduct for $(AS_A, \{d\})$ if and only if

1. $POS(AS_B, \{d\}) = POS(AS_A, \{d\})$.
2. For every proper subset $B' \subseteq B$ the first condition is not true.

Approximation spaces and relative reducts are used in next section.

3 Input Data Transformation Problem

In this section we discuss problem of adequate data transformation for knowledge discovery systems. General scheme of our approach is represented on Figure 1.

3.1 Reduct Approach

In this subsection we discuss the following approach:
1. The data is transformed from clausal logic to decision table format by the iterative checking whether a new attribute adds any information to the decision table.
2. The reducts are computed from obtained decision table.
3. Rules from reducts are generated.

Data represented as a set of clauses can be transformed into attribute-value form, consisting of a number of objects that have certain values for certain attributes. This form is known as the decision table. When certain conditions are not met, the transformation is imperfect, because the expressive power of attribute-value language is insufficient to properly represent some concepts. In cases like that the transformation only leaves a limited knowledge about the problem, usually not enough to discover a satisfactory definition.

The idea of translation was inspired by LINUS system [2, 1]. We start with a decision table directly derived from the target relations positive and negative examples. Assuming we have *n*-ary target predicate, the first *n* attributes in the decision table are variables of the same type as their respective target predicate arguments. Last attribute is the target predicate value - true or false. All positive and negative examples of the target predicate are now put into the decision table. Each example is put in a separate row in the table. Then background knowledge is applied to the decision table. We determine all the possible applications of the background predicates on the arguments of the target relation - the first *n* attributes in the table being constructed, taking into account argument types. Each such application introduces a new Boolean attribute.

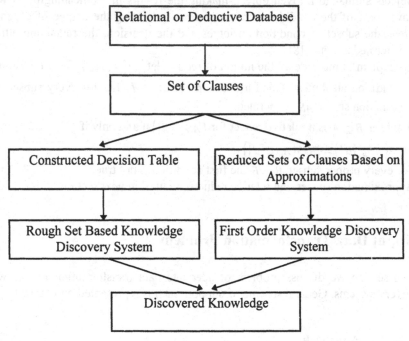

Fig. 1. General Scheme

One can check if a new attribute adds any information to the decision table. Three conditions for adding a new attribute are proposed:

1. $POS\big(AS_{B \cup \{a\}}, \{X_+, X_-\}\big) \supset POS\big(AS_B, \{X_+, X_-\}\big)$. Attribute is added to the decision table if it results in a positive region growth with respect to previously selected attributes.

2. $\dfrac{card\big(\{(x,y) \in X_+ \times X_- : a(x) \neq a(y)\}\big)}{card(X_+ \times X_-)} \geq \theta$, where $\theta \in [0,1]$ is a given real number.

   Attribute is added to the decision table if it introduces some distinction between objects that belong to different non-empty classes X_+ and X_-.

3. $\arg\max\big\{card\big(POS\big(AS_{B \cup \{a\}}, \{X_+, X_-\}\big) - POS\big(AS_B, \{X_+, X_-\}\big)\big)\big\}$. Given several

potential attributes, only the attribute with maximal positive region gain is selected into the decision table.

First two conditions can be applied to a single attribute before it is introduced to the decision table. If this attribute does not meet a condition it is not included in the decision table. The third condition is applied when we have several candidate attributes and must select the one that is potentially best.

In the end we discard the first n nominal attributes as they do not contribute to the problem - they are only used as identifiers and cannot be used in the learning process.

The transformed problem is then analyzed by a rough set based system. First, reducts are computed. Next, decision rules are generated. Although expressed in propositional logic language, the rules are easily converted to first-order logic language.

This approach is not universal and only applies to problems that can be transformed to attribute-value form without the loss of significant data. Counter-examples include problems that employ recursive rules and problems that introduce new variables into their rules, besides the ones that appear in the target predicate. It is important to note that by using a more complicated algorithm to convert these problems to decision table form we may minimize the loss of significant data. This however requires us to introduce into the decision table more than n argument attributes (variables). This greatly increases the number of possible applications of background knowledge on these arguments. Furthermore, we can consider positions of variables in the predicate argument list - this will also generate a lot of new argument attributes. The combined result will be a huge and difficult to comprehend decision table. The effects of applying a rough-set based system on such a table are still being investigated.

3.2 Approximation Space Approach

The approach presented in this subsection consists of the following steps:
1. Selection of potentially important facts from background knowledge.
2. Application of inductive logic programming system such as FOIL [9] or PROGOL [6] to selected clauses.

Such selection is based on the concept of „nominal information", first associated with input data reduction problem in [4, 5]. Nominal information of a fact L is the set of its nominal terms (nominal parameter values). It is denoted as $Nom(L)$.

Nominal information of a set of instances (or a concept) X is the sum of all instances - positive and negative - it consists of:

$$Nom(X) = \bigcup_{L \in X} Nom(L)$$

Selection of representatives (training set reduction) begins with determining the set of instances of target predicates (definitions of which we seek). Such set is denoted as X_{target}.

The selections can be represented as lower and upper approximations of $X_{target} \subseteq U$ in the family of approximation spaces $AS_\# = (U, I_\#, v)$, where $\# \in OP$ and $OP = \{=, \cap, \varepsilon, \subseteq, \supseteq\}$ is the set of operators.

Definition 3.1 Let $AS_\# = \langle U, I_\#, v \rangle$ be an approximation space, where U is the set of clauses with non-empty nominal information.

1. For every $L \in U$ we define $I_\#(L)$, where $\# \in OP$ as

$$I_=(L) = \{L' \in U : Nom(L) = Nom(L')\},$$

$$I_\cap(L) = \{L' \in U : Nom(L) \cap Nom(L') \neq \varnothing\},$$

$$I_\varepsilon(L) = \left\{L' \in U : \frac{card(Nom(L) \cap Nom(L'))}{card(Nom(L) \cup Nom(L'))} \geq \varepsilon\right\}, \text{ where } \varepsilon \in [0,1] \text{ is a parameter,}$$

$$I_\subseteq(L) = \{L' \in U : Nom(L) \subseteq Nom(L')\},$$

$$I_\supseteq(L) = \{L' \in U : Nom(L) \supseteq Nom(L')\}.$$

2. The rough inclusion function is defined as:

$$v(X,Y) = \frac{card(Nom(X) \cap Nom(Y))}{card(Nom(X))}.$$

Each uncertainty function contributes to a different approximation space which results in different kinds of approximations that show different properties.

Proposition 3.2 For every uncertainty function $I_\#$ exists a corresponding relation $\tau_\#$ defined as:

$$(L, L') \in \tau_\# \text{ if and only if } L' \in I_\#(L), \text{ where } \# \in OP.$$

It can be observed that:

1. $\tau_=$ is an equivalence relation.
2. $\tau_\cap$ and τ_ε are tolerance relations (i.e. reflexive and symmetric relations).
3. $\tau_\subseteq$ and $\tau_\supseteq$ are reflexive and transitive relations.

We then define two transformations

$$LOW : \{AS_\# : \# \in OP\} \times P(U) \to P(U) \text{ and } UPP : \{AS_\# : \# \in OP\} \times P(U) \to P(U)$$

based on the lower and upper approximations in $AS_\#$.

Starting with X_{target} we can construct infinite number of approximations by constantly applying one of these transformations first on X_{target} and then on the approximation resulting from the previous step.

Thus, the problem of selection is reduced to constantly applying upper (lower) approximation in the same approximation space to the upper (lower) approximation set obtained in the previous step.

It is worth mentioning that under certain conditions it is possible that $X \subset LOW(AS_\#, X)$, which means that in this approximation space lower approximation has the ability to expand beyond the set it approximates. This may look surprising in comparison to the traditional understanding of approximation spaces and rough sets [8].

The input data reduction problem is then defined as taking into account clauses that are included in $LOW\left(AS_{\#}, X_{target}\right)$. If this approximation appears to be too restrictive, which results in bad quality of discovered knowledge, we then consider $UPP\left(AS_{\#}, X_{target}\right)$. If it also does not meet our expectations, we proceed to consider following approximations: $UPP\left(AS_{\#}, UPP\left(AS_{\#}, X_{target}\right)\right)$ and so on. We can stop when the approximation is sufficient to learn a satisfactory definition of the target concept. Learning is performed with any kind of ILP system.

This approach may be modified by alternating randomly or by a set pattern between the two transformations and obtaining a different kind of sequence.

Since $X_{target} = X_{target}^{+} \cup X_{target}^{-}$ (the union of positive and negative examples of the target relation) we may also consider separate approximations of X_{target}^{+} and X_{target}^{-} which are added after the approximation process. This approach results in a more restrictive approximation (the sets of selected representatives resulting from this approach are subsets of their respective approximations obtained from the whole set X_{target}.

We sketch the algorithm for calculating upper and lower approximations of X_{target}.

```
LOW:=∅; UPP:=∅;
Nominal:=Nom(Xtarget);
for every L in U - X_target  do
begin
  Class:=I_#(L);
  NC:=Nom(Class);
  RoughInclusion:=ν(NC,Nominal);
  if (RoughInclusion=1) then LOW:=LOW∪{L};
  if (RoughInclusion>0) then UPP:=UPP∪{L};
end;
```

Unlike standard rough set approximation calculation this algorithm's time complexity is $O(n^2 m \log m)$ where $n = card\left(U - X_{target}\right)$ is the number of clauses and $m = card(Nom(U))$ is the number of nominal terms. However, in special case of uncertainty function $I_=$ the time can be reduced to $O(nm \log m)$ since we do not need to calculate uncertainty class at all and $NC := Nom(L)$. Other uncertainty functions require us to calculate set intersections or perform other set theoretical operations which are quite time consuming.

Example 3.3 The experimental data set is related to document understanding and has been an object of previous studies, see for example [4]. Predicate data describes 30 single page documents. Background predicates express type, position and alignment of document blocks. Target predicates describe whether a block is one of the five predetermined types: *sender, receiver, logo, reference, date*. First lower approximation and first, second and third upper approximations were considered. By applying approximations in different approximation spaces, several levels of data reduction were obtained. In this data set approximation spaces were divided into four groups, each displaying different data reduction levels. Overall there were eight data levels, ranging from an empty set to a full input data set. Figure 2 shows the results for different approximation space groups and eight possible reduction levels resulting from four previously mentioned approximations. Bars with different patterns represent the gain in input data resulting from applying the next approximation. Experiments with FOIL system show that any non-empty approximation is sufficient to obtain satisfactory definitions of the target predicates (accuracy above 90%).

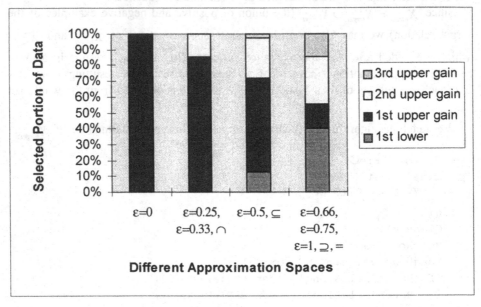

Fig. 2. Four Approximation Space Groups and Eight Approximation Levels

Conclusions

This paper has presented two approaches which aim at overcoming the difficulty met by knowledge discovery systems namely the huge amount of data. Both approaches aim at throwing away facts that are unimportant to the target concept and leaving facts that are potentially necessary. Such process can also be described as selection of representatives. First approach, based on the rough set theory concept of reducts can only be applied to a certain class of problems that can be transformed into attribute-value form without the loss of significant data. The results are quite promising and new ways to transform clauses into attribute values are still being investigated. Second approach uses another rough set theory concept, namely the approximation spaces. By employing a new kind of approximation space we are able to select clauses that are more relevant to the problem. If the selection appears to be too restrictive approximation can be used in multiple passes, each of them expanding the clause set in a way that includes only the most relevant facts from the ones that were previously thrown out. The facts that are totally irrelevant to the problem are never considered.

Acknowledgments. This work has been supported by the grant no 8 T11C 023 15 from State Committee for Scientific Research (KBN).

References

1. Dzeroski S.: Inductive Logic Programming and Knowledge Discovery in Databases, (eds.) U. M. Fayyad, G. Piatetsky-Shapiro, P. Smyth, R. Uthurusamy, Advances in Knowledge Discovery & Data Mining, The MIT Press, 1996, pp. 117-152.
2. Lavrac N., Dzeroski S., Grobelnik M.: Learning Non-Recursive Definitions of Relations with LINUS, Proceedings of Fifth European Working Session on Learning, 1991, pp. 265-281.
3. Lavrac N., Gamberger D., Turney P.: A Relevancy Filter for Constructive Induction, IEEE Intelligent Systems and Their Applications, 13(2), March/April 1998, pp. 50-56.
4. Martienne E., Quafafou M.: Learning Logical Descriptions for Document Understanding: a Rough Sets-based Approach, Proceedings of the International Conference on Rough Sets and Current Trends in Computing, Warsaw, Poland, June 22-26, 1998, Lecture Notes in Artificial Intelligence 1424, Springer Verlag, pp. 202-209.
5. Martienne E., Quafafou M.: Vagueness and Data Reduction in Concept Learning, Proceedings of the 13th European Conference on Artificial Intelligence (ECAI-98), Brighton, UK, August 23-28, 1998.
6. Muggleton S.: Inverse Entailment and Progol, New Generation Computing, 13, 1995, pp. 245-286.
7. Ohrn A., Komorowski J., Skowron A., Synak P.: The Design and Implementation of a Knowledge Discovery Toolkit Based on Rough Sets - The Rosetta System, (eds.) L. Polkowski, A. Skowron, Rough Sets in Knowledge Discovery, Physica-Verlag, Heidelberg 1998.
8. Pawlak Z.: Rough Sets. Theoretical Aspects of Reasoning about Data, Kluwer Academic Publishers, 1991.
9. Quinlan J.R.: Learning Logical Definitions from Relations, Machine Learning, 5, 1990, pp. 239-266.
10. Skowron A., Stepaniuk J.: Generalized Approximation Spaces, Proceedings of the Third International Workshop on Rough Sets and Soft Computing, San Jose, November 10-12, 1994, pp. 156-163.
11. Skowron A., Stepaniuk J.: Tolerance Approximation Spaces, Fundamenta Informaticae, 27, 1996, pp. 245-253.
12. Stepaniuk J.: Approximation Spaces, Reducts and Representatives, (eds.) L. Polkowski, A. Skowron, Rough Sets in Knowledge Discovery, Physica-Verlag, Heidelberg 1998.
13. Tsumoto S.: Extraction of Experts' Decision Process from Clinical Databases Using Rough Set Model, PKDD'97, Trondheim, Norway, June 1997, Lecture Notes in Artificial Intelligence 1263, Springer Verlag, pp. 58-67.
14. Ziarko W., Shan N.: KDD-R: A Comprehensive System for Knowledge Discovery in Databases Using Rough Sets, Proceedings of the Third International Workshop on Rough Sets and Soft Computing, San Jose, November 10-12, 1994, pp. 164-173.

Conceptual Knowledge Discovery in Databases Using Formal Concept Analysis Methods

Gerd Stumme[1], Rudolf Wille[1], Uta Wille[2]

[1] Technische Universität Darmstadt, Fachbereich Mathematik, D-64289 Darmstadt,
Germany, {stumme, wille}@mathematik.tu-darmstadt.de
[2] IBM Research Division, Zurich Research Laboratory, CH-8803 Rüschlikon,
Switzerland, wille_u@jelmoli.ch

In this paper we discuss *Conceptual Knowledge Discovery in Databases* (*CKDD*) as it is developing in the field of *Conceptual Knowledge Processing* (cf. [29],[30]). Conceptual Knowledge Processing is based on the mathematical theory of *Formal Concept Analysis* which has become a successful theory for data analysis during the last 18 years. This approach relies on the pragmatic philosophy of Ch. S. Peirce [15] who claims that we can only analyze and argue within restricted contexts where we always rely on pre-knowledge and common sense. The development of Formal Concept Analysis led to the software system TOSCANA, which is presented as a CKDD tool in this paper. TOSCANA is a flexible navigation tool that allows dynamic browsing through and zooming into the data. It supports the exploration of large databases by visualizing conceptual aspects inherent to the data. We want to clarify that CKDD can be understood as a human-centered approach of Knowledge Discovery in Databases. The actual discussion about human-centered Knowledge Discovery is therefore briefly summarized in Section 1.

1 Human-Centered Knowledge Discovery

Knowledge Discovery in Databases (*KDD*) is aimed at the development of methods, techniques, and tools that support human analysts in the overall process of discovering useful information and knowledge in databases. Many real-world knowledge discovery tasks are both too complex to be accessible by simply applying a single learning or data mining algorithm and too knowledge-intensive to be performed without repeated participation of the domain expert. Therefore, knowledge discovery in databases is considered an interactive and iterative process between a human and a database that may strongly involve background knowledge of the analyzing domain expert. This process-centered view of KDD is the overall theme and contribution of the volume *"Advances in Knowledge Discovery and Data Mining"* [7].

According to R. S. Brachman and T. Anand [3], much attention and effort has been focused on the development of data-mining techniques but only a minor effort has been devoted to the development of tools that support the analyst in the overall discovery task. They see a clear need to emphasize the processorientation of KDD tasks and argue in favor of a more human-centered approach for a successful development of knowledge-discovery support tools (see also [24], p. 564). All in all, human-centered KDD refers to the constitutive character of human interpretation for the discovery of knowledge, and stresses the complex, interactive process of KDD as being lead by human thought.

Real-world knowledge-discovery applications obviously vary in terms of underlying data, complexity, the amount of human involvement required, and their degree of possible automation of parts of the discovery process. In most applications, however, an indispensable part of the discovery process is that the analyst explores the data and sifts through the raw data to become familiar with it and to get a feel for what the data may cover. Often an explicit specification of what one is looking for only arises during an interactive process of data exploration, analysis, and segmentation. R. S. Brachman et al. introduced the notion of *Data Archaeology* for KDD tasks in which a precise specification of the discovery strategy, the crucial questions, and the basic goals of the task have to be elaborated during such an unpredictable interactive exploration of the data [4]. Data Archaeology can be considered a highly human-centered process of asking, exploring, analyzing, interpreting, and learning in interaction with the underlying database.

Emphasizing the KDD process, comprehensive support of the analyst has to be provided that, according to [3], should be embedded into a knowledge-discovery *support environment*. A support environment should especially support the overall process of human-centered KDD, including Data Archaeology involved in many KDD applications. In this paper, we investigate and discuss how the process of human-centered KDD can be supported by *Formal Concept Analysis* methods. This is done with regard to the basic requirements formulated for human-centered KDD support tools.

In order to formulate requirements for knowledge discovery support tools, it is necessary to reflect the underlying understanding of knowledge. A human-centered approach to KDD that supports the overall KDD process should be based on a comprehensive notion of knowledge a part of human thought rather than on a restrictive formalization as it is used for the evaluation of automated knowledge-discovery or data-mining findings (for example [6], p. 8). The *landscape paradigm* of knowledge underlying *conceptual knowledge processing* as described in [30] provides such a comprehensive and human-centered notion of knowledge. Although there is some similarity with the archaeology metaphor, the landscape paradigm places more emphasizes on the intersubjective character of knowledge. Following Peirce's pragmatic philosophy, knowledge is understood as always being incomplete, formed and continuously assured by human argumentation within an intersubjective community of communication (cf. [30]).

Knowledge discovery based on such an understanding of knowledge should support knowledge communication as a part of the KDD process, both with respect to the dialog between user and system and also as a part of human communication and argumentation. This presupposes a high transparency of the discovery process and a representation of its (interim) findings that supports human argumentation to establish intersubjectively assured knowledge. Further fundamental requirements for human-centered KDD support tools have been stated by R. S. Brachman and T. Anand (see [3], p. 53). In addition to tools that support the individual phases of the KDD process, they basically demand support for the coupling of the overall process, for exploratory Data Archaeology, and some help in deciding what discovery techniques to choose. Most of the content of these claims is covered by the more explicit and detailed requirements formulated already in [4]. Requirements 1 to 5 of the subsequent list are explicitly stated in [4], p. 164, while the remaining requirements are implicit in [3] and [4].

1. The system should represent and present to the user the underlying domain in a natural and appropriate fashion. Objects from the domain should be easily incorporated into queries.

2. The domain representation should be extendible by the addition of new categories formed from queries. These categories (and their representative individuals) must be usable in subsequent queries.

3. It should be easy to form tentative segmentations of data, to investigate the segments, and to re-segment quickly and easily. There should be a powerful repertoire of viewing and analysis methods, and these methods should be applicable to segments.

4. Analysts should be supported in recognizing and abstracting common analysis (segmenting and viewing) patterns. These patterns must be easy to apply and modify.

5. There should be facilities for monitoring changes in classes or categories over time.

6. The system should increase the transparency of the KDD process, and document its different stages.

7. Analysis tools should take advantage of explicitly represented background knowledge of domain experts, but should also activate the implicit knowledge of experts.

8. The system should allow highly flexible processes of knowledge discovery respecting the open and procedural nature of productive human thinking. This means in particular the support of intersubjective communication and argumentation.

Before discussing Conceptual Knowledge Discovery in Databases with regard to these requirements in Section 3, we introduce some basic notions and ideas of *Formal Concept Analysis* and *conceptual data systems* in the next section.

2 Formal Concept Analysis

Concepts are necessary for expressing human knowledge. Therefore, the process of discovering knowledge in databases benefits from a comprehensive formalization of concepts which can be activated to communicatively represent knowledge coded in databases. *Formal Concept Analysis* ([27],[28],[5]) offers such a formalization by mathematizing concepts that are understood as units of thought constituted by their extension and intension. To allow a mathematical description of extensions and intensions, Formal Concept Analysis always starts with a *formal context* defined as a triple (G, M, I), where G is a set of *(formal) objects*, M is a set of *(formal) attributes*, and I is a binary relation between G and M (i.e. $I \subseteq G \times M$); in general, gIm $(\Leftrightarrow (g, m) \in I)$ is read: "the object g *has* the attribute m". In Figure 1, a formal context is described by a table in which the crosses represent the binary relation I between the object set G (comprising the gates of Terminal 1 at Frankfurt Airport) and the attribute set M (consisting of certain gate types). A *formal concept* of a formal context (G, M, I) is defined as a pair (A, B) with $A \subseteq G$ and $B \subseteq M$ such that (A, B) is maximal with the property $A \times B \subseteq I$; the sets A and B are called the *extent* and the *intent* of the formal concept (A, B). The *subconcept–superconcept relation* is formalized by $(A_1, B_1) \leq (A_2, B_2) :\Longleftrightarrow A_1 \subseteq A_2 \ (\Longleftrightarrow B_1 \supseteq B_2)$. The set of all concepts of a context (G, M, I) together with the order relation $\leq$ is always a complete lattice, called the *concept lattice* of (G, M, I) and denoted by $\mathfrak{B}(G, M, I)$.

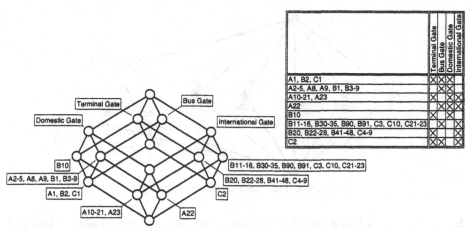

Fig. 1. A formal context concerning gates at Frankfurt Airport and its concept lattice

In this example, the intents of the formal context are exactly the subsets of its attribute set; hence its concept lattice is a 16-element Boolean lattice, as can be seen in Figure 1, which visualizes the concept lattice by a (*labeled*) *line diagram*. In a line diagram of a concept lattice, the name of an object g is always attached to the circle representing the smallest concept with g in its extent (denoted by γg); dually, the name of an attribute m is always attached to the circle representing the largest concept with m in its intent (denoted by μm). This labelling allows us to read the context relation from the diagram because $g I m \iff \gamma g \le \mu m$, in words: *the object g has the attribute m if and only if there is an ascending path from the circle representing γg to the circle representing γm.* The extent and intent of each concept (A, B) can also be recognized because $A = \{g \in G \mid \gamma g \le (A, B)\}$ and $B = \{m \in M \mid (A, B) \le \mu m\}$. For example, the circle in the line diagram of Figure 1 labeled "A2–5,..." represents the concept with the extent {A1, A2, A3, A4, A5, A8, A9, A22, B1, B2, B3, B4, B5, B6, B7, B8, B9, C1} and the intent {Domestic Gate, Bus Gate}. A typical information one can obtain from such a diagram is the fact that gates A10 to A23 provide the flexibility of being used either as Domestic or International Gate, but that with the exception of bus gate A22 they all are terminal gates only.

Graphically represented concept lattices have proven to be extremely useful in discovering and understanding conceptual relationships in given data. Therefore a theory of "conceptual data systems" has been developed to activate concept lattices as query structures for databases. A *conceptual data system* consists of a (relational) database and a collection of formal contexts, called *conceptual scales*, together with line diagrams of their concept lattices; such systems are implemented with the management system TOSCANA (see [20],[26]). For a chosen conceptual scale, TOSCANA presents a line diagram of the corresponding concept lattice indicating all objects stored in the database in their relationships to the attributes of the scale. For instance, as result of a TOSCANA query, Figure 3 shows the concept lattice of the conceptual scale *Runway* indicating as objects 18939 takeoffs at Frankfurt Airport (during one specific month). These objects are classified according to their runways, which are taken as attributes of the scale. The power of the TOSCANA systems lies in the possibility to refine a presented concept lattice by another one so that one obtains either a nested line diagram of a combination of

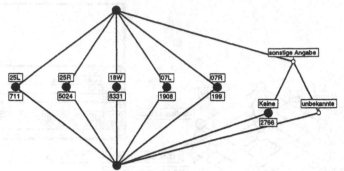

Fig. 2. The query structure *Runway*

both lattices or a line diagram of the second lattice refining a specific concept of the first; the latter alternative may be used for zooming further and further, which potentially allows us to navigate through the entire database.

3 Conceptual Knowledge Discovery in Databases

Conceptual data systems activated by the management system TOSCANA can be considered as *knowledge discovery support environments* that promote human-centered discovery processes and representations of their findings. In this section, we want to discuss how such processes of conceptual knowledge discovery fulfil the requirements listed in Section 1. As illustrating example, we use a TOSCANA system established by U. Kaufmann [10] for exploring data of the information system INFO-80 of the "Flughafen Frankfurt Main AG". this information system supports planning, realization, and control of business transactions related to flight movements at Frankfurt Airport.

In a TOSCANA system, the *objects* of the underlying domain are stored structurally in a relational database so that they can be activated by SQL-statements for establishing updated *conceptual scales*. The objects are represented for the user in line diagrams of the concept lattices of conceptual scales as demonstrated in Figure 3. In general, the objects are first listed in quantities describing the size of the extents of the represented concepts. For instance, in Figure 3 the number 8331 attached to the circle labelled "18W" informs that there were 8331 takeoffs on Runway 18 West. If one wants more specific information about objects, one can obtain the object names for an extent by clicking on the attached number, or even more information about a single object by clicking on its name. Of course, larger numbers as in Figure 3 first have to be differentiated by further scales before considering single objects. But the distribution of the quantities may be already informative: in our example the number 8331 indicates that more than 40% of all takeoffs are from Runway 18 West; this high proportion is interesting because there was a strong controversy about the construction of this runway regarding noise pollution.

Our discussion shows that the first requirement of appropriate object representations is fulfilled in TOSCANA systems. The second requirement of extendibility of categorical structures is already realized by the great flexibility in forming conceptual scales; even during the process of discovery new insights may give rise to further conceptual scales. The third requirement of meaningful data segmentations

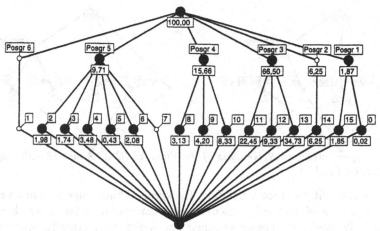

Fig. 3. The query structure *Wingspan Code and Position Size*

is also fulfilled because the conceptual scales and their combinations yield an almost unlimited multitude of conceptual segmentations and with that a powerful repertoire of different views for exploring and analyzing data. This flexible repertoire supports analysts in recognizing and abstracting the interpretable patterns for which the fourth requirement asks.

Let us demonstrate some of the discussed abilities of TOSCANA systems by continuing the investigation of Runway 18 West. In Figure 3 we zoom into the concept node labelled "18W" with the conceptual scale *Wingspan Code and Position Size*. Then we can study the size of the 8331 planes that took off from 18 West within the resulting line diagram shown in Figure 3. The Position Sizes indicate, in increasing order, the size of the docking position of the plane prior to takeoff, while the Wingspan Codes decrease by increasing wingspan (Code 0 stands for 'helicopter'). The size of the extents is described by percentages instead of quantities. From the diagram we obtain that most of the machines that took off from Runway 18 West had position size 4 or 5, hence are rather large. This might lead to the hypothesis that those machines contribute overproportionally to the noise pollution. We test this hypothesis by zooming into the two concept nodes labelled *Posgr 5* and *Posgr 4* with the scale *Noise Class of the Plane by ICAO-Annex 16*. The two line diagrams in Figure 4 indicate that for both position sizes more than 95% of the planes that took off from Runway 18 West are quite silent (as classified by Chapter 3 of the Chicago Treaty). Hence the hypothesis is not supported by the data. Summarizing our investigation, we can conclude that the planes taking off from Runway 18 West are overproportionally large, but that more than 95% of them are categorized as silent.

TOSCANA systems offer also facilities for fulfilling the other requirements listed. Changes in classes or categories over time may be documented in specific scales so that they can be easily monitored. Processes of knowledge discovery are developing in a network of conceptual scales that yields increasing transparency of the process and can be used for documenting the different phases of the process. K. Mackensen and U. Wille have even shown in [14] how such processes may be understood as

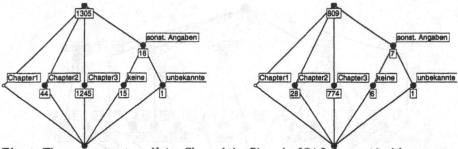

Fig. 4. The query structure *Noise Class of the Plane by ICAO-Annex 16* with respect to position sizes P4 and P5

procedures of qualitative theory building. Background knowledge of domain experts enters the process of knowledge discovery via conceptual scales in which experts have explicitly coded formal aspects of their knowledge in structurally representing a certain theme, thereby also making connections to their implicit knowledge. Overall, a TOSCANA system offers a conceptually shaped landscape of structurally coded knowledge allowing diverse excursions, during which a learning process yields an increasingly better understanding of what to collect and where to continue (cf. [30]). The graphical representation of interesting parts of the landscape, in particular, supports intersubjective communication and argumentation.

4 Applications

TOSCANA systems have been successfully elaborated for many purposes in different research areas, but also on the commercial level. Its range covers a variety of applications, that incorporate knowledge discovery. For instance, TOSCANA systems have been established for *analyzing* data of children with diabetes [20], for *investigating* international cooperations [11], for *exploring* laws and regulations in civil engineering [13], for *retrieving* books in a library [12], [17], for *assisting* engineers in designing pipings [25], for *developing* qualitative theories in music esthetics [14], for *studying* semantics of speech-act verbs [8], and for *examining* the medical nomenclature system SNOMED [18]. As a Conceptual Knowledge Discovery tool, TOSCANA was used to investigate deficiencies of the control system of the incineration plant Darmstadt [9]. One of the leading German mail-order companies is currently implementing a prototype of a TOSCANA system for its customer database, which shall be compared to statistical KDD tools.

Conceptual data systems can also be understood as On-Line Analytical Processing (OLAP) tools [22]. Roughly, the conceptual scales can be regarded as dimensions of a multi-dimensional data cube. The zooming-in on one of the concepts of a scale as described in the previous section corresponds to 'slicing' the data cube. 'Rotating' and 'Drill-Down' are also supported. Figure 6 shows how different scales can be combined and represented in a nested line diagram to visualize dependencies between different 'dimensions'. Here the positions of the aircraft are compared to the positions of the assigned baggage conveyors. In this application, it is not of interest to obtain general propositions, but to detect special cases. For instance, there are four aircraft that docked at Terminal 2, while their assigned baggage conveyors are in Terminal 1. Vice versa, 180 aircrafts at Terminal 1 were assigned conveyors in Terminal 2. The 7+17 cases in which the aircraft docks at one of the two terminals,

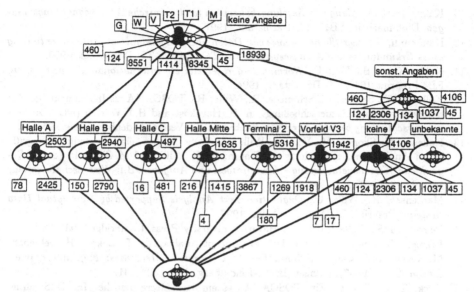

Fig. 5. Nested line diagram of the scales *Position of baggage conveyor* and *Positions*

while the assigned conveyor is on the apron, should also be considered. In all these cases, one can drill down to the original data by clicking on the number to obtain the flight movement numbers, which in turn lead to the data set stored in the INFO-80 system.

Further research in Conceptual Knowledge Processing aims at developing *conceptual knowledge systems* by extending the functionalities of conceptual data systems, especially by logic-based components. As Formal Concept Analysis and Description Logics are closely related and have similar purposes (see, e. g., [4],[19]), first steps in integrating both theories have been made ([1], [2], [16], [21]). For hybrid knowledge processing, an extension of conceptual data systems is foreseen by incorporating statistical and computational components [23]. This indicates a promising development in terms of extending TOSCANA systems toward a wider range of CKDD applications.

References

1. Baader, F., Computing a Minimal Representation of the Subsumption Lattice of all Conjunctions of Concepts Defined in a Terminology. In: *Proc. of KRUSE '95.* August 11–13, 1995, 168–178
2. Berg, H., *Terminologische Begriffslogik.* Diplomarbeit, FB4, TU Darmstadt, 1997.
3. Brachman, R.J., Anand, T., The Process of Knowledge Discovery in Databases. In [7]
4. Brachman, R.J. et. al., Integrated Support for Data Archaeology. *Int. J. of Intelligent and Cooperative Information Systems,* **2**(2), 1993, 159–185.
5. Ganter, B., Wille, R., *Formale Begriffsanalyse: Mathematische Grundlagen.* Berlin-Heidelberg: Springer-Verlag, 1996 (English translation to appear).
6. Fayyad, U.M., Piatetsky-Shapiro, G., Smyth, P., From Data Mining to Knowledge Discovery: An Overview. In [7]
7. Fayyad, U.M., Piatetsky-Shapiro, G., Smyth, P., Uthurusamy, R., Eds. *Advances in Knowledge Discovery and Data Mining.* AAAI/MIT Press, Cambridge 1996.
8. Grosskopf, A., Harras, G., *Eine TOSCANA-Anwendung für Sprechaktverben des Deutschen.* FB4-Preprint, TU Darmstadt 1998.

9. Kalix, E., *Entwicklung von Regelungskonzepten für thermische Abfallbehandlungsanlagen*. Diplomarbeit, FB13, TU Darmstadt, 1997.
10. Kaufmann, U., *Begriffliche Analyse von Daten über Flugereignisse — Implementierung eines Erkundungs- und Analysesystems mit TOSCANA*. TU Darmstadt, 1996.
11. Kohler-Koch, B., Vogt F., *Normen und regelgeleitete internationale Kooperationen*. FB4-Preprint 1632, TU Darmstadt, 1994.
12. Kollewe, W., Sander, C., Schmiede, R., Wille, R., TOSCANA als Instrument der der bibliothekarischen Sacherschließung. In: H. Havekost and H.J. Wätjen (eds.), *Aufbau und Erschließung begrifflicher Datenbanken*. (BIS)-Verlag, Oldenburg, 1995, 95-114.
13. Kollewe, W., Skorsky, M., Vogt, F., Wille, R., TOSCANA — ein Werkzeug zur begrifflichen Analyse und Erkundung von Daten. In: R. Wille and M. Zickwolff (eds.), *Begriffliche Wissensverarbeitung – Grundfragen und Aufgaben*. B.I.-Wissenschaftsverlag, Mannheim, 1994, 267-288.
14. Mackensen, K., Wille, U., *Qualitative Text Analysis Supported by Conceptual Data Systems*. Preprint, ZUMA, Mannheim, 1997.
15. Peirce, Ch. S., *Collected Papers*. Havard University Press, Cambridge, 1931-35.
16. Prediger, S., Logical Scaling in Formal Concept Analysis. In: D. Lukose, H. Delugach, M. Keeler, L. Searle, J. F. Sowa (eds.): *Conceptual Structures: Fulfilling Peirce's Dream*. LNAI **1257**, Springer, Berlin-Heidelberg, 1997, 332-341.
17. Rock, T., Wille, R., Ein TOSCANA-System zur Literatursuche. In: G. Stumme and R. Wille (eds.): *Begriffliche Wissensverarbeitung: Methoden und Anwendungen*. Springer, Berlin-Heidelberg (to appear)
18. Roth-Hintz, M., Mieth, M, Wetter, T., Strahringer, S., Groh, B., Wille, R., Investigating SNOMED by Formal Concept Analysis. Submitted to: *Artificial Intelligence in Medicine*.
19. Selfridge, P. D., Srivastava, D., Wilson, L. O., IDEA: Interactive Data Exploration and Analysis. SIGMOD '96, Montreal, Canada 1996
20. Scheich, P., Skorsky, M., Vogt, F., Wachter, C., Wille, R., Conceptual Data Systems. In: O. Opitz, B. Lausen, R. Klar (eds.): *Information and Classification*. Springer, Berlin-Heidelberg, 1993, 72-84.
21. Stumme, G., The Concept Classification of a Terminology Extended by Conjunction and Disjunction. In: N. Foo, R. Goebel (eds.): *PRICAI'96: Topics in Artificial Intelligence*. LNAI **1114**, Springer, Berlin-Heidelberg, 1996, 121-131
22. Stumme, G., Conceptual Information Systems and Conceptual On-Line Analytical Processing. *Proc. of FODO '98*. Springer, Heidelberg 1998 (submitted)
23. Stumme, G., Wolff, K.E., Computing in Conceptual Data Systems with Relational Structures. In In: *Proc. of KRUSE '97*. Vancouver, August 11-13, 1997, 206-219
24. Uthurusamy, R., From Data Mining to Knowledge Discovery: Current Challenges and Future Directions. In [7]
25. Vogel, N., *Ein begriffliches Erkundungssystem für Rohrleitungen*. TU Darmstadt, 1995.
26. Vogt, F., Wille, R., TOSCANA — A Graphical Tool for Analyzing and Exploring Data. In R. Tamassia, I. G. Tollis (eds.): *Graph Drawing '94*. LNCS **894**. Springer, Berlin-Heidelberg, 1995, 226-233.
27. Wille, R., Restructuring Lattice Theory: An Approach Based on Hierarchies of Concepts. In I. Rival (ed.): *Ordered Sets*. Boston-Dordrecht: Reidel, 1982, 445-470.
28. Wille, R., Concept Lattices and Conceptual Knowledge Systems. *Computers & Mathematics with Applications*, *23*, 1992, 493-515.
29. Wille, R., Begriffliche Datensysteme als Werkzeug der Wissenskommunikation. In H. H. Zimmermann, H.-D. Luckhardt, A. Schulz (eds.): *Mensch und Maschine - Informationelle Schnittstellen der Kommunikation*. Univ.-Verl. Konstanz, 1992, 63-73.
30. Wille, R., Conceptual Landscapes of Knowledge: A Pragmatic Paradigm for Knowledge Processing. In: *Proc. of KRUSE '97*. Vancouver, August 11-13, 1997, 2-13

CLASITEX⁺: A Tool for Knowledge Discovery from Texts

José Francisco Martínez Trinidad[1]

Beatriz Beltrán Martínez[3]

Adolfo Guzmán Arenas[1]

José Ruiz Shulcloper[1,2]

[1]Centro de Investigación en Computación, I. P. N. Mexico City
[2]Instituto de Cibernética, Matemática y Física, CITMA, Cuba.
[3]Facultad de Ciencias de la Computación, Benemérita Universidad Autónoma de Puebla, Mexico.
email: {jruiz,fmartine,aguzman}@pollux.cic.ipn.mx

Abstract. In this work the CLASITEX+ system for discovers the most important themes treated in a text written in Spanish or English is presented. This system works on the basis of trees of concepts and find: a) the most frequent concepts in the text, b) the relation between these concepts computing the co-ocurrence into the sentences that conform the text. Also CLASITEX+ can give us a distribution map of the most frequent concepts in the text An important characteristic of the system is the amount of concepts in Spanish and English handled by the system, also the execution time in the document analysis is very acceptable.

1 Introduction

Last years are remarkable in the rapid growth of available knowledge through electronic media. Traditional data handling methods are becoming less and less capable to fulfil the demands of this information deluge. Therefore, several strategies have been proposed to do fast recovery, search and in general intelligent "analysis" of the information. All these strategies can lie on what is called Data Mining. Most of the existing work has been done on structured (i. e., numeric) databases. Nevertheless, a large portion of available information is in collection of texts written in Spanish, English, or other natural languages (histories, newspaper articles, email messages, web pages, etc.).

The problem to find interesting things in a collection of documents has been termed by Ronnen Feldman and H. Hirsh [1] as "knowledge discovery from text" and the term "text mining" has been used to refer to research in this arena. It is thus very interesting and worthwhile to develop tools to extract non-trivial information from a non-structured (i. e., textual) data base in a reasonable time.

Without any doubt, the most important works in text mining and text knowledge extraction are those developed by Ronnen Feldman´s group [1,2]; among them the KDT system analyzes and browses non-structured text collections. Each document in the collection is labeled by a set of keywords organized in a hierarchical structure.

The hierarchy of concepts is the central data structure in KDT´s architecture. The system considers that a concept is a key word. The concept hierarchy (i, e, the word hierarchy) is an acyclic directed graph where each concept is labeled by a unique name. An edge from concept A to B denotes that A is more general than B. This means that it works only with inclusion relations. The hierarchy contains only those concepts of interest to the user, and he builds it by hand.

The KDT system gives the user the possibility to browse the textual database selecting key words from the hierarchy and watching their distribution with respect to other classes or sets of key words. Each document is labeled by a set of concepts that are those appearing in its contents. In KDT these sets of concepts constitute the only information extracted from a document; each set denotes the joint occurrence of its members in the document.

KDT summarizes and analyzes the contents of the set of words labeling the documents, taking into account for this purpose the probability distribution of the daughter concepts.

A concept (node) C in the hierarchy denotes a discrete random variable whose possible values are its children. $P(C=c_i)$ denotes the distribution of the random variable C. The event $C= c_i$ is the proportion of documents annotated with c_i. $P(C=c_i)$ is the proportion of documents annotated with c_i among all documents annotated with any daughter of C. In this work the associated distribution is considered as a powerful way for browsing the data and for summarize texts and to identify interesting patterns in the data. KDT gives the possibility to the users for compare distributions of similar keywords and view the results using tables and graphs. Finally KDT searches for irregular distributions, correlations, and associations based in conditions and thresholds supplied by the user.

FACT is other system developed by this group for knowledge discovery from texts. It discovers association-patterns of occurrence amongst keywords labeling the items in a collection of textual documents. In addition, when background knowledge is available about the keywords labeling the documents, FACT uses this information to specify constraints on the desired results of the query process. This system takes as input three sources of information. The first is a collection of textual documents on which the discovery process takes place. Each document must be labeled by a set of keywords representing the topics of the document, since this approach begins with the assumption borrowed from the Information retrieval literature. In addition to that, FACT also takes as input background knowledge about the keywords for its discovery process. To be usable such knowledge must define unary and binary predicates over the keywords labeling the documents, representing properties and relations between them. Finally, FACT allows to the user specify a query using a keyword and predicate vocabulary via a collection of menus in a simple graphical user interface.

In both before mentioned systems the document collection must be labeled by keywords. In the case of KDT a typical work session start either loading a class hierarchy from a file or by building a new hierarchy based on the collection of tags of all the documents. It is very important emphasizes that proceed in this way occasions that words equally important that the keywords and that was not considered remains out side of the process of discovery.

On the other hand FACT also requires that the collection of documents be labeled by keywords since the process of co-ocurrence discovery is realized on the basis of this sets of keywords. Something that should note is in the case of this system that does not consider the document in the discovery process. Everything turns around the keywords (more frequent words), so if the indexing process was not carry out conveniently we can not guarantee that the final result be the expected by the user.

In this work we present a system that discovers the concepts (themes or topics) most important treated by a written document in English or Spanish [4], this system works on the basis of trees of concepts. Besides it finds the relationship between the most important concepts in the text computing the co-ocurrence of apparition (of the most important concepts) in the sentences (paragraphs, sections, etc.) which conforms the texts. The system can give us a co-ocurrence distribution map of the most important concepts in the document. Finally this system in the discovery process of the most important concepts in a document read or traverses the text completely.

2 Clasitex$^+$

CLASITEX$^+$ is a system that analyzes a text in Spanish or English and discover the principal themes that are treated in the text. An important characteristic of the system is the use of a knowledge base constituted by trees of concepts.

The fundamental assumption in the system is that in a text the most repeated concept is the central theme of the same. Note that the most repeated concept is not necessarily the most repeated word, since a concept may have associated more than one word, i.e., many words can vote by one concept.

By term we will understand a set of one or more words. So we have that a term could represent several concepts or meanings. The concepts on the other hand by definition are not ambiguous. If a term introduce polisemia and the number of different meanings is N, then that term generates N different concepts. With these concepts we will work.

A tree of concepts is an acyclic graph in which each node is a term that represent to a concept and the edges represents relationships between the concepts. Examples of the concepts considered by CLASITEX$^+$ are "home", "Mexican Revolution", "National Polytechnic Institute", "Discoverer of the America", etc.

In CLASITEX$^+$ text files are used to represent the trees of concepts. Each file represents a subtree with depth one, where the file name is the father's name in the subtree and each one of the children appears in a line of the text file, as is showed in Fig. 1. So we have subtrees of a single level (depth one) in each file. The way in order to create new subtrees is the following:

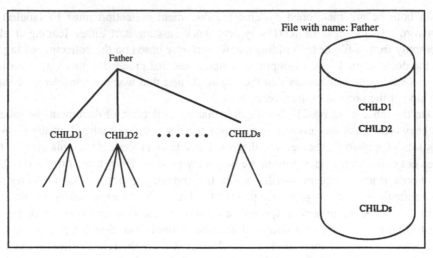

Fig. 1. Representation of a tree of concepts in file.

1. We have various directories named arbol1, arbol2, arbol3, etc., in directory arbol1 are all the trees whose children consists of a single word, in directory arbol2 are all the trees whose children have two words, and so successively.
2. If exists words of different longitude in a subtree, then in the respective directories we should create files with the same name
3. The files should be created with the following format:
   <word><dot>
   <word><space><word><dot>
   <word><space><word><space><word><dot>, etc.

After creating the trees, are created other files named dictionaries, one for each arbol directory in dependence of the concept longitude. In these files are all the concepts in alphabetical order and the list of all the concepts that votes by him (the list of all their children). Besides, It exists terms that we know priori does not have any meaning (item, personal pronouns, prepositions, etc). These are placed in other file and do not vote for no one.

The trees were generated in this way in order to consider the polisemia problem in the terms. So, since a term may have different semantic meanings, each one of them will represent one different concept. For example the term star have meanings in the sense: astronomy, badge, famous person; then were utilized the concepts astronomy-star, badge-star, famous-person-star and were constructed the respective trees for each concept.

The considered semantic relationships in CLASITEX⁺ to construct the trees of concepts are the following: inclusion, ownership, synonymous, conjugations, suggests, evoke, etc.

The most important module in CLASITEX⁺ is where the analysis of the document is realized. By analysis of a document we mean to say the determination of the principal themes (concepts) in a document. In this task are considered all the trees of concepts that has been given like knowledge base for the system, and the system gets

Input: File with text to analyze.

      DICCIONARIO-s= {(c, $concept$) / |c|=s}

      where: c is a string of characters

            |c| is the number of terms separated with one space in the string c.

            DICCIONARIO-s is a file containing all the terms c such that |c|=s associated to concept.

            SIN_SENTIDO is a file containing without sense terms.

Output: File (.cue) containing the concepts found in the text and their corresponding voting.

      File (.res) containing the concepts for the which a term of the text votes.

      File (.des) containing without sense terms in the text.

Variables: $cadena$ is a string of characters.

          s is |$cadena$| (number of characters in $cadena$).

          $índice$ is a pointer to the text.

          N is the maximal longitude of a term.

Step 1: Pointing the variable $índice$ to the beginning of the file to analyze.

Step 2: While not end of file

      Step 2.1: $s \leftarrow N$.

      Step 2.2: If s>0 then do

            Step 2.2.1: Take $cadena$ (a string) of longitude s starting from $índice$.

            Step 2.2.2: If $cadena$ exists in DICCIONARIO-s then

                    voting for the respective node.

                    $índice \leftarrow índice + s$.

                    go to step 2.1

            Step 2.2.3: Else

                  Step 2.2.3.1: If (s=1) and ($cadena$ exists in SIN_SENTIDO) then

                          $índice \leftarrow índice + s$.

                          go to step 2.1

                  Step 2.2.3.2: Else

                        write ($cadena$).

                        $s \leftarrow s$-1.

                        go to step 2.2.

      Step 2.3: Else

            $índice \leftarrow índice$+1

            go to step 2.1

Fig. 2. Algorithm for discovers the most important concepts in a text.

the main concepts that appears in the text. For this task is necessary travel the complete document, and we should search not only isolated words but pair, trios, quartets of words, in general terms, verifying for each term if it denotes or not a concept. If denotes some concept, then one vote is given to the corresponding concept. As final result of this process we will have some concepts receive more votes than other and are precisely these which without a doubt constitutes or denotes themes in the text, the algorithm in CLASITEX⁺ is given in Fig. 2.

The CLASITEX⁺ system was programmed in C standard so is very portable. Besides, this system at the same time that reads or traverse a document, process it, i.e., eliminates numbers, punctuation sings and converts to lower letters the capital letters, so it is not necessary create temporal additional files.

In order to improve the speed in the voting process is convenient maintain the dictionaries of concepts and the without sense terms in memory. In this way the access to hard disk diminishes, and this benefits the velocity of the system. In order to maintain the dictionaries in memory was proposed the following data structure: An array of indexes with the letters from *a* to *z* (in ASCII code), all the combinations of two letters, the accented vowels and the letter ñ (in the Spanish case) was considered. Each one of these index points to a single link list whose nodes contain a concept that begins with these letters and besides all the concepts that vote for it, if some one index does not have associated concepts to him, this point to null. The before mentioned structure is showed in Fig. 3.

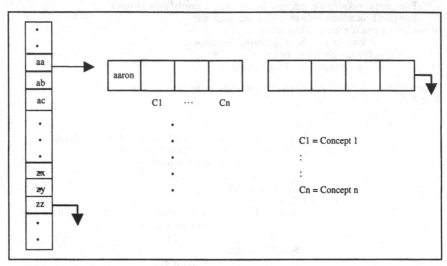

Fig. 3. Data structure for handling concepts in memory.

As result of the discovery process of the most important themes treated in a document, CLASITEX⁺ gets a set of concepts ordered of the most frequent at least frequent. In order to discover what concepts are related, the system carries out an analysis in the co-ocurrence of apparition of the most important concepts in the sentences conforming the text. Here we are supposing if two concepts appear in the same sentence, then these are related, and if the frequency of co-ocurrence of these concepts is high then we can affirm these concepts are very related in the document. The analysis of the co-ocurrence may be carrying out by pairs, trios, and quartets of concepts in the sentences. CLASITEX⁺ can give us a co-ocurrence distribution map of the most important concepts and their relations in the sentences, paragraphs, and sections.

The system considers the accents and the letter ñ (in Spanish case), eliminating the ambiguity that is produced in some concepts when are not considered.

The current number of concepts in Spanish that handle the system is approximately 72,000 that include areas such as: Biology, Computation, Physics, Mathematics, Medicine, Geography, etc. These concepts are of general knowledge, are not specialized.

The process to discover the most important themes in a document discussed previously is very general, so it is possible apply this same methodology independently of the idiom. If we want to find the important themes that treat a document written in English, only we need the trees of concepts in English. In CLASITEX⁺ was considered the option for work analyzing documents in English by the system, so now the system handles 83,513 concepts of general knowledge in English.

3 Examples

Due to space limitations we show the results of CLASITEX⁺ in a little simple text taken of "Discover the world of science" magazine [3]. Naturally that the introduced methodology has a lot value when we have many documents and these have a large content.

Table 1. Concepts discovered by CLASITEX⁺.

space-exploration&rocketry. 18	tools&equipment. 3
celestial-bodies. 17	tools,tests,units&scales. 3
celestial-phenomena&points. 6	large,tall,fat.. 3
electricity&electronics. 5	genetics,heredity&evolution. 2
principles-of-mechanics,waves. 4	fabrics&cloth. 2
beautiful,attractive,well-formed. 4	quantities-relationships. 2
types-of-ship&types-of-boats. 4	labor. 2
maps&cartography. 3	the-earth. 2
earth's-atmosphere. 3	materials,formations. 2
publishing. 3	elements. 2
forecasting&meteorology. 3	measures&standards-of-time. 2

SATURN, 2004

Ten or twenty years a go, interplanetary space probes where built like battleships: big, rugged, bristling with instruments - and costing a boatload of money. Although NASA has been phasing out such missions, only in October did it finally launch its last: the Cassini probe to Saturn.

By 2004, if all goes well, Cassini will park itself in orbit around Saturn loop around and around, taking readings and snapping close-ups of the planet, its gossamer rings, and its 18 moons - the some sort out work its cousin Galileo is now doing at Jupiter. Like Galileo, Cassini is two probes in one. While the main craft orbits Saturn a second probe come the European - built Huygens, will detach and fall into the atmosphere of Titan, Saturn's largest moon. Titan is a world into itself, nearly as big as Mars, it has an atmosphere that astronomers think is laced with organic chemicals - the building blocks of life. "There are only a few solid bodies in the solar system with thick atmospheres - Earth,Venus, and Titan", says planetary scientist Jonathan Lunine the University Arizona in Tucson. "A Titan is the best model for the Earth prior to the time when life began".

Cassini also resembles Galileo in that it carries radioactive plutonium - 72 pounds of the poisonous stuff, which provides heart to power the probe beyond Mars. The risk of that much plutonium being accidentally released into the atmosphere, either at launch or when Cassini flies by Earth for a gravity assist in August of 1999, drew a great deal of protest, as did the 1989 launch of Galileo. But in a perfect reply, Cassini headed of into deep space without a serious hitch.

The most important concepts discovered by CLASITEX⁺ are the showed in the Table 1.

CLASITEX⁺ takes 1.15 seconds in order to discover the most important concepts. From the previous result we have that the most frequent concepts are: 1)space-exploration&rocketry, 2)celestial-bodies, 3)celestial phenomena&points and 4)electricity&electronics.

Now computing the co-ocurrence between pairs of concepts we can find how are related these concepts.

Table 2. Co-ocurrence of apparition of the most important concepts in the sentences conforming the text.

Sentences	Pairs of concepts				
	1,2	1,3	1,4	2,3	3,4
Ten or twenty years a go...					
Although NASA has been...	1	1			
By 2004, if all...	1	1		1	
Like Galileo...					
While the main...	1	1	1	1	1
Titan is a world...	1			1	
"There are only....	1			1	
"A Titan is...					
Cassini also...					
The risk of...	1	1		1	
But in a perfect...					
Total	6	4	1	5	1

So from the analysis of co-ocurrence (see Table 2), we can see that the related concepts are:

space-exploration&rocketry and *celestial-bodies*
celestial-bodies and *celestial-phenomena&points*
space-exploration&rocketry and *celestial-phenomena&points*

So the final user can easily see that the analyzed text treat about the space exploration of celestial bodies, also about celestial bodies, phenomena and celestial points, and finally about space exploration of phenomenon and celestial points. All the before in automatic way and in little seconds. Besides CLASITEX⁺ gives the possibility of locating exactly within the text, the zones where the most important related concepts appear.

4 Conclusions

In this work was presented the CLASITEX$^+$ system, where some strategies were introduced for handle trees of concepts in memory and increase the speed in the analysis of a document (written in Spanish or English). The system discovers the most important concepts (main themes) treated in a document, and also finds which of those concepts are related computing the co-ocurrence of apparition of the same in the sentences of the document, in an acceptable time. Other important aspect in the system is the amount of concepts in Spanish and English.

This work constitutes a step more in the analysis of texts or non-structured data. In future work improvements in the strategy to voting will be introduced, we will introduce a semantic similarity measure between concepts that consider the relative position of the concepts within the tree. This will help us to give a weight to each concept in the voting process, this weight will be in function of the semantic similarity and, therefore, will reduce the ambiguity problem. Besides will be solved problems such as: establish order between the secondary themes of a document; prepare a summary of the fundamental contents in a document; describe tendencies or the conceptual evolution in time of an information source emitting a set of documents; reveal the conceptual nexus between them, etc.

This work was partially financed by Dirección de Estudios de Posgrado e Investigación del Instituto Politécnico Nacional and the CONACyT Projects No.3757P-A9608 and REDI of Mexico.

References

[1]Feldman R. and Hirsh H. "Mining association in text in the presence of background knowledge". In the Proceedings of the Second International Conference on Knowledge Discovery and Data Mining, Portland Oregon, August, 343-346 (1996).

[2]Feldman R. and Ido Dagan. "Knowledge Discovery in textual databeses (KDT) ". In the Proceedings of the first Int. Conf. On Data Mining and Knowledge Discovery (KDD95), pp. 112-117, Montreal, Aug 1995.

[3]Flamsteed S. "Saturn, 2004". Discover, The world of science, pp. 76, January 1998.

[4]Guzmán A.A. "Finding the main themes in a spanish document". Journal Expert Systems and Applicacions, Vol.14, No.1, January (1998).

[5]Rijsbergen C.J., et al. "Information retrieval". Second Edition 1979, http://www.dcs.gla.ac.uk/Keith/Preface.html.

[6]Salton G. "Automatic Text Processing: The transformation, Analysis and Retrieval of Information by Computer". Addison-Wesley Publishing Company (1989).

Discovery of Approximate Medical Knowledge Based on Rough Set Model

Shusaku Tsumoto

Department of Information Medicine, Medical Research Institute,
Tokyo Medical and Dental University
1-5-45 Yushima, Bunkyo-ku Tokyo 113 Japan
E-mail: tsumoto@computer.org

Abstract. One of the most important problems on rule induction methods is that extracted rules do not plausibly represent information on experts' decision processes, which makes rule interpretation by domain experts difficult. This paper first discusses the characteristics of medical reasoning and defines positive and negative rules which models medical experts' rules. Then, algorithms for induction of positive and negative rules are introduced. The proposed method was evaluated on medical databases, the experimental results of which show that induced rules correctly represented experts' knowledge and several interesting patterns were discovered.

1 Introduction

Rule induction methods are classified into two categories, induction of deterministic rules and probabilistic ones[2, 3, 5, 7]. While deterministic rules are supported by positive examples, probabilistic ones are supported by large positive examples and small negative samples. That is, both kinds of rules select positively one decision if a case satisfies their conditional parts.

However, domain experts do not use only positive reasoning but also negative reasoning, since a domain is not always deterministic. For example, when a patient does not have a headache, migraine should not be suspected: negative reasoning plays an important role in cutting the search space of a differential diagnosis[7].[1] Therefore, negative rules should be induced from databases in order to induce rules which will be easier for domain experts to interpret: induction of plausible rules will be important for an interaction between domain experts and rule induction methods.

In this paper, first, the characteristics of medical reasoning are focused and two kinds of rules, positive rules and negative rules, are defined as a model of medical reasoning. Both rules, whose supporting sets correspond to the lower and

---

[1] The essential point is that if extracted patterns do not reflect experts' reasoning process, domain experts have difficulties in interpreting them. Without interpretation of domain experts, a discovery procedure would not proceed, which also means that the interaction between human experts and computers is indispensable to computer-assisted discovery.

upper approximation in rough sets[3], are defined as deterministic rules with two measures, classification accuracy and coverage. Then, algorithms for induction of positive and negative rules are introduced, which are defined as search procedures using accuracy and coverage as evaluation functions. The proposed method was evaluated on medical databases, the experimental results of which show that induced rules correctly represented experts' knowledge and several interesting patterns were discovered.

2 Focusing Mechanism

One of the characteristics in medical reasoning is a focusing mechanism, which is used to select the final diagnosis from many candidates[7]. For example, in differential diagnosis of headache, more than 60 diseases will be checked by present history, physical examinations and laboratory examinations. In diagnostic procedures, a candidate is excluded if a symptom necessary to diagnose is not observed.

This style of reasoning consists of the following two kinds of reasoning processes: exclusive reasoning and inclusive reasoning. [2] The diagnostic procedure will proceed as follows: first, exclusive reasoning excludes a disease from candidates when a patient does not have a symptom which is necessary to diagnose that disease. Secondly, inclusive reasoning suspects a disease in the output of the exclusive process when a patient has symptoms specific to a disease. These two steps are modeled as usage of two kinds of rules, negative rules (exclusive rules) and positive rules, the former of which corresponds to exclusive reasoning and the latter of which corresponds to inclusive reasoning. In the next two subsections, these two rules are represented as special kinds of probabilistic rules.

3 Definition of Rules

3.1 Rough Sets

In the following sections, we use the following notations of rough set theory[3], which is illustrated by a small database shown in Table 1, collecting the patients who complained of headache. First, a combination of attribute-value pairs, corresponding to a complex in AQ terminology[6], is denoted by a formula R. For example, $[location = whole] \wedge [nausea = no]$ will be one formula, denoted by $R = [location = whole] \wedge [nausea = no]$.

Secondly, a set of samples which satisfy R is denoted by $[x]_R$, corresponding to a star in AQ terminology. For example, the set, $[x]_{[location=whole]}$, each member of which satisfies $[location = whole]$, is equal to $\{2,4,5,6\}$, which shows that the second, fourth, fifth and sixth case (In the following, the numbers in a set are used to represent each record number). These relations can be also extended to multivariate cases, such as such as $[x]_{[location=whole] \wedge [nausea=no]} = \{2,5\}$ and

---

[2] Relations this diagnostic model with another diagnostic model are discussed in [8].

Table 1. An Example of Database

No.	age	location	nature	prodrome	nausea	M1	class
1	50-59	occular	persistent	no	no	yes	m.c.h.
2	40-49	whole	persistent	no	no	yes	m.c.h.
3	40-49	lateral	throbbing	no	yes	no	migra
4	40-49	whole	throbbing	yes	yes	no	migra
5	40-49	whole	radiating	no	no	yes	m.c.h.
6	50-59	whole	persistent	no	yes	yes	psycho

DEFINITIONS. M1: tenderness of M1, m.c.h.: muscle contraction headache, migra: migraine, psycho: psychological pain.

$[x]_{[location=whole] \lor [nausea=no]} = \{1, 2, 4, 5, 6\}$, where $\land$ and $\lor$ denote "and" and "or" respectively. Finally, U, which stands for "Universe", denotes all training samples. In the framework of rough set theory, the set $\{2,5\}$ is called *strictly definable* by the former conjunction, and also called *roughly definable* by the latter disjunctive formula. Therefore, the classification of training samples D can be viewed as a search for the best set $[x]_R$ which is supported by the relation R. In this way, we can define the characteristics of classification in the set-theoretic framework.

For further information on rough set theory, readers could refer to [3, 9].

3.2 Classification Accuracy and Coverage

Classification accuracy and coverage (true positive rate) are defined as:

$$\alpha_R(D) = \frac{|[x]_R \cap D|}{|[x]_R|}, \text{ and } \kappa_R(D) = \frac{|[x]_R \cap D|}{|D|},$$

where $|A|$, $\alpha_R(D)$ and $\kappa_R(D)$ denote the cardinality of a set A, a classification accuracy of R as to classification of D and a coverage, or a true positive rate of R to D, respectively. In the above example, when R and D are set to $[nau = 1]$ and $[class = migraine]$, $\alpha_R(D) = 2/3 = 0.67$ and $\kappa_R(D) = 2/2 = 1.0$.

It is notable that $\alpha_R(D)$ measures the degree of the sufficiency of a proposition, $R \to D$, and that $\kappa_R(D)$ measures the degree of its necessity. For example, if $\alpha_R(D)$ is equal to 1.0, then $R \to D$ is true. On the other hand, if $\kappa_R(D)$ is equal to 1.0, then $D \to R$ is true. Thus, if both measures are 1.0, then $R \leftrightarrow D$.

3.3 Probabilistic Rules

By the use of accuracy and coverage, a probabilistic rule is defined as:

$$R \xrightarrow{\alpha, \kappa} d \quad s.t. \quad R = \land_j [a_j = v_k], \alpha_R(D) \geq \delta_\alpha \text{ and } \kappa_R(D) \geq \delta_\kappa,$$

This rule is a kind of probabilistic proposition with two statistical measures, which is an extension of Ziarko's variable precision model(VPRS) [9].[3]

It is also notable that both a positive rule and a negative rule are defined as special cases of this rule, as shown in the next subsections.

3.4 Positive Rules

A positive rule is defined as a rule supported by only positive examples, the classification accuracy of which is equal to 1.0. It is notable that the set supporting this rule corresponds to a subset of the lower approximation of a target concept, which is introduced in rough sets[3]. Thus, a positive rule is represented as:

$$R \rightarrow d \quad s.t. \quad R = \wedge_j [a_j = v_k], \quad \alpha_R(D) = 1.0$$

In the above example, one positive rule of "m.c.h." is:

$$[nausea = no] \rightarrow m.c.h. \quad \alpha = 3/3 = 1.0.$$

This positive rule is often called a deterministic rule. However, in this paper, we use a term, positive (deterministic) rules, because a deterministic rule which is supported only by negative examples, called a negative rule, is introduced as in the next subsection.

3.5 Negative Rules

Before defining a negative rule, let us first introduce an exclusive rule, the contrapositive of a negative rule[7]. An exclusive rule is defined as a rule supported by all the positive examples, the coverage of which is equal to 1.0.[4] It is notable that the set supporting a exclusive rule corresponds to the upper approximation of a target concept, which is introduced in rough sets[3]. Thus, an exclusive rule is represented as:

$$R \rightarrow d \quad s.t. \quad R = \vee_j [a_j = v_k], \quad \kappa_R(D) = 1.0.$$

In the above example, exclusive rule of "m.c.h." is:

$$[M1 = yes] \vee [nau = no] \rightarrow m.c.h. \quad \kappa = 1.0,$$

From the viewpoint of propositional logic, an exclusive rule should be represented as:

$$d \rightarrow \vee_j [a_j = v_k],$$

because the condition of an exclusive rule corresponds to the necessity condition of conclusion d. Thus, it is easy to see that a negative rule is defined as the contrapositive of an exclusive rule:

$$\wedge_j \neg [a_j = v_k] \rightarrow \neg d,$$

---

[3] This probabilistic rule is also a kind of *Rough Modus Ponens*[4].
[4] An exclusive rule represents the necessity condition of a decision.

which means that if a case does not satisfy any attribute value pairs in the condition of a negative rules, then we can exclude a decision d from candidates. For example, the negative rule of m.c.h. is:

$$\neg[M1 = yes] \wedge \neg[nausea = no] \rightarrow \neg m.c.h.$$

In summary, a negative rule is defined as:

$$\wedge_j \neg[a_j = v_k] \rightarrow \neg d \quad s.t. \quad \forall[a_j = v_k] \; \kappa_{[a_j = v_k]}(D) = 1.0,$$

where D denotes a set of samples which belong to a class d.

Negative rules should be also included in a category of deterministic rules, since their coverage, a measure of negative concepts is equal to 1.0. It is also notable that the set supporting a negative rule corresponds to a subset of negative region, which is introduced in rough sets[3].

4 Algorithms for Rule Induction

The contrapositive of a negative rule, an exclusive rule is induced as an exclusive rule by the modification of the algorithm introduced in PRIMEROSE-REX[7], as shown in Figure 1. Negative rules are derived as the contrapositive of induced exclusive rules. On the other hand, positive rules are induced as inclusive rules by the algorithm introduced in PRIMEROSE-REX[7], as shown in Figure 2. For induction of positive rules, the threshold of accuracy and coverage is set to 1.0 and 0.0, respectively.

5 Experimental Results

5.1 Performance of Rules Obtained

For experimental evaluation, a new system, called PRIMEROSE-REX2 (Probabilistic Rule Induction Method for Rules of Expert System ver 2.0), is developed, where the algorithms discussed in Section 4 are implemented. PRIMEROSE-REX2 was applied to the following three medical domains: headache(RHINOS domain), whose training samples consist of 1477 samples, 10 classes and 20 attributes, cerebulovasular diseases, whose training samples consist of 620 samples, 15 classes and 25 attributes, and meningitis, whose training samples consists of 213 samples, 3 classes and 27 attributes.

The experiments were performed by the following three procedures. First, these samples were randomly splits into new training samples and new test samples. Second, using the new training samples, PRIMEROSE-REX2 induced positive and negative rules. Third, the induced results were tested by the new test samples. These procedures were repeated for 100 times and average all the estimators over 100 trials.

Experimental results are shown in Table 2. The first and second row show the results obtained by using PRIMROSE-REX2: the results in the first row

procedure *Exclusive and Negative Rules*;
  var
    L : *List*; /* A list of elementary attribute-value pairs */
  begin
    $L := P_0$; /* P_0: A list of elementary attribute-value pairs given in a database */
    while $(L \neq \{\})$ **do**
      begin
        Select one pair $[a_i = v_j]$ from L;
        if $([x]_{[a_i=v_j]} \cap D \neq \phi)$ **then do** /* D: positive examples of a target class d */
          begin
            $L_{ir} := L_{ir} + [a_i = v_j]$; /* Candidates for Positive Rules */
            if $(\kappa_{[a_i=v_j]}(D) = 1.0)$
            then $R_{er} := R_{er} \wedge [a_i = v_j]$; /* Include $[a_i = v_j]$ in a list of Exclusive Rule */
          end
        $L := L - [a_i = v_j]$;
      end
    Construct Negative Rules:
      Take the contrapositive of R_{er}.
end {*Exclusive and Negative Rules*};

Fig. 1. Induction of Exclusive and Negative Rules

Table 2. Experimental Results (Accuracy: Averaged)

Method	Headache	CVD	Meningitis
PRIMEROSE-REX2 (Positive+Negative)	91.3%	89.3%	92.5%
PRIMEROSE-REX2 (Positive)	68.3%	71.3%	74.5%
Experts	95.0%	92.9%	93.2%

were derived by using both positive and negative rules and those in the second row were derived by only positive rules. The third row shows the results derived from medical experts. These results show that the combination of positive and negative rules outperforms positive rules, although it is a litle worse than medical experts' rules.

6 What is Discovered ?

6.1 Positive Rules in Meningitis

In the domain of meningitis, the following positive rules, which medical experts do not expect, are obtained.

$$[WBC < 12000]\&[Sex = Female]\&[Age < 40]\&[CSF\_CELL < 1000] \rightarrow Virus$$
$$[Age \geq 40]\&[WBC \geq 8000]\&[Sex = Male]\&[CSF\_CELL \geq 1000] \rightarrow Bacteria$$

```
procedure Positive Rules;
  var
    i : integer;    M, Lᵢ : List;
  begin
    L₁ := Lᵢᵣ;
    /* Lᵢᵣ: A list of candidates generated by induction of exclusive rules */
    i := 1;   M := {};
    for i := 1 to n do /* n: Total number of attributes given in a database */
      begin
        while ( Lᵢ ≠ {} ) do
          begin
            Select one pair R = ∧[aᵢ = vⱼ] from Lᵢ;
            Lᵢ := Lᵢ - {R};
            if   (αR(D) > δₐ)
                then  do Sᵢᵣ := Sᵢᵣ + {R}; /* Include R in a list of the Positive Rules */
            else M := M + {R};
          end
        Lᵢ₊₁ := (A list of the whole combination of the conjunction formulae in M);
      end
  end {Positive Rules};
```

Fig. 2. Induction of Positive Rules

The most interesting points are that these rules have information about age and sex, which often seems to be unimportant attributes for differential diagnosis.

The first discovery is that women do not often suffer from bacterial infection, compared with men, since such relationships between sex and meningitis has not been discussed in medical context[1]. Examined the database of meningitis closely, it is found that most of the above patients suffer from chronic diseases, such as DM, LC, and sinusitis, which are the risk factors of bacterial meningitis. The second discovery is that [age < 40] is also an important factor not to suspect viral meningitis, which also matches the fact that most old people suffer from chronic diseases.

These results were also re-evaluted in medical practice. Recently, the above two rules were checked by additional 21 cases who suffered from meningitis (15 cases: viral and 6 cases: bacterial meningitis.) Surprisingly, the above rules misclassfied only three cases (two are viral, and the other is bacterial), that is, the total accuracy is equal to $18/21 = 85.7\%$ and the accuracies for viral and bacterial meningitis are equal to $13/15 = 86.7\%$ and $5/6 = 83.3\%$. The reasons of misclassification are the following: a case of bacterial infection is a patient who have a severe immunodeficiency, although he is very young. Two cases of viral infection are patients who also have suffered from herpes zoster. It is notable that even those misclassficiation cases can be explained from the viewpoint of the immunodeficiency: that is, it is confirmed that immunodefiency is a key word for menigitis.

The validation of these rules is still ongoing, which will be reported in the near future.

6.2 Positive and Negative Rules in CVD

Concerning the database on CVD, several interesting rules are derived. The most interesting results are the following positive and negative rules for thalamus hemorrahge:

$$[Sex = Female]\&[Hemiparesis = Left]\&[LOC : positive] \rightarrow Thalamus$$
$$\neg[Risk : Hypertension]\&\neg[Sensory = no] \rightarrow \neg Thalamus$$

Interestingly, LOC(loss of consciousness) under the condition of $[Sex = Female]\&[Hemiparesis = Left]$ is an important factor to diagnose thalamic damage. In this domain, any strong correlations between these attributes and others, like the database of meningitis, have not been found yet. It will be our future work to find what factor will be behind these rules.

7 Discussion

As discussed in Section 4, positive (PR) and negative rules (NR) are:

$$PR : \wedge_j[a_j = v_k] \rightarrow d \quad s.t \quad \alpha_{\wedge_j[a_j=v_k]}(D) = 1.0$$
$$NR : \wedge_j\neg[a_j = v_k] \rightarrow \neg d \quad s.t. \quad \forall[a_j = v_k] \quad \kappa_{[a_j=v_k]}(D) = 1.0.$$

Positive rules are exactly equivalent to a deterministic rules, which are defined in [3]. So, the disjunction of positive rules corresponds to the positive region of a target concept (decision attribute). On the other hand, negative rules correspond to the negative region of a target concept. From this viewpoint, probabilistic rules correspond to the combination of the boundary region and the positive region (mainly the boundary region).

Thus our approach, the combination of positive and negative deterministic rules captures the target concept as the combination of positive and negative information. Interestingly, our experiment shows that the combination outperforms the usage of only positive rules, which suggests that we need also negative information to achieve higher accuracy. So, although our method is very simple, it captures the important aspect of experts' reasoning and points out that we should examine the role of negative information in experts' decision more closely.

Another aspect of experts' reasoning is fuzzy or probabilistic: in the rough set community, the problems of deterministic rules are pointed by Ziarko[9], who introduces Variable Precision Rough Set Model (VPRS model). VPRS model extends the positive concept with the precision of classification accuracy: a relation, the classification accuracy of which is larger than a given precision (threshold), will be regarded as positive. Thus, in this model, rules of high accuracy are included in an extended positive region. Analogously, we can also extend the negative concept with the precision of coverage, which will make an extended negative region. The combination of those positive and negative rules will extend the approach introduced in this paper, which is expected to gain the performance or to extract knowledge about experts' decision more correctly. Thus, it will be a future work to check whether the combination of extended positive and negative rules will outperform that of positive and negative deterministic rules.

Another interest is a measure of boundary region: a measure of positive information is accuracy and one of negative information is coverage. Probabilistic rules can be measured by the combination of accuracy and coverage[7, 8], but the combination of two measures is difficult to compare each rule: to measure the quality of boundary. It will also be one of the imporant future research directions.

8 Conclusions

In this paper, the characteristics of two measures, classification accuracy and coverage is discussed, which shows that both measures are dual and that accuracy and coverage are measures of both positive and negative rules, respectively. Then, an algorithm for induction of positive and negative rules is introduced. The proposed method was evaluated on medical databases, the experimental results of which show that induced rules correctly represented experts' knowledge and several interesting patterns were discovered.

References

1. Adams RD. and Victor M. *Principles of Neurology*, 5th edition, New York, McGraw-Hill. 1993.
2. Michalski, R. S., Mozetic, I., Hong, J., and Lavrac, N. The Multi-Purpose Incremental Learning System AQ15 and its Testing Application to Three Medical Domains. *Proceedings of the fifth National Conference on Artificial Intelligence*, 1041-1045, AAAI Press, Palo Alto, CA, 1986.
3. Pawlak, Z. *Rough Sets*. Kluwer Academic Publishers, Dordrecht, 1991.
4. Pawlak, Z. Rough Modus Ponens. *Proceedings of IPMU'98* , Paris, 1998.
5. Quinlan, J.R. *C4.5 - Programs for Machine Learning*, Morgan Kaufmann, CA, 1993.
6. Shavlik, J. W. and Dietterich, T.G. (eds.) *Readings in Machine Learning*, CA: Morgan Kaufmann, 1990.
7. Tsumoto, S. and Tanaka, H. Automated Discovery of Medical Expert System Rules from Clinical Databases based on Rough Sets. Proceedings of the Second International Conference on Knowledge Discovery and Data Mining 96, pp.63-69, AAAI Press, 1996.
8. Tsumoto, S. Modelling Medical Diagnostic Rules based on Rough Sets, *Rough Sets and Current Trends in Computing*, Lecture Note in Artificial Intelligence, 1998.
9. Ziarko, W. Variable Precision Rough Set Model. *Journal of Computer and System Sciences*, **46**, 39-59, 1993.

Scalable, High-Performance Data Mining with Parallel Processing

Alex Alves Freitas

CEFET-PR, Dep. de Informatica (DAINF)
Av. Sete de Setembro, 3165
Curitiba - PR 80230-901
BRAZIL
alex@dainf.cefetpr.br
http://www.dainf.cefetpr.br/ alex

Abstract

Parallel processing seems to be the great hope to speed up and scale up data mining algorithms, in order to cope with the huge size of real-world databases and data warehouses. However, most projects on parallel data mining have focused on the parallelization of a single kind of algorithm or knowledge discovery paradigm. This tutorial will present a considerably broader view of the area of parallel data mining. In particular, it will discuss the parallelization of algorithms of four different knowledge discovery paradigms, namely rule induction, instance-based learning (or nearest neighbours), genetic algorithms and neural networks. In addition, this tutorial will address both the use of "general- purpose" parallel machines and the use of commercially-available parallel database servers. Different parallelization strategies will be discussed and compared, for each of the four above- mentioned knowledge discovery paradigms.

Practical Text Mining

Ronen Feldman

Data Mining Laboratory
Department of Mathematics and Computer Science
Bar-Ilan University
Ramat-Gan Israel 52900
feldman@cs.biu.ac.il

Abstract

Knowledge Discovery in Databases (KDD) focuses on the computerized exploration of large amounts of data and on the discovery of interesting patterns
within them. While most work on KDD has been concerned with structured
databases, there has been little work on handling the huge amount of information that is available only in unstructured textual form. In this tutorial we will
present the general theory of Text Mining and will demonstrate several systems
that use these principles to enable interactive exploration of large textual collections. We view Text Mining as a combination of Information Retrieval methods
and Data Mining methods. We will describe generic techniques for text categorization and information extraction that are used by these systems. The systems
that will be presented are KDT which is system for Knowledge Discovery in
Texts, FACT, which discovers associations amongst keywords labeling the items
in a collection of textual documents, and Text Explorer which is a system that
provides a high level language for interactive exploration of textual collections.
We will present a general architecture for text mining and will outline the algorithms and data structures behind the systems. We will give special emphasis to
incremental algorithms and to efficient data structures. The Tutorial will cover
the state of the art in this rapidly growing area of research.

Industrial Applications of Data Mining

Gholamreza Nakhaeizadeh

Daimler-Benz, Research and Technology 3
Postfach 2360, Ulm, Germany
Nakhaeizadeh@dbag.ulm.daimlerbenz.com

Abstract

In the recent years Data Mining has found a lot of applications in industry and commerce. Some aspects of such applications in Marketing, Quality Management and Risk Management will be discussed:

1.Marketing Applications
Development of a Predictive Modelling process within the project "Customer Relationship Management" (CRM). The aim is to improve the relationship with customers. Among others customer care and marketing activities need to be better adapted to the needs of (prospective) customers. The outcome of the analysis is a predictive model which can be embedded and used in an operative system.

Development of Adequate Information Models supporting Marketing Research to find out the opinion of customers in respect to products and the service quality and to inform the related departments adequately and timely. To this end since some years several data sources have been exploited and data analysis reveals the inability of the existing information models to differentiate significantly between products and service quality respectively. The main task is the development of data mining method providing sufficient information models for products and services.

Development of Forecast Models for Warranty Costs. The main aim is to develop the forecast models for warranty costs that are caused by legal and voluntary regulations. One of the essential targets is the implementation of a highly automated planning process which is capable to improve forecast accuracy. Besides the classical statistical models, other forecasting models based on neural nets are examined.

2. Quality Management
Development of an Early Warning System using Data Mining. The aim is to provide methods that allow an early prediction of fault rates. This should enable the initiation of corrective actions as early as possible. This leads to early identification and detection if the quality goals are violated. During the analysis of the domain, several potential applications are identified and the three most important of them are realized. The solutions is embedded in a unified interactive environment.

3. Risk management

Increasing globalization efforts in international trade and high fluctuations makes risk analysis of financial markets an inevitable feature of corporate risk management. Given the large interest of the treasury department of companies for the future development of interest rates and exchange rates, the main emphasis is laid on the development of robust and reliable quantitative forecasting methods for currencies, interest rates and yield curves, respectively

Author Index

Lecture Notes in Artificial Intelligence (LNAI)

Lecture Notes in Computer Science